Encyclopaedia of Child
for Southern Africa

from birth to adolescence

W.E.B. EDGE

 DAVID PHILIP

Cape Town Johannesburg London

First published 1986 by David Philip, Publisher (Pty) Ltd, 217 Werdmuller Centre, Claremont, 7700, South Africa

Distributed in the UK and Europe by Global Book Resources Ltd, 7 Bury Place, London WC1A 26A

ISBN 0 86486 042 0

SECOND IMPRESSION (WITH CORRECTIONS) 1988

GRATEFUL ACKNOWLEDGEMENTS ARE DUE TO THE SOUTH AFRICAN CHRISTMAS STAMP FUND FOR PERMISSION TO REPRODUCE THE FRONT COVER PHOTOGRAPHS, WHICH WERE USED FOR THEIR 1977 SERIES OF CHRISTMAS STAMPS. THE SOUTH AFRICAN CHRISTMAS STAMP FUND HAS SINCE ITS INAUGURATION IN 1929 BEEN CONCERNED IN RAISING FUNDS TO HELP PREVENT AND CONTROL TUBERCULOSIS.

PRINTED BY GALVIN & SALES, 170 BUITENGRAGT, CAPE TOWN

Foreword

A quiet, but nonetheless highly significant revolution has occurred over recent years. People now are no longer content to be passively informed on health matters by professionals, but seek actively to educate themselves on every aspect of health and illness. This has resulted in a burgeoning literature directed at the layman, not least in the field of infant and child health. This is all to the good. There can be no better investment for the future than assuring our children optimal care, nurture and development, and what better way of achieving this than by disseminating such knowledge as widely as possible?

Dr Edge is an able and experienced paediatrician who has devoted a lifetime to a busy paediatric practice. He is in an excellent position to know the type of questions that parents need answering about their children's problems. There are many paediatricians with similar experience, but very few have shown the enthusiasm, perseverance and single-mindedness required to set down their knowledge and experience in writing for the layman. Even fewer have Dr Edge's ability to explain technical problems in a simple and lucid manner. His answers reflect modern thinking across a broad range of topics. This contribution is a particularly novel one in that the information is set down in easily accessible alphabetical format. Throughout the book run threads of urbane wisdom and humour that will make the Encyclopaedia a delight to savour and consult.

M. A. KIBEL
Stella and Paul Loewenstein Professor of Child Health
University of Cape Town

Author's Preface

Today's parents are very different from the parents of yesteryear. So are today's doctors. With the advent of ever more potent drugs the doctor is able to treat disease infinitely more effectively than he ever has before. Not all diseases, however, are treatable and much medication is administered inappropriately, extravagantly and ineffectively. While the doctor prescribes more and more medication, the patient or parent – who often simply wants reassurance or an explanation – becomes more alarmed by the chemist's bill than by the original symptoms. Today's parents want to understand the nature of their children's illness and not just have them treated. Unfortunately the doctor is often too busy to give such explanations, and the communication gap causes a deterioration in doctor-patient relationships.

It is in the hope of to some extent bridging this gap that this book has been written. It is directed at the parents who do not simply want to be told how to bath the baby or put on a napkin; they may know these things but they often do not know when it is necessary to consult a doctor, nor do they understand why their son should get asthma nor what they should do if he wets his bed, is bitten by a snake, has schooling difficulties or complains of tummyaches. Should their daughter become seriously ill they will want to understand her illness and not just hand her trustingly to hospital or doctor, only to retrieve her when she is better. Much illness can be managed perfectly satisfactorily without medical help but some guidance is required and it is hoped that this book will fulfil this need. Inevitably there will be omissions and the author would be grateful for any suggestions so that deficiencies may be corrected in future editions.

Apart from parents, others involved in the care of children such as nurses and particularly clinic workers may find some help in these pages. Comments and suggestions from such workers would be warmly welcomed.

For easy reference the book has been written in dictionary form. Though something is gained, inevitably something is lost and this does make the book less readable. It does, however, make 'dipping' easy and cross references make it unnecessary to read the book from end to end.

Raising children is hard work, expensive and often anxious but it should for the most part be fun. If this book helps to increase your enjoyment of your child its major aim will have been fulfilled. If it makes a contribution to your child's health, that will be a most satisfying bonus.

TO MY TEACHERS — THE CHILDREN

Note to the Second Impression

AIDS

With the widespread publicity given to this appalling condition, few people can be unaware of its ravages and its threat. AIDS is due to infection with a specific virus, the human immuno-deficiency virus (HIV). This invades the defence cells of the body leading to severe and progressive impairment of the immuné system with a resultant tendency to unusual infections, a tendency to the development of unusual malignant tumours, general wasting and frequently progressive degeneration of the brain. The virus is acquired only on intimate contact or by injection of blood or its products.

Originally the condition appeared to be confined to male homosexuals, drug-abusers and haemophiliacs who had been given contaminated blood products. The virus is, however, also spread by normal heterosexual contact and this is the main mode of spread in Africa. As the result of promiscuity and prostitution an estimated 2 million people harbour the virus in Central and West Africa and it is moving south at an alarming rate. A woman harbouring the virus stands about a 50 per cent chance of passing the disease on to her baby *in utero*. Congenitally acquired infection is basically similar to the disease in adults though the infections encountered are rather different. A syndrome of embryopathy with congenital abnormalities of the head and face has been described but is questionable. The majority of affected babies exhibit progressive brain damage as well as a predisposition to unusual infections.

Parents may worry that their children could acquire the virus innocently via, for example, contaminated articles. This is not so. Acquisition by blood transfusion or injection of blood products is now virtually eliminated as a result of screening of all donors. Acquisition by kissing is highly unlikely for although the virus is present in saliva as in other body fluids the concentration is very low and saliva has a protective effect. Sexual abuse of children, male or female, is a much greater threat.

Once acquired, the virus remains dormant for a long time, producing no symptoms. The first manifestation of disease is usually enlargement of the lymph glands – 'AIDS-related complex'. Thereafter gradual deterioration occurs, with infections such as pneumonia (often due to an unusual organism known as pneumocystitis) and fungal invasion being common. Malignant tumours may develop and progressive dementia frequently precedes death.

Because of their suppressed immunity children with AIDS should not receive live virus vaccines (e.g. Measles and Poliomyelitis). Killed vaccines are safe. On exposure to measles and chickenpox passive immunity can be given in the form of appropriate *gammaglobulin.

Treatment of AIDS is as yet unsatisfactory but is being intensively researched. The most promising drug so far is AZT. There is no preventive vaccine. The only way to avoid AIDS is by avoiding intimate contact with carriers of the virus.

DIABETES

A recent development in the management of Diabetes has been the introduction of the Novopen, which is a portable, cartridge-loaded syringe allowing administration of insulin several times a day without any fussing. The insulin is given in a dose calculated to cover the anticipated meal, and at night a long-acting insulin is given to cover the night hours. Control can be monitored by blood glucose estimations, and relatively painless finger prickers as well as electronic glucose-level readers are available. This type of tight control is suitable for older children and adults but with younger children one still has to compromise with less frequent injections and urine testing, with blood glucose estimations being kept to a minimum. As in most situations a sensible balanced approach is better than a maniacal quest for perfection, for perfection is rarely attained, and the main products of an overzealous approach are anxiety and unhappiness. Diabetic control should be as good as is compatible with a normal happy existence.

ABDOMEN

This contains the abdominal viscera, namely stomach, intestines, liver, spleen, pancreas and kidneys. It is continuous below with the pelvis, which is occupied by the bladder, rectum and internal genital organs of the female. Because these important structures are found here, the abdomen is the site of many childhood symptoms, particularly pain.

Abdominal distension. It is normal for small children to have fairly protuberant tummies. Factors causing true distension may be accumulation of excess fluid, gas (usually as the result of fermentation processes in conditions of impaired diges- tion, such as coeliac disease), or enlargement of the various organs such as the liver or kidneys owing to disease, especially tumours. Ovarian cysts may rise out of the pelvis into the abdomen, and of course in the older girl pregnancy is always a possibility. Severe constipation, especially when associated with abnormalities of the bowel, may produce gross distension of the large intestine. If your child's tummy appears distended, feel it, and if any lumps are palpable report to your doctor without delay. Simple distension is not urgent but should be checked anyway. Distension with pain and especially with repeated vomiting calls for prompt medical assessment.

Abdominal pain. This is probably the commonest complaint in childhood and few children escape tummyaches at some time or another. Acute abdominal pain may be due to many causes, including bowel obstruction, inflammatory disease such as appendicitis, and bowel irritation from toxic substances or infection – in which case it is usually accompanied by diarrhoea. If severe vomiting is present, or if the abdomen is decidedly distended or acutely tender, the child should be checked as a matter of some urgency and it is better not to give any medication until prescribed by a doctor as this may confuse the picture.

Recurrent abdominal pain is extremely common and is often emotional; a common example is the child with regular morning tummyaches as the result of some anxiety about school. In only about 6 per cent of cases of recurrent abdominal pain is an organic cause identifiable. This does not mean of course that the other cases are not genuine or inevitably caused by emotion. Many children seem to react to any adversity through their tummies. It is common for instance for the child with tonsillitis to complain of a tummyache rather than a sore throat. Children localise pain rather poorly and whereas, for example, an adult with kidney trouble will usually complain of pain in the back, in the child this is usually referred to the abdomen. Unless the pattern of abdominal pain clearly indicates an emotional origin it is wise for you to have the child checked by a doctor, who will probably want to have urine and stool specimens examined and may advise further investigation if this is warranted. Over-investigation however often serves merely to focus more attention upon the child's complaints and fortify them. Once it has been established that no significant organic disease is present, as little attention as possible should be paid to the pain. You can help the doctor considerably by carefully observing the pattern of the complaints, noting whether they are related to any other symptoms such as constipation or urinary disturbance; and it would be wise to take specimens of urine and stool with you to the doctor so that time is not lost.

Specific food allergies may cause recurrent pain, and in such cases parents' observations are all-important.

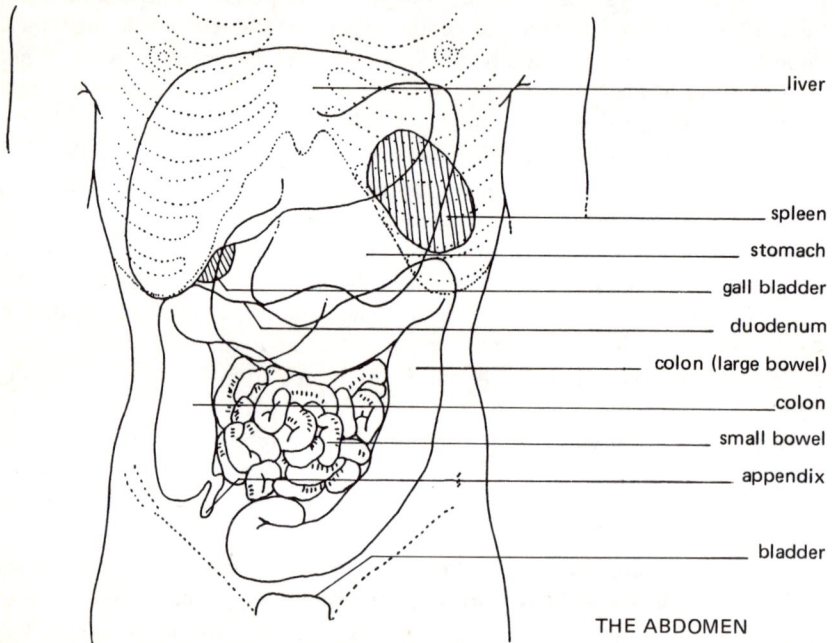

liver
spleen
stomach
gall bladder
duodenum
colon (large bowel)
colon
small bowel
appendix
bladder

THE ABDOMEN

ABSENCES
A name often applied to short periods of unresponsiveness characteristic of petit mal. (See *epilepsy.)

ACIDOSIS
A condition in which the body fluids are excessively acid. The normal degree of acidity as measured by the pH is about 7,4. In acidotic states this falls. The body is always producing acids in the general metabolic processes and particularly as the result of muscular activity. These acids are removed in two ways:

(1) via the urine, which is usually acid;
(2) via the lungs, in the form of carbon dioxide.

There are thus two main forms of acidosis, metabolic and respiratory. Acidosis also occurs in uncontrolled diabetes and in certain other metabolic derangements.

In lay minds 'acidity' is associated with an irritating urine and excoriation in the napkin area, and is often attributed to the ingestion of acid fruits and juices. This is a complete misconception. Certain individuals may have a specific intolerance for foodstuffs like acid fruits and juices, but in most cases the association is fortuitous. 'Acidity', like 'wind', has become a traditional cultural villain. It deserves exoneration.

ACNE

This extremely common skin disease of adolescence particularly affects the face but often also the back and upper chest. It is basically due to plugging of the hair follicles by blackheads and to leakage of the secretion of the sebaceous glands into the skin, causing severe irritation. The hair follicles then become infected, with the formation of pimples, and after the pimples have discharged there is often residual scarring. The condition is usually self-limiting but may continue for many years. Occasionally it is seen in newborn babies.

Treatment of acne is not simple. The skin should be gently cleansed and the blackheads (comedones) very gently expressed but excessive squeezing should be avoided. Removal of the sebaceous plugs is helped by preparations such as tretinoin and sulphur-containing creams, which produce mild peeling. Various preparations are employed to prevent infection, including topical antibacterial agents, and it is common practice to use long-term antibiotics, particularly tetracycline, which is especially effective against the germs inhabiting the hair follicles. Because acne is associated with puberty and the secretion of male hormones (produced by both males and females), preparations which suppress such hormones are often extremely effective but these must be used only under strict medical supervision. Sunlight or ultra-violet light in limited dosage is often helpful but over-exposure should be avoided. The emotional accompaniments of acne are often severe and require considerable sympathetic parental support. Emotional disturbance often aggravates acne and attention to this aspect may be helpful.

ADDER

See *snakebite

ADDITIVES

The numerous chemical substances added to commercially prepared foodstuffs, such as dyes, preservatives and flavouring agents, have reached such concentrations in the modern diet that the average per capita consumption of such chemicals in the United States is about 5 kg per annum. It is small wonder therefore that alarm has been expressed regarding the potential harm of such substances. In children they have been accused of causing hyperactivity and there is a little evidence to suggest that this might be so in the very, very occasional child. Food additives have to pass strict tests and controls before being permitted but it is worth getting into the habit of reading the labels on food packages and avoiding foods with many additives.

ADENOIDS

These structures are similar to the tonsils and form part of a ring of protective tissue at the back of the nose and mouth. Enlargement of the adenoids leads to difficulty in breathing and may predispose the child to ear infection. The adenoids are often removed together with the tonsils in states of chronic or frequently recurring infection. Such operations are undesirable in the very young child and are in general performed far too often. Adenoidal enlargement is frequently secondary to chronic nasal allergy and removal of the adenoids in such circumstances does nothing to alleviate the basic trouble.

ADOPTION

About 10 per cent of couples will find, usually to their great distress, that they are infertile. In most cases there will be a fairly definite cause and a third of these will be due to male infertility. In many cases, however, no cause is apparent and it is only after years of trying that the couple realise that pregnancy is unlikely to occur. Some of the causes are fairly readily reversible or can at least be helped and it is assumed that if your marriage has proved infertile you will have sought expert medical help. In cases of established infertility, adoption may be the only answer. It is essential that both parents agree on and are happy about such a decision and adoption should never be considered as a repair mechanism for a shaky marriage. Not only will it simply not work but it brings a third and totally innocent person into the unhappy situation. If, however, after due reflection you decide to try to adopt a child you should waste no time before contacting an appropriate adoption agency, for since the advent of the contraceptive pill very few babies, relatively speaking, are now available for adoption. You will almost certainly have to wait a year or two before you get a child. The laws of the country are strict and adoptive children not only have to conform to the race of the adopting parents but their religion, socio-economic status and physical characteristics have to be considered as well, and this may cause extra delay. You may therefore be tempted to explore alternative routes for acquiring a baby and unfortunately there are still people who will exploit this situation, often for their own gain. You will be well advised to deal with no-one other than a recognised adoption agency, who will select a baby for you who will match you in every possible way and who will have been medically examined to assess the suitability for adoption.

Having set the machinery in motion you will probably become impatient during the waiting period but this is a time for preparation and anticipation and a time you should enjoy together, fortifying your attitudes and preparing for the happy event. The occasional woman has even been able to stimulate her breasts to lactate and has successfully breastfed her adopted baby! Men have greater difficulty than women in accepting adoption as a solution to infertility, feeling that this is in some way a slur on their virility. Once they have managed to overcome these feelings, however, they are usually just as enthusiastic and as grateful as their wives.

Adopting an older child. For the couple who have left it rather late or for those that already have older children, the optimum solution is often adoption of an older child and these are often more readily available than newborn babies. There may be some initial difficulties in adjustment for both the child and the adopting parents but these are seldom of long duration and the end result is usually excellent, with firm bonds being forged between parent and child.

Telling the child she is adopted. There are some parents who find it impossible to tell their children that they are adopted and in this way they may do great harm. Others have every intention of telling the child but are terrified of doing so and therefore often do it clumsily. Others may go to the opposite extreme and refer to the child always as 'our adopted baby' instead of simply 'our baby'. All these faulty approaches are rooted in parental insecurity. If you accept your child for what she is, she will accept you in the same way. Many a child wonders at some stage whether she might be adopted, particularly when her parents appear to her to be utterly incomprehensible. Almost always some opportunity will present itself for informing your child rather casually, and certainly unemotionally, that she is adopted, but it can be made quite clear to her that it is on this account that she is loved all the more. It is important to be honest at all times with children, for the truth will eventually emerge somehow and the child's respect for you will then inevitably drop. As the child grows older she may demand more information regarding her adoption and these matters should be discussed freely and openly in a manner appropriate to her understanding. There will inevitably be times when she thinks that her own parents would have treated her better, just as there will inevitably be times when you will wonder whether other parents wouldn't have been more appropriate for her, but provided you have built up your relationship on love such occasions should be rare and brief. Whenever you feel that your child might perhaps be inappropriate for you, look around at your friends and see to what extent their children differ from each other and from the parents. Genetic factors play little part in the creation of family bonds. This is not to say that differences in character might not at times give rise to misunderstanding and unhappiness, but you must accept your child for what she is and not for what you might want her to be.

AGGRESSION

A certain degree of aggressiveness is normal in children, as in adults, and no doubt contributes to self-preservation. Unusual aggressiveness often stems from jealousy, for example of the toddler towards the new baby, who becomes the victim of eye-poking and toe-biting, or of the older child towards siblings who are more competent or more popular. Excessive aggression is frequently found in children with brain-damage, when it is often associated with impulsivity, poor concentration and *hyperactivity.

ALBINISM

This is a rare condition in which pigment-producing cells are absent. The skin is extremely fair, the hair colourless, and pigment is also lacking in the eyes, leading to an intolerance of strong light. The condition is inherited as a Mendelian recessive (see *genetics), the parents usually being unaffected but 25 per cent of the children being afflicted with the condition. The skin should be protected from excessive exposure to the sun, which not only causes severe burning but frequently leads to skin cancer, and the eyes should be protected by wearing a hat and dark-glasses.

ALBUMIN

Albumin is one of the major classes of protein in the body. Because of its somewhat smaller molecular size, it may leak through into the urine in disease states of the kidney, causing albuminuria. This might be revealed as a persistent froth on the urine when it is passed. Low levels of blood albumin are found in malnutrition, in severe liver disease, in kidney diseases such as nephrosis where albumin is lost in the urine, and in rarer conditions where protein is lost through the bowel. The blood albumin exerts an osmotic effect, retaining fluid in the blood vessels, and when the protein level falls critically, fluid is lost into the tissues, producing oedema.

ALCOHOL

In addition to the unmeasurable social misery it causes and the 80 per cent of road accidents for which it is responsible, alcohol may also have a damaging effect on the foetus. Babies born of alcoholic mothers tend to be small in size with small heads and brains and they may suffer varying degrees of mental retardation. The face is peculiar with a somewhat undeveloped mid-face and a featureless upper lip. There may be other accompanying deformities. In spite of these horrifying effects, modest consumption of alcohol during pregnancy does not appear to be harmful, though there are some who would ban it completely. Alcohol is not excreted in any significant amount in the milk and normal social consumption is therefore not contraindicated during lactation. Remember, however, that children are taught more by example than anything else and if we are to reduce the ravages of alcohol the consumption of this social poison will have to be reduced.

ALKALOSIS

A condition in which the body fluids are more alkaline than is normal. The degree of acidity or alkalinity is expressed as pH, the normal blood pH being about 7,4. As alkalinity increases the pH rises. Alkalotic states may result from excessive ingestion of alkalies, such as sodium bicarbonate, or from loss of acid, as in persistent vomiting.

ALLERGY

About 10 per cent of people in Western societies are afflicted with some sort of allergic trouble. (Some authorities put the figure as high as 20 per cent.) The incidence in less developed societies appears to be very much lower. Whether this is the result of a true genetic difference or whether it is due to a simpler existence with less opportunity for contact with harmful allergenic substances is difficult to say. There appears to be some evidence that as the black African adopts a Westernised life style the incidence of Western diseases, including allergies, increases.

What is allergy? Allergy is an altered reaction on the part of the body to contact with a foreign substance (known as the allergen). The normal defences of the body involve several mechanisms for getting rid of foreign material. Often it is simply removed by scavenging cells. Sometimes chemical substances are produced which combine with the foreign material, rendering it innocuous. Other chemicals may be produced which stimulate the appetite of the scavenging cells (opsonins).

The allergic diseases are largely hereditarily determined; if one parent is allergic there is about a 30 per cent chance of any child being similarly affected, and if both parents are allergic the chances are doubled. Allergic troubles include eczema, allergic rhinitis, asthma, urticaria and angio-oedema, which are together known as the *atopic diseases*. There is little set pattern of inheritance, a parent with eczema, for example, perhaps having a child whose skin is perfectly normal but who will develop asthma. Despite the hereditary nature of atopic disease, children will often develop allergic problems when there is no family background.

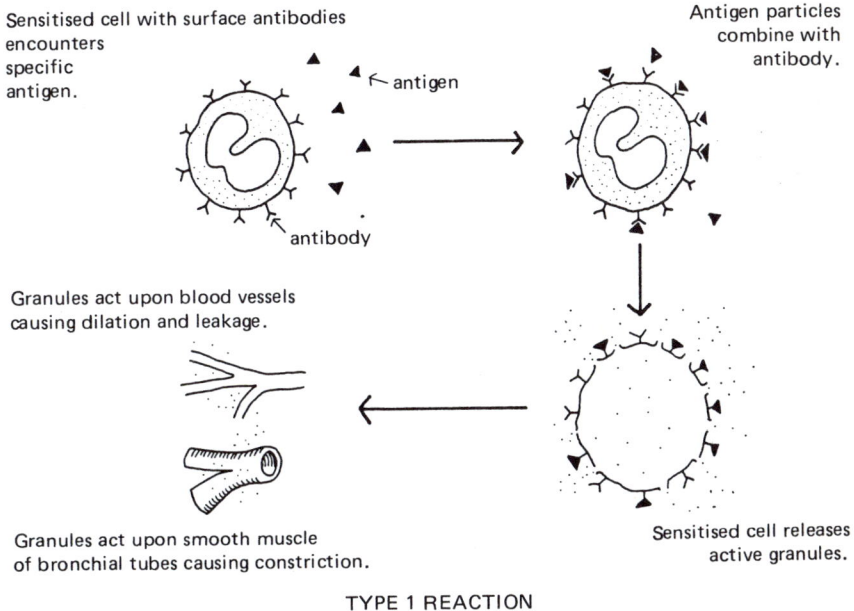

Sensitised cell with surface antibodies encounters specific antigen.

← antigen

antibody

Antigen particles combine with antibody.

Granules act upon blood vessels causing dilation and leakage.

Granules act upon smooth muscle of bronchial tubes causing constriction.

Sensitised cell releases active granules.

TYPE 1 REACTION

Types of allergic response
Type 1 reaction. There are 4 main types of allergic reaction, the most important being Type 1, which is predominantly involved in the atopic diseases. The sequence of events is illustrated in the figure. Atopic subjects have an excess of a specific antibody known as Immunoglobulin E (IgE), which adheres to the surface of certain cells known as mast cells which are widely distributed throughout the body. When such cells encounter a specific antigen, a reaction takes place which liberates the chemical granules within the cell, the most well-known and potent of which is histamine. This has the effect of dilating small blood-vessels and increasing their permeability, and of causing contraction of the smooth muscle in the walls of the bronchial tubes. Similar reactions may occur in the nose, producing the symptoms of hayfever, with profuse outpouring of mucus and swelling of the mucosal lining, and in the gut, causing an inflammatory reaction of the intestinal lining, with abdominal pain and bowel disturbance. Dilation of the blood-vessels of the skin causes urticaria, or hives, and leakage of fluid from the blood-vessels may cause the swellings of *angio-oedema (or angioneurotic oedema). Severe generalised reactions are known as anaphylaxis, which may lead to collapse and death.

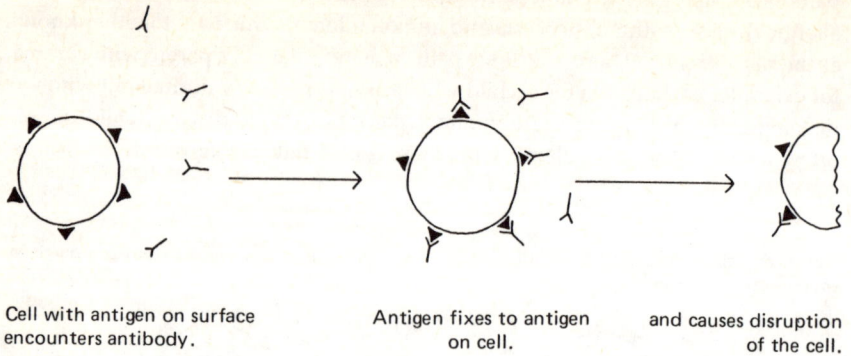

Cell with antigen on surface encounters antibody.   Antigen fixes to antigen on cell.   and causes disruption of the cell.

Type 2 reaction. In this type of response the situation is reversed. The cell surface contains antigen, and when this antigen encounters the appropriate antibody, the cell surface is destroyed. This may be accompanied by agglutination of the cells. A good example of this process is the anaemia caused in new-born babies by the Rhesus factor. This latter is an antigen present on the red blood-cells of some 85 per cent of the population but absent in those who are Rhesus negative. When such a Rhesus negative person encounters the Rhesus antibody, for example by blood transfusion or by leakage of Rhesus positive cells from her baby *in utero*, she will produce the appropriate antibodies to destroy the antigen. These of course do not affect her own Rhesus negative blood-cells. They may, however, pass through the placenta into the baby's circulation and destroy the baby's blood. (See *Rhesus.)

TYPE 3 REACTION

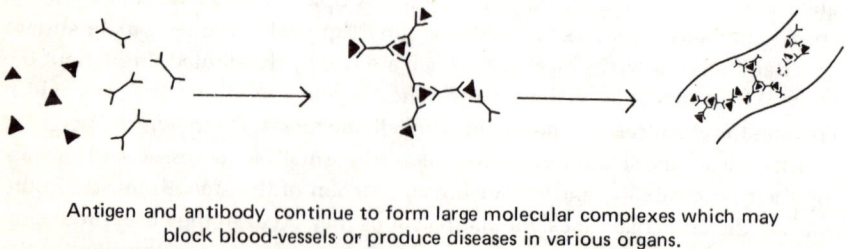

Antigen and antibody continue to form large molecular complexes which may block blood-vessels or produce diseases in various organs.

Type 3 reaction. In this situation both antigen and antibody are freely circulating but combine to form large molecular complexes which may block the blood capillaries and interfere generally with cellular function. Serum sickness is an example of a disease caused by such reactions.

Particles of antigen attract specific cells,
causing an inflamatory reaction.

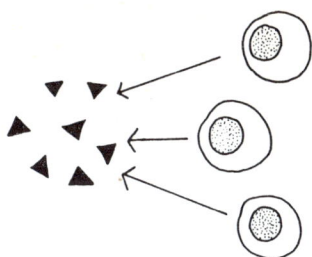

Type 4 reaction. Certain of the defence cells are sensitised to foreign substances and are attracted to any accumulation of such substance, giving rise to an inflammatory reaction. This is the mechanism involved in rejection of foreign tissue grafts. It is responsible for most forms of contact dermatitis and also for positive tuberculin tests, which indicate a previous experience of tuberculo-protein.

For further information, see under specific diseases, such as *asthma, *eczema, *rhinitis, *urticaria, etc.

Food allergy

This is less certain territory and many symptoms are attributed to an allergy to ingestants when there is little factual foundation for this. Nevertheless, the condition does exist, even though the situation may be difficult to prove. Skin tests, which are extremely useful in pinpointing respiratory allergens, are of little value when it comes to ingestants. RASTs (radioallergosorbent tests), which detect specific IgE antibodies, are perhaps more reliable.

Milk allergy in infancy. There is no doubt that some babies tolerate artificial feeds poorly. There are even some who seem to be intolerant of their mother's breast milk but this situation is very rare, so if you are breastfeeding your baby and encounter difficulties, don't jump to the conclusion that this means that your baby is unable to tolerate your breast milk. Some other factor is nearly always responsible.

The artificially fed baby, who is usually given some form of cow's milk, may show various symptoms of intolerance or allergy. The term 'allergy' is appropriate only if immune mechanisms are responsible for the symptoms. Occasionally a baby will react so violently to cow's milk that she collapses with anaphylactic shock. This, however, is extremely rare. The very occasional baby may react sufficiently violently to produce weals where the milk comes into contact with her lips or skin. This again is very rare.

Milder symptoms, however, are not uncommon. The incidence of milk allergy varies greatly from population to population. In Britain it is about 1 per cent. In certain areas of North America it reaches a level of over 10 per cent. In the South African black population it is practically unknown.

Milk allergy may be suspected if the baby shows any or some of the following symptoms:

(1) Chronic upper-respiratory catarrh with a perpetually blocked, snuffly nose, excessive mucoid secretion and often a degree of difficulty in breathing.

(2) Poor feeding, with apparent colic after taking a portion of the feed, manifested by squirming and crying.

(3) Persistent vomiting after feeds, often repetitive, sometimes fairly forceful, and often associated with obvious discomfort.

(4) Persistent diarrhoea not due to infection or other causes.

(5) Infantile eczema.

There are numerous other causes of these symptoms and a diagnosis of milk allergy should not be made lightly or without confirmatory proof if possible. It will naturally be suspected if there is a family background of allergic troubles.

Definitive diagnosis rests on the baby's response to removal of milk from the diet and relapse on its reintroduction. Milk may be replaced with soya substitutes like Isomil, Infasoy, Pro-Sobee. Unfortunately, about 20 per cent of babies allergic to milk will also be allergic to these soya preparations. Other milk substitutes (Allergilac, Nutramigen) have had the milk protein so altered that the allergic potential is reduced to a minimum. Extreme cases may require a meat-based formula.

Cow's milk may be replaced by other animal milks, the best of course being human milk, although this is usually difficult to obtain, but goat's milk or ass's milk may solve the problem. Their allergenicity, however, is very similar to that of cow's milk.

If the symptoms subside after introduction of the non-cow's-milk feed, the diagnosis still requires further confirmation by reintroducing cow's milk to see whether the symptoms return. If this isn't done, coincidence cannot be ruled out and the baby may be kept on a difficult or expensive feed for an unnecessarily long time.

Less severe cases of milk intolerance may be solved by giving a feed based on cow's milk but one in which the protein has been denatured to some extent. Evaporated milk, such as Carnation, is heated to a high temperature in the evaporation process and is thereby rendered appreciably less allergenic. The same applies to dried acidified milks like Pelargon. Such feeds are therefore worth a trial in a baby who shows minor manifestations of milk intolerance.

Milk allergy in babies seldom persists longer than 6 to 8 months. After a few months on the appropriate feed, therefore, an attempt should be made to reintroduce milk and if this is not immediately tolerated, further attempts should be made every 6 weeks or so.

Eventually nearly all these children will tolerate milk perfectly satisfactorily. Introduction of other foods seldom poses a significant problem but all new foodstuffs should be introduced one at a time so that any intolerance is immediately detected.

Particular care should be taken with the introduction of egg, especially the white of egg, which is highly allergenic, and it is best to leave this until the child is about 1 year old.

The baby who has shown clear milk allergy will subsequently have to be watched closely for the development of other allergic manifestations, including the later digestive upsets.

Later digestive allergic manifestations. Abdominal symptoms are common in children, so common that it must be the rare child indeed who escapes attacks of abdominal pain, vomiting and diarrhoea.

Many children complain of recurrent abdominal pains, but in only about 6 per cent of these is a definite organic cause established. Many digestive upsets must be due to the ingestion of some irritating foodstuff, and some of the recurrent symptoms are almost certainly due to intestinal allergy.

Nevertheless, the situation is extremely difficult to prove. When other clearly allergic symptoms accompany the abdominal complaints, for instance urticaria, their allergic basis is better established, but in the absence of definite allergic manifestations, the association must remain somewhat speculative.

An allergic cause becomes decidedly suspicious when the symptoms regularly follow the eating of any particular substance, especially such well-known causes of allergic troubles as citrus fruits, strawberries, tomatoes, chocolate, nuts, eggs, fish, shellfish, pork, and so on. You'll therefore have to watch for this and if any particular foodstuff seems to be the cause of the recurring symptoms, it should naturally be eliminated.

In more difficult cases, where there's a strong suspicion of allergy as a cause, particularly where other symptoms such as urticaria accompany the abdominal complaints, an elimination diet may have to be introduced to sort out the problem.

Elimination diet. Initially only a basic intake of hypoallergenic foods is allowed — soya-milk substitutes, rice, lamb (and perhaps chicken), vegetables such as carrots, potatoes, broccoli, and fruits such as apple, pear, banana, plum. After a few days other foodstuffs are added one at a time, keeping until last the common allergic culprits such as milk, egg, fish, shellfish, pork, tomatoes, strawberries, nuts and chocolate.

AMMONIA (IN URINE)

Urine which has been passed for some time, particularly in napkins, almost always develops a smell of ammonia due to the splitting of urea by germs. This renders the urine alkaline and it used to be thought that this was the common cause of ordinary napkin rashes. This has recently been shown not to be the case. Recommendations that the napkins be rinsed in a dilute acid solution such as dilute vinegar are therefore probably valueless; any benefit attributed to rinsing was probably due to increased attentiveness together with more frequent changing of napkins. Contact with wet napkins, particularly when the humidity is increased by overlying plastic, will certainly cause irritation. (See *napkins.)

AMNIOTIC FLUID

This is a fluid which surrounds the baby while it is still in the uterus. It originates from many sources, both maternal and foetal. The baby passes urine into the amniotic fluid and also swallows it. The fluid therefore may be diminished when the foetal kidneys are not working properly and it may be in excess when there is blockage of the baby's digestive tract.

A specimen of fluid is often withdrawn for diagnostic purposes during the early months to make sure there are no foetal abnormalities, particularly chromosomal abnormalities such as Down's syndrome. Such tests involve growing the foetal cells and analysing their chromosomal content. In the case of several rare conditions checks can be made to ensure they do not exist by rather elaborate chemical tests on the amniotic fluid, one of the most important being Tay-Sachs disease, which is relatively common in Ashkenazi Jews. Later in pregnancy, tests for foetal maturity, particularly adequate lung development, may be very valuable, especially when early induction of labour or Caesarean section is planned. The procedure of removing a sample of amniotic fluid, amniocentesis, carries a very slight risk for the pregnancy.

AMOEBA

This is a single-celled organism of which there are many species. The common amoeba causing disease — Entamoeba histolytica — is widespread but particularly rife and aggressive in tropical and semi-tropical areas. It invades the lining of the large bowel, causing ulceration and dysenteric symptoms — diarrhoea with blood and mucus in the stools. It may enter the bloodstream and cause abscesses, particularly in the liver, and these may reach an enormous size.

Amoebiasis usually responds well to treatment with metronidazole. Other drugs are sometimes required. Occasionally, particularly in black Africans, the disease is fulminating, causing severe destruction of the colon, and in such cases the mortality is high.

ANAEMIA

This implies an inadequacy of the red blood-corpuscles, which form the bulk of the cellular content of the blood. The blood also contains white blood-cells of several types, which are responsible for body defences, and platelets, which assist in blood-clotting. The cellular elements are suspended in the plasma, which itself is almost colourless. It is the red cells therefore which give the skin and mucous membranes, as well as the blood, a red or pink colour. Although pallor is characteristic of anaemia it can be a very deceptive sign. The best places to evaluate it are the conjunctiva of the eyelid, the mucous membranes of the mouth and the tongue, and the finger nail beds.

The blood-cells are manufactured in the red bone marrow and in the case of the red blood-cells they are replaced at about 1 per cent per day, the average red-cell life being 120 days. Anaemia may result from some defect in the manufacturing process, such as depression of the bone marrow by toxic substances, or radiation or invasion by, for example, tumour tissue. Occasionally the marrow is simply congenitally deficient. In order for red cells to be produced, certain chemical substrates are essential and dominant amongst these is iron. Iron-deficiency anaemia is common in pre-term babies, who rapidly exhaust their iron stores, in infants who are denied iron-containing foods and consume mostly milk, and in older children of the poorer members of the community for whom iron-containing foods are simply too expensive. Iron deficiency is fairly common among vegetarians, as some of the best sources of iron are meat and eggs. Iron may of course also be lost through bleeding, and chronic iron deficiency is therefore common in women or girls with excessive menstrual loss. Blood may also be lost through repeated nose-bleeds, bleeding from the gastro-intestinal tract, etc. In the case of blood loss this should of course be corrected. Where dietary iron is deficient it should be replaced with appropriate foods and iron-containing medicines. Other substances are also essential for red-cell production; one of these is folic acid, which is found in the leaves of vegetables and which is often deficient in the diet of the black African living largely on maize. Vitamin C affects the metabolism of iron and is often required to correct iron-deficiency-related anaemia. In pre-term babies lack of vitamin E may cause anaemia.

In addition to reduced production and haemorrhage, anaemia may result from an excessive rate of blood destruction. Normally the red blood-cells are destroyed at the same rate as the blood is being rebuilt, namely at about 1 per cent per day. Increased destruction may be the result of excessively fragile blood-cells due to a congenital defect affecting either the red-cell wall (such as the condition known as congenital spherocytosis) or the haemoglobin molecule (as in sickle-cell disease). Destruction of red cells may also be brought about by the production of abnormal antibodies, for example in *Rhesus haemolytic disease. Very rarely the body may produce antibodies against its own red blood-cells, causing an acute acquired haemolytic anaemia.

If a child is found to be anaemic, it is essential that an accurate diagnosis be made as to the cause, and treatment be instituted appropriately. It is not sufficient simply to give a 'tonic' and hope for the best.

ANAPHYLAXIS

This is a severe generalised reaction to a foreign substance, such as horse-serum or other animal sera, stings from bees, wasps and hornets, injected drugs such as penicillin in sensitive individuals, and occasionally from ingestion of allergens such as egg, milk, shellfish and nuts. Symptoms usually begin with apprehension, headache, dizziness, sweating, urticaria and breathing difficulty, and progress to collapse, with an impalpable pulse, profuse sweating, unconsciousness and possibly death.

The greatest dangers are associated with the giving of serum, such as for snakebite, and stings from insects. If such an event is followed by the symptoms enumerated above, the patient should be given an immediate injection of adrenaline: 0,25 ml for a small child and 0,5 ml for a large child, plus an injectible antihistamine preparation (e.g. mepyramine, chlorpheniramine, promethazine or clemastine) and a corticosteroid such as soluble hydrocortisone, betamethasone, dexamethasone or methylprednisolone. Should the patient stop breathing, artificial respiration should be carried out until spontaneous breathing recommences. Expert medical assistance should be sought as soon as possible.

People who have shown severe sensitivity reactions to Hymenoptera (bees, wasps, hornets) should always have these drugs available or they should be desensitised to the insect venom.

ANGIO-OEDEMA OR ANGIO-NEUROTIC OEDEMA

This is an allergic manifestation, taking the form of fairly large swellings, usually involving the soft tissues of the eye, face or genital regions and often associated with urticaria. The swellings persist for several hours and then subside slowly. Often trauma is an initiating factor. When the swelling involves the floor of the mouth or the larynx, respiratory obstruction may occur and the condition is then extremely dangerous. In other areas it is simply a nuisance. Identifying the allergic cause may be extremely difficult. Treatment consists of the administration of adrenaline by injection in severe cases, especially with threatening suffocation, and otherwise antihistamine drugs or corticosteroids. (See *urticaria.)

ANIMALS

Children have a natural love for animals which should be applauded even if the occasional 'pet' they bring home is untraditional and seemingly unworthy of great affection! Common pets such as dogs and cats are to be encouraged, except in the case of the child who is severely allergic to their hair. It is of course important to have your pets protected against common diseases which may afflict them, including rabies. The older child must learn that if she has the privilege and joy of having a pet she must also undertake some of the care.

Some parasitic diseases are spread by household pets, including sandworms (from the larva of the dog hookworm), toxocariasis (caused by a dog roundworm), hydatid disease (caused by a small dog-tapeworm, with its intermediate phase normally in sheep), and toxoplasmosis, which is spread largely by cats. Birds of the parrot family may spread the respiratory infection, psittacosis. Mice, rats and hamsters are relatively safe.

ANOREXIA

A temporary loss of appetite is a natural accompaniment to almost any illness and need not cause concern. Mothers often feel that their children will come to considerable harm if they do not eat for a few days. This is not so. Fluids of course are essential and especially if there are excessive losses due to fever or diarrhoea. Longstanding anorexia associated with significant weight loss is of course a more serious problem and will require medical assessment. Anorexia nervosa is a serious condition, usually afflicting adolescent girls; it is sometimes the result of absurdly excessive slimming campaigns but is often a manifestation of deep emotional turmoil. Prolonged medical and psychological help is usually required.

ANTENATAL CARE

From the time that a woman knows she is pregnant she should consult a doctor to make sure that her health is optimal for her growing baby. It may seem unnecessary to seek medical advice for a situation which is after all perfectly natural, but there are hazards to both mother and baby in pregnancy and the earlier these are detected the better. From the mother's point of view a doctor will want to check for conditions such as heart disease, which may be considerably aggravated by pregnancy, kidney disease, which may pose a grave threat, high blood pressure, diabetes and infections. Of the infections, those which most often cause harm to the foetus are syphilis and German measles. The latter is harmful only during the first 4 months of pregnancy and the earlier it occurs the more devastating is its effect. You should of course have been immunised against German measles either as an infant or as a teenager. Unfortunately, however, many women are still susceptible. The disease is not always recognisable, for infection does not always produce the characteristic rash. If, therefore, you should be exposed to German measles, make sure that blood tests are taken to determine whether you have acquired the virus.

It is wise for you not to smoke during pregnancy and consumption of alcohol should be extremely modest. Smoking reduces foetal size, including brain size, and heavy consumption of alcohol can be quite disastrous. (See *alcohol.) Exposure to X-rays during the early months of pregnancy should be avoided.

With respect to the baby, certain congenital abnormalities can be detected antenatally. In particular, neural-tube defects (spina bifida and anencephaly, in which either the spinal cord or the brain are unformed and lie open to the exterior) may be detected by means of chemical tests on the mother's blood or the amniotic fluid obtained by amniocentesis, or by ultrasound scanning. The latter procedure is quite harmless and may give valuable information regarding the foetus and the site of the placenta. Blood tests on the mother should be done to exclude syphilis and to determine her blood groups, particularly the Rhesus blood group, and if she is Rhesus negative and the baby's father Rhesus positive, repeat blood tests will have to be done during pregnancy to determine the presence of antibodies to the Rhesus factor. The baby should not be subjected to any potential toxins and no drugs or medicines should be taken without your doctor's explicit permission. The baby is well protected from trauma and only penetrating injuries are likely to be damaging. Diabetes in the mother somewhat increases the risk of congenital abnormalities in the baby; other ill-effects of diabetes, in particular excessive foetal size, are related to the degree of diabetic control, which therefore should be meticulous during pregnancy. Any significant deterioration in your health during pregnancy should be reported immediately to your doctor.

ANTIBIOTICS

There is no doubt that these wonder drugs are grossly abused and it would be of benefit to your child, yourselves, your pocket and your doctor if you put up a certain resistance to their administration. Antibiotics are of value only in cases of infection with the larger infective agents, in other words, bacteria. They are quite useless against viruses, which cause the bulk of minor infections. The first antibiotic, penicillin, is still the most effective in cases of infection with susceptible organisms. It has, however, a limited range and, unfortunately, germs such as staphylococcus (a common cause of abscesses) and gonococcus (the causal agent of gonorrhoea), readily become resistant to penicillin by the production of an enzyme, penicillinase, which destroys it. Modifications of penicillin have therefore been evolved which have increased the spectrum of activity, and some are unaffected by penicillinase. Unfortunately, these more expensive derivatives tend to be used inappropriately when simple penicillin would be best, for example in tonsillitis.

Penicillin was followed by broader-spectrum antibiotics, such as the tetracyclines and chloramphenicol. Only after many years of use was it realised that the tetracyclines produced staining of the teeth in young children, with a tendency to cause dental caries, and they are also deposited in bone although with no obvious ill effect. Chloramphenicol on occasion produces severe blood disorders which can be fatal. The newer antibiotics are much safer and most have a broad spectrum of activity, but they are expensive and where possible they should be used only when laboratory tests have determined the sensitivity of the infecting organism.

There is a widespread misconception that patients may become resistant to antibiotics. People cannot become resistant to antibiotics, although they may of course become sensitive to them, responding to their administration with undesirable side-effects. It is only the germs which develop resistance. But this is a very serious problem and a powerful reason not to use antibiotics indiscriminately. It took little time for staphylococci to learn the tricks of resistance and other germs have not been slow to follow their example! Even the pneumococcus, which was thought always to be sensitive to penicillin, has recently evolved resistant strains. Where resistance is a likely problem, two or more antimicrobial agents are sometimes given simultaneously, as in the management of tuberculosis, where the administration of one agent alone very frequently leads to resistance. In the case of very serious infections such as meningitis, it is common practice to give more than one antibiotic until the nature and sensitivity of the organism is known.

In certain situations, antibiotics may be given for prolonged periods, such as in the preventive management of rheumatic fever or in frequently recurring tonsillitis. The administration of penicillin in these situations is entirely innocuous. The cause of these troubles is the streptococcal germ, which fortunately is always penicillin-sensitive and, except in cases of penicillin sensitivity on the part of the patient, such medication is extremely well tolerated. Tetracyclines are often given for long periods in cases of severe acne. Tuberculosis may require treatment of 6 months to 2 years. In all these situations you may be sure that the risk of ill-effect from treatment is negligible compared with the benefit to be obtained.

Antibiotics are the most potent weapons in the doctor's armamentarium. You do not however use a gun to get rid of a cockroach. Antibiotics can be wonderful and life-saving but they are used with abandon and extravagance. Over 100 preparations are available, which is a reflection more of the value of the market than of the need for preparations. Fortunately, the public is becoming more critical and many a parent is now more anxious about the frequent medication the child is receiving, than about the frequent, relatively minor illnesses for which expensive, unnecessary and often potentially harmful treatment is being given.

ANTIBODIES

These are complex chemical substances produced by the defence cells of the body in response to the presence of a foreign substance which is known as an antigen. Antibodies are extremely specific for the antigen which provoked their formation and do not give a general protective cover. Once an antibody has been produced in response to an antigenic stimulus, the level tends to wane, but the sensitised cells persist and when antigen is again encountered there is a rapid outpouring of antibody. This is the mechanism whereby second attacks of the common infections such as measles and chickenpox are prevented. Antibody production is stimulated artificially by administration of vaccines, which may be of various types. (See *immunity.)

Antibodies are not always beneficial. They may be responsible for severe allergic reactions, they may cause blood destruction, as in Rhesus haemolytic disease, and they may sometimes be formed against the body's own cells in a distorted immunological response. Antibodies may be given in the form of a concentrated serum to counteract the effect of a toxin, as in the treatment of diphtheria, tetanus or snakebite, giving a temporary so-called passive immunity.

ANTISPASMODICS

These are drugs given to relax the spasm of the smooth muscle found in the viscera, such as the bowel and bronchial tubes. Such drugs commonly act by stimulation or paralysis of the nerve suppy to the muscle fibres. The original bowel antispasmodic was atropine, but more modern preparations such as dicyclomine are now more popular. In excessive dosage such drugs can produce side-effects such as rapid heart rate, dry mouth and dilatation of the pupil. Bronchial antispasmodics are of a different type. (See *asthma.)

ANUS

Fortunately, children do not suffer from anal troubles as frequently as adults, who have a tendency to constipation and piles.

Imperforate anus. This is a condition in which the anal canal fails to develop properly so that the bowel cannot empty itself. Various degrees of severity are encountered but all require surgical treatment as soon as the defect is detected.

Anal fissure. This is a tear in the lining of the anal canal, usually the result of passing hard, constipated stools. It causes pain, which in turn makes the child reluctant to pass his motions and leads to perpetuation of the constipation. Bleeding may occur, but if blood is found on the stool it is always superficial and never mixed in with the stool, thus distinguishing it from other forms of bowel bleeding. The fissure may occasionally become chronic and require surgical treatment but nearly all cases will heal satisfactorily, provided the repeated trauma of passing constipated stools is alleviated. Treatment therefore consists of administering a suitable laxative, which should be given regularly until healing is complete, and thereafter gradually reduced. (See *constipation.)

Anal irritation. This may result from contact with stool which has been incompletely wiped from the perianal skin and this simply calls for suitable hygienic measures. Perianal itching is often due to *threadworms, and treatment then consists of the removal of these by administration of a suitable vermifuge.

APGAR SCORE

A widely used scoring system for evaluation of the state of the newborn baby. 0, 1 or 2 marks are allotted for colour, heart rate, respiratory effort, response to stimulus, and muscle tone and movement. The test is commonly applied at 1 minute and 5 minutes after birth. Low scores at 5 minutes are an indication for follow-up assessment, though only 4 per cent of babies with scores of 4 or less have subsequent problems. The test can be criticised not only on this account but also because colour is not of great relevance and the baby requiring rapid resuscitation at birth should be dealt with immediately without bothering with a 1 minute Apgar rating.

APNOEA

This means an arrest of breathing, no matter what the cause. Apnoeic attacks are particularly common in premature babies and in sick neonates with conditions such as intracranial bleeding, severe infections, low blood-sugar levels, or in association with convulsions. Babies liable to such attacks therefore are usually carefully monitored and often require simple stimulation to make them breathe again. Apnoeic attacks can be prevented to a considerable extent by appropriate medication.

APPENDICITIS

This is probably the most feared abdominal condition and most parents faced with a child with abdominal pain will wonder whether it isn't her appendix. This organ is a little blind-ended appendage to the caecum and its function is not entirely clear. It contains a great amount of lymphatic tissue, the cells of which are to a great extent responsible for the body's defences. Just as the tonsils and adenoids guard the entrance to the digestive tract so the appendix seems in some way to guard the entrance to the large bowel, which teems with micro-organisms. Faecal concretions may form in the appendix and cause obstruction, which leads to inflammation, but acute appendicitis is often unassociated with obstruction. The symptoms in adults and older children are fairly typical, with pain commencing in the central abdomen and subsequently settling in the appendiceal area on the right. A rather low-grade temperature is present and vomiting may occur. Palpation of the abdomen reveals tenderness in the right lower region. A child presenting with these features therefore should be seen by a doctor. In very small children the picture is much more obscure and the diagnosis is often not made before the appendix actually bursts. Treatment of acute appendicitis consists of removal of the offending organ, but if an abscess has formed the surgeon will probably wait until this has subsided, with or without drainage, before performing an appendicectomy.

Appendiceal colic may be produced by concretions causing partial obstruction without actual inflammation. The appendix may also be involved in bilharzia.

Acute appendicitis can be simulated by other less serious conditions, such as mesenteric adenitis, and it may happen therefore that an operation performed in good faith and with adequate indication may reveal a perfectly normal appendix. The so-called 'grumbling appendix' is an obscure entity, the validity of which many doctors refuse to recognise. It has to be admitted however that there is the very occasional child with persistent abdominal pain whose symptoms are completely relieved after the appendix is removed. This, however, does not justify the speculative appendicectomies so frequently and regrettably performed.

APPETITE

Few parents seem to be satisfied with their children's appetites and the lengths to which parents will go in order to get their children to eat more than is necessary is astounding. In the healthy child, appetite is self-regulatory, and provided the child is not losing weight you should pay no attention to her appetite. Frequently the lean, active child seems to exist on hardly anything and even the obese child often seems to eat remarkably little. Appetite will diminish with almost any significant illness but this need cause no alarm as the child rapidly makes up for it once she is better. So-called tonics and appetite stimulants have hardly any place in medicine. Like vitamins, cough mixtures and numerous other medications they are given largely to make the parent feel better rather than to benefit the child.

Attempts to force a child to eat are utterly misguided and any anxiety demonstrated about a child's appetite immediately puts a powerful weapon into her hands which she will use without mercy. (See *feeding problems.)

ARTIFICIAL RESPIRATION

It is as well to know how to perform effective artificial respiration as one never knows when it may prove necessary. It is often administered inadvisedly and unnecessarily, such as during convulsions, but anybody who is not breathing because of, for example, suffocation, electric shock or drowning, should be given artificial respiration until spontaneous breathing is established. It must be realised that the brain cells will survive for only about 2 minutes after their oxygen supply is cut off and therefore no time must be wasted in dealing with a patient who is not breathing.

Mouth-to-mouth resuscitation is the method of choice and is much more effective than older methods involving chest compression. Any obstruction to breathing should first be removed, and in the case of drowning the child should first be put on her tummy and the chest compressed a few times. She is then turned onto her back and the head is tilted backwards. In the case of a very small child the operator's mouth should be placed over the mouth and nose of the victim. In a larger child or adult the nose must be pinched in order to seal it, and the operator's mouth placed over the open mouth of the victim. Air is then blown into the victim's chest, which should be seen to rise. The quantity blown will naturally depend upon the size of the child, and remember that harm can be done by overdistending the lungs. In the case of a small baby a small puff using the mouth rather than the lungs is sufficient. After inflating the victim's lungs, the operator's mouth is then removed and the lungs allowed to deflate, which will take a few seconds. Rhythmical resuscitation is then continued at about 15 blows of air per minute until the child begins to breathe. Thereafter the victim should be watched to make sure that she maintains a pink colour and that breathing continues.

If the victim's heart is not beating this is not necessarily a sign that she is irreversibly dead. Cardiac massage as well as artificial respiration should be performed for several minutes before giving up. To perform cardiac massage, the patient should be on a firm surface and not, for example, on a soft bed. The 'heel' of one hand is placed over the lower chest and the other hand on top of it and regular, firm compressions are given every 1 – 2 seconds. It is almost impossible for one person to perform artificial respiration and cardiac massage at the same time but the two procedures should be alternated as best as possible. If no heart beat has returned after 5 minutes and the victim's pupils are widely dilated, there is no point in making further efforts.

ASPHYXIA

This implies defective respiration leading to inadequate blood oxygenation. The causes are numerous, and include poisonous gases, respiratory obstruction, lung disease and ineffective respiratory movements. Choking on a foreign body is a common cause and you should know how to deal with it. (See *choking.)

Neonatal asphyxia implies impaired oxygenation of the baby during or immediately after birth. In milder forms the baby recovers spontaneously with increasing respirations as oxygenation improves. Increasing asphyxia is manifested by diminished respiratory effort and a progressively slowing and weakening pulse. The baby becomes pale, limp and unresponsive. Unless energetic measures are taken to oxygenate the baby at this stage recovery is unlikely. If there is no medical help and you have to deal with such a crisis yourself, try to clear the baby's air passages by holding her head down and compressing the chest a few times and then perform mouth-to-mouth resuscitation, as described under *artificial respiration.

ASPIRIN

A useful medication for relief of pain and fever but it has to some extent been replaced by paracetamol, which is somewhat safer. Aspirin may cause severe gastric irritation, with ulceration and bleeding. Excessive dosage may cause ringing in the ears, and poisoning may result in gross disturbance of the body chemistry, leading to collapse, coma and even death. If aspirin poisoning is suspected, the child should be made to vomit and you should then either consult your doctor or take the child to hospital.

ASTHMA

This is the most serious of the atopic diseases, frequently following upon eczema and allergic rhinitis. During infancy, asthma often isn't recognised as such and it is usually only after 3 or 4 years of repeated trouble that it becomes clear that the 'bronchitis' is really asthma.

A family history of allergy, or of preceding eczema, milk intolerance or chronic rhinitis should alert you to the possibility that the child is having recurrent asthma rather than repeated bronchitis. In the small child, the symptoms of these conditions are almost indistinguishable. In the older child and adult, the recurrent attacks of wheezing are characteristic.

The causes of asthma

Basically, asthma is an allergic disease caused by the inhalation of various allergens, the commonest being house dust, dust mites, animal danders, feathers, moulds and various pollens. Foodstuffs are of little importance except in the occasional individual. It isn't uncommon, however, for certain dietary items, particularly synthetic fruit juices preserved with sulphur dioxide, and cold foods such as ice cream, to act as triggering mechanisms for asthmatic attacks.

Other triggering mechanisms may be: exposure to irritating gases or fumes; sudden changes in temperature; abrupt changes in weather; drugs such as aspirin; and exercise — though it's important to distinguish between asthma which is revealed by exertion because of the sudden need for extra oxygen, the breathlessness disappearing as soon as the exertion ceases, and true exercise-induced asthma in which the symptoms are brought on by exertion and persist after its termination.

Infection is a common accompaniment of asthma and may sometimes be responsible for precipitating attacks. In other cases, the infection follows the initial allergic insult, which damages the defence mechanisms.

It is often difficult to be sure whether infection is present or not: what, for example, appears to be an initial cold may, in fact, be simply an acute exacerbation of allergic rhinitis, and the signs of bronchitis are difficult to distinguish from those of pure asthma.

If he does suspect infection to be present, your doctor will probably prescribe an antibiotic; such medication, however, should not be given without a good indication and should never be administered except on your doctor's instructions.

The association between emotional stress and asthma is a complex one. The role of emotion in producing asthma has probably been overstressed in the past, but there are certainly some children who react to emotional distress with asthmatic symptoms. On the other hand, a child who has had repeated asthmatic trouble is very likely to have emotional problems secondary to her repeated ill health, loss of schooling and so on.

During a severe asthmatic attack there is a natural reaction of fear, so a calm and confident attitude on the part of attendants and family will help a great deal in restoring emotional balance.

What happens during an asthmatic attack?

As a result of the allergic reaction, histamine and other substances are released which cause:

(1) Contraction of the smooth muscle in the bronchial walls, leading to constriction.

(2) An inflammatory swelling of the mucous lining of the bronchi, leading to further encroachment of the lumen.

(3) Stimulation of the mucus-secreting glands in the bronchi, leading to further obstruction by mucus plugs.

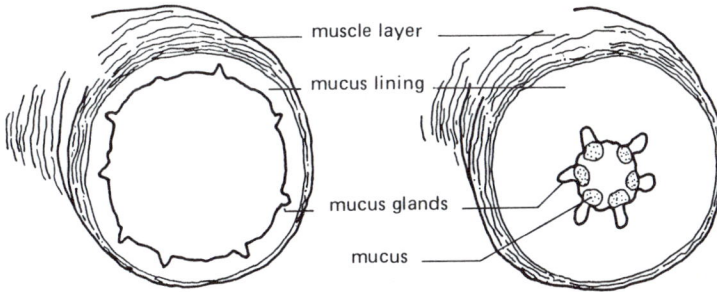

muscle layer

mucus lining

mucus glands

mucus

These three effects augment each other in producing marked obstruction of the airways. Whereas bronchodilator drugs are extremely effective when given early in the attack, later their efficacy is much less and, by this stage, corticosteroids are often the only effective remedy.

Of course, much depends on the extent to which bronchial spasm is causing the obstruction. If much of the latter is due to mucosal swelling and mucus secretion, relaxation of bronchial spasm alone won't accomplish a great deal.

Treatment of the asthmatic attack

It is convenient to consider the treatment of asthma under two headings: (1) treatment of the actual asthmatic attack, and (2) long-term preventive management. These do, of course, overlap to some extent and many of the drugs used are of value in both contexts.

Naturally, you will be guided by your doctor, and it is important that you carry out his instructions to the letter, otherwise he will find it impossible to judge the efficacy of his treatment, which inevitably has to be tailored to each individual according to the response.

It is not possible to detail every preparation used in the treatment of asthma, as there are far too many of them — but you should have some idea of the action of the drugs used so that you may help your doctor assess their efficacy in the case of your particular child.

Bronchodilator drugs. (1) Drugs acting through the nerve supply to the bronchi. The muscle of the bronchial wall is innervated by nerves from the sympathetic system, stimulation via these nerves leading to relaxation and bronchodilatation. The nervous impulses in the sympathetic nervous system are transmitted largely by adrenaline, and this was one of the earliest drugs to be effective in the treatment of asthma.

Unfortunately, adrenaline also produces effects elsewhere, causing a marked increase of heart rate, elevation of blood pressure and other actions which are either irrelevant or, indeed, possibly harmful in the acute asthmatic situation.

Nevertheless, adrenaline and similar drugs, such as isoprenaline, do produce a very marked bronchodilator effect and are still useful preparations. They have, however, been largely superseded by more modern preparations which still have a good bronchodilator effect without the unwanted side-effects of adrenaline.

These drugs may be administered in various ways. They can be inhaled in aerosol form, and give rapid relief provided they are inhaled deep into the bronchial tree. When obstruction is very severe, this may be impossible. Also, small children often don't co-operate sufficiently well to inhale such preparations effectively, although even infants can be given such medication via a cardboard or plastic cup placed over the nose and mouth with the aerosol sprayed through a perforation in the base.

Although these preparations are safe, they should not be over-used, and the limits set by your doctor should be adhered to. The preparations available in this form include: hexoprenaline, orciprenaline, salbutamol, rimiterol, fenoterol, carbuterol and terbutaline. They are of value if used early in the asthmatic attack and are very convenient. Some, however, have an effect of rather short duration and if relief is obtained for only a brief time, it is better to use other medications rather than very frequent inhalations of these aerosols. Salbutamol and fenoterol may be administered as nebulised solutions, and as such are very effective. Home nebulisers are fashionable and therefore over-used. Aerosols properly employed are usually as effective. It is often not realised that the dose administered by nebulisation is on average 25 times the dose of an aerosol.

Several other spray preparations are available but they are less specific and have more marked side-effects than those named above.

Apart from the aerosol sprays, most of these preparations are also available as tablets or syrup to be taken orally, and some are also in injectable form for your doctor's use. They are all effective remedies for relieving bronchospasm and are safe when used in the correct dose.

(2) Theophylline preparations. These preparations act in a completely different manner, having a direct effect on the muscle cells and not operating via the nerve supply. They are very useful, both for the treatment of the acute attack and for prevention, but dosage has to be kept within strict limits as they can be toxic. They

are often included in proprietary asthma remedies and are also available in tablet form, as an alcoholic solution and as suppositories. Absorption of the latter, however, is unpredictable and irregular and makes accurate dosage difficult. Alcoholic solutions are well-absorbed and perhaps therefore preferable when a rapid effect from oral administration is required.

Theophylline is very effective when given by injection but overdosage is, in this case, a risk if these drugs have been administered orally or rectally beforehand. Theophylline preparations and the sympathetic stimulant bronchodilators do augment each other's effects and are often therefore given in conjunction.

Drugs used to reduce the mucosal swelling. Unfortunately, although the antihistamine drugs might be expected to reduce the mucosal swelling, they are in fact extremely disappointing in asthma and have no place in its treatment. Corticosteroids, however, are extremely effective in suppressing the allergic response and are of great value in the management of severe asthmatic attacks.

The public has a rightful fear of cortisone-like drugs, but when administered over a short time they are very safe and if the response to simple bronchodilator drugs isn't immediate, there should be little hesitation in resorting to steroid administration — particularly as the effect is not immediate but usually delayed for several hours.

Numerous preparations are available and they can be given in the form of tablets, syrup or by injection. High doses are usually needed for the first day or two, with rapid reduction thereafter.

Corticosteroids are also of value prophylactically but, if given for prolonged periods, they tend to produce side-effects and prolonged administration is therefore kept to a minimum. However, if your doctor has advised the use of these drugs for acute asthmatic attacks, you should not hesitate to use them.

Treatment to remove obstructing mucus. Good hydration is the most important factor in helping to liquefy the tenacious mucus which is secreted into the bronchi during an asthmatic attack. If the patient is unable to take adequate fluid by mouth, then this has to be given intravenously.

Humidifying the inspired air is of little value, as by the time this reaches the bronchi it has been fully humidified by the moist upper airways. And although there are several preparations available which help to liquefy mucus, they do not really act rapidly enough to be of value in the treatment of acute asthma.

Psychological measures. When dealing with a fearful, often exhausted asthmatic patient, it is essential to maintain an attitude of calm and confidence, and particularly so with children. You may feel extremely anxious yourself but you must try not to show it. Do meticulously what your doctor has instructed and if the response of your patient is not satisfactory then do not hesitate to call your doctor, no matter what the time.

The most favourable time for treating an asthmatic attack is at its start. Once it is fully established, it becomes much more difficult to break. If the response to home treatment is not satisfactory, hospitalisation may become necessary. Severe asthma can be a real medical emergency, demanding the most intensive treatment, so do not hesitate if you feel concerned about your child's progress.

The long-term preventive treatment of asthma

The logical and most desirable preventive measure in any situation is, of course, removal of the cause, when this is known. In many cases of asthma, the cause can be determined with some certainty and steps to remove or avoid it usually lead to considerable improvement.

Many children, however, need additional help in the form of continuous prophylactic treatment, and this often causes great concern to parents who feel that their children should not be having so much medication. However, there is virtually no danger from properly medically supervised prophylactic therapy. Long-continued asthma, on the other hand, is decidedly dangerous as it may lead to progressive lung destruction. So if continuous treatment is necessary to prevent asthma adequately in your child, please accept this as being infinitely preferable to the risks of continuing asthma.

Removal of the cause — environmental control. Identification of the specific allergic basis for asthma in any individual is usually possible after the age of 3 or 4 years, by studying the details of the patient's history, augmented by appropriate skin tests.

Skin tests, however, are by no means infallible, and the observations of parents are often of greater value in determining the basic cause and the various triggering factors which may precipitate attacks.

Generally speaking, the most common underlying allergy is that of house dust and house-dust mites. House dust consists of numerous substances — fibres from upholstery and carpets, insect deposits and degradation products, moulds and so on. It should not be confused with grit, which may blow in from outside and which, although perhaps an irritant, is not allergenic.

The most important constituent of house dust is the dust mite which, in spite of its lowly status, goes by the impressive name of *dermatophagoides pteronyssinus*. This tiny mite lives on a diet of shed human skin scales. Heavy populations of the mite are therefore found in bedding, particularly mattresses and pillows, but the mites and their excreta, which are also allergenic, are distributed widely through the dust in the average home.

The mite thrives best in humid, warm conditions and this accounts for much of the climatic influence on asthmatic incidence.

If house dust or mite sensitivity is suspected as the basis for asthma — and particularly if this can be proven by skin testing — then measures should be taken immediately to rid the home, and particularly the patient's room, of dust and mites. This is not easy. Meticulous attention to detail is required. (See *house dust.)

Other allergens commonly responsible for asthma — animal danders, feathers, and so on — are relatively easily avoided. Even if specific sensitivity isn't shown towards household pets, these are generally undesirable as they often harbour large amounts of dust in their coats.

Food allergy is rarely of significance in asthma but, as mentioned above, certain foods may act as triggering agents and if this is seen to be the case such substances should naturally be avoided. Skin-testing for various foodstuffs is of little or no value in this situation.

Prophylactic bronchodilator drugs. Both the sympathetic stimulant drugs and theophylline preparations are of value in the routine medical prophylaxis of asthma. Such drugs may be administered orally, or by inhalation. Furthermore, exercise-induced asthma is usually preventable by inhalation of a bronchodilator aerosol just prior to the exertion.

There are numerous proprietary preparations, consisting of combinations of bronchodilator drugs, often with an antihistamine to relieve accompanying allergic rhinitis. Some of these preparations, in the form of slowly absorbed tablets, are designed to give a long period of action, and these are often of considerable value, particularly at night.

All these medications should of course be taken only on your doctor's instructions and they should not be augmented by further medication of your own.

Drugs with a preventive action. (1) Disodium cromoglycate (Lomudal). This preparation interferes with the allergic response and is effective in the prevention of asthma in about 60 per cent of patients. Unfortunately, the drug is not absorbed and therefore has to be administered by inhalation. It is presented in the form of a powder in a capsule and the inhalation is performed with the aid of a special 'spinhaler', which ejects the powder from the perforated capsule only while the patient is forcibly breathing in. Even small children can be taught to use the spinhaler effectively. It is also available as an aerosol and as a solution for nebulisation.

Inhalations are usually given 4 times a day but this can often be reduced to no more than twice daily. There are no side-effects, apart from occasional mild throat irritation.

Ketotifin is an oral preparation with cell-stabilising properties. It may have a place in management of certain cases.

(2) Corticosteroids. In the past these drugs often had to be given for fairly long periods in obstinate cases of frequent or continuous asthma and they still occasionally have to be used in this way in otherwise unresponsive patients. Given orally, however, they do tend to produce undesirable side-effects and their use is therefore kept to a minimum.

Parents are rightly frightened by the prospects of long-term corticosteroid treatment but, on the other hand, they should equally be frightened by asthma. If your doctor judges it necessary to put your child on long-term prophylaxis with corticosteroid drugs it is because he judges this to be safer than continued severe asthma, and you should accept his opinion.

Beclomethasone (Becotide, Viarox) is a corticosteroid effective by inhalation and presented as a metered dosage, pressurised aerosol. The nasal preparations are highly effective in the prevention of allergic rhinitis and the pulmonary inhalers are also of great value in the prevention of asthma. The dose is so small that side-effects are not found.

Inhalations are usually given initially 4 times a day but can often be subsequently reduced to 2 or 3 times daily. Although the inhaler is designed to be held in the lips, children sometimes find difficulty in co-ordinating a deep breath with the puff of the inhaler. More effective inhalation is often accomplished by holding the inhaler near to the widely opened mouth and giving the puff as the child commences a deep breath. A 'spacer' between the aerosol and the mouth also increases the efficiency of inhalation.

Alternatively, a hole may be cut in the base of a cardboard or plastic cup and the rim then placed over the child's nose and mouth, and several puffs given. There need be no fear regarding long-continued administration of these preparations.

Hyposensitisation. Where the allergic spectrum of the patient is fairly clearly established and avoidance of the offending allergens is impossible or has proved ineffective, a course of hyposensitising injections may be indicated. Effectivity, however, is only about 40 per cent. As a rule, such treatment is not administered to children under the age of 5 or 6 years, but there are exceptions.

Dust and dust mite antigens are the commonest components of such vaccines, which should not contain a multiplicity of products. You must, of course, be guided by your doctor as to the advisability of attempted hyposensitisation.

Occasionally, severe reactions may occur and after each injection your child should remain at the doctor's surgery for about 30 minutes in case treatment for such a reaction becomes necessary.

The actual mechanism of hyposensitisation is not entirely clear. It probably depends on the stimulation of production of a type of antibody (IgG) different from the reagin responsible for the allergic response. Such antibodies react with and neutralise the antigen before it has a chance to react with the reagin to cause liberation of histamine and other active principles.

Before closing this section on the treatment of asthma, it is worth repeating that in cases where asthmatic attacks are very frequent or continuous, their prevention by means of continuous medication becomes imperative and long-term adminis-tration of appropriate drugs should not cause anxiety.

ATHETOSIS

This is a condition associated with cerebral palsy in which writhing movements of the limbs, particularly the hands and arms, lead to severe disability in manipula-tion. Athetosis is less commonly seen nowadays, as one of the commonest causes in the past was severe jaundice in the neonatal period and this is now controlled. Athetoid movements are not seen during the first year of life; they disappear during sleep and are increased by any voluntary attempts at fine movement. They are often associated with a degree of spasticity. Children with athetoid cerebral palsy are often of normal intelligence but they may have associated impairment of hearing. (See *cerebral palsy.)

ATHLETE'S FOOT

This is due to a fungal infection of the skin and is therefore almost confined to those who wear shoes which cause the retention of excessive moisture. Fungi thrive only in a hot, humid environment. The condition is easily recognised by the typical pale, soggy skin between the toes, often associated with painful cracking and sometimes associated with tense, itchy blisters on the soles. The condition is fairly readily cured by application of suitable fungicidal remedies, of which many are available in the form of lotions, ointments or powders. The condition is, however, very likely to recur, particularly in hot weather, and in such a case substituting sandals for shoes or, even better, going barefoot may provide the only satisfactory answer.

AUTISM

This is a rare condition, poorly understood, in which the young child appears to retreat from contact with the world in general and people in particular into a confined world of her own. Communication is extremely difficult and the child seeks safety in her world of meaningless and maddening repetition. There is confusion and disagreement regarding the handling of autistic children but attempts must be made to penetrate any chink in the wall they build about themselves. With a patient and loving approach many can be helped to break down the barriers. The outlook in each case, however, is very uncertain.

BABY BOUNCER

This gimmicky piece of apparatus may provide amusement for a child from about 7 months of age but it is not to be regarded as an essential element in the modern home. It is not injurious to the normal baby but neither does it provide any developmental advantage.

BABY WALKERS

These enable a child to get around in the upright position appreciably earlier than he could without their aid. They therefore expand his world and make life more interesting. On the other hand they are by no means free from danger, particularly if the child has access to stairs. If your child is in a walker, therefore, always make sure that he is in a safe area. Walkers do not produce deformities of the limbs or back.

BALDNESS

Bald patches in children may be due to several causes:

Alopecia areata. One or more, more-or-less circular bald areas may appear fairly suddenly, the scalp skin being clean and shiny with no evidence of irritation. Occasionally the whole scalp may be involved. The cause is unknown. We are all losing hairs at a rate of about 100 a day and it would appear that in these bald areas all the hair follicles get into step and the hairs are shed at the same time. The condition is almost always self-limiting, the new hair often being rather fair but gradually assuming the normal colour. Treatment is usually unnecessary but injection of steroids into the scalp does appear to have a beneficial effect. Minoxidil, a blood-pressure-reducing drug, has hirsutism as a side-effect and has been used topically with success.

Trichotillomania. Children often pull their hair to some extent, but this may reach pathological proportions and bald areas are produced as a result. Sometimes the hair is eaten and then it may form an obstructing mat in the stomach. If simple admonishment does not cure the habit, psychological help may be necessary.

Ringworm. This is a fungus infection of the scalp, distinguishable from alopecia areata by the obvious inflammation of the skin and the presence of broken hairs. (See *ringworm.)

BATHING

Far too much is made of baby-bathing, as though it were a ritual fraught with danger and difficulty. The majority of babies in the world never see a bath and they survive thoroughly well, because the skin has a remarkable ability to care for itself. On the other hand, in a modern society it would be almost inconceivable not to bath one's baby daily. Let it then be fun.

A few tips might be helpful. If possible, have a working top with everything prepared before the baby is put in the bath, a towel to put him on and dry him with afterwards, and clothes to dress him with before he chills. The bath should be a safe one and the water pleasantly warm (about 30°C). Traditionally, the temperature is tested with the elbow but a hand is just as informative. Hold the baby firmly while lifting him in and out of the bath, supporting the top end with a hand holding his shoulder and the wrist supporting the head and neck and hold his ankles with the other hand, the index finger being placed between the legs. The face is best washed with water, using cotton-wool swabs or a cloth, and this is most conveniently done on the working top rather than in the bath. The head should be rinsed each bath time and shampooed two or three times a week. Pay particular attention to the fontanelle or 'soft spot', which some mothers are afraid to handle and which as a result accumulates a lot of scale which simply has to be removed mechanically. Baby shampoos which are non-irritating to the eyes are an advantage. In cases of scalp disease, special shampoos may be necessary. Soaping of the rest of the body is often easier performed on the working top and the soap then washed off. Trying to soap the baby in the bath is often an impossible task. Pay special attention to the creases, such as the neck, under the arms and the groins, where skin debris tends to accumulate and cause irritation. These areas must be well dried after the bath by using a dabbing rather than a rubbing motion. The navel, if still raw, may be simply dabbed dry or it may be dried with a cotton-wool swab soaked in surgical spirit. If you use a baby powder do so sparingly and do not sprinkle it near the baby's face. Refrain from sticking cotton-wool buds into the baby's various orifices. It suffices to wipe away anything you can see. Ear wax will come out naturally if given the opportunity and pushing cleaning utensils into the ear simply packs the wax against the eardrum, possibly causing damage and certainly making it impossible for the doctor to see the ear when it might be important for him to do so. The nose, likewise, should simply be wiped clear, as the delicate lining membranes are likely to be damaged by any attempt at probing. Nails are more easily cut while the baby is asleep.

At first the baby is rather scared of being bathed but rapidly comes to enjoy it. At this stage he should be allowed to splash and play, but always remember that the bath is a dangerous place and never, never leave the baby unattended.

BATTERING

Battered babies are nothing new, but increased publicity has been given to this problem since its more widespread recognition. It may occur in all classes of society but is more common among the poor and unprivileged where overcrowding, alcoholism and general roughness make life more difficult. Injuries may be inflicted by mother, father or both. Other forms of child abuse short of actual physical damage are also extremely common. The child may be presented as having injured himself by a fall or other accident but the multiplicity of injuries, particularly bony injuries with evidence of their having occurred at different times, makes non-accidental injury a fair certainty.

In dealing with this problem, medical, social and legal authorities attempt to take a non-punitive approach, doing their best to help the parents in their state of inadequacy. There must indeed be few parents who have not got near to inflicting injury on their child as the result of desperation and exhaustion. In the case of battering parents, the normal controls have gone. They often basically care for their children and bitterly regret their misdeeds. The child, of course, has to be protected but, given reasonable parental improvement, he is then better back with his family than in a 'home' or place of safety. Battering parents have usually had unsatisfactory childhoods themselves, lacking normal parental affection, and these traits may be perpetuated for generations. If you ever feel close to battering you child (1) go away from him for a time to cool off and (2) discuss the problem openly with your spouse, a friend, doctor or social agency. Don't be ashamed of your feelings — they are probably quite normal.

BCG (BACILLE CALMETTE GUÉRIN)

This is a vaccine against tuberculosis, consisting of a suspension of live, attenuated (i.e. weakened) tubercle bacilli. It is usually administered by a multiple skin-prick method and it is normal for a reaction to appear in the injection sites after about 3 weeks and persist for a couple of months. There may be some enlargement of the local lymph glands draining the vaccination area. Very, very rarely it may produce more significant reactions, particularly in children with immunological deficiencies. The protection given by the vaccine seems to vary from community to community. It is certainly highly advisable in areas where tuberculosis is a significant problem, and is therefore usually administered to babies shortly after birth and repeated in childhood. BCG vaccination is compulsory in South Africa.

BEDWETTING

The age at which control of the bladder is achieved varies considerably from child to child. Most will become dry during the day by 18 months and will achieve night dryness between 2 and 3 years of age, but at the age of 3 some 25 per cent of children are still wetting their beds and it is only if the habit persists to about 4 years that one can consider it to be a problem. Even at 4 years, about 10 per cent of children are still bedwetting. Parental attitudes vary greatly, some being extremely tolerant and doing nothing to assist their child, others, having little knowledge of what is normal, adopting a punitive attitude, which is both unjustifiable and harmful. If your child does have a bedwetting problem it is only fair to both of you to do something about it. Take him to your doctor for a physical check and remember to take a freshly voided urine specimen at the same time. Most children will have normal habits by day but some seem to have a rather small bladder capacity and it might be helpful for your doctor if you could measure the quantity of urine passed on each occasion over a 24-hour period and record the time and quantity.

Only rarely is an organic abnormality present. There are some children with, for example, misplaced ureters, who will wet all the time, others may have incontinence due to neurological defects. Most bedwetters, however, are perfectly healthy and normal and the cause of the affliction is generally unknown. The role of emotional disturbance as a cause of bedwetting has been greatly exaggerated. When this is a factor, it is usually in the case of the older child who has achieved a period of dryness, and in whom emotional trauma has caused reversion to an infantile pattern of behaviour. It must be realised that children do not wet their beds deliberately. Punishment does not help, nor do reward systems, which in fact are unfair to the child in that they reward him for activities which he is unable to control. Once improvement has been obtained, however, the keeping of a calendar is often encouraging to the child and may reinforce improvement. Do not institute such a calendar until there is reason to believe that the child will get satisfaction and enjoyment rather than simple frustration from keeping it.

Medicinal treatment is often very effective. Drugs producing bladder relaxation through the nerve supply, such as emepronium and oxybutynim, are sometimes helpful, but the most popular preparation is probably imipramine, which is effective in some 80 per cent of cases of primary enuresis. Exactly how it acts is incompletely understood. The dosage and time of administration are often all-important and it is often necessary to give a dose at bedtime, followed by a second dose when the child is lifted to empty his bladder at the parents' bedtime. If effective, the medication is usually kept up for 6 weeks or so and then stopped to see whether improvement is maintained. Repeat courses can be given if relapse occurs. Such treatment, however, must be under medical supervision.

Cases resistant to these relatively simple measures are often helped by the electric buzzer, and sometimes the combination of these two forms of treatment is more effective than either one alone. The buzzer is designed to wake the child as soon as the first few drops of urine are passed. He is then expected to get up and empty his bladder. Eventually he becomes conditioned to empty the bladder before the alarm goes off. This may, however, take several months of treatment. There are very few children who will not be helped by some form of management. Do not, therefore, accept your child's bedwetting too complacently. Remember that it is unpleasant for him, too. For the child at boarding-school it can be disastrous. Everything possible should therefore be done to resolve the problem.

BEE STINGS
See *stings

BEHAVIOUR
Every parent probably has some idea of normal children's behaviour but even when they expect the worst they are often still unpleasantly surprised! It is important to realise that behaviour is basically directed towards survival. The small child therefore is utterly self-centred. He is discovering the world and as far as he is concerned the world is his. The idea of sharing never enters his mind. For survival he is of course dependent upon his parents, and particularly his mother, who therefore becomes his most treasured possession. When he finds that he has to share her with others this may cause considerable conflict in his mind. Eventually, of course, he learns that sharing is to his advantage and he then begins to play co-operatively with other children instead of simply gathering all he can and saying 'mine'.

Gradually the child will accept increasing distance from his mother in his keenness to explore his environment, but will keep requiring reassurance of her presence and protection.

Survival for the young child is of course dependent upon the protection of the home. Severe insecurity is therefore produced by anything which seems to him to threaten the home environment. Parental discord is one of the greatest of these threats. It is normal for parents to have differences, but these can be expressed in civilised terms and the child reassured that such differences are normal and are in no way a threat to his security. Children require warmth and affection and some parents, particularly those who have themselves been unloved to some extent, may have difficulty cuddling their children. Try to make a habit of expressing your love physically as well as verbally. Gradually, as the child's dependence upon his parents for security diminishes, his survival is dependent more upon his own efforts. Eventually, at adolescence, his desire for independence may bring him into increasing conflict with his protective home environment. This is a demanding time for parents, requiring great patience and tolerance, but the rewards when their child eventually reaches adulthood are proportionately great. (See also *emotional development.)

Behavioural disturbances. These are dealt with under individual items, e.g. *thumb-sucking, *tantrums, *masturbation.

Behavioural modification. Much parental activity is directed towards modifying the behaviour of their children and making it more socially acceptable. The self-centred pursuits of the young child cannot be allowed free rein and parental sanity demands that some restraints be imposed. There was a time when psychologists were advocating that children be given unlimited opportunity for self-expression. The disastrous results soon led to their backpedalling on this matter. Children will accept almost any restriction provided it is basically fair, in other words provided that the parents accept the same sort of restrictions for themselves — and the limits of acceptable behaviour must remain constant. A child cannot possibly learn if the rules are always changing. Behaviour modification is best achieved by encouraging the child's good behaviour and ignoring rather than punishing the bad. The child soon learns that he profits better from doing what is acceptable than from persisting with unrewarding activity. There are of course limits to unacceptable behaviour, and discipline may demand occasional punitive action. Punishment, however, should never be severe, it should always be prompt and therefore associated with the crime, and it should be brief. It should be carried out by whichever parent happens to be present at the time and not delayed until, for example, father's return home from work. (See *discipline.)

BEREAVEMENT
Children suffer from bereavement, just as adults do, although their reactions inevitably will be determined by their degree of maturity. The loss of a parent is of course an overwhelming disaster, but the loss of a sibling or friend may be a very traumatic experience for a child and may even cause symptoms which seem out of proportion to the degree of tragedy. Older children will require a period of mourning to get over their bereavement. They will be greatly helped by being able to talk about things rather than being forced to mourn silently and alone. They will require considerable comforting, but the greatest comfort will be to know that you share their loss. Bereavement may be the child's first encounter with death and may provide a good opportunity for discussion of the whole subject of death. Such

discussion should be honest and frank but of course appropriate to the child's understanding. Parents may find it awkward to discuss death with their children, just as they may find it embarrassing to discuss sex, but reluctance to discuss these topics will make the child look elsewhere for answers and lead to a progressive decline in communication between parent and child.

BILHARZIA

An estimated 3 to 4 million people in South Africa suffer from this infestation. The disease is due to a schistosome, a small fluke-like parasite which lives in the bloodstream, particularly in the small veins of the bladder and the large intestine. There are 2 main types, *Schistosoma haematobium*, which predominantly affects the bladder and usually manifests as the passage of blood in the urine, and *Schistosoma mansoni*, which predominantly affects the bowel and has few, if any, symptoms but may cause some degree of diarrhoea, and the passage of blood and mucus in the stools. In the East, a third type is known as *Schistosoma japonicum*. Other forms of schistosomiasis are common in animals and one such form, *Schistosoma mattheei*, may infest humans.

The life-cycle of the parasite demands an intermediate host in the form of a fresh-water snail. The disease is acquired by bathing in water in which such snails exist and which has been contaminated by human excreta. The eggs of the parasite are passed in the urine or stools and, soon after reaching water, rupture to release the contained miracidium, which then enters the body of a suitable snail and forms a cyst, which in turn releases numerous cercariae. These escape into the water, where they may survive for some 48 hours, and if they encounter a suitable host they penetrate the skin, enter the bloodstream and are swept to the liver where they develop into adult forms. When these have reached the egg-laying stage they migrate down the veins to the bladder and bowel.

Some hours or days after exposure to infected water there may be itching as the result of skin reaction to penetration by the cercariae. Some weeks later there may be fever and general malaise, often with urticarial rashes and enlargement of the liver. These symptoms settle and some 2 months after acquisition of the disease the specific symptom of blood in the urine or stools appears. Characteristically, the blood is more concentrated in the urine at the end of the act of micturition. Heavy infestations lead to thickening of the bladder, with loss of elasticity, and the bladder wall may calcify. Obstruction to the ureters may lead to severe kidney damage. The liver may become progressively destroyed. Bilharzia occasionally affects unusual organs such as the lungs, with secondary effects on the heart and the central nervous system, causing epilepsy or paralysis. Bilharzia may predispose to cancer.

Treatment. Several effective remedies are available. *S. haematobium* may be successfully treated with niridazole, and for *S. mansoni*, oxamniquine is effective. Both forms of bilharzia may be treated with praziquantel.

BIRTH

Next to conception, birth can be the most exciting, significant, as well as the most dangerous event in anybody's life. It is as well to remember, however, that the baby's existence began 9 months previously and that by the time of birth the most miraculous progress has been made from a single microscopic cell to a well-formed baby. Birth involves a profound change in life-style for the baby, whose cushioned, intra-uterine existence with passive nutrition and oxygenation via the placenta has to become an independent life which will continue only as the result of his own respiratory and digestive efforts.

The birth process

This occurs in 3 stages:

(1) Dilatation of the cervix. Before the onset of labour, the entrance to the womb, called the cervix, is closed and before the baby can be expelled the cervix has to dilate. This is achieved by rhythmically recurring uterine muscular activity, which stretches the lower part of the uterus and which uses the presenting part of the baby, usually the head, as a further dilating agent. Eventually the cervix becomes completely effaced and the baby's head then passes through into the vagina. The first stage of labour usually lasts several hours, but in women who have previously had babies it may occur remarkably rapidly and with no discomfort.

(2) Expulsion of the baby. With continued uterine muscular activity, the baby's head is gradually pushed down the birth canal. During this stage, uterine action is supplemented by voluntary efforts on the part of the mother, who uses her abdominal muscles to push the baby out. The hormonal influences during pregnancy have softened the tissues of the vagina and vulva so that they distend very readily. After the baby's head is born, the residual pressure on the chest and abdomen squeeze out the normal secretions from the baby's nose and mouth, so that when he breathes he does not inhale these accumulations. In Caesarean births and in breech deliveries this squeezing act does not take place and the baby is more likely to have respiratory troubles from aspiration of secretions, unless these are removed artificially by suction. When the head has been delivered, the arms are usually released by the obstetrician or midwife, and the baby's trunk and legs follow rapidly.

(3) Delivery of the placenta (afterbirth). This is usually expelled by one or two further contractions of the uterus, but its delivery is often assisted by the obstetrician or midwife.

Recent years have shown some new fashions in birth, with an increase in popularity of home delivery, deliveries in various positions, deliveries under conditions of extreme silence and subdued lighting, and even deliveries under water. Whatever circumstances you may fancy, let your baby's birth be simply the most wonderful event in your life. It is an event to be experienced if possible by both parents, and the father's part in the process need not be entirely passive. He can give great comfort and encouragement to his partner, and his presence at the delivery has been shown to have a significant bonding effect.

Birth-marks

Apart from bruises, skin blemishes present at birth or shortly after birth are called birth-marks, though they have nothing to do with the birth process. They are of several types.

(1) The simple naevus. Most white-skinned babies have pink marks at the back of the neck, on the upper eyelids or in the centre of the forehead which, though sometimes quite prominent, are of no importance whatever and which always disappear, usually within a matter of a few months.

(2) **Strawberry naevi.** These are not present at birth but appear shortly afterwards and may increase in size for several months before receding and eventually disappearing. The naevus is raised above the skin surface and it may be a bright red colour, giving rise to its name of strawberry naevus. Such birth-marks are often multiple. Occasionally they are extremely large and may then predispose to bleeding. As a rule, they begin to blanch towards the end of the first year and usually disappear by the age of 3.

(3) **The port-wine stain** may occur anywhere on the body, but is often found on the face, where it tends to be rather disfiguring. Though initially flat, it later becomes raised and more conspicuous. Such blemishes can usually be concealed effectively with the help of masking cosmetics. They do not resolve spontaneously.

(4) **Pigmented naevi.** These vary greatly in colour and size, some are flat, some raised and some hairy. They do not regress spontaneously and the more unsightly ones may have to be surgically removed. They do not become malignant in childhood but in adults any change in appearance of a pigmented mole should lead to medical evaluation.

(5) **Mongolian spots.** In darker-skinned races, bluish pigmented areas, particularly over the buttocks and back, are extremely common. They may resemble bruises but are not elevated. They are of no consequence and will eventually disappear.

Birth injuries

Considering the violence of the birth process it is perhaps surprising that birth injuries are not more common. Most significant injuries will be immediately apparent and if they are of any consequence your doctor will almost certainly discuss them with you. Even what seem to be major injuries, such as broken bones, usually heal very rapidly.

Head-moulding. Virtually all babies born vaginally have their heads squeezed into a rather elongated shape, which may appear somewhat frightening but which corrects itself very rapidly. The deformation is usually exaggerated by the presence of the *caput succedaneum*, a puffy swollen area of the scalp over the presenting part which led the way through the birth canal. This subsides within about 24 hours. Severe moulding may occasionally lead to tearing of blood-vessels inside the skull but such bleeding is not common and usually clears up without aftereffect. If there is any suggestion of brain involvement your doctor will tell you, so please do not worry unnecessarily. Later deformities of the skull may be due to posture (many babies lie with their heads on one side, causing flattening and often marked asymmetry which, however, corrects itself once the baby becomes more mobile), or inequality in head growth due to premature fusion of the skull bones. This condition may require correction and your doctor should therefore be consulted.

Bleeding. During the birth of the head, small blood-vessels under the scalp are frequently ruptured, leading to bleeding on the surface of the skull bones. This forms a soft lump which may achieve a rather alarming size. It always disappears eventually, even if it becomes ossified to some extent in the process. No treatment is required. Such haemorrhages may increase the tendency for jaundice to develop.

As a result of congestion during the birth process, haemorrhages into the eyes may occur. These appear alarming but are of no consequence and they will disappear spontaneously. They may be accompanied by tiny haemorrhages into the skin.

Bleeding may occur from the cord if this is inadequately clamped or tied, and such haemorrhages occasionally are so profuse as to necessitate a blood transfusion. Slight bleeding after the cord separates is common and need cause no alarm.

Injuries to bones. The clavicle or collar-bone is quite often fractured, particularly when difficulty is experienced in delivering the shoulder. Such fractures may not be evident immediately and may be revealed only when a lump forms in the clavicle as the result of healing. No treatment is required as these fractures always heal satisfactorily. Occasionally other bones are broken, such as the humerus (upper-arm bone) or femur (thigh bone). Such fractures require a short period of immobilisation but always heal well.

Injuries to nerves. Nerves may be injured by pressure or by stretching. One-sided weakness of the face is not uncommon as the result of pressure on the facial nerve. The baby's mouth is distorted when he cries and he may have difficulty in closing the eye. This condition always resolves satisfactorily. The nerves to the arm may be injured as the result of traction on the shoulder, particularly in breech deliveries, resulting in Erb's palsy. The arm and hand hang close to the side, the elbow cannot be bent and there is weakness of the hand. This condition almost always clears up completely.

Brain injury. This is the most dreaded result of birth trauma and it may arise from several situations, such as direct trauma, interference with the oxygen supply, pressure due to swelling of the brain or bleeding inside the head. The premature baby whose skull bones are soft and who is liable to respiratory problems is at greater risk than the full-term baby. Recent evidence obtained by scanning shows that bleeding is relatively common and surprisingly rarely leaves any after-effect. The baby's brain is much more resistant to insult than is the adult brain. Do not therefore worry unnecessarily. Your doctor will tell you if there is need for real anxiety.

BITES

See *dog bites, *insects, *scorpion stings, *snakebite, *spider bites, etc.

BLACKHEADS

These are the solidified secretions of the sebaceous (oily) glands of the skin, which are stimulated to secrete rather excessively at puberty. The pigment is not dirt and washing will neither prevent nor get rid of blackheads. These should be very gently expressed so as to unblock the glands, which otherwise become irritated and lead to *acne.

BLADDER

This is a muscular reservoir that holds the urine, which is being produced perpetually by the kidneys from where it trickles down the ureters. It empties via the urethra to the exterior. Bladder control is achieved usually by day at 15 to 18 months and by night by 2 to 3 years, but there is wide variation. Girls, as in most things, are rather quicker than boys. Bladder capacity varies and when this is small the child may have to pass urine frequently during the day and may wet his bed to a later age. (See *bedwetting.) Training the bladder to hold more by postponing urination as long as possible during the day sometimes helps. Increased frequency of urination is also usual when the bladder is irritated, for example by infection. (See *urinary infections.) Bladder function may be severely impaired in bilharzia.

BLEEDING

When blood-vessels are ruptured there is inevitably some leakage of blood, which may be external with blood loss, or internal, in which case the blood is reabsorbed and the iron reused. Excessive bleeding is prevented by contraction of the vessel walls and by clotting of the blood, producing a plug. Abnormal bleeding may therefore result from abnormality of the vessels, as in scurvy, or from some impairment of the clotting mechanism. This clotting mechanism is a very complex process initiated by tissue injury, which causes a cascade of chemical changes involving at least 12 coagulation factors, resulting in the production of fibrin filaments; these form a mesh which entraps the blood cells, producing the clot. As the fibrin threads contract, the blood cells are squeezed out and the clot becomes smaller, until eventually it is absorbed.

External bleeding is readily obvious and can usually be controlled by pressure over the injury or, in very severe cases, by pressure over the artery supplying the bleeding area. Nose-bleeds are usually controllable by simple pressure over the bleeding nostril, maintained for 10 to 20 minutes. If blood loss is severe, the patient becomes pale and shocked, and is then in need of urgent medical attention. Before attempting to transport a patient, however, make sure that the bleeding is under control.

Internal bleeding may be the result of trauma, such as to the liver, spleen or other organ, and, being invisible, may be deceptive. The patient may rapidly become shocked. If internal bleeding is suspected, lose no time in getting the patient to a hospital.

Abnormal bleeding may or may not be associated with trauma. Nose-bleeds are common in children and may be caused by picking the nose, although they often start spontaneously. Some of the vessels on the nasal septum are very superficial and bleed readily. In such cases, cauterisation should cure the condition. Abnormal bruising is an indication of some blood disturbance and requires appropriate investigation. It must be realised, however, that children do lead traumatic lives, and bruises, particularly on the shins, are very common. If, however, the bruising appears to be out of keeping with the degree of trauma, consult your doctor.

BLINDNESS

Blindness in babies is difficult to detect until they are able to follow reasonably well, when it may be noticed that the eyes are not focusing and tend to rove aimlessly. Certain ocular conditions causing blindness, such as cataract, may be detected by examination of the eyes at birth. Should you notice that the pupil of an eye is white or grey instead of black you must report this to your doctor immediately. Blindness may result from many causes, which include opacities, such as cataract, within the eye, preventing light falling on the retina; diseases of the retina or of the nerves leading from the eye to the brain; interference with the visual tracts within the brain itself; and disturbances of the part of the brain which interprets the visual signals, i.e. the visual cortex, which is situated right at the back of the brain. The elucidation of visual difficulties therefore may be very complex. If you suspect at any stage that your child is not seeing properly, take him to your doctor to be checked. It is better to worry him unnecessarily than to miss an important condition.

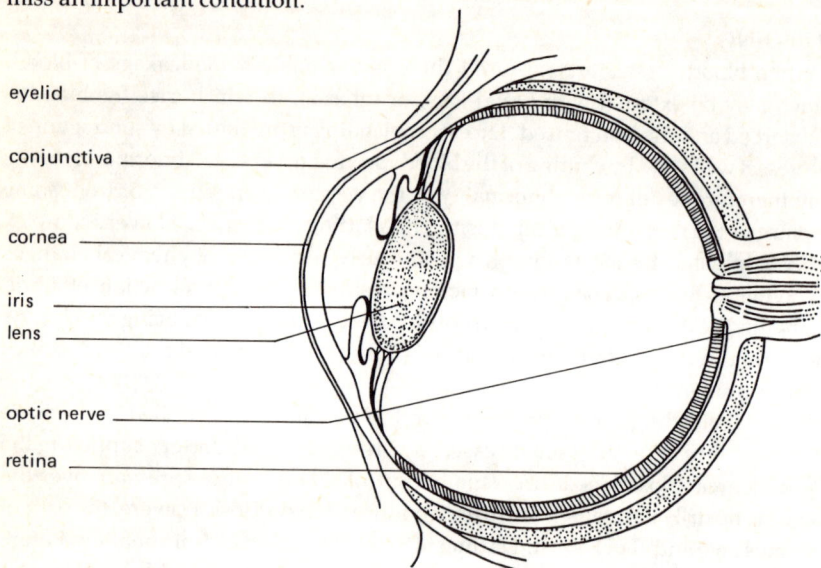

eyelid
conjunctiva
cornea
iris
lens
optic nerve
retina

Colour blindness. This is almost confined to boys, of whom it afflicts some 8 per cent. It is due to the failure of development of some of the cones in the retina, which distinguish the various wavelengths of light that we interpret as colours. Persons with only 2 types of cone instead of 3 will have difficulty in distinguishing between red and green, and their vision will be akin to what you see on a television screen when one of the colours fails. The condition is not usually recognised until the child is at school, when his colour difficulty usually becomes apparent. The greatest handicap associated with the condition is in interpreting traffic signals.

BLISTER BEETLE

This beetle, also known as the CMR beetle (because its colours are those of the Cape Mounted Rifles Regiment), causes rather severe skin irritation on direct contact. Small children touching the beetle may spread the poison elsewhere, particularly to the lips. The blisters may persist for several days but there is no systemic reaction. Soothing applications such as calamine lotion may be applied but they do nothing to alter the course of the reaction. The poison is similar to that of the cantharides beetle or Spanish fly.

BLOOD

Blood is the organ of distribution in the body and it performs many vital functions. The dramatic red colour is due to the presence in the red blood-cells of the iron-containing pigment, haemoglobin, which is responsible for oxygen transport. There are 4 to 5 million red blood-cells in each cubic millimetre of blood. The average adult has a blood volume of about 5 litres, giving a total red-cell count of 20 to 25 billion. In children, the blood volume averages about 80 ml per kilogram body weight. Blood-cells are not static objects, for they are continuously being destroyed and replaced. The average red cell lasts for 120 days, while white cells survive only a few days, as do the platelets. All these elements are suspended in the plasma, which contains, amongst other things, protein, salts and glucose, and which supplies nutrient substances to the whole body; it also carries waste-products from the various tissues to the organs of excretion, such as the kidneys, liver and lungs. Because there is continuous interchange between the tissues and the blood, the latter is a very useful reflection of the state of the whole body. Blood-samples are therefore frequently taken for analysis and yield extremely valuable information, not only about the state of the blood but about other tissues as well.

The white cells (leucocytes) of the blood are of several types. Some contain chemical granules which are readily recognisable on staining and these are referred to as granulocytes, of which there are 3 different types. The cells free of granules may be large (monocytes) or small (lymphocytes). All the white cells are concerned with body defence. They are not only present in the blood but also migrate to and from the tissues. The white-cell count is generally a useful indicator in infections. The so-called polymorphonuclear granulocytes are usually increased in septic infection, whereas virus infections produce no such response. In allergic states and invasion by the larger parasites, a special type of granulocyte, which takes up red stains and is therefore called an eosinophil, increases in number. In glandular fever there is an excess of large and rather modified lymphocytes.

The blood platelets are concerned with clotting and arrest of haemorrhage. (See *bleeding.) They are tiny fragments of large cells present in the bone marrow, where all the blood cells are manufactured.

The blood, being a complex organ, is liable to many disorders. These will be found listed under the respective conditions, e.g. *anaemia, *bleeding, *jaundice, *leukaemia.

BLUENESS

When the haemoglobin (the red oxygen-carrying pigment in the blood) gives up its oxygen, it loses its bright-red colour and becomes relatively blue. Blueness or cyanosis therefore implies an excess of de-oxygenated haemoglobin in the blood. Blueness can of course be due to other factors, such as pigment, the normal skin pigments being responsible for the blue mongolian spots seen in dark-skinned babies, and the blueness of bruising, which is due to extravasated blood. When blueness is localised, for example to the extremities, it implies stagnation of the circulation in these areas. This may be due to cold, venous congestion or arterial obstruction (which will also produce pallor). When blueness is generalised it means that there is a considerable increase of de-oxygenated haemoglobin in the whole blood. This may be due to inadequate oxygenation in the lungs or it may result from admixture of blue venous blood with the arterial blood, as occurs in congenital heart abnormalities. Very occasionally, generalised blueness may be due to chemical effects on the blood itself, as in methaemoglobinaemia, which may be congenital or may result from poisoning by, for example, nitrites and aniline dyes. Aniline dyes, used in marking inks, have caused epidemics of methaemoglobinaemia, leading to cyanosis, in nurseries when napkins have not been washed after marking.

BOILS

A boil is the result of infection of a hair follicle by a staphylococcal germ. The infection comes from the skin and not via the blood, as is commonly thought. Boils occur in thoroughly healthy people and are not a manifestation of a rundown state. Often several members of a family will have recurring boils because they have acquired the same staphylococcal germ. It must be realised that most people harbour staphylococci on their skins, in their throats and very commonly in the nose. There are, however, many different types of staphylococci, some more vicious than others.

Treatment of boils. Once a boil has formed, very little can be done to alter its course. If given at an early stage, appropriate antibiotics may kill off the germs and thereby slightly reduce the period of discomfort but they are in fact seldom indicated and never solve the problem of recurrent boils. What you put on the boil does not seem to matter much. It is wise to cover it with a plaster, which protects it from abrasion and injury and absorbs the pus when the boil discharges, thus preventing contamination of the surrounding skin. Beyond this nothing is indicated. Squeezing boils may well lead to the infection spreading. Boils on the face should never be squeezed. Elsewhere, once the boil has ripened, evacuation of the pus may be assisted by gentle pressure away from the boil. Once the core has been expelled the boil heals rapidly.

Recurrent boils. Because the infection enters from outside, the only way to prevent boils is by protecting the skin. Various bactericidal soaps are advocated but they are generally disappointing. The only remedy which is really effective is the use of a 3 per cent hexochloraphene detergent cream, which should be continued for at least a month after the last boil.

BONDING

The creation of emotional ties between parent and child is a continuous process which begins even before birth. The bonding begins from the time the pregnancy is confirmed and is strongly reinforced when the mother begins to feel the baby moving inside her. Strong bonds are formed immediately after birth, and obstetricians are now aware of the need for a mother to see and feel her baby immediately after it is born. Most babies open their eyes very soon after birth, and eye-to-eye contact with the parents at this stage is important. Although the baby's vision is initially a little vague, and he has difficulty in focusing and following, he will nevertheless fix quite intently on a face from birth. Further contact with the baby, and especially breastfeeding, leads to the establishment of further strong bonds, increased by the baby's dependence upon parental care. Mothers who are separated from their babies in the early stages because of prematurity or illness in one or the other, lack this early bonding, and although later contact will compensate to a great extent, there is a higher incidence of problems in such families. If, therefore, for some reason you have to be separated from your newborn baby make sure that contact is re-established as soon as possible and that you and your baby can see and feel each other as much as possible. Although the original work on bonding stressed the importance of early contact at birth, this has not subsequently been confirmed. If you missed out on this early contact, do not feel deprived. It is by no means essential to satisfactory continued bonding.

BONES

Because of their hardness and durability one tends to regard bones as something rather inert. In fact, like nearly all body tissues they are highly active, being continuously destroyed and rebuilt. There is therefore a regular turnover of calcium, phosphorus and other salts between the bones and the blood. Bones therefore are living structures, not fossils.

Fractures. Children, leading the active lives they do, break bones fairly frequently. These almost always heal very satisfactorily with a short period of immobilisation. Because the bones are more springy than those of adults the fracture of a long bone is often incomplete, giving rise to the so-called greenstick fracture in which there is no significant displacement of the bone-ends and for which very little treatment is therefore necessary.

Compound fractures, in which the fracture communicates with the surface through a breach in the skin, are extremely serious injuries and require immediate hospitalisation. No forceful attempts should be made to realign the bones as the risk of infection may thereby be increased, but the limb should be splinted to reduce pain and the open wound covered with a sterile dressing.

Abnormal bone growth. There are many abnormalities of bone growth, producing dwarfism or deformities. Some abnormalities of bone-formation result in brittle bones — a severe form of this is characterised by fractures before birth, which give rise to severe deformities of the limbs; a less severe form appears rather later when the child begins to lead a more traumatic existence. There is no treatment for this condition apart from management of the fractures, but fortunately the bones do tend to become stronger with the advent of puberty.

BOREDOM

This is one of the cardinal sins! When one considers the exciting world we live in and the short span of three score years and ten in which we have to explore it, no one should ever be bored. Children left to their own devices very seldom are, but we inflict boredom upon them by imposing ridiculous restraints. Go into an African homestead and you will never find a bored child. From the earliest age, a baby is strapped to his mother's back, where he gets a good view of the world about him as well as the comfort of her close presence. As a toddler he has almost unlimited liberty and a little later he has duties which occupy much of his day. Babies who are brought up in pampered surroundings, however, are often bored and this is a common cause of excessive crying. Small children, with their short attention spans, get bored because they are hindered in their explorations and older children are bored largely because adults set such a bad example. However mundane life may appear to be, it need never be boring, and to inflict boredom on a child is a particularly vile cruelty. Especially as, given half a chance, he could make your own life so exciting!

BOTTLES

Feeding-bottles are fairly well standardised these days, and the exact shape is of no importance. All have a single hole at one end for the teat, and you should make sure that when assembled the feeding-bottle allows air to flow into the bottle as the milk flows out, otherwise a vacuum is produced and the baby may suck laboriously for little reward.

The main choice in bottles lies between glass and plastic. Glass is easier to clean but is of course fragile. The softer plastic bottles are much more difficult to clean satisfactorily and often become thoroughly unsightly. The more expensive hard plastic bottles are a good compromise. Teats are more important than bottles. Single-holed teats are often rather slow and the baby may then stop feeding from exhaustion before his hunger is completely satisfied. Too large a hole on the other hand may cause choking. (See *teats.)

Bottle-feeding. When breastfeeding is impossible for one reason or another you may be quite sure that bottle-feeding will pose no great problem. During the early months it is essential to ensure sterility. (See *sterilisation.) Some feeds can be prepared in the bottle, but many milk powders do not dissolve very readily and it is as well then to do the mixing in a bowl or jug and then fill the bottles. You may find it more convenient to prepare the day's feeds at one sitting, in which case you will need 5 or 6 bottles, or you may prefer to prepare each feed individually. It doesn't matter. Filled bottles should preferably be stored in a refrigerator, as unless feeds have been subjected to terminal sterilisation there is always a chance of contamination, and bacteria in the milk will multiply rapidly at room temperature, particularly in hot climates. It is quite unnecessary to rewarm the feed before giving it to the baby. Do not therefore be hoodwinked into buying a lot of unnecessary apparatus for this purpose.

When giving a feed it is better to have the baby in a near-sitting position so that if he does accumulate air in the stomach he can bring it up when he wants to do so. It is a common habit to break the baby from his feed periodically in order to wind him. This is quite unnecessary. If the baby becomes uncomfortable with wind he will stop feeding of his own accord and he may then be winded. Many babies find it very irritating to have teats removed when they have just happily got going and some protest so much that they will refuse to feed further. (See *wind.)

How much should you give? This question should be directed at the baby. He can have as much as he wants and it is wise to have a little milk left in the bottle so that you are certain he has had enough. Those who are mathematically inclined may like to know that the average baby in the early months of life will require 150 to 180 ml of milk per kilogram of body weight per day, but appetites vary considerably and no baby should be forced to obey these rules. There are some who are satisfied and will thrive satisfactorily on considerably less and there are many gluttonous babies who will demand appreciably more. Provided the feed is suitable you cannot overfeed your baby. This is not to say that qualitative overfeeding is equally mythological. If the milk is unsuitable — too much salt or protein, for example — it is possible to give an excess of such substances. But provided the formulation is correct the total quantity of feed can be left to the baby.

If your baby leaves an appreciable amount of milk in the bottle, there is no need to throw it away, provided it can be kept in a refrigerator until the next feed. If this is not possible it is wiser to dispose of the feed after a short while, as contamination will inevitably be present.

How long should bottle-feeding continue? By 9 or 10 months it should be possible to give the baby a fairly tidy feed by cup, and thereafter the cup will play an increasingly interesting and important part in his life. It is wise to get rid of bottles by the time the baby is a year old. If permitted much beyond this age they become increasingly difficult to remove and they tend to produce tooth deformity and, if filled with sugared drinks, lead to dreadful dental decay.

There is some evidence that drinking from a bottle while lying down predisposes to ear infections. In this position, a little milk is often regurgitated into the back of the nose and may cause irritation of the openings of the Eustachian tube, which leads to the ear. It is better therefore to feed your baby in an upright position. Bottles given at night often lead to considerable sleep disturbance. When a bottle is given each time a baby stirs, an excess of fluid is consumed necessitating the passage of large volumes of urine, which in turn causes discomfort and wakefulness. Some babies may consume 5 or 6 bottles of fluid a night in this way. Only when the bottle is removed, perhaps at the cost of 1 or 2 nights of increased fretfulness which are well worth the price, does the situation improve dramatically.

BOWELS

The small bowel is the site of food digestion and absorption. The absorptive surface, which in the adult is about the size of a rugby field, is the scene of tremendous chemical activity. The highly active cells lining the bowel have to be replaced every few days. With such high levels of activity it is understandable that disturbances are likely to produce fairly severe symptoms, usually in the form of diarrhoea and abdominal pain. The large bowel, which commences at the caecum (to which the appendix is attached), is the site of considerable water absorption, reducing the voluminous fluid content of the small bowel to relatively dry, normal stools. The large bowel is populated by hordes of bacteria, which form a considerable part of the stool mass.

It is normal for a certain amount of gas to be present in the bowel; part of this is swallowed air and part is the result of fermentation processes. A wide variety of gases is therefore encountered, such as nitrogen, sulphur dioxide, methane and acetylene. These gases have to be removed, and thus it is normal for flatus to be passed, the average frequency being about 13 times a day. Children are somewhat less discreet in their habits than adults and may therefore give the impression of passing an excessive amount of wind. This is usually a misconception.

Bowel habits vary considerably. A breastfed baby may have a stool with each feed or may go for more than 10 days without having a bowel movement. The stools, however, are always soft. Later, as a greater variety of food is consumed, bowel habits are to some extent dependent upon the diet. Many Western diets are deficient in roughage and lead to constipation. For disturbances of bowel function see *constipation, *diarrhoea, *dysentery.

BRAIN

From conception through to the age of 2 years, the brain grows more rapidly than any other part of the body. This makes it particularly vulnerable to damage from various causes, such as oxygen lack, maternal alcoholism and smoking, virus infection and possibly malnutrition. Developmental progress in the infant is largely dependent upon brain maturation. There are certain well-defined areas of the brain associated with specific functions but large areas, presumably related to higher cerebral functions, are ill-understood. (See figure.)

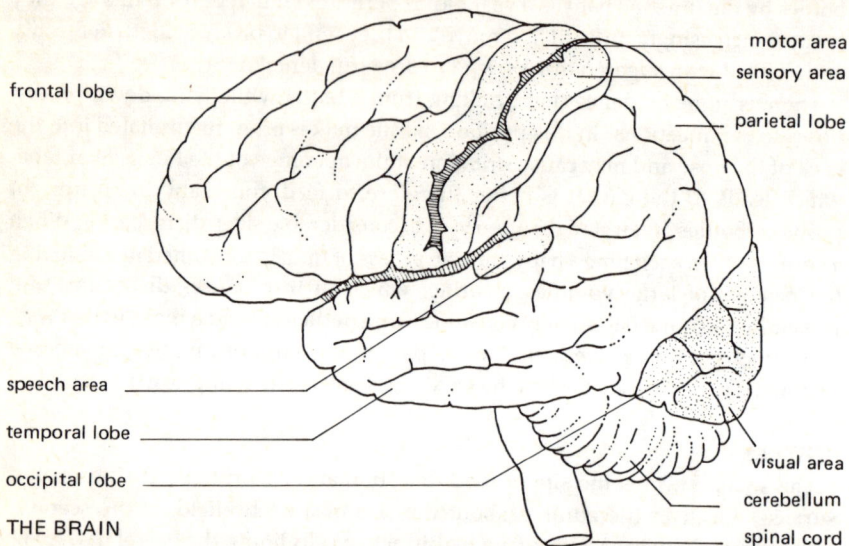

THE BRAIN

Brain-damage. This may result from a variety of influences occurring either before, during or after birth. Diffuse brain-damage results in developmental delay and impairment of intelligence. These features may be accompanied by evidence of localised brain involvement, for example locomotor dysfunction (such as spastic cerebral palsy), speech difficulties, deafness, blindness, etc.

To distinguish between brain-damage occurring before, during or after birth is often difficult and indeed may be impossible. Examples of antenatal damaging factors are: congenital malformations of the brain, irradiation, chemical poisons such as alcohol or cytotoxic drugs, severe maternal disease, placental insufficiency, and infections such as rubella and other viruses or toxoplasmosis. Brain-damage during birth may be due to direct trauma, bleeding into or around the brain, or oxygen lack. The latter not uncommonly also leads to bleeding, particularly in premature babies. Postnatal damage may be due to many factors — trauma, chemical poisons, metabolic disturbances such as low blood-sugar levels, degenerative diseases (many of which are hereditary), *meningitis, *encephalitis, *hydrocephalus (water on the brain), craniostenosis (in which the skull bones fuse prematurely), drugs, poisons, etc. Brain-damage may be associated with *cerebral palsy and/or *epilepsy.

Brain-damaged patients often reveal behavioural characteristics such as hyperactivity, poor attention span, easy distractibility, disciplinary problems, learning difficulties, temper outbursts, aggressiveness and anti-social behaviour. Many children exhibiting such traits have been labelled brain-damaged with little or no justification. Parents often welcome such a diagnosis, feeling that it exonerates them from some imagined blame. Usually such labelling does not help the child and often leads to inappropriate therapeutic measures. Some children unquestionably are brain-damaged, but beware of this diagnosis. (See *hyperactivity, *school, *epilepsy.)

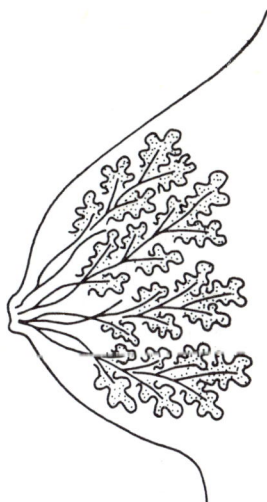

BREAST ANATOMY

BREAST

The anatomy of the breast is illustrated in the figure. Each breast has about 20 lobes of glandular tissue, each with a duct opening separately on the nipple. Before the duct opens, it dilates to form a milk reservoir lying under the areola (the pigmented part of the breast around the nipple). Breast development at puberty is induced by the female sex-hormones, oestrogen and progesterone. Lactation is stimulated by a hormone from a pituitary gland called prolactin. During suckling, stimulation of the nipple area releases another pituitary hormone, which causes contraction of the glandular tissue of the breast — which may be felt as a tingling — and this causes the draught reflex, also known as the let-down reflex, enabling the milk to flow. At the same time, this hormone (oxytocin) also stimulates the uterine muscle to contract, and these contractions may be a little uncomfortable.

Towards the end of pregnancy, the breasts begin to secrete colostrum, which differs from mature milk in having a very high protein content. For the first 2 to 3 days after birth, colostrum will continue to be secreted until the milk comes in. During this time the baby should be put to the breast regularly, for it is thought that there is some immunological gain from his having the colostrum; suckling also helps to clear the ducts as well as to protrude the nipple, which because of its confined existence is often somewhat flat. True inverted nipples are very rare.

On about the third day after delivery there is a surge in breast activity, and the breasts may be very uncomfortable as a result of engorgement. The baby may find it difficult to get hold of the nipple if the areolar region is very swollen and his attempts may result in abrasion or cracking of the nipple, which is very painful and which may predispose to infection. Getting over this stage will call for a little tolerance and patience. The breasts should be gently expressed by massaging towards the nipple, followed by compression of the areolar region, but great care must be taken not to compound the problems by bruising. Your doctor may wish to deflate the breasts using artificial oxytocin or small doses of oestrogens or prolactin inhibitors. This is such an important stage in getting breastfeeding established that any significant difficulties should be discussed with your doctor.

Once lactation is established the main stimulus to further milk production is emptying of the breasts. The baby's requirements and efforts will therefore largely govern the quantity of milk produced. There is, however, a limit, and the average mother will not produce more than about 800 ml of milk a day.

Mothers are often concerned about the appearance of their milk, which may look pale-blue and watery. This is quite normal. The fat content of the milk varies greatly. The hind-milk (the milk produced late during the feed) has a much higher fat content than the fore-milk. The amount varies to some extent from feed to feed and day to day but overall the baby gets what he needs, even from poorly nourished mothers. Do not ever imagine therefore that your 'milk has turned to water', as one so often hears. This is just not possible.

BREASTFEEDING

It is absurd that one should have to preach the virtues of such a natural thing as breastfeeding, but so-called civilisation has brought with it an unnaturalness that has severely threatened normal behaviour. The modern mother fortunately is well aware of the advantages breastfeeding brings her baby and she will discover through experience that there are advantages for herself as well. From the baby's point of view, human milk is admirably suited to his needs, whereas other milks, however modified, can never quite compare. Breast milk, being delivered at source, does not become contaminated and although it is not completely sterile, germs shared between baby and mother are usually harmless. There are several substances in mother's milk which protect the baby's bowel from infection. A breastfed baby never becomes constipated. Milk allergy is practically unknown in breastfed babies, although there is some evidence that foreign proteins ingested by the mother may appear in her milk in very low concentration. The cost of breastfeeding is negligible and represents a considerable saving compared with the cost of feeding a baby artificially. From the mother's point of view, breastfeeding is a satisfying and rewarding experience. The breasts are sensual organs and their purposeful use should be decidedly pleasurable. There are some unfortunate women who have a distaste for breastfeeding and they are to be pitied, for they miss out on one of the great pleasures in life. The naked contact between baby and mother also provides a powerful bonding influence. There is therefore every reason for a mother to breastfeed her baby. Some are discouraged by the fear that this may spoil the shape of the breasts. This is not the case. Pregnancy is associated with breast enlargement and when this recedes there may be a degree of residual slackness which is not increased by breastfeeding. Sometimes, indeed, the reverse seems to be true. An added advantage is that mothers who breastfeed tend to lose the excess weight gained in pregnancy faster than women who do not breastfeed. Adequate support for the heavier breast is desirable both during pregnancy and during lactation.

The act of suckling involves a double action on the part of the baby. When feeding, the baby will take not only the nipple but most of the areolar region into his mouth, so that the milk sinusoids lie between his jaws. These sinusoids are rhythmically compressed by his jaw movements, alternating with powerful sucking, which draws the milk from the nipple. The flow is aided by the maternal draught reflex. The average baby will practically empty a breast in 5 minutes and certainly in 10. Milk is, however, continuously being produced so that further efforts may bring him some small reward. If, however, the baby is not satisfied after 20 minutes of feeding it is unlikely that the mother's lactation is adequate.

Technique of breastfeeding

The less sophisticated mother feeds her baby anywhere and anytime and there is rarely any problem. The Westernised woman unfortunately often feels embarrassed about exposing herself, and breastfeeding then becomes a less spontaneous and more secretive exercise. Whatever your attitudes, you should feel comfortable while breastfeeding your baby, for discomfort, physical or emotional, is likely to impede lactation and inhibit the let-down reflex. The baby is held to the breast in a comfortable position so that he has access to the nipple. There is no need to thrust the nipple into his mouth. He will find it perfectly well, provided he is interested in feeding. Unfortunately, in hospital babies are expected to feed at regular times and often they are simply not ready. Well-meaning nurses then try to force the nipple into his mouth and to wake him up by flicking his feet or inflicting other minor irritations on him, usually to no avail. The baby is then accused of being uncooperative, mother is accused of being incompetent, and in an atmosphere of anger and frustration baby is eventually removed. Some time later he will probably awake and want a feed but as it is not feeding time he will be left to cry until he eventually settles from exhaustion. It is now, however, that the next feed is 'due' and the whole process starts again. After a couple of days of this sort of performance, mother usually feels thoroughly depressed by the whole business and is ready to give up. In this she is sometimes encouraged by nurses and doctors, who should know better. If you encounter difficulties such as these in the first few days, please be patient. Try feeding the baby strictly on demand with no extras and accept the fact that sometimes lactation takes many days to become established, that during this time it is normal for the baby to lose weight and that you may have to put up with a certain amount of breast discomfort from engorgement, but given the right attitudes there is absolutely no reason why you should not satisfactorily breastfeed your baby.

How long should the baby be allowed to suckle? There should be no strict rules, but a baby sucking well will probably empty a breast in 5 to 10 minutes. Suckling beyond 15 minutes is likely to cause nipple troubles. Most babies, however, having emptied one breast will indicate that they are no longer being rewarded for their efforts, by letting go of the nipple. They should then be put to the other breast and allowed to take what they want from that. The breasts should be alternated each feed so that one breast is emptied completely. If the supply of milk is profuse, the baby may be satisfied by feeding at one breast alone. In such a case, it is wise to express the other breast so that engorgement does not occur. If there is a breast-milk bank in your area you may wish to contribute to this and your efforts will then be greatly appreciated. Eventually the milk supply adjusts to the baby's needs.

Weak or premature babies may tire before they have taken in enough for their needs. This will be indicated by unsatisfactory weight gain. If there is a problem of this nature your doctor will almost certainly be supervising matters and will advise you appropriately.

How often should baby be put to the breast? There is no doubt that things go much more smoothly if the baby is allowed to demand-feed, at least in the early weeks. Unless there are specific problems, most babies will have settled into a fairly regular routine by 4 weeks of age, usually feeding more or less 4-hourly. This does not mean, however, that every baby should be subjected to a 4-hourly routine. Babies vary considerably, not only in size but also in appetite, and some will demand much more than others. Once lactation is fully established it should not be necessary to feed baby at shorter intervals than about 2½ hours and if baby is demanding more frequently it suggests that the milk supply is probably inadequate. Infrequent feeding sometimes causes concern to mothers but if baby is prepared to go appreciably longer than 4 hours, especially at night, this should be counted a blessing, provided that baby is thriving satisfactorily. Night feeds are usually demanded for the first 6 to 8 weeks but it should be left to the baby to decide when to give up his night feed. Trying to replace a night feed with glucose water, as is sometimes advised in an attempt to get the baby to abandon the night feed, is utterly misguided. The usual result is to produce an angry, hungry baby, a distraught, confused mother and a tired and frustrated father. Be natural in feeding your baby. Let him have what he asks for and ignore any well-meant but misguided advice that offends your commonsense and natural inclinations.

After the first few weeks you may try to guide your baby into feeding-times that are convenient to yourself, by waking him a little early if this suits your timetable or coaxing him to wait longer if it is inconvenient to feed him immediately, but there should be no rigidity and no unnecessary unhappiness to either of you.

How long should breastfeeding be continued? Provided both you and your baby are happily enjoying breastfeeding, this should be continued as long as you wish, and if possible until baby can be weaned from the breast onto a cup, thus avoiding bottles altogether. Most babies will take to a cup between 6 and 8 months of age, by which time they are also enjoying a considerable variety of foods. Baby will usually indicate his enjoyment of and willingness to take from the cup, and the breastfeeds are then progressively eliminated. There should, however, be no rigid insistence upon a set programme.

There are some babies who indicate their desire to wean themselves from the breast much earlier, often around the fourth or fifth month. These are enterprising babies who are keen to experience other foods, and they should be allowed to satisfy their wants. If your baby shows more interest in his solids than he does in the breast, give him as much and as great a variety of solid food as he is willing to take. Mothers often imagine that there is something magical about milk and that babies should have a set quantity per day. There is hardly anything in milk that cannot be supplied by other foods. Mothers often worry unnecessarily, too, about fluid intake. No baby will allow himself to become dehydrated or even thirsty without indicating his distress, unless he is gravely ill. Milk is about 90 per cent water, but even so-called solids contain about 80 per cent water, so if he is eating satisfactorily your baby is already ingesting a considerable amount of fluid and you may rely upon him to satisfy his fluid needs, provided you offer him an adequate quantity. (See *weaning.)

The working mother and breastfeeding

Many mothers abandon breastfeeding too readily, simply because they have to return to work. This is often unnecessary. She may, in fact, be able to take baby to work with her and breastfeed him there. Provided the distance is not too great, she may be able to nip home for breastfeeds. If this is not possible, baby at least can be put to the breast when she is at home, and even if only 2 or 3 breastfeeds are given per day, lactation usually continues satisfactorily. A determined mother will usually gain the respect of as well as suitable concessions from her employer, so do not be afraid to exhibit some enterprise. Both you and your baby are likely to gain.

Difficulties in breastfeeding

(1) Nipple problems. Occasionally, a nipple is truly inverted and cannot be coaxed into any degree of protrusion. This is very rare. Most nipples regarded as inverted are simply flat, often the result of restrictive underwear, and if given a chance they will assume perfectly normal form and function. The flat nipple should be dealt with during pregnancy by taking the pressure off, if necessary by wearing nipple shields, which encourage the nipple to protrude. Protrusion can also be encouraged by suitable manipulation, pulling the nipple out between finger and thumb. Even if at the time of birth the nipples are still flat they can usually be made to protrude to some extent and once the baby latches on this helps tremendously. If baby is unable to fix onto the nipple, the breast tends to become engorged and this compounds the problem. The baby should still be encouraged to suck and the breast gently expressed to reduce the degree of engorgement. Using a feeding nipple-shield may help to reduce the swelling and pull the nipple out. Once this has been accomplished, the baby should then be encouraged to suckle direct from the breast, as feeding via a shield is relatively inefficient.

Cracks and abrasions of the nipple are common and are often associated with the difficulties described above. If the baby cannot draw the nipple well into the mouth he tends to gnaw at it, increasing the irritation. As always, prevention is better than cure and it has been found that frequent short feeds are less damaging to the nipple than less frequent, prolonged feeds. Demand-feeding, therefore, even if it be as frequent as 2-hourly, usually helps to solve the problem. If the nipple becomes really sore owing to abrasion or cracking, breastfeeding should be temporarily abandoned and the milk expressed in order to give the nipple a chance to heal. What is applied to the nipple is of relatively little importance, provided it is not irritating and does not delay healing even further. Bland applications may be soothing but there is nothing which actually speeds the rate of healing. Usually 24 hours' rest is all that is required for re-epithelialisation.

To prevent cracked nipples, various antenatal programmes have been recommended. Too vigorous attempts at nipple-hardening probably do more harm than good and lead to brittleness of the skin. Most women would rightly object to brushing their nipples with a nailbrush! Gentle antenatal massage with an emollient cream will at least do no harm. The abandonment of unnecessarily restrictive underclothing has been a thoroughly good thing for nipples, which previously suffered too confined an existence.

(2) Breast engorgement. This has already been discussed. It is normal for the breast to be engorged to some extent and often to an uncomfortable degree during the early days of lactation. The best treatment for the condition is to continue breastfeeding, if possible on demand, as frequently as the baby will co-operate, in order to reduce the engorgement as rapidly as possible. This may be augmented if necessary by gentle expression of the breasts. To achieve this, the breasts are first massaged gently from the periphery towards the areola, and the milk which has then accumulated in the milk sinusoids is expressed by compression of the areolar region between the thumb and forefinger. This should never be allowed to become painful. If engorgement reaches such a level that manual expression becomes impossible, there might be justification for temporary partial suppression of lactation by medication. Stimulation of milk ejection by artificial pituitary-gland hormone is also sometimes helpful when the natural draught reflex is suppressed by discomfort and anxiety. Difficulties due to engorgement are almost always temporary and soluble, and never justify the abandonment of breastfeeding.

(3) Inflammation of the breasts. Infection of the breast (mastitis) is common and may arise at any time. Cracked nipples and breast engorgement are strong predisposing factors. If allowed to progress, a breast abscess will eventually form which will then require surgical drainage. It is important therefore to treat mastitis in the early stages. If you experience any localised engorgement with pain and tenderness, particularly if the overlying skin should be reddened or if the discomfort is associated with fever or shivering, your doctor should be consulted immediately. Prompt antibiotic treatment will almost certainly suppress the condition before an abscess has had time to form. If the breast does become inflamed, it is important that regular emptying continue, and usually it is safe to allow the baby to suckle. If your doctor advises against this, the breasts should be regularly expressed, if necessary with the aid of a breast pump. It is worth repeating that the main factor in achieving a satisfactory outcome is early treatment.

Neonatal mastitis

Newborn babies in the early days and weeks of life often exhibit enlargement of the breasts, from which so-called witch's milk can be expressed. This is a benign and self-limiting condition and the breasts should be left entirely alone. Any manipulation may lead to infection; this is evidenced by increased swelling, redness and tenderness, and the baby may be feverish. If you suspect that infection has supervened, consult your doctor without delay.

BREATH-HOLDING ATTACKS

These episodes, which are very alarming to parents, may be confused with convulsions, but there are very clear differences. A breath-holding attack always follows some annoyance to the child, be it physical injury (which may be extremely minor), frustration or sheer anger. The sequence of events is typical. The child takes a breath as though intending to scream, but is then unable to emit a noise or exhale and simply continues to hold his breath, becoming congested in the face, eventually turning blue and finally losing consciousness and becoming limp. At this stage the throat relaxes and the child is then able to breathe, usually initially in a series of gasps but eventually more normally. Occasionally, in the later stages of the attack the child may pass into a mild convulsive state with the eyes turning up and some stiffening of the body, before he relaxes into the typical limpness which heralds recovery. The frequency of breath-holding attacks varies considerably, some children repeating the performance several times a day. Attacks seldom begin before the age of 6 months and usually cease by the age of 3 to 4 years.

What should you do? If you are quite sure that your child is having nothing more serious than breath-holding spells, you may be completely reassured that they are harmless and that the child will always recover. It may be possible in the early stages of an attack to distract the child out of it but this is rarely successful. There should on no account be any exhibition of panic or anxiety. Physical means of distraction such as throwing cold water over the child are valueless and usually bad for the carpet. Some people advocate sticking a finger into the child's mouth and hooking his tongue forward. This may release the spasm but it is an unnecessary manoeuvre and you are quite likely to get bitten. While the child is still conscious you should make it quite clear that you are utterly unimpressed by his performance and you should ignore him totally. He should never be allowed to benefit from these episodes as this simply encourages their repetition. Although the attacks usually occur in the presence of a parent, other people who handle the child, such as grandparents or nursery-school teachers, should be instructed to exhibit the same lack of concern. A child who is presented with a consistently negative pattern of response will realise that the performances are unprofitable and they will then cease. In the case of the child having very frequent breath-holding attacks these may be diminished to some extent by sedation but in general this is undesirable and usually unnecessary.

BRONCHITIS

This is an inflammation of the bronchial tubes, which may be caused by the breathing in of physical or chemical irritants but much more commonly by infections due to viruses or bacteria. In children, viruses are a much more frequent cause of respiratory infections than are the larger bacteria, but the latter are often secondary invaders in primary virus infections.

Because the lining of the bronchial tubes becomes swollen, the lumen may be appreciably narrowed and a degree of bronchial obstruction may result. This is increased by the accumulation of inflammatory secretions. These secretions are normally removed by ciliary action. The cells lining the mucous membrane have fine hair-like projections which waft the mucus up into the larger tubes, from where it is coughed out. In bronchitis this protective action is impeded and secretions may therefore accumulate.

The symptoms of bronchitis are cough, fever and sometimes breathing difficulty with wheezing. In the infant whose bronchial tubes are very narrow, wheezing is often a prominent symptom and the condition is frequently referred to as wheezy bronchitis, or sometimes asthmatic bronchitis. In many of the viral infections and particularly commonly in measles, the whole of the respiratory tract is involved and the condition is then referred to as laryngo-tracheo-bronchitis.

Because of the wheezing which accompanies it, bronchitis in children is often confused with asthma and indeed it may be impossible to differentiate between the two until the regularly recurring nature of asthmatic attacks makes this diagnosis clear. Asthmatic attacks in children under the age of 3 are, however, very frequently mislabelled bronchitis even by experienced doctors. When 'bronchitis' recurs unacceptably frequently, either there is a predisposing cause or the condition is asthma.

Treatment of bronchitis. Because it is impossible to distinguish clinically between viral and bacteriological causes, antibiotics are usually administered. These may be combined with a bronchodilator if there appears to be some element of bronchospasm, and medications may be given which help to liquefy the obstructing secretions and aid their removal. Cough mixtures are of very little value and if secretions are present they must be removed, therefore suppression of the cough is undesirable. Physiotherapy is often administered but its efficacy is questionable.

BRUISING

A bruise is the result of the discolouration produced by blood leaking out of the blood-vessels into the tissues. It is usually due to trauma but bruising may occur spontaneously in conditions where the blood-vessels are abnormally weak and permeable or where there is some deficiency in the blood-clotting mechanism. (See *bleeding.) Spontaneous or unusually easy bruising, therefore, demands investigation.

BURNS

Burns of the skin may be produced by dry heat (including sunburn), wet heat (scalds) or other hot fluids, strong chemicals, electricity and radiation. Apart from the most superficial burns, their severity is judged more by the extent than by the depth. Burns involving 50 per cent or more of the body surface are often fatal. The depth of the burn is of course also of importance. In first-degree burns there is simply reddening of the skin without blister formation, but there may be a degree of subsequent peeling. In second-degree burns the upper layers of the skin are destroyed and blisters form as the result of exudation from the lower skin layers. The blisters eventually rupture, the dead skin is shed and healing then progresses from below with no significant resultant scarring. In third-degree burns, where the deeper layers of the skin are destroyed, healing cannot take place except by ingrowth of skin from the surrounding area (unless skin is grafted onto the denuded area) and scarring is usually severe. Before healing takes place there is continuous loss of body fluids from the raw areas and there is a constant risk of infection. Because of these severe dangers, namely shock, loss of body nutrients and infection, the management of severe burns demands a high level of medical skill.

What to do if your child is burnt. Immediate plunging of the affected part into cold water is relieving and may reduce the degree of injury. Small wounds should simply be protected with a sterile dressing. Blisters should be left intact until they rupture spontaneously, as they form a good protective cover and usually by the time the blister ruptures the underlying skin has almost healed. Deep burns, such as from hot metal objects, electric toasters or stoves, should be seen by a doctor as there may be extensive tissue injury, and scarring may lead to impaired function, particularly in areas such as the hand. The most severe burns occur when the clothes catch alight, and this is a particular danger with modern synthetic flammable materials. Should this happen, extinguish the flames by wrapping the child immediately in a sheet, blanket or almost any accessible material. If possible, dowse the child with cold water and then wrap him in a clean sheet and rush him to the nearest hospital or doctor. Do not waste time trying to remove pieces of charred material which though unsightly are sterile and therefore harmless. Do not apply anything to the burn areas as this will do no particular good and may make subsequent surgical cleaning more difficult.

Any extensive burn will be accompanied by shock, manifested by restlessness, thirst and a rapid, feeble pulse. Keep the child as calm as possible, do not warm him excessively and keep him flat rather than upright. It is wiser to administer nothing by mouth, as an anaesthetic may be required for cleaning and dressing of the burns. If, however, there is to be a long delay in reaching hospital then generous quantities of warm fluids should be offered.

Prevention of burns. It goes without saying that children should be protected from naked flames at all times and from a young age they should be made aware of the dangers of stoves, electric plugs, etc. The latter should be of the safety type so that things cannot be poked in. Pot handles should not be allowed to project temptingly over the sides of the stove. Matches and lighters should be kept well out of children's reach until they are of a responsible age. Burns should be almost entirely preventable, and yet continue to be one of the most common accidents, simply because the most elementary precautions are neglected. The occasional accident will always happen and in such a case there should be no excessive self-recrimination; but burns do occur far too frequently and must constantly be guarded against.

CAESAREAN SECTION

This method of delivery has become increasingly common, and with modern anaesthesia and technique it provides a safe solution to most obstetrical problems. If fully anaesthetised the mother of course misses the birth of her baby, and Caesarean section under epidural analgesia is therefore achieving increasing popularity. Local anaesthetic is injected into the spine and causes numbness of the lower half of the body. Although some sensation is retained, the operation is quite painless and most mothers are thrilled to witness the arrival of their child.

Cutting the uterus does cause some weakness in the uterine muscle and a limit is therefore usually placed on the number of Caesarean sections a woman may have, the precise number depending upon the state of the uterine scar.

The baby born by Caesarean section may require suctioning to clear the secretions from nose, throat and possibly stomach, as the normal squeezing action which occurs in vaginal delivery is lost. As a rule, however, the baby cries immediately and can be handed straight to the mother.

CALCIUM

This essential element is found mostly in the bones and teeth, only a very tiny proportion of body calcium being present in other tissues and the blood. There is, however, a constant turnover of calcium in the body and a minimum daily intake is required to maintain balance and to provide for growth. A baby needs about 0,5 g of calcium a day, and a rapidly growing teenager 1,5 g. Calcium is found in many foodstuffs, but particularly in milk. Although the calcium content of human milk is much lower than that of cow's milk (30 mg compared with 140 mg per 100 ml), breast-milk calcium is much better absorbed and deficiency does not occur in breastfed babies.

Calcium absorption is dependent upon adequate *vitamin D, and deficiency of this vitamin therefore leads to calcium loss, with softening of the bones and poor tooth-formation, a condition known as rickets. This is common among premature babies who have not been given supplements of vitamin D, and may also occur in older children with dietary deficiencies. (See *rickets.) The average diet contains adequate calcium, and supplements, which are popular with the public, are unnecessary for a well-nourished person. There are, however, cases of rickets in rural black children due to insufficient calcium in the diet.

CALORIES

This measure of energy has given way to the kilojoule in scientific circles, but most people are still more comfortable with calories. One calorie equals 4,2 kilojoules. Caloric needs vary from age to age and individual to individual, the average requirement in young infants being 100 to 120 calories per kilogram body weight. Premature babies require rather more. By adolescence the average calorie requirement has fallen to about 70 per kilogram body weight. The calorie content of breast milk and cow's milk is the same, namely 70 per 100 ml, and most infant formulae are similar in caloric value. Skimmed milk has a low caloric value of about 40. The caloric values of some common foodstuffs are listed below (in calories per 100g).

Cereals		Fats		liver	140
bread	250	butter	720	mutton	208
maize-meal	350	cooking-oil	880	pork	280
pasta	370	margarine	720		
rice	380	mayonnaise	720	**Nuts**	500-600
wheat	336	vegetable fat	880		
				Vegetables	
Confectionery		**Fruit**		avocado	125
cakes	300–400	apple	53	beetroot	31
honey	300	apricots	47	cabbage	28
jam	280	bananas	39	carrot	42
milk chocolate	516	dates	273	cauliflower	21
sugar	380	grapes	59	green beans	25
		mango	44	dried beans	340
		orange	35	green peas	67
Dairy products		pawpaw	26	maize	90
cheese	350–400	pineapple	27	onion	28
egg	163			potato	65
milk	67	**Fruit juices**	45-65	pumpkin	33
				spinach	23
Dried fruits		**Meats (raw)**		squash	13
dates	273	beef	197	sweetpotato	113
peaches	263	chicken	154	tomato	22
prunes	256	fish (raw)	73		
raisins	290				

CANCER

Though the term cancer really refers to a malignant growth originating in epithelial (surface) tissues, it is now used to embrace all forms of malignancy, including, for example, cancer of the blood (*leukaemia) and cancer of the connective tissues (sarcoma). In children over the age of 2 years, cancer is the second most common cause of death in Western societies, the commonest being accidents. Modern cancer treatment offers a real hope of cure in a high proportion of cases; for example, a 60 per cent cure rate in the common type of childhood leukaemia.

CAR SAFETY

It is impossible to protect your children totally from all accidents, but certain precautions will appreciably reduce the danger to them. Small children should be strapped in high-quality safety-chairs, anchored to the car. The adult seat-belt is of no protective value to a small child. A toddler should never be allowed to sit beside you on the front seat or in your lap. Should you have an accident it would be quite impossible for you to restrain her and she would almost certainly fly through the windscreen. Furthermore, in this position she may fiddle with the controls and also prove a real menace by distracting you from your driving. Get her used from the beginning to sitting in her safety-chair. Older children should have appropriate safety-belts and should be well-disciplined in their use. On long journeys see that they have something to do so they do not become bored, restless and a distracting influence on the driver.

Car-door locks should be of the safety type so that they are not inadvertently opened. Always watch out for small hands when closing car doors. Finger injuries are common and extremely painful, though usually not damaging.

CAR-SICKNESS

We do not know why some people are afflicted with motion sickness and others appear to be immune. If your child regularly becomes car-sick on a journey, consult your doctor, who will almost certainly be able to help by recommending an appropriate antiemetic medicine.

CARBOHYDRATE

A major class of foodstuff, consisting of carbon, hydrogen and oxygen, and providing the main source of energy in the average diet. Starch and sugar are the chief entities. Carbohydrate foods are relatively cheap and therefore constitute the major items in the diet of the poor and the ignorant, often resulting in severe malnutrition.

CARIES

This is the commonest disease of Western man, and seems unquestionably to be related to diet, and in particular to the overconsumption of refined sugars and starches, which promote the proliferation of acid-producing micro-organisms in the dental plaque. The fine starches adhere to the teeth, and although sugars should be rapidly removed by the saliva, the eating of sweets, particularly of the sort that adhere to the teeth, and the sucking at endless bottles of sugared fluids, provide ideal conditions for the caries-producing germs.

Some teeth are more resistant to caries than others. The poorly calcified teeth of many premature babies decay rapidly. Teeth which have been injured by tetracycline drugs also have poor resistance. On the other hand, resistance to caries can be enhanced by *fluoride.

Caries can be discouraged by regular cleaning of the teeth, particularly meticulous removal of food debris between the teeth by the use of wooden probes and dental floss. Brushing is valuable, but nylon bristles can be damaging and they should therefore be soft, and brushing movements confined to a vertical up-and-down motion.

It is a sad observation that the teeth of the indigenous black population, which used to be almost completely free of caries, have deteriorated so badly with the acquisition of Western dietary habits, particularly with the consumption of commercially milled grains and refined sugars. 'Bottle-rot' caries in small children is rife as the result of protracted bottle-feeding. Bottles should be removed by the age of 1 year.

CAROTENAEMIA

Overconsumption of yellow vegetables and fruits, such as carrots, pumpkin and occasionally oranges, may lead to an accumulation of the yellow pigment, carotene, which stains the skin. This is most marked where the skin is thick, namely the palms of the hands and soles of the feet. The eyes do not turn yellow. The condition is quite harmless and requires no treatment, but to restore normal appearances the intake of yellow foods should be restricted. The condition is easily distinguished from jaundice by the lack of involvement of the eyes and the normal colour of the urine.

CASEIN

This is a protein found in milk, particularly cow's milk — which contains 5 times as much casein as does human milk. During digestion the casein is coagulated and forms a tough curd, which is difficult to digest. Such curds may appear in the stools of a baby fed on cow's milk. They do not do any particular harm but indicate that digestion is incomplete.

CATARRH

This term is applied to inflammation of a mucous membrane and most commonly refers to the nose. A simple cold is a catarrhal state, but the term is more often used when symptoms are long standing. Chronic nasal catarrh is most commonly allergic in origin. (See *colds, *rhinitis and *allergy.) Catarrhal symptoms consist of nasal obstruction, often making it impossible for the child to blow the nose, nasal discharge — usually of a thin, clear mucus — sneezing, sniffing, itching and snoring. In babies, such symptoms may be the result of milk allergy but in older children they are usually due to inhalation of allergens such as dust and pollens. Small babies often have noisy breathing owing simply to the fact that the nasal passages are narrow, and for this situation no treatment is required.

Catarrhal symptoms confined to one nostril, and particularly when associated with an unpleasant odour and perhaps bloodstained discharge, should make one suspicious of a foreign body in the nose. Small and sometimes not so small children push all sorts of objects into their various orifices, the most popular objects being beans and bits of plastic.

Chronic nasal catarrh should not be neglected, as it is usually readily amenable to treatment. Chronic nasal blockage leads to mouth-breathing, which may predispose to throat infections and asthma. There may be an accompanying hearing loss and these children may do poorly at school until their catarrh is relieved.

CEPHALHAEMATOMA

This is a common condition in newborn babies due to bleeding between a skull bone and the overlying membrane. A lump forms which may achieve a rather alarming size. It is strictly confined to the area of the underlying bone but more than one such lump may be present. Even the largest lumps, however, eventually disappear and they require no treatment. Sometimes they become hard and ossified before being absorbed, but the bone will ultimately realign satisfactorily.

More rarely, bleeding occurs beneath the scalp and is then much more extensive, causing a puffy swelling of the whole scalp area, usually associated with 'black eyes'. The loss of blood may be considerable and such babies often have to have a blood transfusion. This condition, known as subaponeurotic cephalhaematoma, is much more common in black babies than others and this is thought to be due to subtle differences in scalp structure.

CEREALS

Ceres was the Greek goddess of wheat but she has given her name to any food derived from grassy seeds, namely barley, oats, rye, rice, maize, sorghum, etc. Such cereals form the basis of most diets because of their relative cheapness and easy cultivation. Whole cereals do contain appreciable amounts of protein, some fat and other essential food substances, but modern milling processes usually remove these valuable ingredients, leaving almost pure starch, which has little nutritive value.

Cereals are often the first non-milk foods to be offered to babies and they are usually well tolerated. The occasional child will, however, show intolerance, the most common type being sensitivity to gluten, a protein found especially in wheat — giving rise to a state of malabsorption known as *coeliac disease.

Breakfast cereals are popular because of their palatability. Many are almost pure carbohydrate and of poor nutritional value. There is some virtue in having a bran-containing cereal to increase the fibre content of the diet, which will help to combat constipation and certain other bowel troubles.

CEREBRAL PALSY

This is not an entity in itself but a group of very variable conditions, all characterised by some disorder of motor function acquired before the nervous system has achieved full maturity. The brain may be damaged antenatally, during the birth process, or later in life. (See *brain-damage.) Most cases are the result of some degree of asphyxia at birth. The damage is then usually symmetrical and fairly diffuse, the resultant effect being generalised spasticity associated with varying degrees of mental retardation. The brain-damage may, however, be more localised and symptoms may be confined to one side of the body, resulting in what is known as a hemiplegia. Paralysis may not be the dominant feature, and in such cases difficulty in coordination may be the major handicap — so-called ataxic cerebral palsy, which may sometimes be predominantly unilateral. Whereas increase of muscle tone is a marked feature in the spastic type, in the ataxic type there may, especially in the early stages, be decrease in muscle tone, or floppiness. In a minority of cases involuntary movements are a feature and these may be of several types. These 'dyskinesias' include dystonia (in which there is imbalance of muscle tone), choreiform movements resembling those of St Vitus's dance, athetoid types characterised by writhing movements, and tremors. Any of these various dysfunctions may involve one, two, three or all four limbs. The degree of mental impairment varies widely and there may be added handicaps such as visual difficulty or blindness, hearing loss, etc. The possible permutations are almost limitless and a diagnosis of 'cerebral palsy' is therefore meaningless unless qualified by a description of the specific handicaps.

The diagnosis of cerebral palsy may be difficult in the first few months of life. Such children, even those who are subsequently spastic, may initially be rather floppy. Developmental progress is usually slow and there may be feeding difficulties. Later the more specific features associated with muscular weakness become apparent. It is important that hearing loss be recognised early so that if possible it can be corrected and special training begun. Cerebral palsy can almost always be recognised by the age of 6 months although the full-blown picture may not be established until considerably later.

The management of cerebral palsy involves many facets, and a team of doctors, physiotherapists, occupational therapists, special teachers, psychologists, speech therapists and social workers is required to give the child the best opportunity and the family the maximum of support. The more affluent societies have well-established cerebral-palsy schools which provide all aspects of care but which are of course extremely expensive. At home the child should be given as much stimulation as possible, physical help in exploring his environment and in exercising his skills. Exercises prescribed by physiotherapists can be continued at home to encourage balanced movements and prevent contractures and deformities. At a later stage, surgical measures may be required to release contracted muscles or restore muscle balance, and in some cases elaborate neuro-surgical techniques may be useful in diminishing muscle spasm.

Whenever possible the child with cerebral palsy should attend a normal school but this will obviously depend upon the degree of disability present. Many of the therapies are difficult to evaluate, especially in the case of children, whose normal growth and development usually lead to spontaneous improvement. Many treatments are applied with considerably more enthusiasm than critical appraisal and the field is wide open for the charlatan and the crank. Expectations have to be realistic. Many a handicapped child, however, will compensate for one disability by high achievement in a different area, and most victims of cerebral palsy, apart from those who are severely mentally retarded, will lead happy and fulfilling lives.

CHEST

The major contents of the chest cavity are shown in the diagram. The ribs, with their attached muscles, form the framework of the chest, and the contents are separated from the abdominal cavity by the diaphragm. Anteriorly the ribs are attached to the sternum or breastbone by flexible cartilaginous extensions. Posteriorly they are hinged to the spine. Normal quiet breathing is almost entirely diaphragmatic but the chest capacity can be considerably increased by elevation of the ribs. Only inspiration requires muscular effort, expiration being effected by the elastic recoil of the lungs. Forced expiration, as, for example, in coughing is performed by contraction of the abdominal muscles.

Chest deformities. These may be congenital and associated with malformation of, for example, the spine, or they may be acquired as the result of disease of the thoracic contents. Congenital heart disease may produce a bulge in the sternal region. Obstruction to the respiratory passages requires an increased inspiratory effort and this may lead to depression of the sternum, which occasionally may reach an extreme degree and require corrective surgery. Where the bones are particularly soft, as in rickets, the ribs may collapse and the sternum may be pushed forward, leading to a pigeon-chest deformity. Difficulties in expiration lead to trapping of air within the lungs, and the chest then becomes overdistended and barrel-shaped. Any significant chest deformity should obviously be medically assessed. Parents are often worried by prominence of the little bit of cartilage at the lower end of the sternum but this is quite normal.

THE CHEST

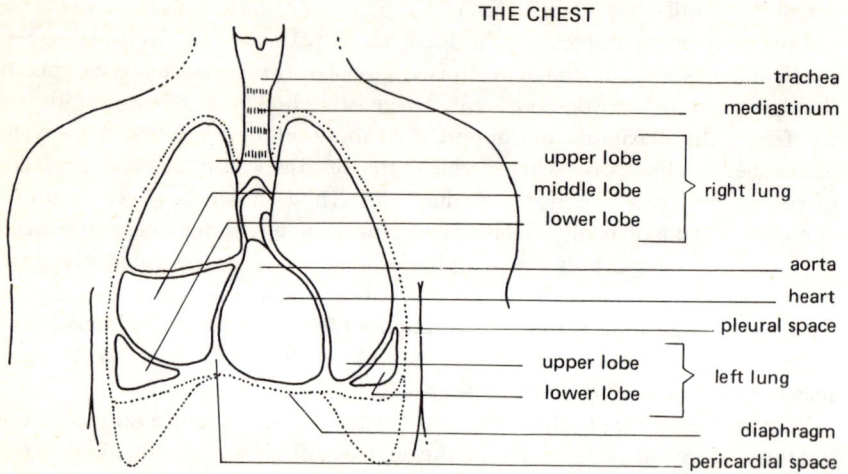

- trachea
- mediastinum
- upper lobe
- middle lobe
- lower lobe
- right lung
- aorta
- heart
- pleural space
- upper lobe
- lower lobe
- left lung
- diaphragm
- pericardial space

CHICKENPOX

This is a usually mild, easily recognisable condition caused by a virus which also causes shingles or herpes zoster. The incubation period is 11 – 21 days, usually about 2 weeks. The characteristic eruption may be preceded for 24 hours or so by mild fever and malaise, which may continue thereafter for a few days. Often, however, the spots are the first sign of the disease. They appear rapidly, initially as small red spots, which develop into thin-walled blisters which rupture easily, leaving a scab. Crops of spots erupt over several days, and one of the characteristic features of the disease is the presence of spots in various stages of development. The extent of the rash is extremely variable, from 1 or 2 spots to a profuse eruption, accompanied sometimes by fairly high fever. The spots may appear in the mouth and occasionally in the eye. They are characteristically itchy, and scratching may lead to secondary infection which may then cause residual scarring. In rare cases the disease may be complicated by meningo-encephalitis, in which unsteadiness of gait is the commonest manifestation. Recovery from meningo-encephalitis is usually complete.

Treatment. This is directed towards relieving itching and preventing scratching. The nails should be cut short and kept clean. A soothing lotion such as calamine may be dabbed on the spots and in severe cases oral medication may be prescribed to relieve the itch. Chickenpox may be severe in the child afflicted with eczema, and such children should avoid exposure to infection. The disease may be danger-ous in the child whose immunity is suppressed, such as the child under treatment for leukaemia or other malignancies, and more active treatment may be required in such cases. Such children can be protected if they are exposed to the disease by administration of specific immunoglobulin (ZIG). A viral vaccine is in the course of preparation.

CHILBLAINS
It is not known why some people develop chilblains on exposure to cold. Chilblains consist of painful, itching, red swellings on the fingers, sometimes the toes, and the ears or nose. Scratching may lead to infection. There is no specific cure for the condition, which should be prevented by avoiding unnecessary exposure to cold and by wearing gloves.

CHILD ABUSE
This may take various forms, the most widely publicised being physical violence, though subtler forms of abuse are probably more frequent. (See *battering.) Burning, for example with a lighted cigarette, often accompanies physical assault. Psychological abuse may vary, from instilling unnecessary fears to inflicting distorted beliefs, which may cripple a child's normal social adjustment or lead to religious, racial or other group intolerance. Such abuse of a child's mind is as heinous as physical injury, because attitudes tend to persist for life.

Sexual abuse of children is much more common than is generally realised. The more horrifying cases do hit the newspaper headlines but lesser degrees of abuse are widespread. Older girls are often forced into incestuous relationships and are too afraid to defend themselves.

If you have reason to believe that a child is being abused in any significant way, report the situation to your local social agency, such as Child Welfare Society, who will look into the matter discreetly and without prejudice.

CHILDBIRTH
See *birth

CHOKING
There are few more alarming experiences than sudden obstruction of the airways. When this occurs in the region of the throat or larynx it may be due to one of a number of factors — spasm of the muscles as the result of sudden irritation from, for example, irritant gases or foreign bodies; actual blockage of the airway by foreign material; swelling of the tissues as the result of inflammation or allergy; or pressure from outside, as in strangulation.

Sudden airways obstruction is of course an extreme emergency. Some of the causes may be difficult to overcome without special facilities but everyone should know what to do in the case of choking on food. This happens most often in restaurants, and the commonest cause is a tough piece of meat. Should you encounter such a situation, apply what is termed the 'Heimlich hug'. Stand behind the unfortunate victim, put your arms around his abdomen and then give a sharp and forceful heave backwards and upwards. This pushes the diaphragm up, expels the residual air in the lungs with considerable force and almost always dislodges the obstructing particle. Many a life has been saved in this way.

Incomplete obstruction may result from a foreign body lodging in the larynx or lower down in one of the bronchial tubes. Following the initial choking episode there may be repeated coughing, noisy breathing, hoarseness of the voice or breathing difficulty. Such symptoms suggest that the foreign body has been inhaled and this situation must be taken very seriously. A foreign body, particularly one of vegetable origin, lodged in a bronchus may lead to progressive lung destruction. If, therefore, you have any doubt whatever about a foreign body still being present in the respiratory tract you must consult a doctor. You must also be very insistent because there may be very few signs of trouble while considerable damage is being done. The commonest foreign bodies to be inhaled are peanuts, which should not be given to small children because of this danger, and bits of plastic from toys. Such objects do not show up on X-ray and this fact may postpone their detection.

Occasionally a foreign body such as a coin may get stuck in the oesophagus or gullet, where it may press on the trachea or create an inflammatory reaction which involves the trachea, causing respiratory symptoms. Because of the multiple causes of breathing difficulty this is a symptom which demands urgent medical evaluation. Temporary choking and gagging often occur in small children who put the most unlikely objects in their mouths during this oral phase of development. Usually the foreign matter is expelled by the child's own efforts. Occasionally some help may be required; try first to remove the foreign body with a finger. If this fails, perform the Heimlich hug. This is more effective than the traditional reaction of holding the child upside-down and thumping.

CHOLERA

This is an acute infectious diarrhoeal disease characterised by the passage of very profuse, frequent, watery stools, resulting in severe fluid loss. Essential salts are also lost in the stools and must be replaced. Without appropriate treatment the disease carries a high mortality. As the infection is confined to man and is not shared by other animals, the disease is spread only as a result of poor hygiene. Poor sanitation results in pollution of water supplies, and such contamination causes severe outbreaks of the disease. Sporadic spread may be caused by flies and contaminated food.

The incubation period varies from several hours to 3 days. The first symptom is acute diarrhoea, unassociated as a rule with abdominal pain. Vomiting may supervene and there may be muscular cramps as the result of salt loss. As dehydration progresses, the eyes become sunken, the mouth dry, the skin inelastic, the pulse rapid and thin, and the urinary output diminished. Failure to rehydrate the patient will result in progressive deterioration and death.

Treatment consists primarily in replacing the lost water and salts. This may require intravenous infusion, but oral rehydration treatment should be initiated as early as possible. A simple and suitable fluid consists of one litre of water to which is added 1 teaspoonful of common salt and 4 tablespoons of sugar (see *dehydration). Such fluid should be given frequently and in as large a volume as can be tolerated until the patient can be admitted to hospital. Further treatment consists in administration of an appropriate antibacterial agent, such as tetracycline.

Prevention of the disease consists primarily of providing hygienic water supplies. Those who are dependent upon river water should take the precaution of sterilising the water, either by boiling or by chlorination.

A vaccine is available which may give limited protection but it cannot be relied upon to prevent the disease. Vaccination is compulsory when travelling to countries where cholera is endemic but do not imagine that this will give you adequate protective cover. Hygienic measures are much more important.

CHOREA (ST VITUS'S DANCE)

The term chorea means the recurrence of jerky, involuntary movements, usually occurring in random fashion and affecting most of the body. Occasionally it may be unilateral or largely confined to one limb. It occurs in one of the less common forms of cerebral palsy and may then be combined with *athetosis. Usually, however, chorea is the result of an inflammatory reaction in the brain and is one of the rheumatic manifestations. Though rarely associated with the joint pains typical of that condition, there is fairly often involvement of the heart. (See *rheumatic fever.) In addition to the involuntary movements, which are jerky, unpredictable and may lead to severe disability, the patient with chorea also usually exhibits emotional lability and slurred speech. Before the disease is recognised, the child may well be punished for clumsiness or bad writing. Rheumatic chorea is more common in girls than boys, occurs usually between the ages of 5 and 15, and often has a tendency to relapse. The duration of the condition is unpredictable, averaging about 10 weeks but often lasting considerably longer.

Treatment. The severely afflicted child may have to be nursed in a padded cot to prevent injury. Most cases however are milder and bedrest need not be imposed unless there is accompanying acute rheumatic heart disease. Sedative drugs are often useful in reducing the severity of symptoms, and of these haloperidol is the most effective. As in cases of *rheumatic fever, patients with chorea should be kept on prophylactic treatment with penicillin for many years in order to prevent recurrences. Such a programme may initially alarm you, but such treatment is in fact extremely safe and may well prevent severe heart damage.

CHROMOSOMES

The 46 chromosomes, which are contained within the nucleus of every human cell (except the red blood-cells, from which the nucleus has been extruded) are illustrated in the figure. The 22 pairs of autosomes are arranged in 7 groups, with the sex chromosomes — XX for females or XY for males — being separate. Chemically, the chromosomes consist of DNA (deoxyribose nucleic acid), which contains the genetic code and determines our inherited characteristics. Many of these genes have now been mapped onto individual chromosomes. The X chromosome lends itself particularly readily to such mapping, as conditions determined by it (e.g. *haemophilia and *colour-blindness) will as a rule be manifested only in males and not in females, who have a compensatory normal X chromosome.

Chromosomal abnormalities are a common cause of abortion, and in viable children hundreds of chromosomal defects have now been recognised. One of the commonest of these is *Down's syndrome, which is due to an extra (trisomy) chromosome 21. Other trisomies usually produce severe defects, with the excep-

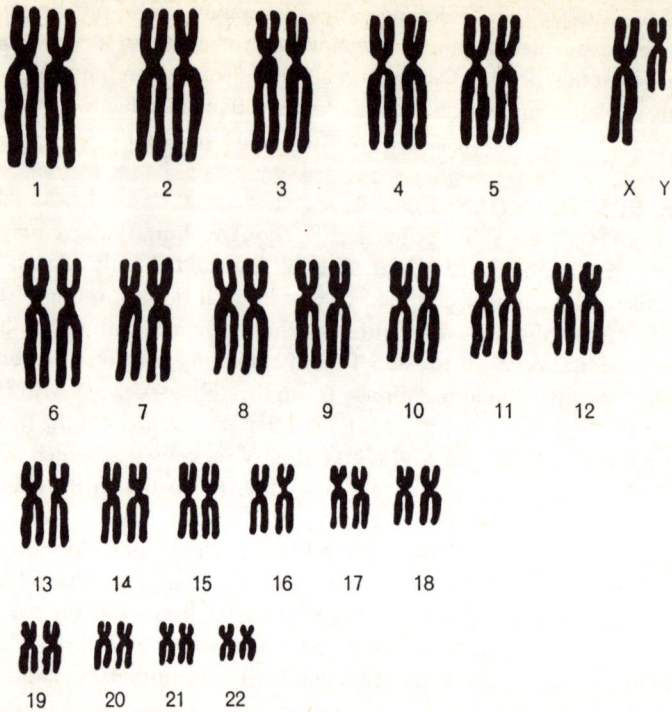

THE NORMAL HUMAN CHROMOSOMES (MALE)

tion of the sex chromosomes, where an abnormal number (aneuploidy) is compatible with relatively subtle physical abnormalities, for example *Turner's syndrome and *Klinefelter's syndrome.

Trisomy for a specific chromosome may be the result of faulty meiosis. Meiosis is the process by which the chromosomal content of the germ cells (ova and sperms) is halved, each daughter cell then normally having 23 chromosomes.

Occasionally both members of a chromosome pair, for example number 21, will pass to one daughter cell (the other receiving none and being then non-viable). When such a germ cell is fertilised, the resulting zygote will contain 3 chromosomes (i.e. trisomy) number 21. Such a process is known as non-dysjunction. The other mechanism for production of trisomies is known as translocation. Here the extra chromosome is stuck onto another normal chromosome and therefore follows it into the daughter cell. When this cell becomes fertilised there is again triplication of the genetic material of chromosome 21 (in the case of Down's syndrome). This is a much less common mechanism but important to identify, for if one of the parents has a balanced translocation the chances of producing an abnormal baby are about 1:6. (See *Down's syndrome.)

Chromosomal abnormalities can be detected by taking a sample of the *liquor amnii* antenatally, and culturing the baby's cells. This might be indicated where there is a history of previous abnormalities and it is also indicated in the prospective mother aged 36 years or more, in whom the chances of bearing a child with

Down's syndrome are appreciably increased above the random frequency of 1:600 (over the age of 40 the risk is increased 10 times).

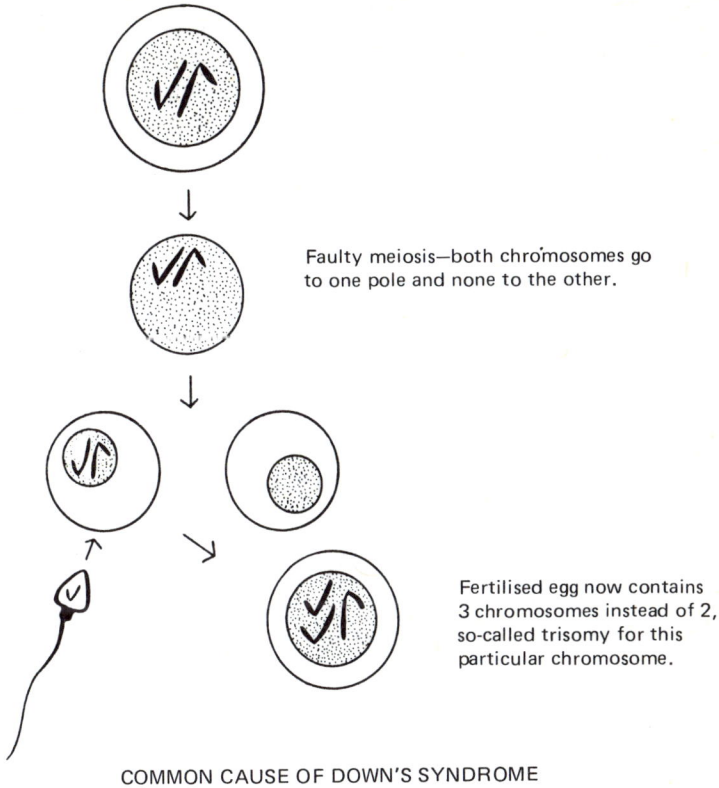

Faulty meiosis—both chromosomes go to one pole and none to the other.

Fertilised egg now contains 3 chromosomes instead of 2, so-called trisomy for this particular chromosome.

COMMON CAUSE OF DOWN'S SYNDROME

CIRCUMCISION

Ritual circumcision arose in response to hygienic necessity. Where desert conditions prevail the accumulation of desquamated skin scales (smegma) and sand leads to severe irritation, which may eventually predispose to cancerous change, not only of the penis but, it would seem, sometimes also of the cervix of cohabiting women. Under such conditions, therefore, there can be no doubt that circumcision is a most excellent operation, and if done expertly it carries very little risk. There may, however, occasionally be damage to the head of the penis, too much of the foreskin is occasionally removed, and there may be severe bleeding. Such troubles, however, should be extremely rare.

Where adequate hygienic facilities exist there is virtually no medical indication for circumcision. Unfortunately many people, including doctors, are unaware of the normal appearance of the foreskin, which is often long and narrow and quite impossible to retract sufficiently to reveal even a small portion of the underlying glans. The inner portion of the foreskin is stuck down to the glans for many years and any forceful attempt at separation will result in pain and bleeding. Forceful stretching of the foreskin at an early age may lead to scar formation and narrowing, with retractile difficulties later. If what appears to be a tight foreskin is pulled out instead of pushed back, it is usually apparent that the channel is very adequate and if the infant passes urine the resultant stream is even more convincing. Foreskins should be left alone and retracted, for washing purposes, only as far as they go with complete comfort.

The practice of ritual adolescent circumcision common among African tribes can only be utterly condemned. It is extremely painful and fraught with severe danger. Irreversible mutilation is common and infection may result in loss of the genital organs. It goes without saying that if circumcision is required it should be done with adequate surgical skill.

With so much effort directed towards its removal one may ask what function the foreskin serves. It is there to protect the underlying head of the penis, which in the uncircumcised male is covered with an extremely thin and sensitive skin. After circumcision the skin thickens and sensitivity diminishes. This does not lessen sexual drive but it does lessen sexual pleasure. Before you have your baby boy circumcised, therefore, you might ask yourself whether you have the right to deprive him in this way.

Female circumcision, in which the labia minora and clitoris are removed, is mentioned only because it still happens. There can be few more hideous and mutilating traditions. (See also *foreskin.)

CLEFT LIP AND CLEFT PALATE

These deformities occur in about 1:800 births. They are unsightly, and because of this are an initial shock to parents, who, however, can be reassured that the results of modern surgery are so good that hardly any residual deformity will persist. The clefts may be midline or lateral and may involve the lip and/or variable degrees of the palate. There is a very definite familial incidence.

Cleft lip (harelip) is usually repaired initially at 2 to 3 months of age but secondary operations may be necessary for fine adjustments. The cleft palate is sometimes treated with orthodontic occlusive apparatus, although the benefits from this are rather questionable. Surgical repair is usually undertaken between 12 and 18 months of age. There is usually some need for subsequent orthodontic attention and for speech therapy.

Feeding the baby who has a cleft lip alone, usually presents no problem, and such babies should be breastfed. A cleft of the palate makes sucking difficult, and although in some cases breastfeeding may be successful, problems must be anticipated. These babies can swallow fairly normally and the problem therefore is to deliver the milk into the back of the throat. This can be done by spoon, but these babies do very well with a soft teat in which a cross-cut has been made so that it requires only compression and no sucking action for the milk to be delivered. Special hooded teats are manufactured, but are quite useless.

CLOTHING

From infancy to adolescence most children are overdressed. The newborn baby starts life with a layette which is often unnecessarily elaborate and which is further augmented by gifts from relatives and friends, so that mother is hard pressed to use all the clothes before the baby grows out of them. It is natural for a mother to be proud of her baby and to want to show him or her off to best advantage, but dressing should nevertheless be simple and appropriate to climate and temperature. Overdressing leads to excessive sweating, skin rashes, irritability and excessive thirst. Do not for a moment imagine that by putting an unnecessary vest on a child you are going to protect her from 'catching cold'. Colds are acquired from people and not from exposure. Naturally, in cold weather clothing must be appropriately warm, but you can best judge what is suitable for your baby by looking at what you feel comfortable in yourself. Premature babies are rather special as they tend to lose heat very readily and they therefore have to be kept better insulated than mature babies. They are unlikely to overheat as a result of their own internal heat production. Older children will usually shed excessive clothing but they are frequently forced, particularly by oversolicitous grandmothers, to retain vests and jerseys which simply irritate the active, energetic young child, who generates a considerable amount of heat which has to be lost to the environment. Let your older child therefore judge for herself what is appropriate in the way of clothing. The rebelliousness of adolescence of course is often manifested by outrageous clothes, which may simply have to be tolerated with good humour until the phase is passed. Clothing should above all be functional and comfortable.

CLUBFOOT

This deformity occurs in about 1 per 1 000 births, and in 50 per cent of cases it is bilateral. In the commonest type the foot turns inwards, often with the toes pointing down (talipes equinovarus). In the less common variety the foot is turned out and the toes point upward (talipes calcaneovalgus).

These abnormalities should be dealt with as soon as possible after birth. Regular manipulation overcorrecting the deformities may suffice but splinting is often necessary. If the condition is not rapidly corrected, serial plaster-of-paris splints may be necessary. Occasionally operative measures are required to overcome the more severe components of the deformity. As a general rule, the deformities are readily corrected and the end result is excellent.

CLUMSINESS

Children, like adults, vary considerably in their skills, just as they do in their sizes, shapes and mental abilities. Some are naturally athletic, good at games, graceful in their movements and are able to draw and write beautifully. Other are 'Woody Allens'. Skills can be improved by practice but there is an inborn limit of the extent to which they can be affected. Most clumsy children are perfectly normal, however irritating and occasionally expensive their clumsiness may be. Ridicule and nagging are not likely to help the situation and good-humoured tolerance and encouragement are preferable attitudes.

Abnormally clumsy children may possibly be suffering from some brain dysfunction, such as mild ataxic cerebral palsy. Clumsiness appearing later may be due to *chorea or damage to the co-ordinating centres in the brain from, for example, encephalitis, meningitis or tumour. Such abnormal clumsiness should be fairly obvious.

The clumsy child often experiences schooling difficulties, especially when her writing is particularly bad. It not infrequently happens that too much meaning is attached to clumsiness, and rather misguided therapeutic measures are taken in the hope that these will improve school performance. Nobody ever learns to read by walking the plank or throwing a ball.

If your child appears to you unduly clumsy, by all means have her examined by a doctor, if only for your own reassurance. Acquired clumsiness always calls for a medical opinion.

COBRA
See *snakebite

COELIAC DISEASE
This disease is due to inability to handle gluten, a protein found in wheat and to a lesser extent in rye. This leads to a failure in digestion and absorption, and the stools become large, offensive, pale and fatty. The child fails to thrive and may actually lose weight. The muscles waste, subcutaneous fat disappears and the skin becomes wrinkled. The children are also characteristically miserable, with poor appetite. The digestive lining of the upper intestine is flattened and atrophied. Symptoms begin only after cereals have been added to the diet but may thereafter make their appearance at almost any age. Sometimes fairly long, spontaneous remissions occur. Secondary nutritional deficiencies such as anaemia and rickets are common.

Treatment entails the exclusion of wheat and rye gluten from the diet (oats and barley also contain some gluten but this is usually tolerated). The sensitivity to gluten does vary somewhat but it is wise initially to exclude gluten completely. Parents of children with coeliac disease are recommended to join the Food Allergy and Intolerance Society, and useful recipes as well as general advice will be found in the book *A Gluten-free Guide for Southern Africa* by Carole Smollan (publisher, Maskew Miller). (See also *gluten.)

The response of the child with coeliac disease (or gluten enteropathy, which is a more accurate term) to a gluten-free diet is usually prompt, symptoms improving within a week or so and weight-gain occurring rapidly. During this phase, extra vitamins may be required, particularly vitamin D to protect against rickets as bone growth improves. Once the condition is diagnosed with certainty, gluten should be avoided for life, although some patients will tolerate small amounts for fairly long periods. Cases of transient gluten intolerance have been recorded but are very rare.

COLDS
Everyone has experienced colds and knows only too well their unpleasant symptoms. There is however considerable popular misconception as to their nature. They are virus infections, acquired from other people harbouring the

virus, and they are most definitely not *caused* by failure to wear a vest, by getting the feet wet, washing the hair, exposure to wind or any of the other common misbeliefs. Colds are most common in small children after the passive immunity which they have obtained from the mother has worn off. (See *immunity.) Experience of one cold virus will give future protection only to that specific virus and to none of the other cold viruses, of which there are some 200 known at present. It is small wonder therefore that children in the early years, especially those living in towns, average 6–8 colds per year. People do vary greatly in their tendency to catch colds and in the severity of their symptoms, and these differences are as yet unexplained.

Cold symptoms may begin in the nose or the throat and the irritation rapidly spreads to involve the whole of these areas, with the resultant profuse nasal discharge, which is initially watery and subsequently thicker, and sneezing, coughing, sore throat and perhaps some degree of fever. Inflammation may spread to the nasal sinuses, to the ears or down into the chest, causing bronchitis or even pneumonia. Because the mucous membrane is intensely irritated, its defensive capabilities are impaired and secondary infection by bacteria may then occur. Such bacterial complications may be amenable to antibiotic treatment but this will in no way alter the course of the primary virus infection. In the absence of complication, therefore, treatment of colds should be kept to a minimum. Clothing should be comfortable but not excessive, though frank chilling should be avoided. Dry air is irritating, particularly to the patient who is mouth-breathing as the result of nasal obstruction, and steam inhalations with or without the addition of such things as menthol or Friar's Balsam are often soothing. Hot drinks have a similar effect. Aspirin or paracetamol may be given for relief of sore throat or alleviation of fever if this is present, but such medications should not be given simply as a routine. Cough mixtures and decongestant medications are of very little value. Nasal obstruction may be relieved by the use of decongestant nosedrops, and these are particularly useful in babies who have difficulty in breathing and feeding, but they should not be overused and the period of administration should not exceed 4 or 5 days except on explicit medical instructions, as the habitual use of nose-drops of this type may damage the nasal mucous membrane. A mild sedative at night will help the patient and also indirectly benefit the other family members.

Colds have to be distinguished from other causes of nasal irritation such as allergy, congenital syphilis in babies and foreign bodies in the nose. The distinction between frequently recurring colds and allergic rhinitis in small children is often extremely difficult and of course the two often go hand-in-hand.

With ordinary uncomplicated colds there is no need to consult your doctor. If, however, the child is unexpectedly ill, is running a significant temperature, has a chesty cough or complains of earache, or if in the older child purulent nasal secretions continue for an excessive time in association with headache which suggests sinusitis, then medical opinion should be sought.

Finally, let it be said again that there is no way of preventing colds apart from avoiding people harbouring the viruses. The giving of so-called tonics, extra vitamins (including vitamin C), the removal of tonsils and adenoids, will be of no value. Because of the multiplicity of viruses responsible, an effective vaccine is impossible to prepare. Colds simply have to be accepted as an unpleasant part of life.

COLD SORES
See *herpes simplex

COLIC
Colic is, by definition, any intermittent spasmodic pain resulting from spasm of a hollow viscus. It most commonly arises from the bowel but may arise from the hollow structures such as the ureters and gall bladder. The severest forms of colic are due to obstruction. Less severe forms may result from irritation due to inflammation or allergy.

Infantile colic. This diagnosis is often assumed without justification. Many babies cry rather excessively and this may occur particularly at one time of the day, usually in the evenings. This habit tends to wane after the age of 3 months and this feature has given rise to the appellation '3-month colic'. The fact that the baby draws up her legs when she cries does not mean that she has a tummyache. It is simply the natural thing for a baby to do when she cries. Much of what is called colic is in fact hunger. This applies particularly to the breastfed baby, for the milk supply at the end of an exhausting day is often diminished and, in addition to being tired, mother may also be tense and anxious to get the baby settled before she has to cope with her husband's return, prepare the supper or cope with entertainment. It is difficult under such circumstances to relax, and the let-down reflex is therefore impaired and the baby may well, as a result of all these factors, have an unsatisfying feed. Before accusing the baby of having colic, therefore, try to ensure that her evening feed is adequate in all respects. Many babies seem to be particularly hungry at this time of day. Our own second child would not settle in the evening until she had had a double feed and there are many babies like this. If your baby is being breastfed and seems to be hungry at this time of day it is far better to offer her a *complementary feed by bottle and ensure her satisfaction and happiness than to let her cry endlessly. This does not endanger breastfeeding but actually encourages it, as both mother and baby are happy.

Even quite young babies may cry from sheer loneliness. It is natural for a baby to enjoy the comfort of her mother's nearness. If therefore your baby has a fretful period, rather than resorting to medications try putting her in a sling so that she can enjoy the comfort of your presence.

If in spite of these simple measures the baby continues crying and no other cause is apparent, the accusation of colic becomes more firmly based. This is often supposed to result from the presence of 'wind in the bowel'. It is quite normal for the bowel to contain a fair amount of gas. An excess of gas can be uncomfortable but if the baby is being fed in a sitting position and kept upright for a short period after the feed, so that she can bring up any excess of gas in the stomach, it is unlikely that she has much uncomfortable gas in the bowel. It is normal for babies to pass flatus (see *bowels) and this therefore does not indicate that 'wind' is causing symptoms. Much medication is given to babies to help them bring up winds. Such treatment is fatuous and futile. All that need be done is to keep the baby erect so that she can burp if she wants to.

Genuine colic does seem to occur in babies intolerant of certain feeds, particularly cows' milk. One often finds however that feeds are changed rather senselessly and confusion is added to expense. In the breastfed baby colic has been attributed to foreign proteins, particularly cows' milk protein, being absorbed intact by the mother and excreted into the milk. The evidence for this is very limited and the notion is rather unjustifiably popular. Nevertheless it does give mothers something harmless to try before resorting to more desperate measures, and to take yourself off milk and cheese for a short period does not entail great hardship (though you should make sure you are still getting adequate nutrition). Other foodstuffs are highly unlikely to cause trouble. If your baby is being artificially fed and seems unhappy it might be worth trying a change of feed, but this should be done in logical steps. If, as is probable, she is on a modified cows'-milk-based feed there is no point in trying another preparation which is almost identical. You might in the first place try an evaporated milk, or an acidified milk such as Pelargon. Continuation of symptoms, especially if there is a family history of allergy, would then justify a change to a different type of feed, such as a soya-based milk substitute. More elaborate manipulations may be made by your doctor if your baby is seriously suspected of having an allergic problem. (See also *allergy.)

Relief from colic may be obtained by administration of antispasmodic drugs. If these are successful the evidence for colic is increased. The most popular preparation is dicyclomine, of which there are several proprietary brands, no one being significantly better than another. Because of a few adverse incidents the manufacturers of dicyclomine preparations have warned against their use in young infants. This fear is greatly exaggerated. Traditional gripe water has virtually no pharmacological effects at all. Babies seem to like the taste and it is at least fairly harmless, but these virtues hardly justify its ridiculous popularity.

If your baby appears to be 'colicky' do try to be sensible about it. Consider the other possible causes of fretfulness and try to eliminate them. If the baby remains excessively distressed, by all means consult your doctor but remember that he too may feel somewhat frustrated by a situation in which a definite diagnosis is often just not possible.

COLOSTRUM
During the final weeks of pregnancy and more especially during the first 2–3 days after birth, the breasts secrete small quantities of this protein-rich fluid. The small quantity gives it little nutritional value but there may be some benefit to the baby in the protective substances, particularly immunoglobulins, that colostrum contains. The main advantage of putting the baby to the breast during this period, however, lies in the resultant stimulation of lactation (see *breast) and the reciprocal emotional satisfaction of close contact between mother and child.

COLOUR-BLINDNESS
This is most often hereditary, but may occasionally be acquired, and it is then usually due to serious disease of the retina or optic nerve. Normal colour vision depends upon the presence and normal function of 3 different types of visual cones in the retina of the eye, one for each of the primary colours. In the

commonest hereditary form of colour-blindness there is an inability to distinguish red and green, but occasionally all colour vision is affected and only black and white can be perceived.

The hereditary form of colour-blindness is due to an abnormal gene carried on the X chromosome. It is inherited as a Mendelian recessive, and the presence of a normal X chromosome therefore prevents the abnormality from occurring. In females with XX chromosomes, therefore, the condition is extremely rare whereas in males it is not uncommon (about 8 per cent).

The condition is often recognisable at about the age of 5 years when the child should be able to distinguish colours with accuracy. It may become apparent only when the child is obviously confused by traffic lights. Sometimes, however, the child compensates by the knowledge that the 'go' light is always at the bottom, and the condition may escape notice until the child himself complains of difficulty in distinguishing red from green. There is no treatment for the hereditary condition.

COMFORTERS

See *dummies

COMFORT OBJECTS

Many children have a favourite blanket, cloth, fluffy material or other object from which they derive comfort, particularly when under stress or when they are going to sleep. Unless the comfort object if particularly revolting, this situation can be regarded as temporary and benign and not worthy therefore of great attention. The child will eventually give up her comfort cloth, or whatever it is, either when it has disintegrated or when she has achieved greater maturity. There is little point in fighting her about it or ridiculing her when her addiction is doing no harm and is in any case going to end. If, however, the child appears seriously disturbed or the comfort needs persist to an age which is unacceptable then perhaps you should do something about it. Ask your doctor whether he thinks there is really a problem.

COMPLEMENTARY FEEDS

A complementary feed is an additional bottle-feed given after a breastfeed when the quantity obtained from the breast is deemed insufficient. Complementary feeds are in general preferred to supplementary feeds (bottles given in place of breastfeeds), as the regular and more frequent suckling provides a better stimulus to continued lactation. When complementary feeds are given, the baby should be allowed to take what she wants rather than a fixed quantity.

CONGENITAL ABNORMALITIES

These are considered under the individual conditions, such as *birthmarks, *clubfoot, *cleft lip and cleft palate, *dislocation of the hip, *hydrocephalus, *spina bifida, etc. The risk of significant congenital abnormality in any random pregnancy is between 1 and 2 per cent. This may seem high but when the complexity of human development from a single fertilised cell is considered it is in fact astonishing that it usually happens so smoothly and perfectly. The more severe abnormalities often end up as miscarriages, and the basic defect is then not usually recognised. Many congenital conditions can now be recognised antenatally either by amniocentesis or occasionally by simpler tests, for example the detection of spina bifida by finding an increase in the mother's blood-level of alpha-foeto-protein. If there is a strong history in your family of congenital conditions your doctor should be informed so that appropriate steps may be taken.

CONJUNCTIVITIS

The eyes (except for the cornea) and the inner surfaces of the eyelids are covered by a delicate membrane known as the conjunctiva. Inflammation of this membrane is therefore called conjunctivitis. This may be due to a variety of causes — chemical irritation, desiccation and trauma from wind, foreign bodies, and invading organisms such as viruses and bacteria. These conditions are all of relatively short duration. More chronic or recurrent conjunctivitis is likely to be allergic and is often associated with hayfever. In tropical countries a particularly vicious type of chronic conjunctivitis is trachoma, the result of infection with chlamydia, a large-sized virus.

Conjunctivitis is particularly common in newborn babies but in the first day or two actual infection is often not present. Later it is often due to a staphylococcus, and antibiotic treatment then becomes necessary. The baby's eyes can also become infected with gonorrhoea and this type of conjunctivitis is particularly severe. More chronic cases of neonatal conjunctivitis may be due to chlamydia. Subsequent watery eyes are often associated with blockage of the tearducts. Unilateral conjunctivitis is almost always due to a foreign body and this should be diligently sought and removed.

Treatment of conjunctivitis depends upon the cause. Topical antibiotics instilled into the eye are useful when bacterial infection is present. Irrigation of the eye with water, or preferably sterile saline, suffices in milder cases. Chlamydial infections respond to tetracycline.

CONSTIPATION

The refined nature of the average Western diet, combined with the sedentary lives led by most people, ensures that constipation is one of the most popular complaints. It is by no means confined to adults or to females. Constipation is characterised by the passage not just of infrequent but, more particularly, of hard stools. The frequency is of relative unimportance. Breastfed babies may well go for 1 or even 2 weeks without a stool but when it is eventually passed it is of perfectly normal soft consistency. An artificially fed baby, however, who had not had a stool for an equivalent time would inevitably pass hard pebbles or chalky masses. In older children constipation often presents with frequent, small, liquid stools or with soiling. Constipation may of course be a symptom of significant bowel disease, and its sudden onset associated with abdominal distension or vomiting is of ominous significance. Chronic constipation with enormous dilatation of the large bowel may be the result of congenital deficiency in the nerve supply to the bowel, a condition known as Hirschsprung's disease. Thyroid deficiency is also an occasional cause of chronic constipation. As a rule, however, constipation is not due to bowel abnormality but to faulty dietary habits. Beyond infancy the stool frequency varies a great deal, as does stool consistency, but the stools should never become hard and uncomfortable. Such stools imply that there has been an excessive absorption of water in the large bowel, leaving only the dry residue. Natural foods contain a considerable amount of cellulose, which is not digestible and which therefore adds to the stool bulk and helps maintain a normal consistency. In recent years we have come to realise that bran is an important article of diet, but the bran has been completely removed from most of today's milled cereals.

Some cases of constipation are simply imaginary and based on the assumption that the bowels should move daily or even twice daily. As stated above, the frequency doesn't matter. It is the character of the stool that is important. If defaecation causes discomfort it is only natural that the child will try to hold the stools in, and a vicious circle is then established, for each time the bowels move more discomfort is produced, sometimes with actual tearing of the anus, resulting in bleeding from a fissure, and the child becomes less and less willing to part with her stools. Eventually enormous masses may be retained. Some bowel content must then leak past and, because with perpetual distension rectal sensation is diminished, incontinence results. This is a common form of presentation of constipation in children.

Treatment of constipation depends upon its cause. In babies a change of feed may be beneficial but the commonly recommended manoeuvres, such as giving extra water or adding sugar to the feeds, are valueless. Syrup or honey is rather more effective but a fair amount has to be given, for example ½ to 1 teaspoonful to each bottle. If this does not work, a simple laxative such as Magnesia, which has the effect of retaining water and therefore making the stools softer, may be given and may be required in a small dose daily. This is far better than giving explosive doses every few days. Rather than using artificial laxatives, however, it is preferable to use natural preparations and the addition of, for example, prunes to the diet is often helpful. Other fruits and vegetables are often disappointing in their effect.

The older child presenting with constipation will usually not be relieved until the obstructing stools are removed. These she will be reluctant to pass unless helped, for example, by an enema. Very effective disposable small-volume enemas are available. Once evacuated the bowel may regain its rhythmicity without further help, apart from a diet providing adequate roughage. In more severe cases, however, it is necessary to ensure regular, comfortably passed stools by administering a daily laxative for a time and then very gradually reducing the daily dose. Senna is a useful preparation for this purpose.

Although one deplores excessive parental interest in children's stools, for such obsession is often the cause of trouble, nevertheless when true constipation is present it should be adequately managed. There is no place whatever for the traditional weekly 'clear out' and as a general rule laxatives should not be given to children except on medical instruction.

CONTRACEPTION

Following the birth of your baby you may wish to defer further pregnancy, and some form of contraception then becomes desirable. Do not rely on breastfeeding to accomplish this. The pill may to some extent reduce lactation, and other forms of contraception may therefore be preferable, such as an intrauterine device.

Discuss this problem with your doctor.

Contraception and the teenager. Except in the most rigid societies where virginity can still more or less be relied upon, the age at which sexual activity begins is progressively falling. Parents are naturally concerned to avoid unwanted pregnancy in their teenage daughters. If you have managed to maintain a frank and open relationship with your children in which sexual matters are freely discussed they will probably have sufficient understanding to assume a responsible attitude. Although both boys and girls should be imbued with sufficient respect for one another to avoid the appalling hurt of unwanted pregnancy, nevertheless with today's freedoms chastity is a tall order. If therefore you suspect that your daughter is sexually active, try to discuss things with her. You may be shocked at her answers but that is preferable to being shocked by pregnancy.

CONVULSIONS

Convulsions occur in about 6 per cent of children and are therefore fairly commonplace They are nevertheless extremely alarming to parents. In the young child, convulsions are usually associated with fever and are then almost always benign. Only a very small proportion of such children, about 3 per cent, may go on to have epilepsy. Although the manifestations are similar, simple feverish convulsions and epilepsy are very different matters. Convulsions may occur in the neonatal period and are then most commonly due to birth injury or to metabolic disturbances such as low blood-sugar or low blood-calcium levels. Although alarming they usually carry a good prognosis.

Febrile convulsions usually occur in the age 6 months to 3 years. They are seldom seen after the age of 5. They mostly occur at the onset of a feverish illness when the temperature rises rapidly. The actual convulsive level varies from child to child but is usually over 39°C. The convulsion may well be the first indication that fever is present. In a typical convulsion the child goes stiff, loses consciousness and has difficulty in breathing because of spasm of the respiratory muscles. As a result of this she may become blue, and because it is impossible for her to swallow saliva, it accumulates and she may froth at the mouth. Jerking movements may occur and these are usually bilateral and symmetrical. The jaw participates in these movements and the tongue may be bitten, but it is rarely severely injured and strenuous efforts do not need to be made to protect it. The convulsion itself usually lasts one-half to 2 minutes and then passes off, the child becoming limp and then gradually regaining consciousness. She is likely to remain drowsy for a variable time. Convulsions may recur during the same feverish illness but this is rather uncommon. About 30 to 40 per cent of children who have had one febrile convulsion will have subsequent ones, and recurrence is more likely if the first occurred under the age of 1 year.

What to do? First of all don't panic. It is extremely frightening as a parent to witness your child having a convulsion but the probability is that it will last for no longer than 2 minutes and during this time all you have to do is to prevent injury. Put the child on a surface where she can't fall off, and prevent the head from being banged. Limb movements need not be restrained. Try to keep the child in a prone or semi-prone position with the head to the side so that secretions drain out instead of being inhaled. If there are champing movements of the jaws the tongue can be protected by inserting, for example, a folded handkerchief between the teeth but do not use a hard object and do not use your finger! Do not try to apply artificial respiration as this will simply predispose to respiratory infection by blowing secretions down into the chest. The child will breathe again once the convulsion has ceased. Initially such breathing is of a gasping nature but rapidly becomes rhythmical and regular. If the child is feverish, which she almost certainly is, try to cool her down by removing the clothing, putting on a fan, and if necessary sponging her down with cool water or applying towels soaked in cool water. When she is conscious, an antipyretic drug such as aspirin or paracetamol may be given, but do not on any account try to pour anything into the mouth of an unconscious person.

Unpleasant features of convulsions, suggesting that they are not of simple febrile nature, are: a duration of more than 10 minutes, asymmetrical features, and preceding or subsequent neurological abnormalities. After any first convulsion it is wise for the child to be examined medically and your doctor may feel it necessary to do certain investigations such as a lumbar puncture, especially if there is any suspicion of meningitis. Subsequent convulsions, however, provided they have no worrisome features, can be managed perfectly well by you at home.

Prevention of convulsions. The most important preventive measure is control of high fever. If a child has had a previous convulsion, her temperature should be watched closely during feverish illnesses and not allowed to rise above 39°C. Fever may be controlled by exposure, fanning, application of cool water and antipyretic drugs — salicylates, paracetamol or mefenamic acid. If, in spite of such measures, a child continues to have unacceptably frequent convulsions she may be put onto anticonvulsant medication with phenobarbitone or valproate, which are the only effective anticonvulsants in this situation. Alternatively, medication may be confined to febrile periods, and diazepam is then the most effective preparation. This can be given by mouth to the conscious patient but is also very rapidly absorbed per rectum. It can be used in this way for termination of convulsions should these continue beyond about 5 minutes. A doctor wishing to terminate a convulsion usually gives such a drug intravenously and it is then immediately effective.

CORTICOSTEROIDS

This group of drugs is based on cortisone, which is a natural secretion of the adrenal gland and which is essential for life; failure to produce cortisone is manifested by cardiovascular collapse (shock), low blood-sugar level and loss of salt. Corticosteroids are therefore used for replacement therapy in states of adrenal insufficiency, but are more commonly employed for their powerful anti-inflammatory effect. They are also of great value in allergic conditions and may be administered topically, for example as creams or ointments for eczema or as aerosol sprays for allergic rhinitis and asthma. They are potent immunosuppressives and are used in treating malignancies, such as leukaemia.

Prolonged administration of corticosteroids suppresses the normal adrenal secretion, and sudden cessation of administration may therefore result in a steroid-deficient state. Long courses of treatment are therefore terminated by gradual dose reduction. Short courses have no such suppressive effect and can be terminated quite abruptly.

Side-effects of corticosteroids are considerable. They produce rounding of the face, obesity, particularly of the trunk, stretch marks in the skin, elevation of blood pressure, a diabetic-like state, duodenal ulceration and mental changes. Prolonged treatment is therefore not embarked upon lightly and only when the benefit is likely to outweigh the undesirable effects.

COT DEATH (SUDDEN INFANT DEATH SYNDROME)

Considerable publicity has been given to this situation, which is indeed a shocking experience for parents, though its incidence is extremely low. Most cot deaths occur in babies 2 to 6 months of age. Some of these have had neonatal problems which might have acted as a warning to the possibility of sudden death later, but most babies are perfectly healthy and are simply found dead. It used to be thought that such deaths were due to inadvertent suffocation, but this is rarely the case. Many are due to overwhelming infection such as pneumonia or septicaemia. Some have been thought to be due to inhalation of small quantities of milk in a child who is allergic and develops a sudden bronchial reaction. Most cases go unexplained. Parents tend to feel unnecessary guilt and it is not uncommon for one to blame the other quite unjustifiably. If such a tragedy should happen to you, accept that nothing could have been done to prevent it and that therefore no one is to blame. Accept, too, that the chances of its happening again are infinitesimally small and not worthy of consideration.

Missed sudden deaths cause even more anxiety than sudden death itself. It may happen that a baby is found very nearly dead but is fortunately resuscitated in time. Naturally the parents of such a baby live in dread that it might happen again and they watch the baby day and night. This puts an intolerable strain on them and on their relationship. The best solution to this situation is for them to have a monitor which would alarm them should the baby's breathing cease. Such monitors are available and may be obtainable from your local hospital.

COUGH

This most common complaint has many causes. Most coughs are associated with simple upper-respiratory infections and are due to irritation of the throat, either by infection itself or by the trickling down of mucus from the back of the nose. A croupy cough is associated with laryngitis and a brassy cough with tracheal irritation. Bronchitis usually causes a productive cough, and an inhaled foreign body a very distressing cough. Whooping cough gives rise to typical spasms with a tendency to choke and vomit. Sometimes people cough simply from habit. The nature of the cough therefore often gives a good clue to its origin. Coughing normally serves a purpose in protecting the lower respiratory tract, and therefore it should not be suppressed.

In spite of the abundance of cough-mixtures it has to be accepted that treatment of coughs is largely ineffective. Treatment should be directed at the cause rather than the cough. There are some cough-suppressant drugs, one of the most effective being pholcodine, and such a preparation may have some value in the treatment of useless coughs such as pertussis. More benefit, however, is often obtained from simple sedation, as the disturbance is always more marked at night.

Allergic coughs are common and may be the sole manifestation of an allergic state, although frequently there is accompanying allergic nose-trouble. When due to domestic allergens, allergic coughs tend to be worse at night, and they may be associated with snoring (due to nasal obstruction), early morning sneezing and mouth-breathing. Treatment directed towards the underlying allergy is usually remarkably effective.

CRADLE CAP

This is due to the accumulation of skin secretions and desquamated skin scales, and it is particularly marked in seborrhoeic states in which the skin secretions are increased. Mothers are often afraid to cleanse the fontanelle region of the scalp, and scalp debris then tends to accumulate in this region. The condition is usually preventable by adequate shampooing and fairly vigorous removal of scalp scales. If these are difficult to remove, a soft nail-brush may be used instead of a flannel. If the scales are hard they may be softened beforehand by application of liquid paraffin or other light oil a few hours before shampooing, but such oils should not be left on the scalp as they will increase the severity of the condition. In very severe cases special shampoos may be required and in frank seborrhoeic states steroid lotions are of value.

CRETINISM

Thyroid deficiency, either congenital or arising at an early age, results in poor growth of all body tissues including the brain, and cretins are therefore both short and mentally subnormal. They have characteristically coarse features, and the infant cretin in addition has a gruff, leathery voice, dry skin and hair, and often an umbilical hernia. Congenital thyroid deficiency is usually not recognisable at birth and by the time diagnosis is made at the age of a few months irreparable harm has been done. This is a period of rapid brain growth and if such growth is impeded by thyroid lack it is never rectified later, no matter how much thyroid is given. Congenital thyroid deficiency occurs in about 1:4000 births, though the incidence appears to be appreciably lower in black Africans. Because it is so important to diagnose thyroid deficiency as early as possible, many countries now have compulsory screening tests on every neonate. Such tests are available and should be applied to every newborn baby. The test is simple and requires only the collection of a few drops of blood on about the fourth day of life. Such testing should be obligatory. (See *thyroid.)

CROUP

This is a most frightening condition, resulting from obstruction of the airway at the level of the larynx, usually as the result of infection, most commonly due to viruses. Laryngeal obstruction can, however, also result from foreign bodies in the larynx, other types of inflammation such as diphtheria, and allergic reactions. Viral croup may be associated with a cold but often begins fairly abruptly, and typically at night. The child awakes with breathing difficulty, noisy breathing, the noise being characteristically on inspiration rather than expiration, and hoarseness of the voice. Because of the obstruction, increased respiratory efforts have to be made and this leads to drawing in of the sternum and lower ribs on inspiration.

The child is understandably very frightened and becomes restless and distressed. The pulse rate may rise to high levels and if the obstruction is severe she may become blue. Such signs indicate an urgent need for relief and the child should be rushed to hospital without delay. Milder cases are often relieved by simply moistening the inspired air by boiling a kettle and directing the steam towards the child with a covering towel, but beware of burns and scalds, particularly with a restless small child. Alternatively, the child can be sat over the bath while hot water is run into it. However apprehensive you may feel yourself try to remain calm so as to instil calm confidence in the child, for increased anxiety will make her much worse. Do not hesitate to contact your doctor no matter what the hour. By the time laryngitis has produced sufficient obstruction to cause breathing difficulty, the diameter of the larynx has been reduced to something like 2 mm, and any further encroachment can be disastrous. Regard it therefore very seriously.

Croup may recur but frequent recurrences should make one suspicious of allergy as a cause. Whereas corticosteroid drugs are of little value in infective croup they are often very effective in allergic croup. Other medications are not of great value, but special inhalations of, for example, adrenaline, which can be administered in hospital, are often effective.

Whereas viral croup usually afflicts children between the ages of 18 months and 4 years, similar symptoms affecting older children suggest the possibility of *epiglottitis. This is a very serious condition which demands immediate hospitalisation. For diphtheritic croup see *diphtheria.

CRYING

Excessive crying in babies is of course a subjective impression, and some parents are much more tolerant than others. Crying is the only means a baby has of expressing her displeasure. This may result from physical discomfort, hunger or simply loneliness. The possible causes of physical discomfort are endless but most are readily detectible. Remember that simple things like too tight a napkin can become very uncomfortable after a time and clothing should therefore be loose and adapted to the temperature. Excessive cold or warmth may make a baby unhappy. When the cause of a baby's crying is not apparent she is often accused of having *colic or 'wind'. This may possibly be so but much so-called colic is hunger, so please see that your baby is adequately fed according to her ideas and not yours before you start giving her anti-colic medications. Make sure, too, that your baby is not crying from lack of maternal contact. She may be quite happy if you carry her about in a sling on your front or back and this is not 'spoiling her'. It is simply fulfilling a very natural need.

A sudden change in baby's behaviour, with excessive crying particularly if this is associated with fever, vomiting or other significant symptom, probably calls for medical assessment.

The somewhat older infant who cries excessively, particularly at night, can be an exhausting problem. (See *sleep.) Such children are often unhappy because they have not received a great deal of parental affection when they behave well, and much of their crying is therefore simply attention-seeking. Such crying should not be rewarded but there should be adequate compensation, with attention given when the child is behaving acceptably. This may be difficult for the harassed mother but is very essential in managing the problem.

The older child who cries excessively almost certainly has a reason. She may experience jealousy of a younger sibling, she may feel insecure as the result of parental friction or she may have problems in relationships at pre-school or school. You should try to determine her problems, understand them and deal with them if possible. It is no good just saying, 'Don't be a cry-baby.' It may be that her problem will turn out to be insoluble but at least it would have been brought out into the open and considered sympathetically, which is all she probably wants.

You may not be able to interpret your child's crying every time, and failure to do so should not make you feel inadequate or guilty. If your child's crying is getting you down don't just ignore the situation and hope for the best. The best probably won't materialise. If there really is a problem go and discuss it with your doctor.

CUTS AND MINOR INJURIES

The body has a remarkable ability for healing itself and most minor injuries require no real attention. Every child should receive prophylactic tetanus immunisations, and even severely contaminated wounds will not then give rise to this dread disease. Dirty cuts should be cleansed with running water from a tap but clean cuts have usually bled sufficiently to remove any dirt. If a cut is long and gaping it will probably require stitching and you should then take your child to your doctor. The edges of smaller cuts can be well approximated, once bleeding has ceased, with strips of porous plaster. The approximated edges of the cut heal rapidly with little scab and scar formation. If infection supervenes, however, healing is delayed. If a wound has been stitched and then becomes inflamed and messy the stitches will probably have to be removed and healing allowed to progress more slowly from the bottom.

There is an almost universal desire to treat cuts and abrasions with antiseptics. These are quite unnecessary. Anything that stings simply adds to the child's discomfort and many antiseptics will destroy the body cells as well as bacteria and therefore delay healing. As in most situations nature cares for us far more efficiently than we do ourselves.

CYSTIC FIBROSIS

This genetically determined disease is transmitted as a Mendelian autosomal recessive and has an incidence in white people of about 1:2 500. It is considerably rarer in other races and is unknown in the black African. There is an unusually high incidence in the Afrikaners of Namibia. The condition affects multiple glands, particularly those of the bronchi and of the pancreas, whose secretions become extremely viscid and cause obstruction of the ducts. This leads to repeated lung infection and to pancreatic insufficiency, with the passage of undigested fatty stools. The sweat glands are also affected and produce a sweat high in sodium and chloride. This provides one of the most reliable tests for the disease.

Cystic fibrosis has a variable severity, but as a rule affected children thrive poorly and repeated pneumonia leads to progressive lung destruction. Modern management has greatly improved the expected life-span but the long-term outlook is nevertheless poor.

CYSTITIS

Inflammation of the bladder may form part of a general urinary-tract infection or it may be isolated. Cystitis is more common in girls than boys, probably because the short urethra makes it an easier target for ascending infection. The symptoms of cystitis are increased frequency in passing urine, and discomfort, usually burning, during the act. The urine may be cloudy and sometimes smells of ammonia. Treatment consists of appropriate antibacterial therapy and the correction of any mechanical abnormalities that may be leading to stagnation, which predisposes to infection. (See *urinary-tract infections.)

DANDRUFF

Skin is being shed perpetually from the whole surface of the body, including the scalp. Usually this comes off in very fine scales which are almost invisible. When the skin scales become stuck together by the natural secretions they form larger particles, which in the baby appear as *cradle cap and which in the adult are shed as dandruff. The treatment and prevention of dandruff depends upon regular scalp cleansing. Special shampoos are available for the more severe conditions and these are usually very effective. The scalp, like the rest of the skin, adjusts to climatic factors and to the treatment it receives and it is wise therefore for the latter to be as consistent as possible.

DEAFNESS

Deafness may be partial or complete, unilateral or bilateral. About 1 in every 1 000 children is born deaf, sometimes with other associated abnormalities but often as an isolated handicap. Deafness may also result from severe jaundice in the neonatal period, or from disease of the ears, and it is a common sequel to meningitis. Drugs such as streptomycin may produce deafness.

Deaf babies do produce sounds but because they are largely non-responsive and non-imitative, the vocal repertoire, even by the age of 6 months, is appreciably diminished. From birth the normal baby may startle at a loud noise. At about 3 months he will usually turn towards the side of the noise. Elaborate tests involving evoked response audiometry are available for infants suspected of being deaf. It is important that deafness be diagnosed as early as possible so that appropriate steps can be taken to compensate for it. If, therefore, you suspect that your baby might be deaf do not delay in having him checked.

Deafness in the older child is commonly the result of repeated ear infections. If secretions are allowed to remain in the middle ear they tend to gum up the conductive mechanism. Every child who is having schooling difficulties should have his hearing checked — much apparent inattentiveness is due to hearing loss. The child with significant deafness will require special education at one of the appropriate schools.

DEATH

It is natural for adults to try to protect their children from the knowledge of death and they usually feel as embarrassed answering questions on this subject as they do about sex. Death is an inevitable end to life and there is no reason why children should not be made aware of this fact. They usually first encounter death in a relative or a pet and they will then require some consolation in their sadness, but death should not be distorted or excessively euphemised. Whatever your religious beliefs you will naturally try to convey these to your children but if your children doubt and question you should try to answer them honestly and frankly with detail appropriate to the child's understanding.

The dying child. Many children who are severely ill and especially those in hospital may question whether they are going to die. As a rule you will be able to reassure them with complete honesty that they are not. Even a child with leukaemia who may be undergoing rather horrifying treatment can usually be assured that the treatment will be succesful, if not in eliminating his disease completely, at least in restoring health, and an air of optimism should then prevail. But what about the child who is really dying? Most adults are afraid of death and therefore assume that their children will inevitably be so too. If, however, the child has been brought up to regard death as a natural thing, he may well have little fear of it and may welcome it as a release from the sufferings he might have endured. If so the possibility of death should not be denied but neither need it be accentuated. It may be very difficult to discuss such topics unemotionally but it may well be helpful to child as well as parent to attempt to do so. So much will depend upon the individual personalities.

DEHYDRATION

Dehydration implies the loss not only of water but also of essential salts, and the resulting derangements in body metabolism may be very complex. We are always losing a certain amount of fluid in urine, sweat, breath and stools but these losses may become excessive, for example, in extremely hot conditions, in diabetic states or as the result of diarrhoea. Abnormal losses may result from protracted vomiting, and occasionally fluid may be lost as the result of surgical drainage. In children the most common cause of dehydration is gastro-enteritis, in which fluid is lost both in the diarrhoeic stools and from vomiting. Because stools are largely alkaline, and because the fluid loss leads to inefficient kidney function, a state of acidosis frequently develops. If more salt is lost than water the body becomes salt-depleted and the dehydration is then called hypotonic. If proportionate amounts of salt and fluid are lost the dehydration is isotonic, and if more water is lost than salt the dehydration is hypertonic. In infants the latter may be extremely serious, often resulting in brain damage.

The dehydrated child presents a fairly characteristic picture, with sunken eyes, dry mouth, excessive thirst, inelastic skin and, in the case of infants, a depressed fontanelle. Little or no urine is usually passed and that which is produced is extremely concentrated.

Management. Any significant degree of dehydration is an emergency, requiring prompt restoration of body-water and salts. This is best accomplished in hospital, but if you cannot get immediate medical help try to get in as much fluid as the child will retain, giving small amounts frequently. An easily prepared suitable fluid would be 1 level teaspoonful of salt and 4 tablespoons of sugar to 1 litre of water. A more appropriate solution, particularly in acidotic states, is ½ teaspoonful salt, ¼ teaspoonful potassium chloride, ½ teaspoonful baking soda (sodium bicarbonate) and 4 tablespoonfuls of sugar (sucrose or glucose) to 1 litre of water. Proprietary electrolyte preparations are available and are suitable for most situations.

If oral fluids are not tolerated it may be possible to suppress vomiting by administration of an antiemetic drug (e.g. promazine) but it is usually safer to rehydrate the child with intravenous fluids. Vomiting usually ceases once hydration is restored to normal. (See *gastro-enteritis, *diabetes, etc.)

DELIRIUM

Any person with high fever may become delirious as a result of irritation of the brain. This does not imply any damage. It is particularly common in *typhoid fever and may occur with almost any of the children's infectious diseases. Some degree of delirium is usual in infections involving the brain itself, such as encephalitis, meningitis and cerebral malaria. Delirium may be seen as a side-effect from some drugs. Treatment is not usually required for delirium itself, but is directed towards the underlying condition. The severely disturbed patient, however, may require appropriate sedation.

DENTAL DECAY

See *caries

DEPRESSION

A degree of depression is common in mothers a few days after delivery, so-called 'fourth-day blues' or 'mothers' weeps'. This state is due to a combination of factors. There are severe endocrine dislocations, similar to those occurring with menstruation but much more exaggerated. The mother has been through 9 months of anticipation with the climax of delivery and has for a brief spell been the centre of attention, receiving flowers, gifts and congratulations. She has had the new joy of her baby. Then suddenly the excitement is over. She probably has some degree of breast-engorgement and may be worried about the baby's feeding. Her husband is probably complaining about her absence and feeling sorry for himself. The prospect of being wholly responsible for the new being to whom she has given life may daunt her and so she feels depressed. This is however usually a fleeting situation lasting only a few days. If it persists, and particularly if it should get worse, then you must without hesitation consult your doctor, for you may well need help.

Depression does not afflict adults only. Children also may become depressed, perhaps as a reaction to an obviously depressing situation such as domestic strife or severe illness or loss of mother; they may become depressed as the result of unjustified guilt feelings, or there may be no obvious cause. In addition to depression of mood the child tends to withdraw from normal activities, complain of tiredness and may relapse into infantile behaviour such as thumb-sucking. If such symptoms are persistent you should consult your doctor.

DEPRIVATION

We are all perhaps deprived in some way, for no one can have everything, but significant deprivation implies the infliction of an obstacle to full development. Even small babies brought up in institutions with little in the way of individual attention develop at a slower rate, and their ultimate achievements tend to be less than those of the more fortunate. Children in a normal family situation may be emotionally deprived if the parents are unable to relate to them satisfactorily. Deprivation of luxuries is not important, in fact children of wealthy parents are often deprived in other respects, particularly of the company of their business- and socially-occupied parents. The parent who as a child has himself not had a satisfactory home life often finds it very difficult to establish one for his children.

Educational deprivation is rife. This is true particularly for the poorer sections of the community but also for some of the more affluent. The quality of education depends upon the teacher and this should be judged not on academic qualifications alone but on his or her ability to perpetuate a child's natural inquisitiveness and to provide as many questions as answers. If your child is not being stimulated at school, do everything you can to remedy the situation.

DERMATITIS

Inflammation of the skin may result from many causes: physical and chemical irritation, allergy, infection, etc. Only a few specific forms of dermatitis will be considered here. For ammoniacal dermatitis see below under napkin dermatitis. For atopic dermatitis see *eczema.

Contact dermatitis. This is an allergic reaction (Type 4, see *allergy) to contact with specific chemical substances. These may be medications such as antihistamines, anaesthetic ointments, cosmetics or dyes, or plants, such as *Rhus.* The reaction is not immediate but is usually delayed for 1 to 2 days. There then appears an acute eczematous type of eruption in the area of contact, followed by a sensitivity reaction elsewhere. Distribution of the initial lesions usually suggests the type of contact. Future exposure should obviously be avoided. Local application of corticosteroids is usually relieving, but in severe reactions systemic steroids may be required.

Napkin dermatitis. Several factors may be involved in the production of rashes in the napkin area, but the commonest cause is simple contact with irritating urine. At one time it was thought that this was due to ammonia formation as the result of breakdown of urea by germs normally present, and it was advocated that to counteract the alkalinity of ammonia the napkins should be washed in a dilute acid solution, for example of vinegar. It has now been demonstrated that this is not valid. If a napkin rash is present, contact with wet napkins should certainly be reduced to an absolute minimum and the napkins left off as far as possible. This usually suffices to clear the condition. It is usually apparent whether the napkins alone are responsible for the rash, for it is then confined to the areas in contact with the napkin and the creases are spared. Frequently, however, there is superimposed fungal infection and this invades the creases. In such cases an anti-fungal preparation is indicated. Simple dyes such as gentian violet or dilute mercurochrome solution are effective, but they do discolour the napkins. More elegant preparations contain nystatin, clotrimazole, miconazole, haloprogin, or similar substances, and these usually work well. Severe forms of napkin dermatitis often respond best to a paste containing hydrocortisone and vioform. The fundamental thing in treating, however, is to reduce napkin contact. Plastic pants and plastic-covered disposable napkins are best not used during times of active dermatitis.

Seborrhoeic dermatitis. This condition commonly begins during the first 2 months of life. Associated with cradle cap there is a napkin eruption and irritation of the skin folds of the axillae, neck and behind the ears. It is fundamental to clear the scalp (see *cradle cap), and the other areas of dermatitis usually respond well to topical steroid preparations.

For other forms of dermatitis see *impetigo.

DESENSITISATION

Chronic allergic conditions such as hayfever and asthma are often treated by desensitisation or hyposensitisation, which consists of the administration of gradually increasing doses of the antigenic substance in the hope that tolerance will thereby be improved. Once an adequate dose has been reached, maintenance injections are required for up to 2 years. Such treatment is effective in 40–50 per cent of cases and is of greater value in the case of pollen sensitivity (where exposure is usually unpreventable) than in allergies due to domestic allergens, in which case environmental modification is the most favourable approach. Desensitisation depends upon the production of a different type of antibody (IgG), which deals with the antigen before it has time to react with IgE. It is the latter reaction which causes the common allergic responses. (See *allergy.)

As desensitisation involves a series of injections, it is undesirable for small children and is usually contraindicated in children under 6 years of age. It may be considered for older children if other forms of management have failed. It should never be used as a first line of treatment and the need for it is in fact extremely limited.

DEVELOPMENT

The most important thing there is to know about child development is that there is a wide range of normality. Initial studies in this area brought forth a rather rigid concept of 'milestones' of development and it was expected that every child should pass these at a set age. The general pattern of development is fairly constant but the rate is very varied. Naturally you would be concerned if your child seemed to be developing appreciably more slowly than others. You would not be concerned, but would in fact be rather pleased, if he were developing more rapidly than the average. The fact that this is possible implies immediately that there is a wide range of normality on either side of the mean, just as there is a wide range of normality in physical growth or any other potential. If you are worried you should by all means consult an expert.

Most modern parents have some idea of the stages of development of children and of the times at which various skills are acquired. There may, however, be as much significance in the manner in which a particular skill is performed as in the time of its attainment. Sitting, for example, may mean many things, from maintaining a sitting posture for a few seconds to sitting with complete stability and being able to reach for objects on all sides. The transition from the former to the latter type of sitting will take 2 to 3 months. Similarly, one may ask what is meant by crawling. Creeping along on the elbows trailing the legs behind, crawling on hands or knees, or crawling in the bear position? This progressive development will also take about 3 months. Admittedly, a child's development often appears to proceed in small leaps and although there would seem to be a considerable difference between, for example, walking and not walking, nevertheless the concept of 'milestones' is a poor one. 'Stepping-stones' has been suggested as a better alternative, and this does at least imply that one has got to reach one stone before stepping to the next. Any distortion of developmental progress is often of greater significance than a mere variation in rate.

Development is largely dependent upon anatomical maturation of the nervous system. This progresses from the head down, so that voluntary control is progressively established over the eyes, face, arms, hands, back and legs, in this order. If this sequence is not followed it suggests strongly that there is some abnormality of the nervous system. The speed of maturation may be influenced by many factors, the most important being the child's individual make-up. In general, premature babies must be expected to develop somewhat later than full-term babies, although when considered from the age of conception rather than the age of birth their development is often rather advanced. Girls tend to develop rather more rapidly than boys, and black children, on the whole, develop more rapidly than white. The child's personality often makes a difference. The rather timid child who on commencing to walk falls rather badly, may be put off trying again for several weeks. Deprivation has a very definite deleterious effect. Children in institutions who receive little in the way of affection and encouragement tend to develop more slowly than those in normal families. Physical handicaps, such as blindness, deafness, cerebral palsy, will produce fairly specific distortions in developmental progress.

The baby at birth. The degree of development of the nervous system at birth permits a limited repertoire of activity. The newborn baby is able not only to suck and swallow but to root for the nipple without this being placed directly in his mouth. He yawns, hiccups, sighs, sneezes and stretches. He displays rather crude primitive reflexes, prominent among which is the startle response which consists of a grimace, rapid outstretching of the arms and hands followed by a slower grasping movement forwards, and similar movements of the legs. This startle reflex persists for 2 to 3 months and then disappears. The grasp reflex is also characteristic of this age, and the baby may hold on sufficiently strongly to be pulled up by his own grasping efforts. If put on his feet, the baby will display walking movements. When lying at rest with the head turned to one side, the limbs on that side tend to be stretched out whereas those on the opposite side are flexed. The newborn baby is unable to express pleasure but make his displeasure very apparent by crying.

The eyes and vision. The newborn baby obviously sees, and will fix his gaze more on a face than on any other object. This eye-to-eye contact with the parents is thought to be important in the bonding process. He will fix also on a bright object but will be unable to follow it through more than a few degrees. By the age of a month he displays much more visual interest and is capable of following an object through a limited range but not across the midline from one side to the other. Visible tears are produced at about this time. At 6 weeks he will follow a face fairly intently and it is at about this age that he responds with a smile. By 2 months the eyes focus more accurately and he will follow an object through a fairly wide range. By 3 months this is extended to the whole range of ocular movement. At this age, too, he is obviously excited by the sight of a new object and makes thrashing movements of the arms in a crude attempt to grasp. He takes a considerable interest in his hands, looking at them intently, and is obviously fascinated by their movement. He is able to pluck at his clothes, which adds to this interest. Hand–eye co-ordination progresses rapidly until, at about 4–5 months, he is able to grasp a toy with some accuracy. He has now entered the oral phase of development and everything he finds is put to the mouth. By 6 months he responds to any new visual stimulus with great interest, turning head and body to get as good a view as possible and trying to reach out. Fast-moving objects, however, still elude him, but by the age of 2 years visual development appears to be complete.

Hearing. In the first few days of life, the newborn baby displays hardly any response to noise. This is probably because the ear canals are still filled with fluid. As this drains, the eardrum mobilises and he then responds to a sudden, loud sound with a startle reflex. By 2 to 3 months of age he will begin to turn his head towards a sound, so that hearing in each ear can be tested to some extent. His repertoire of sounds is thereafter increasingly determined by imitation of noises he hears. By about 8 months he will respond to his name. Comprehension of speech thereafter advances rapidly and by the age of 1 year he understands a considerable amount and will be saying a few meaningful words.

Control of body position. For the first few weeks of life, the newborn baby tends to maintain the folded-up position he occupies inside his mother's womb. When put in the prone position he retains this flexed position with his head turned to one side. Feeble attempts may be made to lift his head but he can support it only momentarily. By 4 weeks he maintains a rather less flexed position and is able to lift his chin up for a few seconds. By 8 weeks he can lift his head well and look forward, and the legs are now stretched out behind him. At 12 weeks he can pick up not only his head but also his shoulders and support himself on his elbows with the legs completely straight. A month later he can lift up his chest and his arms. By 6 months he delights in pushing himself up on his outstretched arms and looking about. By now he is also an expert in rolling. Mothers are often taken unawares by the baby's first roll and are filled with guilt when the baby falls off the table while she turns to fetch a clean napkin. Fortunately babies are very resilient.

DEVELOPMENT IN THE PRONE POSITION

By about 8 months the baby is usually trying to crawl, although his initial efforts send him backwards rather than forwards. His expertise improves rapidly and he is soon able to get around at a fair rate, trailing his legs behind him in seal-like fashion. He uses his legs more and more, however, and by 9 or 10 months is usually crawling on hands and knees. Just before walking he may go through a period of crawling like a bear on hands and feet, but this stage is sometimes omitted. Some babies never crawl. They shuffle about on their bottoms in the sitting position and sometimes do this so effectively that walking is somewhat delayed.

Sitting. The newborn baby, if pulled up in a sitting position, displays a variable amount of head lag, and when he is upright he is quite unable to control the head, which flops about backwards and forwards and from side-to-side. Head control is progressively achieved over the next 3 months and this control extends to the upper spine, which is held much straighter by this age, although the lower part still tends to curve forward. The baby will, however, enjoy being propped up so that he can see the world around him. By 6 months, if put in a sitting position he will be able to maintain this for a short while by putting his hands in front of him for extra support. He will still tend to totter over to one or other side. A month later he will probably be able to sit erect with straight spine. By 8 to 8½ months he will be able to lean forward and grasp a toy. A month later he will have complete stability in the sitting position and be able to turn from side-to-side without falling.

DEVELOPMENT IN THE SITTING POSITION

Progress towards walking. We have seen that the newborn baby if held in the upright position will make some reflex walking movements, but these are not voluntarily controlled. He is completely slumped and takes no weight on his feet. With progression of voluntary control he first achieves stability of the head and neck, until at 3 months he can control his head fully. His spinal muscles become progressively stronger and at about 5 months of age he takes some weight on his legs. At 6 months he takes a fair amount of his weight but if not held will tend to sag at the hips and knees. A month later, however, he will take all his weight and try to bounce. By 9 months he will probably be able to stand if he is able to hold onto something stable, but he cannot of his own accord pull himself into a standing position. His initial efforts to do so are clumsy, and repeated falls may discourage the more timid child. At about 11 months he will get himself into a standing position and walk sideways, holding on. With both hands held he will step out forwards. By about 12 months he will be able to walk with one hand held, and a month later will probably take his first free steps. The age of achieving this, however, is extremely variable, some babies being able to walk as early as 8 months and others achieving this only at 18 months. The early gait is very unstable, the legs being kept wide apart, the steps are irregular, the arms are held up for balance and the direction is somewhat unpredictable. Progress is punctuated by frequent tumbles. The average child at 15 months is still unable to turn a corner but tends to fall down and then start again in a new direction. By the age of 2 he is sufficiently stable to be able to kick at a ball. By 3 he can walk up stairs in normal adult fashion, but to come down he still needs to put both feet on each step.

Development of manipulation. The early grasp reflex of the newborn baby, which is associated with a tendency for the hands to remain closed, persists for about 2 months. At 3 months the baby becomes excited by the sight of a new object and clearly would like to take it but is able only to make thrashing movements of the arms. If something is put into his hand he will retain it for a few seconds before letting go. He does manage to pull at his clothing and this seems to give him great pleasure. He spends a lot of time looking at his hands and at about 4 months he is able to get his hands together and play with them. At about this time he will make clumsy grasping efforts, and his skill then rapidly improves. Everything he is able to find is put to the mouth and explored for taste and texture. Initially, both hands are used together for grasping, and such efforts are made with the whole hand rather than with the fingers and thumb. At about 6 months he begins to transfer objects from hand to hand, inspecting them and handling them before finally tasting them. If offered a second toy while still clutching the first he will tend to drop the former in order to go for the latter, but by about 8 months he will retain his grasp on the first and then clutch onto both. By 9 months his grasp has become more delicate and he now employs his thumb and fingers to pick up small objects. Shortly after this he discovers the joy of dropping things. At 8 months a dropped toy is immediately forgotten as though it no longer existed, but at 10 to 11 months he drops things deliberately and waits for them to be returned. Before he is a year old he will enjoy putting things in and out of containers. Shortly after a year he can put one block on top of another and by the age of 2 can build his blocks into towers of 4 to 6, depending upon the size and stability of the blocks, plastic ones being decidedly inferior for building purposes to the old wooden ones.

From the age of about 6 months, the baby will be keen to hold his own bottle and shortly after this he will want to help in manipulating his food. A certain amount of mess is unavoidable. The baby will want to pat his food, dip his hands into it and smear it over everything accessible. His initial efforts with the spoon tip the contents into his lap or onto the floor, but he should nevertheless be allowed to 'help' with the feeding, as refusal to do so may result in angry food rejection. His expertise improves with practice and by 15 months he will probably be able to feed himself reasonably well with a spoon. He will also be able to use a cup, still, however, with some spillage, but by 18 months he should be able to handle a cup safely. At 2 he will probably be able to put on his socks and shoes, not necessarily on the right feet, and he will not be able to do up the buckles until a year or so later. By 2½ he will probably be able to remove his pants and will be fully toilet-trained. By 3 to 4 years he should be dressing and undressing almost fully.

Speech development. From about 6 weeks of age, when the baby usually begins smiling, he also expresses pleasure with gurgling noises followed soon after by cooing vowel sounds. Thereafter he responds increasingly to conversation with a variety of noises and at about 6 to 7 months he introduces consonant sounds such as B, D and K, combining these with the vowel sounds into single syllables such as ba, da. A month or so later these syllables tend to be repeated making baba, dada, mama sounds, which at this stage are not meaningful but which subsequently become so irrespective of the family language. At the age of 1 year the average child is saying 3 to 6 words with some meaning. Over the next 6 months or so he indulges in profuse babbling in imitation of speech. His language becomes gradually more defined and at 2 years of age he will probably be making 2- to 3-word

1 2 3 4 5 6 7 8 9 12 15 18

19-24 months
- Puts 3 words together (pronoun, verb, object)
- Listens to stories with pictures
- Turns pages by self
- Tells immediate experiences
- Imitates household tasks
- Helps to undress
- Handles spoon well
- Builds 6 block tower
- Imitates horizontal stroke
- Circular scribbling
- Opens doors
- Walks up and down stairs, one step at a time
- Runs well

16-18 months
- Understands simple verbal commands
- 10 word vocabulary
- Names a few pictures in book
- Feeds self with some spilling
- Hugs doll or bear
- Builds 3-4 block tower
- Strokes imitatively with pencil
- Scribbles spontaneously
- Walks fast, runs stiffly
- Climbs into adult chair
- Walks upstairs with one hand held

15 mo
- Jargon
- Builds 2 block tower
- Shows or offers toys

13-14 m
- Speaks 3-6 words (including names)
- Enjoys "putting in and taking out"
- Imitates scribbling
- Walks alone

12 mo.
- Understands "give it to me"
- Says 2 words plus "mama and dada"
- Dangles toy by string
- Walks with one hand held

11 mo.
- Holds out toy but does not let go
- Walks around furniture
- Walks with both hands held
- Stands alone

10 m.
- Waves "bye" or plays "pat-a-cake"
- Says "dada and mamma"
- Explores and pokes around on toy

9 months
- Parachute reaction present
- Bangs 2 toys together
- Grasps crumb with thumb/index finger
- Pulls self to standing; stands supported
- Crawls or creeps on hands and knees

8 months
- Consonant sounds (da, ba, ga, ka)
- Tries to pick up crumb by raking with thumb, 2nd and 3rd fingers
- Handles toy in each hand
- Pivots in prone using arms
- Sits alone steadily

7 mo.
- Vowel sounds in a series
- Bangs table with a toy
- Transfers toy from hand to hand
- Sits briefly placed on hard surface

6 mo.
- Sits with assistance
- "Talks" to toys spontaneously
- Reaches out, grasps toy with 1 hand

5 mo.
- Squeals
- Brings hands to midline; finger play
- No head lag when pulled to sit

4 mo.
- Rolls over both ways
- Laughs aloud
- Puts toys to mouth
- Prone: lifts head high, chest up

3 months
- Rolls prone to supine or reverse
- Coos and chuckles
- Eyes follow moving objects all planes
- Searches for sound with eyes
- Actively holds rattle placed in hand
- Prone: holds head up at 45°, sustains

2 months
- Eyes follow moving person around
- Smiles socially when stimulated
- Follows rattle with eyes past midline
- Head erect & bobbing, sitting supported
- Prone: lifts head half way, recurrently

1 mo.
- Reduces activity when talked to
- Focuses on rattle in line of vision
- Prone: lifts head briefly

1 2 3 4 5 6 7 8 9 12 15 18
CHRONOLOGICAL AGE IN MONTHS

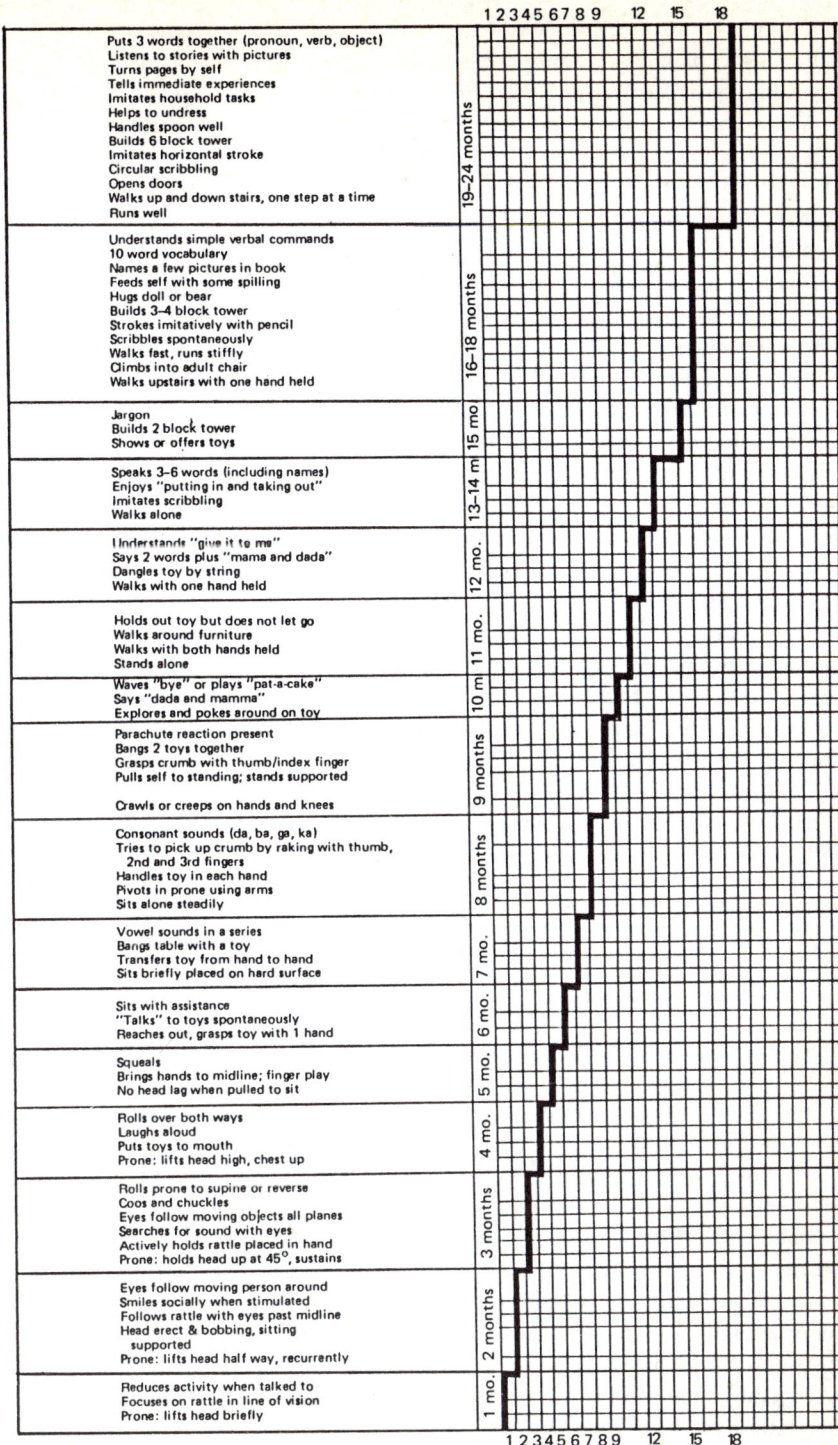

KANSAS INFANT DEVELOPMENT SCREEN
(KIDS)
University of Kansas Medical Center

sentences. Thereafter, speech development is rapid, and talking is almost incessant. The exploratory nature of the toddler gives rise to constant chatter and questioning, which may be exhausting but which demands response.

Although speech development is often a good guide to the child's mentality, this is by no means infallible. Speech development is extremely variable. Many children do not talk until after the age of 3 and it may be comforting to know that Albert Einstein did not talk until he was 4. If speech is delayed it is important to establish that hearing is normal, and an unusually silent baby should be suspected of possible deafness. Speech defects such as lisping, mispronunciation and stammering are common in the first few years and as a rule need not cause anxiety before the age of about 4. Parents should make a practice of speaking clearly and normally to their children and not indulging in silly baby-talk, which the children often rather despise. Parents tend to underestimate their children's understanding and talk down to them instead of using straight-forward language. A child's intellectual development depends a great deal upon his exposure to language, and the richer this is the better. This applies of course to the child's whole environment. The more varied, interesting and stimulating this is the more he is likely to respond. The first year is largely concentrated on oral gratification, but he is developing receptive skills in other sensory areas, particularly visual and auditory, as well as practical skills in achieving mobility and manipulation. This does not mean that he should be provided with all the most expensive, brightly coloured, noisy and elaborate toys. A few homely items from the kitchen are just as intriguing as specific toys and when you are too busy to talk to him let him at least have the pleasure of music. (See *emotional development.)

For those interested in developmental screening, the simple Kansas chart is illustrated. Remember, however, that these are average ages of accomplishment and that the range of normality is considerable.

DIABETES

There are two main types of diabetes — diabetes insipidus, in which large quantities of very dilute sugar-free urine are passed, and diabetes mellitus or sweet diabetes, in which the urine contains sugar. This type of diabetes is much more common and when the term is used unqualified the diabetes is assumed to be mellitus.

Diabetes insipidus may be due to failure of production of the antidiuretic hormone by the pituitary gland, or it may be the result of unresponsiveness on the part of the kidneys to this hormone. These conditions will not be considered because of their rarity.

Diabetes mellitus is due to failure of the pancreas to produce insulin. The pancreatic gland has a double function. It produces digestive enzymes, which it secretes into the upper intestine, and in addition it produces endocrine secretions, dominant among which is insulin, whose main function is to promote the utilisation and storage of glucose, thus lowering the blood-glucose level. In the absence of insulin, glucose is not satisfactorily metabolised and the blood-level therefore rises. Associated with this there is a generalised metabolic disturbance involving the incomplete utilisation of fats and the accumulation of fatty acids, which gives rise to the state of ketoacidosis. When this is present, acetone can be smelt in the breath and ketones detected in the urine. Because of the increased production of urine, and the vomiting which is often present, hydration is progressively impaired and the patient looks extremely sunken. Ketosis causes increased respiration and 'air hunger'. The patient becomes progressively drowsy and confused and eventually loses consciousness. It is in this stage that many young diabetics present for the first time. They may, however, present simply with excessive thirst and abnormal urinary output, including sometimes bedwetting and loss of weight.

Management. The fundamental need for the juvenile diabetic is for insulin. This has to be given by injection, and in the early stages of treatment rather frequent injections may be necessary. These will, however, diminish until the child is eventually on 1 or 2 injections daily. If given with a very fine needle such injections are almost painless, and as soon as possible the child should be taught how to give his own injections, thus giving him complete independence. Several types of insulin are available with varying duration of activity, short-acting preparations lasting about 6 hours, medium-acting about 15 hours and the long-acting up to 30 hours; the last however are very infrequently used. It is impossible to adjust the insulin dose with complete precision but as good control as possible should be aimed at in order to prevent the long-term complications of diabetes, which affect predominantly the eyes, the blood-vessels and the nerves.

Some degree of dietary control is essential if wild fluctuations in blood-sugar levels are to be avoided. Meals should be small, limited in carbohydrate content and the food intake distributed as evenly as possible throughout the day by giving snacks between meals and at bedtime. It is as well initially to consult tables giving the carbohydrate values of foods, such as those prepared by the British Diabetic Association. It is important to realise, however, that the form in which the carbohydrate is taken is of great importance. Sugars are rapidly absorbed, as are pure starches, but when buffered, for example with bran, as in wholewheat bread, the absorption is much slower. Sugar in fruit, such as apples, is absorbed much more slowly and is therefore more readily handled by the diabetic. As far as possible, natural foods should therefore be given. Because of the vascular complications, margerine high in polyunsaturates is probably preferable to butter.

Although sugar substitutes are useful, the diabetic patient should be encouraged to develop non-sweet tastes. For special occasions, sugar-free diabetic drinks should replace the popular sucrose-containing 'cold drinks', which are in any case an abomination.

Regular urine-testing is essential for the diabetic, but once stability has been achieved it is usually not necessary to test more than once a day in the morning, with more frequent checks once a week. When control is lost it may be necessary to check blood-sugar levels, and this can be done easily using a drop of blood from a finger-prick and the Dextrostix, Visidex or Haemogluco test-strips. Regular blood-glucose monitoring can be of value in obtaining finer diabetic control especially in adults, but for small children this is impractical. If the urine contains an appreciable amount of glucose it should also be tested for ketones.

Diabetic coma. There are two types of coma associated with diabetes. The first, due to hyperglycaemia (i.e. a high blood-sugar level) and ketoacidosis, has already been described. The second type, due to hypoglycaemia, occurs when there is an excess of insulin and insufficient carbohydrate. Hunger, dizziness and light-headedness are common early symptoms. The skin is moist and there may be tremor or unsteadiness. Difficulty in focusing the eyes may be accompanied by an actual squint. The child becomes confused, often resistant, and eventually loses consciousness, and there may be convulsions. These symptoms are usually of sudden onset and therefore distinguishable from those of hyperglycaemic ketoacidosis, which usually supervenes more gradually. The management of hypoglycaemia would depend upon its severity. In the early stages a simple sweet or spoon of sugar should be followed by a light meal and if the child is confused or drowsy a sugar or glucose solution, 3 teaspoonfuls to a cup of water, or juice should be given. If he is unconscious, it is unwise to try and give anything by mouth and the glucose should preferably be given intravenously. An alternative is to inject Glucagon, which is another pancreatic hormone that elevates the blood-glucose level. If hypoglycaemia occurs with any frequency the dose or type of insulin requires modification.

Ketoacidosis, as indicated earlier, requires urgent insulin administration and in addition the correcting of dehydration by administering appropriate fluids and salt. In the stuporose patient this will require intravenous administration, and hospitalisation will then be necessary. Ketoacidosis is often precipitated in the previously well-controlled diabetic by infection, and this will also require appropriate treatment. Children who are giving their own injections may of course forget their insulin or give an incorrect dose, and this possibility must always be checked.

After initiating of insulin treatment in the new diabetic there is usually a diminishing need, and the dose administered has to be reduced over the first several weeks and may actually reach zero for a time. This however is only a temporary situation, indicating a partial recovery of pancreatic function. Insulin injections will almost certainly be required again.

The diabetic child should lead a perfectly normal life, provided his insulin is taken regularly and he pays reasonable attention to his diet. Exercise helps to reduce the blood-sugar level, and when strenuous exercise is contemplated the insulin dose may have to be reduced. Regular daily physical activity of some sort is as desirable as in the normal child. Diabetics should not, however, embark on dangerous activities unaccompanied. They should be identified with a suitable bracelet indicating that they are diabetics and they should always have available a couple of sweets to take should they develop hypoglycaemic symptoms.

Syringes sometimes cause problems, but the simple disposable diabetic syringe with fine needle attached is admirable and nothing more elaborate is required. Children who have difficulty in giving their own injections may prefer the automatic injector, but this is an extravagance which is hardly justifiable. Syringes do not need to be meticulously sterilised. It is quite safe after giving the injection to put the syringe, with the needle protected, in the refrigerator and leave it there until the next injection is due, and this can be continued for 2 months quite safely before the syringe need be changed. Nor is it necessary to sterilise the skin. A wipe with a spirit swab achieves absolutely nothing and more elaborate manoeuvres are unnecessary.

It is advisable for every diabetic to join the Diabetic Association, which gives its members a great deal of practical help.

Maternal diabetes. Diabetes tends to reduce fertility, but nevertheless many diabetic women successfully have families. It is essential that the diabetes be controlled as accurately as possible during pregnancy in order to avoid harmful effects on the foetus. There is a slightly increased incidence of congenital abnormalities but this is not sufficiently high to cause anxiety. Poorly controlled maternal diabetes usually causes excessive growth of the foetus, although some babies remain small. The baby is often delivered somewhat prematurely and then, in spite of his large size, behaves in a manner appropriate to his period of gestation. When the mother's diabetes has been well controlled hardly any difficulty is experienced with the baby. When control is less perfect the baby commonly develops hypoglycaemia (low blood-sugar) within a short time of birth. If severe, this can be damaging and babies are therefore usually protected by giving them glucose orally or intravenously for the first day or two of life. Thereafter there is usually no problem. Babies born prematurely may suffer from the respiratory distress syndrome, as well as the other hazards of prematurity, but these problems are transient and usually successfully handled.

It must be stressed that the most important factor in the successful outcome of pregnancy in a diabetic woman is good control during her pregnancy.

DIAPERS
See *napkins

DIARRHOEA
Looseness of the stools, with increased frequency, is one of the commonest symptoms in childhood. Most cases are mild, shortlived, self-limiting and in need of no treatment. The severity of diarrhoea, however, varies greatly and in very severe cases dehydration and death can supervene within a matter of hours. Gastro-enteritis is the commonest cause of death in small children in undeveloped countries.

Diarrhoea has many causes. It may be diet-related and due to irritation of the bowel by toxic substances inadvertently ingested, or the result of inability on the part of the bowel to digest and absorb specific foodstuffs, for example lactose intolerance and coeliac disease, or it may be due to specific intestinal allergies. The most common cause is some infection of the bowel due to viruses, bacteria or protozoa such as amoebae and giardia. The larger parasites, such as whipworms and bilharzia, may cause dysentery. Sometimes in small children diarrhoea appears to be associated with infection outside the intestines, but it is more probable that the same virus has caused an enteritis as well as predisposing to, for example, ear infection. Excessive nervousness can cause diarrhoea, as may endocrine disturbance such as thyrotoxicosis. Occasionally, what appears to be diarrhoea is really a manifestation of *constipation. If the small bowel is predominantly involved, the intestinal contents are propelled at an excessive rate and the stools are then often green. This is because the bile, which normally changes to a brown colour during its passage down the intestine, has not had time to be so altered. If the large bowel is severely irritated and inflamed there is an excess of mucus in the stool, and this may be associated with bleeding. (See *dysentery.) The exaggerated contractions of the muscular wall of the bowel give rise to cramps, which are usually felt vaguely over the abdomen and not localised, though colonic pain is situated lower than upper intestinal pain. Vomiting often accompanies the diarrhoea and the condition is then known as gastro-enteritis. The exact cause of gastro-enteritis is most often not determined. Many cases are due to virus infections, particularly in winter, and one particularly common agent, the Rotavirus (so-called because it resembles a wheel) can be readily identified by special stool tests. In summer a higher proportion of cases is due to infection with specific bacteria, such as the food-poisoning organisms (Salmonellae) or the dysenteric group (Shigellae).

The severity of the condition depends to a great extent on whether vomiting is present or not, for if the child is vomiting and is unable to make good the stool losses of water and salts he may rapidly become dehydrated. If there is no vomiting and the child appears well there is little need to worry, and normal feeds can be continued with the addition of extra fluids to satisfy the child's thirst. If the child appears ill, is running a high temperature, is vomiting, is exhibiting signs of dehydration with sunken eyes, sunken fontanelle, inelastic skin and dry mouth, or if the stools contain blood, then you must seek medical help. The significantly dehydrated child will almost certainly require hospital admission and probably intravenous fluids. Until such time as you are able to get him to a doctor you should try to get in as much fluid as possible, giving either fruit juice or the type of fluid described under *dehydration.

Medicines have little part to play in the treatment of acute diarrhoeal states. If vomiting is present they will be poorly tolerated and may make matters worse. It is, however, sometimes possible to suppress the vomiting with antiemetic drugs given by injection. The diarrhoea is almost always self-limiting. Medicines to reduce the bowel motility are contraindicated, particularly in children, as they may mask fluid losses by allowing large amounts of fluid to accumulate in the bowel lumen. Furthermore, if there is a bowel irritant it is better that this be expelled than retained. Some of these medications are frankly dangerous in children. Preparations such as chalk, pectin and kaolin may improve the appearance of the stools by increasing the residue but they do not diminish fluid loss and they are of absolutely no value. Antibiotics are ineffective in virus infections and often prolong the disease, even in bacterial infections such as Salmonellae. They may have a place in the treatment of acute bacterial dysentery but this also is usually a self-limiting disease. Conditions such as amoebiasis, however, do require active treatment. The majority of cases of diarrhoea will cease spontaneously and need only fluid and electrolyte management.

Chronic diarrhoea. This is common in the toddler age-group, and often the cause is undetermined — so-called 'toddler diarrhoea'. The stools are excessively soft and usually contain easily recognisable food particles. In spite of this apparent 'indigestion' the child thrives perfectly well and is usually quite happy. The condition requires no treatment but if the symptoms are embarrassing there may be justification for treating this particular type of diarrhoea with a drug to reduce bowel motility, such as loperamide, in appropriate dosage. Chronic diarrhoea is commonly due to a small intestinal parasite, *Giardia lamblia*, a unicellular flagellate which inhabits the upper bowel and which does not always appear on stool testing. It is often worth treating speculatively for this condition without trying to prove the existence of the parasite with stool tests. Chronic diarrhoea with foul, pale, fatty stools may be due to *coeliac disease, *cystic fibrosis or, occasionally, specific food (e.g. milk) intolerance. A recently recognised cause of persistent diarrhoea is excessive consumption of apple juice. Rarer causes of chronic diarrhoea are congenital abnormalities of the bowel, operative resection of a significant portion of the bowel, and diseases such as *ulcerative colitis. Diarrhoea almost always accompanies severe malnutrition, and is then due to several factors: infection, atrophy of the bowel-lining and deficiency of the digestive enzymes. All children with chronic diarrhoea should be seen by a doctor.

DIET

The main nutritional requirements provided by food are protein, required for growth and maintenance of healthy body tissues, carbohydrate, required for energy purposes, and fat, used largely for energy storage but with some fatty acids being essential for health. Numerous elements are required such as iron, calcium, phosphorus, sodium, chloride, and potassium, and some are essential although only in small quantities, for example, magnesium, zinc, copper and fluorine. Vitamins are chemical substances essential for normal metabolism which the body is unable to manufacture from simpler compounds, and which therefore have to be obtained from the diet.

It is unlikely that the children of readers of this book will suffer from any dietary deficiency. Provided a child is given a reasonably balanced intake of natural foodstuffs no extras need be given. Huge sums of money are wasted annually in the purchase of vitamins and tonics for children who have no need of them. Not only is such practice wasteful but it may be psychologically harmful in persuading a child who is perfectly well that he is in need of medicine. Unfortunately, doctors are much to blame in creating the illusion that there is a magical medicinal answer to every problem. In contrast to the more privileged members of society, the bulk of the world's population lead a precarious dietary existence, and in southern Africa the incidence of severe malnutrition, particularly among children, is appalling. This is due not solely to poverty but also to ignorance. Staple foods such as maize-meal, which are severely deficient in protein and other essential nutrients, continue to be given to children as virtually the sole article of diet. The addition of readily available, inexpensive, high protein foods, such as beans, would go a long way towards preventing the malnutritional ravages among the poor.

Special diets. There are few indications for special diets for children, who in general should be encouraged, but certainly not forced, to eat as wide a variety of foods as possible. Diabetic children have to have some restrictions imposed upon their intake of carbohydrates, sufferers from coeliac disease have to avoid gluten, some rare metabolic disorders, for example, phenylketonuria, demand very special diets excluding specific amino acids, and obese children should have their calorie intake reduced. (See *calories.) Fad diets so popular among adults have no place in the world of children. (See also *feeding.)

DIPHTHERIA

This is a specific infectious disease caused by a bacillus which usually invades the throat, nose or larynx but may involve other areas. It produces a powerful toxin which severely damages the adjacent tissues, giving rise to a membrane of greyish-white appearance, which is typical of the disease. The toxin also spreads to other parts of the body, affecting particularly the heart and the peripheral nerves. Other organs, such as liver and kidneys, may also be involved.

The incubation period is 2 to 7 days. Initial symptoms are fever, malaise and headache. The throat is inflamed and the lymph glands of the neck enlarge, producing considerable swelling. The inflammation commonly involves the larynx, causing breathing difficulty, and unless the obstruction is relieved death may well supervene. (See *croup.) Secondary infection such as pneumonia may occur. The heart is commonly affected by the toxin, resulting in heart failure and possibly death. If the child survives he may develop paralysis as the result of nerve involvement, usually from the 3rd to the 8th week after onset of the disease. This paralysis often involves the throat, causing difficulty in swallowing, and also the eyes and diaphragm.

Treatment consists of administration of the specific antitoxin, penicillin, to kill off the bacteria; maintenance of the airway, which often entails bypassing the larynx by means of a tracheostomy; and supportive treatment for the complications. With adequate treatment the mortality rate is fairly low.

Prevention. Diphtheria should not exist, for it is readily prevented by administration of the appropriate vaccine, which consists of a toxoid (i.e. a modified toxin) which promotes the formation by the body of specific antitoxin. The toxoid is usually combined with whooping-cough vaccine and tetanus toxoid, and administered from the 3rd month of life in 3 initial injections at 6–8 weekly intervals, with booster doses at about 18 months and 5 years. It is absolutely essential to have your child immunised against diphtheria. Not to do so is criminally irresponsible.

DIRT-EATING
See *pica

DISCHARGE
Vaginal discharge is common in baby girls in the first few days of life. It may consist solely of rather thick mucus, or there may occasionally be actual bleeding, which is the equivalent of menstrual bleeding and due to the hormonal changes which have occurred with delivery and which also commonly cause breast enlargement and milk secretion. This discharge is of no importance and requires no management apart from general cleanliness.

Later vaginal discharge may be due to infection, foreign bodies, threadworms or, in the pubertal girl, the normal increased vaginal secretions. (See *vaginal discharge.)

DISCIPLINE
Much has been written and said about this subject and the disciplinary pendulum continues to swing to and fro. Parents' attitudes towards discipline will inevitably be coloured by their own experiences. If these were satisfactory they will tend to perpetuate the attitudes of their own parents and if unsatisfactory they will probably try to remedy the defects as they see them, but it is surprising to what

extent overtly bad disciplinary attitudes are perpetuated from generation to generation.

Discipline means different things to different people. To some it may be equated with punishment, which is quite wrong for it involves much more than this. Disciplining your child largely means giving the example and the opportunity for self-discipline, so that he may fit in happily with society. The means by which this is achieved will inevitably vary depending upon the character of the parents, the character of the child and the nature of the environment. It will also be governed by the age of the child and the parents' knowledge of normal development. Behaviour which is normal at 18 months may be thoroughly inappropriate at 4.

The exploratory toddler will have to be disciplined for the sake of his own safety. He must be taught that electric plugs are dangerous and are not to be touched, that he must not dig a knife into the toaster, that the pot handles projecting from the stove so temptingly are full of danger and that if he pulls the cat's tail he is likely to get scratched. It is almost always possible to communicate these warnings by tone of voice without recourse to physical punishment, but the occasional light tap may be necessary to reinforce taboos. It should never be necessary to inflict significant physical hurt on a child. Many animals cuff their children in training but they never hurt them.

The school-going child has a considerable amount of discipline forced upon him by the school, some of it good and sensible, much of it pointless and silly. It is only natural that children should revolt against rules which they find senseless, and if too many petty rules are imposed there may well be a complete breakdown in discipline from sheer revulsion for the whole system. Rules should therefore have a reasonable basis. They should apply to everybody so that the child does not feel victimised, they should be fair and they should be constant. No child can learn if the rules change from day to day. Children are generally happier working within well-defined limits of behaviour, and if tempted to err beyond these limits they will expect to have to pay some retribution. Punishment, however, should never be severe or vindictive, it should be immediate, appropriate, shortlived and effective. A popular method of punishment is 'time out', in which the child is deprived of interesting activity for a short period, say 2 minutes, which he must spend, for example, sitting in a particular chair. He may occasionally be sent to his room but he should not be sent to bed, and it is not a good idea to banish him to the toilet. It may be difficult to avoid the odd smack but this need never be really painful, and it should be given with the hand and never an implement, so that you are well aware of the force you are using. A child will accept these punishments and benefit from them, provided they seem to him just, and particularly if they are administered infrequently, for the more a child is punished the less effective punishment becomes. If a child seems to need punishing often, something is seriously amiss and you should consult someone about it. Once the price has been paid the whole thing should be forgotten and friendly relationships restored. On no account should punishment be delayed until father gets home, and there is no place for continued harping and grumbling.

The teenager may present a more difficult problem. Rebelliousness is normal at this age and there should be a progressive relaxation of parental control, but still with well-defined limits of behaviour. The adolescent will accept such limits more readily if he sees that his parents also accept certain limits, but if it is clear to him that there is hypocrisy involved in what is expected of him, he cannot be blamed if he loses a certain amount of respect for his parents, and therefore a respect for discipline. This is a time when contact with your child has to be maximal, when doors have to be opened not closed, when living together should be mutually stimulating and not a perpetual strain. It is a time of interest and opportunity but it is a time also of criticism and judgement, and training and discipline will be best achieved by example rather than dictatorship.

DISLOCATION

Congenital dislocation of the hip. This is a relatively common condition, 6 times more common in girls than in boys and affecting the left hip more than the right. There is a high incidence in babies presenting by the breech. The severity of the condition varies from simple ligamentous laxity, producing a dislocatable hip, many of which recover spontaneously without treatment, to a gross abnormality in which the hip joint is severely malformed. The practice of swaddling appears to increase the incidence, which is particularly high in northern Italy and also in some North American Indian tribes. Where, however, the infant is carried astride the back with the legs in an abducted position, for example in the black African, the incidence is particularly low.

Every newborn baby should be examined for the possibility of dislocated hips and if these are found, appropriate treatment should be instituted. In the simpler cases it suffices to keep the thighs abducted, and this can be achieved fairly simply be reversing the napkins. If this proves inadequate a special abduction splint will be required. Persistent dislocation, or those associated with malformation of the hip joint, will probably require operative treatment.

Dislocation of the head of the radius. This is a fairly common injury, produced usually by picking the child up with one arm, a usual manoeuvre when a small child is being slung onto the mother's back. The radius (one of the long forearm bones) is pulled out of its ligament near the elbow joint, and in addition to local pain there is limitation of joint movement. The condition may correct itself spontaneously but the dislocation can be readily corrected by the appropriate manipulation, with immediate relief of symptoms.

DIVORCE

In a society where the divorce rate is approaching 50 per cent it might be thought that children would be becoming immune to this situation, which is almost becoming the norm. The effect on children depends of course a great deal upon their age and, to a much greater extent, upon parental attitudes. Where the divorce is simply the culmination of many years of unhappiness and strife the child's security will have been destroyed long before the divorce itself and the latter may come as a relief. Where the divorce is precipitated to legitimise a sudden extra-marital affair, it may come as a profound shock to a sensitive teenager. One can therefore hardly generalise about the effects of divorce on children, except to say that they are profound and usually damaging. It is important, therefore, if you are contemplating separation or divorce, to explain to your children the reasons behind it. Children can be made to understand that their security is not severely threatened, that they are still loved by both parents even though the parents' love for each other may have disintegrated and, above all, that both parents continue to care. It can be pointed out that it is because they care that the divorce is taking place, for there is no point in trying to stick together in perpetual disharmony or in silent, sullen resentment 'for the sake of the children'. If, however, there is the slightest possibility of preserving your marriage and restoring to it some of the happiness which you originally anticipated, then don't give it up too readily. In every marriage, as in every life, there are ups and downs, and however unbearable some of the downs may appear to be, the next up may surprisingly bring quite extraordinary enrichment. The sticky periods will demand patience, tact, tolerance, sacrifice and humility, but may it not be worth it?

If there is absolutely no alternative to divorce, do see that your children are not used as weapons with which to bludgeon your opponent. Don't use them as convenient auditory receptacles for vilification of your ex-spouse. Remember that your children identify with both of you. By humiliating their father or mother you humiliate them — and have they not already suffered enough? It may be difficult to be loyal to someone who has caused you such hurt that love has evaporated or turned to hate, but for the sake of the children you can try. If your marriage, for which you had such high hopes, should end in divorce, let it at least be clean and surgical and not allowed to fester. Try to see things through the eyes of your children and let the devastation be as restrained as possible.

DOG-BITES

These wounds are usually not very serious, although they may be fairly penetrating, and often become infected. Dog-bites on the face may be disfiguring and are usually best attended to by a doctor. Bites elsewhere should simply be washed clean and protected by a small dressing until a healing scab has formed.

Tetanus may occur after dog-bites but there is little risk of this if a child has been immunised. A booster tetanus injection may be advisable if the immunisation status is doubtful. Rabies is the most feared complication of dog-bite, but the behaviour of the dog should indicate whether this is a possibility. If the dog is your own it will be fairly clear whether or not it is rabid, but in outbreaks of this disease a child may well be bitten by a stray dog that cannot be identified. In such cases it is safer to embark upon vaccine treatment, as once the disease is manifest it is inevitably fatal. (See *rabies.)

DOWN'S SYNDROME

This condition, also known as mongolism, is one of the most common congenital abnormalities, occurring in about 1:600 births but increasing in frequency with advancing maternal age. It is due to a chromosomal abnormality (see *chromosomes), the normal number of 46 chromosomes being increased to 47 by the presence of an extra chromosome, number 21 (trisomy 21). This abnormality arises at the time of conception and affects every cell of the body. This makes the condition completely incurable. The trisomic state arises, as a rule, because of faulty meiosis in the formation of the ovum, which, like the sperms, normally has only half the number of chromosomes in the other body cells, namely 23. If, however, meiosis is defective, one of the daughter cells may contain 2 chromosomes number 21, and when this ovum is fertilised there are then 3. (See figure.) A very small number of trisomies are due to what is called a balanced translocation in the parent, an important situation to identify, for in this case the chances of having a second trisomic child are as high as 1:6. (See *chromosomes.)

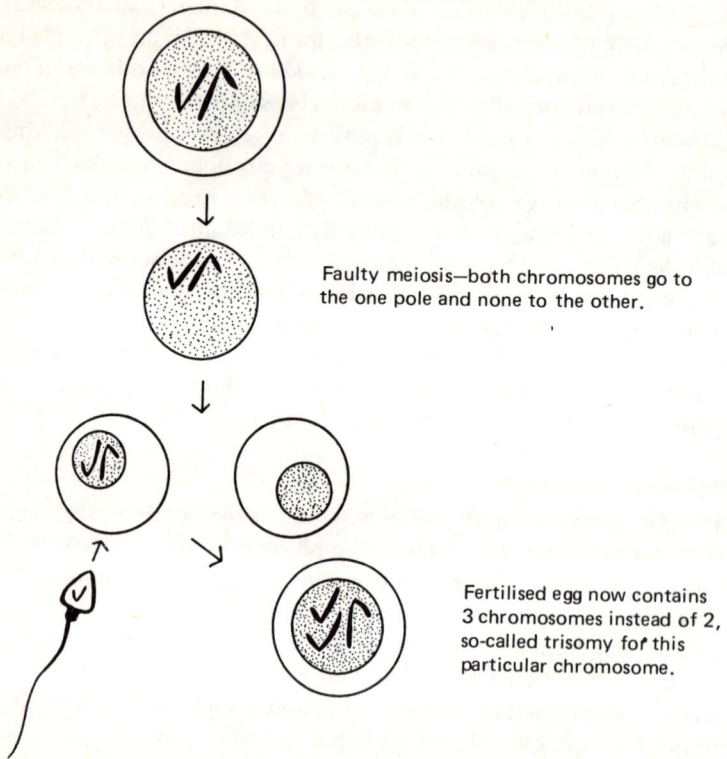

Faulty meiosis—both chromosomes go to the one pole and none to the other.

Fertilised egg now contains 3 chromosomes instead of 2, so-called trisomy for this particular chromosome.

DOWN'S SYNDROME

The child with Down's syndrome displays characteristic features, which are usually identifiable at birth. The head is rather small and round, the eyes slant in mongoloid fashion, and there is often a ring of small white specks in the iris. The mouth is down-turned and the tongue large. The ears tend to be small and misshapen. There is excessive loose skin in the neck. The hands are stubby, show a characteristic single transverse palmar crease, and the fifth finger is often short and incurving. There are characteristic features of the fine hand creases. There is usually a rather wide cleft between the great toe and the others. The baby's general muscle tone is poor, causing limpness and relative inactivity. Abnormalities of the heart are present in about 20 per cent of cases. Mental retardation is invariably present, the average IQ being about 50, but these children are usually quiet and good-humoured.

In the early months and years, the child with Down's syndrome requires no special care or management. If a heart defect is present this may predispose to pneumonia, and in any case such children are more prone to infection than the normal child. Development will inevitably be slow, and with increasing age, therefore, the difference becomes more and more conspicuous. By school-going age it is clear that the child will not benefit from a normal school curriculum, but he will nevertheless profit from a degree of formal education, and the acquisition of even elementary reading and writing will help to enlarge his world considerably. A great deal of supportive help will be required for parents, and advice regarding, for example, special school placement will be best obtained through the Mental Health Society.

DPT

DPT is otherwise known as DWT or triple antigen, and is a vaccine against diphtheria, whooping-cough (pertussis) and tetanus. It should be administered to all babies (with the exception of the pertussis component, which may be omitted in babies with neurological problems), commencing at 3 months of age and repeated at 6- to 8-week intervals for 3 doses. Subsequent boosters are given at about 18 months and 5 years. Excellent immunity is obtained to diphtheria and tetanus, and 60 to 80 per cent protection against whooping-cough.

Reactions to the vaccine are usually due to the pertussis component. Local pain and swelling are common, but unimportant. A nodule at the injection site may persist for a long time. Fever and irritability during the first 24 hours are frequent. More severe reactions should be reported.

DROWNING

The sadly high incidence of accidental drowning is a reflection as much of opulence as of carelessness, for as many such accidents occur in private pools as elsewhere. Whatever mechanical precautions are taken they are just never infallible, and the determination with which small children will head for water makes it imperative that they be watched the whole time. The best precaution against drowning, of course, is to teach your child to swim. This can be done from the age of about 6 months and a child so trained can often swim before he can walk. This, however, does not inevitably protect him, nor does it protect other children, and if you are in the fortunate position of having your own pool, for your own peace of mind have it protected as safely as possible with a fence that is unscalable and under which it is not possible to burrow, and a gate that is child- and fool-proof.

There are differences between fresh- and sea-water drowning, which are important for proper subsequent management, but, from your point of view, if a near-drowning accident should occur, the important thing is to get the child breathing again as rapidly as possible. The small child should be held upside down for a short while, to drain as much water from the air passages as possible, and the larger child put on his tummy and the chest squeezed a few times. Thereafter the child should be placed on his back, and mouth-to-mouth respiration performed until regular, spontaneous respiration is established. (See *artificial respiration.) He will almost certainly be cold as a result of exposure, and he should then be wrapped in warm blankets and taken to the doctor or hospital as a matter of urgency. If respirations should fail, artificial respiration should be reapplied as necessary en route.

DRUGS

Though the term 'drug' may be applied to any medicine, it is commonly associated with narcotics, and it may be that this association is a good thing if it serves to remind people that drugs are to be treated with respect and not to be consumed without good reason.

Drug abuse among young people has been a phenomenon that has more or less paralleled the general increase in consumption of medicines of all sorts. The production of really potent medications has been a feature of the last 50 years or so. People have always sought magic as an answer to their problems, and in recent decades they appear to have found a certain amount, with pills to relieve pain, pills to relieve depression, pills to relieve insomnia, pills for constipation, pills for diarrhoea and, greatest joy of all, pills for contraception. Is it any wonder therefore that young people brought up in such an atmosphere want to try the various drugs they have heard of? And sometimes of course they get hooked.

If you are to help your child avoid the drug menace, it is no good avoiding the subject in the hope that it will never arise. You will set a good example by not abusing drugs yourself, be these medicines, tobacco or, the most dangerous of all, alcohol. It is a good idea to discuss freely and repeatedly the problem of drug abuse, and to let your child feel free to open such discussions should he so wish. If he gets into undesirable company, try to steer him out of it, though this will require great tact and patience, and if he seems to be in danger, seek help before the situation becomes irretrievable.

DUMMIES

Most people, including paediatricians, feel obliged to condemn dummies as being unhygienic, unaesthetic and sometimes damaging, while at the same time unashamedly giving them to their own infants. There is no doubt that a dummy can be useful in pacifying a baby who is crying. Unfortunately, the baby cannot tell us why he finds a dummy soothing, but at an age where gratification is almost entirely oral it presumably bluffs him to some extent. It would perhaps be better to find out why the baby is crying. If he is hungry it would be better to give him something other than rubber. If it is from loneliness, he would be better comforted by closeness to his mother, for example, by using a sling.

Are dummies harmful? Though dummies must be regarded as unhygienic, by the time a child is able to find and replace the dummy, which has perhaps fallen on the floor, he is probably grubbing around and mouthing far more noxious objects. Perpetually dipping the dummy in syrups is certainly bad for the teeth once these have appeared. Dipping in glycerin of borax has caused convulsions. Distortion of the teeth can occur from prolonged use of dummies. It would be wise, therefore, to get rid of dummies by the time teeth have erupted, and the baby should at this age in any case be given a more stimulating occupation than sucking a dummy.

It is often asked whether, if a child is going to suck something, it is preferable for him to suck a dummy or his thumb. Opinion is almost equally divided on the subject and it therefore probably does not matter. The dummy can at least be thrown away, whereas the thumb cannot. On the other hand, the thumb does not get lost and is always immediately available. The question begs the true problem, which is why the child beyond the first few months of life needs to suck anything at all. The answer is usually that he is bored, and the correct approach therefore is to provide him with greater interest and distraction.

DUST
See *house dust

DWARFISM
Significantly impaired growth may result from many factors. It may simply be constitutional and a reflection of the parental size, it may be due to disease, particularly of the kidneys, which results in retarded growth, or to rickets. It may be associated with other congenital abnormalities, and among these a whole variety of syndromes is recognised. It may be due to specific abnormalities of bone formation, such as achondroplasia, or it may be the result of endocrine deficiency particularly of the growth hormone secreted by the pituitary gland. Lack of thyroid also results in poor growth, and long-continued administration of cortico-steroid drugs likewise suppresses growth.

Achondroplasia is one of the commonest conditions, and most circus dwarfs belong to this category. The abnormal bone development affects particularly the upper arms and thighs and the base of the skull, so that the forehead is prominent and the nose rather depressed. This condition is inherited as a Mendelian domi-nant, and the chances of offspring being affected are therefore 1:2. Many cases, however, are new mutants, arising without preceding family history. There is no treatment for this condition.

Pituitary dwarfs may be the result of pure growth-hormone deficiency, but frequently other endocrine abnormalities, such as thyroid deficiency, accompany the condition. These children grow very slowly from the beginning but their body proportions are not distorted. Growth can be improved by administration of human growth-hormone which, however, is very expensive and which tends to lose its efficacy after 2–3 years of treatment.

DYSENTERY
This term is applied to diarrhoea with the presence of blood and mucus in the stool. It implies a severe irritation of the large bowel. This may be the result of chemical poisons such as heavy metals and phosphorus (very unlikely in chil-dren), bacterial infection with dysenteric organisms (Shigella and Salmonella), amoebic infection common in the tropics and subtropics, certain parasites such as whipworms, and rare conditions of uncertain origin such as ulcerative colitis.

The acute bacillary dysenteries are of abrupt onset, often associated with fever, and there is profuse bloody diarrhoea which lasts for 3–4 days and will then usually terminate spontaneously. These infections can be very severe resulting in dehydration and shock and requiring prompt intravenous fluid replacement. The excreta are highly infectious and should be disposed of with great care to prevent contamination. Regular hand-washing is essential after attention to such a patient. Occasionally, the patient may continue to excrete the offending bacteria in a carrier state after symptoms have subsided.

Amoebic dysentery is due to invasion of the colonic lining by a small unicellular parasite, the *Entamoeba histolytica*. This produces ulceration of the lining of the colon. In severe cases such ulceration may almost destroy the whole lining, and in the worst cases perforation of the bowel may occur. Most cases, however, are milder, and some 5 per cent of the population harbour the parasite without symptoms. The amoeba may enter the bloodstream and be carried to the liver, where it proliferates, producing large amoebic abscesses. These give rise to fever, abdominal pain and liver tenderness, and occasionally jaundice. In nearly half of the cases of such metastatic amoebiasis there is no history of preceding dysentery. The treatment of amoebiasis, whether bowel or metastatic, is administration of a suitable amoebicidal drug such as metronidazole.

Whipworm dysentery is common in young African children. The worms, which have a long, thin, anterior segment, burrow into the colon, causing bleeding and irritation. This is a chronic condition and the blood loss is often sufficient to produce severe anaemia. The worms are fairly readily dislodged by modern vermicidal drugs. (See *worms.)

DYSLEXIA

This simply means difficulty in reading, and may be applied to a child who, having normal intelligence and normal vision and being exposed to adequate teaching methods, nevertheless fails to make proper progress in reading and writing. His speech is usually normal and his understanding of the spoken word unimpaired but there is a breakdown in the complicated connections which relate words to visual symbols. Seldom is there any identifiable brain disease or destruction.

The dyslexic child stands in great danger of being labelled lazy or stupid if his problem is not recognised relatively early. He develops a poor self-image and gives up trying, thus compounding the problem. If recognised early, however, the application of special teaching methods will greatly help the dyslexic child and he may eventually achieve complete competence. Occasionally such children continue to have extreme difficulty with reading and writing throughout their lives. There are nevertheless numerous instances of people who have been extremely successful in spite of such a handicap. If you suspect that your child is not progressing satisfactorily, take the matter up with his teachers. (See 'schooling problems' under *school.)

EAR

The anatomy of the right ear is illustrated in the figure. Note that the eardrum completely separates the external auditory canal from the middle ear. The middle ear communicates with the nasal cavity via the eustachian tube. Sound vibrations impinging on the eardrum are transmitted through the tiny bones of the middle ear to the cochlea, where they are converted into nervous impulses.

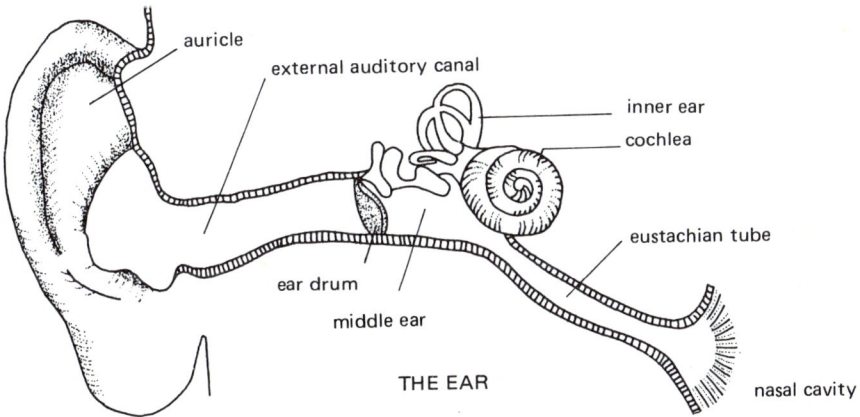

THE EAR

Diseases of the ear are common in children. The external ear may be inflamed as the result of chemical irritation, for example from swimming pools; infection may be introduced through foreign bodies (and children find an astonishing range of objects to push in their ears); or infections such as boils may arise, which are extremely painful because the skin of the canal, being firmly adherent to the surrounding bone, cannot stretch.

Most infections of the ear in small children arise in the middle ear, and are the result of obstruction to the eustachian tube by colds originating in the nose. The eustachian tube becomes swollen and blocked, and if inflammatory secretions accumulate in the middle ear they may burst through the eardrum, causing a discharge. Such infections may subside spontaneously, but usually require treatment. Recurrent otitis media (middle-ear infection) is common in children under the age of 2 years, and although parents may become disheartened by the situation the condition does usually resolve without any long-term damage.

Recurrent otitis media is often treated by insertion of *grommets, small plastic tubes placed through the eardrum to ensure equalisation of pressure between the middle ear and the atmosphere. They are greatly abused, put in far too readily and far too young. But they do have value.

Sometimes, secretions in the middle ear, if allowed to persist, tend to glue up the ossicles, with resultant hearing loss. The eardrum is sometimes almost completely destroyed by chronic middle-ear infection and may have to be reconstructed surgically (tympanoplasty).

As well as by acute infections of the nose, eustachian block may be caused by enlargement of the adenoids, though such enlargement is usually secondary to repeated infections or nasal allergy. Infants given bottles in the supine position often regurgitate a little milk into the back of the nose and up the eustachian tube, and this may well predispose to ear infection. It is better to feed your baby sitting up.

Ear wax is a normal product of the skin glands of the auditory canal. It tends to work its way to the surface, but poking in the ears often causes retention, and the habit of cleaning the ears with cotton-buds pushed into the canal cannot be too strongly condemned. Excessive wax can be removed by special instruments or by syringing, but a discharging ear should never be syringed. When the wax is excessively hard, making removal difficult, it can be softened with cerumolytic ear drops.

EATING

Eating habits are largely culturally determined and governed by the availability of foodstuffs. Children's eating patterns will be to a great extent a reflection of parental example. Although children may dislike certain food tastes, in general food fads are created by parents and they should therefore be avoided by introducing to your child as wide a variety of foods as is possible from the beginning of mixed feeding. The child should never be forced to eat; meals should be a gastronomic pleasure and a happy family reunion. No child will allow herself to starve in the presence of food. Appetite may of course be depressed by disease, but most feeding problems are parent-made. (See *feeding.)

ECZEMA

This is a distressing condition of very varying severity, beginning as a rule in infancy, during the first few months of life, and usually running a relapsing course until some time during the second year, when 50 per cent of cases clear completely. The others continue to have residual trouble, usually confined to the crease areas of the joints, particularly the elbows and knees but also sometimes the wrists and ankles, and this may continue for several years. Many of these children go on to have allergic nose troubles, and about 50 per cent of them will eventually have asthma.

Although some babies will develop eczema while still entirely breastfed, many develop their first trouble a variable time after the introduction of artificial feeds, particularly cow's milk.

Milk allergy is probably an important cause in such cases and the removal of milk from the diet often leads to great improvement. Other foodstuffs, such as eggs, are often poorly tolerated by such infants, producing digestive upsets as well as exacerbations of the eczema. Other foreign protein substances such as wool are also frequently harmful. Contact with woollen socks, woollen carpets, and sometimes grass in older children, may lead to persistence of the eczema in the ankle regions.

You should therefore take careful note of any foodstuffs or possible contact substances which might be aggravating the condition, and these should be removed.

Eczema frequently begins on the face, usually on the cheeks and forehead as a red, spotty, often weeping eruption which then spreads to the limbs, chest and neck, and frequently produces weeping cracks around the ears.

In its later stages the eczema tends to be drier with some scaling and much thickening of the skin, but the severity of the reaction is very variable and the treatment has to be varied accordingly. In all stages the skin is very itchy and the child aggravates the condition by rubbing and scratching. Secondary infection by bacteria or fungi is common, and calls for appropriate treatment.

Treatment of eczema is often difficult and is always a matter for your doctor to decide. His instructions should be followed meticulously. In infants, suspect foodstuffs, such as milk and eggs, are usually removed from the diet, often with excellent response. Soya bean preparations can be used as a milk substitute, but there are also some highly modified milk-based feeds which have little or no allergic ability.

The child should be kept as cool as possible, as heat and sweating usually aggravate the condition. Clothing should be non-irritating and consist of light cotton garments rather than wool. Anything which irritates the eczema should, of course, be avoided. Soap is sometimes aggravating and soap substitutes or mild detergents are usually better. Unfortunately many of these children are at the dirty, crawling stage and require thorough cleaning. In the smaller infant, bland baths of water or saline are usually adequate.

Numerous preparations are available as applications to the skin. In the wet, weeping stage, drying agents are usually used, whereas when the skin is dry and scaly, creams or ointments are preferable. Simple astringent lotions containing lead or zinc are useful, and ichthyol or tar preparations help to relieve itching.

The most effective applications, however, are topical corticosteroids, which may be applied as lotions, creams, ointments or pastes depending on the phase and position of the eczema. These are usually highly effective preparations but should be used only under close medical supervision.

In very severe cases it may occasionally be necessary to use systemic corticosteroids to obtain an initial adequate response. Where secondary infection is a problem, antibacterial substances are usually incorporated in the topical application, and occasionally systemic antibiotics may have to be given.

Itching may be relieved by administration of antihistamines, and sometimes sedation is necessary, particularly at night, to suppress scratching. Splinting may also occasionally be required and for this purpose light cardboard tubes are usually effective.

The course of eczema is very unpredictable, so you mustn't become impatient with treatment which is largely suppressive rather than curative and may have to continue for a long time.

Chickenpox can be very unpleasant in the eczematous child and exposure should be vigorously avoided.

Inoculations against diphtheria, whooping-cough, tetanus and poliomyelitis should be carried out normally. In fact, it is better for the allergic child to have such protection so that the administration of serum, for instance in the child exposed to possible tetanus or diphtheria, can be obviated. The administration of such serum to allergic subjects is extremely dangerous.

EDUCATION

Your child is being educated almost from the moment of birth and it is the duty as well as the pleasure of parents to bring to their children in the pre-school years as much stimulation and information as is possible. A child may drive you mad with her eternal 'whys', but if you do your best to answer her you will probably be astonished at how much you gain in the process.

A considerable amount of knowledge and skill is acquired if a child attends a pre-primary school, but formal education begins at school entry. Parents may at this stage feel somewhat superseded and excluded by the educationalists, but they should at all times take a keen interest in their child's progress and if they feel this is not entirely satisfactory there should be no hesitation whatever in taking the matter up with the teachers. Parents are expected to help to a considerable extent in the first years of schooling but they should of course never do a child's work for her. When it comes to preparing projects, they may advise and provide materials but the work should be left to the child. When the child is in senior school the parents will probably be able to contribute little, but should nevertheless maintain a continual interest in the child's progress, and encourage as wide a field of learning as possible. When the child reaches the tertiary educational level the parents will have little to do except pay! This should be done with pleasure and without any reference to the hardships and privations which may be involved. No child should be made to feel guilty about the process of being educated. For educational difficulties see 'schooling problems' under *school.

ELECTRIC BURNS & SHOCK

Electric burns are often deceptive, for though small in area they may be very penetrating. In the hand particularly they may involve vital structures such as nerves and tendons, and it is wise therefore to have such a burn examined by a doctor in the early stages.

A strong electric current passing through the body causes sudden generalised muscle spasm, unconsciousness and often cardiac arrest. Do not assume that the patient is dead. Once she has been removed from the electrical danger, apply artificial respiration, and if there is no heart beat employ cardiac massage for 2–3 minutes as described under *artificial respiration.

ELECTROCARDIOGRAM (ECG)

This is a record of the electrical activity of the heart. It gives very useful information on cardiac function, particularly on enlargement of the various cardiac cavities, abnormalities of rhythm and, more particularly in the older patient, evidence of inadequate oxygenation of the heart muscle. It can be of value in general conditions such as thyroid disturbances, and it may give warning of body-salt disturbances, especially of calcium and potassium. The standard ECG is recorded from 12 different leads so as to give as complete a picture as possible of overall cardiac activity.

ELECTROENCEPHALOGRAM (EEG)

This is a record of the electrical activity of the brain. The brain consists of billions of nerve cells, each with dozens of connections, and it must be appreciated therefore that the recording of the electrical activity of the brain as a whole tells one very little about the functioning of specific groups of neurones. It is rather like trying to find out about waves by studying the tides. Nevertheless, the EEG has some uses. Its main value is in epilepsy, and particularly in petit-mal epilepsy where the pattern is specific. It may reveal localised epileptic discharges confirming clinical diagnosis, but what is important is whether the patient is having fits, and not what her EEG looks like. An EEG should never be 'treated', that is, no patient should be treated on the basis of EEG findings alone. At least 10 per cent of perfectly normal people will have what appears to be an abnormal EEG.

The EEG has become a regrettably popular investigation in the case of children with learning disabilities. There is no specific pattern in this situation and the EEG is quite valueless, except possibly as confirmatory evidence in cases of suspected petit mal. This, however, is invariably apparent clinically. Other forms of blank periods, for example daydreaming, may however be confused with petit mal, and an EEG may then resolve the problem. Using the EEG automatically for children with learning problems is not only unjustified but may be misleading and positively harmful.

The technique of recording an EEG is simple. Electrodes are simply stuck onto the scalp and there is no discomfort whatever. The patient does, however, have to be quiet and co-operative and smaller children therefore will require sedation.

EMOTIONAL DEVELOPMENT

Emotional development is clearly bound up with mental and physical development. It is important for parents to be aware of emotional developmental processes, for so many childhood problems are due to emotional and behavioural disturbances rather than to any strictly physical complaints. Traditional Freudian psychology recognises 5 main stages of development:

(1) The oral stage. This occupies the first year or so of life and is called this because most of the baby's exploration and gratification is related to her mouth. As soon as she is able to reach for objects she puts them to her mouth, which is at this stage a most important sensory organ. At first the baby is hardly aware of her mother as a separate being. She is there as a constant source of food, warmth and comfort. After a few weeks she is able to distinguish her mother from others and rapidly comes to recognise her other features such as voice, smell and mood. If her experience of her mother has been an unsatisfying one, particularly with regard to feeding, she may become resentful of her, and such an agitated, protesting baby may settle happily in the arms of someone else after several futile hours spent by a tense mother trying to settle her. For the first 5 months or so a baby will accept almost anyone as a mother substitute and separation at this age therefore is not a great problem. Thereafter, the baby's awareness of, dependence upon and attachment to her mother increases and separation becomes more and more traumatic.

Fear of strangers becomes apparent at about 9–10 months and the reassurance of mother's presence is constantly sought. Gradually, the toddler ventures further afield.

During the latter part of the first year the child's personality begins to take shape. An extremely active child intent on exploring every corner of her environment who is excessively restrained may become frustrated and aggressive, and such unendearing behaviour may provoke the parents as well as exhaust them. Further restrictive practices on their part may establish a vicious circle which is difficult to break. The more placid, friendly child will probably receive more affection but may also receive less stimulation.

During the oral phase of development, feeding habits become established, and mishandling at this stage may lead to significant problems (see *feeding). Feeding should be fun and no child should ever be forced to eat.

(2) The anal stage. This phase, which occupies the second year or so of life, is so called because during this period elimination patterns are evolved and continence is achieved. The child thus learns a degree of co-operation. She also learns that she has control not only over her body functions but to a considerable extent over her environment and the people in it. She learns that she has a will, and nothing becomes more satisfying than inflicting it on others. This discovery of will leads to the typical negativistic attitude of the 2-year-old. She will be determined, for instance, to practise her skill with the teaspoon, even though her efforts result in more food getting onto the floor than into her mouth. If denied the opportunity, however, she may well react with angry food refusal, and the stage is then set for frustrating feeding problems. The child of this age has to learn that co-operation brings rewards. This applies particularly to toilet-training, which should never be a forced procedure but simply a co-operative evolution. Certain restrictions on behaviour have to be imposed in the interests of her own safety and for the preservation of property, as well as parental sanity. Behaviour modification should be effected as far as possible by ignoring undesirable behaviour and rewarding acceptable behaviour with expressions of suitable pleasure. Punishment is rarely necessary. While protecting her from significant danger, it is wise to let her learn from experience that certain activities are hazardous. Parents should not insist upon total docility. Children at this age display remarkable determination and, as far as possible, head-on clashes should be avoided, either by diversion or by offering her a choice in which both alternatives are acceptable to yourself. By offering her a choice you enable her to save face. Above all it is important that parental attitudes and the rules of life should be consistent. A child can never learn if the rules change from day to day.

In the battle of wills, which is inevitable at this stage, you should not be afraid to display your own determination. A child does not thrive in an atmosphere of parental weakness and vacillation. If a clash is unavoidable you must see that you win it and never, therefore, enter a conflict with your child which you cannot win, for example over eating. It is natural that when defeated a small child will express anger, and she should then be comforted and not provoked, and the whole situation forgotten as rapidly as possible. Temper tantrums should be totally ignored, as any attention paid to them simply encourages their repetition.

(3) The genital stage. This occupies most of the pre-school period, from 3 to 6 years of age. This sees tremendous development, particularly in group activities. Whereas the infant forms one of a pair with her mother, the pre-school child learns to co-operate with others in a group situation, either at home with brothers and sisters, or with playmates. She has to adjust to sharing mother's affection with other members of the family and to sharing her material possessions. Whereas the infant demands immediate gratification of all needs, the older child has to learn to accept postponement of gratification. She has now become aware of the future as well as of the present. At about 3, the child becomes aware of her sex and develops thereafter a considerable interest in the other sex. Embarrassing questions may be asked in rather inappropriate situations but these should be answered as accurately and as matter-of-factly as possible. There may develop particular attachments to the opposite-sex parent, and abnormal persistence of such attachments may lead later to the Oedipus and Electra complexes.

The new-found sexual awareness of the children at this age is accompanied by a degree of eroticism. They are well aware that fondling the genitals is quite different in sensation from fondling other parts of the body. The parent who adopts a scolding, forbidding attitude may do considerable harm by sowing the seeds of sexual guilt, and this may lead later to a distorted pattern of sexual behaviour. Masturbation is common in both sexes. Parents are often horrified at the sexuality of their small children but it should be realised that this is quite normal, and they should take the opportunity to explain sexual matters, with detail appropriate to the child's understanding. There should never be any suggestion of sexual guilt. What is a child to think when she is told that sexual activity is everything undesirable, and she herself is the living evidence of her parents' own sexuality? Guilt often occupies an increasingly important part of the child's feelings at this age and may invade all sorts of unexpected areas. Where, for example, there is parental discord, a child often feels herself to be the cause, and her inexpressible guilt adds greatly to her insecurity. As more and more is expected of her, and her shortcomings become increasingly apparent, she may also be imbued with guilt, and this may lead to depression. It is important, therefore, to dwell on the positive aspects of life, praising the child's virtues rather than harping on her shortcomings.

Incessant questioning is characteristic of this age, and all reasonable questions should be satisfactorily answered in a manner appropriate to the child's understanding. The child will not, however, want answers embellished with unnecessary details, which she will usually find boring. Answers are in any case likely to be misinterpreted by the child to conform to her own thoughts and observations. The pre-school child's world is full of charm and fantasy and this should as far as possible be preserved without unnecessary realism.

(4) The latent phase. This occupies the first half of the schoolgoing period, namely 6 to 12 years. Sexual and other fantasies of the genital stage become replaced by realistic occupations, with formal learning and competitive peer relationships. The teacher becomes a dominant feature in the child's life and much effort goes into trying to please her. Shortcomings in this respect may give rise to considerable anxiety, often manifested by physical complaints, such as early-morning tummyaches. Learning habits become established in the early school years, and if these are unsatisfactory the pattern may be set for ongoing difficul-

ties. Problems should therefore be dealt with early. Physical symptoms presenting at this age are so often emotional, and the real cause inapparent to the child herself, so that information may have to be sought from other sources such as teachers and friends.

The child in the early school years is still incapable of much abstract thought. Concepts such as honesty, faithfulness, loyalty and love, have rather little meaning to the pre-adolescent child. Habits of behaviour, however, become well-established at this age and set the pattern for future attitudes, for example towards industry, competition and friendship. Self-esteem is extremely important and a child's confidence can easily be destroyed by failure to achieve. It is essential that children be given adequate recognition for even small achievements and thereby encouraged, rather than having teachers and parents harping always on their deficiencies. There are some parents who, by lavishing excessive praise, turn their children into conceited horrors, but such children nevertheless are encouraged to achieve, even at the price of considerable unpopularity.

Although described as latent, this phase is extremely important in determining the child's future characteristics. One child may sail through this period without problems, another will encounter difficulties in adjustment to school but will be greatly strengthened by overcoming these satisfactorily. Another may have her spirit broken or become depressed as a result of difficulties with which she is unable to cope. It is important that parents' expectations of their children be realistic and they must not express disappointment if a child's achievements fall short of or are different from their hopes. It is important, too, that parents maintain their own integrity, for nothing will more effectively destroy a child's confidence in life than to have her parents revealed as hypocrites who, while expecting their children to embrace all the virtues, themselves display few of them.

(5) Puberty and adolescence. The turmoil of this age will probably still be sufficiently fresh in the memories of most parents to enable them to adopt a reasonably sympathetic attitude towards their own children. In addition to the problems of her own physical change, the adolescent has to adapt to the new adult role she is called upon to play, with severance of the dependence she has thus far had on her parents. She has to decide upon a career, her attitudes towards society become defined, and she has to sort out her sexual problems. In these days of changing modes there may be considerable conflict between adolescent ideas and those of their parents. A degree of rebellion is normal but this may become exaggerated if family relationships have been unsatisfactory and there is mistrust on both sides. Family loyalties may be severely strained. It is difficult for parents to achieve the fine balance required between the provision of security and the simultaneous progressive granting of independence. Parental restraints are essential but they should be reasonable, acceptable and malleable. They will then be respected by the adolescent even though she may feel obliged to rebel against them. She will not respect you for excessive indulgence, bribery or hypocrisy. It may be difficult at times to preserve a sense of humour, yet this is essential. Adolescence is an exciting time, not only for the youngsters but also for their parents, and few things are more rewarding than guiding a child successfully through this period of such remarkable development.

EMOTIONAL DISTURBANCES

Many of these are considered under their appropriate headings, for example, *nail-biting, *enuresis, *stealing. Basically, the ingredients for such disturbances are conflict and anxiety. Conflict arises when the child finds herself in a situation which she realises is unacceptable and in which the emotional content cannot be directly expressed. The emotions are then redirected along more acceptable paths, employing several mechanisms which are well recognised, for example:

Repression. Unacceptable thoughts are simply repressed but the emotional content bursts out in inappropriate ways. For example, an adopted child learning of her adoption may find it quite intolerable that her own mother might not have wanted her. In repressing such thoughts her emotions find expression in hostility towards her adoptive parents. They, in turn, find it difficult to accept such reaction when they have given the child both care and affection. The child, being aware of this, develops a sense of guilt, which again she finds inexpressible and this leads to further resentment and hostility. A vicious circle of the interaction becomes established, which may end in severe conflict between child and parents. The solution to such a situation demands great understanding, patience and forbearance and may well require expert psychological help.

Regression. When a 3-year-old child who has been the centre of attention suddenly finds herself with a baby sister or brother on whom a considerable amount of parental care is inevitably focused, she develops feelings of jealousy mingled with hatred, but to these she cannot give direct expression. Her desire is to direct more parental attention onto herself, and because to her it is apparent that infantile behaviour attracts such attention she regresses into babyish habits such as wetting and soiling. This may well gain her attention which is not particularly to her liking, but it is better than no attention at all. It is only when it becomes clear to her that more appropriate behaviour is better rewarded than her regressive expressions that the latter will cease.

Denial. This is a common defence mechanism in an intolerable situation. The young child confronted, for example, with the death of a parent may deny the actuality completely and behave as though nothing has happened. Another form of denial commonly seen is in the case of the child who, having clearly committed a misdemeanour and confronted with irrefutable evidence, continues to deny any knowledge of it. Even though this may generate further punishment, the denial will be continued until a more sympathetic attitude is adopted by the parents or authorities and the fear of dire punishment has receded.

Displacement. A young child who is jealous of a sibling who displays greater ability then she does is unable to express her hostility directly, but instead displaces it towards others and becomes generally aggressive towards her peers. This is also a common reaction in children experiencing schooling problems.

Projection. The child who is unable to accept her own hostile feelings, for example towards a stepfather, will project these feelings onto others, and she will then imagine that the stepfather is hostile towards her, even though this may initially be far from true. A child's behaviour however is often sufficient to produce genuine resentment on the part of the stepfather and thus a vicious cycle of reactions may be set in motion and only arrested by expert intervention.

Sublimation. This is the most acceptable of all the compensating mechanisms and in fact accounts for a great deal of human creativity. Sexual curiosity may in this fashion be diverted into a passion for general learning, and much civilised behaviour may be the result of sublimation of baser drives.

The patterns of emotional disturbances are almost limitless but most will be recognisable as being due to the above mechanisms. Fortunately, many of the minor aberrations are self-limiting and expert psychological help is not required. If, however, severe behavioural disturbances are present, no time should be lost in seeking adequate help.

ENCEPHALITIS

Encephalitis, or inflammation of the brain, may arise from many different causes. Often it is due to viruses with a specific predilection for the central nervous system. It may arise as a complication of the infectious diseases, for example measles, mumps and chickenpox. Measles encephalitis occurs in about 1 per 1 000 cases and may be very severe, often leaving residual damage. A slowly progressive form of disease, subacute sclerosing panencephalitis, may occur many years after the attack of measles. A degree of brain inflammation always accompanies meningitis, and localised infection may occur with bacterial invasion, causing a brain abscess. Encephalitis may also result from parasitic invasion, for example malaria and tapeworm. Many toxic states give rise to a similar picture of 'encephalopathy', but this is not quite the same as encephalitis.

There has been much discussion regarding the encephalitis of whooping-cough vaccination. Though this may rarely occur, the dangers have probably been exaggerated. Most suspected cases have not been substantiated on further investigation. As a precaution, however, pertussis vaccine is usually not given to children who have had convulsions or who have had another form of encephalitis. A history of convulsions in first-degree relatives is regarded by some authorities as a contraindication, but this is probably unjustified.

ENURESIS

See *bedwetting

EPIGLOTTITIS

An inflammatory condition of the epiglottis, a little cartilaginous projection at the base of the tongue. When this becomes inflamed it causes severe respiratory obstruction, with noisy breathing and considerable apprehension. It afflicts children usually from 2 to 6 years of age, whereas the more common viral croup occurs as a rule in younger children. No time should be lost in getting a child with this condition into hospital.

EPILEPSY (see also *convulsions)

Epilepsy is a condition in which repeated episodes of disorganised central nervous system activity result in states of altered consciousness or motor or sensory dysfunction. Various classifications have been attempted but the main categories observed in children are:

(1) Petit-mal attacks. These are momentary lapses of consciousness, in which the child stops whatever she might be doing for a few seconds and then carries on as if there had been no interruption. There is no falling, involuntary movement or incontinence. They occur usually from the age of about 6 years to early adulthood, often ceasing after adolescence. The attacks may occur many times a day and in such cases may interfere with learning. The EEG usually shows a characteristic pattern. Attacks can often be precipitated by over-breathing, which can be used to confirm the diagnosis. Treatment is usually very successful, the most effective drugs being Valproate and Ethosuximide.

(2) **Grand mal, or major epilepsy.** Several types of seizure are recognised, the commonest being the typical tonic, clonic convulsion, which most people will recognise as a fit. The patient may sense the onset of the seizure with an aura, and may emit a frightened cry before she falls to the ground, with the body in a state of generalised muscle spasm, and total loss of consciousness. Breathing is impossible at this stage, which usually lasts only a few seconds before passing into the clonic stage, in which repeated movements of muscles are made — including those of the tongue and jaw — which may result in the tongue being bitten. Incontinence is common. Breathing is irregular and inadequate and the patient turns blue. This stage usually lasts up to a few minutes. The patient then relaxes, breathing is re-established and consciousness is regained after several minutes. Thereafter the patient usually lapses into sleep, after which there is full recovery. Occasionally, the epileptic state may be maintained for a long period until terminated by appropriate medical treatment — so-called status epilepticus.

There are several variations of major epileptic attacks:

(a) Tonic attacks. These consist of the tonic phase only, without clonic movements. They are also known as myoclonic seizures.

(b) Infantile spasms. These are abrupt, brief episodes during which the child adopts a flexed attitude, which gives rise to the descriptive term of Salaam seizures. They may occur in runs, particularly when the child is drowsy. The condition is usually associated with severe brain disease, and the EEG is often characteristically chaotic.

(c) Akinetic attacks or drop attacks. Here the patient has neither a tonic nor a clonic phase but simply collapses without any involuntary movements.

(3) **Focal epilepsy.** These originate in a specific area of the brain, but the abnormal activity may spread and terminate in a full-blown grand-mal attack. The initial manifestations may be motor or sensory, beginning often in an extremity and then 'marching' proximally. Such epilepsy arises in a focus in the motor or sensory area of the brain. (See *brain.)

Temporal lobe epilepsy. This may give rise to a great variety of symptoms, varying from grand-mal seizures, preceded by peculiar auras, to outbursts of abnormal behaviour. Sometimes visceral symptoms predominate — so-called abdominal epilepsy.

Causes of epilepsy

These are numerous and include hereditary factors, developmental abnormalities of the brain, brain injury as the result of birth or later trauma, injury as the result of oxygen lack, toxic and infective states, degenerative diseases of the nervous system, and brain tumours. Metabolic disturbances may precipitate fits, e.g. hypoglycaemia (low blood sugar), hypocalcaemia (low blood calcium), al-

117 «» E

kalosis. Occlusion of blood-vessels (strokes) often causes fits in adults and may also occur in children. The commonest cause of convulsions in children is simple fever (see *convulsions). Only 2–4 per cent of children presenting with simple feverish convulsions will go on to have epilepsy.

Treatment of epilepsy

Individual fits do not usually last more than a few minutes and during this time the patient has simply to be protected from injury. She should be turned to the side so that saliva and vomitus do not accumulate in the mouth and become inhaled. If the tongue is being bitten, a piece of wood or non-traumatising material may be inserted between the teeth. If status epilepticus occurs, with one fit passing straight into another, then this must be terminated and a doctor should be called. An intravenous injection of diazepam or clonazepam is usually extremely effective. The former drug can also be administered rectally and is rapidly absorbed by this route. Your doctor may equip you with rectal diazepam for home use.

The long-term management of epilepsy consists of identifying, and if possible removing, any causative factors, and administration of appropriate anticonvulsant drugs, the most commonly used being phenobarbitone, phenytoin, primidone and carbamazepine, the last being particularly useful for focal, and especially temporal lobe, attacks. It is recommended that every epileptic or parent of an epileptic child join the South African National Epilepsy League.

EPSTEIN'S PEARLS

These are small white spots on the palate, near the midline at the junction of hard and soft palates, commonly seen in newborn babies, and persisting for a few weeks. They are of absolutely no significance but must be distinguished from thrush.

EUSTACHIAN TUBE

See *ear

EYES

The anatomy of the eye is illustrated in the figure. Tears are produced by the lacrimal gland, which is situated above and outside the eye, and they flow naturally towards the inner aspect, where they drain through the lacrimal ducts via small openings on the upper and lower lids. The ducts initially lead to a small chamber called the lacrimal sac, situated near the inner corner of the eye, and this in turn is ducted into the nose. At birth the eyes are relatively big compared with the rest of the body. Congenital defects include microphthalmia (small eye) and cataract (an opacification of the lens). One of the commoner causes of these abnormalities is congenital rubella.

Vision is present at birth and the baby will concentrate fairly closely on a face but will show little interest in other objects. By 3 months or so she should focus well and follow completely. (See *development.)

Conjunctivitis is discussed under that heading. Recurrent conjunctivitis is often associated with a blocked tearduct, and in such cases it may be helpful to express the ducts by squeezing over the inner angle of the eye before inserting any medication. Blocked ducts usually recanalise spontaneously before the age of

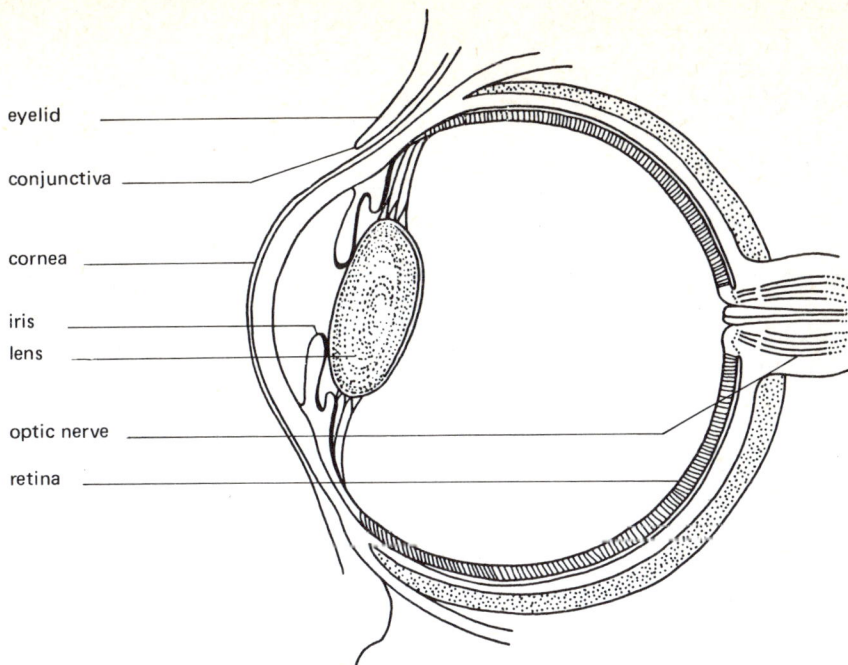

eyelid

conjunctiva

cornea

iris
lens

optic nerve

retina

6 months. If they are then still blocked, an opthalmological opinion should be sought, as they will probably require probing.

Squint, or strabismus, is of two main types. It may be due to weakness of one or more of the eye muscles so that certain movements of that eye are deficient (paralytic squint) or it may be due to a visual difficulty and inability to focus the eyes satisfactorily so that one eye tends to wander (concomitant squint). Very young babies often squint intermittently but if this persists to the age of 6 months the baby should be seen medically.

False squints are common. The baby with marked epicanthic folds (folds of skin at the inner aspect of the eye), giving rise to an excessively broad-looking nasal bridge, often appears to squint when she looks to one or other side. This is an illusion but if you have any doubt let your doctor check the situation. (See *squint.)

Defective vision is common, the most frequent disability being short-sightedness (myopia). This usually becomes apparent when the child can no longer see the blackboard adequately at school. If there is any suggestion of a visual defect you will naturally have your child accurately tested.

Foreign bodies in the eye. It is common for specks of dust to cause irritation, but these are usually removed by the natural tears. A foreign body under the lids can often be removed by turning the lids out and wiping the speck away with a corner of a handkerchief. To evert the upper lid, the patient should look down to her feet, then grasp the lid and eyelashes between finger and thumb, and in this way the lid is fairly easily turned inside out. If the foreign body is not revealed by these manoeuvres it may be flushed out using an eyebath. If simple means do not dislodge the foreign body, take the child rapidly to the doctor or hospital. Penetrating injuries of the eye are a grave emergency and require immediate hospital attention. (See also *styes.)

FAECES

The art of stool-gazing is perhaps practised excessively by parents but nevertheless it is useful to know what is normal and acceptable at various ages.

The newborn baby passes meconium, which is a thick, dark-green, tarry substance with a high bile content. After a couple of days the stools change to a transitional type which is often somewhat loose and mucoid and which gives place after a further day or two to the normal milk stools, the character of which depends a great deal on the type of feed. If the baby is breastfed the stools tend to be very soft and of a bright-yellow colour. The frequency varies enormously, from a stool at every feed to a stool every 10 days or more. Even with such infrequent defaecation the stools never become hard.

The stool of the artificially fed baby is generally lighter-coloured and firmer. Greenish or greyish stools are quite common in the baby fed on modified milk feeds, and provided the consistency is normal the colour is of little importance. The artificially fed baby may become constipated, and a regular more-or-less daily bowel movement is therefore desirable. (See *constipation.) Soya feeds often give rise to dark putty-like stools. Whereas the stools of the breast-fed baby are acid in reaction, those of the artificially fed baby are alkaline.

As a greater variety of foodstuffs enters the diet, so the child's stools become more akin to adult stools. Concern is often expressed by mothers because they are able to recognise undigested vegetable particles, such as peas, carrots, maize, etc., in the small child's stool. This is quite normal and is not a sign of impaired digestion.

Toddlers are often fascinated by their faeces and expect you to share in their admiration of their products. During the training period it is permissible to express pleasure at your child's co-operation but there is no need to lavish praise on him for performing a perfectly normal function. Be as matter-of-fact about excretory mechanisms as possible.

FAINTING

This is common in school-age children and often causes quite unnecessary anxiety. Fainting usually occurs in the standing position and also not uncommonly with prolonged kneeling. It never occurs while the child is active. The condition is due to a loss of tone in the blood-vessels, which permits the blood pressure to fall, and an inadequate quantity of blood then reaches the brain. There is not immediate loss of consciousness, for this is heralded by a feeling of lightheadedness, associated with pallor and often sweating. When a child feels he is going to faint he should be allowed to sit down with the head in a lowered position between the knees and he will then usually recover within a few minutes. The child who has fainted should be taken into the fresh air, and his clothing loosened, and he should be left horizontal until he feels better. There is no need for any continued rest once recovery has occurred and the child should return to normal activities. Some children may faint repeatedly at, for example, school assembly, and in such cases they should be permitted to sit down. It is important to avoid any unnecessary fussing so that the child does not begin to regard himself as abnormal or ill. By all means let your doctor check him but having been reassured that the attacks are simple faints there should be no further display of anxiety.

FAT
Fat is a major food constituent consisting of fatty acids combined with glycerol. Fats have to be broken down by the digestive enzymes into their constituent fractions before they can be absorbed, and impaired digestion, as in cystic fibrosis, coeliac disease, etc., is often characterised by fatty stools. Fat has more than twice the calorie value of carbohydrate or protein (9 calories per gram) and fat stores therefore form useful reserves of energy. Most of the body fat is of this nature, namely metabolically inactive calorie reserve, but a small proportion, the brown fat, is metabolically active and this is of some importance in the small pre-term baby whose insulating storage fat is deficient.

An excessive intake of animal fat is associated with degeneration of the blood-vessels, and it has therefore become fashionable to replace butter with margarine, most brands of which consist largely of unsaturated fats of vegetable origin. Not all vegetable fats however are 'safe', notably coconut oil. Whereas the link between high blood-cholesterol levels and coronary heart disease is indisputable, the specific danger of animal fats in this regard is not quite proven.

FATNESS
See *obesity

FEARS
Adults as well as children display a great variety of fears, some quite reasonable and healthy but many unreasonable and imaginary. There is inevitably a fear of the unknown, and for a child, whose knowledge is limited, the unknown is proportionally greater than it is for an adult. Such fears can only be handled with sympathy and explanation and a demonstration that the fear is unfounded. There are many fears which persist, however, for example fears of storms, spiders, lifts and dentists, even when the benign nature of the feared entity has been repeatedly demonstrated. Such phobias may occasionally be traced to an original frightening experience but usually the problem does not warrant profound psychological analysis.

Parental attitudes are of great importance in controlling a child's fears, for there is little hope of convincing him that an electrical storm is simply exciting when at the first peal of thunder you dive under the bed. It is better if you can carry the child to a window where he can witness the storm, and teach him to count the intervals between lightning and thunder so that it becomes enjoyable rather than frightening. Fear of the dark is understandable in small children and in such cases complete darkness should be avoided by provision of a night light. This however should shed no frightening shadows on the walls.

Somatic symptoms, e.g. tummyaches, headaches and vomiting, are often due to fear reactions, often associated with school. The child may be reluctant to admit to the problems facing him, but every effort should be made to unearth them if there is a suspicion of an emotional cause.

Many specific phobias occur in adults, most of which can be related to alarming experiences in childhood. Such fears are often fortified by incorrect handling, such as ridicule or exposing the child repeatedly to the frightening object or situation in the hope that this will cure him. A frightened child needs comfort, reassurance and understanding, and his fears will be best eliminated by explanation and example.

FEBRILE CONVULSIONS
See *convulsions

FEEDING (see also *feeding problems, *food)
It is unfortunate that infant feeding has become such an apparently complicated and difficult subject for mothers. Other animals find no difficulty in feeding their young and in teaching them to search for food. Why has the human made it such a problem? Much of the blame must regrettably be placed on the medical and allied professions who, armed with much science and even more pseudo-science, have tried to inflict rigid patterns of feeding on their unfortunate victims. At least all are now united in advocating breastfeeding for the young baby. Problems are nevertheless encountered even in such a natural situation. (See *breastfeeding.)

Artificial feeding
The baby who cannot be totally breastfed will almost certainly thrive perfectly satisfactorily on a substitute feed, provided this is of a reasonable constitution. Many excellent milk-based baby feeds are available, the constitution of many closely approaching that of breast milk. The competitive striving of manufacturers to produce a product ever closer in chemical composition to breast milk has probably been unnecessary and misguided. Except in the case of premature and very small babies the child's digestive tract is capable of handling a great variety of foodstuffs, and the kidneys are usually able to make the necessary adjustments to compensate for imbalance in the intake of salts and other constituents which may occasionally lead to trouble. Babies thrived for a long time on cows' milk and other animal milks with very little modification. This is not to deny the validity of scientific advances but these must be kept in perspective, and ridiculous and functionally insignificant dietary modifications and adjustments should not be allowed to complicate life unnecessarily. There are times when real expertise in baby feeding is required. Much of the advice handed out by clinics and doctors is scientifically invalid and unnecessary. If therefore the advice conflicts with your commonsense do not hesitate to question it.

Equipment
When buying bottles and teats do not try to save money by buying inferior-quality products which you will have to replace after a short time. Glass is more easily cleaned than plastic but of course it breaks. If you settle for plastic get a good

quality which will not deteriorate with repeated sterilisation. (See *bottles.) Teats come in a variety of shapes and degrees of firmness but these features matter very little. What does matter is the ability of the teat to let the milk out. Some with only one hole are very slow and the baby may exhaust himself sucking before he is satisfied. The human nipple has 20 holes and a strongly sucking baby will get his feed at a considerable rate. A single-hole teat often gets blocked, especially with flocculated feeds such as Pelargon, and it is wiser therefore to have 2 or 3 holes. Extra holes can be made by plunging in a fine, red-hot needle. (See *teats.) Most teats have valve holes which prevent a vacuum from developing in the bottle. See that these work properly, and do not screw the cap on so tightly that the vent holes are occluded. If the bottle is held upside-down, milk should drip from the teat at about 1 drop per second. Teats may need special modification in the case of very weak babies or those with mechanical difficulties, such as cleft palate, where there is difficulty in sucking. Such babies usually feed satisfactorily if the teat is cross-cut so that milk flows from it when it is compressed and very little sucking action is then required.

Sterilisation of bottles and teats

Because babies have a low resistance to infection and because the artificially fed baby does not have the benefit of the protective factors present in breast milk, it is essential that the feeds be as free as possible of harmful germs. The feeding equipment therefore should not only be clean but virtually sterile. There are two main ways of achieving sterility, namely by boiling or by chemical sterilisation, which is most safely achieved by soaking the equipment in a hypochlorite solution.

(1) **Boiling.** Sterilisation by boiling may again be achieved in 2 ways. The bottles and teats may be boiled, and the feed, carefully prepared so as to prevent contamination, then added and the bottles sealed. This method does not ensure complete sterility and it is wise therefore to store the bottles in a refrigerator unless they are used soon after preparation. In hospital, the method of terminal sterilisation is usually employed and this may be done at home by preparing the feeds in the bottles, capping them loosely, and standing them upright in a boiler so that their tops are not submerged — they are then brought to boiling-point for some 10 minutes. After cooling, the caps are screwed down firmly and the contents are then quite sterile and may be stored without refrigeration for at least 24 hours.

Needless to say, before any method of sterilisation the bottles and teats should be very thoroughly cleaned. The teats may be rubbed with a little coarse salt to remove milk residues, and clean water should be ejected through the teat holes to ensure their cleanliness and patency.

(2) **Chemical sterilisation (Milton method).** This is convenient and reliable if meticulous attention is paid to detail. Special containers are obtainable which simplify the complete submersion of both bottles and teats in the Milton solution, which must be prepared according to the manufacturer's instructions. No bubbles must be allowed to remain in the equipment as these would prevent contact between the solution and the surfaces of bottles and teats, which is essential for sterilisation. There is no need to rinse the bottles before filling them with the feed, as the hypochlorite solution is reduced to completely harmless salt on contact with

milk. Once the feed has been added to the bottle, because the former is not completely sterile, it is wise to store the feed in a refrigerator unless it is used almost immediately.

Preparation of the feed

Nearly all dried-milk feeds are prepared by adding 1 level measure of powder to 25 ml of water. The water should be boiled to ensure sterility, particularly if its source is in any way suspect. The feed may be prepared in a clean jug, preferably sterilised by filling with boiled water and allowing to stand for a few minutes. Most modern milk powders dissolve readily and require only a little stirring. Be careful to avoid clots, as these may block the teats and cause the baby considerable distress. If clotting is a problem a mechanical beater is a great help.

If only one bottle is being prepared there is no objection to putting the requisite volume of boiled water into the bottle, adding the appropriate amount of milk powder, capping and shaking.

It is possible for milk powders to become contaminated and containers should always be sealed after use and should not be left opened for long periods of time.

Quantity of feeds

Feeding-tables, as for example on tins of the various baby milks, should be taken as a guide only and not strictly adhered to (though instructions about the proportion of powder to water should be followed exactly). Babies' appetites vary enormously and the baby should determine the volume of his feed as well as the frequency. Unfortunately, the bogy of overfeeding is constantly being raised, with the result that thousands of babies are being made miserable by underfeeding. If left to his own devices the baby will take what he needs. A little milk should therefore be left in the bottle when he has taken what he wants. Only in this way can you be certain that he has had enough.

During the first few months of life the average baby requires between 150 and 170 ml per kilogram of body weight per day. A 4 kg baby therefore will probably be taking 600 to 700 ml of milk daily, probably in 6 feeds of 125 ml each. At some feeds he may take appreciably less, at others he may demand rather more. Some babies are especially hungry in the evenings, and much so-called evening colic is simply hunger. Provided your baby is well, you need not be afraid to feed him and to feed him all he will take. Be prepared to listen to your baby and ignore the advice of granny, aunty, the clinic sister and the doctor if this conflicts with what your baby is trying to tell you.

Rewarming the feed

This is quite unnecessary. Even small premature babies will accept and tolerate a bottle taken straight from the refrigerator. There is therefore no need to waste your money on bottle-warmers or insulators.

What milk should you use?

The fact that so many baby-milk feeds are available is sufficient proof that no one is significantly better than the other. A glance at the Table under *milk shows that there is very little difference in the basic constituents of the various milk feeds. What you choose therefore will probably be best determined by cost. Do not imagine that because a product is higher priced it is necessarily better than its rivals. It is customary to use one of the highly modified cows'-milk-based feeds for babies during the first few months of life. These preparations have vitamins and iron added and they therefore constitute complete foods for the small baby. You may if you wish continue with such feeds for as long as milk constitutes a significant part of the baby's diet, but if you wish to change to ordinary cows' milk after the first 3 to 4 months of your baby's life there is no objection to your doing so. Raw cows' milk should always be brought to the boil in order to ensure its safety, but pasteurised or sterilised milk is safe without boiling unless it has been opened and possibly contaminated. Whole cows' milk is contraindicated in small babies because of its high protein and salt contents. Somewhat paradoxically, perhaps, it is at present fashionable to feed premature babies on milks with a slightly higher protein and salt content than those closely simulating breast milk. In fact nobody really knows what the optimum feed is for a premature baby. Babies with heart troubles should in general have a low salt intake and babies with allergic troubles will probably be given a non-milk feed such as a soya preparation. If a baby from a highly allergic family has to be artificially fed, there is some virtue in starting with a soya feed right from the beginning. With these few exceptions the average baby can be given any reasonable feed.

Technique of bottle-feeding

There is no great skill required in giving a baby a bottle. Both you and the baby should, however, be comfortable and it is better to have him in a semi-sitting position so that air does not accumulate excessively in the stomach and does not pass on into the bowel. If he is sitting up the baby can burp whenever he wants. Furthermore, in the sitting position less milk is regurgitated into the back of the nose, a situation which may predispose to ear infection. (See *ear.) Once the baby is sucking, see that the air valves in the teat are working satisfactorily, as evidenced by a stream of bubbles coming into the bottle otherwise the baby may be sucking against a vacuum and getting little reward. He should be allowed to continue sucking until he stops voluntarily, when the bottle may be removed, and he may be winded by sitting up, or put against the shoulder and gently patted. Mothers often break the feed too frequently in order to wind the baby and this may make him very annoyed. Far too much disturbance is attributed to 'wind'. It is of course a convenient thing to blame and constitutes a ready culprit for every ill which precedes teething. (See *wind.) If the feeds are unduly protracted make sure that the teat holes are adequate. (See *teats.) Bottle-feeding, like breastfeeding, should be a happy experience for both parent and baby, and there is at least the advantage that father can participate more actively in the fun.

Never prop-feed your baby, i.e. never lie him down with the bottle propped so that he can suck at it without active supervision and assistance. This is a dangerous practice which may lead to choking, aspiration of the feed and pneumonia. However busy you may be always take the time to feed your baby in the proper manner.

What is to be done with the leftovers?

Once the baby has sucked at the bottle, the contents are to some extent contaminated, though of course with the baby's own germs. Milk provides a very good culture medium for bacteria, and if left at room temperature the milk will rapidly become very significantly contaminated. Refrigeration, however, will largely prevent bacterial growth, and it is quite safe to put the bottle back into the refrigerator for use at the next feed. Longer periods of storage should not be allowed and if refrigeration is impossible the feed residue should be discarded.

Times of feeding

In the early weeks of life, feeding times should not be rigid. The baby should be demand-fed as far as possible, as this leads to greater contentment and also to more enthusiastic sucking if the baby is given a feed when he is hungry. Premature babies may require waking, as otherwise they may take in an insufficient quantity, but the average vigorous baby can be depended upon to fend for himself very adequately. After the age of about 4 weeks, a baby usually settles into a routine and the feeds can then be given at times convenient to yourself, usually 4-hourly during the day. Night feeds should be continued as long as the baby wants them. As a rule, it is convenient to feed the baby at about 10 p.m. when mother wants to go to bed, and there is no objection to his being wakened for this feed. If he wakes during the night it is better to satisfy him with a milk feed rather than trying to fool him with water. Such a ruse will not make him give up the night feed and will simply make him angry and you exhausted. When he is ready to abandon the night feed he will do so.

Weaning off the bottle

The average baby will be able to drink from a cup by 7 to 8 months, and from this time on he should be encouraged to take more and more of his fluids in this way. It is wise to get rid of the bottle completely by the age of 1 year as it otherwise becomes an addiction and increasingly difficult to remove. Prolonged bottle-feeding is not only graceless but leads to dental deformation and tooth decay, particularly when sugared drinks are given. Much nocturnal disturbance is caused by prolonged bottle-feeding. The baby who has several bottles a night passes huge quantities of urine, requires frequent changing and on each occasion is settled with yet another bottle. Once this vicious cycle has been interrupted by removal of the bottle, the baby usually sleeps peacefully.

Introduction of solids

Milk will provide all the baby's requirements for a few months but thereafter it is an incomplete food. Furthermore, there is a limit to the amount of breast milk a mother can produce. It is usually in the region of 800 ml per day, so that once a baby has reached a weight of around 6 kg it is unlikely that he will get adequate nourishment from the breast alone. The introduction of solids therefore should be based on the individual situation. Fashions come and go. At present we are in a phase of late introduction of solids. Twenty years ago a mother could not compete in the clinic stakes unless she could boast that her baby was eating baked beans and sardines by 3 weeks. Most babies survive happily no matter what the fashion may be at the time. If you listen to your baby he will tell you what he wants. The large baby with a birth weight of 5 kg is clearly going to need solids much earlier than his punier colleagues who may be content to drift on for 5 or 6 months with nothing but breast milk. The average 4-month baby who has begun to grasp and bring everything to his mouth to taste is demonstrating that he is ready for new foods. From now on he will want to taste anything edible and most things inedible too. A variety of foodstuffs presented relatively early on will prevent faddy tastes from developing. It must be realised that the baby's digestive system is capable of handling any foodstuff digestible by adults, the only exception being starch during the first 6 weeks of life. You can therefore give him anything, provided it is in a form that he can swallow, although long before he has teeth a baby will chew very effectively with his gums. The first teeth anyway are for biting and not for chewing.

The baby's first reaction to solids given by spoon is one of puzzlement. He has been used to milk being delivered at the back of his mouth and his first inclination when confronted with a spoonful of porridge in the front of his mouth is to spit it out. He very soon realises, however, that the food is good and his enjoyment of it is henceforth obvious.

There is far too much caution in the introduction of solids, for although some items, such as egg, may upset a baby and should therefore be introduced with due care, the quantity of other foods need not be restricted. It is wise to introduce one item at a time so that if there is any suggestion of intolerance it will be clear what to suspect. However, once the baby has accepted the food he should be allowed to have as much as he likes. There should, nevertheless, be a limit on the intake of fattening foods in the case of the overweight baby, whose meals should consist largely of vegetables, fruit and meat, with cereal perhaps once a day.

By the time the average baby is ready for solids he has probably settled down into a programme of 4-hourly feeds, 4 to 5 per day. There need be no rules regarding the times at which solids are given. Many mothers introduce them first before the 10 a.m. feed and a little later before the 6 p.m. feed, but you can do what suits you and your baby, and once he is taking a fair quantity, introduce 3 meals a day. Solids are usually given before the bottle, but if the baby is thirsty he should be offered his milk first. Be relaxed about the whole business and let it be fun for both of you. If it is, then you are doing the right thing.

In the early stages it is convenient to use the proprietary foods, of which there is a tremendous variety, all of which are nutritionally sound. Fresh fruits, however, are valuable and it is easy enough to prepare mashed banana, pawpaw, apple purée, etc. Once the baby is taking a fair quantity you will probably want to prepare your own vegetables, and the addition of meat or liver adds valuable iron and protein. Mothers are sometimes concerned because vegetable particles can be recognised in the infant's stool. This is quite normal and is due simply to the fact that cellulose is not digestible by human beings. Egg is a valuable source of protein and minerals, especially iron, and although it should be introduced with caution, once tolerance is established an egg may be given every day or every other day. Gradually, the foods should be less finely prepared so that the baby becomes accustomed to handling lumps and chewing. There are some, however, who tend to choke and vomit on even small lumps, and they will require their food to be sieved or liquidised for rather longer. By 6 months of age the baby will be keen to hold something and suck at it. Biscuits and rusks are popular but usually end up as a squashy mess all over everything. Biscuits and other highly refined preparations are thoroughly bad for the teeth and should be discouraged. A piece of steak, cheese or fruit is much to be preferred. Sweet tastes should not be encouraged and sugared drinks are an abomination, especially when given by bottle for they then lead to dreadful dental decay. Unsweetened, pure fruit juice does not have this effect, and is also a good source of vitamin C.

By 1 year of age your baby should be eating nearly everything that other members of the family have, and there should be little need to prepare things especially for him. For a couple of months he will probably have wanted to 'help' with his feeding, though it is only by about 15 months that he will get a spoonful of food into his mouth without spillage. Self-feeding, however messy, should nevertheless be encouraged and the baby brought to independence as soon as possible.

Weaning onto the cup

Even small babies can be quite satisfactorily fed from a cup or small glass, but this becomes much easier after the age of about 6 months. From this time on, an increasing proportion of the baby's fluids should be given by cup so that he becomes accustomed to it. A non-spill feeding cup is useful in preventing mess and loss before the baby's skills are adequately developed. If breastfeeding can be continued through to about the 9th month, there is every advantage in weaning the baby straight onto a cup and avoiding the bottle stage completely. In any case it is wise to get rid of bottles by the time a baby is a year old. (See *bottles.) An excessive consumption of milk depresses an infant's appetite for other foods and is a common cause of iron-deficiency anaemia. Mothers of such children often perpetuate the bottle-feeds, fearing that their children will otherwise get insufficient nourishment. They should of course do the very reverse — get rid of the bottle and allow the child to become hungry. There is a widespread misconception that there is something magical about milk which makes it essential for children. It can indeed be a valuable source of protein and other essential food substances, but it is by no means essential and is in fact to some extent to be discouraged if the child has access to enough other foods.

The need for specific food supplements

Proprietary baby foods are fortified with vitamins and iron, and supplements of such substances need therefore not be given except in the case of premature babies, who may need additional quantities. A baby fed on a non-fortified milk, such as ordinary cows' milk, will have an insecure vitamin intake and it is wise therefore in such cases for vitamin supplements, particularly vitamin C and vitamin D, to be added until the baby is on a mixed diet. (See *vitamins.) Cows' milk not only is deficient in iron but also hampers its absorption and sometimes increases its loss, so that iron deficiency is common in cows'-milk-fed babies after the first few months of life. Iron supplements may therefore be required. Breast milk contains little iron but what there is is so well absorbed that breastfed babies hardly ever become iron deficient. (See *iron.) In fluoride-deficient areas, additional fluoride should be given in order to prevent dental decay. (See *fluoride.)

FEEDING PROBLEMS

Feeding problems in the breastfed baby

Provided the mother's lactation is adequate, the nipples satisfactory and the baby able to suck, there should be no problems with regard to breastfeeding. (For problems at the breast see *breast.) A breastfed baby who is unhappy should be assumed in the first instance to be not getting enough. This may be due to a temporary deficiency in lactation, which will usually be corrected by demand-feeding and adequate rest. The best stimulation for milk production is regular and complete emptying of the breasts. Other measures are of little or no value. There is no benefit from an over-consumption of fluid, be it in the form of milk, stout, Coca-Cola or any other popular beverage. A variety of stimulants to lactation have been popular through the ages and you may take your choice from peanuts, lucerne, powdered earthworms, cuttlefish soup, sea slugs, silkworms in wine, ground pearls and breast-milk enemas, and many more. Forget the quest for magic and be practical. If the baby is clearly hungry and is taking all you can produce, you will for a time have to accept some complementation of the breastfeeding by offering a bottle after each breastfeed and allowing the baby to help himself. With the diminution in anxiety and tension, lactation will almost certainly improve and it may well then be possible to dispense with the extra bottle-feeds.

Is breast milk ever unsuitable for the baby? Once lactation is established, the milk appears rather watery, and many a mother has abandoned breastfeeding in the fear that it was insufficiently nutritious for her baby. This is completely wrong. Even in severely undernourished mothers, breast milk, though varying in quality, is still adequate nutritionally.

Can a baby be intolerant of his mother's milk? This is such a rare situation that the answer should be no. There is, however, the very rare baby with significant digestive symptoms which disappear when the baby is put on an artificial feed. You should, however, not abandon breastfeeding without consulting your doctor and having his agreement. There is a little evidence to suggest that certain proteins, such as cows'-milk protein, may occasionally be absorbed intact into the mother's bloodstream and excreted in her milk. The quantities involved are minute and very unlikely to affect any but the most exquisitely sensitive baby. The idea has become unfortunately popular as a cause of infantile colic (see *colic) but it does at least provide the mother of a fretful baby with a harmless manoeuvre (removal of milk and dairy products from her own diet) before she is tempted to abandon breastfeeding.

Overfeeding in the breastfed baby does not exist. For other difficulties that may be encountered see *colic, *wind, *vomiting, etc.

Feeding problems in the artificially fed baby

Many of the problems encountered in the artificially fed baby are related to mechanical difficulties with *bottles and *teats.

Underfeeding. This is the commonest cause of dissatisfaction in the baby and is often due to an inadequate teat hole or a poorly functioning valve mechanism, so that the baby sucks strenuously until he is tired but has not yet received a sufficient reward for his labours. He may settle for a time from exhaustion and then wake up hungry after a short period, demanding more food. With bottle-feeding it is of course possible to see exactly how much the baby has taken. This may appear to be adequate, but unfortunately it tells one nothing about the baby's satisfaction. If the baby is persistently unhappy, therefore, and seems to be hungry, pay attention to the teats and bottle and allow the baby to demand-feed. Most problems will be solved by such simple commonsense measures. If not there may be reason to change the feed.

Overfeeding. This bogy still lurks in the minds of many people but, as in the case of the breastfed baby, in general it can be ignored. Babies' appetites vary greatly. Likewise, although the average baby gains somewhere in the region of 200 g per week, the rate of gain varies widely, the larger babies tending to gain more rapidly than the smaller ones. It is utterly unreasonable to diagnose overfeeding simply because a baby is gaining weight more rapidly than the average. A baby whose tendency is to gain weight at such a rate will be rendered utterly miserable if his food intake is cut down in order to make him gain at the average rate. Do not worry about overfeeding. Provided you are giving him the right sort of food you can let him take as much as he wants.

The above statements, while true, do require some qualification. There is some evidence, by no means conclusive, that fat babies do tend to grow into fat adults, and obesity is unquestionably unhealthy. The over-fat baby therefore might well require his intake of fattening foods, particularly carbohydrates and fats, curtailed but they should then be replaced with satisfying quantities of less fattening foods, and he should not be allowed to go hungry. Similarly, it is possible to give too much of certain constituents in the diet, such as sodium (salt), particularly to small babies who may not be able to make the necessary adjustments. Whole cows' milk, which has a high sodium content, is therefore not a suitable feed for a small baby. An excess of sugar is most undesirable, not only because of its intrinsic calorie content but also because the cultivation of sweet tastes perpetuates the overingestion of carbohydrates, and sugar and refined starches are responsible for most of the dental decay seen in young children. If extra drinks are required it is better to give either water or unadulterated fruit juices.

Feeding problems in the older child

It is astonishing how few parents are satisfied with the quantity of food their children eat. There are a few who in these days of rising inflation feel their children eat too much, but most parents seem to think that their children should eat more than they do. You may be quite sure that a child who is not ill will consume as much food as he needs, provided the food is available. There is absolutely no need to try and force him. As soon as he is capable of doing so a child should feed himself, no matter how messy the process. A small child may go off his food after the spoon has been used for administration of some vile medicine but his suspicions will not last for long. There should be no fussing, for his hunger will soon drive him to eat again. If forcible attempts are made to feed him he will almost certainly resist and if feeding is allowed to take on the character of a contest the child will always win. This is a situation you must not allow to happen. A child who is ill may well go off his food but it should be fairly clear to you in such a case that there is a reason. If in doubt by all means consult your doctor. It is, however, usually the thoroughly well-nourished and extremely healthy child who is brought with the complaint that 'he doesn't eat a thing'. Very often such children are consuming huge quantities of milk which the misguided mother encourages so that 'at least he gets something in'. Excessive milk consumption after babyhood often causes anaemia and constipation, and although there is good reason to encourage a consumption of 2 to 3 glasses a day in order to ensure an adequate intake of proteins and calcium, there is no need for more.

On no account let meals become a battle. The child between the ages of 1 and 3 years is intensely negativistic and will oppose almost anything you try to force upon him. If he has only to shut his mouth to get his parents to perform the most absurd antics in order to get food into him which he wants to eat anyway, he will extract the maximum of satisfaction from the situation. Just don't give him a chance. His food should be put before him and he should be given a reasonable time in which to eat it, after which it is calmly taken away. Snacks between meals should be restricted and should consist of healthy foods rather than biscuits and sweets, and if he has elected not to eat his meal he should not be allowed to compensate by filling up with snacks.

It is of course often irritating to the small child deeply involved in play activity to have this interrupted for a meal. Mealtimes should therefore be announced as something exciting rather than an end to play. Once at table he is expected to devote his attentions to eating but mealtimes should also be fun and an opportunity for the family to gather together in mutual enjoyment.

If, in spite of correct attitudes, food refusal persists, and particularly if the child is losing weight, then you should seek medical advice.

FEVER

A rise in body temperature may be due to many causes but the most common by far is infection. It is wrong to regard fever as an undesirable thing. Most of the germs causing infection are very sensitive to temperature levels and a significant rise in temperature may well help to eliminate them. A high temperature is often accompanied by a feeling of discomfort but the only danger associated with fever (except where this reaches an astronomical level) is the possibility of convulsions, occurring in young children usually from 6 months to 4 years of age. (See *convulsions.) In older children and adults there is no need to treat fever simply because it is there. In the convulsive age group, however, and particularly if a child has had a previous convulsion, the temperature should if possible be kept below 39°C. This may be achieved by stripping the child, fanning him, sponging him with cool water or placing him in a cool bath, and by administration of antipyretic drugs such as paracetamol, aspirin and mefanamic acid. It is more important of course to determine the cause of the fever and to deal with this appropriately. (See also *heat stroke.)

FITS

See *epilepsy, *convulsions

FLAT FEET

The infant normally appears to have flat feet because of the amount of fat in the sole. In the older child, the degree of development of the foot arch is very variable and many people have flat feet without suffering the slightest disability. Probably more problems are created by the highly arched foot. It is highly questionable whether remedial measures for 'flat feet' — be these in the form of special footwear or exercises — are of the slightest benefit, and so-called arch supports usually produce nothing but discomfort. Beware therefore of over-enthusiastic treatment for what is probably a normal condition.

FLEAS

These ubiquitous pests seldom cause serious disease but their bites may be confused with other rashes. Flea-bites are itchy and usually occur in groups, particularly on the trunk, in small children. They are also common on the extremities, and sensitivity to flea-bites is the usual cause of *papular urticaria. This eruption consists of small papules and vesicles, particularly on the lower extremities, and scratching may lead to infection, producing sores. It is fundamental in treating the condition to eliminate the fleas, not only from the household pets but also from their breeding-places in carpets and floors where, particularly in warm climates, fleas may become permanently established, hopping on to any convenient bypasser, human or animal, for the necessary meals. Relatively simple domestic insecticides may suffice but in obstinate cases of infestation professional fumigation may be necessary.

Fleas may transmit typhus and plague.

FLUORIDE

Despite the incontestable evidence that adequate fluoride does protect the teeth from dental decay there has been much argument about the artificial fluoridation of water supplies. The fluoride content of drinking water in southern Africa is in general inadequate and extra fluoride should therefore be given to children from early age in order to protect both their deciduous and their permanent teeth. You should, however, be guided by your dentist, who will know the local fluoride situation. Where this is not deficient extra fluoride should not be given, as an excess may be harmful.

FONTANELLE

The anterior fontanelle is commonly known as the 'soft spot' in a baby's head. It is more or less diamond-shaped and is of very variable size. The posterior fontanelle lies towards the back of the cranium and is triangular in shape and much smaller. Sometimes there is an extra fontanelle between the two. The anterior fontanelle normally becomes progressively smaller, and closes as a rule between 6 months and 18 months of age. The posterior fontanelle may be closed at birth but may persist up to 6 months.

The tension of the fontanelle is a useful indicator of the pressure inside the head. It tends to sink in states of dehydration, constituting a useful sign in such conditions as gastro-enteritis. In conditions such as meningitis the fontanelle becomes tense. An elevated fontanelle is also seen in cases of bleeding into the cranial cavity, brain tumours, hydrocephalus (water on the brain), rickets and certain poisonings, e.g. vitamin A.

Early closure of the fontanelle may be due to the skull bones fusing too early (craniostenosis) and delayed closure may be due to a variety of causes, e.g. hydrocephalus, rickets and thyroid deficiency.

Mothers are often afraid to wash the fontanelle area of the scalp, with the result that skin debris accumulates. The gap between the bones in the fontanelle region is covered by a very tough fibrous membrane and it is quite impossible to do any damage by even vigorous washing.

FOOD (see also *diet and *feeding)

It goes without saying that food is essential for life, and starvation has killed many more people than have wars. Two-thirds of the world's population at present is undernourished.

Most people distinguish between good food and bad food not on the basis of its taste or on the art with which it is prepared but on their assessment of its nutritional value. Such assessments may be very inaccurate. Vegetables, for example, are regarded as 'healthy' whereas their nutritive value is poor, although they are desirable for the provision of fibre and also vitamin C. The latter is however largely destroyed by cooking. Similar remarks apply to fruits, which, because of their higher sugar content, provide more calories. Protein is essential for growth and health, and the high-protein foods such as meat, eggs, milk, cheese, and fish are generally and justifiably held in high regard. They are however very expensive foodstuffs and often consumed in excess by the affluent. The average adult requires no more than 1 g per kilogram of body mass per day of high-class protein and a growing child twice this quantity. Protein in excess of about 4 g per kilogram of body mass per day is simply used as fuel and there are cheaper forms of fuel.

Because of their relatively low cost, cereals are the most widely consumed foodstuffs, and whole cereals are very nutritious. Unfortunately, they are so mutilated by modern milling that what is left in most cereal foods is simply carbohydrate. This applies particularly to maize, which when used as a staple food without more nourishing supplements leads to severe *malnutrition.

There are no foods which are unsuitable for even very small children, who should be introduced at an early age to a varied dietary intake. (See *feeding and *feeding problems.)

Food additives. See *additives

Food refusal. See *feeding problems

FOOD-POISONING

This is of two main types — chemical and bacterial. Food can of course be contaminated with a variety of chemical substances, some of which will lead to acute gastro-intestinal upsets with nausea, vomiting and diarrhoea, closely resembling the results of bacterial contamination. Other chemical poisons may have very different effects, e.g. insecticides. (See *poisoning.)

Bacterial food-contamination may result in a direct toxic effect if the bacteria have proliferated in the food and produced a toxic substance. Certain staphylococci may do this. Symptoms occur very soon after ingestion and consist of vomiting and diarrhoea, often leading to severe dehydration and general toxicity. Other forms of contamination result in the ingestion of live organisms which then propagate in the bowel, e.g. Salmonella-poisoning. In such cases the onset is delayed some 12 to 24 hours after ingestion. In addition to diarrhoea and vomiting there may be accompanying fever, and patients are often severely ill, requiring treatment in hospital. Food-poisoning must always be suspected when several people develop similar symptoms after ingestion of a common foodstuff.

Rarer forms of poisoning include botulism, this being the result of contamination by a bacillus which produces a neurotoxin leading to paralysis. Botulism is most commonly due to contamination of canned foods but may also occur in infants, in which case the bacillus is present in the bowel, sometimes introduced by honey. Symptoms include constipation and weakness to a degree requiring artificial ventilation, and may persist for many weeks.

Another rare cause of food-poisoning is the 'Red Tide'. A minute marine organism which causes discolouration of the sea contaminates shellfish, and ingestion of the latter leads to severe neurological disturbances with profound weakness, which may be fatal.

FORCEPS DELIVERY

When the progress of a baby's head down the birth canal becomes arrested, delivery may be hastened by applying forceps or by using the vacuum extractor. Although the use of forceps may result in some superficial bruising of the baby's scalp, it does not damage the baby's skull or brain, for the forceps, correctly applied, rather protect the baby's head from being squashed. Any brain-damage which might be apparent after a forceps delivery is more probably due to the condition which made assistance necessary rather than to the application of forceps itself.

FOREIGN BODIES

Young children display considerable enterprise and imagination in the selection of foreign bodies to push into their various orifices. The nose is probably the most popular receptacle for such items as beans, peas, small stones, paper and plastic. A unilateral nasal discharge, particularly if offensive, should make one suspect a foreign body. Similar articles may be pushed into ears, which are also commonly traumatised by sticks, hair-pins, or other items used for attempts at cleaning. Inhaled foreign bodies are the most dangerous for they may cause severe respiratory obstruction if lodged in the larynx, or they may cause severe lung disease if they are inhaled deeper down into one of the bronchi. Common items here are peanuts (which should not be given to small children because of this danger) and bits of plastic. Foreign bodies may get stuck in the oesophagus or gullet and may then give rise to difficulties in swallowing and sometimes respiratory symptoms. The commonest such items are coins, which fortunately will be revealed by X-ray, whereas most other foreign bodies are not.

The other popular place for foreign bodies is the vagina of a small girl, who may experiment with a great variety of articles. Occasionally objects may be pushed up the urethra into the bladder. A persistent vaginal discharge, particularly if offensive and irritating, is highly suggestive of a foreign body.

FORESKIN (see also *circumcision)

It is remarkable that males have for so long acquiesced in the removal of an integral part of their most treasured possession. The foreskin serves to protect the glans of the penis, which in its covered state is an exquisitely sensitive structure. Babies' foreskins vary greatly in length and apparent tightness. Occasionally a baby is born without a foreskin or with the lower part missing so that if forms a hood rather than a sheath.

Normally the foreskin is stuck down to the underlying glans of the penis for many years, and complete detachment may not occur until puberty. Separation is not always uniform and pearly collections of smegma may periodically occur. These may cause temporary irritation but they will be discharged spontaneously and require nothing more than normal washing with retraction of the foreskin only to the point of comfort and not beyond. The foreskin may not be fully retractable for very many years and no force should be exerted in trying to retract it. Forceful retraction leads to tearing, and subsequent healing, if associated with scar formation, may make retraction impossible and necessitate circumcision. If proper care is given circumcision is hardly ever necessary. In conditions where hygiene is difficult, however, it may save a great deal of discomfort. The accumulation of smegma leads to irritation and this may predispose to cancer, not only of the penis but possibly also of the cervix of sexual partners. Where it is not possible to wash adequately, circumcision may therefore be advantageous and this was no doubt the origin of ritual circumcision of Jews and Muslims in extremely arid regions. With modern hygienic facilities the foreskin should lead a much less threatened existence.

FORMULA
This American term for an artificial-milk feed is a hangover from the era when baby feeds were prescribed in various dilutions and contortions according to the pseudo-scientific whim of the consultant. The simpler terms 'feed' or 'milk' are preferred.

FRACTURES
It is not possible to describe the nature and treatment of every possible fracture but some common types are:

(1) Fractures in the newborn baby
Fractures of the skull may result from pressure on the bones by the maternal bony parts and sometimes by imperfectly applied instruments. The bones, being soft, dent rather than break, giving rise to a so-called pond fracture. There is rarely any significant damage to the underlying brain. Although such fractures may realign spontaneously the more severe ones may require elevation.

Fracture of the clavicle or collar bone. This is a common injury in the newborn baby, often produced during delivery of the shoulders. The condition is usually revealed by the baby's not moving one arm as well as the other, and the irregularity in the bone may then be felt. Sometimes such a fracture is not recognised until the healing process produces a lump in the bone. There is very rarely any complicating damage to the blood-vessels and nerves which lie under the clavicle. Healing is always satisfactory, even without immobilisation.

Fracture of the humerus. The upper-arm bone may easily be broken by pressure on the arm in an attempt to deliver the shoulders. There is usually an audible snap, the arm is subsequently immobile and passive movement is obviously painful. There may be some shortening and deformity of the arm compared with the other side. For adequate healing of such a fracture the bone-ends must be immobilised, but this is simply achieved by strapping the arm to the chest wall for about 3 weeks.

Fracture of the femur. This occurs most commonly in breech presentation. As in the case of the humerus there is usually an audible snap when the bone breaks and the baby subsequently does not move the affected leg. Shortening and some deformity of the thigh are usually apparent and passive movements are painful. Because the muscles of the thigh tend to pull the bone-ends into an overriding position, some traction may have to be exerted on the limb by putting the baby in a 'gallows' splint for a few weeks. If left alone, however, the bone reunites and remodels perfectly well and the modern trend is not to treat these fractures.

Healing of all the above fractures is usually most satisfactory and if alignment is not quite perfect the bone usually remodels with no residual deformity.

(2) Greenstick fractures

In young children the bones are not as rigid as in adults, and fractures are often incomplete. There is pain at the site of the fracture but no deformity of the limb. Confirmation of a fracture may require X-ray examination. Immobilisation is not required but further trauma must be prevented during healing and, in the case of fractures of the lower limbs, weight-bearing must be avoided until healing is complete.

(3) Simple fractures

These are closed fractures in which there is no communication between the bone-ends and a skin wound. The commonest sites are the clavicle, the lower end of the radius near the wrist, the elbow region, the mid-humerus and, in the lower limb, the bones just above the ankle, spiral fractures of the tibia from torsion movements, and the midshaft of the femur. All these fractures require appropriate immobilisation under medical supervision.

Skull fractures are common as a result of falls, motor-vehicle injuries, etc., but simple crack fractures are in themselves unimportant and they are a poor indicator of underlying brain injury. Depressed fractures of the skull, however, inevitably damage the underlying brain to some extent and usually require surgical elevation. Fractures of the base of the skull, which may result in bleeding or leakage of cerebrospinal fluid from the ears or nose, are usually the result of severe trauma and are very serious.

(4) Compound fractures

These are associated with damage to the overlying skin so that contamination of the fracture site occurs readily. The broken bone-ends may project through the skin wound. These are very serious injuries. Handling should be kept to a minimum and the limb immobilised by splinting or, in the case of the leg, bandaging it to the other leg. The skin wound should be left untouched as far as possible or covered with a simple sterile dressing.

While awaiting transport to hospital the patient should be treated for *shock and will almost certainly require some pain relief. If, however, he is likely to require an anaesthetic and there will be little delay in receiving hospital attention, avoid giving anything by mouth.

FRIENDS

Man is a social animal and, next to parents, friends are the most important items in the child's life. His taste in friends may not always please you but do not let this be too apparent. You will probably try to influence him to some extent but do not try to choose his friends for him, for you will surely not succeed and an imperfect friend is better than none.

Some children have few friends, other many. The loss of a very special friend may be highly traumatic for a time, but the friend is usually replaced fairly quickly. Whether you approve of them or not, do encourage your children's friends to come to your home, where at least you can observe the association. A friend who is having a bad influence on your child may be in serious need of friendly help himself and, although it may be difficult to generate such altruistic feelings, this possibility should be kept in mind, as you may be able to do a great deal of good.

Imaginary friends are common in the pre-school years and their 'existence' may worry parents who feel that their child should have a more realistic attitude. The imaginary friend often shares the same minor imperfections as the child so that he can be blamed instead of the real culprit. There is no harm in this situation and the 'friend' should be tolerated with good humour, for his life is not likely to be a long one.

GALACTAGOGUES

A galactagogue is any agent or drug which increases the secretion of milk. Farmers appear to have had much more success in attempts to improve milk supply than have doctors. From time immemorial a variety of products has been advocated (see *feeding problems) but there is little evidence that anything is convincingly successful. Modern favourites are sulpiride and metoclopramide. Whatever you might be tempted to take, take with a large dose of faith and it may then do some good. The only proven stimulus to lactation is regular and adequate emptying of the breasts, preferably by a vigorously suckling baby. Demand-feeding solves many of the minor difficulties associated with inadequate lactation.

GAMMAGLOBULIN

This is a fraction of the body proteins containing most of the immunoglobulins, which are the antibodies responsible for immunity. The newborn baby is protected by gammaglobulins which have passed through the placenta from the maternal circulation. These progressively wane, and the infant goes through a period where the gammaglobulins are normally low. This is physiological and demands no treatment, although gammaglobulin is often mistakenly administered to such children.

Rarely, gammaglobulins are not produced in adequate concentration, leading to a condition known as hypogammaglobulinaemia or, in the case of total absence, agammaglobulinaemia. In such conditions the regular injection of gammaglobulin helps to restore immunity.

Gammaglobulin may also be administered as a preventive measure to weakly children exposed to measles, and as a prophylactic against infectious jaundice. (See also *immunoglobulins.)

GANGRENE

This implies death of tissue, often of an extremity, as a result of interference with the blood supply. In children this is seen only as a result of trauma. Gas gangrene is due to infection by a specific germ resembling the tetanus bacillus.

GARGLES

This rather old-fashioned habit is of little value. The act of gargling simply keeps the medicament away from the throat, which is usually the target area. A sore throat is better relieved by sucking a soothing lozenge or sipping a soothing liquid, both of which allow maximum contact between the medication and the painful or inflamed throat. (See also *tonsillitis.)

GARGOYLISM

An unflattering term for the rare condition of mucopolysaccharide disturbance characterised by physical deformities which have been fancied to resemble some of the gargoyles of medieval cathedrals.

GASTRO-ENTERITIS

This implies irritation or inflammation of the gastro-intestinal tract. The associated symptoms are vomiting, diarrhoea and often there is abdominal colicky pain. There may be associated fever and if the symptoms are severe they may lead to dehydration. The diagnosis is one to be made by your doctor rather than by yourself. You may however quite reasonably be tempted to make the diagnosis when your baby presents with the typical symptoms, and whether or not the diagnosis is correct matters little, provided the management is appropriate.

In the case of the small infant, the combination of vomiting and diarrhoea, leading as often happens to significant dehydration with or without the associated acidosis, electrolyte disturbances and convulsions which frequently accompany gastro enteritis, makes this one of the most hazardous as well as one of the commonest infections in the community. The dangers are often greatly increased by inappropriate attention. The feverish child is wrapped up so that his temperature goes even higher, leading to convulsions and further fluid loss. The fluids administered often contain the wrong ingredients, leading to further electrolyte disturbances. Aspirin is often given to relieve fever and this increases the tendency to acidosis. Finally, medications are often administered which are not only valueless but harmful.

Until seen by a doctor the child with gastro-enteritic symptoms should be given only an appropriate solution of sugar and electrolytes in small frequent quantities to the limit of his tolerance. If feverish he should be kept cool by exposure and cool sponging. No medicines should be given. Appropriate oral solutions are discussed under *dehydration. (See also *diarrhoea.)

GENES

We now know that genes are relatively short, chemical segments of chromosomes which are responsible for coding the synthesis of certain proteins or their fractions. Many of the genes have now been mapped onto individual chromosomes. Genetic chemical engineering however does not as yet enable us to correct genetic defects.

Because chromosomes (with the exception of the sex chromosomes) occur in pairs, an abnormal gene will only express itself if it is dominant or, in the case of a recessive, if there is no normal gene present to compensate for it, as in the case of some sex-linked conditions such as haemophilia. In general, however, recessively inherited conditions are revealed only when both genes are abnormal, as in the homozygote (see *genetics). The individual with one abnormal gene may be detectable by tests sufficiently sensitive to demonstrate a minor abnormality not clinically recognisable.

GENETICS

The mode of inheritance of most common genetic conditions is illustrated in the following diagrams.

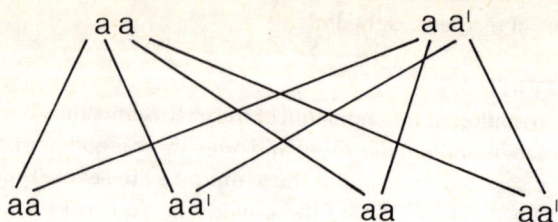

(1) If one parent is normal (aa) and the other parent carries one abnormal gene (aa-), then of the resulting offspring 50 per cent will be normal and 50 per cent will carry the abnormal gene. If the abnormal gene is a dominant it will then be expressed in these 50 per cent of offspring. If a recessive it will be inapparent but they will be carriers of the condition, which would reveal itself should they mate with another carrier, as in (2).

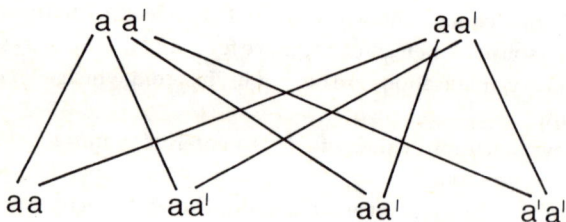

(2) Represents the situation where both parents are carriers of an abnormal gene. If the gene is a recessive both parents will seem normal, as will 75 per cent of their offspring. The remaining 25 per cent, however, being homozygous for the abnormal gene, will manifest the abnormality. 50 per cent of all offspring will be carriers of the condition. If the gene is a dominant one, then 75 per cent of the offspring will manifest the abnormality, two-thirds of them being heterozygous and one-third homozygous for the condition.

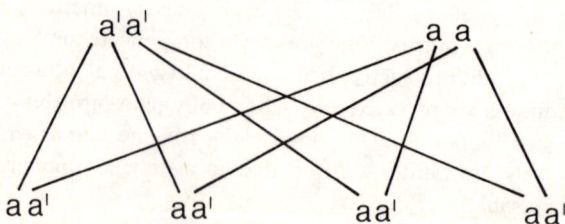

(3) Represents the situation where one parent is homozygous for the abnormal gene and the other parent is normal. All the offspring of such a union will be carriers but none will be clinically affected if the condition is a recessive.

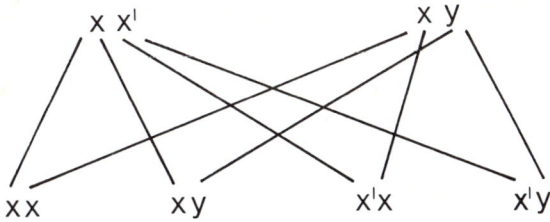

(4) Illustrates the inheritance of a sex-linked condition in which the abnormal gene is present on the X chromosome. If this is a recessive, females having two X chromosomes will compensate for the abnormality and the latter is then unexpressed. Any males, however, who inherit the abnormal gene will manifest the disease state, as there is only a Y and no normal X chromosome to compensate for the abnormality. In such a union, half the males will manifest the disease and half the females will be carriers. Many conditions are inherited in this way, the best known perhaps being *haemophilia.

Should you come from a family where genetically inherited disease is present or should you give birth to an offspring with a genetically determined condition you will probably seek help from an expert to discuss the chances of propagating the abnormality. It is not for such an advisor to tell you what to do but simply to put the risks clearly to you in order that you may make the wisest decision.

GENITALS

In the first weeks of foetal development the genitalia are undifferentiated, but under the influence of male hormones secreted by the foetal testes in the male, the external genital organs develop along male lines. At birth it is usually quite clear that the child is either a boy or a girl but it does rarely happen that the external genitalia are indeterminate. This may be due to true hermaphroditism in which both testicular and ovarian tissue is present (a condition surprisingly common in the African). It may be due to masculinisation of a female infant or to feminisation of a male infant. Sorting out these problems is often a very complex undertaking.

Baby girls often exhibit fairly profuse mucoid vaginal discharge in the first few days of life and this may be accompanied by some bleeding as the result of the influence of maternal hormones. This situation need cause no anxiety, is self-limiting and requires no treatment.

It is not uncommon for the labia minora (the small lips) to be fused together leaving only a tiny opening for the passage of urine. Such a situation may predispose to urinary infection and it is desirable that the anatomy be corrected. Fortunately the adhesions are very thin and easily split.

Baby boys at birth may appear to have rather large genitalia but these then tend to diminish in size. The foreskin may appear long and narrow but if the urinary stream is normal there is no problem. (See *foreskin.) The testicles are often very mobile and may bounce in and out of the scrotum. If they are incompletely descended and never found in the scrotum they may require surgical correction between 2 and 4 years of age. (See *testes.) The penis in fat babies often appears very tiny because most of the shaft is buried in a fat pad. This you will probably be able to determine for yourself, but if you are worried, by all means consult your doctor.

Care of the genitals should not present a significant problem. Babies of both sexes should be washed normally and children should be taught to look after their own bodies with normal hygienic care but nothing very special. The foreskin should be retracted only as far as it goes with complete comfort. In the case of girls it is normal for a small quantity of bath water to enter the vagina but this will do no harm.

It is normal for small children to be curious about their genital organs and when at the age of about 3 they are aware of sexual differences the interest is increased. Any questions that arise should be dealt with simply, unemotionally and as explicitly as is appropriate for the child's age.

GENTIAN VIOLET

This dye, usually presented as a 1 per cent aqueous solution, is a useful and inexpensive preparation for the treatment particularly of fungal infections. It is effective in the case of oral thrush, when it should be applied twice a day and not more often, as excessive application may cause irritation and ulceration of the delicate mucous membrane. It may be used on the skin but is rather unflattering. It is very effective in the treatment of vaginal thrush, but then requires expert application.

GERMAN MEASLES

See *rubella

GIARDIA

This unicellular flagellate is a common intestinal parasite, which may or may not produce symptoms. Children with abdominal pains are often treated speculatively for giardiasis with considerable success. The parasite often causes a chronic diarrhoea with sloppy, pale, unpleasant stools and, as stool examination reveals the parasite in only about 50 per cent of cases, it is common practice to treat children suffering from such symptoms for the possibility of giardiasis before investigating the diarrhoea in greater depth. If the child responds, a great deal of effort and expense has been saved. If she does not, little has been lost.

Several medications are of value in treating giardiasis, the most popular being metronidazole.

GLANDS

These are secretory organs which are divided into two main categories.

(1) The *exocrine glands,* whose secretions are directed to the exterior, e.g. breast, pancreas, sweat glands.

(2) The *endocrine glands* whose secretions are absorbed into the bloodstream and

then circulate around the body, e.g. the pituitary, thyroid, adrenal glands. In addition to its exocrine function of producing digestive juices, the pancreas also has an endocrine function, secreting insulin and glucagon. The gonads, in addition to producing ova or sperms, secrete sex hormones. The upper intestinal epithelium, in addition to its absorptive function, secretes digestive enzymes and also produces endocrine secretions having a regulatory effect upon other portions of the digestive tract. The endocrine system is therefore a very complex one.

Lymph glands, better called lymph nodes, do not have a secretory function. They act as filters in the lymphatic system. The glands are situated in groups in the neck, axillae and groins, where they are readily palpable especially in young children, who have a great deal of lymphatic tissue. There are also numerous lymph nodes in the abdomen and the chest. Lymph nodes enlarge with infection and usually then become painful and tender, and in suppurative infections they may form abscesses requiring surgical drainage. Tuberculosis often affects lymph nodes.

GLANDULAR FEVER

This is a specific but very variable disease caused by a particular virus (the Epstein-Barr virus). Symptoms consist of fever, malaise, sore throat, enlargement of the lymph nodes particularly of the neck, and sometimes a rash. Occasionally the liver is involved, causing jaundice, and there are other rarer manifestations. The blood count shows a characteristic picture and there is a heterophile antibody test which is usually positive after about one week of symptoms but which in small children is usually negative.

The duration of symptoms is very variable but the disease does tend to be shorter in children than in adults, who often remain feeling unwell for many weeks and sometimes months. There is no specific treatment for this disease.

GLOBULIN

Globulin is one of the two main classes of protein in the body, the other being albumin which has a lower molecular weight. By various techniques the globulins can be fractionated and the globulin pattern is helpful in identifying some disease states. Probably the most important globulins are the so-called gammaglobulins, which contain most of the antibodies required for immunological reactions. These are called immunoglobulins or Igs. They in turn can be further subdivided into IgG, IgA, IgM, IgE, etc. (See *immunoglobulins.)

GLUCOSE

This is a simple sugar (monosaccharide) which forms the basis for most of the energy required by the body. Other sugars are converted to glucose before they can be utilised. Glucose is rapidly absorbed and is therefore almost immediately available for energy purposes. From a practical point of view, however, it has little advantage in this respect over the much cheaper sucrose or ordinary cane sugar. There is never a need for you to buy glucose. Even in conditions such as gastroenteritis, where sugar and salt solutions are required temporarily, sucrose is just as effective in providing energy and in assisting the absorption of salt. In the case of healthy children, refined sugars are to be avoided as much as possible as they have no nutritional value, apart from their calorie content.

GLUTEN

A protein found in wheat and rye and to a less significant extent also in oats and barley, sensitivity to which results in *coeliac disease. Children and adults with a sensitivity to gluten develop an atrophic condition of the bowel-lining, which leads to impaired absorption of foodstuffs and a chronic diarrhoeal state, the stools being typically large, pale, foul and fatty. Nutritional failure leads to weight loss and general debility. Removal of gluten from the diet results in fairly rapid correction of all these abnormalities.

Because of its known effect in producing coeliac disease, gluten sometimes gets blamed for other symptoms. This is illogical and unjustifiable. The only indication for a gluten-free diet is coeliac disease.

GOATS' MILK

Being very similar in composition to cows' milk, goats' milk achieves varying popularity as a substitute for the latter when there is a suspicion of cows'-milk allergy or intolerance. When readily available it is well worth trying. It is however just as possible to be allergic to the protein in goats' milk as that in cows' milk, and this is impossible to predict. Like any other animal milk, goats' milk should be boiled or pasteurised before being consumed, particularly as goats may spread brucellosis or undulant fever.

GONORRHOEA

This common venereal disease may be spread to children by direct sexual contact and any girl with acute vulvo-vaginitis should be tested for gonorrhoea because of this possibility. Males are less likely to be molested but are not of course immune. The causative germ is the gonococcus. An infected mother may transmit the disease to her baby and it then usually affects the eyes, causing a severe conjunctivitis with profuse purulent discharge. This condition requires prompt treatment to avoid damage to the eye with resultant loss of vision.

The gonococcus, which originally was extremely sensitive to penicillin, has exhibited progressive resistance to antibiotics and in some areas now poses a serious therapeutic problem. Like all venereal diseases, gonorrhoea has become rife with the surge in adolescent promiscuity. In the female it may lead to serious inflammation of the pelvic organs with consequent sterility, and in the male it produces not only an acutely uncomfortable inflammation of the urethra but may also spread to involve the testicles, with resultant damage. The disease may also spread elsewhere, particularly to joints.

GRANDPARENTS

Like any other group of people, grandparents differ widely among themselves and it is impossible therefore to generalise. Some are an absolute joy to both younger generations, others are an infernal nuisance. All are probably concerned about their grandchild's welfare but in their efforts to promote it they may do considerable harm. Grandparents are therefore to be kept under very firm control.

They should not be allowed to 'take over', for your child is your responsibility and granny will not be to blame if things go wrong. On the other hand, grandparents have a great deal to offer, not least in terms of experience. They may be in a position to render very real assistance to young parents, perhaps financially, perhaps physically in relieving them of some of the burdens and allowing them the occasional respite from family cares. They should not be abused however. Remember that older people tire, and an hour or two with a boisterous grandchild may be more than enough. There are some grandparents on the other hand who are extraordinarily possessive and who achieve a closer relationship with the grandchild than do her own parents. This may be the result of financial necessity or it may be the result of the extended family situation in which granny reigns as queen. It may be difficult for young parents not to submit to this sort of regime but it should be possible for them to retain control while encouraging the healthy and affectionate relationship between grandparent and grandchild. This is often a very valuable one for both, particularly when the parents are very busy and unable to give their offspring as much attention and affection as they might wish. Children, sensing the lesser pressures on grandparents, often confide in them more readily and express their thoughts more willingly than to their parents. In return, grandparents may have a very stimulating effect upon their grandchildren, being able to devote time that the parents cannot afford. It will pay you therefore to use grandparents wisely.

GRAZES

Small children are always grazing themselves and the larger child often inflicts fairly extensive superficial injuries upon himself by tumbling off his bicycle. Such abrasions are often contaminated by soil and they should then be washed with fairly liberal quantities of clean water. No application is necessary, no matter how great the temptation to dab them with some vivid antiseptic. The crust which forms will be shed when healing is complete and until then it should be left alone.

Even a superficial injury may be contaminated by tetanus germs and it is therefore important to maintain tetanus immunisation.

GREED

Some children as well as adults are naturally greedier than others but excessive greed is often a compensation for deprivation in other areas or a manifestation of general insecurity. Appetite of course varies considerably and provided the child is not gaining excessive weight you need not be perturbed. If your child seems abnormally greedy try to find out whether there is some emotional reason for it, and if there appears to be a significant problem, consult your doctor.

GRIPES

See *colic

GROIN

This, being a moist area, is a favourite site for fungal overgrowth, as may occur in some napkin rashes in infants or as 'Dobie itch' in older children and adults. In this condition there is a confluent inflammation of the skin with redness, thickening and itching in the pants area. The condition is infectious and often produces outbreaks in schools, camps, etc. Treatment is by application of an appropriate anti-fungal medication.

Swellings in the groin are common. In boys the testicles are often highly mobile and may retract up into the groin leaving the scrotum empty, which provides the main clue to the diagnosis. An incompletely descended testicle may also be felt in the groin, but this does not enter the scrotum when the child is warm and relaxed. Hernias may occur in both boys and girls though they are much more common in the former. They may come and go and can be difficult to diagnose with certainty if they are not seen. An inguinal hernia even in a small baby will not resolve spontaneously and should be surgically corrected as soon as possible. The other common swelling in the groin is an enlarged lymph node, usually as a result of infection of the leg or buttock regions. Such a swelling is common in tick bite fever. A progressively enlarging lymph gland in any area should be seen by a doctor.

GROMMETS

These are small plastic tubes which may be inserted through the eardrum in order to provide a communication between the middle ear and the outside air. This prevents pressure changes within the middle ear that may occur as a result of blockage of the Eustachian tubes, which provide the normal communication between the middle ear and the nasal cavity. Grommets are usually inserted in cases of recurrent otitis media in an attempt to prevent further episodes of such trouble. The tubes tend to be extruded after a variable time and the finding of a grommet on the child's pillow need not therefore cause you alarm. There is a tendency for grommets to be overused.

GROWING PAINS

Pains in the legs are common in young children and are usually unassociated with any disease. Though not due to growing, they occur in the growing child and if they must have a name, 'growing pains' at least implies that they are innocent. The pains may occur after particularly vigorous activity, are most common at the end of the day or at night and are usually located in the calves and less frequently in the thighs. There is no associated spasm of the muscles, as in true cramp. The pain may be very severe and sufficient to make the child cry bitterly but the duration is usually only a matter of minutes. There is usually no point therefore in administering any pain-relieving drug such as aspirin, for the pain has usually disappeared before the drug can take effect. Rubbing the aching part seems to help and at least gives the impression that something is being done. Do not assume that because nothing is detectably the matter with the limb that the pain is not genuine. It almost certainly is and the child should not be accused of malingering.

Growing pains have to be distinguished from pains due to disease of bone, joints or muscles but in such cases the pain is usually of longer duration or constantly present and is often associated with a limp. If you have any doubt, by all means consult your doctor so that you may be reassured that no organic disease is present. You may however have experienced growing pains yourself and well remember their features and be able therefore to diagnose with some confidence similar pains in your child. In severe cases where the pains occur regularly at night, waking the child from sleep, there may be justification for trying the effect of a Disprin or other mild analgesic administered at bedtime. The child can be reassured that eventually her growing pains will cease.

GROWTH

In spite of being such an obvious and inevitable feature of childhood, growth never ceases to interest and sometimes concern parents and other adult family members. The second question asked after a baby is born is inevitably, 'How much does she weigh?' and the first embarrassing remark that auntie always makes is, 'My! how you have grown.' It is to some extent regrettable that growth, being a physical characteristic, is measurable, for the mother's emotions tend to go up and down with the scales, and whereas fall-off in growth may be a salutary sign that all is not well, frequent and fanatical weighing often causes needless anxiety. It is important to realise that growth rates differ from child to child and there is a wide range of normality. This is illustrated by the accompanying charts, which show the growth changes in 95 per cent of normal children. Comparative values of height and mass are much more informative than either alone, and serial measurements are of far greater value than isolated ones. If a child's growth curve is out of line with the normal trend then the situation probably demands evaluation.

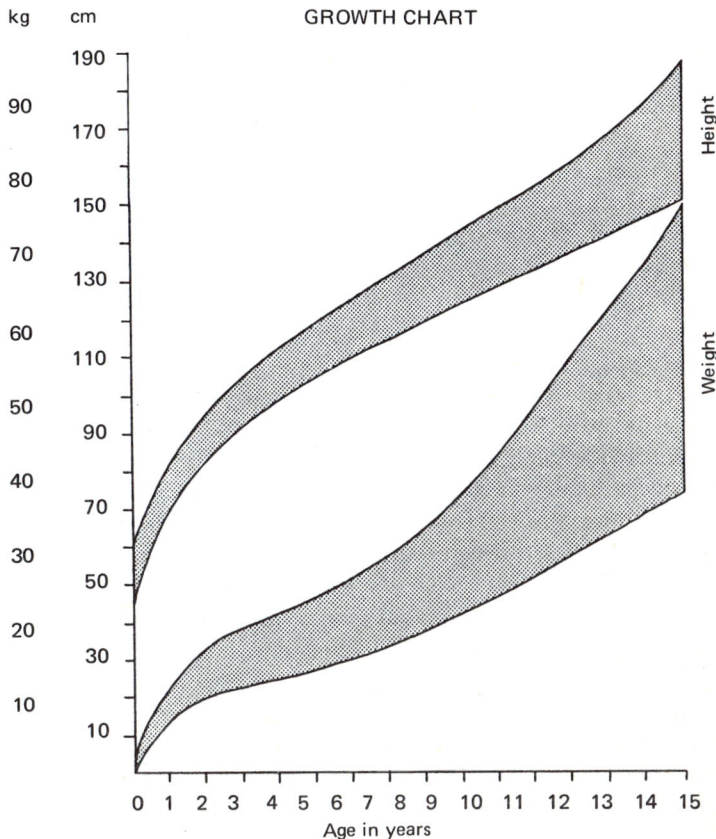

GROWTH CHART

A glance at the curves suffices to show that growth is not uniform. It is most rapid in the first 2 years of life, then steadies down until puberty, when a second growth spurt occurs, which is earlier in girls than in boys. Different tissues have very different growth rates. The brain for example grows very rapidly during intra-uterine life and for the first 2 years. As a result of this, body proportions change considerably. At birth the head occupies ¼ of the total body length, whereas in the adult the proportion is only ⅛. Lymphatic tissue concerned with body defence grows extremely rapidly in young childhood, so that the child of 10 has twice as much lymphatic tissue as an adult. It is normal therefore for tonsils and lymph nodes to be prominent in children. After the age of 10 these tissues regress. The genital organs remain infantile until puberty, when there is very sudden enlargement which is quite out of step with all other tissues. It is important to realise that these changes in body configuration, e.g. from the chubby bow-legged baby to the spindly knock-kneed 5-year-old, are quite normal.

Growth is of course influenced by genetic factors but the influence of parental size is significant only after the age of 3 to 4 years. Racial factors are also of some importance and no one would expect a pigmy to turn into a giant, but much of what was thought to be racial influence has been shown to be environmental. Japanese in Japan, for example, tend to be short whereas Japanese in California are as large as other Americans.

Growth is considerably influenced by nutrition. Deficiency of calories leads to generalised wasting whereas deficiency of protein is characterised by retarded linear growth. Growth may be impaired by almost any chronic disease and stunting may result from the deformities of, for example, rickets. Growth is to a great extent controlled by the endocrine system and in particular by the growth hormone secreted by the anterior pituitary gland, deficiency of which leads to severe dwarfing, and it is also considerably influenced by thyroid from the thyroid gland, deficiency of which leads to *cretinism.

Maternal diabetes usually causes overgrowth of the baby, resulting in large birth size owing to the excess of sugar available.

In addition to simple height and mass, other measurements are sometimes of considerable value. In particular the circumference of the head in the first few months of life is a good indicator of brain growth. Occasionally the skull bones knit together too early, halting brain expansion. This requires surgical correction. On the other hand excessively rapid head growth usually denotes water on the brain and this too may require surgical intervention. A graph of normal head growth is therefore included. Remember that this includes only 95 per cent of normal children and it is possible therefore for a measurement to be outside the shaded area and still normal. Premature babies must have allowance made for their degree of prematurity, and babies who are small at birth, with heads in proportions to their other dimensions, tend on the whole to remain small. The large-headed, thin, 'light for dates' babies, on the other hand, tend to put on weight rapidly and their head growth is normal.

Inadequate growth. If a child is growing abnormally slowly she should unquestionably be seen by a doctor and she may well require elaborate investigation to determine the cause. Malnutrition, endocrine abnormalities and chronic diseases of the heart, chest, kidneys and digestive system will have to be checked for, to

HEAD CIRCUMFERENCE IN THE FIRST THREE YEARS

cm

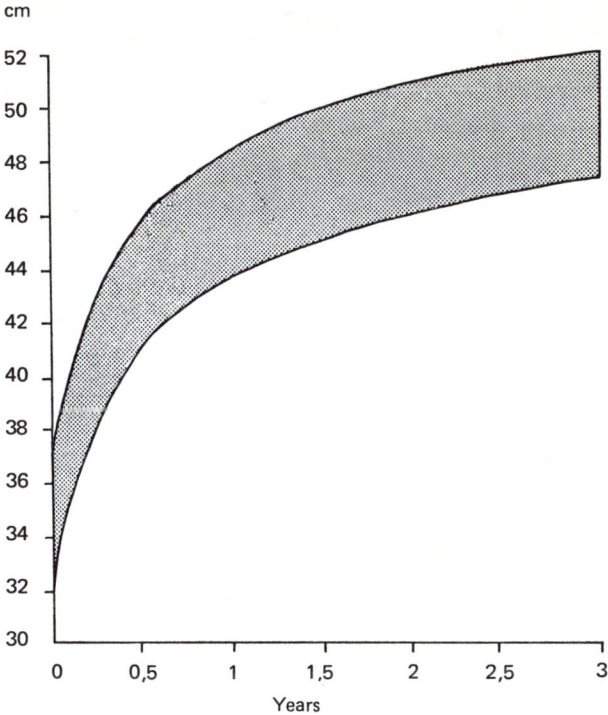

Years

discover whether they exist. There are many abnormalities of bone which may be responsible for short stature.

Excessive growth. This may be an embarrassment, especially in girls, and it is possible, if treatment is initiated before puberty, to slow down the growth rate and reduce the eventual height. Once puberty is complete however very little residual growth occurs and treatment at this stage is of no avail. Excessive growth may be due to overproduction of pituitary growth hormone and this will require rectification. Most big people, however, are simply big and not abnormal.

GUMS

Before the eruption of the teeth a baby is able to chew even quite hard foods as well as other articles with his gums. During eruption of a tooth there may be a little reddening of the gum and minor discomfort, but teething should not be blamed for significant symptoms. The gums are usually healthy structures and resistant to infection except in the neighbourhood of a tooth. It is infection of the tooth which causes a 'gum boil'. The gums may be generally inflamed in herpetic stomatitis (see *herpes), they may demonstrate a blue line in lead poisoning, they may bleed in scurvy and they may become overgrown as a side effect of treatment with phenytoin for epilepsy. Otherwise they give rise to very little trouble.

GYMNASTICS

While providing a most aesthetic athletic pursuit, gymnastics does also provide an opportunity for injury. Most of the injuries are simple strains and sprains which heal rapidly, but fractures of the elbow are relatively common from falls on the outstretched arm, and more chronic afflictions of the wrist joint and sometimes the lower limb joints also occur. Excessive arching of the back may lead to slipping of the vertebrae, and this may give rise to chronic back pain and disability. Like most activities, sensible enthusiasm is fine but excessive competitiveness may be dangerous.

HAEMOGLOBIN

This is the pigment in the red blood-cells which is responsible for transport of oxygen. It consists of an iron-containing fraction, haem, linked to a protein globin. The red cells are continuously being destroyed and replaced, and in the process the haemoglobin is broken down. The iron of the haem is retained but the remaining fraction is turned to bile and excreted by the liver.

There are various forms of haemoglobin with very minor chemical differences which, however, may have a considerable effect. Before birth the dominant haemoglobin is foetal haemoglobin, which is well suited to the relatively low oxygen tensions of foetal life. After birth this is relatively inefficient and it is progressively replaced by adult haemoglobin. Many abnormal forms of haemoglobin are known, such as haemoglobin C, D, E, etc., the general effect of which is to reduce the lifespan of the red blood-cells. Haemoglobin S is responsible for sickle-cell anaemia.

The haemoglobin level in the blood is easily measured, a low level indicating anaemia. Mean adult levels are — males 15,5 g per 100 ml, females 14 g per 100 ml, with a variation of about 2,5 g on either side. The haemoglobin level is high at birth but falls to a nadir at about 3 months of age, when the mean is 11,5, and thereafter it slowly rises to reach adult levels at about 6 years. Ignorance of these facts often causes infants to be diagnosed as anaemic when they are not.

HAEMOLYTIC DISEASE OF NEWBORN

See *jaundice, *Rhesus

HAEMOPHILIA

A hereditary condition characterised by excessive bleeding due to deficiency of one of the blood-clotting factors. Classical haemophilia is due to lack of Factor VIII (anti-haemophilic globulin) and is indistinguishable clinically from deficiency of Factor IX or Christmas disease (named after the first patient described with this condition, a 5-year-old boy called Christmas). The abnormality in both forms of haemophilia is carried on the X chromosome, and the disease is therefore usually manifest only in the male but is carried by the female (see *genetics). Because the blood cannot clot, bleeding even after very minor injury is persistent and severe blood loss may occur, necessitating transfusion in addition to replacement of the missing factor. Characteristically, bleeding also occurs into joints even after minor injury, and repeated bleeding leads to severe destruction of joints and loss of function, with severe crippling.

The treatment of haemophilia consists of replacing the missing coagulation factor. Concentrates of these factors are available and in severe cases they should be administered regularly every week or so, to prevent (in particular) the joint destruction which is otherwise almost inevitable. In milder cases it may suffice to administer the missing factor only when injury has produced significant bleeding.

It is not inevitable that the mother of a haemophiliac is a carrier, for some 25 per cent of cases are new mutations without antecedent family history. Carriers can usually be detected by appropriate blood tests, and genetic counselling may then be given. It is now possible by means of foetoscopy to sample foetal blood and therefore detect the condition in the foetus at a stage where abortion is still possible. With less refined techniques it is possible to determine the sex of the foetus but indiscriminate abortion of male foetuses involves a 50 per cent wastage, and non-abortion of female foetuses simply perpetuates the disease, as 50 per cent will be carriers.

HAIR

Hair, like the skin of which it is an appendage, is continuously being replaced, each hair follicle going through a cycle of growth and rest after the fully grown hair is shed. This normal shedding results in the loss of about 100 hairs a day.

Newborn babies have varying amounts of hair, much of which is often shed after the first few weeks, the secondary hair growth often being of a different character. When sexual hair appears at puberty the scalp hair again often changes, becoming coarser and sometimes wavy. Hair characteristics are of course varied and very individual.

Hair quality is influenced by nutrition, particularly protein malnutrition in which it becomes thin and depigmented, by disease such as ringworm, and by endocrine disturbances such as lack of thyroid in which the hair is characteristically straight, sparse and dry. There are also rare congenital abnormalities of the hair. Being a relatively tough appendage, the hair requires little special care beyond ordinary cleanliness. For the causes of scalp hair loss see *baldness.

HANDICAPS

These are considered under the individual items, e.g. *cerebral palsy, *blindness, *deafness, *mental handicap, etc.

HANDEDNESS

Preference for one or other hand may be exhibited sometime during the second 6 months of life but clear dominance is often not shown until 2 to 3 years of age and sometimes later; 8 to 10 per cent of people are lefthanded. No attempt should be made to change the handedness exhibited by a child.

HANDS AND HAND USE

See *development of manipulation

HARELIP

Clefts of the lip and palate are relatively common (about 1 per 1 000 births). Because the centre portion of the upper lip is developed as a projection downwards from the nose and because a cleft is the result of failure of union of the processes which form the lip, the deformity is always to one or other side of the filtrum. The extent of the cleft varies, from a slight indentation to a deep cleft into the nostril which is continuous with a cleft of the palate. The deformity may be bilateral, and this is particularly disfiguring. Fortunately, however, surgical repair of the various clefts leaves an excellent cosmetic result. These deformities tend to some extent to be familial and the risk of having a second child with similar deformity is about 1:25. The risk of a parent with a cleft having an affected offspring is about 1:33.

Harelips are usually repaired at about the age of 3 months when the baby is reasonably established. Feeding does not usually present a great problem unless a palatal cleft is also present. Most of these babies can be satisfactorily breastfed but if this proves impossible a cross-cut teat is usually the most satisfactory. (See *cleft lip and cleft palate, and *feeding.)

HAYFEVER
See *rhinitis

HEAD-BANGING
Rhythmical movements of various sorts are often performed by small children as a soothing mechanism usually indulged in before going to sleep. Head-banging is a rather extreme form, often causing persistent forehead bruising though the child never does himself any severe harm. Banging on the cot is often noisy and disturbing to others but if the cot is removed the child is likely to bang his head on the wall.

Head-banging almost certainly stems from a degree of insecurity and attempts should be made to determine the cause if possible and to remedy it. The banging itself should as far as possible be ignored. The cot may be padded to reduce the degree of trauma and the amount of noise but appeals and threats will do no good. The child should be stimulated as much as possible and not subjected to long periods of boredom during which his only amusement is banging. The habit may persist for a year or two but usually does not require deep psychological assistance.

HEAD INJURIES
Because of the relatively large size of their heads, infants who fall stand a much greater chance of banging the head than adults. Head injuries at any age, however, and of whatever cause, are to be feared — largely because of the possibility of injury to the brain. Superficial injuries are rarely of any great consequence. The scalp when lacerated will bleed profusely but this can usually be arrested by simple pressure, using something like a folded handkerchief as a pad. If the wound is gaping it will require stitching but small wounds will heal perfectly satisfactorily if left alone. Severe blows may cause fracture of the skull bones but a simple crack fracture does not add to the gravity of the situation and requires no treatment. A depressed fracture will probably require surgical elevation. Fractures of the base of the skull are far more serious and may be indicated by a leakage of blood or cerebrospinal fluid from the ear or nose. If such signs are present, therefore, a doctor must be consulted.

The mildest form of injury to the brain is simple concussion. This is associated with a short period of unconsciousness and the child may subsequently be a little unsteady and vomit once or twice, usually recovering completely after a sleep. There is a widespread misconception that following a head injury the patient should be kept awake. This is based on the fact that bleeding into the head may occur relatively slowly and that after a period of relative normality the patient may lapse into a coma because of increasing pressure within the head. Such a situation will not be prevented by keeping the patient awake and there is therefore absolutely no logic in trying to prevent him from sleeping if this is what he wishes to do. If, however, he seems unusually deeply asleep, for example snoring when this is not his habit or showing strange irregularities in his breathing, or if he is unusually difficult to arouse, then one must suspect that there might be some internal haemorrhage and a doctor should be consulted. Simple concussion does not leave any aftermath but it may well be that there is some undetectable damage because repeated concussion, as suffered by boxers, may lead to eventual mental deterioration.

More severe head injury may result in some degree of contusion, i.e. bruising of the brain, and in such cases the period of unconsciousness may be somewhat longer and recovery more delayed. There is, however, no specific treatment for this situation. It is inevitable that some brain cells will be damaged but the effects are usually undetectable.

Injury to a blood-vessel may result in progressive bleeding, usually into one of the spaces superficial to the brain rather than into the brain substance itself, and this may lead to progressive deterioration in consciousness and abnormalities which indicate focal brain damage. Any patient with a serious head injury is therefore usually kept under observation for a day or two to make sure that such a situation, should it develop, is detected immediately, for surgical evacuation of the blood clot will then be necessary. The exact localisation of such haemorrhage is nowadays readily and accurately detected by means of CT scanning.

Severe brain injury may leave residual troubles in the form of behavioural disorders, including the hyperkinetic syndrome, personality changes, mental deterioration and epilepsy. Most head injuries, however, are transient and innocent.

HEADACHE

Many people seem to regard headaches as an adult prerogative. In fact headaches in children are not uncommon, particularly in schoolgoing children. In childhood it is rather more important than in the case of adults to make sure there is no organic cause, and in particular no such conditions as intracranial tumour, but the bulk of children's headaches are benign and their cause no less mysterious than in the case of adults. Many headaches are of simple tension type and related to the stress of schoolwork. Such headaches fairly typically come on at school and are absent over weekends and during school holidays. True migraine is not uncommon in children, particularly those with a family background of similar troubles. Such headaches are usually situated in the front of the head, are often unilateral but not necessarily so, and may be associated with visual disturbances although this is not essential. Sometimes they are accompanied by abdominal symptoms, so-called abdominal migraine. The typical migrainous headache leads to vomiting, which may produce relief (see *migraine).

Headaches due to intracranial tumours occur characteristically on waking in the morning, and are usually associated with nausea and vomiting. Signs of neurological disturbance are often late in appearing.

The treatment of headache depends largely on its type. Where emotional factors are the cause, the reason for the child's nervous tension should be sought and relieved. The occasional tablet of paracetamol or aspirin preparation is not likely to be harmful but one should not encourage recourse to pill-swallowing for every minor symptom. Migrainous headaches can usually be relieved by the combination of an analgesic such as aspirin with an antiemetic taken early in the attack. Several preparations are available for prophylactic use if attacks are frequent. These include phenobarbitone and other anticonvulsant drugs, pizotifen, clonidine and propranalol, but the latter medications are seldom indicated in children.

HEARING
See *deafness and *ear

HEART
The heart is indeed a wonderful organ, maintaining its steady beat approximately 100 000 times a day throughout life. Structurally it is divided into 4 chambers. The right atrium receives blood from the whole body except the lungs, pushes it through to the right ventricle, which then ejects it through the lungs, where it is oxygenated. It is then returned to the left atrium, which delivers it to the left ventricle, which in turn pushes it out through the aorta to the whole body. In foetal life the lungs are of course functionless, and are bypassed by the *ductus arteriosus*, which normally closes soon after birth. It may occasionally remain open and then require surgical closure. During foetal life there is a communication between the two atria which normally closes when the lungs are expanded by the baby's first breath.

Congenital abnormalities of the heart
These are of 2 main types:

Cyanotic, in which the baby is blue because deoxygenated blood is mixed with the arterial blood. This may result from a variety of anomalies, the most common of which is known as Fallot's tetralogy. Here a hole in the heart is combined with narrowing of the pulmonary artery leading to the lungs, and a misplaced aorta. This abnormality can be totally corrected by modern surgery. Blueness presenting in the first days of life is most commonly due to a switchover in the great arteries leaving the ventricles. Life is then dependent upon shunts between the two sides of the heart and these can be increased by temporary life-saving procedures until definitive correction is attempted. There are many different types of cyanotic congenital heart disease, all requiring elaborate investigation at special centres for their elucidation. Nearly all can be helped, if not totally corrected, by surgery.

Acyanotic. Congenital abnormalities not associated with blueness comprise simple holes in the heart, most of which eventually close spontaneously; narrowing of the great arteries (pulmonary stenosis, aortic stenosis and coarctation of the aorta); persistence of the *ductus arteriosus;* and a variety of less frequent abnormalities. As in the case of cyanotic heart disease, most of these are amenable to surgery. The management of congenital heart disease has been one of the most remarkable medical advances in the last 30 years.

Certain germs which gain access to the bloodstream may settle in abnormal areas of the heart, causing the condition known as bacterial endocarditis, and it is for this reason that children with heart disease are protected during dental manipulations, tonsillectomy, etc., with penicillin.

Diseases of the heart

The most important condition affecting the heart in children is rheumatic fever. Although this disease has declined remarkably in the Western world since streptococcal sore throats have been treated with penicillin, it nevertheless still flourishes in the poor and unprivileged members of the community. Rheumatic fever used to be a disease of temperate climates. It now flourishes in tropical and subtropical areas. When it affects the heart it may injure the cardiac muscle, causing heart failure, or it may produce inflammation of the heart valves, leading to subsequent deformity and incompetence, and this puts the heart at a mechanical disadvantage. Not all cases of rheumatic fever are complicated by heart involvement, but this is the greatest risk, and it is therefore important to prevent recurrences after a child has had rheumatic fever. This can be achieved by the regular administration of penicillin, which prevents reinfection with the specific streptococcal germs that cause rheumatic fever. Fortunately these germs never become resistant to penicillin. The penicillin may be given orally or, rather more effectively, by monthly injection of a long-acting intramuscular preparation. The duration of its administration will vary according to the severity of the case and the age of the child at the onset of the disease. The risk of recurrences is greatest in the first 3 to 5 years after an attack so the minimum duration of penicillin prophylaxis will be 5 years. Very often it is given for life.

Many viruses may affect the heart muscle, causing heart failure, and heart involvement is a not uncommon complication of diphtheria. Heart attacks, i.e. coronary occlusion, are not unknown in children. Arterial degeneration begins early in life; and in families prone to coronary disease, particularly those with very high cholesterol levels, dietary prophylactic measures should probably start in childhood.

HEAT RASH

There is a widespread tendency for mothers to overwrap their babies even in hot climates, and the colonial era lingers on with babies clad in bonnets and woollies when their indigenous counterparts are happy in a string of beads. Overheating leads to excessive perspiration and this may cause irritation of the skin, particularly the face and scalp, shoulder regions, chest and the creases. Both prevention and cure require only removal of the excessive clothing. In very irritated areas calamine lotion is soothing but usually no application is necessary.

HEAT STROKE

Excessive exposure to the sun, particularly when associated with exertion, may lead to an elevation in the body temperature to the point of illness, with headache and vomiting as the dominant symptoms. Excessive loss of fluid and salts may complicate the picture. Heat stroke is rare in children, who usually have sufficient sense to avoid exertion in the hot sun.

HEIGHT
See *growth

HEPATITIS
Inflammation of the liver may be due to many causes. Localised infection giving rise to abscess formation may be due to various bacteria or, more commonly in southern Africa, to the amoeba. More diffuse hepatitis associated with jaundice may be due to congenital syphilis. In newborn babies certain viruses acquired from the mother may cause diffuse hepatitis, e.g. herpes and the cytomegalo virus. Yellow fever is a serious form of viral hepatitis spread by mosquitoes. By far the commonest causes of hepatitis, however, are the viruses of infectious jaundice. These are of at least 3 types — A and B, both of which have been recognised, and others which, because they have not been specifically recognised, are simply called non A–non B. Type A hepatitis is usually spread by the faecal-oral route, i.e. ingestion of contaminated water, food, etc. It has an incubation period which averages 4 weeks but which varies appreciably. The severity of illness is very variable, some cases not being jaundiced at all and simply feeling off-colour, others becoming deeply jaundiced and some dying from liver failure. In children the disease is usually fairly mild and recovery is complete. It does not go on to a chronic stage, as may happen with hepatitis B. If, however, there has been much destruction by the disease there may be resultant scarring (cirrhosis).

The hepatitis B virus may persist in the blood for a long time and infection therefore usually occurs from the blood of an infected person, e.g. by transfusion, use of contaminated syringes or needles, and it may be sexually transmitted. Bed-bugs are thought to be a possible vector. The virus is also transmitted readily from mother to baby during or shortly after birth. The incubation period ranges from 2 to 7 months, with an average of 4 months. The clinical picture is indistinguishable from hepatitis A. Some 10 per cent of patients fail to clear the virus from the blood, and a high proportion of these continue with low-grade chronic hepatitis which may eventually produce severe liver destruction. This chronic hepatitis does respond to treatment with corticosteroids with or without other immunosuppressive drugs.

There is no treatment for ordinary infective hepatitis. Exercise is not harmful and dietary factors are unimportant. Hospitalisation is necessary only if the patient is severely ill with the possibility of liver failure, otherwise he is better nursed at home. In hepatitis A the virus is excreted for only about one week after onset of symptoms, and prolonged isolation is therefore unnecessary.

Prevention of hepatitis can be accomplished by administration of gammaglobulin concentrates. In the case of hepatitis A ordinary gammaglobulin is sufficient, but to prevent hepatitis B, a hyperimmune globulin should be administered immediately after exposure. A vaccine is now available for prevention of hepatitis B. Infants of carrier mothers should be protected by administration of hyperimmune globulin at birth, followed by repeated doses of vaccine.

HEREDITY
See *genetics

HERNIA

The protrusion of any visceral structure through an abnormal opening is known as a hernia. Common sites of herniation are:

(1) Umbilical hernia. Large hernias in the region of the umbilicus are sometimes present at birth — a so-called coele. The more common umbilical hernia is apparent in the early months and may progressively enlarge, particularly in the case of a fretful baby. These hernias may reach a large size, especially in African children, nevertheless they virtually always regress and operative correction is seldom indicated. If the hernia is still present at the age of 5 years, when it may be something of an embarrassment to the child, then a doctor should be consulted. Strapping the hernia is futile, but actual inversion of the hernia with retentive strapping, if performed in the early weeks, may sometimes lead to more rapid resolution.

(2) Inguinal hernias. In the course of foetal life, the testicle descends from an intra-abdominal position, through the lower abdominal wall, to take up its final position in the scrotum, dragging with it a tubular extension of the peritoneal cavity. Normally this seals off, but it may persist, giving rise to either an accumulation of fluid around the testicle (a coele) or a hernia, if bowel or other abdominal content finds its way into the abnormal sac. These may therefore present at a very young age. Much later in life, herniation may result from weakness of the abdominal muscles in the inguinal region. Inguinal hernias are much more common in boys than in girls, but they do occur in the latter and occasionally it is an ovary which protrudes through into the hernial sac.

The danger of an inguinal hernia is entrapment and strangulation of the protruded bowel. Although this does not commonly occur in babies it is always a possibility and the hernia should therefore be surgically repaired as early as possible.

(3) Diaphragmatic hernia. Congenital defects in the diaphragm may permit massive herniation of abdominal contents into the chest, causing respiratory difficulty at birth or, if the condition is less severe, digestive symptoms may predominate. Herniation of the stomach into the chest may cause vomiting with severe irritation of the lower oesophagus, and the resultant chronic bleeding may cause severe anaemia. These are not common conditions.

HERPES SIMPLEX

There are two herpes viruses, type 1 being primarily oral and type 2 primarily genital, but their areas of operation are to some extent interchangeable. The initial infection of the herpes virus 1 causes an acute inflammation of the mouth, with ulcers which may be present on and inside the lips, on the gums, inside the cheeks, on the tongue and on the palate. The severity varies greatly, some children having only one or two ulcers and others having almost confluent ulceration of the whole mouth. Similar lesions may also occur on the skin around the mouth and on the chin, and infection may be transferred to the hands by sucking. The virus may also affect the eye, producing ulceration of the cornea. Children with an initial attack of herpes are usually intensely miserable, are unable to eat and reluctant to drink. Fever may be high and persist for many days. In severe cases it is necessary to feed by tube until the child is willing to drink, which fortunately occurs before the ulcers have completely healed. The condition lasts about 10 days and no treatment alters its course. The mouth should be kept clean by rinsing and the use of, for example, an oral spray, which helps to restore freshness; mouthwashes with a mild topical anaesthetic effect give some relief. Sedation at night is justifiable. Antibiotics are valueless, and topical application such as gentian violet may simply increase discomfort. This is one of the most frustrating conditions to treat.

After the initial attack of herpes, the virus often lingers in the skin and mucous membrane, to break out again causing recurrent 'cold sores' during periods of infection or debility. Adults with such lesions should realise that they are infectious.

Genital herpes has become a most serious venereal disease because it is untreatable. Antiviral drugs are disappointing but Acyclovir is of some value. A mother with genital herpes may pass the infection to her newborn child and the virus may then produce widespread disease. Adolescents should be warned of the dangers of genital herpes, which is probably causing more misery in the world today than all the other venereal diseases put together.

HERPES ZOSTER

This is due to the same virus that causes chickenpox. The virus appears to lurk in certain nerves and then break out into the area supplied by that nerve, causing an eruption of vesicles similar to the rash of chickenpox but in a localised area. Herpes zoster, also known as shingles, is rare in children but may afflict those whose immunity is suppressed, particularly by anti-cancer drugs. Such patients can be protected by administration of a hyperimmune serum, namely Zoster Immune Globulin. Shingles is an unpleasant condition in elderly people, for it is often very painful, the pain persisting after the eruption has settled. In children, fortunately, it is much less uncomfortable.

HICCUPS

Hiccups are common if not universal in small babies and may even occur *in utero*. While often distressing to mothers they cause no particular discomfort to the baby and are in any case self-limiting. They may occur with feeds or, on the other hand, may be terminated by a feed. In any case they are of no importance. Later in life, protracted hiccups are very distressing. Simple manoeuvres are sometimes successful in arresting them, e.g. drinking a glass of water or holding the breath for as long as possible, or perhaps even trying to drink while bending down. Hiccups can often be terminated by facing the unfortunate patient, placing both hands across the shoulders with the thumbs under the collar bones and exerting firm pressure for about 1 minute.

HIP

For congenital dislocation of the hip see *dislocation.

HIVES

See *urticaria

HOARSENESS

This may be due to various afflictions of the vocal chords, the commonest being inflammation due to a variety of respiratory viruses. It is therefore a common accompaniment of colds, non-specific sore throats and influenza. It may be the first sign of impending croup and whereas hoarseness in itself is of no great consequence, any associated difficulty in breathing must be taken very seriously. Other infections of the larynx, e.g. diphtheria, may be very serious indeed.

HOOKWORMS

See *worms

HORMONES

These are chemical substances which are secreted by the endocrine glands and which circulate in the bloodstream and influence the body processes, either generally or in specific target organs remotely situated from the secreting gland itself. The pituitary gland, for example, secretes a great number of hormones, and by this means exerts control over the thyroid, the adrenal glands and the gonads (testicles and ovaries). It also secretes growth hormone, which determines the rate of body growth and has a controlling effect on water excretion by the kidney. The thyroid gland secretes thyroxin, which controls the rate of general body metabolism. The adrenal gland secretes adrenalin, which produces an energy surge preparing the body for fight or flight, and the outside layer of the adrenals secretes cortisone and a certain amount of male hormone similar to that secreted by the testes. The ovaries secrete oestrogen and progesterone, which cause the cyclical changes in the uterine lining. The pancreas secretes insulin, which regulates sugar metabolism. Hormones are extremely potent chemical messengers of which only very small quantities are required to produce profound effects. Hormonal imbalance may result from deficient secretion, excessive secretion or the artificial administration of hormone products. There are many situations where children require hormone administration. It is important in such cases that you realise that the dose has to be very, very finely adjusted and you must therefore meticulously obey the doctor's instructions.

HOSPITAL

Although hospitals have lost a great deal of their frightening aspect, admission to hospital for a child, be it on an emergency basis or for some planned therapy, is always traumatic to some extent. Often, however, it is the parents who suffer much more than the child, and your own attitudes will largely determine the degree of disturbance which your child experiences. If you are obviously upset, unduly fussy or clearly fearful, your child will sense this and adopt similar attitudes. It will be helpful if you can adopt a calm and matter-of-fact confidence which will convey to your child the impression that going to hospital is really quite a normal event.

The influence of age. Babies in the first year of life may suffer to some extent from the so-called maternal deprivation syndrome if they lose contact with mother for any appreciable period, but small babies readily take to any mother substitute and nurses are trained these days to administer not only medicine, food and general care but also affection. After the age of 1 year, separation becomes increasingly stressful until the age of 4 or 5 years when the child becomes more reasonable and will accept explanations. Although it is to be anticipated that children of this age will be disturbed by hospitalisation, it is surprising how often they settle down quite happily, often to the disappointment of oversolicitous parents! After the age of 5, and once the initial adjustments have been made, children often find hospitalisation fun. They may regret being discharged.

Preparation for hospital. Where admission is non-urgent and hospitalisation is planned for surgery, investigation or treatment, the child over 3 years of age should have things explained to him. This should be done not only unemotionally and with the conviction that it is in his best interests, but also truthfully. There is no need to dwell on any gruesome aspects but nor is it wise to paint an over-rosy picture bearing little resemblance to reality. If your child has had a friend in hospital who quite enjoyed the experience it may be helpful to remind him. If your child has had unpleasant symptoms which will be terminated by treatment, dwell on the positive aspects and the benefit to be expected. Whereas the small child is more fearful of parting with parents, the older child may be more fearful of pain, and it will be reassuring to him to be told that in these days of efficient medications hardly any pain is felt, but admit that there may be a little discomfort at times if this is likely to be the case. On no account be dishonest with him.

When the time comes to go to hospital he should help to prepare his things, and one or two favourite toys may accompany him. Let it be quite clear that he is going to hospital, and do not indulge in any subterfuge or he will lose his trust in you. Many hospitals allow a preview so that the child can acquaint himself with the ward before he is admitted and this may actually make him look forward to the experience.

Hospital visiting. To minimise the disturbance, and particularly if the hospital stay is to be a short one, you may be allowed to accompany your child into hospital and stay with him. This would usually meet with your doctor's approval but there may be situations where the child would be better off in a Children's Ward. You should accept your doctor's opinion regarding the optimum arrangements. Most institutions nowadays are liberal with regard to visiting hours and you should try to visit your child daily when this is possible. He will soon become adjusted to the routine and will look forward to your regular visits. Let these be happy occasions and avoid exhibiting anxiety or distress yourself. The occasional little surprise will bring joy but do not be ridiculously overindulgent simply because your child is in hospital, and try to treat him as normally as you would at home. When the time comes for the end of the visit, let it be quite clear that you are leaving, but stress that you will be back again the next day (if you will be — never make promises you cannot keep). If you are able to stay with him until he falls asleep you may then steal away, but do not try to avoid parting by pretending to be called to the telephone and just not returning to say goodbye. Always, always be honest with your child.

After hospital. In the young child, a certain amount of disturbance after hospitalisation is to be expected. He may become more clinging and fearful, he may revert to rather immature behaviour, his toilet-training may be disturbed, he may have difficulties in sleeping and may experience nightmares. Such symptoms should be treated with gentle understanding but without excessive fussing. There should be no relaxation of normal discipline. A reasonable amount of sympathy is comforting but no child (or adult for that matter) should be allowed to profit unduly from illness. Sometimes the other children in the household are rather more upset than the patient, for they may be jealous of the attention he has received. A little explanation, patience and commonsense will deal with these problems.

All experience is valuable and hospitalisation, though sometimes unpleasant, can always be turned to profit. The young patient will have achieved an extra degree of maturity and independence, and the overclinging parent may realise after a period of separation that relationships with the child are improved by a less close attachment. Do not think of hospitalisation therefore as a potential disaster. It may be an opportunity.

HOUSE DUST

This, together with the house dust mite, is responsible for the bulk of respiratory allergies. It consists of many ingredients, such as fibre particles from carpets, upholstery, etc., insect deposits and residues, all sorts of degradation products, and moulds. It should not be confused with sand and grit, which are non-allergenic. Probably the most important ingredient is the *house dust mite. In cases of respiratory allergy in which house-dust and dust-mite sensitivity is considered to be an important factor, every effort should be made to reduce exposure to these allergens. To rid a home or even one room of dust is not easy but it is often well worthwhile, as symptoms may thereby be quite dramatically reduced and the need for preventive medication disappear.

How to prepare and keep a dust-free room

(1) Cleaning the room. First, everything movable should be taken from the room, including pictures, rugs and curtains. If there is a built-in cupboard it should be scrubbed out and the whole room made dust-tight by closing all holes or cracks in the walls, ceiling and floor.

It is not necessary to supply heat for a room intended as a bedroom, indeed this is undesirable as any source of heat tends to collect and circulate dust. Once the room is tightly closed to dust, it should be cleaned thoroughly with soap and water and a damp cloth. Get every speck of dust from floors, walls and ceilings, from moulding strips above windows and doors, from cracks in the floor, on light fixtures, around pipes, and so on. Picture-rails and box pelmets should be removed if possible. A vacuum cleaner may be used to rid the room of large dust particles but this should be followed by a damp cloth for fine cleaning.

(2) Furnishing the room. Furniture can be returned after it has been completely freed of dust by cleaning with soap and water and a damp cloth. The bed should be dismantled completely and carefully cleaned throughout. Springs should be carefully wiped with a damp cloth.

Only the following furniture should be permitted in the child's room: a bed, a small table, a simple wooden chair or two, and a chest of drawers (if the child's clothes cannot be kept in some other place, which is preferable). All these items should be carefully cleaned inside and out, and should be of a type that is easily kept clean.

The mattress of the child's bed should be encased in plastic material and if there is a spring-box then it too should be covered with plastic. Pillows should also have a plastic cover. Foam pillows and mattresses are desirable but they should be covered with plastic material anyway unless they're absolutely new. Plastic coverings for mattresses and pillows for allergic patients are available in many large stores, and special mattresses and pillows are available in most centres. Synthetic fibre or cotton blankets are better than wool for the allergic child. If wool must be used it should be kept from the child by one or two layers of sheet so that the wool doesn't touch the child or have a chance to add dust to the room.

Blankets should be washed frequently. Woollen clothes are better avoided by the allergic child and should be kept out of the room in any case. Other things to avoid are rugs, upholstered furniture, curtains and draperies, bookcases, venetian blinds and anything else that is likely to make or harbour dust.

Stuffed toys should not be permitted. Any toys allowed should be made of wood, metal or plastic and they should always be kept meticulously clean.

The bed should be kept covered during the day with an impervious bedspread, which is then carefully removed from the room at night so as not to disturb any dust which may have fallen on it during the day.

If there are cracks in the floor which collect dust these should be filled and the floor covered from wall to wall with vinyl. The floor should be washed or wet-mopped and never dry-swept. Pets should not be allowed into an allergic child's room. Preferably they should be kept out of the house altogether.

Keeping it that way. If the above things are carefully done you will have a room which is:

(i) As free as possible of dust.

(ii) As free as possible of things that make dust.

(iii) As free as possible of things that hold dust.

To keep it this way:

(a) Keep windows and doors closed as much as possible, but the windows may be opened at night.

(b) Go over the room each day with a damp cloth, removing dust from all exposed surfaces.

(c) Once a week go over the entire room just as you did at first, cleaning every bit of room and furniture with a damp cloth.

(d) Encourage the child to dress and undress in another place if possible and use the bedroom only for sleeping.

(e) Keep the rest of the house as dust free as possible by the measures outlined above and by frequent careful damp-cloth cleaning, avoiding any dry-dusting and dry-sweeping.

A vacuum cleaner should be used for removal of coarse dirt particles but it is insufficient on its own for fine cleaning.

HOUSE DUST MITE (DERMATOPHAGOIDES)

This microscopic creature, together with its products — including faeces, has been recognised in recent years as the most important allergenic constituent of house dust, and probably the commonest cause of respiratory allergic symptoms worldwide. It feeds on a diet of shed human skin scales, and large numbers of mites are therefore found in bedding, particularly mattresses and pillows, with less dense populations in house dust generally. The hot, humid conditions found along the coast tend to favour proliferation of the mites and many asthma sufferers therefore tend to be worse at the coast.

It is impossible to eliminate the mites but they can be contained by encasing mattresses and pillows in plastic covers, which are not uncomfortable provided the plastic is of suitable type and the covers are well made. A spray is available for mattresses, which may reduce the concentration of mites. The dust-freeing measures outlined above should reduce the mite population to insignificant proportions. It is possible to desensitise to the dust mite using a specific vaccine but such desensitisation is often disappointing in its effectiveness.

HUNGER

Half the world's population is in a chronic state of hunger, but for these geographical, demographic and political problems a book such as this has no solution. The older child can complain of hunger and make his needs known and it becomes a problem therefore only in the infant. Much of babies' distress attributed to colic, wind or other imaginary ills is really hunger. Mothers, not realising that babies' appetites vary considerably, are often afraid to feed their infants otherwise than is recommended strictly by the clinic or the tin. Such instructions may be taken as guides but the ultimate decision should be left to the baby who, given the opportunity, will take what he wants and needs. Much distress has been caused by the myth of quantitative overfeeding. If your baby is fretful without other symptoms, assume first that he is hungry. If he doesn't settle with more food then look for other possibilities and if necessary consult your doctor. (See also *appetite and *feeding.)

HYALINE MEMBRANE DISEASE

See *respiratory distress

HYDROCEPHALUS

Normally there is a constant production, flow and absorption of cerebrospinal fluid through the cavities and over the surface of the brain and spinal cord. In the baby the pressure in this fluid system is reflected by the tension of the fontanelle. In parts of its course the fluid has to pass through very small orifices and if these become obstructed the flow of fluid is impaired, pressure builds up and the volume of fluid increases. This may occur before birth, causing congenital hydrocephalus, it may occur shortly after birth as the result of bleeding or infection, or it may occur at any stage as the result of obstruction by tumour, etc. If the increased pressure occurs before the skull bones have united, the head grows excessively in size, the fontanelle becomes very large and there may be spaces between the skull bones. At first the pressure is high and the fontanelle therefore tense but as the head increases in size the pressure tends to diminish. The brain becomes stretched and distorted and there is usually some degree of brain destruction. In some cases, however, quite marked hydrocephalus may be present with normal intelligence. One of the reasons for measuring the head circumference of babies is the early detection of hydrocephalus.

Although many cases will arrest spontaneously (up to 60 per cent), the rate of head growth will determine the need for corrective measures. A baby presenting with such trouble will probably require a brain scan to determine the exact type and degree of hydrocephalus and in all but the mildest cases surgical correction will probably be necessary. This is achieved by shunting the excess fluid via a thin tube with a delicate valve mechanism into the bloodstream or into the peritoneal cavity. Such operations are usually very effective but they are not trouble-free. The tubes quite frequently block and then have to be replaced and infection is an ever-present danger.

Hydrocephalus may be associated with other abnormalities such as spina bifida and is a common complication of surgical treatment of the latter condition. With modern facilities, however, the outlook for the child with hydrocephalus, provided he is treated in time and has not suffered damage from a primary cause such as severe intracranial bleeding, meningitis or brain tumour, is good.

HYDROCOELE

This is a collection of fluid around a testicle. It is fairly common in babies and is then due to patency of the tube connecting the peritoneal cavity with the potential space surrounding the testicles, which normally seals off during the descent of the testis. (See *hernia.) The majority of such infantile hydrocoeles clear up spontaneously during the first year of life. If they persist beyond this time, surgical correction may be necessary. Hydrocoeles occurring later may be due to disease of the testis and a medical opinion must always be sought.

HYPERACTIVITY

Hyperactivity, or the hyperkinetic syndrome, tends to be attached as a label more and more frequently to children whose activity level may or may not be abnormal. Judgement after all is in the eye of the beholder and adult tolerance varies considerably. It is perfectly normal for young children to be hyperactive by older standards, and exactly when such activity reaches levels which may be considered abnormal is impossible to define. By the time a child gets to school he should have settled sufficiently to be able to concentrate reasonably well and to limit his activities to acceptable levels. Some perfectly normal children, however, are still highly active, fidgety, readily distracted and with a poor concentration span — all features characteristic of the hyperkinetic syndrome. Because many children who have suffered brain damage as a result of birth difficulties, head trauma, infections such as encephalitis and meningitis, etc., exhibit hyperkinetic behavioural characteristics, it became fashionable in the 1960s to label all such children as being 'Minimally Cerebrally Damaged' — even though no such damage could be demonstrated either clinically or pathologically when the opportunity arose. We now realise that there are many causes of hyperkinetic behaviour. It may be perfectly normal — as it is in the majority of cases. It may be a manifestation of general immaturity, for rates of maturation vary considerably. Girls mature more rapidly than boys, and it is significant that hyperactivity is found at least 4 times as often in boys as in girls. It is difficult to believe that boys are 4 times more likely to suffer brain damage. Hyperactive behaviour is commonly the result of emotional disturbance and insecurity. It may be the result of, rather than the prime cause of, poor scholastic performance. Hyperactivity may be a result of brain damage but it is significant that in children known to be brain-damaged, e.g. with cerebral palsy, the incidence of hyperkinesis is not particularly high. Dietary factors have been incriminated and it would appear that in the very, very occasional child dietary restrictions can be helpful. But the evidence is slender, uncritical and uncontrolled and is largely rejected by medical opinion. We are, however, very ignorant regarding brain chemistry. There are over 30 known chemicals produced in the brain which act as neuro-transmitters. The balance between these can certainly be affected by drugs and may well be influenced by dietary factors. At present, however, we are floundering in the dark.

What are the features of the truly hyperactive child? As babies these children are often fractious and non-cuddly. As toddlers they may be difficult to manage because of exaggerated negativism. Excessive activity may be apparent within the first few years but is often not recognised until later. In contrast to the normal active child, who may achieve a great deal, the excessive activity of the hyperactive child is largely undirected and purposeless. He therefore accomplishes very little, most tasks being uncompleted, and he flits unsuccessfully from one passing interest to another. This becomes particularly apparent at school, where he is unable to concentrate adequately and is easily distracted from even the simplest task by the slightest external stimulus. He is restless and fidgety, resistant to discipline, always in trouble with authority, often aggressive, uninhibited in his behaviour, particularly in the presence of adults, and sometimes destructive. Many of these characteristics can be applied to perfectly normal children and the difference is often simply one of degree and appropriateness for age. Opinion therefore often varies as to whether a child is truly hyperkinetic or not. The term is in any case perhaps a bad one, as it stresses only one feature of behaviour. Nearly 100 alternative terms have been given to the syndrome. Currently favoured is 'Attention Deficit Disorder'. This is a fairly innocuous label, which does have the virtue of stressing one of the main problems from an educational viewpoint. Most experts know what they mean when they talk about the hyperkinetic syndrome. Many would disagree about the diagnostic labelling of individual children. There is often severe disagreement regarding causation. Individual prejudices here become manifest with, for example, behavioural psychologists tending to favour emotional disturbance, educational psychologists, aided by doctors, often postulating hypothetical brain damage (usually when there is no evidence of such) and the faddists blaming the diet. Other experts often become involved and almost inevitably find troubles in their own areas. Optometrists diagnose minor ocular imbalance and prescribe glasses, neurologists do electroencephalograms and treat for 'epilepsy', physiotherapists and occupational therapists give various exercises to promote coordination. If there is confusion in the diagnostic field there is even greater confusion in the therapeutic field. Parents faced with this problem therefore would be wise not to embrace with wholehearted enthusiasm unreasonable and biased conclusions and recommendations from solitary experts simply because such solutions may appeal to them. Parents are often filled with guilt feelings, and to have something to blame is a relief and an exoneration. The parent who, following an interview with a neurologist with regard to a highly active but perfectly normal son, was heard to remark, 'What a relief it is to know that he is brain damaged', is not unique. If you are faced with this problem in your child, by shopping around you will get any opinion you want. It would be best to accept what seems to you the sanest rather than the most comfortable diagnosis.

Medical treatment of the hyperkinetic child. There are several drugs which will often help to reduce restlessness, increase concentration ability and improve school performance. The most popular of these is methylphenidate but pemoline is an alternative with the possible advantage of a once-a-day dose. Dosage has to be tailored to the individual and directed towards the effect desired. The dose which makes the teacher's life most bearable is not necessarily the dose which best improves the pupil's performance. Any drug administered should be carefully evaluated, with control periods on and off medication, and administration should be continued only if there is clear evidence of benefit. Far too many children are put on drugs without the slightest evidence that they are being helped.

What is the eventual outlook for the hyperkinetic child? Most such children eventually settle down, usually round about puberty, and those who have required medication may well be able to dispense with it at this time. Some, however, will continue to benefit for many further years. It is essential that medication be periodically withdrawn to determine its need.

For other aspects of management see *schooling problems.

HYPOCHLORITE

See *Milton

HYSTERIA

In this condition, physical illness is simulated, for example blindness, paralysis of one or more limbs, disturbances of gait, or convulsions. The pattern of manifestations is bizarre, however, and usually recognisable as non-genuine. Often, however, the child's state is fortified by unnecessary investigations to rule out the possibility of physical disease. Hysterical manifestations are more common in the adolescent but do occur in younger children and they are seen in all racial groups, perhaps being commoner in Indians and Africans than in others. Girls are more often affected than boys. Treatment consists of explaining the true nature of the symptoms to the child and getting to the bottom of the emotional disturbance which precipitated the hysterical reaction.

ICHTHYOSIS

This is a condition in which the skin is excessively dry and scaly, resembling that of a fish. There are various forms, inherited in different ways, some improving with age, others remaining unaltered and some worsening. An expert opinion is desirable in all cases.

IMMUNITY

Resistance to disease depends upon complex body defence mechanisms, which are of two main types. Certain cells, such as the white cells of the blood, are scavengers whose main duty is to attack and devour invading organisms. Such cells are attracted to sites of infection, and their concentration in such areas sets up an inflammatory reaction. There are two main cell types responsible for such cellular defence, the granulocytes, which deal with such infections as tonsillitis and boils, and the lymphocytes, which are involved in more chronic inflammatory processes such as tuberculosis and graft rejection. Some of the lymphocytes transform into so-called plasma cells, which are responsible for producing antibodies. There are several other cell types involved in immunological processes but the details are too complex to be discussed in a book of this nature. The whole subject of immunity is growing rapidly.

Besides setting up a cellular immune response, foreign substances, be they invading micro-organisms or chemical substances, are likely to provoke a humoral immune response, involving the production of specific antibodies which help to neutralise the foreign particles or make them more delectable for the scavenging cells. Antibodies are proteins which belong to the globulin fraction and are therefore known as immunoglobulins. They can be divided into various types, depending on their molecular size and other characteristics. Thus we have IgG, IgA, IgE, etc.

The foetus passively acquires IgG-type antibodies from the mother and these protect the newborn baby from a variety of diseases. They are, however, progressively destroyed and by the age of 5 or 6 months such passive immunity has completely waned. IgA and IgM antibodies do not pass through the placenta and the baby therefore has to make these for herself. Elevated IgM antibodies at birth are indicative of intra-uterine infection. IgE antibodies, also known as reagins, are associated with the atopic diseases such as eczema, asthma and hayfever, and are the agents responsible for the type 1 allergic response (see *allergy).

Immunity varies to some extent from individual to individual and such minor differences remain largely unexplained. Severe immunological defects do occasionally occur, involving the cellular component or the humoral component or both. Deficiency of immunoglobulins can be largely corrected by injection of gammaglobulin, but there is a period of physiological hypogammaglobulinaemia in infancy which requires no treatment.

Immunological responses are impaired in malnutrition, which depresses cellular immunity; after infections, particularly measles; and in states of general debility. Emotion may also have an influence. Immunity may be artificially suppressed by drugs such as corticosteroids and other drugs used for cancer treatment or in the management of host rejection after organ transplantation.

Artificial immunity

This can be achieved in two ways.

Passive immunity can be induced by the administration of appropriate antibodies produced from another source, either human or animal. The antibodies in the serum are concentrated into a small volume to be injected either intramuscularly or intravenously. Such antibodies are progressively destroyed, and because they were not produced by the host, immunity progressively wanes. Such passive immunity may be used in the prevention or treatment of measles, diphtheria, tetanus, snakebite, and for the prevention of sensitisation of the Rhesus negative mother should she have a Rhesus positive baby. Animal sera are dangerous, as the recipient may be sensitised to the animal proteins and a second dose might produce disastrous effects. Wherever possible, therefore, human products are used, for example tetanus hyperimmune globulin has now replaced horse serum.

Active immunity is induced by exposing the subject to a modified form of antigen so that antibody is produced without the acquisition of disease. The antigen may consist of a killed suspension of the virus or bacteria (e.g. Salk polio vaccine, pertussis vaccine, typhoid vaccine) or a suspension of live but attenuated micro-organisms (e.g. polio vaccine, BCG); or the antigen may consist not of the micro-organism itself but of its toxic products, in which case a modified toxin (toxoid) is administered (e.g. diphtheria and tetanus immunisations). (See *immunisation.)

IMMUNISATION

Every child should be protected by artificial immunisation from tuberculosis, diphtheria, tetanus, whooping cough, poliomyelitis and measles. Protection is also offered against mumps and rubella, and certainly every girl should be protected against rubella by the time she has reached puberty. At times of special risk, other vaccinations may be desirable, such as cholera or yellow fever.

BCG **(the bacillus of Calmette and Guérin)** is a live bacterial vaccine prepared from tubercle bacilli which have been attenuated to a degree where they are capable of causing only an insignificant local reaction. It is administered as a rule by a multiple puncture apparatus, usually onto the right upper arm. A reaction takes place after a few weeks and may persist for a few months. It should be administered soon after birth, as protection is not obtained until the reaction has taken place. The efficacy of BCG appears to vary considerably with the type of population; studies in Britain showed an 85–90 per cent protection rate, whereas a subsequent large series in India showed no protection. There is no danger from the vaccine except in the severely immunologically compromised individual. BCG vaccination is compulsory.

Diphtheria, whooping cough and tetanus immunisations (DPT or DWT or Triple Antigen). This combined vaccine consists of diphtheria toxoid, tetanus toxoid and killed pertussis bacteria. It gives excellent protection against diphtheria and tetanus, and significant but incomplete protection against whooping cough. Injections are usually commenced at 3 months of age and 3 are given at intervals of 6 to 8 weeks, with a booster at from 18 months to 3 years. Longer intervals between doses do not reduce the efficacy and it is not necessary to restart the course because of undue delay in administering second or third doses. A further booster of diphtheria and tetanus vaccine is given before school entry. The vaccine is given by subcutaneous injection, and local reactions are fairly common and may result in a persistent lump at the site of injection which may last many months. During the first 24 hours or so after administration there may be appreciable fever and irritability. More severe reactions occasionally occur and are then due to the whooping cough component. Much publicity has been given to the risks of encephalitis as the result of pertussis immunisation but most cases have been unsubstantiated and the risk is extremely small; nevertheless the pertussis component is usually omitted if there is a history of brain disease or convulsions.

Tetanus immunity should be maintained throughout life, with boosters given every 5 to 10 years. This, however, is seldom done. Fortunately, immunity can be rapidly restimulated by administration of toxoid at the time of an injury, and in the previously immunised person administration of serum is unnecessary. It is wise therefore for everybody to know his immunisation status so as to avoid the unnecessary administration of potentially dangerous substances.

Poliomyelitis immunisation. Most countries employ the attenuated live vaccine, which is administered by mouth and which contains all 3 polio viruses. The vaccine is usually given simultaneously with DPT. The universal administration of poliomyelitis vaccine should eliminate the disease, which unfortunately and quite unnecessarily still occurs, particularly in the summer months. Some countries still favour the Salk vaccine, which is a killed vaccine administered by injection and which is also very effective.

Measles immunisation. Measles vaccine consists of a live attenuated virus. It is administered by subcutaneous injection and gives longlasting protection in about 97 per cent of cases, provided the vaccine has been kept refrigerated, which is necessary for its potency. Unfortunately, this requirement is not always fulfilled and the vaccine then becomes unreliable. A more heat-stable vaccine is now available.

The age of administration depends upon the population risk. Where there is little likelihood of a child acquiring measles in early infancy, vaccination is best delayed until after the age of 13 months as the response is then optimal. In communities where exposure at a younger age is a greater likelihood, and particularly populations in whom, because of malnutrition and other debilitating conditions, measles is a devastating disease, vaccination is usually given earlier, from the age of 6 months, with a subsequent booster. Measles vaccine may produce a mild feverish illness, sometimes with a rash, 7 to 10 days after administration. This mild measles-like illness is never accompanied by the complications of wild measles and is a small price to pay for immunity to a disease which carries a high morbidity and significant mortality.

Rubella (German measles) vaccination. This is an attenuated live virus vaccine given by injection; as a rule it provokes no reaction, although very occasionally limb pains may occur several weeks after administration. Attitudes to rubella vaccination differ considerably. The American plan is to immunise all young children, and the vaccine is usually incorporated with measles vaccine and mumps vaccine — the 'MMR'. Rubella cannot be considered a serious disease in childhood, and its main danger is the possibility of damage to the foetus should a mother acquire rubella in early pregnancy. It is therefore only really necessary to immunise girls. Although it seems that protection will probably be lifelong, we cannot yet be certain. Antibody levels do wane progressively until sometimes they are undetectable. It would seem therefore that there is much to be said for the British plan, which is to immunise schoolgirls at puberty. This of course is unnecessary if they have had definite rubella. Immunisation in the teenager will certainly protect her during her fertile years and this is probably therefore the safer course.

Mumps vaccination. This attenuated live virus vaccine is often combined with the vaccines for measles and rubella. Childhood mumps, though uncomfortable, is rarely serious even when complicated by meningo-encephalitis or pancreatitis. In the adult, however, involvement of the gonads can be very unpleasant. We are as yet unsure of the duration of immunity produced by the vaccine, although the probability is that it will be lifelong. It is nevertheless possible that early vaccination, while protecting the child and young adult, may lead to susceptibility in later life. The advisability of administering mumps vaccine at an early age is therefore still somewhat questionable and it may be better preserved for older children who have not had mumps.

IMMUNOGLOBULINS.

These are a specific class of protein, to which the antibodies produced by immunological processes belong. They are subdivided, depending upon molecular size and other features, into various types, e.g. IgA, IgM, IgG, IgE, etc. IgG antibodies are in the highest concentration and these, being of relatively small molecular size, are able to traverse the placenta and achieve a high concentration in the foetal blood. They give the baby passive protection, lasting several months, from a variety of diseases including measles. IgM and IgA antibodies do not traverse the placenta and the baby therefore has to make these herself. Concentrations at birth are normally extremely low. An elevated IgM level in the newborn baby is indicative of intra-uterine infection. IgE antibodies, also known as reagins, are responsible for the type 1 allergic response (see *allergy) and an elevated level is indicative of an atopic state. IgE levels are also raised in parasitic infestations.

Concentrates of specific immunoglobulins are available for the treatment of certain diseases, e.g. tetanus, herpes zoster.

IMPETIGO

This is an infectious skin condition commonly due to a streptococcal germ. It may be superimposed upon other skin troubles such as scabies, eczema and papular urticaria. The infection is readily spread via the fingers, and insect bites therefore easily become impetiginised as a result of scratching. It is common on the face, around the nose and mouth, but may occur at any site. The lesions start as small spots, and develop into blisters which rupture easily, leaving a yellowish crust. The condition usually clears satisfactorily with appropriate antibacterial applications, but when it is profuse a systemic antibiotic, usually simple penicillin, may be indicated.

Impetigo, and in particular impetiginised scabies, is a common cause of *nephritis, especially in the African population.

INCONTINENCE

Incontinence of bowels or bladder is a distressing situation for both child and parent. The situation is often greatly worsened by wrong parental attitudes.

Faecal incontinence. Prolongation of soiling beyond the age at which a child is expected to be clean may be due to faulty training habits and excessive attention to the bowels, with forced potting producing negative results. Diarrhoea may produce incontinence simply because fluid stools are more difficult to retain and there is excessive urgency. Such a situation, however, is very temporary. Incontinence may be due to disease of the rectum or anus or impairment of the nerve supply, as in spina bifida. However, most cases of faecal incontinence in childhood are due simply to severe constipation. A large cannonball stool forms in the rectum, which the child is reluctant to pass. Fluid stool from above leaks past this obstructing mass and, because of reduced sensitivity of the rectum and anus, soiling then occurs. Correction of the constipation leads to cure of the incontinence. (See *constipation.)

Urinary incontinence. Continuous leakage may be due to a misplaced ureter or to neurological defects, but incontinence is usually intermittent. Wetting by day may be due simply to forgetfulness, to reluctance to use a strange toilet, to irritation of the genitals or bladder, to urinary infection, and occasionally to the production of a grossly excessive quantity of urine. Management will obviously depend upon the cause. For nocturnal incontinence see *bedwetting.

INCUBATORS

There is nothing magical about an incubator, which is simply a box providing warmth, humidity and isolation. Premature and sickly babies tend to lose heat easily and often cannot be kept warm by simple wrapping. An external heat source is then necessary. The incubator, while keeping the baby warm, allows full visibility. The atmosphere can be modified, for example by addition of extra oxygen for babies with respiratory difficulties. Incubators are of particular value in colder climates and often tend to be used unnecessarily in the warm, humid coastal regions. They are not without danger. Though built-in alarms should prevent most accidents, incubators do occasionally fail, allowing babies to chill, and occasionally they overheat, with equally severe consequences. Like all medical apparatus they should be used with discrimination and under expert supervision.

Parents tend to react to incubators much as people do to oxygen administration, fearing that they imply a grave situation. This is not the case. Incubators are used largely so that the baby may be observed and not for any great therapeutic advantage. Do not conclude therefore that your baby is sick simply because she has been put in an incubator. If you are worried, discuss matters with your doctor.

INFECTION

It is little over a hundred years since micro-organisms were first discovered and an explanation was found for so many diseases. With greater understanding of infections, and particularly since the advent of antibiotics, increasing control has been obtained over infections and they no longer pose the same threat. Virus infections, however, still have to be conquered. The common infecting agents are:

(1) **Viruses.** These are more like complex chemicals than living organisms. They contain either RNA or DNA, and have to make use of living cells in order to propagate. They cause a wide variety of diseases, such as the common cold and other respiratory infections, gastro-enteritis, hepatitis, meningo-encephalitis, poliomyelitis, and such simple things as warts.

(2) **Rickettsia.** These organisms are larger than viruses but smaller than bacteria. They cause, for example, typhus fever and tick-bite fever. They are susceptible to certain antibiotics, such as tetracyclines.

(3) **Bacteria.** These come in a variety of shapes and sizes and are responsible for a great number of diseases, such as tonsillitis, pneumonia, boils and abscesses, meningitis, tetanus, plague, tuberculosis and leprosy. Most are susceptible to appropriate antibiotics but many eventually acquire resistance.

(4) **Spirochaetes.** These are rather larger organisms with a corkscrew shape, but behave much as the other bacteria. They cause diseases such as syphilis and yaws, relapsing fever, rat-bite fever and trench mouth. They are in general sensitive to antibiotics, particularly penicillin.

(5) **Fungi.** Most fungal infections are superficial, for example, athlete's foot, ringworm and thrush. Some fungi cause pneumonia and some may spread elsewhere, producing for example meningitis.

(6) **Protozoa.** These are small unicellular parasites, which include the amoeba, which may cause dysentery or liver abscesses; the malarial parasites; trypanosomes, which cause sleeping sickness, etc.

(7) **Metazoa.** These are the larger, multicellular parasites such as the intestinal worms, bilharzial flukes and hydatids. Invasion by these larger organisms is usually referred to as infestation rather than infection.

INFECTIOUS DISEASES

These are considered under their respective names, e.g. *chickenpox, *measles, *rubella, etc.

INJECTIONS

Injections should be avoided in children whenever possible, but unfortunately they are still often given thoughtlessly and unnecessarily. If, however, a child is vomiting, essential drugs may have to be given by injection and there are of course some preparations, such as insulin, which cannot be given by any other route. Antibiotics which have to be given in high doses for prolonged periods can usually be given intravenously, which obviates the pain of repeated injections.

Injections may be given into various sites. The most superficial is an intradermal injection, in which the substance is given into the skin itself, using a very fine needle. With subcutaneous injection, delivery is made into the fat lying deep to the skin. Absorption from this site is relatively slow. From an intramuscular injection, absorption is rather more rapid. If an immediate effect is required, injection may be made into a vein, but such injections should not be made by untrained persons.

It may be necessary for you to inject your child subcutaneously, as in the case of a diabetic, or intramuscularly, for example to administer snakebite serum. Intramuscular injections should be given with a fairly long needle and into a large muscle, e.g. the front and outer aspect of the thigh or the upper, outer quadrant of the buttock (see diagram). Other parts of the buttock should not be used for fear of injuring important nerves.

PREFERRED SITE FOR INTRAMUSCULAR INJECTION

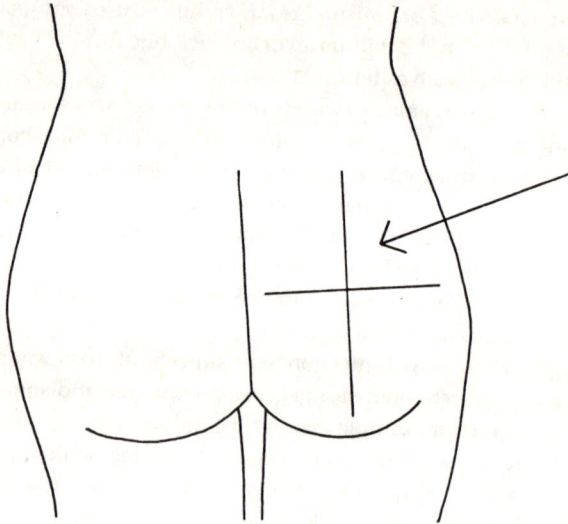

INJURIES

Minor abrasions, cuts and bruises are common in children and usually require no particular attention. Cuts and lacerations which are gaping should be seen by a doctor as they may require stitching, but usually adequate approximation of the edges can be obtained once bleeding has ceased by applying appropriate sticking-plaster strips. Bleeding should be minimised by direct pressure on the wound or, if a large artery is involved, by pressure on the artery above the injured site. Severe injuries are accompanied by shock, and this should be appropriately managed. (See *shock.) The severely injured patient should be moved as little as possible, to avoid further damage to vital structures. (For head injuries see *head injury, and for bone injuries see *fractures.)

INSECTS

Insects are important as vectors of disease, e.g. mosquitoes for malaria and yellow fever, fleas and lice for typhus, ticks (not really insects) for tick bite fever and relapsing fever. Other insects are important as parasites, e.g. lice, and others bite or sting with varying ferocity, e.g. fleas, mosquitoes, bees, wasps and hornets. Flea and mosquito bites tend to produce more severe reactions in small children than in adults. Scratching often leads to infection. Flea bites on the trunk are usually recognisable because of their grouped patterns. On the legs they may give rise to multiple itchy spots known as *papular urticaria. Mosquito bites usually occur on exposed surfaces, especially the face and arms. Insect-repellant sprays, creams and lotions are a valuable protection against insect bites, but have to be reapplied every few hours.

Venomous insect stings are very unpleasant and painful and may be dangerous to the sensitive person. If your child should have had a severe systemic reaction to an insect sting, you should discuss with your doctor the advisability of desensitisation or of having available for your own use appropriate drugs to administer in such a crisis. Such drugs would be adrenalin, an antihistamine preparation and an injectible corticosteroid. (See *anaphylaxis and *stings.)

INSOMNIA

Difficulty with sleeping may afflict older children as the result of anxieties, e.g. over school, over parental discord or over difficult peer relationships. In such a situation the cause of the insomnia should be sought and dealt with. Sleep disturbances in infants and small children are of a different nature and are due either to physical distress, bad habits or simple attention seeking. (See *sleep disturbance.)

INSULIN

This vitally important hormone, largely responsible for controlling the metabolism of sugar, is secreted by small clumps of cells in the pancreas, known as the Islets of Langerhans. The remainder of the pancreas is devoted to producing digestive enzymes, which are secreted into the duodenum. The output of insulin is stimulated by a carbohydrate meal, which raises the blood sugar level. Insulin controls this level by encouraging the conversion of glucose into a storage form, known as glycogen, in the liver and muscles.

In diabetes, insulin has to be administered artificially by injection. (See *diabetes.) Ordinary soluble insulin has a rapid action extending over only some 7 hours. The effect can be prolonged by chemical modification, particularly by the addition of zinc, producing long-acting insulin preparations, and various combinations of short- and long-acting insulins are available. All preparations are now standardised at 100 units per ml. Insulin may be of beef or pork origin (the latter more closely resembling human insulin) and it is also manufactured by recombinant DNA technology which produces true human insulin.

Insulin overdosage leads to a fall in blood sugar level (hypoglycaemia) characterised by hunger, dizziness, lightheadedness, sweating, unsteadiness, tremor, visual disturbances, confusion and eventual loss of consciousness. Convulsions may occur. Treatment consists of urgent administration of sugar. (See *diabetes.)

INTELLIGENCE

Though universally understood, intelligence is difficult to define but may be most closely equated with quickness in understanding. It is measured by a variety of intelligence tests adjusted for age, and from these the mental age of the child is derived. The intelligence quotient, or IQ, is calculated as the mental age divided by the chronological age and multiplied by 100. The IQ should not change significantly throughout life. Minor variations do occur, however, as the result of indisposition, emotional upset, lack of co-operation, etc., and a figure should never be taken as absolute. The psychologist administering the test always allows for the child's condition at the time. IQ testing in a handicapped child may be extremely difficult, for many such children possessing good intelligence are unable to express it.

Children with low intelligence who are incapable of following the normal school curriculum will obviously require special schooling. Children of exceptionally high intelligence are almost as great a problem. They are liable to be bored by school, so much so that their results are often poor. They require a great deal of extra stimulation which the school as a rule cannot provide. Many of the large centres have associations for gifted children and these can be of great value in providing extra stimulus. The child of exceptionally high intelligence should be kept as normal as possible in her general activities and peer relationships, but this is sometimes difficult. She often prefers the company of much older children or adults. This naturally should not be denied her if it is the only way she can achieve the stimulus she seeks.

INTUSSUSCEPTION

In this condition, a portion of bowel is forced into an adjacent portion of bowel in telescopic fashion. The inner portion becomes swollen as a result of venous obstruction, and eventually the blood supply may be cut off, causing gangrene of that portion of the bowel. Before this happens there is usually bleeding, and the stools may consist simply of blood and mucus. Intussusception causes obstruction of the bowel, with vomiting and usually some abdominal distension. It is characterised by severe bouts of colic, the infant screaming and becoming pale with each episode. A small child behaving in this fashion therefore should be suspected as possibly having intussusception and she should be medically examined. As the commonest site of intussusception is in the region of the caecum, a barium enema will usually reveal the condition, and if this examination is done early enough it may be curative. As a rule, however, surgery is necessary to restore the anatomy to normal. If gangrene of the bowel has occurred this portion will have to be removed, hence the importance of examining the condition of the bowel except in the very earliest cases. Occasionally, subacute intussusception occurs without bowel obstruction but with recurring abdominal colic. This is a rare situation.

IRON

Although iron deficiency is usually associated with anaemia, iron is an essential constituent of many body enzymes, and deficiency of iron is therefore manifested in many other ways, e.g. general debility, loss of appetite, poor growth, pica, irritability, poor schoolwork, muscular weakness and immunological depression with a tendency to excessive infection. Because of her rapid growth rate the infant requires relatively large quantities of iron. Although the amount of iron in breast milk is rather low it is nevertheless extremely well absorbed, and iron deficiency rarely occurs in the fully breastfed, full-term baby. The premature baby, who lacks iron stores at birth, readily becomes iron deficient. An excessive intake of cows' milk often leads to iron deficiency. Protein malnutrition is frequently associated with iron lack. At a later age, iron deficiency may result from dietary deficiency or from excessive loss, e.g. as a result of infestation with hookworms, whipworms or bilharzia.

Iron deficiency is easily corrected by administration of iron but the cause should always be determined so that recurrence does not occur. (See also *blood and *haemoglobin.)

ITCHING

This distressing symptom may be due to external irritants, e.g. insect bites and scabies, and to diseases of the skin such as eczema and urticaria; and it may occasionally be associated with systemic conditions such as severe jaundice and certain malignancies. Scratching is the natural response to itching, and although this may sometimes bring relief it may also perpetuate the itch and, although treatment in general should be directed at the cause, the itching itself may require relief. Soothing applications such as Calamine lotion or, in the case of eczema, steroid preparations, usually afford considerable relief. Many of the antihistamine drugs are helpful, such as promethazine, and their mild sedative effect is often an advantage in this situation. (See *eczema, *scabies, *urticaria.)

JAUNDICE

The green pigment, bile, is produced as the result of breakdown of red blood-cells, a process which is continuously going on, resulting in the destruction of about 1 per cent of the red cell population each day. The bile produced is excreted by the liver via the bile ducts into the intestine. As a result of further chemical changes the colour is altered to brown, the normal stool colour. Jaundice is due to an excess of bile in the blood. This may result from:

(1) Increased red-cell breakdown. An excessive rate of bile production can be the result of increased red-cell breakdown. Of this there may be many causes, including congenital abnormalities of the red cells, e.g. hereditary spherocytosis, congenital abnormalities of the *haemoglobin, infections such as septicaemia and malaria, and certain poisons or drugs which may destroy the red blood-cells. In newborn babies, severe jaundice may result from red-cell antibodies produced by the mother which traverse the placenta and destroy the baby's blood. Such antibodies are directed against the specific antigens on the baby's red blood-cells, the most important of which are the A and B antigens and the Rhesus antigens. Although naturally occurring antibodies are present in all people lacking the specific A or B antigen, these are of large molecular size and do not pass through the placenta. Normally, therefore, a Group 0 mother carrying a Group A or B baby will not have any problem. If, however, as the result of sensitisation to the A or B antigens, she produces a particular type of 'immune' antibody, this may pass through the placenta and cause excessive destruction of the baby's red cells, as occurs in the Rhesus situation. (See *Rhesus.) As a result of the excessive destruction of the baby's blood cells, combined with the immaturity of the baby's liver, severe jaundice may result.

(2) Liver disease. Any serious diffuse disease of the liver is likely to be associated with jaundice, e.g. infectious hepatitis, congenital syphilis, yellow fever. Poisons and certain drugs may produce severe liver injury with resultant jaundice. Newborn babies have immature liver function and for the first few days of life have difficulty in excreting bile, with the result that at least 50 per cent of babies become jaundiced to some extent. Where there is an added load of bilirubin, as in haemolytic disease, the disability of the liver in excreting bile adds greatly to the problem.

The bile produced in the breakdown of red blood-cells is initially largely fat-soluble. In order for it to be excreted, the liver combines it with glycuronic acid to form a water-soluble compound. The enzyme responsible for this conjugation is lacking in the early newborn period. The bile which accumulates, therefore, is of the unconjugated type and this renders it noxious in high concentration, particularly to brain cells. The main danger of severe jaundice in the neonatal period therefore is to the brain. (See *kernicterus.)

(3) Obstruction of the bile ducts. This type of jaundice is common in adults as a result of, for example, gallstones or cancer. In babies, part of the bile duct system may be absent. Rarely, the ducts may be compressed by cysts or tumours. In such cases a relentless obstructive-type jaundice occurs, which if unrelieved results in eventual liver damage. It is always important to check for this type of jaundice, for surgery offers the only hope of cure. In cases of congenital obliteration of the bile ducts, however, the chances of surgical success are limited.

Most cases of neonatal jaundice are relatively mild and require no treatment. Precise diagnosis is, however, very important. The depth of jaundice is often difficult to judge clinically and blood tests are usually performed to determine the exact blood bilirubin level. Depending on this result, and on the assessment of other relevant factors, for example associated prematurity or evidence of haemolytic disease, your doctor may decide to treat the baby with phototherapy, which converts the bile in and under the skin to a harmless form and helps to prevent an excessive rise in bilirubin level in the blood. Phototherapy, because of its convenience and safety, is perhaps somewhat overused.

In severe cases of jaundice, where the bilirubin level threatens to achieve potentially dangerous heights, an exchange blood transfusion may be necessary.

JEALOUSY

This universal human emotion is most commonly and most powerfully precipitated in childhood by the arrival of a younger sibling. Children react less markedly over the age of 4 or 5 years, especially if there is an intervening offspring, for jealousy is mainly directed towards the child immediately younger. Jealousy manifestations vary greatly. There may be quite clear demonstrations of dislike and antagonism, with deliberate attempts to hurt the new baby, or the manifestations may be more subtle with expressions of affection when the parents are present but surreptitious attempts to harm or to hurt when no one is watching. Other children may revert to inappropriate behaviour, particularly infantile patterns, for example with soiling and wetting when they see that attention is paid to the new baby on this account (see *emotional development). Once a jealousy situation is established it may persist for a very long time, even into adulthood, particularly if the younger sibling is rather more attractive or successful than the older. Every care should therefore be taken by parents to reduce jealousy feelings, though these cannot be entirely eliminated.

Whatever the age gap, you will no doubt have warned your child during your pregnancy that a younger sibling is on the way. It is better not to do this unnecessarily early, as a small child's time scale does not encourage patience. When the new baby does arrive, the elder child should not experience unnecessary dislocation in his normal routine, and particularly not anything which he may interpret as victimisation. Introduce the new baby to him rather casually and without expecting him to be filled with admiration. You must continue to give him his rightful share of affection, and any behavioural aberrations must be treated with understanding, but there should be no gross relaxation in discipline or ridiculous tolerance of unacceptable behaviour. As always, it is good behaviour which should be rewarded and the bad largely ignored. You can stress his seniority by granting some privileges appropriate to his age, but do not stoop to bribery. Accept that some degree of jealousy is inevitable and normal but with sympathetic yet sensible attitudes there should be no very significant dislocation.

JOINTS

The common conditions affecting joints are dislocation, inflammation of various types, and bleeding into the joint. Degenerative conditions are common in old age. For congenital dislocation of the hip, and dislocation of the head of the radius, see *dislocation. For bleeding into joints see *haemophilia.

Joint pains are not uncommon in childhood and are sometimes simply rather atypical growing pains in which the child localises the discomfort rather poorly. Inflammation of the joints may be due to many conditions. *Rheumatic fever is characterised by pains which flit from joint to joint, staying only a day or two in each site. It follows a streptococcal throat infection, and may be accompanied by heart involvement. (See *rheumatic fever.) Rheumatoid arthritis also involves multiple joints, although it may start in just one or two. Several other diseases may be complicated by joint involvement, e.g. brucellosis, lupus, gonorrhoea and rubella. Tuberculosis may spread to joints, particularly hip and knee. Bacteria gaining access to the bloodstream may settle in a joint, causing a septic arthritis, which is a very serious condition. A common condition affecting the hip in young children is what is known as transient synovitis, the cause of which is unknown but which may be related to relatively mild trauma and which settles completely with rest. Joint symptoms are to be taken seriously in children and a doctor's opinion should always be sought.

KERNICTERUS

Severe jaundice in newborn babies may produce damage to brain cells, particularly those in the primitive nuclei at the base of the brain, which then become stained with bile. This is the condition known as kernicterus. It is in order to prevent this that significant neonatal jaundice is watched carefully and treated when necessary with phototherapy or exchange blood transfusion. There is no set level of bilirubin in the blood at which kernicterus occurs. In small premature babies it may occur at quite low levels of jaundice, and the mechanism in such cases may be rather different from the simple bile toxicity in the full-term baby. The initial symptoms of kernicterus are mild, with lethargy, poor feeding and floppiness. Subsequently, the baby becomes stiff and arched with inco-ordinate eye movements and often fever. If the baby survives, there is often a degree of subsequent deafness, associated with a particular form of cerebral palsy known as *athetosis, characterised by writhing limb movements, and the deciduous teeth may be stained green. The early symptoms are often reversible if prompt treatment is given. The later symptoms, however, imply that brain damage has occurred. With the decline in Rhesus haemolytic disease, and the improved management of jaundice with phototherapy, kernicterus is rare nowadays, but it does still occur, particularly in African babies, in whom the jaundice is often difficult to detect and who may thus be brought to hospital with the damage already done.

KIDNEYS

Each kidney consists of about a million units called nephrons, which are responsible for ridding the blood of waste products. Each nephron commences with a glomerulus, a tiny round bunch of capillaries, from which filtered fluid passes into the next portion of the nephron, the tubule, while the blood cells and protein are withheld in the blood. In the tubule the filtrate is concentrated. It is then excreted via collecting tubules which open up via the pyramids into the pelvis of the kidney, and the urine then goes down the ureter into the bladder. The lower end of the ureter traverses the bladder wall obliquely, forming a valve which normally prevents backflow of urine up the ureter. Incompetence of this valve mechanism is a common cause of kidney infection.

Congenital abnormalities of the kidneys and ureters are relatively common. One kidney may be absent, both may lie on the same side, there may be double kidneys, and sometimes the kidneys are fused into a horseshoe shape. Any of these abnormalities may predispose to infection. If the urine becomes infected, and particularly if there is stasis or backflow, the infection may spread into the

cortex ——————————

pyramid ——————————

—————— pelvis

—————— ureter

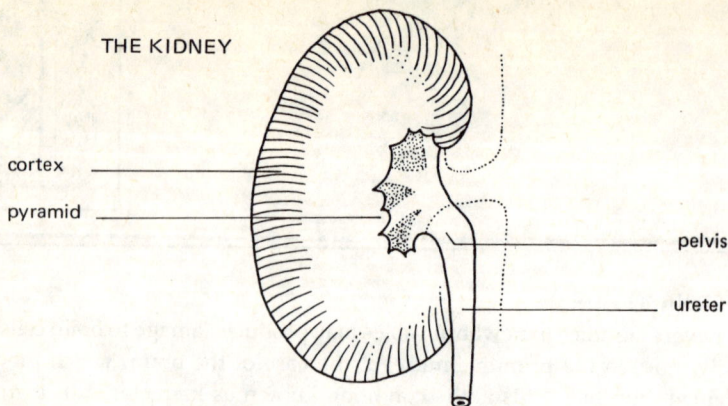

tubules and destroy that portion of the kidney, with resultant scarring. It is highly important, therefore, that urinary infection in children should be detected as early as possible and dealt with appropriately, otherwise the kidneys may become progressively destroyed. Pyelitis is manifested in older children by high fever, often rigors, pain in the back or sometimes in the flank or abdomen, usually accompanied by some disturbance of urination such as pain, burning or increased frequency. The urine may be murky and may contain blood. In infants and small children the symptoms are less typical and may not suggest kidney disease at all. Fever, vomiting, fretfulness, diarrhoea and occasionally jaundice are the usual presenting symptoms in infants, who may also have a febrile convulsion. All children with fever for which there is no obvious cause should have the urine examined.

Urinary infection usually responds promptly to appropriate antibiotic treatment but it is always wise to check for any predisposing cause by radiological examination of the kidneys. This may be done by injecting an opaque dye intravenously, the resulting pyelogram revealing the anatomy of the kidney, ureters and bladder as well as giving a good idea of kidney function. Cases suspected of having ureteric reflux are investigated by injecting an opaque dye into the bladder and then getting the child to pass urine under X-ray visualisation. Reflux tends to diminish with age, but severe cases, particularly if associated with recurrent urinary tract infection, will probably require operation to restore ureteric competence by re-implanting the ureter into the bladder.

Other common kidney conditions in childhood are nephritis and the nephrotic syndrome, or *nephrosis. Bilharzia may affect the kidney by causing obstruction of the ureter. As in any form of obstruction, the pressure then increases, the pelvis of the kidney dilates and the kidney tissue itself becomes stretched and eventually to a great extent destroyed. This condition is known as hydronephrosis. It is a common result of congenital obstructions, particularly in baby boys, in whom the commonest cause is the presence of urethral valves which impede the urinary stream.

It should be mentioned that analgesic drugs may severely damage the kidney, and although the quantities usually given to children appear to be safe this is an added reason for keeping medication to a minimum and discouraging the habit of pill-swallowing for every minor symptom.

KNOCK-KNEES

What appears to be excessive angulation at the knees is common in the pre-school child and nearly all cases correct themselves spontaneously. The over-weight child should have his diet restricted but usually no specific treatment is necessary. In severe cases, however, one should make sure that disease of the bones does not exist, particularly rickets, which, while uncommon in the white child, is not rare in other races. The ordinary case of knock-knees is often associated with flat feet, and although this may cause an unflattering, unathletic appearance you can be almost certain that by the age of 8 to 10 years the condition will have resolved. In severe cases, by all means consult your doctor.

KLINEFELTER'S SYNDROME

This is a rare condition in males which is due to a sex chromosomal abnormality, the chromosomal make-up being XXY. Such patients are usually tall with long limbs, some degree of breast enlargement, small testicles, a delay in secondary sexual maturation and often some degree of mental retardation.

KOPLIK'S SPOTS

These are small white spots found inside the mouth in the early stages of measles, just before and at the time of eruption of the rash. They are found particularly inside the cheeks but also inside the lower lip. They are specific for measles and, if seen, a confident diagnosis can be made before the rash appears.

KWASHIORKOR

This term is thought to originate from a West African word meaning red-headed boy, and to refer therefore to the hair discolouration which is a feature of the condition. Kwashiorkor is a severe form of malnutrition, primarily due to protein deficiency but often associated with deficiencies of other food factors, including calories. When affected children are grossly underweight, the condition is referred to as marasmic kwashiorkor. Such malnutrition is common in various areas of the world including Africa, South America, the Caribbean and the Far East. Poverty and ignorance are the main causes.

The child with fully developed kwashiorkor presents a pathetic picture. There is generalised swelling of the body, which may become so marked that the eyes cannot be opened. The skin is lustreless with areas of dark pigmentation, cracking in places, and often with excoriation, particularly in the napkin area. The hair is depigmented, thin and easily pulled out. The demeanour is characterised by perpetual irritability and apathy. Other features commonly present are inflammation of the mouth; anaemia (which may be severe and is usually due to a combination of deficiencies of iron, protein and folic acid); dryness and irritation of the eyes, sometimes leading to ulceration of the cornea. There is fatty change in the liver leading to enlargement of this organ. Infections such as pneumonia and gastro-enteritis are frequent and often seem to precipitate the kwashiorkor symptoms. Measles is a common cause of death in such children. There is generalised muscle wasting, which may not be apparent initially because of the excessive accumulation of fluid. Associated with the wasting there is loss of essential salts such as potassium and magnesium. Brain damage is disputed but probable.

Treatment consists essentially in giving a diet adequate in protein and calories. Vitamin deficiencies may also have to be corrected, and additional iron, potassium and magnesium are often required. Initiation of treatment is best undertaken in hospital, especially when significant infection is present.

LACTASE

This enzyme, secreted by the cells of the intestinal lining, splits lactose — the sugar found in milk — into its two monosaccharide components, glucose and galactose. (See *lactose.) When the enzyme is missing, lactose cannot be absorbed and tends to cause diarrhoea. The absence of lactase may be a congenital abnormality but it is often reduced temporarily after an attack of gastro-enteritis. In such cases, reintroduction of milk into the diet reprecipitates diarrhoea. If lactose is then found in the stool, milk should be withheld for a short period until the bowel has recovered.

Lactase tends to diminish with age, for after infancy milk becomes a somewhat unnatural food. The enzyme is usually absent in adult Africans who, knowing that whole milk is poorly tolerated, prefer to consume it in the form of maas, which, as a result of the fermentation process, has nearly all the original lactose reduced to lactic acid.

LACTOSE

This is the sugar found in milk. Like sucrose and maltose it is a disaccharide consisting of joined molecules of glucose and galactose. In its intact form it cannot be absorbed and utilised. It is split into its monosaccharide components by lactase (see above), which is secreted by the intestinal epithelium. Unabsorbed lactose passes through the bowel, and because of its osmotic effect increases the water content of the stool, causing diarrhoea.

Lactose intolerance is a not uncommon cause of persistent diarrhoea in newborn babies. Transient lactose intolerance is common after gastro-enteritis and it is also a feature of protein malnutrition.

LANGUAGE

Language development (see also *development). From shortly after the time at which a baby smiles, at around 6 weeks, he will begin to make pleasant cooing sounds which progressively increase in variety, until at the age of 6 months or so he is putting consonant and vowel sounds together in the form of da, ma, ba, pa, etc. These sounds, when repeated, become his first words which, initially probably meaningless, soon acquire specific meanings as mama, dada, baba, etc. Thereafter he experiments a great deal with new sounds, creating a babbling in imitation of adult speech. By the age of a year he will have a few very definite words. At about 18 months, on average, he will learn to put two words together such as 'mummy come' and by 2 years of age he will make three-word sentences. Thereafter, his use of language advances rapidly. It must be appreciated that these are average ages and that there is a wide variation in the rate of language development. Albert Einstein did not speak until he was 4. An unusually silent baby should be suspected of possible deafness and if there is significant retardation in speech development you should consult your doctor.

A child who has not been exposed to speech cannot learn language. At the other end of the scale, it does appear that the more a child is exposed to language, the more rapid is his speech development. It is important therefore to talk to your baby and to read to him even before his comprehension is complete. Young children also appreciate rhythm and therefore love even nonsensical nursery rhymes and any sort of song. You can refine their tastes later.

Retarded speech development. This always gives rise to anxiety but need not necessarily do so, because of the wide variation of what is normal. The child who is a late talker should, however, be examined carefully for deafness and it is important to evaluate his other developmental characteristics to make sure that intelligence is normal. The institutionalised or otherwise deprived child may be slow simply because of lack of stimulation. The battered child may be too terrified to speak.

Growing up with more than one language. Educationists seem to agree that a child should not be deliberately taught a second language until his mother tongue is well established. There is no reason, however, why his father tongue should not be established at the same time, for small children will find it possible to acquire two languages simultaneously without significant confusion, particularly if they are consistently spoken by different parents or attendants. Such a child will readily receive a message in one language from mother and transmit it in the other language to father or to the nanny. In spite of earlier opinions to the contrary, this does not appear to slow down the rate of language development or reduce vocabulary. If therefore there is more than one language in the home let your child profit from this exposure and do not artificially contrive to make the home unilingual.

LANUGO

This is the fine downy hair found particularly in premature babies, most prominently on the back. It is shed fairly rapidly after birth.

LARYNGITIS (see also *croup)

Inflammation of the larynx or voice box may be due to many factors, the commonest being the respiratory viruses. The larynx is rarely involved on its own and there may be accompanying sore throat or spread of the infection downwards to produce tracheitis and bronchitis, the complex then being known as laryngo-tracheo-bronchitis. In this condition, in addition to the loss of voice and cough of laryngitis, there may be accompanying wheezing. Other infecting agents may cause laryngitis, the most serious being *diphtheria. Laryngitis may also be due to physical agents, e.g. inhalation of steam from the spout of a boiling kettle, or chemical irritants. Because the larynx is the narrowest part of the airway, swelling in this region may cause severe obstruction to the breathing, this usually being accompanied by an inspiratory noise, and the condition is then known as croup. Croup characteristically begins fairly abruptly at night and can be a most alarming condition. For management see *croup.

LAXATIVES (see *constipation)

In this constipated modern world laxatives are abused as much as vitamins and tranquillisers. Highly refined diets such as afflict most of us tend to produce constipation, but the remedy as a rule lies not in laxatives but in suitable dietary corrections, with a regular intake of bran and other roughage to increase the stool bulk and moisture content. Laxatives are rarely necessary. They may be indicated in cases of obstinate constipation and should then be taken daily in a dose sufficient to normalise the stools for a few weeks. The dose should then be gradually reduced. Routine administration of laxatives for a weekly 'clean-out' has no justification. If your child has the correct diet he should never have to take a laxative.

LAZINESS

Most children possess a super-abundance of energy. If your child appears to be lazy it is probably because he is unhappy or bored and you should therefore try to get at the root of the problem. Apparent laziness may be the result of debilitating disease but it should be apparent to you if the child is frankly ill. Low energy levels may be associated with thyroid deficiency. Laziness at school may be due to many factors, including poor teaching, pupil–teacher conflict, learning difficulties, poor peer relationships or general unhappiness. It is not sufficient to punish the child for being lazy. The cause of the problem must be determined.

LEAD POISONING

This used to be common when lead was used in paint and lead pipes used in plumbing but it is now rare, although the lead in petrol fumes is causing concern in heavily polluted areas. Lead poisoning produces gastro-intestinal symptoms with abdominal pain and vomiting, it causes a chronic anaemia and may affect the nervous system with irritability, drowsiness, convulsions and coma, as well as peripheral paralysis, particularly of the wrist, as a result of nerve toxicity. Low-grade lead poisoning is suspected of causing mental dullness. The diagnosis is proved by estimating the blood lead level and by demonstrating depositions of lead in the bones on X-ray examination.

LEARNING PROBLEMS

See *schooling problems

LEFT-HANDEDNESS

This should not be regarded as an abnormality, for some 8–10 per cent of boys are left-handed and a slightly smaller percentage of girls. Often such children are ambidextrous, playing, for example, left-handed tennis but right-handed cricket. Brain lateralisation is often mixed. Whereas in right-handed persons the centre for speech is in the left side of the brain, in the majority of left-handed subjects it is also in the left cerebral hemisphere, being only occasionally on the right.

No attempt should be made to change the handedness of a child as this will usually simply cause frustration and do no good. The child who displays very early lateralisation should be examined to make sure that there is nothing the matter with the opposite side, e.g. unilateral cerebral palsy.

LEUKAEMIA

This is a cancerous condition of the white blood-cells, which proliferate at the expense initially of the other blood components and eventually at the expense of the whole body. In spite of its rarity it has achieved a great deal of publicity and is therefore often feared by parents. Initial manifestations are usually anaemia, together with a bleeding tendency. There may be bone pains, fever and general malaise. There are various different types of leukaemia, each carrying a different outlook. Virtually all can be helped by modern treatment, and about 50 per cent can be cured. Treatment is unpleasant, consisting of corticosteroids and cytotoxic drugs administered systemically and also initially by lumbar puncture, together with deep X-ray therapy to the head in order to prevent central nervous system recurrences. Treatment has to be continued for a minimum of 2 years.

LICE

Infestation with lice is common in poorer communities where facilities for hygiene are inadequate.

Head lice. They are usually confined to the scalp region but they may extend to other hairy areas. Because they are blood-sucking insects they cause a degree of scalp irritation. The lice are usually visible but are often not as conspicuous as the eggs (the nits), which are tiny white spots attached to the hairs and difficult to remove. Lice spread fairly readily from person to person on close contact and outbreaks of head-lice infestation are common in schools.

Treatment consists of shampooing with a shampoo containing either gamma benzene hexachloride or malathion. The nits are difficult to kill, but may be removed by patient fine-combing.

Body lice. These are less common than head lice but they tend to spread in conditions of overcrowding with poor facilities for washing. The lice live largely in clothing, with periodic sorties for feeding on the non-hairy skin. They may be responsible for spreading typhus fever (due to a rickettsial organism) and they are also the vectors for louse-borne relapsing fever (due to a large corkscrew-like spirochete).

Body lice may be treated with benzyl-benzoate or gamma benzene hexachloride or malathion applications, and clothes should be either boiled or burnt.

Pubic lice (crabs). These are spread by close, usually venereal, contact and are therefore not likely to be encountered in children. Very occasionally they inhabit the eyelashes.

LIMB PAINS

See *growing-pains

LIMPING

A limp is usually due to pain but may also be due to bony or neuromuscular asymmetry in the lower limbs. Painful causes, which may vary from a thorn in the foot to tuberculosis of the hip, are usually fairly easily located, although the small child may localise discomfort very poorly. Furthermore, painful conditions in the hip are often referred to the knee and vice versa. Longstanding limps are commonly due to cerebral palsy, limb asymmetry and poliomyelitis. Limps of recent onset should be suspected of being traumatic or due to such hip conditions as transient synovitis, *Perthés disease, etc. If the child is feverish and ill, inflammation of the bone (osteitis) or of the joint (septic arthritis) should be suspected, and in such cases medical attention is urgent to make the diagnosis.

LISPING

This is to some extent normal in small children and in the older child who has lost his upper front teeth. It is never due to 'tongue-tie'. Persistent lisping should be evaluated and corrected by a speech therapist.

LOW BIRTH-WEIGHT BABIES

Babies who are small at birth may have been born prematurely or may simply be small. Even premature (pre-term) babies may be inappropriately light. All babies who lie below the 10th percentile for weight, no matter what their period of gestation may be, are referred to as 'light for dates' or 'small for gestational age' (SGA) babies. The distinction between a purely pre-term small baby and the SGA baby is an important one, for they behave very differently and their respective risks are dissimilar. Assessment of gestational age is vital in making this distinction. This can be done with fair accuracy on the basis of the baby's physical features and his neuromuscular development. The SGA baby is more mature than his physical size would suggest and he may for example suck well from the beginning, whereas a purely pre-term baby of equivalent size would have to be fed by tube.

SGA babies can to some extent be divided into two groups: those normally proportioned babies who have simply grown slowly throughout foetal life and in whom this is probably attributable to foetal rather than placental factors, and those who display evidence of recent poor growth, being relatively long and thin with head size appropriate for gestational age. These babies tend to put on weight rapidly after birth and demand large feeds. Their eventual size tends to be normal, whereas the first type of compact SGA baby tends to remain small.

The particular hazards faced by these various types of low birth-weight babies differ considerably. A premature baby is faced with respiratory problems due to lung immaturity. Vessels are fragile and bleeding is common. There is an increased incidence of jaundice due to liver immaturity. Infections are relatively common, the premature birth sometimes being precipitated by infection, or the baby's relatively poor resistance contributing to it. Because of inadequate iron stores, premature babies often become anaemic. In contrast, the SGA baby may face respiratory troubles due to aspiration of meconium. Blood-sugar levels may fall severely and such babies are usually therefore given extra glucose from shortly after delivery. SGA babies often have an excess of blood and this occasionally requires adjustment.

The eventual outlook for the SGA baby depends to some extent on the cause of the condition. If the baby is simply genetically small he will differ in no way from the large, full-term baby. Certain communities, e.g. Indians, tend to have smaller babies than others. The baby may be small as the result of maternal disease, such as high blood-pressure or chronic kidney conditions, and these factors may have been operating throughout most of pregnancy, causing the baby to grow more slowly. Other situations may cause intra-uterine malnutrition of the baby only during the latter part of pregnancy, as in maternal toxaemia, and in such cases the baby may not be undergrown but may simply be thin. These babies as a rule do well once they are released from the hostile intra-uterine environment. Babies whose low birth-size is the result of maternal alcoholism or excessive smoking have a good immediate prospect for survival, but brain growth is likely to be impaired to a variable extent and the baby's intelligence proportionately reduced. The importance of restricting alcohol consumption and smoking during pregnancy cannot be overemphasised. For further discussion of the pre-term baby see *prematurity.

LUMBAR PUNCTURE

This procedure has an unfortunate reputation in the public mind but in skilled hands it is almost painless. It is used to sample the cerebrospinal fluid which fills the cavities in and around the brain and spinal cord. With the patient well flexed, either lying on his side or in a sitting position, a needle is inserted between two lower lumbar vertebrae into the spinal canal. Pressure readings may be taken and a specimen of fluid is withdrawn for analysis. Lumbar puncture is essential for the diagnosis of meningitis and encephalitis.

LUNGS

The lungs consist of minute air spaces, called alveoli, with very thin walls through which the blood circulating in the lung capillaries comes into close contact with the inspired air. Gaseous exchange readily takes place, oxygen being absorbed into the blood and carbon dioxide removed. The right lung is divided into 3 separate lobes and the left lung into 2. Each lobe has several so-called bronchopulmonary segments, each supplied by its own bronchus, pulmonary artery and pulmonary vein.

The lungs at birth are solid structures but with the first few breaths air is drawn down the bronchial tubes into the alveoli, which then become permanently expanded. Such expansion is dependent upon a detergent-like fluid secreted by the lung tissue, which reduces the surface tension and prevents the alveoli from collapsing. In premature babies this substance — known as surfactant — is lacking and the resultant difficulty in maintaining lung alveolar expansion leads to the condition known as respiratory distress or hyaline membrane disease. Because during intra-uterine life, the surfactant leaks out into the liquor, the liquor can be sampled to determine the degree of lung maturity of the foetus and the prospects for safe delivery.

For diseases of the lungs see *bronchitis, *pneumonia, *cystic fibrosis, etc.

LYING

Deliberate lying must be distinguished from the fanciful imagery of the young child, who may recount endless stories from his world of fantasy. There is no harm in such fantasy and indeed it is to be encouraged, provided there is also a progressive realisation of reality. The quest for truth, however honourable, should not totally displace charm. Likewise, social considerations often demand some distortion of the truth for the sparing of feelings. Do not expect your child to participate in such subterfuges for he will inevitably let you down — especially if from him you have always demanded the truth, the whole truth and nothing but the truth.

True lying occurs only after the child has an established sense of right and wrong and knows it quite well to be wrong. Lies are most commonly told because of fear, whether of discovery or of punishment or both. The young child's fibs are usually obvious, should not be taken too seriously or punished severely. The standards expected of him should be appropriate and if fibbing is excessive these standards should be examined, as well as any other factors which may be operative in causing the child to retreat into such behaviour. This becomes of much greater importance in the older child, whose lies are usually more skilled and often difficult to prove. Lying in such cases is often associated with stealing and can be an attempt on the part of the child to get extra attention or increased popularity. Such behaviour stems often from a basic insecurity and lack of adequate affection. Very frequent lying in the older child should be regarded as a cry for help and every attempt made to get at the root cause. This may require expert psychological assistance.

You cannot of course expect perfect truth from your offspring if you have set them a bad example. Be sure therefore that as far as possible you yourselves are truthful and if from time to time a white lie has to be told let it either be without the child's knowledge or else explain to him the reasons. Hypocrisy will simply lose you your child's respect.

LYMPH GLANDS
See *glands

M

MALARIA

This is one of the most widespread of world diseases, occurring in nearly all tropical countries and in many semi-tropical countries of the Northern Hemisphere. In Africa it extends to Zimbabwe and the northern areas of Botswana, the north-eastern Transvaal, Swaziland and northern Natal. There is a big incidence of cases in Mozambique, where it occurs all the year round. The disease is due to a small parasite of the genus *Plasmodium*, of which there are 4 distinct species. It is spread by anopheline mosquitoes. The parasite has a complicated life cycle both in the mosquito and in man. After infection there is an incubation period of some 7–30 days, depending upon the type of malaria and whether or not prophylactic drugs have been taken. The patient then becomes unwell, with peaks of fever occurring every 48–72 hours in typical cases, though with malignant malaria the cyclical pattern is less clear. The typical malarial attack commences with a cold stage during which the patient shivers while the temperature is mounting; a hot stage during which she is flushed, often delirious with headache, nausea and vomiting; followed by the sweating stage during which the temperature falls and the symptoms wane. The most feared complication is cerebral malaria, in which the patient becomes progressively stuporose and eventually comatose with high fever. The prognosis of this condition is very grave. The diagnosis of malaria is made by finding the malarial parasites in the red blood-cells, and treatment should be instituted as soon as possible. The most commonly used drug is chloroquine, a suitable course for an adult being 4 tablets immediately, 2 tablets 6–8 hours later and then 2 tablets daily for 2 days followed by 2 tablets weekly for 4–6 weeks. Children receive appropriately smaller doses. Unfortunately, chloroquine resistance is on the increase, such cases having been reported from East Africa, and resistance will almost certainly spread south. Cases resistant to chloroquine may be treated with other drugs, preferably quinine.

Malaria prophylaxis. For this purpose chloroquine can be taken, 2 tablets weekly for an adult, but in areas where chloroquine resistance is common a combination of chloroquine and pyrimethamine (Daraclor) or other combination drugs may be preferable. Daraclor syrup is suitable for children; the dose is 10 ml weekly for children of 1–5 years or 5 ml weekly under 1 year. After leaving a malarious area it is essential to continue prophylaxis for a minimum of 4 weeks.

MALFORMATIONS

See *cleft lip & palate, *hydrocephalus, *spina bifida, etc.

MALNUTRITION

Disturbances in nutrition are rife throughout the world. Whereas the bulk of the world's population suffer from undernutrition, a significant proportion in the Western world suffer from overnutrition. Both can be disastrous.

Undernutrition. The combination of poverty and ignorance makes various forms of undernutrition almost universal in the less privileged members of society. Nutritional deficiency is often compounded by parasitic infestation and infection.

Deficiency of calories leads to progressive wasting, and in infants a state of marasmus is said to exist when the body weight has fallen to below 60 per cent of the expected weight. Marasmus is common in African babies in whom breastfeeding has failed for some reason and who are often given artificial feeds in extremely dilute form. The food is not basically unbalanced, it is simply deficient in quantity, and features of protein malnutrition do not therefore appear even though the protein intake is less than optimal. Treatment consists of giving adequate food, but if the starvation is of extreme degree it may be very difficult to restore nutrition, and the mortality rate is then high.

Deficiency of protein leads to a condition known as *kwashiorkor. The diet may or may not be adequate in calorie content but is of poor quality with regard to protein, and the clinical picture produced is typical whether in Africa, South America, India or Italy. The child is apathetic, miserable and irritable, growth is usually retarded depending upon the duration of the malnutrition, the body becomes swollen with excessive fluid, the skin becomes pigmented, lustreless, dry and cracked with areas of peeling, the hair is lustreless, depigmented and thin. Muscle wasting and weakness may be severe, anaemia is common, the mouth is frequently inflamed with ulceration and the eyes may be affected, sometimes with ulceration of the cornea. The liver is enlarged and infiltrated with fat. Vitamin deficiencies are common accompaniments. Infections such as gastro-enteritis and pneumonia occur frequently and are a common cause of death, as is measles. Treatment consists of replenishing the body proteins by suitable dietary means, milk protein being particularly suitable, treating any infection present, correcting anaemia and replacing missing specific food substances. Cases often present so late that kwashiorkor carries a high mortality rate.

It is of course insufficient to treat the child without making efforts to prevent recurrence by educating the parents and rendering social assistance.

Overnutrition. An excess of food leads to *obesity, which carries its own hazards, particularly heart disease. The child who is putting on weight excessively should be checked to make certain that there is no other reason, and her intake of carbohydrate foods, which provide only calories, should then be severely restricted (see *calories).

For vitamin deficiencies, see *vitamins.

MANNERS

If manners maketh man, parents maketh manners. The only way you will teach your child good manners is by setting an example yourself. You may try to instruct her, but without example she will pay little attention. She will of course tend to pick up (inevitably less acceptable) manners from her friends and these you might have to work hard to correct. Too much nagging will be counterproductive but by seeing your consistent example she will realise that good manners are the lubricant of life.

MASTITIS

See *breast

MASTOID

The bone behind the ear consists largely of air-filled cells communicating with the middle ear. When the latter becomes infected, inflammation may spread into the mastoid, causing the condition known as mastoiditis. This used to be a common and very severe complication of otitis media (middle ear infection) but it is now rare and usually responds to timely antibiotic treatment. Surgical excision and drainage are occasionally necessary.

MASTURBATION

Now that this is recognised as an almost universal habit in boys and an extremely common one in girls it can be discussed without embarrassment. Gone are the days when it was said to be the cause of weakness or insanity. In itself it is perfectly harmless and a natural sexual outlet. It is the guilt feelings which may accompany it that do the harm.

Infantile masturbation is not rare and may occur from the age of a few months. The child makes rhythmical movements, either rubbing the thighs together or rubbing the genital area against some object, becoming very intent in the process, often flushed and making grunting sounds. A climax appears to be reached, for the child then frequently falls asleep. Parents often suspect such manifestations as being in the nature of a convulsion and are often horrified to be told that this is no more than infantile masturbation. They can rest assured however that the condition is entirely innocent and will pass with increased distractions.

Masturbation in the older child may start with the accidental discovery that fondling the genitals is pleasurable or by being introduced to the habit by other children. Parental attitudes are all-important in the prevention of destructive guilt feelings. If you are aware of the problem and can freely discuss it with your child, do so, explaining that this is natural, widespread and nothing to be ashamed of, but nevertheless to be kept private. An absorbing interest in other activities will reduce the need for masturbation and these therefore can be encouraged. Children should of course have a knowledge of sexual matters appropriate for their age, a knowledge best given them by their parents (see *sex). Parents should refrain from reacting with horror when they see their children touching their genitals. By all means gently teach them to be discreet but do not drive them into a state of furtive guilt.

MATTRESSES

Mattresses nowadays are made either of foam or of springs and wadding. For the small, light child, foam is very adequate. The mattress support should be firm and sag-free. For babies a mattress should be fairly firm rather than too soft, to prevent possible suffocation. Cot mattresses should fit correctly, leaving no gaps for possible injury.

Mattresses are a menace to the allergic child sensitive to dust and particularly to the dust mite. In such cases the mattress should be encased in a plastic cover. (See *house dust.)

MEALS (see also *food)

Mealtimes should be happy family get-togethers where not only food but also ideas are exchanged. The small child may resent interrupting her fascinating activities in order to eat and she may therefore require a little warning rather than an instant summons, but if mealtimes are pleasant and exciting she will come willingly enough. Although she may be expected to come to the table, no child should be forced to eat. If she refuses to eat what she is given it should be simply removed without a fuss and nothing more given until the next mealtime. Eating problems are created by parents, not by children.

Mealtimes do, however, provide a good opportunity to observe your child, and if poor appetite is combined with weight loss she should be seen by a doctor.

Mealtimes will vary from household to household, some being regular, some haphazard. It really doesn't matter, provided the child gets enough food. The main thing is that they should be pleasant occasions.

MEASLES

This acute infectious disease should be easy enough for you to recognise once the typical rash has appeared, but during the initial few days it may cause much anxiety. The incubation period is 10–12 days and the initial symptoms are those of an increasingly severe cold associated with mounting fever and a dry, irritating cough. The eyes are reddened, giving the child a bleary look, and she may find strong light uncomfortable. For a day or two before the rash appears, *Koplik's spots may be visible inside the mouth. These are small white spots found most commonly inside the cheeks opposite the molar teeth. After about 4 days of illness the rash appears, initially as faint pink spots behind the ears spreading over the forehead and face down to the neck and eventually over the whole body until it reaches the extremities on the second or third day. The rash is typically blotchy but varies considerably in severity. In dark-skinned people the redness is invisible and the rash is almost better felt than seen. The eruption fades in the same sequence in which it developed and is usually followed by brownish discolouration of the skin with fine peeling.

Measles is a miserable disease and unfortunately there is no specific treatment which will reduce its duration. The child should be allowed to please herself with regard to bedrest and there is no need to darken the room unless the child specifically requests it. It is normal for appetite to be suppressed and there may be some diarrhoea. Nourishing fluids should therefore be encouraged. The fever usually subsides 2–3 days after the appearance of the rash, and persisting or mounting fever beyond this time suggests that there might be complications and the child should then be seen by a doctor.

Secondary infection of the ears is common and pneumonia occurs frequently, particularly in African children, who are usually extremely ill with this disease. In about 1:1 000 cases encephalitis (inflammation of the brain) occurs and although this usually subsides spontaneously and satisfactorily, it can occasionally be serious. Persistent fever associated with headache, stiffness of the neck and back, convulsions, delirium or loss of consciousness, call for prompt medical assessment. Very, very occasionally a slowly progressive brain disease may occur many years after the initial measles infection. This is known as subacute sclerosing panencephalitis.

Measles itself, being a virus infection, cannot be treated except symptomatically. When the fever is high, antipyretic drugs such as paracetamol are useful. The mouth should be kept clean by frequent drinks, and if necessary mouthwashes, and the eyes if necessary cleaned with simple water. Antibiotics will be used for bacterial complications but are useless for the measles itself and are of no value given prophylactically. Gammaglobulin given soon after exposure and before the onset of symptoms may prevent or modify the disease, but is indicated only in the case of children whose resistance is likely to be low.

Measles is a preventable disease. The attenuated live virus vaccine should be given to all children who have not had measles after the age of 13 months, and in younger children who are particularly at risk, such as African babies. Because the response to the vaccine in the child aged under 1 year is not very good, repeat vaccination should be carried out at about 15 months. If given within 24 hours of exposure to measles, the vaccine will modify the illness without impairing the subsequent development of full immunity. Measles vaccine is often combined with mumps and rubella vaccine in MMR. (See *immunisation.)

MEASLES – GERMAN
See *rubella

MEATAL ULCER
Circumcised baby boys often develop a small ulcer on the tip of the penis due to irritating contact with wet napkins. This causes pain when the baby passes urine. Napkin contact should be reduced to a minimum and a napkin liner is helpful. The tip of the penis should be protected by frequent application of petroleum jelly or a suitable ointment. Healing usually occurs rapidly with these simple measures.

MEDICINES
Far too much medicine is given to children, just as far too much is taken by adults. Some medicines of course are extremely valuable but much medication is almost useless, much is given for its placebo effect and some is dangerous. Do not therefore demand medicine every time your child is seen by a doctor. Rather be delighted if he says that no medication is necessary.

Giving medicines to small children. This may pose a problem in infants and in older children if the taste is unpleasant. Babies have to be restrained to some extent and the medicine can then simply be put in with a spoon. Any that is rejected is collected from the chin and put back. Small doses can be given by a dropper straight into the mouth. Larger infants may struggle to such an extent that very little is consumed. You must then use your judgement as to whether to give more in order that an adequate dose be retained. Most paediatric medications are suitably flavoured to make them acceptable to small children but occasionally medication is available only in tablet form and in this case the tablet should be crushed and mixed with a spoon of jam or something the child particularly likes. A small tablet can sometimes be hidden in a spoonful of food but the child will usually detect it and her suspicions are then aroused for the future.

Children on regular medication, for example epileptics or diabetics, should be taught to become independent as early as possible and to accept responsibility for their own treatment. They may still, however, require covert supervision for they may deliberately not take their medication because they resent being 'different', or they may simply be forgetful. Regular medication should be taken at a set time and become as automatic as brushing the teeth.

MENINGISMUS

This is the term given to symptoms and signs resembling meningitis but occurring in the absence of that condition. Meningismus may accompany a wide variety of infections, e.g. tonsillitis, ear infection, pneumonia (particularly right upper lobe pneumonia), and urinary infection. Often the diagnosis can only be made with certainty following lumbar puncture. The symptoms subside as the predisposing infection is brought under control.

MENINGITIS

This dreaded diagnosis probably conjures up in your mind visions of a profoundly ill child, likely to die or to survive with appalling sequelae. This used indeed to be the picture in cases of bacterial meningitis before the antibiotic era. Nowadays the position is very, very different.

There are 3 main causes of meningitis — viruses, acute bacterial infections and tuberculosis. All produce rather similar symptoms with fever, headache, vomiting, irritability and photophobia (dislike of light). Convulsions may occur, and in severe cases loss of consciousness may supervene. Irritation of the spine leads to stiffness of the neck and back, and in babies the excessive production of cerebrospinal fluid causes increased tension and often bulging of the fontanelle.

Meningitis is the result of invasion of the cerebrospinal fluid — which surrounds the brain and spinal cord and fills the cavities inside the brain — by the infective agents mentioned above. Access is usually gained via the bloodstream but there may be direct invasion via open wounds of the head, and occasionally infection spreads from contiguous structures such as the sinuses or the ear.

Meningitis in small babies is particularly deceptive as the classical signs are usually lacking. Lethargy and poor feeding are common early symptoms. Any ill baby running an unexplained fever is likely to need lumbar puncture to check for the possibility of meningitis. In small children, who tend to resist examination, the detection of neck and back stiffness may be difficult and is best elicited by trying to get the child to bend his head voluntarily rather than by forcible passive flexion.

Viral meningitis. This is nowadays far more common than bacterial meningitis. Unfortunately, the distinction is often rather difficult and many patients are treated for bacterial infection for the sake of safety. In general, the child with viral meningitis is less ill and the degree of reaction in the cerebrospinal fluid is less marked than in bacterial meningitis. No specific treatment is required and the child usually recovers spontaneously within a few days. Medicines to control vomiting, relieve fever and alleviate headache may be given but often the child needs no medication at all.

Acute bacterial meningitis. This is due to a variety of micro-organisms and often the responsible germ can be isolated from the blood as well as from the cerebrospinal fluid. A particularly infectious form is meningococcal meningitis, which often occurs in epidemics. In young children the haemophilus germ is the most common cause and at all ages the pneumococcus (which is the commonest cause of pneumonia) is a likely candidate. Once the germ has been isolated and its antibiotic sensitivity established, optimal treatment can be given. Until then the patient is usually covered for every likely possibility. Initially, antibiotics are usually given intravenously in order to obtain high blood concentrations without giving repeated injections. Treatment is usually required for 7–10 days.

Tuberculous meningitis. This is very rare in white children but is relatively common in African and coloured children, in whom tuberculosis is still rife. The disease is more insidious in its onset than the acute form of bacterial meningitis but progresses relentlessly if treatment is not rapidly instituted. With modern anti-tuberculous drugs, and provided the diagnosis is made early, the outlook for the patient is good.

It must be reiterated that acute meningitis can be a devastating disease, and the earlier treatment is instituted the better the outlook. Any child displaying symptoms suggestive of meningitis should be taken immediately to a doctor.

MENSTRUATION

The age of onset of menstruation varies greatly but has in general been falling.

Girls approaching puberty should obviously be informed about the changes to expect, so that their first period is not a surprise to them. It is almost inconceivable, however, that nowadays a girl would escape such knowledge. Mothers should help to instil a healthy attitude in their daughters towards the inconveniences of menstruation and not introduce it as 'the curse' or suggest that premenstrual tension might be a problem. Today's more positive attitudes which have made childbirth much more of a pleasure should also relieve menstruation from most of its Victorian hangups.

Informing sons of the cyclical changes of women is perhaps more difficult. It is easier in a mixed family, especially where the daughters are frank.

By the time a boy is taking an interest in girls he should know about their menstrual cycles so that he does not cause embarrassment. Parents who are natural and open with their children should have no difficulty in informing them of the 'facts of life'.

MENTAL HANDICAP

Of all the tragedies afflicting parents, to have a child who is mentally retarded is probably the most difficult to bear. Physical handicaps are not only easier to understand but are usually easier to deal with. Mental handicap tends to generate a feeling of hopelessness and often of guilt. In at least 50 per cent of cases the cause for mental handicap is unknown. Even when it is known it is hardly ever possible that the situation could have been prevented. Should you therefore be one of the unfortunate parents with a mentally handicapped child do not burden yourself with unnecessary guilt. Nor should you put unjustifiable blame on others. Be determined to give the child every opportunity to advance as far as possible and to extract from life all the joy that it can still give. On the other hand, and particularly if you have other children, the attention given to the handicapped one should be balanced and should not deprive the others of the affection and the care to which they are entitled. Time and again families are disrupted and marriages broken by a mother's excessive concentration upon a handicapped child to the neglect of other members of the family. There is a balance in all things, and in a situation such as this there is a great need for wisdom and commonsense as well as love.

The causes of mental deficiency

(1) **Congenital causes.** Some cases may be recognisable at birth because of certain physical characteristics, e.g. *Down's syndrome or Mongolism. One can be quite certain that such a child will be mentally defective to a fairly severe extent. Other types of chromosomal abnormality associated with recognisable physical peculiarities are usually not compatible with long life. In cases of excessively small head size (microcephaly), or water on the brain (hydrocephalus), the degree of mental impairment may be uncertain until the child has grown.

(2) **Trauma.** Damage to the brain at birth may result from bleeding into its substance or from oxygen lack. If this results in gross damage to brain cells the child is likely to have some form of cerebral palsy in addition to mental handicap.

The brain may, of course, also be severely injured after birth, e.g. in motor vehicle accidents, and various degrees of mental impairment may result.

(3) **Metabolic conditions.** There are numerous disturbances in body chemistry which may be associated with mental deficiency. The commonest of these is known as *phenylketonuria, in which an amino acid, phenylalanine, accumulates excessively and damages the brain. There are numerous other very rare biochemical causes. Nearly all such conditions are inherited as Mendelian recessives and tend therefore to be commoner in inbred communities. They are very rare in southern Africa. It is, however, always important to check for this possibility by having the child medically examined, not only because the condition may be treatable but so that the parents can be advised about the risks to further offspring.

(4) **Endocrine abnormalities.** Congenital hypothyroidism is an important cause of mental subnormality, but with screening tests being now available such babies should be identified at birth and treatment instituted immediately. (See *cretinism.)

(5) **Diseases of the brain.** Potentially destructive inflammatory conditions, such as encephalitis and meningitis, may produce varying degrees of brain damage, with resultant impairment of intellect. There are many degenerative brain conditions, some of which are associated with the accumulation of abnormal substances, and many of which have been identified as being due to lack of a specific enzyme. One of the better-known such diseases is Tay-Sachs disease, particularly common in Ashkenazi Jews. Such degenerative conditions are relentless and not amenable to treatment, but fortunately many, including Tay-Sachs disease, can be diagnosed antenatally and the affected foetus then aborted.

Management

If, after adequate investigation, no cause has been found for a child's mental retardation this then has to be accepted as a cruel blow of fate not likely to be repeated. The degree of retardation will have to be assessed and the child's educational programme adjusted to her capacity.

It is important that the child should receive as much normal stimulation as possible and not be left dumped in a dark corner with no interests. Children who are deprived in this way appear retarded when in fact they are not, and every child, no matter what her mentality, deserves to be given the maximum opportunity for development. Absurd stimulatory programmes, however, cannot be endorsed as there is no real evidence of their effectiveness. In the early years it is difficult to prognosticate with regard to the child's eventual attainments, and life is full of surprises. Expectations should be realistic, however, and any undue stress put on the child by overambitious educational programmes is likely to be counter-productive.

Guidance and help may be obtained from assessment agencies, either independent or associated with education departments or special schools, and the Mental Health Society provides a valuable supportive service.

Institutionalisation. Although even the most severely retarded child should be kept at home as long as possible in order to provide the affection and stimulation of a normal home environment, there may nevertheless come a point where for the sake of other members of the family the child will be better placed in an institution. This is a very hard decision for parents to have to make, especially after so much care has often been lavished upon the defective child. However heartbreaking such a decision may be it is essential that the problem be clearly seen and dealt with in as unemotional a manner as is possible. It is not uncommon to find families severely deprived of a mother's attention because of excessive and futile devotion to an abnormal child. Remember that normal children, too, require parental attention and love.

MICROCEPHALY

A condition in which the head and brain fail to grow adequately, resulting in mental retardation and frequently epilepsy. The condition may be the result of primary brain damage or disease, e.g. intra-uterine infection or severe asphyxia at birth, or it may occasionally be the result of premature closure of the skull bones, causing secondary cramping of the brain. This is a very important condition to recognise as appropriate surgery will enable the brain to grow normally. Brain growth is maximal during the first 2 years and the condition must therefore be recognised as early as possible, as compensatory growth will not occur later. The child with microcephalic brain damage is likely to be very severely retarded and to require institutional care.

MILIA

These are small white spots, very common on the skin of the face of newborn babies, particularly on the nose. They are due to accumulated secretions of the sebaceous glands and are of no importance. The spots will disappear spontaneously within a week or two and they require no treatment.

MILK

The basic constitution of human, cow and goat milks as well as the various proprietary milk preparations available will be found in the Table. There are, however, more subtle differences which are at times of considerable importance. Breast milk varies in its constitution from one feed to the next and also during various parts of the feed, much of the fat being produced in the hind milk. The fat

BASIC CONSTITUENTS OF MILK FEEDS

Type of milk	Protein	Fat	Carbo-hydrate	Type of fat	Type of carbohydrate	Added iron?	Added? vitamins?	Salt content
Human	1,25	4,0	7,0	butterfat	lactose	—	—	low
Cow	3,3	3,8	4,7	butterfat	lactose	—	—	high
Goat	3,3	4,1	4,7	butterfat	lactose	—	—	high
'Humanised milks':								
Cow and gate Babymilk	1,8	3,3	6,6	butterfat	lactose	yes	yes	low
Lactogen	2,1	3,1	6,7	butterfat & corn oil	lactose & sucrose	yes	yes	low
Lactogen Full Protein (after 4 months)	3,1	2,75	7,45	butterfat & corn oil	lactose & sucrose maltodextrin	yes	yes	low
Nan	1,65	3,4	7,3	butterfat & veg oil	lactose	yes	yes	low
Pelargon	2,8	2,9	3,7	butterfat & corn oil	lactose	yes	yes	low
Similac	1,8	3,5	7,0	corn & cocoanut oils	lactose	yes	yes	low
SMA	1,5	3,6	7,2	oleo corn & cocoa-nut oils	lactose	yes	yes	low
S.26	1,5	3,6	7,2	oleo corn & cocoa-nut oils	lactose	yes	yes	low
Fat (low):								
Semilko	3,9	1,6	5,6	butterfat	lactose	yes	yes	high
Whole dried milks:								
Klim	3,5	4,0	5,0	butterfat	lactose	yes	A & D	high
Nespray	3,5	4,0	5,0	butterfat	lactose	yes	A & D	high
Evaporated whole milks:								
Carnation	3,5	4,0	5,0	butterfat	lactose	no	no	high
Ideal								high

globules in human milk are much smaller than those in cows' milk and the fat is therefore more readily digestible. The protein in human milk consists to a much greater extent of lactalbumin, whereas cows' milk contains 5 times as much casein as does human milk. This forms a tough curd on digestion in the stomach, and some of the protein may as a result not be absorbed but pass through into the stools as curds. The high salt content of cows' milk makes it an unsuitable feed for small babies but the so-called humanised preparations have the salt content reduced to near breast milk levels. The high phosphorus content of cows' milk impedes the absorption of calcium, and the phosphate content of humanised milks is therefore also lowered.

These various factors make it advantageous to use a humanised milk preparation for the first few months of baby's life if you are not breastfeeding. It does not matter much which you choose. The occasional baby does seem to be happier on one feed than on another but for the most part these preferences are imaginary and there is little to choose between one brand and the next. Your choice therefore will probably best be governed by price. The cost of feeding a baby on anything other than breast milk is considerable, so shop around.

It must be assumed that breast milk is the ideal food for the small human infant. The tiny premature baby may require rather more salt and protein. In general, mammalian milks vary according to the needs of the offspring. For example, rat milk contains 5 times as much protein as human milk and whale milk contains 50 per cent fat. No matter what chemical manipulations are devised it is impossible to make human milk from something else.

Milk allergy. Estimates of the incidence of milk allergy in babies vary from under 1 per cent to over 20 per cent. This being an inexact diagnosis, much lies in the eye of the beholder. The crucial test lies in the alleviation of symptoms by milk removal and their reprecipitation by reintroduction of milk, the experiment being repeated 2 to 3 times with consistent results. Such criteria are usually not met and in the present fashionable climate many, many babies are fed milk substitutes without justification. (See *allergy.)

Milk banks. Breast-milk banks have been established in many large centres and provide a valuable commodity for some babies. There is the occasional baby who will tolerate nothing other than breast milk. Premature babies do well on breast milk, although there is evidence that the tiniest babies require rather more protein and salt than breast milk provides. Without in any way wishing to depress the enthusiasm of those contributing to milk banks, it has to be admitted that most babies will thrive satisfactorily on artificial feeds if their own mother's milk is unavailable, and the overall value of breast-milk banks still has to be proved. Raw breast milk contains protective substances but carries the risk of possible infection. Sterilising the milk by heat destroys most of the protective factors. Most banks therefore settle for a compromise situation in which the milk is heated sufficiently to reduce the bacterial content to safe levels while reducing the damage to protective substances to a minimum. Perfection is just not possible. A mother who has an excess of milk may gain considerable satisfaction from presenting this to a bank or to an individual baby, and in this she deserves nothing but encouragement.

Milk intolerance. Where symptoms are attributable to milk but no strictly allergic mechanism is demonstrable, the term milk intolerance is preferred to milk allergy. The distinction may be important medically but from a practical viewpoint management consists of removing the offending substance. Some children seem poorly tolerant of milk fat, and in such cases a skimmed or partly skimmed preparation is preferable. Intolerance of milk sugar (see *lactose intolerance) is relatively common, and although milk protein is the factor responsible for allergic problems, these are sometimes not clearly identifiable. The term milk intolerance therefore would include cases of milk allergy but not vice versa.

Milk substitutes. In cases of milk allergy or intolerance several substitute products are available. Most of these are based on soya, e.g. Infasoy, Isomil, and Sobee, the chemical constitution of which closely approximates human milk. The two cannot however be equated. There is evidence that premature babies fare less well on soya feeds compared with milk-based feeds, and there is also evidence from Italian studies of impaired immunological status in infants given soya instead of milk. The diagnosis of milk intolerance should therefore be convincing before long-term substitution by a soya preparation is advised. Some 20 per cent of babies allergic to milk will also develop allergy to soya. In such cases, highly modified milk-based feeds, e.g. Nutramigen, may be required, and in exceptional cases meat-based formulae may be necessary. This situation, however, is extremely rare.

MILTON

This is a solution of sodium hypochlorite, which owes its bactericidal properties to the liberation of chlorine. The Milton method of sterilisation for bottles and teats is practical and safe, provided meticulous attention is paid to detail. The solution cannot sterilise anything with which it does not come into direct contact. It is therefore important that the bottles and teats be completely filled with the solution and kept submerged for 3 hours. The containers available from the manufacturer are more practical than household utensils. Bottles do not have to be rinsed after removal from the solution as any residual hypochlorite is rapidly changed to harmless salt on contact with milk. Hypochlorite is a powerful bleaching agent and teats will therefore lose their colour, but this is of no importance. All equipment should of course be meticulously cleaned before any form of sterilisation.

MOBILES

These are a boon to the bored baby and to the harassed parent. They should be hung near enough to catch the baby's attention without of course inviting destruction. It is fun to make them yourself and their production may provide an extra occupation for older children in the family.

MOLES

Known medically as pigmented naevi, moles vary greatly in size, small ones may be regarded as 'beauty spots' but the large hairy naevus may be very disfiguring. For such lesions, the opinion of a plastic surgeon should be sought. Moles hardly ever undergo malignant change in children, but a mole in an adult which undergoes change such as enlargement, irritation or itchiness should be seen promptly.

MONGOL
See *Down's syndrome

MONGOLIAN SPOT
Bluish pigmented areas of varying size may occur in babies of all darker-skinned races. They are most common over the lower back and buttocks but may extend up the trunk and occasionally onto the limbs. They may be mistaken for bruises. Mongolian spots are of absolutely no importance and they eventually fade.

MOOD, MOODINESS
Changes of mood occur in all people but some individuals are much more labile and some more placid. Excessive moodiness is characteristic of the adolescent of both sexes, but in girls the mood often fluctuates with the menstrual cycle. Excessive moodiness in the pre-adolescent child may be due to emotional distress and an attempt should be made to unearth the underlying cause. Excessive and unreasonable moodiness may be very irritating and provoking but it is better handled with patience and forbearance, ignoring the bad moods but enjoying the good and avoiding unnecessary and destructive retaliation. Try to maintain a mutually trusting and receptive attitude so that if something is worrying your child she will come and tell you rather than continuing to suppress her smouldering emotions.

MOSQUITO
There are many varieties of mosquito, the most important being the anopheline carriers of malaria. These are most readily recognised by the fact that when settled the body forms an angle to the surface, whereas other mosquitoes sit with the body parallel to the surface. Only the female mosquito bites. In order to improve the supply of blood she injects an irritant into the skin and it is this which causes the itching and swelling. Mosquito bites occur on exposed areas such as the face and limbs, and they are not grouped. In heavily mosquito-infested areas, protection may be afforded by screening, mosquito nets and appropriate clothing. Insect-repellent sprays and creams are also effective but have to be applied fairly frequently. Insect-repellent vapour strips are also obtainable and appear to be of value.

MOUTH
Most conditions of the mouth are dealt with under other headings. The main congenital abnormalities are *cleft lip and palate.

In the newborn baby, concern may be caused by the normal little white spots in the centre of the palate known as *Epstein's pearls. These are not to be confused with thrush, and they are of no importance. They eventually disappear after several weeks.

Small mucous cysts may occur on the gums; these also disappear spontaneously.

Tongue-tie is now an archaic concept, for it is realised that the frenum of the tongue varies greatly from individual to individual. Though the tongue may appear to be tethered by a short, thick frenum, this is simply a normal variant and requires no interference. The tip of the tongue will eventually mobilise quite sufficiently for normal speech, and 'tongue-tie' does not interfere with suckling in the small baby.

Infections of the mouth are common. Thrush presents as a white coating, often on the tongue and palate and inside the cheeks. It usually responds readily to simple preparations such as gentian violet, but this is unflattering and alternative preparations are nystatin drops or miconazole gel. Herpes causes a severe ulcerative stomatitis and recurrent 'cold sores'. Solitary painful ulcers known as aphthous ulcers occur in both children and adults. Their cause is unknown. The acute discomfort of this condition may be relieved by application of a corticosteroid in a base which enables it to adhere to the oral mucous membrane. Measles produces a diffuse inflammation of the mouth and the typical white Koplik's spots herald the appearance of the rash.

Sore throat is most commonly due to a virus infection. It may be due to tonsillitis, in which case inspection of the throat will reveal the inflamed red tonsils with white spots. It is, however, often not possible to distinguish a virus sore throat from a streptococcal infection and your doctor may therefore feel it wise to play safe and order penicillin. (See *throat.)

Halitosis (bad breath) may be due to tonsillitis or more diffuse mouth infection as well as to rotten teeth in older persons. Halitosis due to onions, garlic, smoking, etc. is readily recognisable. Bad breath is not the result of constipation.

MUCUS

This is a perfectly normal secretion of many organs, e.g. the nose, the bronchial glands, the stomach and the large bowel. Irritation of these organs may lead to an excessive production of mucus, e.g. cold or hayfever, bronchitis and dysentery. When vomiting occurs it is natural that the vomitus should contain mucus, for a great deal is secreted by the lining of the stomach. Normal mucus forms a protective layer over the mucous membrane and it is being continuously produced and removed.

Like everybody else, newborn babies secrete fair quantities of mucus and as they are not very skilled at removing it, it may accumulate to some extent in the nose, causing a moist rattle. This is of no importance. Newborn babies may also vomit mucoid gastric contents during the first day or two of life, this being often accentuated if they have swallowed a significant amount of blood during delivery. In such cases, the stomach may be aspirated or washed out, but these manoeuvres are often performed unnecessarily.

The mucus in *cystic fibrosis is abnormally viscid and causes obstruction of the glands, particularly of the bronchi and of the pancreas.

Thick mucus, as is produced for example in chronic bronchitis, may be thinned by the use of mucolytic agents. Though given often to children with respiratory troubles, these preparations have a very limited place.

MUMPS

This is a virus infection with an incubation period of 2–3 weeks, most commonly 17–18 days. The virus affects predominantly the salivary glands, particularly the parotid gland, which lies between the jawbone and the ear, but it may also affect other organs such as the pancreas, the gonads and the central nervous system.

Mumps is a variable disease. There may be some initial fever and malaise for 1 or 2 days, but the first symptom is usually a painful swelling in one or both of the parotid glands. One side only may be affected or they may be affected in turn. Sometimes no parotid swelling is present but the other salivary glands may be involved, and occasionally there may be, for example, mumps meningitis without any mumps swellings at all. In the average case, the swelling increases over 1–3 days and then slowly subsides, usually within a week. Fever is not usually high. Discomfort is increased by chewing and swallowing, especially anything which increases salivation, such as lemon juice. One attack of mumps gives immunity for life.

Complications consist of:

(1) Meningo-encephalitis. This is usually benign, though unpleasant while it lasts. The picture is one of a viral meningitis (see *meningitis) with headache, fever and vomiting. Symptoms last as a rule for only a few days and subside spontaneously with complete recovery.

(2) Pancreatitis. This causes abdominal pain, often accompanied by vomiting, with tenderness and rigidity of the abdomen.

(3) Testicular inflammation (orchitis). This may occur in up to 20 per cent of post-pubertal males. Usually one testis alone is involved. Because of this, even though the affected testicle may be damaged, sterility is rare.

(4) Deafness. This may occur after mumps and is almost always unilateral, but the affected ear is usually permanently damaged.

Treatment

There is no specific treatment for mumps. Comfort may be obtained from warmth, but poultices are messy and ineffective. Analgesics such as paracetamol give some relief. The mouth should be kept clean by frequent drinks, and food should be bland so as not to stimulate excessive salivation.

Immunisation against mumps (see *immunisation)

The live virus vaccine is usually combined with measles and rubella vaccines and administered to children at about 15 months of age. Although immunity should be longlasting, of this we cannot yet be certain. As mumps is a benign illness in childhood there is no great need for protection and it can well be argued that immunisation should be reserved for boys who have not had mumps, just prior to puberty, in order to protect them from the possible orchitic complications.

MURMURS

The mention of a heart murmur often causes needless anxiety to parents. Some 50 per cent of children will have a murmur at some stage of their lives. The bulk of these are quite innocent, may come and go and need cause no anxiety whatever. A heart murmur does, however, need careful assessment for it may indicate heart disease, and sophisticated investigation may be required for total assessment of the problem. You will have to be guided by your doctor. Do not assume that just because a murmur is heard, some heart abnormality must inevitably be present. If the child has no symptoms the chances are that the murmur is of no significance.

MUSCLES (for muscular pain see *growing-pains)

Diseases of the muscles are uncommon in children, though inflammation (myositis) does rarely occur. Muscle-wasting is usually secondary to disuse or to impairment of the nerve supply, as in poliomyelitis.

Healthy muscles will build up from normal childhood activities and there is no need to inflict specific muscle-building exercises on small children. Later, if a boy wishes to develop his musculature in any particular direction he can do so. Remember that you can't have everything. A 'Mr Universe' with muscles like a prize bull would be incapable of running a marathon. A boy with athletic tendencies must decide what he wants his body to do and then train it appropriately.

MUSIC

Nearly all children love music and this may be a useful form of communication with them. Of course a small child's efforts at musical production may not always fall soothingly on adult ears. Don't give your child a trumpet and ask her to remain silent. Do not be afraid to expose your children to good music at an early age. They may well enjoy it. Simple songs will naturally be easier for them to reproduce but there are many 3- and 4-year-olds who will thoroughly enjoy Brahms.

MYRINGOTOMY

This is an operation by which a hole is made in the eardrum in order to relieve pressure or allow secretions contained in the middle ear to drain. Acute ear infections usually respond well to conservative management and the operation is rarely necessary in such cases. In more chronic situations grommets are usually inserted to prolong the patency of the myringotomy.

NAILS

The fingernails of the newborn baby are soft but quite sharp and if his arms are allowed to thrash about during periods of hunger he may scratch his face quite severely. Nails are best trimmed while the baby is asleep.

White spots under the nails are of no significance. They are not an indication of dietary deficiencies. A reversed curve on the nails — spoon-shaped nails — suggests iron deficiency.

Clubbing of the nails occurs in cyanotic congenital heart disease and chronic chest conditions such as bronchiectasis.

NAIL-BITING

This habit is so common that it should not cause concern unless it is associated with other nervous manifestations. The anxious child commonly bites his nails but then so do many normal children without particular stresses. You will have to judge therefore whether it is a manifestation of anxiety or insecurity, or whether it is simply a rather ugly habit. If the latter, the child should simply be gently discouraged. The habit will almost certainly eventually cease. Painting the nails with vile-tasting substances is simply ineffective. If the nail-biting is part of a general nervous reaction, of which there are other manifestations, then the root cause should be determined, and if possible corrected, as in such cases the habit may persist into adulthood. Profound psychological help is not usually required.

NANNIES

Nannies come in various shapes, sizes, colours and language groups. These aspects are all irrelevant, for what matters is the type of care that a nanny will give your child. Mothers often feel guilty about leaving their children in the care of a nanny, but if this enables the mothers to lead more fulfilling lives and therefore ultimately to be of greater benefit to their families, the positive aspects overwhelmingly eclipse the negative ones. There is nothing unhealthy about the relationship between a small child and his nanny. He is able to distinguish her quite clearly from mother, to split his affections appropriately and to feel secure in the presence of either. However good the nanny may be it is essential that mother retain her position as the number one person in her child's life. This can be achieved only by providing that special care and love which a nanny cannot give.

When choosing a nanny for your child you will pay attention to various factors. She should above all be a loving sort of person with whom your child will feel secure. She should be able to maintain the same hygienic standards as you do yourself. She should be adaptable. Provided you can communicate with her it matters little if she speaks a language other than yours to your child even if initially he shows preference for 'nanny tongue' over mother tongue. As the child grows out of the nursery stage he should receive more and more stimulation from his parents, and by the time he is capable of looking after his own physical needs nanny will have become largely an affectionate memory.

NAPKINS

When buying your layette do not pay too much attention to the lists and advice given to you by commercial undertakings. Work out for yourself what you are likely to need. The amount of clothing will depend largely upon the climate in which you live. The number and type of napkins will depend to a great extent on your washing and drying facilities. Where these are good, your need for towelling napkins will be less. During periods of bad weather when the supply of napkins may run short you can always make do with disposable ones. The latter, though somewhat more expensive overall, are convenient and save a great deal of unpleasant labour. The plastic backing, however, leads to retention of a great deal of moisture, and this may predispose to skin irritation if the baby is not changed frequently. Many mothers use towelling napkins routinely at home and disposables when they take the baby out. This seems a very sensible compromise.

A napkin liner is useful to prevent excessive soiling of the napkins and thus make handling and washing more pleasant. If a liner is not used and the napkin is very soiled, most of the stool should be removed mechanically before putting the napkin to soak.

Washing and rinsing. Whether you wash the napkins by machine or by hand you may prefer to use soap flakes or one of the more potent modern detergents. The latter are more likely to be irritating to the hands and also to the baby if the napkins are inadequately rinsed. Rinsing therefore is rather more important than washing. It is not necessary to sterilise napkins but it may give you a feeling of extra cleanliness to know that they have been sterilised either chemically or by boiling. Given a choice, however, between cleanliness and sterility, most of us would choose the former.

Towelling napkins should not be ironed as this makes them hard.

Changing the napkin. In general this is best done after feeds, for the baby so often wets and soils at feed times. If you change him before the feed you are very likely to have to change him again afterwards. Gently cleanse the baby each time you change him, using either cotton wool or a disposable soft tissue. A little petroleum jelly or zinc and castor oil cream is usually sufficient to give the skin some protection from the excessive moisture. If, however, a napkin rash has developed, more elaborate treatment may be necessary.

Napkin rashes. These are common and need cause you no shame. When you think what the baby's skin has to endure for the first 2 years of life, it is hardly surprising that it occasionally becomes irritated. Napkin rashes are of several types. The commonest, so-called ammonia dermatitis, occurs predominantly upon the convex surfaces coming into contact with the napkin, and the creases are spared. This was thought to be due to excessive ammonia production as the result of bacterial action upon the urea in urine. Ammonia is strongly alkaline. In spite of the tempting nature of this hypothesis, experiments have not confirmed its validity. Any urine that has been passed for some time is inevitably contaminated with germs, and ammonia will inevitably be formed. It has not been shown to be irritating. At the other end of the pH scale, many mothers ascribe napkin rashes to 'acidity'. This is equally invalid. Urine is normally acid, and increasing its acidity does not appear to make it more irritating.

In spite of these remarks, the essential thing in dealing with a common napkin rash is to reduce exposure to urine. Plastic pants should not be worn as these help to retain moisture. The napkin should whenever possible be left off and as much air allowed to the region as is possible. A nappy liner may help to reduce contact when napkins cannot be avoided. In a high proportion of cases, fungal infection is superimposed upon the initial irritation and a fungicidal application is then desirable. Topical corticosteroids are anti-inflammatory and often useful, especially when combined with a fungicidal agent in a pasty base.

Thrush dermatitis commonly infects the napkin area and characteristically produces circular lesions with papery edges. In fungal infection the creases are not spared but are often more severely affected. There may be accompanying oral thrush and there may be inflammation of the creases elsewhere, for example in the neck and armpits. Such rashes should be kept as dry as possible, and although proprietary fungicides are valuable a simple preparation such as ¼ per cent mercurochrome lotion is often equally effective.

Similar rashes extending into the creases occur in seborrhoeic states, and napkin rashes may be associated with a wide variety of other conditions. If the rash does not respond to simple treatment as suggested above, let your doctor see it.

NAUSEA

This commonly precedes or is associated with vomiting. The main causes may be neurological: emotion, increased intracranial pressure, or gastro-intestinal: gastric irritation from over-indulgence, ingestion of toxic substances, food allergy, intestinal obstruction. (See *vomiting.)

NAVEL

Before birth the umbilical cord carries the two arteries and one vein which connect the baby to the placenta. When the cord is severed after birth these structures atrophy and disappear, leaving only a small scar. During the process of separation there may occasionally be a little bleeding but this is usually not severe. The cord stump should be allowed to dry out, and application of surgical spirit is traditional, though probably useless. When applying disposable napkins in the early days make sure that the cord stump is not enclosed in the plastic, as it then remains soggy and most unpleasant.

If the navel remains moist this is probably due to persistence of one of the blood vessel stumps, giving rise to what is called a granuloma — a pale pink, moist, polyp-like structure in the depth of the navel. Cauterisation with silver nitrate usually leads to rapid healing. The cord stump separates after a variable time, usually within 7-10 days, though it may persist for up to 3 weeks.

At certain stages of intra-uterine development other structures also pass through the navel. At one stage the bowel cannot be accommodated in the abdomen and herniates through into the umbilical cord, only to return later in development. Sometimes, however, this does not happen and the bowel remains herniated — a so-called omphalocoele. With conservative surgical management this gradually corrects itself. A duct from the bladder passes through the umbilicus and, though this nearly always seals off, it may persist as a small opening through which urine may be passed. Very rarely, a duct from the bowel may persist and faeces may then be discharged through the umbilicus. If you suspect any of these rare conditions, naturally you will inform your doctor.

Because scar tissue is sometimes weak, the umbilicus may distend to form a hernia. Though usually small, these may sometimes achieve an impressive size, particularly in African children. They nearly always disappear without treatment, usually by the age of 5 years. Surgical treatment is only indicated if the hernia is still present when a child is due to attend school, when it may cause him some embarrassment.

NECK

The symptoms most likely to cause concern in this region are pain and stiffness in the neck, and enlarged glands. A stiff neck, limiting particularly forward bending, is characteristic of *meningitis and *meningismus. Unilateral pain with stiffness is commonly due to involvement of one of the spinal small joints. More chronic pain and stiffness may be due to disease of the spine, e.g. tuberculosis. Irritation of the muscles may be due to inflamed lymph glands. These occur often in association with infection of the nose and throat, but enlargement may be the result of infection elsewhere, e.g. of the scalp, or of specific diseases such as tick bite fever or glandular fever. Inflamed glands may take many weeks to settle down. Occasionally, progressive septic infection leads to abscess formation within the gland, which then has to be drained. Tuberculosis of the neck glands used to be common but is now extremely rare in white children, though it is still seen in less privileged communities, in which tuberculosis is still a problem.

The thyroid gland, which consists of 2 lobes joined by an isthmus lying across the front of the trachea, is often rather conspicuous in puberty as a physiological enlargement. At other times, enlargement may represent overactivity (a toxic goitre) or it may represent an attempt on the part of the gland to produce its secretion under difficult conditions, e.g. iodine lack or enzyme deficiency. Significant thyroid enlargement calls for a medical opinion.

NEPHRITIS

This is an inflammatory condition of the kidneys, usually secondary to infection by the streptococcus, either in the throat or on the skin. The disease has waned appreciably as the result of liberal use of penicillin in the treatment of sore throats. It is, however, still very common in African children and is then often due to secondarily infected scabies.

As a result of the inflammation of the kidney glomeruli, blood and protein leak through into the urine, and the blood may give it a red, brown or smoky appearance. Protein is readily detected on testing. Impaired kidney function leads to the retention of body water due to diminished urinary output, and puffiness of the eyes and generalised body-swelling result. The other characteristic feature of acute nephritis is a rise in blood pressure. This may be severe enough to affect the brain, causing convulsions.

Although a child with acute nephritis can be managed at home, if the blood pressure is significantly elevated he is safer in hospital. The condition is as a rule self-limiting, and nearly all patients recover completely. A few go on to have persistent kidney disease. Treatment consists mainly in limiting the intake of fluid and salts to the quantity with which the kidneys can cope, at the same time preserving as well as possible the child's nutrition. The high blood pressure is dealt with by rest and appropriate hypotensive drugs. The excessive fluid-retention may be treated with diuretic drugs, but while these may increase the output of water they do not basically improve kidney function.

Following an attack of nephritis, blood and protein may be found in the urine for a considerable time — up to a year or two. Your doctor will probably want to follow the child up as long as the urine remains abnormal. Later trouble is very unlikely to supervene.

NEPHROSIS OR NEPHROTIC SYNDROME

In this condition, the kidneys allow protein to leak through into the urine, thus depleting the blood proteins and causing oedema (swelling), particularly of the eyes but also of the body generally. The condition may be associated with various types of kidney disease but in the commonest form seen in children there is hardly any kidney pathology detectable. This is the so-called minimal change nephrotic syndrome. Such children nearly always respond well to treatment with corticosteroids but they may relapse frequently, in which case other forms of treatment might have to be added. The outlook in this condition is good.

For reasons not understood, such minimal change nephrosis is very rare in African children, in whom most cases of nephrotic syndrome are due to fairly severe kidney pathology, with a resultant relatively poor prognosis.

NEWBORN

The newborn (neonatal) period comprises the first 4 weeks of life. This is a period of great adjustment, not only for the baby, whose birth has transferred him from a warm, passive intra-uterine existence to the less cosy outside world in which he has to fend for himself, but also for the parents, whose lives will be very drastically changed by the arrival of this new member of the family. After the first few days of heady excitement there may follow, particularly for the new mother, a period of relative depression. This is so common that 'fourth day blues' or mother's weeps are regarded as normal. Such feelings should be transient and mild. If they are more exaggerated than this you must tell your doctor.

The newborn baby is not necessarily a beautiful sight. He is usually covered with a greasy substance known as vernix caseosa and also with a certain amount of maternal blood. The head is often moulded and may appear grossly misshapen, but this always corrects itself within a few days. A newborn baby's proportions are very different from those of an adult. His head is much larger, occupying one-quarter of his body length instead of the adult one-eighth, and the limbs are relatively short. The baby tends to retain his flexed intra-uterine position.

At birth the baby usually cries vigorously and then settles to sleep. Crying may be repeated when he is bathed. Crying thereafter usually denotes hunger. Most babies pass urine at or shortly after birth, and nearly all will pass meconium within 24 hours. If there is undue delay in either of these functions, and particularly if there is associated abdominal distension, you should mention this to your doctor. Many babies vomit small quantities of mucus during the first day or so but if this is excessive, particularly if there is associated choking, your doctor should be informed. Such symptoms suggest that there might be a swallowing problem as the result, for example, of oesophageal obstruction.

Jaundice is common in the neonatal period but if it appears within the first 24 hours, or if it becomes very deep, you must inform your doctor (see *jaundice).

Commonly encountered conditions in the neonatal period are sticky eyes (see *conjunctivitis), thrush, skin rashes, particularly the common urticaria neonatorum, enlargement of the breasts as the result of the influence of maternal hormones, and vaginal bleeding due to the same cause. Severe infections such as septicaemia and meningitis do occur but are rare, and most babies have no problems at all.

Care of the newborn. The baby should be put to the breast on demand when he cries and no extra fluids need be given unless the climate is particularly hot or the nursery overheated. Babies occasionally run a fever on the third day or so of life if they have lost an unusual amount of fluid. This will be reflected in an excessive weight loss well above the usual 10 per cent of birth weight. Most babies regain their birth weight by the tenth day but some are rather slower. Far too much attention is paid to weight in the early months of life and much needless anxiety caused thereby. Healthy babies should be weighed at birth and when they leave hospital, and any additional weighing inbetween should be only on strict indication.

The baby should naturally be cleaned regularly, but daily bathing is not essential. Topping and tailing is quite sufficient most days. The navel requires no special attention beyond being kept clean. If disposable napkins are used these should not cover the cord stump, as drying is then impeded. The buttocks may be protected with a little petroleum jelly or zinc and castor oil cream. Clothing should be appropriate for the weather, bearing in mind that the smaller the baby the more warmth he requires. There is no objection whatever to taking small babies outdoors, provided they are not exposed to extremes of temperature and are protected from the sun.

The newborn baby's repertoire of activities is somewhat limited. He is able to suckle and to root around for the nipple without its being put in his mouth (the so-called rooting reflex). His only vocal skill is crying. He is able to see and will fix his gaze more on a face than on anything else. He has little control over his large head, which tends therefore to flop around but he can lift it sufficiently when he's lying on his tummy to turn it from side to side. Limb movements are jerky and incoordinate and he displays a marked startle or Moro reflex, produced on almost any strong stimulus. This consists of a facial grimace, a rapid outward stretching of the arms and hands followed by a slower grasping movement forwards with similar movements of the legs. This reflex persists for 2 to 3 months before gradually disappearing. He also displays the grasp reflex, with which anything placed in the hand is grasped tightly. Other activities are yawning, sighing, sneezing, coughing and stretching. He is also rather prone to hiccups, which seem, however, to distress him very little. Do not assume because your baby sneezes he has a cold. This is simply the natural way of trying to clear the nose.

By the end of the newborn period the average baby has settled into an easy routine, with feeding occurring fairly regularly, on average every 4 hours, and most of the time between feeds will still be spent sleeping. The baby will have wakeful periods, however, during which he begins to take an increasing interest in his environment. Particular attention will be paid to mother and some babies will be responding with a smile, though on average this appears only after about 6 weeks.

This is an easy and happy period of childhood. Make the most of it!

NICOTINE
See *smoking

NIGHT DISTURBANCE
See *sleep disturbance

NIGHT LIGHTS
These should be reserved for the child who is afraid of the dark. Such fears are real and will not be helped by a toughening attitude. The child needs reassurance and comfort. A night light therefore is not unreasonable but it should not itself cause further disturbance either by its brightness or by the casting of frightening shadows.

NIGHTMARES AND NIGHT TERRORS
Attempts have been made to distinguish between these, but they should be regarded as the same phenomenon. They occur typically in a child 4 to 8 years old, when imagination is at its height. Within an hour or two of going to sleep the child will scream in terror and may to some extent indicate his fears by shouting things like 'go away'. When you reach him to comfort him he will be found to be not properly awake or responsive, being either still asleep and in the throes of his nightmare or in a state of clouded consciousness. Only by waking him thoroughly will you put an end to the disturbance, for he will then be aware that it was only a dream and his fears will subside. If he is not fully wakened he may return to sleep for a time and then have a repetition of the nightmare.

Although perfectly normal children may be prone to such disturbances they are often precipitated by frightening experiences such as separation from parents, witnessing of accidents and exposure to alarming films and television. If your child is prone to nightmares, therefore, it is wise to avoid such stimulating experiences shortly before bedtime. Excessively frequent nightmares might indicate an emotional situation and justify a consultation with your doctor.

NIPPLES
Though the shape, size and degree of protuberance vary greatly, nearly every nipple will function perfectly well. True inverted nipples are very rare. This deformity cannot be corrected and the mother would be well advised to make no attempt at breastfeeding. Unfortunately, many nipples which are simply flat are

diagnosed as being inverted, and breastfeeding needlessly forsworn. If with manipulation the nipple can be made to project at all, it is not an inverted nipple. Flat nipples are often the result of restrictive underwear and in these modern free-nipple days one expects to find fewer such problems. Flat nipples should be encouraged to protrude by the wearing of nipple shields during pregnancy and by regular gentle massage of the nipple between forefinger and thumb. In this exercise the husband can be a willing help.

When a baby sucks at the breast he takes the whole of the nipple and most of the areola (the pigmented portion surrounding the nipple) into his mouth. This enables him to compress the milk sinusoids as well as suck (see *breastfeeding). The nipple is therefore little traumatised by normal suckling. When, however, the breast is engorged and the baby is unable to draw the nipple out sufficiently, he tends to gnaw at it, and this may cause an abrasion. Being a very painful condition, this causes the mother to tense up, and impedes the draught reflex, thus leading to further breast engorgement. If, therefore, during the early days of feeding a painful crack or abrasion appears, the baby should temporarily be taken off the affected breast, as further nursing will simply increase the damage. Usually only 24 hours is required for the abrasion to heal. During this time the breast must be emptied by some other means, either manual expression or with the help of a breast pump. The baby may be allowed to suckle via a nipple shield but this is a relatively inefficient way of emptying a breast and will probably require augmentation by expression. What is applied to the nipple is of little importance provided that it is not irritating and does not interfere with the natural healing process. Once the trouble has healed the baby should be put back on the breast and if possible on a demand-feeding schedule. It has been shown that frequent feeds are less damaging than less frequent, more protracted feeds.

In order to prevent these nipple troubles, various programmes have been advocated antenatally to toughen up the nipples. Most women will rightly object to scrubbing their nipples with a nail brush. Application of astringents is more likely to lead to brittleness of the skin than to any benefit. Massaging with emollient creams will do no harm but it probably does little good. Most likely simple freedom of the nipple is all that is required. Beware though of 'jogging nipples', if you are given to jogging, for with the enlargement of the breasts during pregnancy there may be additional movement and resultant trauma from clothing.

Bleeding from the nipple is always to be taken seriously. It may clearly be due to a crack and will then cease with healing, but bleeding coming from within the nipple or breast calls for a medical examination. This may be first manifested by the baby's vomiting of blood, and any such symptom occurring after the first 2 days must direct attention to the breast.

NOSE

Nose-bleeding. This may be the result of direct trauma, such as a blow on the nose, in which case the bleeding might be rather alarming but will always stop spontaneously.

Recurrent nose-bleeding is common and usually occurs from the nasal septum, where the vessels are very superficial. It is commoner in drier climates than at the coast. Simple pressure on the nostril will nearly always arrest such bleeding, but it may have to maintained for many minutes. Frequent nose-bleeds of this type will probably be helped by cauterisation of the small vessels on the nasal septum and it is therefore worth seeing your doctor. Bleeding may be the result of local disease, such as a foreign body in the nose, which causes accompanying nasal discharge usually with an unpleasant odour. Nose-bleeding occasionally is a manifestation of a generalised illness such as purpura, rheumatic fever or hypertension.

Nasal discharge. This is most commonly due to a simple cold, in which case the onset is sudden, with associated symptoms of sneezing, coughing, sore throat and perhaps some fever. Persistent nasal discharge is commonly due to allergy. The mucous membrane of the nose is often swollen to such an extent that breathing and blowing are impossible. The discharge is typically a clear mucoid one and there is associated sneezing and nasal itching. There may be irritation of the eyes and perhaps an allergic cough. In small children the distinction between nasal allergy and frequent colds is extremely difficult to make. (See *allergy, *colds, *rhinitis.)

Sinusitis implies the spread of infection from the nose to the paranasal sinuses, which are air-containing spaces within the skull bones, communicating with the nose. When the nose is inflamed the sinus openings become blocked, and infection then creeps in. The symptoms are a heavy feeling in the head, headache, particularly above the eyes, fever and a thick nasal discharge. Blowing the nose often tends to push secretions back into the sinuses. Sniffing, though socially less acceptable, is much more efficient at draining the sinuses. If, therefore, your child wants to sniff, let him. When blowing the nose, both nostrils should not be occluded at the same time but in turn.

Nose drops of the decongestant type are often abused and continued for unacceptably long periods. A baby with an obstructed nose may have difficulty in breathing and in feeding, and at the height of a cold therefore it is legitimate to use nose drops to shrink the nasal lining and reduce secretions. These are best inserted before feeds. Such treatment should never be continued for more than 4 to 5 days at a stretch. Saline irrigations of the nose are harmless but impossible in children. Inhalation of steam is often relieving in conditions such as sinusitis. In allergic rhinitis, relief is usually obtained from cromoglycate drops or sprays, or from beclomethasone aerosols, and side effects are few. Antihistamine drugs may also be helpful. Beware, however, of nasal medications and do not use them without your doctor's instructions.

NURSERY SCHOOL

There is a great deal of benefit to be obtained from nursery schools, not only for the child but also for the mother. Do not imagine, however, that it is essential for a child to attend a nursery school if he is to be prepared for optimum progress when his formal education begins. Nursery school will teach him many things, but things which he would learn anyway in a normal home environment with reasonably stimulating parents. Above all it will teach him to socialise, and if there are not children in the neighbourhood with whom he can play in his pre-school years, then nursery school is a good idea. He will learn that discipline is for everybody, not just for him. Having passed the first two years, when he considers himself the centre of the universe, he will learn to give and take. He will be given the opportunity to channel his energy in a way that does not drive mother to distraction and he will learn that adults, including teachers, are basically kind.

Probably the main advantage of your child going to nursery school, however, is the release it gives you for other activities. Not having the child constantly under your feet probably will make you appreciate and enjoy him more. Your times together will be more precious and more stimulating. There is therefore much to be said for sending your child to a pre-primary school. These are run by qualified persons and have to conform to adequate standards. Nevertheless, each school has its own particular character, and in order to select the one at which your child will be happiest it is wise to speak to as many friends and neighbours as possible.

Children vary greatly in their initial reactions to nursery school, some protesting against the separation from mother for a long while, others being unable to wait to get to school each morning. Do not be upset if your child is reluctant initially. By all means discuss things with the teacher, but have every confidence that he will eventually settle down happily, and when the time comes for him to go to 'proper' school there will be no problem.

OBESITY

This is not as simple a subject as it would seem. While it is true that the only way in which a person can become fat is by eating too much, there are many factors still poorly understood. Fat people do not inevitably eat more than thin people, nor are they necessarily slothful, though eventually their weight precludes much physical activity. There appear to be differences in metabolism between thin people and fat people, the thin ones burning up calories much more readily, while the fat ones store them up. Fundamentally, however, the fat person is consuming too many calories for his particular needs. This applies to fat babies and children as well as adults. The time to tackle obesity is as soon as it becomes manifest and not to wait until the situation has become grotesque.

There has been a certain amount of evidence that fat babies turn into fat adults. There is today less enthusiasm for this idea, but nevertheless the baby who is becoming too fat should have her calorie intake reduced. This means cutting down the pure energy foods, i.e. carbohydrates such as starches and sugars, and reducing the intake of high energy fat (fats and oils have more than twice as many calories per gram as do carbohydrates and proteins). Skimming milk removes half its calorie content. The fat baby therefore should be fed largely on vegetables, fruit, lean meat, fish and low-fat dairy products.

The same principles apply to the child who is obese. All sugars should be eliminated, starches reduced to a minimum and between-meal snacks and sweetened drinks forbidden. Foods to be encouraged are vegetables, excluding potatoes, salads, of which she may eat as much as she likes, lean meat, low-fat cheese and skimmed milk, with plain water as the main drink. Meals can still be made interesting and satisfying and there is absolutely no need for the child to go hungry. She must simply eat the right things and avoid the wrong things (see *calories). Weight reduction need not be abrupt. The very obese child should aim to lose some but then hold her weight static while she grows into it.

Trying to reduce weight is often very disheartening. Initial loss is often good but the curve then tends to flatten out, even with continuation of severe dietary restrictions. It is therefore better not to aim for some preconceived target, for this may be almost unattainable. Disappointment leads to discouragement.

Regular exercise is a considerable help in weight reduction and this need not be particularly strenuous. A long brisk walk is probably better than a game of squash. If parental example can get the child jogging, so much the better.

A regular check should be kept on the weight but this should not be done at absurdly short intervals. Once a month is enough. The child who is conscientious and co-operative should be rewarded (in a non-fattening way!), to reinforce positive attitudes.

ONE-PARENT FAMILY
See *single parent

OPERATIONS
Children, including babies, take surgical operations as a rule extremely well, and you do not therefore have to fear their ability to survive even very major surgery. A child of understanding age about to undergo a surgical operation should have the situation explained to her as factually as possible but naturally without accentuation of gory detail. Her fears of pain, which are very natural, can be allayed by explaining that she will have an anaesthetic and that afterwards she will have medicines to alleviate pain, and that therefore although she must expect some degree of discomfort it should not be at all severe. (See also *hospital.)

OTITIS
Otitis externa. This is an inflammation of the skin of the external canal, which leads down to, but not beyond, the eardrum. (For anatomy of the ear see *ear.) It may result from irritation by secretions discharging through a perforation of the eardrum as the result of otitis media. Sometimes the irritation is due to inadvised trauma as the result of trying to remove wax, and sometimes the condition is associated with swimming. Boils of the external canal are extremely painful, as the skin is tightly adherent to the underlying bone and there is little room for expansion. External otitis is treated with antibacterial and anti-inflammatory topical applications rather than with systemic antibiotics. Swimming is usually discouraged.

Wax is a normal secretion of the ear. It tends to migrate outwards of its own accord. Excessive accumulations may block the canal and cause discomfort. On no account should cotton buds be poked into the ears in order to clean them. This simply impacts the wax and makes its removal impossible.

Otitis media. This implies inflammation of the middle ear, which connects to the back of the nose via the Eustachian tube. With colds, the tube lining becomes inflamed, and with otitis media there is a catarrhal condition of the middle ear which, however, almost always resolves spontaneously.

Sometimes such catarrhal otitis media is complicated by superimposed bacterial infection, causing an exudation of inflammatory secretions into the middle ear; and the build-up of tension if the Eustachian tube is blocked leads to rupture of the eardrum. The ear then discharges. The perforation of the eardrum is usually small and heals completely as the condition subsides. Such acute otitis media is usually treated with an antibiotic but the majority of cases clear without any treatment at all. Occasionally the eardrum is destroyed to a greater extent by persistent infection and there may be damage to the small bones of the middle ear. Repeated infections or persistent discharge from the ear therefore call for expert medical opinion and treatment. With modern surgery, even extensive damage to the structures of the middle ear can be successfully repaired.

Particularly with antibiotic treatment there is a possibility that secretions may be retained within the middle ear, causing a so-called 'glue ear'. This impedes mobility of the eardrum and ossicles, and causes varying degrees of deafness. If you suspect therefore that your child is not hearing as well as before, take her to your doctor. The condition may respond to simple decongestive nose drops directed at re-opening the Eustachian tube, but drainage of the secretions may be necessary.

Recurrent otitis media. This is common in small children under the age of 2 because of the short, straight anatomy of the Eustachian tube. Many children outgrow such troubles without permanent damage to the ears. Your doctor may however feel that active treatment is necessary and may advocate drainage of the middle ear with insertion of *grommets or removal of the adenoids. There has been a trend towards overenthusiastic surgery, and fine judgement is needed about the advisability of such procedures.

OXYGEN

As everybody knows, oxygen is essential for life, as oxygenation is the basis of nearly all energy-producing chemical reactions within the body. Atmospheric oxygen, which constitutes about 20 per cent of the air we breathe, diffuses readily into the blood in the lung capillaries and is then carried by the haemoglobin in the red blood-cells to all the body tissues. With normal lung function, the haemoglobin in the pulmonary capillaries and veins is almost completely saturated with oxygen. With impairment of lung function this may not be the case, and increasing the oxygen tension in the lung alveoli by increasing the oxygen content of the inspired air may correct the oxygen lack in the blood.

This is the basis for giving oxygen under such circumstances. Oxygen is, however, often given thoughtlessly, needlessly or even inadvisedly, simply because nothing better can be thought of. Parents are often deeply concerned if their child is given oxygen, thinking that this heralds disaster. Such is far from the case. If used appropriately, oxygen is a temporary crutch to help over a period of respiratory difficulty which is almost certainly reversible.

Oxygen is not without its dangers. Like every other essential to life — water, salt, vitamins, etc. — an excess can be toxic. In premature babies, unnecessarily high oxygen concentrations are probably the cause of an eye condition known as retrolental fibroplasia, which may cause blindness, and which at one time was probably the commonest cause of blindness in the United States. Excessive oxygen can under certain circumstances actually depress respiration, and prolonged high concentrations almost certainly damage the lungs. Like all other forms of medication, therefore, oxygen administration has to be restrained and appropriate.

OXYTOCIN

This is a hormone secreted by the pituitary gland at the base of the brain, which stimulates the uterine muscle to contract and which also stimulates the muscular tissue of the breast glands, causing the milk to flow. (See *breastfeeding.)

PAIN

Though decidedly unpleasant, pain is one of the most important defence mechanisms, directing attention in no uncertain fashion to where it is needed. It usually ensures rest for the affected part, rest which is so important for healing processes. Acute pain usually has a ready explanation. Recurrent pains are often due to obscure causes and may indeed never have an adequate explanation. For further discussion of recurrent pain see *headache, *abdominal pain, *growing pains, etc.

PALLOR

Parents often worry because their child appears pale, and wonder whether this indicates anaemia. It is true that the anaemic child usually appears pale but the reverse is by no means always correct. Significant anaemia is usually observable in the conjunctiva (the inside of the lower eyelid), the gums and the nails, but even the most experienced doctor finds it difficult to assess anaemia clinically with any accuracy. Fair children often appear pale because of their light skins, and in hot climates many children appear sallow. If you are worried about your child's pallor by all means consult your doctor, who will probably have the blood checked. (See also *anaemia.)

PANCREAS

The pancreatic gland lies deep in the upper abdomen in the curve of the duodenum, with its tail extending to the left. Its duct empties into the duodenum through a common opening with the bile duct from the liver. The pancreas secretes very powerful digestive enzymes which split the protein, fat and carbohydrates of the food into absorbable fractions. In the tail of the pancreas are small islets of different tissue, the so-called islands of Langerhans, the cells of which secrete insulin and also the insulin antagonist, glucagon.

The pancreas is rarely the site of disease in childhood but it may become inflamed in *mumps and it is severely affected in *cystic fibrosis. The insulin-secreting cells of the islands of Langerhans are destroyed in juvenile diabetes, thought usually to be the result of a virus infection in a predisposed person.

PAPULAR URTICARIA

In this condition, crops of itchy spots occur predominantly on the legs but sometimes also on the trunk and arms. Small children react excessively to insect bites and this condition is usually due to sensitivity to fleas. Not every spot which appears is an actual flea bite. The fleas may be acquired from pets but commonly live in carpets or between floor boards, and this explains the predilection for the lower limbs. Scratching of the spots often leads to superimposed infection.

The condition is best treated by getting rid of the fleas with suitable insecticides. Insect repellents can also be used. Other topical applications are of little value unless there is superimposed infection, but antihistamine drugs may help to reduce itching.

PARACETAMOL

This aspirin-like drug is useful for relief of pain and fever. It is probably safer than aspirin, but in high dosage can produce severe liver toxicity. Like all medicines, therefore, it should be used with discretion and with careful attention to dose.

PARALYSIS

Significant paralysis of muscles is usually due to interference with the nerve supply rather than to disease of the muscle itself. Among the more common specific paralytic conditions are:

Erb's palsy. This occurs in newborn babies and is the result of excessive traction on the nerve roots in the neck which supply certain muscles of the arm. The arm lies immobile against the trunk, with the elbow extended and the hand directed backwards with the fingers flexed. The condition is usually transient and full recovery is likely within a few weeks.

Facial paralysis. This may occur in the newborn baby as the result of pressure on the nerves supplying the muscles of the face. The condition is always transient and recovery is complete.

Bell's palsy. A similar condition, occurring at a later age both in children and in adults. There is sudden onset of paralysis of one side of the face, with difficulty in closing the eye on the affected side and pulling of the mouth towards the unaffected side. The facial nerve traverses a long narrow bony canal and the condition is thought to be the result of compression of the nerve by inflammatory swelling. Nearly all cases recover completely, especially in children. There is some evidence that treatment with corticosteroids is of value but the spontaneous recovery rate is so high that the value of treatment is very questionable.

Poliomyelitis. This most dreaded of paralytic diseases is now, thanks to the vaccine, relatively rare. When the viruses were very prolific it used to attack young children and was therefore known as infantile paralysis. With improvement in general hygiene, infection became a later experience, with older children and even adults being affected. As vaccination gives virtually 100 per cent protection there is no excuse for this disease still to exist. (See *poliomyelitis.)

Hysterical paralysis. This may give rise to very bizarre forms of weakness, usually readily recognisable (see *hysteria). See also *cerebral palsy.

PEANUTS

These are particularly dangerous to children because of the risk of inhalation. It is not only their size and smoothness which makes them so easily inhaled but the fact that they are likely to be eaten by the handful during relatively boisterous activities. It is better not to give your children peanuts but if they do want to eat them they should do so sitting quietly at a table and not romping about. Any choking episode occurring while a child is eating peanuts should be taken very seriously. It is possible for an inhaled peanut to remain undetected until severe damage has occurred to the lung. If therefore there is ever a question of a peanut having been inhaled, consult your doctor and insist upon an X-ray examination. This is not always conclusive, for peanuts are not opaque to X-rays, and if there remains a strong suspicion it is safer to have a look. This involves passing a bronchoscope down the trachea under anaesthesia; the foreign body is removed by suction or with forceps.

PENICILLIN (see also *antibiotics)

Penicillin, the original antibiotic discovered by Sir Alexander Fleming, is still the best and safest when the germ responsible for the disease is sensitive to it. The streptococcus that causes tonsillitis, impetigo and may precipitate rheumatic fever and nephritis, is always penicillin sensitive. It nevertheless requires a full 10 days of penicillin treatment to eliminate a streptococcus from the throat. In the prevention of rheumatic fever, penicillin is given daily for years, usually with no ill effect whatever.

Because of the narrow bacterial spectrum of the original penicillin and the emergence of germs resistant to it, e.g. staphylococci, numerous modifications of penicillin have been evolved. Many of these are not destroyed by penicillinase (an enzyme produced by germs resistant to penicillin) and many of these preparations have a wide antibacterial cover. While being extremely valuable when used correctly, they are grossly overprescribed and often squandered on virus infections in which of course they are totally ineffective. The penicillins are relatively non-toxic, reactions consisting usually of skin rashes, but in sensitised individuals alarming and sometimes fatal anaphylactic reactions may occur, particularly on injection.

Though rashes are not uncommon as a side effect of penicillin, particularly with derivatives such as ampicillin, penicillin sensitivity tends to be overdiagnosed. Many of the rashes attributed to the drug are due to the virus for which it has incorrectly been given. Even in established cases of penicillin sensitivity, it has been found that 50 per cent of children have lost their sensitivity after 1 year. When, therefore, penicillin is the antibiotic of choice, it should almost certainly be given.

PENIS

This most treasured male possession should be treated with respect at all ages. There is considerable misconception regarding the normal anatomy of the penis and particularly of the foreskin, which is usually long and tight and adherent to the underlying glans of the penis for many years. Separation gradually occurs in middle childhood. This may be accompanied by a certain amount of irritation due to pockets of smegma but given time and gentle handling there should be no problem. Never should any forcible attempt be made to retract the foreskin, as this will only do damage. It should be pulled back only as far as it goes with comfort for normal cleansing purposes and for the rest it should be left alone. (See *circumcision.)

The size of the penis varies considerably and in plump little boys most of the shaft may be embedded in a large fat pad so that the organ appears very tiny. A true micropenis is extremely rare.

Enlargement of the penis is one of the early signs of puberty. In its flaccid state the adult organ varies greatly in size but when erect these differences are eliminated. When considered in relation to total body size the human penis is larger than that of any other animal. Be understanding therefore of those who regard it with pride!

PERIODIC SYNDROME

Many children experience recurrent attacks of abdominal pain associated with vomiting and often with fever and sometimes headache. When no cause can be determined for such attacks, they are often referred to as the periodic syndrome or cyclical vomiting when this is the dominant symptom. Attacks with headache and abdominal pain may be called abdominal migraine, particularly if there is a family history of migraine.

It is apparent that the diagnosis is inexact and often meaningless and largely a confession of ignorance. Like most unexplained symptoms, there has been a tendency to attribute the periodic syndrome to emotion. This may be correct but there should be more positive evidence of emotional disturbance before accepting this as the sole cause. It is important to investigate possible physical causes such as recurrent urinary infection and food allergies. Such children often end in the hands of the surgeons for removal of a 'grumbling appendix'. The appendix is almost invariably normal but the operation does sometimes cure the symptoms, almost certainly a psychological rather than a physical effect.

If your child has symptoms suggestive of the periodic syndrome without detectable organic cause, try to elicit any emotional factors which may be responsible. Overinvestigation and excessive treatment of such a condition often serves only to reinforce the impression of significant disease. (See *abdominal pain.)

PERITONEUM

This is the thin membrane which lines the abdominal cavity and covers the abdominal viscera. It encloses a potential space known as the peritoneal cavity, which normally contains only a very small quantity of fluid sufficient for lubrication. Inflammation of the peritoneum, known as peritonitis, may result from spread of infection from the outside, as in penetrating injuries of the abdomen, or from rupture of or inflammation of an abdominal viscus, e.g. appendicitis, ruptured duodenal ulcer, etc. Peritonitis is characterised by severe pain, tenderness and rigidity of the abdominal muscles, usually associated with high fever. Such symptoms call for immediate medical attention.

PERTHES' DISEASE

This is a condition affecting the bone of the hip joint. It afflicts children in the age group 4 to 10 years and is 10 times as common in boys as in girls. In 10 per cent of cases it is bilateral. The symptoms are a limp, with pain in the hip region, or sometimes referred to the knee. X-ray changes are characteristic. The condition is self-limiting, though cases inadequately treated often develop arthritis later.

Weight-bearing during the active stage of the disease should be prevented.

PERTUSSIS

Whooping-cough is a most unpleasant disease, particularly in young babies, in whom it may be serious and even life-threatening. The disease is due to a specific germ but there are several virus infections which closely simulate the condition and which are known as parapertussis.

Whooping-cough begins with what appears to be a simple cold but the cough increases in severity, becoming spasmodic, i.e. a series of coughs occur without drawing the breath in. Finally, at the end of such a coughing bout the breath is drawn in rapidly against a still partly closed larynx, and this causes the typical inspiratory whoop. Severe coughing spasms are associated with choking and often with vomiting, and the child may lose a significant amount of weight during the course of the disease. Spasms are precipitated by eating and drinking, physical activity, excitement, changes of environment, irritation from tobacco smoke, etc. The cough tends to be worse at night and the whole family may become thoroughly exhausted. After about 4 weeks the cough usually begins to subside, but symptoms rarely last less than 6 weeks and the distressing cough may recur with subsequent colds or minor infections, giving the impression of a second attack of whooping-cough. The condition is infectious from the onset of symptoms for about 4 weeks.

Complications are not uncommon and include superimposed ear infection, pneumonia, collapse of portions of the lung, convulsions and subsequent lung damage.

Treatment is not very satisfactory. If given early, antibiotics are of value, and if therefore whooping-cough is suspected you should contact your doctor as soon as possible. Cough mixtures are of little use, although a long-acting cough suppressant may be of some help at night. Better effect, however, is usually obtained from sedation. Respiratory irritants should be avoided and although sudden changes of temperature are undesirable, fresh air is not contraindicated. If vomiting is a problem the child should be re-fed immediately after a vomit.

As babies do not inherit any immunity to whooping-cough from their mothers, immunisation should be carried out as early as possible. The vaccine is not 100 per cent effective but usually lessens the severity of the illness. There has been concern regarding the safety of pertussis immunisation but this is generally advocated, except for children who have had convulsions or neurological problems. (See *immunisation.)

PETS

Even the strangest of pets provides a child with interest, responsibility and companionship. During the animistic stage of development animals will be endowed with all sorts of human qualities and therefore provide near-human company without reciprocal demands. Although the keeping of a pet will provide additional work for parents, this should be accepted as being well worthwhile. The child should be encouraged to undertake some of the responsibilities but too much should not be demanded of him. The pet must be a pleasure for everybody.

Though dogs and cats are the most obvious and probably most interesting household pets, almost any animal can fill this role. Dangerous pets such as poisonous snakes, scorpions, etc., should be strongly discouraged but depending upon the type of home and the interest of the child, the range is wide open — from a foal to a beetle. In general, mammals are more interesting than other creatures, and apart from dogs and cats there are rabbits, guinea pigs, hamsters and mice. If such pets are allowed to breed this will provide considerable instruction in reproductive processes. Birds, such as budgies, are attractive pets for more cramped living conditions. Fish can be interesting but are hardly cuddly. Reptiles such as snakes, lizards and tortoises have limited popularity with parents. Invertebrates are too transient.

Are there any dangers from pets? Even docile dogs and cats can inflict bites and scratches and children should be warned not to tease or frighten their pets because of the risk of significant injury. Dogs harbour hookworms, and contact with their faeces can cause larva migrans — creeping eruption or sandworm — due to invasion of the skin by the larvae of the worm. This causes severe itching and scratching but the larva lives only a matter of weeks. Similar larvae very occasionally spread deeper, invading particularly the liver and causing significant fever and ill health, this condition being known as visceral larva migrans. It is, however, very rare. In sheep-farming areas the dog tapeworm causes hydatid cysts in the sheep and these may also occur in man.

Cats may cause cat scratch disease, which is a specific infection causing enlargement and abscess formation of the lymph nodes draining the site of the scratch. Cats are also the main transmitters of toxoplasmosis, which is occasionally transmitted during pregnancy to the foetus, causing brain damage and blindness. Both cats and dogs as well as other furry animals are common causes of allergy. In spite of these possible drawbacks pets are decidedly to be encouraged.

PHENYLKETONURIA

This is one of the commonest congenital disorders of metabolism, resulting from an inability to break down one of the essential amino acids, phenylalanine, which therefore accumulates and which has a toxic effect, particularly on brain cells, causing mental deficiency. The disease is rare (about 1:20 000), but incidence varies. In southern Africa it is extremely uncommon. The disease is readily detectable by simple chemical tests, and routine screening is performed in many countries. If treated early with a low phenylalanine diet, affected children can be normal and it may not be necessary to continue the diet beyond the age of about 12 years. PKU is inherited as a Mendelian recessive and the risk to subsequent children is therefore 1:4.

PHIMOSIS

This is a narrowing of the foreskin to a degree sufficient to preclude its retraction over the glans of the penis. This is a normal state in small boys (see *circumcision), but persistent phimosis is usually due to scarring as the result of ill-advised, forceful retraction in infancy. True phimosis has to be corrected surgically.

PHOTOTHERAPY

Jaundice in new-born babies is frequently treated by exposing the baby to strong light with a particular wave length, which converts the bile to harmless products that are more readily excreted. Because the procedure is harmless it tends perhaps to be overused. The baby's eyes are covered for protection but he is otherwise left naked in order to profit maximally from the exposure to light. Apart from some looseness of the stools there appears to be no side effect. Phototherapy is seldom required for more than 2 to 3 days and is discontinued as soon as the level of bile in the blood has reached a safe figure. After discontinuing phototherapy there is usually slight increase in jaundice but this rebound effect is normal and need not cause you concern.

PHYSIOTHERAPY

In children, physiotherapy is used mainly in the management of cerebral palsy and for certain chronic chest conditions. The physiotherapist is an extremely important member of the team managing cerebral palsy, and the physical rehabilitative programme is largely in her hands. The programme will almost certainly have to be continued at home in order to achieve the best results.

In chronic chest disease where there is an accumulation of secretions, physiotherapy helps in their removal. Though often employed, it has little place in the management of conditions such as pneumonia and asthma.

PICA (DIRT-EATING)

This is a not uncommon habit in small children, to be distinguished from the normal universal tasting exploits of the infant. The child with pica deliberately eats non-food substances such as soil, pebbles, paper, wood, coal, etc. Pica has been related to iron deficiency and the association is strong enough to warrant appropriate blood tests in any child with this symptom. Often correction of the anaemia corrects the pica. The condition may also be associated with worms because the child who eats sand is more likely to pick up worms. It is uncommon for the dirt-eating child actually to poison himself, as his peculiar tastes are usually consistent, the sand-eater eating sand and the coal-eater eating coal. Indiscriminate pica is more characteristic of the severely retarded child.

Pica is occasionally found in adults. I had one patient who solemnly cooked herself a plate of sand each morning for breakfast. Fortunately she did not inflict this habit on her family.

PIGEON-TOES

Many children in the early months of walking tend to toe-in, and this tendency has been increased by the fashion of nursing babies in the prone position (i.e. tummy down) in which the feet are inevitably encouraged to turn either in or out. As a rule the condition corrects itself spontaneously and no treatment is required. Should you feel, however, that your child's deformity is of a degree requiring medical evaluation, by all means take him to your doctor.

PITUITARY GLAND

This small structure situated at the base of the brain secretes a wide variety of hormones. Many of these control the functions of the other endocrine glands, e.g. the thyroid, adrenals and the gonads, particularly the ovaries. Other hormones have different targets; for example prolactin stimulates lactation of the breast, growth hormone stimulates general body growth and anti-diuretic hormone influences the absorption of water by the kidney tubules. Just as the pituitary controls the secretion of other glands, so its own function is to a great extent regulated by the neighbouring part of the brain known as the hypothalamus.

Pituitary deficiency may involve most or all of the pituitary hormones or there may be only single hormone involvement, e.g. growth hormone, which will produce physical stunting. Such deficiency may be congenital or it may result from pathology of the gland, such as tumour formation. Fortunately, disturbances of pituitary function are rare.

PLACENTA

This remarkable organ serves as the baby's digestive tract, lungs, liver and kidneys during intra-uterine existence, allowing exchanges of nutrients and oxygen from mother to baby and of waste products in the reverse direction. It consists of innumerable leaf-like villi, each with a blood supply from the baby, floating in a pool of circulating maternal blood. Placental insufficiency is usually manifested by poor foetal growth, and in such cases tests of placental function are usually performed and pregnancy terminated if these suggest that the baby is at risk. Babies suffering from placental insufficiency are usually 'light for dates' or 'small for gestational age' (SGA) and tend to be thin at birth but with good weight gain thereafter.

The placenta is usually situated in the upper part of the uterus and is therefore expelled after the baby in the third stage of labour. Occasionally the placenta is situated lower down and is then known as a placenta praevia. This may cause bleeding during pregnancy. Nowadays the position of the placenta is readily determined by scanning.

PLASTIC

Though a product of only the last 30 to 40 years, plastics have become such an important part of the modern world that it is difficult to envisage life without them. They are generally inert substances, and poisoning therefore need not be feared. For children, however, certain plastic products do have their dangers.

Plastic bags have caused numerous deaths. A small child is always tempted to pull such a bag over his head and this may give rise to very rapid suffocation. Never therefore leave plastic bags in the vicinity of small children.

Plastic pants are useful as additional waterproof protection but may give rise to excessive moisture retention and therefore predispose to napkin rashes.

Plastic toys are in general both safe and non-allergic. The main danger is that small portions of plastic may be inhaled, such items being the second commonest foreign body extracted from the lungs. Toys for small children should therefore be sturdy and non-chewable.

PNEUMONIA

There are two main types of lung inflammation — bronchopneumonia and lobar or segmental pneumonia. Both types occur in children.

Bronchopneumonia. This is an extension of bronchitis, and because it spreads via the bronchial tubes the pneumonia is patchy and diffuse. The basic infection is often due to a respiratory virus, with bacteria acting as secondary invaders. Such pneumonia is common in measles and, particularly in African children, may be extremely severe and frequently fatal.

Bronchopneumonia tends to occur at the extremes of life when resistance to infection is poor, whereas lobar pneumonia more frequently affects healthy adults. The initial virus infection reduces resistance still further and allows the secondarily invading germs to gain a foothold. A variety of micro-organisms therefore may be involved in causing bronchopneumonia. The condition is recognised by the severe cough, usually accompanied by significant fever and raised respiratory rate. A child with such symptoms should be seen by a doctor. Treatment is primarily by administering appropriate antibiotics likely to deal with the germs concerned. Oxygen may be necessary for the very distressed child with laboured breathing. Most children, however, can be managed satisfactorily at home.

Lobar pneumonia. This is usually due to the pneumococcal germ but may on occasions be due to other organisms. Spread occurs not by the bronchial tubes but by contiguity of lung tissue. Such spread occurs rapidly, and within a short while a segment or lobe or sometimes more than one lobe of the lung is involved. The patient is acutely ill with very high fever, rapid breathing, often with a catch in the breath, and if the pleura becomes inflamed there may be pain which is accentuated by the dry coughing. Adults may cough up a slightly bloodstained 'rusty' sputum but children always swallow any secretions they produce. Sometimes this type of pneumonia is difficult to detect and the child may present simply with an unexplained high fever, the cause of which is only apparent on X-ray examination. Other cases may present with *meningismus, and this is particularly the case with right upper lobe pneumonias.

A particularly unpleasant type of pneumonia caused by the staphylococcus afflicts small children, typically between the ages of 6 months and 2 years, but sometimes later. The condition starts as a lobar pneumonia but is rapidly complicated by inflammation of the pleura, with pus forming around the lung, and often by abscess formation within the lung. Staphylococcal pneumonia takes a long time to heal and requires prolonged antibiotic treatment but eventually recovery is almost always complete.

Pneumococcal pneumonia responds well to simple penicillin but a wide variety of antibiotics may be used in treatment, usually with rapid and excellent effect.

Atypical pneumonias may be due to several different types of micro-organism and specific diagnosis is often difficult. Chronic pneumonia is most commonly due to tuberculosis and this condition always has to be suspected in cases that do not respond promptly and completely to antibiotic treatment.

POISONING

Nearly all poisoning is preventable — in retrospect. The difficulty lies in anticipating the remarkable ability of the small child to discover the most unlikely ingestants. Always therefore keep anything potentially dangerous well out of reach of small children.

Essential medicines should be locked up, and out-of-date medicines should be discarded (but not where a child will find them). Household cleaning agents should be kept above even a climbing child's reach and garden chemicals such as insecticides should be carefully locked away. With the variety of chemicals available in the modern world the possibilities for poisoning are vast. Natural plant poisons are also a menace and children should be taught from the earliest age not to taste anything of which they are unsure. Remember that small children's tastes do not necessarily conform to your own. You might not be tempted to eat a handful of iron tablets or swallow half a cup of paraffin but to the small child these appear to be delicacies, delicacies which unfortunately may be fatal.

In cases of suspected poisoning what should you do?

(1) Try to identify the poison as accurately as possible and the quantity consumed. Do not waste undue time on this however if, as is probable, the poison should be removed. Make the child vomit as soon as possible, for the stomach may empty very rapidly and once the poison has reached the intestine it cannot be removed. Vomiting, if it is indicated, should therefore be induced promptly.

(2) If the poison is an extreme irritant such as a strong alkali or acid, phenol or creosote (all of which may damage the gullet while being vomited) or if it is a volatile substance such as petrol, benzine, paraffin, turpentine, etc. (all of which may damage the lungs by being inhaled during vomiting) vomiting should not be induced but the child may be given a drink of bland fluid such as milk.

(3) In other cases induce vomiting promptly. The child should be given a drink first in order to fill the stomach and dilute the poison. Lie him on his tummy over your knees with a bowl to catch the vomitus and tickle his throat with a finger until vomiting occurs. The procedure should then be repeated to make sure that the stomach is emptied. The giving of emetic drinks such as strong salt solution or mustard in water is usually unsuccessful and the finger is more reliable. Your doctor or hospital may empty the stomach by giving ipecacuanha or by passing a large tube into the stomach and washing it out.

(4) Contact your doctor or hospital in order to get further advice. With certain poisons the child may well need a period of observation. If you take the child to the doctor or hospital take the remnants of the poison with you, or if this is impossible and the nature of the poison is unknown, take a sample of the vomit.

(5) Never assume that because the child appears immediately well he will remain so. Some poisons have a delayed effect, for example on the liver or on the blood, and symptoms in such cases may occur only very much later.

Most of the larger hospitals now have Poison Centres from which detailed information can be obtained and expert advice received. Your doctor will probably make use of such a centre if he should have any doubts. See also *food poisoning.

POLIOMYELITIS

Since the advent of an effective vaccine this disease should be obsolete, but unfortunately it still exists, occurring typically in summer outbreaks. The condition is due to 3 distinct viruses which invade the nerve cells in the spinal cord, producing paralysis of muscles supplied by the affected segments.

The disease is spread either by direct contact through droplet infection or by the faecal–oral route as the result of poor hygiene. Incubation period is 1 to 3 weeks.

In most cases the illness is a minor one with non-specific symptoms such as fever, poor appetite, headache, lassitude and mild diarrhoea. If the virus spreads to the central nervous system the patient may display meningitic signs with vomiting and neck and back stiffness. Polio used to be a common cause of viral (aseptic) meningitis.

Only a small proportion of persons infected go on to the third stage of paralysis. This tends to affect groups of muscles, with very variable distribution. If the diaphragm is involved, breathing becomes impossible and the patient will die unless artificial respiration can be maintained until recovery takes place. Sometimes parts of the brain are involved, a very serious complication. If paralysis occurs it usually reaches its maximum extent within 48 hours. The degree of recovery is unpredictable and may extend over many months. Once the acute stage is over, physiotherapy helps to rebuild paralysed muscles, but if the nerve supply has been destroyed there is no way in which this can be restored.

The management of poliomyelitis therefore is preventive. It is essential that all babies be immunised against this dread disease. If this could be accomplished the virus would probably be eliminated, as has been the case with smallpox.

PORT WINE STAIN

These disfiguring blemishes are unfortunately most common on the face. Unlike the strawberry naevus the port wine stain not only does not disappear but often tends to become more marked and more raised as the child ages. Occasionally it is associated with vascular abnormalities inside the skull. Modern cosmetics skilfully applied help considerably to improve appearances.

POSSETING

This is a term given to the baby who habitually vomits small quantities of milk after every feed. The vomiting is accompanied by no distress (except on the part of mother, who always has a stained dress and who is perpetually cleaning the carpet). This type of vomiting is seldom influenced by any maneouvre such as changing the feed, although thickening with a feed thickener or cereal sometimes helps. The baby thrives satisfactorily and happily but usually continues to vomit for most of the first year.

Simple posseting has to be distinguished from other more serious causes of repeated vomiting such as abnormalities of the gullet. If therefore the baby is not thriving satisfactorily your doctor should be consulted and he may think it wise to have X-ray studies performed. In the case of the happy, thriving baby, however, no such investigation is necessary. See *vomiting.

POST-MATURITY

The baby who outstays his intra-uterine welcome beyond the 41st or 42nd week of pregnancy usually displays features associated with placental insufficiency. He tends to lose weight, becoming long and thin with loose, dry skin. Meconium is often passed in utero, causing staining of the skin and cord. The babies often appear pale with blue hands and feet. The skin tends to crack and peel but once peeling has occurred the underlying skin is normal.

Post-mature babies may occasionally die in utero and most obstetricians therefore will not allow a pregnancy to continue long beyond term. The passage of meconium and its possible aspiration may cause respiratory problems. Post-mature babies are liable to hypoglycaemia (low blood-sugar levels) and should therefore be given feeds from shortly after delivery.

POSTURE

It is normal for the gangly, pre-adolescent child to have a rather drooping posture and some adolescent girls conscious of their breast development may deliberately adopt a droop to lessen the conspicuousness of puberty. These days, however, the tendency is more towards flaunting rather than attempting to hide such female attributes. Some excessively tall children may try to reduce their height by adopting a poor posture. Rather than nagging such individuals it is better to boost their self-confidence — this will do far more to improve their posture than will perpetual irritation, which usually has a reverse effect, particularly on the adolescent. Most children's posture will improve spontaneously and drill-sergeant tactics are usually not required.

POT TRAINING

See *toilet-training

POTASSIUM

This is one of the essential minerals, found predominantly inside the body cells, as opposed to sodium, which is found largely outside in the extra-cellular fluids. Potassium often becomes depleted in diarrhoeal states, in wasting conditions and in protein malnutrition. Potassium therefore usually has to be replaced in such conditions.

PREMATURITY (see also *low birth-weight babies)

The premature (or, better, pre-term) baby is one born before the 37th week of pregnancy. In former times, a birth weight of 2,5 kg or less was adopted as standard for prematurity but this proved unsatisfactory because of the great variability in birth mass. It is of course often not possible to determine with exactitude the length of gestation but the combination of adequate antenatal care plus the baby's features at birth should give a fair assessment of gestational age. The incidence of premature birth varies to some extent from community to community but averages about 6–7 per cent of all births. Babies born before the 26th week of pregnancy are not likely to survive, because of inadequate lung development, but the outlook improves with advancing gestational age, until at 36 weeks the survival rate should be little different from that of the full-term baby.

There are many causes of premature birth. There is a distinct relationship with socio-economic status and also with the quality of antenatal care. Maternal diseases such as infections, kidney disease, diabetes, syphilis and malaria may predispose to premature delivery, and obstetrical problems such as toxaemia of pregnancy, bleeding, excessive liquor, multiple pregnancy and incompetence of the cervix of the uterus are all associated with premature birth. Many cases, however, are without explanation. Sometimes of course the baby is deliberately delivered prematurely in order to remove it from a hostile intra-uterine environment, as in placental insufficiency, Rhesus incompatibility, etc.

Apart from his small size the premature baby has certain physical characteristics which are apparent in proportion to the degree of prematurity. The head is relatively large compared with the rest of the body, the skin is delicate and thin and in the case of extreme prematurity has a gelatinous appearance. Downy hair known as lanugo is present over the back and shoulder regions. During the first few days the baby appears puffy because of excess of fluid and when this is lost the baby appears thinner than ever. There is little subcutaneous fat. The muscles are feeble and the baby tends therefore to lie in a floppy position with the limbs outstretched rather than in the flexed foetal position characteristic of the normal newborn. Movements are infrequent, jerky and feeble. The reflex behaviour exhibited by the full-term baby, such as sucking and rooting, may be absent or very poorly exhibited. Even the smallest babies, however, may cry quite vigorously.

Significant prematurity exposes the baby to many dangers. Because of the limited amount of fat and generally low metabolism such a baby has great difficulty in maintaining a normal body temperature. He is also unable to adjust to excessively high temperatures. Small babies are therefore usually placed in incubators, which will maintain the body heat and still allow continuous observation. Humidity is also controlled so that excessive evaporation of fluid is avoided. The main danger in the early days is related to the poor development of the lungs with lack of a special chemical substance, known as surfactant, which allows the lungs to expand at birth and to maintain their expansion. Premature lungs lacking surfactant tend to collapse and remain solid so that air exchange is impaired and oxygenation difficult to maintain. This condition, known as the *respiratory distress syndrome or, because of pathology usually present, hyaline membrane disease, is a major cause of mortality. Babies severely affected may require artificial ventilation for several days. This, however, carries its own hazards though the results of such management are, in general, good and the baby as a rule is left with no after-effects.

Jaundice is common in premature babies, who are particularly susceptible to the toxic effects of bilirubin and who therefore are treated either with phototherapy or by means of exchange blood transfusion at lower levels of bilirubin than are full-term babies.

During the last few months of pregnancy, protective antibodies pass across the placenta from the mother to the foetus. The premature baby, lacking such substances, is more prone to infection and therefore requires extra protection from contamination. He also has poor reserves of iron and there is a tendency therefore for premature babies to become anaemic. Extra vitamins are also necessary.

Feeding the premature baby presents considerable difficulties because of his feeble sucking abilities, poor swallowing and a tendency to regurgitate and choke. Very small babies therefore are usually fed intravenously for a few days. If sucking and swallowing are poor they may then be fed by a tube passed into the stomach until it is safe to feed them by bottle. The constitution of the feed is important, for kidney function is impaired and the baby has difficulty in correcting an excess of water or salt. The breast milk secreted by mothers giving birth prematurely has a somewhat higher protein content than does that of full-term mothers and is probably the ideal food for the premature baby.

Because the blood vessels are extremely delicate and relatively unsupported, the premature baby tends to bleed easily. This is a particular hazard as far as the brain is concerned, for bleeding may be induced not only by the trauma of delivery but also by oxygen lack. This is common as a consequence of the baby's respiratory difficulties, not only the result of lung immaturity but also of immaturity of the nervous control of respiration. Premature babies tend to have irregular breathing, often with long pauses, and any form of disturbance may cause breathing arrest. They should therefore be handled as little as possible. Oxygen may be required but excessive oxygenation has to be avoided because of the danger to the eyes (see *oxygen).

Home care of the premature baby. If premature birth is expected, every attempt should be made to get the mother to a hospital for delivery but if this is impossible and the baby is born at home the same principles of care apply. The baby must not be allowed to chill. It should be wrapped in warm blankets and placed in a warm place. Maintenance of breathing is essential. It is unlikely that facilities will exist for sucking secretions out of the airway but drainage can be encouraged by turning the baby face down and gently squeezing the chest. Once breathing is established the baby should be handled as little as possible. If, however, breathing should cease, the same manoeuvre can be repeated and if the baby does not start breathing again but becomes progressively blue then mouth-to-mouth respiration should be attempted by placing the mouth over the baby's nose and mouth and giving a few sharp puffs with the floor of the mouth and tongue and without blowing from the lungs, as overinflation may cause severe damage. If respiratory difficulties persist, or if the baby is very small and feeble, immediate transfer to hospital should be arranged. This is best accomplished by a skilled ambulance team equipped with a portable incubator and resuscitative facilities.

The more vigorous babies can be managed successfully at home and may take breastfeeds well from the beginning. Others may require bottle-feeding for a time, but mother can express her milk and keep her lactation going in the hope that the baby will eventually breastfeed.

Babies unable to suck can sometimes be fed by spoon or pipette but this is extremely dangerous because of the danger of choking. Such babies are best managed in hospital. Feeding will initially have to be rather frequent but intervals can be extended as the baby progresses and the feeds increase in volume.

Progress of the premature baby. Physical growth is often initially somewhat disappointing. The baby loses a good deal of fluid and therefore a fair amount of weight, and birth weight is slow to be regained, this often taking up to 3 weeks or more. Thereafter, however, he may gain at more than average rate. It may be 2 or 3 years before he catches up in size to his full-term peers. Allowance must always be made for the degree of prematurity in assessing developmental progress. A baby born 6 weeks prematurely cannot be expected to smile at 8 weeks of age. It is more likely to be 12 weeks. If there have been no complications, the outlook for the pre-term baby is good, but the very small babies who may have suffered oxygen lack or bleeding into the brain have inevitably a relatively high incidence of neurological troubles such as cerebral palsy. Heroic efforts to resuscitate and maintain such babies therefore may not always be justified.

Because of the soft skull bones and the inability of the baby to move his relatively large head, the skull often assumes a peculiar shape, being flattened from side to side. This, however, corrects itself with the passage of time. Premature babies may develop anaemia and vitamin deficiencies, particularly rickets, but such conditions should be prevented by administration of iron and extra vitamins. All in all, with modern management the outlook for the premature baby is thoroughly good.

PRE-SCHOOL EDUCATION
See *nursery school

PRE-TERM BABY
See *prematurity

PRICKLY HEAT
Also known as miliaria. This condition is due to irritation of the skin as the result of retained sweat secretion within the sweat glands. It is usually due to overclothing. The rash is most prominent around the neck, on the face and scalp, upper chest, and groins and armpits. Secondary infection may occur. The essential in treatment is to keep the baby cool and avoid heating and irritating garments such as wool and nylon next to the skin. Calamine lotion may be applied as a cooling and soothing agent.

PROTEIN
These complex chemicals are fundamental to life. They consist of long chains of amino acids which constitute, as it were, the building blocks. There is a continuous turnover of protein in the body. Some of the constituent amino acids can be synthesised from simpler products but some have to be taken in in the food, the so-called essential amino acids. High quality protein is obtained from meat, fish, eggs, cheese and legumes such as beans. Brown bread is also a good source of protein.

The body proteins can be divided into two main classes — albumin and globulin, the latter being of larger molecular size (see *albumin, *globulin). The globulins can be further subdivided (alpha, beta, gamma, etc.). Antibodies which protect against infection belong to the gamma class (see *immuno globulin).

Because protein-rich foods are expensive, protein malnutrition is common (see *malnutrition).

PUBERTY
The changes of puberty, both physical and emotional, are probably still fairly fresh in most parents' minds. What may be less generally understood is the tremendous variability in the age of puberty. This can cause considerable strain on the early developer and great anxiety to the later developer.

Pubertal changes in girls. The first sign of approaching puberty is usually a growth spurt, which commences on average at about 10½ years of age and which continues for about 4 years. The first sign of actual pubertal development is the appearance of breast buds, followed shortly by the appearance of pubic hair. It is common for one breast to start growing before the other and a degree of eventual asymmetry is not rare. The genitalia enlarge and the first period occurs about 2 years after initial changes. The duration of puberty, however, is extremely variable, taking anything from 18 months to 5 or 6 years. Breast buds sometimes occur long before other pubertal changes. In a small proportion of girls, pubic hair growth precedes breast development. The first period may occur any time between 10 and 16 years. Periods are often irregular at first and menstruation does not inevitably denote fertility at this stage. For practical purposes, however, it should be assumed.

Pubertal changes in boys. The first sign of maturation in boys is enlargement of the testicles, which commences any time between 9½ and 13½ years of age and which precedes enlargement of the penis by about a year. Pubic hair begins to grow shortly after the initial testicular enlargement and the growth spurt commences shortly after. Axillary and facial hair appears about 2 years later, when the voice usually breaks. About midway through puberty there is often enlargement of one or both breasts, with some discomfort, and the swelling is occasionally of a degree sufficient to cause embarrassment. It usually however regresses completely. As in girls, the process of puberty may last anything from 2 to 5 years.

Precocious puberty. This is a rare condition, though partial pubertal changes, e.g. breast enlargement, may occur as a normal variant in young girls. True precocious puberty is a matter for concern and your doctor should be consulted.

Delayed puberty. This is usually a normal variant but it may be associated with endocrine glandular deficiency, particularly pituitary deficiency, and distortions of puberty may occur with other abnormalities, e.g. of the gonads. These are complex conditions requiring elaborate investigation.

Psychological problems associated with puberty

The stresses of adolescence will probably be well remembered by most parents. The achievement of adulthood requires 4 basic accomplishments:

(1) the achievement of independence;
(2) the mastery of sexuality;
(3) the mastery of aggression;
(4) achievement of an adequate adult identity.

Most adolescents successfully accomplish these requirements but usually not without some degree of trauma to themselves and to other members of the family, particularly parents. Dealing with an adolescent requires considerable patience and understanding. On the other hand too much patience and understanding and, particularly, excessive permissiveness may actually hamper the adolescent's progress. Conflict is only to be expected when physical and financial dependence extends, as it often must, well beyond physical maturation. The child must be allowed to explore independently, form his own opinions and as far as possible make his own decisions, even while parents are still holding the financial reins.

There are obviously limits beyond which behaviour is unacceptable, and these should be well defined, but within such limits the child should be granted as much independence as possible. He will respect you more for trust than for severity, more for example than for preaching. His clumsy demonstrations of independence, be these in the form of hair style, clothing or behaviour, may be extremely irritating but should be borne with good humour, for with increased maturity he will see their absurdity.

Adolescent sexuality cannot be brushed under the carpet but should be openly discussed, and healthy and responsible attitudes fostered.

Aggressiveness is best sublimated as desire to achieve. In the non-achiever it tends to find its outlet in delinquency and gang warfare. Some form of achievement recognition is essential to everyone, hence the importance of encouraging whatever even small abilities your child may display.

Dealing with the adolescent is not always easy but it should always be characterised by caring; and for much of the time it can be fun.

PUNISHMENT (see also *discipline)

To deny a place for punishment in the rearing of children would be unrealistic, for it is an effective modifier of behaviour if used appropriately. To be effective, however, it should be used infrequently and only after a preliminary warning. It should be appropriate to the misdemeanour and follow it closely in time so that the two are clearly associated. It should not be over-severe or vindictive, or administered to relieve your own feelings rather than to correct the child's behaviour.

Physical punishment. This should be kept within very strict limits. There is no objection to the occasional light smack administered after a warning if unacceptable behaviour persists. Such punishment has the virtue of immediacy, ease of administration and usually effectiveness. Neither parent nor child feels bad about it and happy relationships are soon restored. Carried to excess, however, physical punishment not only loses its effectiveness, and therefore demands increasingly severe applications, but it becomes degrading to both parties and it is destructive of normal loving relationships. Particularly objectionable is the belting by father when he returns home, for some crime committed during the day, which mother should immediately have corrected.

When administering a spank it is better to use the hand rather than an implement of any sort, for it is not necessary to hurt the child in order to make clear your displeasure.

The use of corporal punishment in schools is not to be recommended, although there are times when it might be the best solution to wiping the slate clean and starting again. Generally speaking, it should be possible to correct children without resort to violence.

Other forms of punishment. 'Time out' is an effective corrective measure for the young child, who resents being deprived of his interesting activities. Two to five minutes spent in a particular chair contemplating his crime is usually sufficient to ensure that it is not repeated. Banishing him to his room is at times the only way of enforcing a period of healing separation but remember that your child's room is his haven and it should not become a dungeon. Imprisonment in the toilet or bathroom is unnecessarily frightening for the small child but there are times when there may be no alternative. Such punishment should be of short duration.

Deprivation of privileges is sometimes appropriate but it tends often to be rather too protracted, causing unnecessary resentment and continued family friction.

Let it be said again that, to be effective, punishment should be immediate, of short duration, non-vindictive and appropriate. It should also be inevitable. If a warning has been issued and the crime is repeated, then punishment must follow, otherwise the child will never take you seriously. But always be sure to give the warning first.

PURGATIVES (see also *constipation and *laxatives)

Most laxatives in high doses will produce purging. There is a widespread primitive belief that if the medicine is 'strong' it must inevitably be good, and purgatives therefore occupy a prominent place in the pharmacopoeia of the traditional healer. Purging is in fact never necessary and especially in children it is decidedly contraindicated. Gentle laxatives have a part to play in the management of severe constipation but they should not be used as a ritual.

PUS

This is the debris left after an inflammatory reaction has resulted in the destruction of a certain amount of normal tissue. It consists of the residues of the dead cells as well as the teeming numbers of inflammatory cells which have streamed into the infected area to do battle with the invading germs. An accumulation of pus forms an abscess. Most abscesses are due to infection with germs such as the staphylococcus and streptococcus, but many other types of organism may be responsible. Tuberculosis produces a lower-grade inflammatory reaction and the resulting abscesses are therefore known as cold abscesses.

Pus in any quantity has to find its way to the exterior and be discharged. Surgical drainage of abscesses therefore is usually indicated in order to speed resolution. Smaller quantities of pus will gradually be absorbed.

A purulent discharge may also occur from open surfaces, e.g. the eyes, nose and sinuses, and in females from the vagina. Pus is therefore a normal product of an inflammatory response and should not be regarded as something frightful. Purulent discharges should if possible be kept confined, however, so as to avoid contamination of other areas by the infecting germs.

PYELITIS

Inflammation of the urinary system may occur at various levels. Infection confined to the bladder is known as cystitis. When, as commonly happens if there is urinary stasis, infection spreads up to the pelvis of the kidney, the condition is then known as pyelitis. If the infection actually invades the kidney tissue then the condition is known as pyelonephritis (see *kidney).

Pyelitis is a common disorder. It may afflict small babies, particularly when there is some form of obstruction to the urinary flow, and a major predisposing cause is ureteric reflux. Older children and adults will usually experience some disturbances of urination such as pain, burning or increased frequency, and the urine may be murky or bloodstained. There is usually a high fever, often associated with rigors (shivering attacks), and there may be pain in the back, flanks or abdomen. In small children the symptoms are much less characteristic, with fever, perhaps with a febrile convulsion, vomiting, diarrhoea, fretfulness and very occasionally jaundice. All children with unexplained fever should have the urine examined.

Pyelitis is treated with appropriate antibacterial drugs, and long courses of treatment are not required unless there is frequently relapsing trouble. Once the infection has been cleared it is essential to look for a predisposing cause and your doctor will therefore probably want to have X-ray studies performed.

Pyelitis is particularly common in pregnant women and there is some evidence that if this occurs early in pregnancy it may have a damaging effect on the foetus. If therefore you should have symptoms suggestive of pyelitis, report the matter promptly to your doctor.

PYLORIC STENOSIS

This condition occurs in about 0,3 per cent of white babies but is decidedly less common in African and Indian babies. Boys are affected 4 times as frequently as girls. The dominant symptom is vomiting, which commences usually 2–4 weeks after birth and becomes increasingly forceful so that ultimately every feed is rejected in projectile fashion, often shooting out up to a metre or more. The condition is due to thickening of the muscle at the lower end of the stomach, which then does not permit the stomach contents to pass on into the bowel. The stomach, in an attempt to overcome the obstruction, contracts very forcefully and these contractions can usually be seen as waves passing across the upper part of the abdomen from left to right. If your doctor suspects this condition, he will examine the baby's abdomen in an attempt to feel the lump formed by the thickened muscle. This is best done at a feed and particularly after a vomit.

The treatment of choice for pyloric stenosis is surgical. The tight muscle is divided and the obstruction thereby relieved. Following operation the baby's feeds are stepped up progressively over about 36 hours, but a breastfed baby may be returned immediately to the breast. The results of surgical treatment are excellent.

In cases presenting somewhat later, after the age of 6 weeks, and if the baby's general condition remains good, medical treatment with antispasmodic drugs may be attempted, although most doctors would proceed to surgery as soon as the diagnosis is made. Medical treatment if attempted should not be pursued when symptoms persist for more than a couple of days, so if your doctor embarks on this line of treatment keep in close touch with him and report promptly if things are not satisfactory.

There is a familial incidence of pyloric stenosis, particularly in the children of mothers who have had the condition, so if your baby is vomiting and there is a family history of pyloric stenosis be sure to mention this fact to your doctor.

Q FEVER

This is an infection by a rickettsia organism (similar to that causing *tick bite fever), usually acquired by man from other animals. The organism invades the lungs, causing an atypical type of pneumonia. The disease responds to treatment with tetracycline antibiotics.

QUARANTINE

This is the period for which a patient suffering from an infectious disease continues to shed the causative agent and is therefore capable of spreading the condition to contacts. In general this starts with the onset of first symptoms and ends with recovery, but in, for example, intestinal infections such as poliomyelitis and typhoid fever, the causative virus or bacterium may continue to be shed for some time. There is nowadays much less fuss about quarantine than there used to be. Some enlightened schools no longer isolate cases of the minor infectious diseases such as chickenpox, mumps and rubella at all, but this is not the general policy of education departments. If in doubt, therefore, check with the school.

QUINSY

This is a serious complication of tonsillar infection in which an abscess forms in the neighbourhood of the tonsil, with swelling, difficulty in swallowing and a liability to choke. It is rare nowadays because of the early treatment of tonsillitis with penicillin. Treatment of quinsy requires surgical drainage of the abscess as well as appropriate antibiotics, and hospital management until the condition has subsided.

RABIES

This dread disease is caused by a specific virus which afflicts the brain and which is also found in the salivary glands. It is primarily a condition of other animals and is spread to man by their bites. Almost any animal may spread the disease, but dogs are the main carriers to the human. An affected animal will always behave in peculiar fashion, and such animals are therefore to be strictly avoided. In areas where rabies occurs, household pets should always be immunised

If a child is bitten by a suspected rabid animal the animal should be kept under safe observation for the development of symptoms, and if it sickens it should be killed and the brain sent for examination so that a definite diagnosis can be made. If the animal is found to be rabid, or if circumstances preclude such examination but sufficient suspicion attaches to the bite to make treatment a wise precaution, then the child should be submitted to vaccine therapy. Fortunately modern vaccines are almost totally safe, especially when compared with the older vaccines, which often produced severe reactions.

Symptoms begin a variable time after the bite, anything from 2 weeks up to 1 year but averaging 20 to 40 days. Once symptoms have appeared, treatment is ineffective. It is essential therefore that vaccine therapy be commenced as soon as possible. An initial dose of serum (human anti-rabies immunoglobulin) is given in order to convey some transient passive immunity, and active immunisation is achieved by 5 or 6 doses of human diploid cell rabies vaccine given at increasing intervals over 1 to 3 months. If the suspected animal does not die within 10 days it could not have been rabid at the time of the bite and in such cases vaccine treatment can be stopped. It it obviously important that you report to your doctor immediately should your child be bitten by an animal capable of conveying this terrible disease.

RASHES

The skin, being such a visible organ, probably gives rise to more anxiety than any other. The skin may react to various insults in a similar way so that identical rashes may be due to physical irritation, infections or sensitivity reactions. Often it is not possible to identify with certainty the cause of a skin rash.

Rashes in young babies

Many babies in the early days of life may develop an extensive rash (urticaria neonatorum) seen predominantly on the trunk and consisting of blotchy weals with often a small white spot at the centre. The spots come and go and may persist for 2 or 3 days. They appear to be associated with no discomfort and the rash requires no treatment. It is assumed to be due to the change of environment from warm intra-uterine bath to dry exterior.

Many babies develop a mild spottiness of the face in the early weeks, such eruptions usually clearing spontaneously without specific treatment. There is no point in changing the baby's feed. However tempting it might be to ascribe such rashes to the milk, this is rarely justified. Eczema, however, is a different problem.

Heat rashes are common and are usually due to overclothing. They affect particularly the neck, shoulders, back and axillary regions but may be fairly widespread. They are best treated by exposing the baby as much as possible and applying only light cotton garments. Simple calamine lotion is a suitable application.

Napkin rashes are very common but their specific distribution makes their cause clear (see *napkin rash).

Rashes of the specific infectious diseases

These are usually readily recognisable, though they may be closely imitated by, for example, drug and other sensitivity reactions. For details see *chickenpox, *measles, *roseola, *rubella, *scarlet fever, *tick-bite fever, etc.

Chickenpox. This is not likely to cause confusion, for it is the only infectious disease in which the rash is vesicular, i.e. forms little blisters. The extent of the eruption is very variable but the individual spot is typical, commencing as a tiny blister with reddened base which grows fairly rapidly and which because of its flimsy wall ruptures readily to form a crust. Crops of such lesions occur over many days. The eruption may perhaps be confused with insect bites and with *papular urticaria.

Measles. In this disease the rash appears on about the 4th day of illness, with faint pink spots, first seen behind the ears, spreading over the forehead and face down to the neck and eventually over the whole body. The rash becomes blotchy and the skin is somewhat roughened, enabling the eruption to be felt rather more readily than seen in dark-skinned people.

Roseola infantum. This condition, occurring only in infants, is characterised by a rash which appears after the temperature has subsided, the spots being fairly discrete and smaller than those of measles, apparent first on the trunk and spreading to the arms and neck with only slight involvement of the face and legs. The rash persists for less than a day and leaves no aftermath.

Rubella (German measles). This disease is often difficult to recognise with certainty outside an epidemic. The rash appears about 1 day after the onset of initial symptoms and varies considerably in severity. It is finer than the eruption of measles, commences on the face and progresses to the trunk. The spots are at first discrete but after the first day they may coalesce and cause a generalised reddening somewhat resembling scarlet fever, particularly over the chest. There is no subsequent peeling.

Scarlet fever. After 1 to 3 days of illness a typical red rash is first seen in the neck, armpits and groin regions and rapidly extends to the trunk and the extremities. Apart from the general reddening of the skin there are profuse very fine red spots. The rash does not involve the face; typically the cheeks are flushed and the skin around the mouth remains rather white.

Tick-bite fever. The rash in this condition is very typical, appearing soon after onset of symptoms and consisting of slightly elevated discrete pink spots about

5 mm in diameter, distributed mainly over the limbs and including the palms of the hands and soles of the feet. The other features of the disease make its nature fairly obvious.

For other forms of rash see *eczema, *napkin rashes, *prickly heat, *urticaria, etc.

READING

To encourage reading in children they should be read to from an early age and often. With so much potted entertainment available, reading skills are deteriorating. It is, however, so fundamental a skill that parents who are not perhaps themselves avid readers should do their utmost to instil a love of reading in their children, and this can only be done by reading to them until they are able to fend for themselves. Even very small children enjoy being read to and absorb much more than you might imagine. If you have learnt a foreign language you will realise that one's understanding is far in advance of one's ability of expression. It's the same with a child. Simply because he is not speaking in complicated sentences does not mean that he does not understand them. Choose your reading material so that it is appropriate to his age but let it be stimulating and not too babyish otherwise both of you will become bored. Very small children enjoy rhythm and rhyme no matter how nonsensical the content. They ought, however, to have their reading diets varied with constituents other than simple rhythmic rhyming rubbish.

The older child will tend to follow his own reading tastes but he can be guided and advanced at a more rapid rate than most parents realise. This is not to say that childhood should not be a delight to be enjoyed for itself and not simply regarded as a preparation for adulthood. As far as reading is concerned the accent should be on enjoyment, for only by enjoyment will a child be stimulated to read for himself.

READING DIFFICULTIES

See *dyslexia and *schooling problems

RECTUM

The rectum is the terminal portion of the bowel, in which the faeces are held until they are excreted via the anal canal. A sensation of fullness of the rectum leads to a desire to pass stool. In severely constipated children this sensitivity is to a greater or lesser extent lost, and faeces therefore tend to accumulate. Only by keeping the rectum largely empty, and thus preventing chronic faecal accumulation, is the rectal sensation restored.

Abnormalities of the rectum. Occasionally the anus is imperforate, and the rectum then usually communicates in front with either the urethra in the male infant or with the vagina in baby girls. These abnormalities are complex, depending upon the length of bowel involved, but most are correctible by surgery though in severe cases anal competence cannot be guaranteed.

Hirschsprung's disease is a rare condition in which the nerve supply to the lower bowel is impaired over a varying distance. The paralysed portion of the bowel is unable to propel the faeces onward and constipation results. Cases may present in infancy or much later with chronic constipation and a very distended bowel. Treatment is surgical and consists of removing the defective portion of the bowel, at the same time trying to preserve rectal sensation as far as possible.

Rectal prolapse. Parents are often disconcerted at the sight of a small portion of the mucous lining of the anal canal becoming visible when the child passes a stool. This is quite normal. When the rectum prolapses an appreciable portion of the bowel is expelled through the anus and often does not resolve spontaneously but requires manual replacement. The more the bowel prolapses the more it becomes swollen, and this in turn leads to an increased tendency to prolapse so that a vicious cycle is established. It is important, therefore, to replace any prolapsed bowel immediately and to keep it retained in its proper place, if necessary by strapping the buttocks together. Rectal prolapse is seen most commonly in young children under the age of 5 with malnutrition or inanition, and is usually related to some disturbance of bowel function, either severe constipation or diarrhoea. It may be associated with polyps or with severe whipworm infestation. In such cases the primary cause must obviously be removed. With regular replacement, attention to the child's nutrition and removal of any predisposing factors, the condition usually resolves satisfactorily. Occasionally, however, surgical treatment is necessary.

REFLEXES

When the doctor taps your tendons or scratches your tummy he is testing for certain reflex actions. The baby in the first few months of life exhibits certain primitive reflexes which then disappear. All these are very different entities but basically a reflex is a prompt response to some excitatory stimulus without the intervention of consciousness.

Primitive reflexes (see also *development). The baby at birth exhibits sucking and swallowing reflexes and in addition the rooting reflex, which enables him to find the nipple without this being put directly in his mouth. He exhibits a strong grasp reflex when anything is put in the hand. If held in a walking position he will step out with the walking reflex. In repose with the head turned to one side, the limbs of that side tend to be extended wehreas the opposite limbs are flexed – the tonic neck reflex. If startled in any way he shows the typical Moro response, with grimacing, stretching out of the arms and hands followed by a grasping movement, as if trying to save himself, with similar movements of the legs. All these reflexes normally disappear in the first 2 to 4 months. They are weak or absent in very premature babies but appear as the baby matures. Persistence of primitive reflexes beyond the first few months of life is indicative of abnormality in the central nervous system.

Tendon reflexes. When the tendon of any muscle is tapped, sensory organs within the muscle send impulses via the spinal cord to the nerves supplying that muscle, resulting in a jerk. Some people have very poor tendon reflexes, which can only be demonstrated with some form of augmentation. The absence of tendon reflexes implies some interruption in the nervous reflex arc. Tendon reflexes are characteristically exaggerated in conditions of spasticity associated with disease of the brain, as in cerebral palsy or after a stroke.

Superficial reflexes. Scratching the skin of the abdomen results in a contraction of the underlying muscle. In the male, stimulation of the skin of the groin region and upper thigh results in retraction of the testicle — the cremasteric reflex.

Stroking the outer part of the sole results in a downward movement of the toes. Because the reflex arc is more complex and extends to a higher level than in the case of the tendon reflexes, the superficial reflexes are usually disturbed in states of brain damage.

Conditioned reflexes. When two different stimuli are regularly and repeatedly associated, one stimulus may give rise to the effect normally produced by the other. Pavlov demonstrated this with his famous dogs, who after being presented with food at the ringing of a bell would ultimately salivate with the bell alone. Much of our child training and adaptive behaviour generally depends upon such reflex patterns. Hence the importance of rewarding good behaviour and ignoring the bad.

REGURGITATION

Many babies regurgitate small quantities of milk after nearly every feed. This is associated with no distress except on the part of mother, who smells perpetually sour and who has to keep apologising for the state of the carpet. This type of regurgitation or habitual vomiting, usually associated with a happy, thriving baby, should be completely ignored. It often diminishes as the baby eats more solid foods, and milk thickeners are therefore a popular remedy. Sometimes they work but do not be disappointed if they do not. Eventually, usually towards the end of the first year of life, the regurgitation ceases spontaneously.

More significant vomiting associated with failure to thrive satisfactorily must of course be taken much more seriously. This may be associated with laxity of the lower end of the oesophagus (gullet), enabling food in the stomach to be regurgitated very easily. Such cases are, however, uncommon and in by far the majority of simple regurgitators no abnormality is present. (See also *vomiting.)

REHYDRATION

See *dehydration

RELIGION

A child's beliefs almost always reflect those of his parents and it is seldom that anyone changes his religion. Faith may become more or less ardent but we tend to retain the religion to which we were born. It is wise while instructing your children in your own personal beliefs to imbue also an attitude of tolerance towards other faiths. As your children grow up and question fundamentals more and more, let religious discussion be open, unemotional and unprejudiced so that your children may acquire their faith through understanding and conviction rather than from fear. Many parents drive their children away from themselves by tolerating no religious arguments or questioning. Do not let this tragedy befall you.

RESPIRATORY DISTRESS

Respiratory distress can of course be due to many causes and particularly to any form of obstruction of the respiratory tree, but when doctors speak of the Respiratory Distress Syndrome they refer to a particular condition which affects premature babies and which is one of the major causes of death in such patients. The lungs of the unborn foetus are solid and the airways filled with fluid. With the first few breaths the lungs become expanded with air. The air–fluid interface within the lungs would normally cause severe surface tension problems, leading to almost immediate collapse of the expanded lung alveoli. To overcome this problem the lungs secrete a detergent-like substance known as surfactant. In premature babies, surfactant is deficient and the lungs therefore tend to collapse. There is an accompanying secretion of high-protein fluid into the lung spaces, from which the protein is precipitated to form what are called hyaline membranes. Pathologically therefore this condition is known as hyaline membrane disease. Because blood oxygenation is defective, the baby is often blue. There may be complications such as intracranial bleeding. There are cardiovascular effects, particularly persistent patency of the ductus arteriosus (which in foetal life connects the two main arteries leaving the heart, enabling blood to bypass the lungs). Normally the ductus closes within hours of birth. Persistent patency complicates the respiratory distress situation, throwing a further strain on the baby's breathing.

The condition of Respiratory Distress Syndrome is characterised by rapid laboured breathing persisting beyond 3 hours after birth. Grunting is characteristic and is actually helpful in maintaining ventilation and blood oxygenation. Symptoms usually reach their greatest intensity at about 24 hours of age, persist for about 3 days and then gradually improve.

Milder cases of this condition will do well with simple supplemental oxygen treatment. If, however, this is not enough to improve the baby's oxygenation, or if through exhaustion the baby begins to have attacks in which respirations fail (apnoeic attacks), then more intensive life-saving measures may be required. It may suffice to increase slightly the pressure of the baby's inspired gases in order to maintain alveolar expansion or, in very severe cases, complete artificial ventilation may be required.

The larger babies as a rule do well and are left with no aftermath. Very small babies, however, present great problems, and the incidence of residual neurological troubles such as cerebral palsy is not insignificant. Because of this many doctors feel that vigorous attempts to support life at all costs are often misguided.

RHESUS FACTOR (HAEMOLYTIC DISEASE OF THE NEWBORN)

When, nearly 50 years ago, a specific red cell antigen was found in the blood of the Macacus Rhesus monkey, few people got very excited. It was subsequently shown that about 15 per cent of Europeans have the same antigen, which then became known as the Rhesus factor. Shortly after this it became clear that the Rhesus factor was responsible for many cases of severe jaundice in newborn babies, of a severity often leading to death or, if the baby survived, to be followed by severe anaemia. What is the mechanism of this condition?

If a mother who is Rhesus negative carries a child who is Rhesus positive, no harm will ensue unless the mother becomes immunised to the Rhesus factor. This may result from tiny leakages of the baby's red blood-cells into the maternal circulation, which occasionally happens during pregnancy but more frequently at the time of delivery. The mother may also be immunised as the result of blood transfusions with Rh positive blood. When the mother's immune system encounters this foreign antigen it prepares antibodies against it (see *immunity). These antibodies may diffuse through the placenta into the baby's circulation, where on

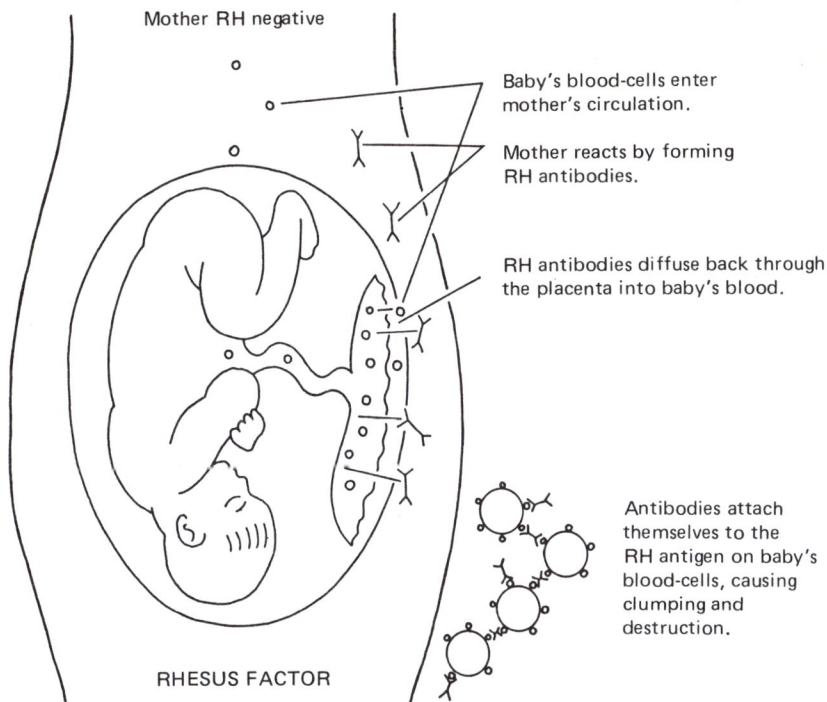

Mother RH negative

Baby's blood-cells enter mother's circulation.

Mother reacts by forming RH antibodies.

RH antibodies diffuse back through the placenta into baby's blood.

Antibodies attach themselves to the RH antigen on baby's blood-cells, causing clumping and destruction.

RHESUS FACTOR

encountering Rhesus positive red blood-cells they cause agglutination and destruction. The baby may therefore become anaemic to a variable degree *in utero*.

The destruction of blood results in the liberation of bile which has to be extracted. This is efficiently done via the placenta before the baby's birth but after delivery the baby's own liver has to cope with the bile load. This it is not used to doing and it takes several days before the requisite enzymes have achieved sufficient concentration to get rid of the bile effectively. During this time the baby becomes increasingly jaundiced. The resultant high levels of bilirubin in the blood may become toxic to the brain cells, which are particularly vulnerable especially in those areas of the brain known as the basal ganglia. When brain cells die as the result of the toxic effect of bilirubin they become bilestained. This gives rise to the name for this condition — kernicterus. Once the liver has become more efficient at bile conjugation and excretion and the dangers of kernicterus are passed, the main hazard to the baby is of progressive anaemia due to the continued destruction of the baby's blood-cells by maternal antibody. This continues for about 2 months but the antibodies then gradually wane and have usually disappeared by 5 months. During this anaemic period the baby may require more than one blood transfusion.

Management. This of course is a matter for your doctor. Every pregnant Rhesus negative woman should have her blood checked periodically during pregnancy to determine whether antibodies have been produced. If these are found, the severity of the situation can be accurately assessed by the strength (titre) of the antibodies and also by examination of the amniotic fluid. In severe cases, early termination of pregnancy may be advised in order to curtail the foetus's exposure to the hostile maternal environment. At birth the severely affected baby is given an exchange blood transfusion in which almost all his Rhesus positive blood is replaced with Rhesus negative blood, which will then not be affected by the antibodies still present. The baby is thus rendered temporarily Rhesus negative. By the time the transfused Rhesus negative red blood-cells are replaced by the baby's own Rhesus positive cells the maternal antibodies will have largely disappeared and there is therefore no subsequent trouble. Babies who become severely jaundiced may require phototherapy and sometimes repeated blood exchanges.

What is the risk to the Rh negative mother? It must be realised that nowadays this is very small. Although in 10 per cent of white pregnancies (less in black people) a Rhesus negative mother will be carrying a Rhesus positive baby, the incidence of haemolytic disease is extremely low. It is very rare for a first baby to be affected at all. Mothers who produce Rh positive babies and who could therefore be immunised to the Rh factor as the result of delivery, are protected by administration of a serum which destroys any baby's blood in their circulation before it has time to exert an antigenic effect. The chances of a woman becoming immunised to the Rhesus factor are therefore very small. Should she, however, have antibodies, the effect on the foetus if Rh positive will depend upon their type and concentration. Regular checks are therefore made throughout pregnancy.

If the father of the baby is also Rhesus negative there is absolutely no risk. If he is what is known as heterozygous, the chances of the baby being Rhesus positive are 50:50. Should he be homozygous the chances are 100 per cent. Even in such situations, however, with modern management there is very little risk of trouble.

If you are Rhesus negative be sure to remind your doctor of this at the time of delivery so that both your and the baby's blood can be taken and checked immediately.

Haemolytic disease due to other blood group factors

With the near-complete disappearance of Rhesus haemolytic disease, most cases of this condition are now due to other blood group antigens, particularly A and B. All persons not having such antigens possess naturally occurring antibodies which would normally destroy such cells should they encounter them. A baby of Group A or B, however, whose mother is say Group 0, is protected from the effect of her naturally occurring antibodies by the fact that these are of large molecular size and are unable to traverse the placenta. Occasionally, such a mother develops immune-type antibodies which do pass through to the baby and which cause symptoms akin to those of Rhesus haemolytic disease, though anaemia is rare and severe jaundice is the main hazard. Phototherapy is usually all that is required for such babies but occasionally replacement transfusion is necessary. Unlike Rhesus haemolytic disease, the condition due to maternal anti-A or anti-B antibodies does not tend to increase in severity with succeeding pregnancies. (See also *jaundice.)

RHEUMATIC FEVER

This disease, once so common in temperate climes, has now almost vanished from Europe and North America and most cases are now found in the tropical and subtropical regions of the world. In southern Africa, rheumatic fever and associated rheumatic heart disease are relatively uncommon among the white community, whereas they are seen not infrequently in other groups.

Rheumatic fever is induced by a preceding streptococcal infection of the throat, not always severe enough to receive medical attention; but the decline in the disease is due largely to the timely treatment of streptococcal throat infections with penicillin.

Apart from fever, which is of variable degree, the dominant symptom of the disease is painful, inflamed joints. The larger joints are usually affected and the pain is characteristically flitting in nature, staying in one joint for 2 to 3 days and then passing to others. In addition to the joints, the heart may be involved, and the heart valves may become distorted through inflammation. The heart muscle may also be affected by the disease and this may lead to heart failure. Sometimes the membrane surrounding the heart (the pericardium) becomes inflamed, causing pain in the front of the chest. Rheumatic nodules may form in tendinous structures, the favourite site being at the back of the elbows and in front of the knees. Very rarely, a specific skin rash (erythema marginatum) may be present. The disease lasts a variable time but seldom less than 8 to 10 weeks, and relapses may occur with further throat infections.

The joint pains respond well to aspirin, which may have to be given in fairly high doses. If the heart is involved with any severity, corticosteroids as well as drugs for heart failure may be required. The most important aspect of treatment, however, lies in the prevention of recurrences and this is achieved by the giving of penicillin on a regular basis to prevent streptococcal infections. It can be administered orally but best results are obtained from regular 3- to 4-weekly injections of a long-acting penicillin. Such prophylactic treatment has to be continued for many years and some doctors advocate its continuation for life. There is hardly ever any ill-effect from such penicillin administration and fortunately the streptococcus does not become resistant to it.

RHEUMATIC HEART DISEASE

All elements of the heart may become inflamed in *rheumatic fever but the main damage left after the disease has subsided is confined to the heart valves. The healing process results in scar tissue being formed in the valves, which normally are very delicate and mobile structures. As the scar tissue hardens, the valve may become incompetent or narrowed or both. The valve most commonly affected is that which lies between the left atrium and the left ventricle of the heart — the mitral valve. The next most commonly affected is the aortic valve lying at the base of the aorta. The valves of the right side of the heart are relatively rarely affected. It is not uncommon to see patients with established chronic rheumatic valvular heart disease who give no history of having had rheumatic fever, and this is particularly so among black people.

Deformed and incompetent valves put an extra strain upon the heart, causing progressive heart failure. Although the heart muscle can to some extent be supported medicinally, the mechanical strain can be lessened only by surgery. Narrowed (stenosed) valves can be dilated, and incompetent valves can sometimes be remodelled to some degree, and a grossly deformed valve can be replaced by a graft or an artificial valve. Such surgery is now commonplace and though it carries significant risks it can be embarked upon with great confidence.

RHEUMATOID DISEASE

Rheumatoid arthritis may occur at any age. In children it is now referred to as juvenile polyarthritis but the disease is of the same nature as that in adults. Although the exact cause is unknown it is thought to be an auto-immune disease in which the body develops antibodies to its own tissues. An acute form of the condition occurs in young children, with nearly all joints being involved and with accompanying fever, enlargement of the lymph glands and spleen, and often a rash. This is the condition described by Still and often referred to as Still's disease. Juvenile arthritis, when it affects older children, may involve many joints or sometimes relatively few. Occasionally the heart is involved, as in rheumatic fever, and there may be eye complications. These diseases run a very fluctuating and unpredictable course. They may burn themselves out fairly rapidly, they may run a relentlessly progressive course, often with much crippling, or there may be relapses with relatively unaffected periods between.

Treatment is not very satisfactory. Anti-inflammatory drugs such as aspirin are used in the first instance but many other preparations are available. Unfortunately, treatment is often rather disappointing and great patience is required from both patient and parents.

RICKETS

Bone consists of cellular matrix in which are deposited calcium salts; these give the bone its rigidity. Rickets is a condition in which there is inadequate deposition of such salts and the bones are therefore weak, tending to bend easily and often to fracture. In children of walking age, deformities such as bow legs or knock-knee are common. In babies there is delayed closure of the fontanelle, softening of the skull bones, enlargement of the ends of the long bones, particularly at the wrist and ankle, and there may be deformities of the chest.

Rickets is most commonly due to lack of vitamin D. Some cases are due to abnormalities of the kidney and these may be familial. They are often resistant to treatment with vitamin D, requiring abnormally high doses. Some cases of rickets in African children appear to be due to a lack of calcium and are cured by a good diet without vitamin D supplementation. (See also *vitamin D.)

RHINITIS

See *colds and *allergy

RINGWORM

This is a fungal infection of the skin, and either the scalp or the smooth skin may be involved. Several fungi are responsible, some being acquired from animals but most from other humans. The condition is contagious but need not cause alarm. On the smooth skin the lesions start as a small spot which grows concentrically to form an enlarging ring with healing at the centre. The active edge is elevated and red. Multiple lesions are often present. In the scalp, ringworm causes patchy baldness, the hairs being dull and broken and the scalp skin covered with greyish scales. Sometimes secondary infection occurs in the ringworm, causing a painful swelling and a very messy scalp.

Ringworms are nowadays readily treated by topical applications of suitable fungicides. In severe cases, tablets may be given by mouth and these are usually very effective and well tolerated.

ROOMING-IN

There is a welcome trend in maternity hospitals towards allowing babies to stay with their mothers most, if not all, of the time. This will not of course apply to mothers who are seriously ill and unable to care for their babies, but for those who are well there are decided advantages. The mother gets to know her baby and achieves greater confidence in handling him than if he is brought only at set feeding hours. The separation of a mother from her newborn child is unnatural. It does not inevitably lead to impaired bonding but it may be that the mother who prefers her baby to be kept away from her in the nursery is the one that tends to bond poorly anyway.

Apart from the joy of having your new baby with you, rooming-in enables you to feed him whenever he is ready, rather than at set hospital times. When fed on demand the baby feeds better and is more content, and at the same time stimulates lactation better. There are thus decided advantages for both of you in rooming-in.

ROSEOLA

This is a common virus infection of infants usually aged 6 months to 2 years. It is characterised by fairly sudden onset of high fever, which in about 10 per cent of cases is associated with a feverish convulsion. After 3 to 4 days the fever subsides abruptly, and at this time a rash appears over the body, commencing on the trunk and spreading to the arms and neck with only slight involvement of the face and legs. The rash is transient, never lasting more than a day. One feature of the disease which may give a clue to the diagnosis before the appearance of the rash, is enlargement of the lymph glands at the back of the head. Your doctor may suspect the condition if these glands are enlarged but the diagnosis can only be made with certainty in retrospect, after the fever has subsided and the rash appeared.

There is no treatment for this condition apart from symptomatic management with, for example, paracetamol, to reduce the fever.

ROUNDWORMS

See *worms

RUBELLA (GERMAN MEASLES)

This mild virus disease is of little consequence except when it is acquired by women during the first 4 months of pregnancy. The incubation period is 2 to 3 weeks. There may be one or two days of malaise with some fever but constitutional symptoms are usually very mild. The lymph glands, particularly at the back of the head and the neck, enlarge as a rule before the rash appears and this may persist for some time. The rash varies a great deal but typically commences on the face and behind the ears, spreading to the trunk. The flat pink spots are initially discrete but after the first day they may coalesce and the patient then simply appears flushed. At this stage the disease may be confused with scarlet fever but the other features of the latter condition are absent and the enlarged glands usually give a clue to the diagnosis. The rash persists for only about 2 days.

Because of the risk to the foetus it is important to recognise German measles with accuracy so that patients may avoid contact with pregnant women. Unfortunately it is often not possible to be certain on clinical grounds alone. Furthermore, many people have the disease without displaying the typical symptoms. In doubtful cases the disease can be confirmed by blood tests and where there is danger of exposure in early pregnancy these should be done on the suspect as well as on the woman at risk.

Vaccination against rubella is highly effective (see *immunisation). It may be given to small children but they do not really need protection against so mild a disease. Because the antibodies tend to wane, children vaccinated early in life should probably be revaccinated at puberty. Any girl who has not definitely had rubella by the age of 12 or 13 should then be given the vaccine. Women in early pregnancy should not be vaccinated, for although the attenuated virus has not been responsible for foetal abnormalities, it has been found to traverse the placenta. Women at risk may be protected to some extent by an injection of *gammaglobulin.

Rubella embryopathy. There is a high risk to the foetus if a mother acquires rubella during the first 2 months of pregnancy, the risk declining in the third month and even more so in the fourth month, and after the fourth month there is no ill effect. Infected infants may continue to shed the virus for a very long time, up to a year, and are therefore a risk to pregnant contacts (the infectivity period of the acquired disease is from 5 days before the rash appears until 1 week afterwards).

The characteristic effects of rubella on the foetus are low birth-weight, brain abnormalities, deafness and cataracts of the eye, often associated with poor eye development. Although the cataracts are often present at birth this is not necessarily so. Further abnormalities affect the heart, and the liver may be involved, causing jaundice. There is no treatment available for the congenitally acquired disease. Prevention therefore is of extreme importance. It achieves an almost greater importance in people with darker skins in whom rubella is not recognisable and in whom therefore rubella embryopathy is relatively common.

RUPTURE

This is the popular term for a *hernia.

RUSKS

These are popular items of food for the baby of about 6 months of age who is able to hold something and chew at it. Whether he has teeth or not he will make steady if soggy progress until the residue is a squashy mess in his hands and a far from neat plaster on everything in the vicinity. It is only fair to add that almost any item of food at this age suffers the same inelegant fate. Rusks are not to be encouraged for the child with teeth. The same applies to biscuits, cake and any other fine-flour food. Much dental decay is caused by such refined starches and sugars. From a dental point of view, therefore, it is better to give your baby a piece of cheese, steak or apple on which to exercise his gums or display his early dental skills.

SAINT VITUS'S DANCE
See *chorea

SALT
Common salt — sodium chloride — is an important inorganic constituent of the body, being found predominantly in the extra-cellular fluid. The chief intracellular ion is potassium. The body becomes depleted of salts in conditions of dehydration associated, for example, with gastro-enteritis, and in restoring body fluids it is important to include the necessary salts. (See *dehydration.)

An excess of salt is undesirable, and high levels in the body can be extremely dangerous, producing disastrous effects on the brain. Chronic excessive salt ingestion may be related to high blood pressure. Severe salt depletion leads to generalised weakness and possibly cramps. Salt concentrations may be severely disturbed in diseases of the adrenal gland. (See also *sodium.)

SANDWORM
This condition is due to the larva of the dog hookworm and sometimes the cat hookworm. The parasite is acquired by contact with the animal's excreta. In warm, humid conditions the larvae emerge from the eggs and burrow into the skin. Because the parasite is not wholly adapted to man, the larvae do not develop fully but simply continue to burrow under the skin for many weeks before they eventually die. This causes severe irritation and much scratching. The aimless tracks of the parasite make the condition easy to diagnose.

Treatment of sandworms with topical applications such as phenol is not satisfactory, as the skin has to be destroyed to an appreciable depth to reach the parasite, which is always at least a centimetre beyond the visible end of the track. The most effective treatment is thiobendazole given by mouth, but its incorporation in an ointment for topical use is also valuable. Prevention, however, is better than cure and small children should not be allowed to play about in moist sand which has been fouled by dogs or cats.

SCABIES
This common skin disease is caused by a tiny mite which burrows into the skin, causing severe irritation and itching. Scratching often leads to superimposed infection. Such infected scabies is a not uncommon cause of nephritis, especially in black children. Scabies spreads by direct contact from person to person, and it is common for several members, or indeed all the members, of a household to be afflicted simultaneously. It is important that all those affected be treated at the

same time as otherwise the condition will continue to spread.

Scabies may affect any part of the skin apart from the face and scalp in adults. In babies, however, the face is not immune. Characteristic sites in older children are the webs between the fingers, but itching is usually widespread. Sometimes the characteristic tiny white burrows can be seen in the inflamed skin.

Several effective treatments are available for scabies, e.g. benzyl-benzoate emulsion and gamma benzene hexachloride. These are best applied after a hot bath or shower, with gentle scrubbing to open the burrows.

SCALDS (see also *burns)

Hot water may produce burns of first, second or third degree but there is never of course actual charring of tissue. When the skin is completely destroyed, however, there may be severe resultant scarring.

Scalds in small children usually result from the child's natural curiosity and the tempting nature of the teapot, kettle or pot on the stove. Such dangers should be foreseen and such objects kept out of range, but children can be very quick, and constant vigilance is required.

Should your child be scalded, the immediate application of cold water may help to reduce the damage. It is better to douse the child promptly with cold water rather than to struggle trying to remove hot clothes. Blisters should be left intact. Simple reddening of the skin should be left untreated. If the scalds are extensive or deep, consult your doctor or take the child to hospital. Do not put anything on denuded areas. This will simply cause unnecessary irritation and will do no good. Small scalded areas not requiring expert attention should simply be covered with a sterile protective dressing until healing takes place.

SCALP

The small baby usually has her head washed every bath-time, though it is not necessary to use a shampoo on each occasion. If there is any suggestion of accumulation of skin debris, however, shampooing should be regular and fairly vigorous so that the scalp scales are removed (see *cradle cap). Pay particular attention to the fontanelle, which many mothers are afraid to clean adequately. In older children the frequency of scalp cleansing will depend much upon the climate, the need being increased in hot, sweaty conditions. Most scalp troubles are due simply to inadequate scalp cleansing.

For diseases of the scalp see *baldness, *lice, *ringworm, etc.

SCARLET FEVER

This disease is considerably less common than it used to be. Basically, scarlet fever is tonsillitis caused by a specific streptococcal germ which produces a toxin that in turn produces a rash. The incubation period of the disease is 2–7 days. Initial symptoms are headache, fever, sore throat and often vomiting, followed within 24–72 hours by the typical rash. This begins in the neck, armpits, groins and upper chest and then extends to the rest of the trunk and the extremities. Superimposed upon a generalised flushing of the skin there are very fine red spots. These are particularly marked in the groin regions. The cheeks are flushed but the skin around the mouth remains very pale. The fever persists for up to a week. The throat is very inflamed and the tongue is characteristic, being coated in the early stages of the disease and subsequently stripping to leave a very red strawberry-like appearance. The neck glands are often enlarged. After the disease has subsided there is usually some peeling of the skin, particularly of the fingers.

Scarlet fever should be treated with penicillin, which not only eliminates the causative streptococcus but also prevents the complication of nephritis (inflammation of the kidneys), which is the main anxiety in this condition. It is important to examine the urine in the later stages of the disease and for a week or two afterwards, and if it appears to contain blood you must inform your doctor.

SCHOOL

Commencing school is one of the big events in a child's life. She may be very excited about it but it will be an excitement nearly always tinged with fear. If she has attended a pre-primary school she will be much less daunted, for she will be used to separation from her parents, but for a child confronted with school for the first time having never been away from her parents, this can be a very frightening prospect. Others of course look forward to school with such enthusiasm and are so outgoing in nature that they present no problem. Judge your child sympathetically and, particularly if she is of a somewhat timid nature, ensure that she has a friend or two to accompany her to school when she starts. This will make all the difference to her confidence.

The regulation age for school entry varies from country to country. It has little influence upon eventual academic achievement. The child should enter school when she is ready for formal learning, and in this, children vary as they do in other features. The regulation age of 5½ to 6½ years will suit most children but there are a few who are ready earlier and some who are not school-ready when the appointed time comes. If you have doubts about your child's school-readiness, have her assessed from this point of view. It is usually better to delay a child's school-entry by a year rather than allow her to flounder hopelessly and become discouraged.

Children should enjoy school, especially in the early years. The young child is keen to learn and is excited by her new discoveries and abilities. Parents can help a great deal by taking a real interest when she recounts the day's happenings at school, and thus maintaining enthusiasm and excitement. At times parents may feel overburdened with homework and believe they are expected to do the teacher's job. Try not to give the impression that homework is a bother and a bore, for this attitude will then be transmitted to your child. Homework should be fun — even when it isn't! It is legitimate to help your child with projects but not to do them for her. Parental products may get a good mark but they will not teach her how to find information, collate it and arrange it attractively and interestingly, which is the object of a project. Doing it for her will simply prove a handicap in the long run.

Boarding versus day school

Although the majority of children attend day schools near home, you may be tempted to consider sending your child to boarding school in the belief that this will give her better opportunities or because you yourself have been to a boarding school and feel that you benefited from the experience. There may be more specific reasons — if your child is being difficult, undisciplined, not settling to work satisfactorily, indulging in undesirable pursuits or keeping bad company. These may all be legitimate reasons for putting her in an environment in which she will have less opportunity for such activities, and her timetable will be structured appropriately in an atmosphere where everyone has to conform to the same rules.

Private boarding schools are extremely expensive and you would need to be satisfied in your own mind that this is money well spent. Some children, particularly the outgoing and sporty types, thrive in boarding schools, whereas others, perhaps more timid, will find greater opportunities if kept at home. However much you may perhaps wish it, your child may not be at all like you. Make your choice of school therefore on the basis of the child's best interests, and avoid particularly any snobbish considerations, which one fears often do influence parents considerably.

School phobia

Few children admit to liking school, even though they are in fact perfectly happy there, and realise that an education is not only the best investment for their future but is also a privilege which they should not squander. If your child is really unhappy at school or fearful of attending, there is a reason. This reason may not immediately be revealed but may take a great deal of unearthing. Every effort, however, should be made to reveal it for only then is it possible to deal with the problem. It may be based on an inability to cope with the schoolwork, on difficulties with the teachers, or more probably on difficulties in personal relationships with other pupils. If you cannot get out of your child the reasons for her school phobia, discuss the problem with her teacher or school principal, and if the problem cannot be rapidly resolved do not hesitate to seek the help of an expert, such as a psychologist, as delay in resolution will simply compound the difficulties.

SCHOOLING PROBLEMS

Some 10–15 per cent of pupils encounter some sort of educational difficulty. Many of these are minor and readily resolved but about half of them are severe and demand expert assistance. There are many causes. Prominent among these are the following:

Defects of vision and hearing. These often go undetected for some time before the child eventually complains that she cannot see the blackboard or that she cannot hear the teacher. In all cases of difficulty, therefore, it is very important that vision and hearing should be adequately tested.

Cultural deprivation. A child coming from a poor home or institution where there is little intellectual stimulation is much more likely to have difficulties in assimilation compared with the child from a stimulating environment. On the other hand there are examples of children from humble backgrounds who have shone brilliantly.

Teacher problems. Poor teaching, inappropriate teaching methods and pupil–teacher conflict account for a great many educational difficulties. The 'Look and Say' method of teaching reading, for example, while it suits the majority of children perfectly well, does not suit all; it is often the more logically minded child, who would be better taught in a basically phonetic way, who does poorly in a general class. Such a child, perhaps intellectually very bright, who gets a poor foundation in Class 1 and 2, may continue to struggle for several years thereafter until her difficulty is recognised and appropriately handled, by which time however much ground has often been lost. Such difficulties should be recognised early and appropriate remedial measures taken.

Emotional problems. The insecure child lacking confidence often makes poor progress, and her difficulties are then compounded by further emotional reactions to her poor performance. Such a child will need considerable emotional support and psychological help.

Poor motivation. Many children are accused of poor motivation when the prime problem is really poor stimulation. The child who lacks interest and motivation presents a difficult problem, for while the label is easy to apply, the cure for poor motivation is elusive. Nothing succeeds like success, and it is only when the child begins to see that she is making progress and begins to get satisfaction from achievement that motivation is likely to improve.

Intelligence level. This is obviously of prime importance in determining scholastic progress. It must be realised, however, that IQ assessments are often inaccurate and can be influenced by a child's attitude or state of health at the time of the test. Although the tester usually makes allowances for adverse factors, nevertheless the results of IQ tests performed on the same child at different times can vary quite considerably. They should not therefore be taken at absolute face value. Intelligence testing, however, is imperative in the case of the child experiencing significant schooling difficulties.

Neurological problems. Brain-damage may result in a lowered intelligence, the hyperkinetic syndrome, cerebral palsy with its physical handicaps, or epilepsy. These conditions may be clearly recognisable or may be of rather subtle presentation.

Epilepsy is often diagnosed and treated in children who have never had any form of fit. Such treatment is usually inappropriate. The frequent blank spells of petit-mal epilepsy may result in loss of a significant amount of sensory input and such attacks therefore must be treated. Many teachers, however, conscious of these problems, tend to diagnose petit-mal epilepsy when a child is simply indulging in daydreaming. If petit-mal is suspected, an EEG examination should be performed, as the tracing in this condition is quite specific. Whereas in children with severe learning disabilities the EEG is more commonly abnormal than in the general population, there is nevertheless no specific pattern associated with this situation, and the EEG has been grossly overrated as a means of investigating such problems. It is in fact rarely indicated. Treatment with anticonvulsant drugs almost always has some side-effect, usually in the form of sedation, and this may adversely affect this child's school performance. It is important, therefore, to confine such treatment to children with definite epileptic symptoms.

The detection of so-called 'soft cerebral signs' in the form, for example, of minor co-ordination difficulties, has been fashionable as an indicator of 'Minimal Cerebral Damage'. This concept is pathologically unproven and clinically tenuous (see also *hyperactivity). Children with frank cerebral palsy who are known to be brain-damaged do not very commonly display the features attributed to 'Minimal Cerebral Damage'. Furthermore it is difficult to accept that 4 to 6 times as many boys as girls should be minimally cerebrally damaged. This concept therefore is falling into disrepute.

Other medical conditions such as thyroid deficiency should be checked for by medical examination and, if necessary, specific function tests. Children with severe allergies often seem to have a concentration problem and may have associated hearing impairment. Appropriate treatment of such conditions may result in marked improvement in school performance.

Dietary factors. These are currently in vogue in certain areas as being the cause of the hyperkinetic syndrome and although controlled studies have failed to substantiate such concepts there is the very, very occasional child who seems to benefit from an appropriate elimination diet. High doses of vitamins have been fashionable but are neither beneficial nor without danger. Food additives, salicylates, trace elements, sugar and various other dietary components have been blamed for deleterious effects, with little scientific backing and largely anecdotal evidence. Parents of children with severe schooling problems tend to clutch at any straw proffered, and this is very understandable. Whereas it is entirely reasonable to 'try anything', provided it is harmless, the effects of such anythings should be critically evaluated, and if benefit is lacking the obstinate pursuance of these attempts at therapy cannot be encouraged.

Adequate evaluation of the child with significant schooling problems requires a team approach. No one person can be an expert in intelligence assessment, remedial teaching, orthoptics, audiometry, psychological evaluation, medical assessment, physiotherapy, occupational therapy, speech therapy, etc. Obviously such a team requires co-ordination, and a doctor or paediatrician is probably the person best equipped to fulfil such a role. The doctor is also the only person who can prescribe appropriate medication should this be indicated. Such medication should, like every other therapeutic modality, be critically evaluated and continued only if there is clear evidence of benefit. It should furthermore be interrupted periodically to determine the need for its continuation. Medication is indicated in only a small proportion of children with learning difficulties, and tends to be used inappropriately, uncritically and excessively. (See also *dyslexia and *hyperactivity.)

SCORPION STINGS

These unpleasant creatures occur in the more arid regions and, though usually found under stones, may accidentally be trodden upon. The larger specimens with smaller tails are less venomous than the smaller scorpions with large tails. The sting causes very severe burning pain but no tissue destruction. Small children may require medical attention because of shock. A cold compress applied locally will help to relieve pain and swelling to some extent, and supportive treatment may be necessary in more severe cases. If, therefore, the child appears ill she should be seen by a doctor.

SCRATCHING

The natural response to an itch is to scratch. Unfortunately, sometimes the scratching itself increases the itch and a vicious circle of itch, scratch, itch, scratch is set up. To interrupt this the scratching must be controlled. This situation is particularly common with eczema. In some nervously disposed individuals, scratching is the initial problem and a chronic dermatitis is induced by the habit. When scratching must be prevented it is sometimes possible to do this with appropriate splinting, for example tubular cardboard splints on the arms or bandaging the hands in small infants. Itching may be relieved by topical applications such as calamine lotion or steroid preparations, and some of the antihistamine drugs have an itch-relieving effect. Sedation is also useful when scratching occurs at night.

Scratching often leads to secondary infection, particularly in young children with insect bites or scabies, and it is important therefore to maintain general cleanliness and keep the nails cut short.

Generalised itching is sometimes a manifestation of serious disease, such as severe jaundice and certain malignancies. In such cases relieving the itch poses a difficult problem.

SCREAMING

This rather more urgent form of crying must not be interpreted always as indicating pain. It may be the result simply of anger, and even small babies get angry. When no physical cause is apparent, screaming is often put down to abdominal pain, and colic is a convenient scapegoat which will satisfy all but the most critical people (see *crying and *colic).

The onset of sudden screaming attacks in a child who was previously healthy and well behaved does demand an explanation, and if there is a suggestion of severe abdominal pain, obstruction of the bowel due to, for example, intussusception should be suspected. Screaming attacks associated with vomiting are particularly suspicious and always demand medical evaluation.

SCURF

See *dandruff

SCURVY

This disease state is due to lack of vitamin C. In the adult it manifests itself as bleeding, particularly from the gums, which become spongy with a tendency in severe protracted cases for the teeth to fall out. Bleeding may occur into muscles or other sites, causing painful swellings which may become secondarily infected.

Infantile scurvy is seen most commonly in babies in the second half of the first year of life when vitamin C may not yet have been introduced into their diet in the form of fresh fruit and vegetables or frank vitamin supplements. The gums are affected only if teeth have erupted. Bleeding occurs usually around the ends of the long bones, resulting in severe pain and immobility with resentment of movement. The bleeding tends to lift the covering membrane (periosteum) from the underlying bone and there may be dislocations of the bone ends. Scurvy may be mistaken for bone infection (osteomyelitis). The condition responds rapidly to administration of vitamin C.

SEBORRHOEA

See *dermatitis and *cradle cap

SEX

The distortions and hypocrisy of the Victorian era have left a legacy which still influences sexual thought and habit today. No sooner had one generation more or less succeeded in throwing off the Victorian mantle and exposing sex for what it is, than the next generation, rejoicing in the sexual freedom afforded by the contraceptive pill, threw the whole sexual scene into chaos. Parents are no longer educating their children, their children are educating them. The role of the parent in sex education therefore is now almost confined to the small child, and even then there may be a feeling of inadequacy as well as embarrassment. If, however, you manage to maintain an open and healthy relationship you will be able to guide your child successfully and happily through the difficulties of adolescence.

By the age of 3 the child knows whether he or she is a little boy or a little girl and is very interested in the difference. She will soon want to know where babies come from and when she begins to ask questions these should be answered directly and clearly but without unnecessary embellishment, which will simply confuse her and obscure the answer she immediately wants. Once she has absorbed the fact that babies grow inside their mothers she will want to know how on earth the baby gets out. Although it may be difficult to explain this simply and without embarrassment, her question does demand a straightforward answer and this should be given. She will next want to know how the baby got in; again the answers should not be unnecessarily detailed but as her knowledge increases and the questions become more searching they should be answered frankly and adequately so that she will come to you for further information and not seek this elsewhere. If you have managed to keep the whole question open you should be able to educate your child progressively so that he or she approaches puberty in a state of adequate readiness. The secret is at all times to give answers appropriate to the child's demands and understanding.

At puberty your child is liable to be more secretive and less open with you about any problems she may have. By this stage, however, a girl should be fully informed about menstruation, female sexual responses and the problems she is likely to encounter in relationships with boys, whose sexual needs may seem more urgent but whose demands should by no means always be met. There is a great need for closeness between mother and daughter at this time and the average girl will welcome sympathetic discussion of her problems. If it becomes clear that she is determined to be sexually active it is far better that she go onto the pill than risk the disasters of pregnancy. The question of chastity and the adolescent young adult is a highly personal matter which individuals have to decide for themselves. The decision should be made thoughtfully and responsibly rather than left to the winds of chance. At least every adolescent should have been imbued with sufficient sense of respect for the other sex to not wish to cause harm. If you can achieve this with your child in today's world you will have done well.

Formal sexual education in schools is now widely practised. Parents should not regard this as absolving them from any responsibility in this area. A small child's initial sex instruction must come from the parents. The more scientific information offered in school is a useful addendum but on no account should it replace parental information and guidance.

Intersex

Occasionally a baby is born with genital organs which cannot clearly be called male or female. The absolute determinant of sex is the presence of testes or ovaries. There are, however, other sex indicators, e.g. the sex chromosomes, in which the possession of a Y chromosome indicates a male whereas two X chromosomes indicate a female. Such tests, however, are not always a reliable indication as to the best gender role to be allocated to the child. Generally speaking, if an adequate phallus is not present a baby is best reared as a girl.

Children with ambiguous genitals may have testes or ovaries or sometimes both. In the first case they are referred to as male pseudohermaphrodites, in the second as female pseudohermaphrodites and in the third as true hermaphrodites. When testicular tissue is present and the child is to be reared as a girl, the testes are best removed. In true hermaphrodites the inappropriate gonad (testis or ovary) should be removed. These are all complex medical problems which demand full discussion and explanation between doctor and parent.

SHINGLES

See *herpes zoster

SHOCK

This is a state characterised by inadequate blood circulation. Nervous shock may result from severe emotional upset. The condition is transient, and as there is no loss of body fluid it is readily reversible and requires no specific treatment, a little rest and a warm drink being all that is needed.

More severe shock may result from severe infection, e.g. septicaemia, physical trauma (particularly bony injury), blood loss from any cause, and burns, especially when these are extensive — the area being more important than the depth. Shock may also result from loss of fluid in severe vomiting and diarrhoea, as well as poisoning, including snakebite and bee stings.

The shocked child is pale and usually cold but the skin is moist. There may be restlessness progressing to delirium and eventual loss of consciousness. Thirst is often extreme but drinks should not be given if there is a possibility of the child's requiring an anaesthetic in the near future, for example for reduction of fractures or treatment of burns. The pulse is feeble and usually rapid and may be difficult to find. First aid treatment of shock should be limited to keeping the patient flat or in a slightly head-down position in order to maintain the circulation of blood to the brain. Excessive warmth should not be applied and covering with a light blanket is sufficient. Drinks should be given only if there is no question of the need of an anaesthetic but if the latter is likely to be delayed, e.g. a prolonged ambulance journey, it is better to give fluids than allow the child to die of shock. Optimally, fluids should be administered intravenously.

Needless to say, a severely shocked child, no matter what the cause, is in need of urgent medical attention and is probably best transported to hospital as rapidly as possible.

SHOES

Shoes are unnecessary for small children, who usually walk better without them. If you feel compelled to buy them for climatic, geographical or social reasons let them at least be comfortable and sensible with stable flat soles and no or low heels. Unfortunately, as with most clothing, the manufacturers determine fashion, and even small children are sometimes pushed into footwear which, while seemingly a suitable introduction to the precarious pedestals later to be inflicted upon the unfortunate victims, nevertheless are thoroughly undesirable. Many orthopaedic problems in later life are caused solely by bad shoes. It is a pity that commonsense does not always equate with ideas of elegance. If you want your children to have healthy feet let them go bare foot as long as possible.

SHYNESS

If your child is excessively shy do not attempt to cure her by throwing her into the deep end, as it were, and hoping that once you have disappeared she will come out of her shell and enjoy the party. It is more probable that she will thoroughly hate the party and refuse to go to another. Shyness should be respected but helped. This is best done by increasing your child's confidence, staying with her when she needs you and selecting for her one or two playmates with whom she feels completely comfortable. Larger groups will be progressively tolerated as her confidence increases. Above all do not ridicule her, for this could be extremely destructive. Time improves most things and shyness is no exception.

SINGLE PARENT

Single-parent families may arise as the result of divorce, bereavement or the unmarried mother. These are all very different situations.

Divorce. The effects of divorce will depend a great deal upon the children's ages and upon parental attitudes. (See *divorce.) The mother will usually be given custody of young children and the trauma of the divorce itself is then often compounded by the fact that mother has to work and is able to give her children less attention than before. A mother should fight strongly for her rights and not accept a settlement which puts an excessive financial strain upon her. One is often tempted to accept anything for the sake of peace or dignity — don't do it!

Do avoid disparaging remarks about their father or mother, whose parental role, after all, cannot be obliterated. Help them rather to retain affection for the other parent, who is important to them, even though they may see him or her very little.

Should mother remarry, of course, a third parental figure enters the scene and, provided relationships are good, there is every possibility that stepfather will occupy an increasingly important role in the child's life. Father may as a result feel rejected to some extent but he should try to accept that for the children to have a healthy close relationship with the man with whom they have most frequent and close contact is from their point of view a most desirable situation.

The single-parent family as result of bereavement. This situation will pose a tremendous strain upon both surviving parent and children, who have to suffer the trauma of bereavement in addition to the ongoing problems of the single-parent situation. There can of course be a great deal of mutual comfort when the children are old enough to understand. When younger children are involved, one hopes that grandparents or close family friends can be a support during the initial period of devastation. Children as well as adults have to mourn and should be allowed to do so. They should not be discouraged from expressing their grief and exteriorising it. There is a natural reluctance to talk about the dead parent in the fear that this will upset the child. This should not be the case; the child needs to talk out her sadness, to receive comfort, but at the same time to be encouraged towards a philosophical acceptance that life goes on and that death after all is the lot of everyone and is the only certainty in our futures. Finally there is the very real hope that the young parent will remarry and a complete family will be re-established.

The unmarried mother. In spite of the simplicity and free availability of modern contraception there is still a high incidence of illegitimate births, especially among schoolgirls who have not had the courage, wisdom or foresight to admit their sexuality and take appropriate precautions. The occasional 'accident' still occurs in an older age group but most young women leading an active sex life are able to fend off unwanted pregnancy. The occasional young woman deliberately wants a child but no husband. No matter what the underlying reason might be, the plight of the unwed mother is an unenviable one, filled with potential tragedy for herself and for her child. It is extremely difficult for a woman to bring up a child entirely on her own, especially if she has to work, and for the child the situation is no easier. Every child needs two parents and, particularly for boys, the lack of a father figure can be crippling. In general, therefore, it is far wiser for a baby born into this situation to be given for adoption rather than that the mother and child should suffer the strains of the single-parent situation through all the years of dependency. There is an unfortunate tendency at present for young girls to keep their illegitimate babies, and only later do they discover to what extent their lives have been ruined by this decision. *Adoption is by no means free of problems but it is a better solution from all points of view. Studies have demonstrated clearly that illegitimate children do better when adopted than when retained by their unmarried mothers – and there is no doubt whatever that the mothers do better.

SINUSES

The sinuses are air spaces in the bones of the head, which communicate with the nasal cavity. In the small baby these are absent or poorly formed and sinusitis is therefore not a problem. The school-going and older child may develop sinusitis as a complication of a cold, and sinus involvement is not infrequent in cases of chronic allergic rhinitis. Acute sinusitis presents with pain in the sinus area, fever, nasal discharge and cough. This requires prompt treatment with appropriate antibiotics and decongestant nasal drops. Steaming is also helpful in loosening secretions and opening up the nose. More chronic sinus involvement is seen in association with allergic nose trouble and is a not uncommon cause of headache. Unfortunately, the underlying nasal allergy often passes unrecognised and much treatment is administered for sinusitis without the basic problem being tackled. A child hardly ever requires surgery for sinusitis and if this is proposed it would be advisable to have a second opinion.

SKIN

The skin is a remarkably adaptable organ but its adaptability is limited and at times it cannot cope with the insults we hurl at it. Over the evolutionary aeons the degree of skin pigment has adapted to the degree of sun exposure and the fair Viking is a more suitable inhabitant of Scandinavia than is the Turk, the Negro a more appropriate inhabitant of Central Africa than the fair Scot. With the massive population migrations of the last few centuries the pattern of skin colour no longer follows lines of latitude but exhibits a kaleidoscopic non-pattern unrelated to helio-radiation. The skin still does its best to adapt to climatic factors but there are severe genetic limits. In general, the more pigmented skin is tougher than the fair integuments of the Northern European, in whom skin problems are therefore more common.

Skin diseases. See *acne, *dermatitis, *eczema, *rashes, etc.

SLEEP

Sleep requirements vary considerably from individual to individual and children are no exception in this. Babies in the early weeks of life spend most of the time between feeds asleep but they do have waking periods which increase progressively, particularly by day, whereas the night-time sleeping period becomes extended, till by the third month it occupies an average 7 to 8 hours. The total sleeping period per day diminishes from an average of 19 hours at 4 weeks, to 15 hours at 6 months and 12 hours at 1 year, at which stage the child is having one or two daytime naps.

Sleep is essential for birds and mammals. Other life forms have periods of inertia, which, however, are not necessary for survival. In the human two distinct forms of sleep have been recognised, one characterised by tranquillity and inactive electro-encephalogram (EEG) and absence of dreaming, the other characterised by rapid eye movements (and hence known as REM sleep), an active EEG and dreaming. It is REM sleep which appears to be essential for continued normal brain function. Children, unless they are ill, will nearly always get their needed quota of sleep. Unfortunately this does not always apply to parents!

Sleeping position is of little importance. The last 20 to 30 years have witnessed a rising popularity for the prone position, both because it was suggested that babies slept for longer periods this way and also because it was thought to be safer should the baby vomit. As babies in any position turn their heads to the side there is little extra safety in lying prone. The most marked effect of this position is on the feet, which are forced to turn either in or out and there may be considerable temporary deformity. This is however always self-corrective and requires no treatment, though it might be wise to lie the baby on her side or back rather than continue to increase the deformity, which will probably worry you and sometimes worries doctors. The best thing is to try your baby out and see which position she prefers. If the baby is swaddled and unable to move she may become very uncomfortable in one position and therefore cry simply to have her position changed. Many babies cry simply from loneliness and will be perfectly happy if harnessed to mother's back or front.

Where should the child sleep at night? This will depend upon the facilities available. Most parents prefer not to be disturbed by their children at night and the latter are therefore put in a separate room from the age of a few weeks. Other parents would like to do this but simply have not got the accommodation. It really doesn't matter. The average young child sleeps sufficiently deeply not to be disturbed by parental nocturnal activities and privacy therefore is not as a rule severely impaired.

Sleep problems. These, it should be realised, are extremely common and while inevitably a cause of exhaustion, need not be a cause of anxiety. During the early weeks of the baby's life she will require night feeds, and it is far better to feed her when she wakes than to try to bluff her with water or sugared water in the hope that this will encourage her to abandon the night feed. It will in fact do the very reverse, for the baby will inevitably be dissatisfied and will continue to clamour for what she wants. When the baby is ready to give up her night feed she will do so. By 3 months most babies are sleeping through. There follows as a rule a period of reasonable tranquillity except when the baby is upset by illness. During the second half of the first year, however, many infants develop inconsiderate nocturnal habits, waking frequently but settling down as a rule fairly readily with perhaps a drink and some demonstration of affectionate reassurance.

At this age a child is ruthlessly demanding of maternal attention and it is wise not to let this get out of hand. Once the baby has been made comfortable further attention should cease and it should be made quite clear that the nights are expected to be for sleeping. It helps a great deal if the child is in her own room so that the parents are not disturbed by every movement and murmur, but such accommodation is not universally available. It may be tempting to bring the disturbing child into your own bed. There is nothing fundamentally the matter with this but it should be clearly realised that each time this is done the child is being encouraged in this direction and it is a direction extremely difficult to reverse. If you enjoy having your child in bed with you by all means do so but be prepared then for her to stay until she has reached the age where she will voluntarily leave. If you prefer to keep your privacy then insist on this from the beginning and do not allow any deviations except for the most compelling reasons. A child will adjust to almost any pattern but it is only when there is consistency that she can be expected to learn and adjust appropriately. How can she be expected to learn if when on one occasion that she cries she is cuddled and taken into mommy's bed and on another occasion the door is firmly closed upon her and she is left to cry it out? Either approach may be appropriate but not both.

During the early months of life much of a baby's crying is attributed to 'wind' or 'colic' and a few months later teething becomes the ready culprit. Such scapegoats may satisfy the uncritical few but if we are honest we will have to admit that most times we do not know why a baby cries excessively. (See *crying, *colic, etc.) Clearly every attempt must be made to identify the cause of a baby's distress and in this your doctor will undoubtedly help, but if a definite cause cannot be pinpointed do not feel that this is due to incompetence. For such is the rule rather than the exception.

As the child develops a greater degree of independence, and particularly in the negativistic years in which she is trying to assert herself, sleep refusal, like food refusal, may become a handy and reliable weapon with which to bludgeon her parents. This applies particularly if there has been inconsistency in parental handling. When the child knows she will not get away with something she will give up trying. At this age, problems may involve going to sleep or subsequent waking and crying. Both should be handled with absolute consistency. Most children develop a bedtime ritual and this need not be discouraged. If kept within reasonable proportions it often helps the child to settle rapidly. The ritual if uncontrolled, however, may become so complicated as to occupy an hour or two. It is not necessary for the child to say goodnight to every item in the house, to tuck every toy up for the night or to have 10 drinks of water. She should be encouraged to have one or two familiar and particularly dear toys in bed with her. It is a good idea to read her a short story and then say goodnight. That then must very definitely be the end.

If the child wakes subsequently during the night, attention should be kept to a minimum. If she wakes screaming, apparently having had a bad dream, she will require some comforting but should then fall off to sleep without too much fuss. Physical comfort should be ensured by changing her if necessary or offering her a drink (by cup not by bottle), and it should then be made quite clear that no further attention will be given. Repeated nocturnal disturbance is simply reinforced by an excess of attention on the part of oversolicitous parents. Once bad habits have been allowed to form they are much more difficult to reverse and considerable fortitude and determination may be required. The wise course therefore is to insist on correct habits from the beginning and not to allow a problem situation to develop.

Sleep problems in the older child are likely to be due to anxiety. This may originate from domestic unhappiness, from problems at school or as the result of difficulties with personal relationships. Seldom are these severe enough to cause long-term insomnia. Nevertheless, the older child who is having sleeping difficulty should have her problems explored sympathetically, and if you as parent are unable to get to the root of the trouble you should not hesitate to invoke the help of a doctor or psychologist. (See also *nightmares.)

Sleep walking. This is an uncommon condition, which achieves its maximum incidence in mid-childhood. It is nearly always related to some anxiety or tension in the child and every attempt therefore should be made to unearth such a cause. Although the sleepwalker rarely sustains significant injury this is nevertheless possible, and appropriate precautions should be taken to prevent, for example, falls from heights. The degree of complexity of activity varies considerably from case to case, some children simply getting up and standing by the bed for a few moments and then lying down again, others walking fairly far afield and undertaking other forms of activity.

The sleepwalking child should be gently led back to bed and she will almost certainly settle down without waking. As indicated above, in cases of repeated sleepwalking an emotional cause should be sought.

SLOWNESS

Slow development in infancy is characteristic of mental handicap but delay in purely motor function may be due to a disordered function of nerves or muscles, or perhaps even bony deformities, unassociated with mental subnormality. In such cases the child's social and linguistic development will probably be normal. It is important therefore that a child displaying slow development in any particular area be carefully assessed from all aspects. (See *cerebral palsy, *development, *mental handicap.)

Slow feeding. Some babies and many small children are slow feeders, sometimes simply because their appetites are small but often because they are far more interested in their surroundings than in their food. Many children have never experienced hunger, having always had their meals provided frequently and regularly. Parents in general worry far too much about what their children eat. A child in the midst of plenty will not starve and there is never any need to force children to eat against their wishes (see *feeding). A reasonable time should be set aside for meals, which should be happy events in a home and not periods of stress and strain. Once a child has lost interest in a meal and starts simply playing with her food instead of eating it, her plate should be removed and the meal considered at an end. The child who is able to feed herself entirely should always be allowed to do so without help and the baby who is just beginning to use a spoon should be given one to manipulate so that she has the feeling that she is helping the process. If her contributions are not directed along such positive channels, they are likely to become negativistic and result in food refusal and endless dawdling.

SMACKING
See "punishment and *discipline

SMALL HEAD
See *microcephaly

SMALLPOX
This disease no longer exists and smallpox vaccination is no longer necessary. The elimination of smallpox is one of the triumphs of preventive medicine.

SMEGMA
When two skin surfaces are closely opposed, as between the foreskin and the underlying glans of the penis, it is normal for skin debris to accumulate. Secondary infection of such accumulations with bacteria and fungi may produce an odour and sometimes a degree of irritation. In girls, smegma may accumulate to a lesser degree within the folds of the labia. With ordinary cleansing, however, smegma should never be a problem.

In small boys the foreskin is adherent to the glans and natural separation occurs only after several years. Because such separation occurs somewhat irregularly there may be small pockets formed and these may cause minor irritation before the contents are extruded. Most boys handle this problem for themselves but some may need reassurance that there is nothing abnormal about their condition.

SMILING
This landmark in a baby's progress usually takes place between 6 and 8 weeks of age but many babies smile much earlier, some within a week or two of birth. Delay in smiling may be a result of social deprivation, as in the institutionalised child; sensory defect, for example blindness; muscular weakness of the facial muscles or interference with their nerve supply; or it more commonly forms part of the picture of general mental retardation. Allowance must of course always be made for the premature baby.

SMOKE

The deleterious effects of cigarette smoking are widely known but some people continue to prefer to blind themselves to reality. Few of us would question their right to harm themselves but most would dispute their right to harm their children. Smoking during pregnancy has been shown to reduce birth size and almost certainly has a harmful effect on all tissues including the brain. Children are often forced into a position of passive smoking when their parents indulge in the habit in confined environments and the resulting irritation aggravates their colds, coughs and asthma. If the child later on emulates her parents' smoking habits she exposes herself to grave dangers in the form of chronic bronchitis and lung cancer. Fortunately many children are revolted by their parents' smoking and do not follow their example.

SNAKEBITE

Of the 140-odd types of snake in southern Africa only 14 are dangerously poisonous. It is wise therefore for people living in country areas to know their snakes, for the majority of snakebites are harmless and as treatment with serum is by no means free of danger it should be administered only when there is reasonable certainty regarding the poisonous nature of the bite. Those who live in snake-infested areas would be well advised to buy one of the excellent books available on the subject and to obtain from the Department of Health their useful booklet, *Poisonous South African Snakes and Snakebite*. It is also wise to keep on stock for immediate use 4 to 6 ampoules of snakebite serum with syringes and needles for administration, and you should learn from suitably qualified persons how to give an intramuscular or, better, an intravenous injection.

The dangerous snakes can be divided into:

(1) The adders (including the puffadder, berg-adder, night-adder, burrowing adder and gaboon adder).

(2) The front-fanged snakes (which include the cobras, e.g. Cape cobra, Egyptian cobra, spitting cobra and rinkhals as well as the mambas).

(3) The back-fanged snakes (including the boomslang and the bird snake).

An expert will be able to identify a snake if it can be produced, but when children are the victims identification is usually impossible and only a guess can be made from the child's description. It is therefore often easier to determine whether the bite has been poisonous by the appearance of symptoms. Local symptoms in the region of the bite usually appear rapidly — within minutes — and systemic symptoms, e.g. with cobra and mamba bites, also appear rapidly. Boomslang poison has a delayed effect but bites by this snake are extremely uncommon. For practical purposes, if no reaction has occurred within 1 hour of the bite the snake was not poisonous.

The adders

These are the most common causes of poisonous snakebite. In decreasing order of importance and severity they are the puffadder, burrowing adder, berg-adder, horned adder and night-adder.

The puffadder. This is easily recognised because of its fat and slothful appearance. Its sluggish movements, however, belie its rapid bite. Its venom is extremely toxic, causing extensive local tissue destruction and severe pain. There is also a somewhat delayed effect on the blood. In known cases of puffadder bite, anti-venom should be given as soon as possible, the dose being a minimum of 20 ml, preferably given intravenously but, if this is impossible, intramuscularly. Tourniquets should not be applied, as this is likely to increase the local tissue destruction.

The berg-adder. This well-patterned greyish snake is slimmer and much more excitable than his cousin the puffadder. The venom produces relatively little local reaction, although there is some pain and swelling, but the most notable toxic effect is on the nervous system. There is usually paralysis of the eye muscles, and there may be other manifestations such as dizziness and difficulty in swallowing. Such symptoms usually persist for a few days only but occasionally may last up to 2 weeks. These symptoms are not life-threatening and no specific treatment is necessary. Anti-venom serum is ineffective and its use is therefore contraindicated.

Night-adder. The venom of the night-adder resembles that of the puffadder but is much less potent. It produces local irritation but usually no tissue destruction. Treatment with serum therefore is not required. Unfortunately, however, the identity of the snake is often in doubt and if the possibility exists of puffadder bite, early administration of serum is advisable.

The burrowing adder. Because of this snake's adaptation to a burrowing existence, the fangs are peculiar and the snake is not able to bite in normal fashion but sweeps the head backwards in a horizontal arc so as to impale one fang only in the victim. This snake is a glossy black colour and usually comes out at night, especially in wet conditions. The poison causes fairly severe local reaction but may also cause general effects, with nausea, vomiting, abdominal pain and sweating and, in addition, neurological disturbances such as paralysis of the pupil, deafness and difficulty in swallowing. Although there is no good evidence of the value of polyvalent anti-venom it should probably be administered in cases of burrowing adder bites.

The gaboon adder. This is a large, vividly coloured snake whose habitat is fortunately confined to the north-eastern regions of South Africa and neighbouring Mozambique. The poison is extremely potent and a gaboon adder bite is a grave emergency. A dose of 40–60 ml of anti-serum should be administered immediately, preferably intravenously, and the patient admitted to hospital as soon as possible.

The front-fanged snakes

The cobras and mambas are the cause of virtually all early deaths from snake-bite. There are 18 species and sub-species in this group and of these 10 are highly dangerous. They are long, rapidly moving snakes and fairly easily identified, the cobras and rinkhals by the striking position they adopt and their hoods, and the mambas by their size and colour. The poison of the front-fanged snakes causes only slight local reaction and its main effect is on the nervous system, producing paralysis, particularly of the muscles of respiration. Death occurs within minutes or up to 24 hours. Patients who survive beyond this time should recover completely. Because it is important to prevent spread of the poison until anti-serum can be given, a tourniquet can be used to prevent the circulation of blood in the bitten limb, but remember that tourniquets can be extremely dangerous and should be loosened at least half-hourly for a few minutes, to prevent gangrene.

Once the patient has been given anti-venom the tourniquet must be removed. A dose of 40 ml of anti-venom should be administered intravenously as soon as possible. Respiration must be maintained, artificially if necessary, and the patient transported rapidly to hospital.

Egyptian cobra. This snake, which may grow up to about 2,5 m in length, is interesting in that it has two colour phases — one in which it is banded in alternate yellow and black bands, the latter being the wider, and a uniform phase in which it is evenly brown or black. It often lives in abandoned ant nests.

Cape cobra. This snake, growing up to about 2 m in length, inhabits the more arid regions and varies greatly in colour, from black to ivory with intervening shades of brown, yellow and speckled. It inhabits rodent burrows and may enter buildings, being little disturbed by human proximity.

Spitting cobras. Three varieties of cobras and the rinkhals can eject venom up to a distance of about 2,5 m and they are remarkably skilled at aiming at the eye. The venom is intensely irritating, and spitting is usually sufficient to provide the snake's defence. Further provocation, however, will lead to biting. The poison is rather more locally irritating than other cobra venoms but its main effect is still on the nervous system. The treatment of a bite is therefore as for other cobras. Venom in the eye should be washed out with liberal quantities of water. There is no point in adding serum or instilling serum into the eye, as this may cause further irritation and does no good.

Rinkhals. This snake is rather fatter than the true cobra and rarely achieves a length much over 1 m. Its name derives from the 2 or 3 pale bands which lie just under the hood. In addition to its hissing and spitting behaviour it is also an expert at feigning dead. From this position however it will strike rapidly if too closely approached. Treatment both for the eyes and for bites is as for the cobras.

Black mamba. Contrary to popular belief, the black mamba is a rather shy snake but it is rightly feared because of the extremely toxic nature of its venom, death within minutes of a bite having been recorded. It is widely distributed over southern Africa. Average length is about 2 m but it may grow to well over 3 m. The inside of the mouth is black but the body is usually a dark grey or dark brown. Because of its large size the snake can rear to a considerable height and bites may therefore occur on the trunk rather than on the leg.

Green mamba. This is a thinner snake, usually about 2 m in length, and is found in the sub-tropical coastal belt only. Because it lives strictly in trees, bites are not very common. The venom is similar to that of the black mamba but less virulent.

Other front-fanged snakes. Included in this group are the coral snakes, the shield-nosed snakes, the garter snakes and sea-snakes. Bites from these snakes are very rare.

Summary of treatment for attacks by front-fanged snakes:

(1) For spitting snakes wash out the eyes with liberal quantities of water.

(2) For bites by these snakes,

(a) Apply a tourniquet immediately but remember to release it every ½ hour and to remove it as soon as anti-venom has been administered.

(b) Give anti-venom to a total of 40 ml as soon as possible, preferably intravenously but otherwise intramuscularly.

(3) Get the patient to hospital as soon as possible, as supportive treatment will almost certainly be necessary. Meanwhile, maintain respiration.

The back-fanged snakes

Although this family includes 45 species, only 2 are of importance for human beings as far as bites are concerned, namely the boomslang and the bird snake. Bites from these creatures are rare. Because the fangs are situated at the back of the mouth, such snakes tend to hang on to their victim and have to be forcefully removed. The poison of these snake is slow-acting and affects the blood, causing extensive bleeding. The ordinary polyvalent anti-venom has no effect on the toxin of the back-fanged snakes. A special serum is, however, available for boomslang bites and should be obtained if there is little doubt about the identity of the snake.

Boomslang. These snakes are usually bright green and achieve a length of about 1,5 m. The colour, however, varies considerably, some being black with yellow belly and others varying shades of brown to brick red.

Bird snake. This is a very slender snake which rather resembles a dried twig. When provoked it inflates the front half of its body. The poison of this snake has the same effect as that of the boomslang but there is no appropriate anti-venom available. Treatment is supportive and requires hospital care.

In the management of snakebite in children no less anti-venom should be given than in the case of an adult. In patients suspected of being allergic to horse serum, a very small quantity should first be administered to determine reactions before administering the whole dose. It is wise to have in addition to the serum some adrenaline and also an injectible corticosteroid in case of severe reactions.

SNEEZING

Though commonly associated with a cold or with nasal irritation as the result of inhalation of irritants, e.g. pepper, sneezing is often a perfectly normal activity, especially in babies. Do not imagine therefore each time your baby sneezes that she has a cold. It is simply a natural way of clearing the nose. Chronic sneezing is usually a manifestation of allergic rhinitis and when this is seasonal it may be called hayfever (see *rhinitis).

SNUFFLES, SNUFFLING

Snuffles is the term given to the inflammation of the nose due to congenital syphilis. This presents as a chronic nasal discharge in babies, often associated with other syphilitic manifestations, particularly bony involvement. Untreated, the condition may persist for months. It eventually leads to destruction of the nasal bones, giving rise to the typical saddle nose in later childhood.

Simple snuffling is common in babies and may persist for many months, requiring no treatment. More severe nasal catarrh is sometimes due to milk allergy.

SODIUM

One of the most important elements in the body, sodium is found largely in the extracellular fluids, as opposed to potassium which is largely an intracellular ion. Loss of water leading to dehydration is accompanied by a variable sodium loss (see *dehydration, *salt).

SOILING

Soiling with faeces beyond the age at which one expects the child to be toilet-trained may be due to retarded development, to mechanical incompetence of the anus, as may be found in spina bifida, to severe diarrhoeal states with loss of control, or more commonly to *constipation, and sometimes it is associated with severe emotional disturbance. The management will obviously depend upon the cause. It is a symptom which should not be ignored, as delay in seeking correct treatment will inevitably aggravate the situation. Soiling therefore is always to be taken seriously.

SORES

Children are rather prone to skin infections and may develop multiple sores, sometimes of the face (*impetigo) and often of the legs and other areas. Such infections are usually spread by scratching and the predisposing cause is therefore frequently an itchy condition such as scabies, tick bites or irritation from grass. Such sores on the legs are commonly referred to as Natal sores, a wholly unjustifiable accusation! Skin infections of this type, particularly when associated with scabies, and especially in African children, are a common cause of nephritis.

Treatment consists of gently removing the scabs by soaking, and applying an antiseptic preparation, e.g. mercurochrome lotion (not the tincture) or a cream such as clioquinol. Occasionally an antibiotic may have to be administered to control spread.

Deeper-seated skin infections are in the nature of boils and these present a rather different problem. (See *boils.)

SORE THROAT

When one considers that the throat is the gateway to both the respiratory and the digestive tracts, and the enormous volumes of air, food and fluid which pass through it daily, it is not surprising that sore throat is one of the most common complaints. This may occasionally arise as the result of trauma or chemical irritation but is usually due to infection. Many viruses infect the throat, often in conjunction with the nose, producing general upper respiratory infection, and the streptococcus may cause diffuse throat infection in addition to septic tonsillitis. Many germs are found in the throat but usually reside there happily without causing disease.

It is important to determine if possible the cause of a sore throat, for whereas the common virus infections require no specific treatment, a streptococcal infection should be treated with penicillin in adequate doses for 10 days. Unfortunately, clinical assessment is very inaccurate, being correct in only about 60 per cent of cases. Bacteriological investigation is helpful but is expensive and often impractical. To be on the safe side, therefore, doctors often treat with penicillin and this has justification in that the complications of streptococcal infection, namely nephritis and rheumatic fever, are thereby prevented. However, to treat every sore throat with penicillin is unnecessarily extravagant and unwise. If the child basically has a cold, of which the sore throat is only part, you have no need to take her to a doctor. (See *colds.) For the ordinary sore throat a soothing pastille is all that is required.

SOYA BEANS

Like other legumes, soya beans are an excellent and cheap source of protein.

Many meat substitutes are now made of soya, which also forms the basis for several proprietary milk substitutes for children allergic to or intolerant of cows' milk.

SOYA 'MILKS'

Proprietary milk substitutes based on soya protein with added fats and carbohydrate include Infasoy, Isomil and Prosobee. These preparations contain added vitamins and iron and are therefore complete feeds for the small infant. They are prepared in the same way as other dried-milk preparations. Babies with milk allergy or lactose intolerance are usually put on a soya feed and generally this solves the problem. However, up to 20 per cent of babies allergic to milk will also develop allergy to soya.

It is common practice when a baby is unhappy on a milk feed to try a change to a soya feed, and occasionally this helps. It is, however, wise to perform the experiment at least twice to make sure that the improvement observed is not due to coincidence. There is currently a craze for milk allergy, and soya feeds have become unnecessarily fashionable. They are not a panacea for every problem (see *allergy). Unless your child is clearly better on a soya feed she should probably have milk. Where there is a strong family history of allergy a baby should ideally be breastfed for at least the first 6 months. If this is impossible there is some justification for withholding cows' milk for this time, as there is evidence that sensitisation is thereby reduced.

SPASTICITY

All muscles have a certain inherent tone; that is, they are not completely flaccid even when relaxed. Muscle tone is governed through the nerve supply. When the nerve fibres from the brain to the spinal cord are interrupted, the tone of muscles supplied by such nerve fibres increases and spasticity results. This is seen in people who have had strokes and is common in children who suffer from *cerebral palsy, most of whom display some degree of spasticity. This considerably impedes normal muscle function and is difficult to overcome with either physiotherapy or drugs. Considerable success is obtained in some cases, however, by selective section of the nerve roots in the spine.

SPEECH

Of all the attributes which distinguish man from lower animals, speech is the most important, and all human cultures are dependent upon the spoken and written word for their perpetuation.

Speech development. From the age of about 6 weeks, a baby learns to experiment with pleasant cooing sounds, and at 3 months she will emit a variety of squeals, grunts, gurgles and humming noises. These become progressively refined in imitation of the noises she hears and she will indulge in a 'conversation' in which she is clearly trying to communicate. From 6 to 8 months she will begin to use consonant sounds, so that she creates syllables such as ba, da, ma, pa. A little later she will put two of these together and mama, dada, papa, baba become her first words. At 1 year of age the average baby has a vocabulary of 3 to 4 words, but in addition she does a great deal of babbling. By 18 months she will probably be joining words together, e.g. 'mommy come', and by 2 years she will probably be making 2- to 3-word sentences. As in the case of an adult learning a foreign language, she is able to understand a great deal more than she can say.

The rate of speech development is extremely variable but it may be influenced by several factors. Hearing is particularly important and the unusually silent child should have her hearing checked. The child deprived of exposure to language, such as the institutionalised child, is likely to have slower speech development and a less rich vocabulary than the more verbally privileged child. See to it therefore that your baby has as rich an exposure as possible. Talk to her, sing to her, play with her and laugh with her, read to her and tell her stories. Applaud her progress and add colour to her own efforts at every opportunity. In this way you will enrich and encourage her language development as well as increase your own satisfaction and enjoyment in your child. (See also *development.)

Speech problems. Minor speech defects during the first 3 years or so of life are common and need not at this stage cause anxiety. Lalling, lisping, stuttering, stammering and cluttering have a good chance of spontaneous resolution. If, however, at the age of 4 such speech defects are increasing rather than diminishing in severity, it would be wise to see a speech therapist. Formal speech correction before this age is usually of little value. You can help your child a great deal yourself by speaking distinctly and encouraging her to imitate you. Many young children's thoughts seem to proceed at a rate greater than their ability to put them into words, but with simple speech maturation the difficulties resolve. It is of course always important to have the child tested for partial deafness and other physical abnormalities. Tongue-tie is never a cause of speech defect.

SPIDER-BITES

Few spiders have jaws strong enough to bite and even fewer are venomous. Most notorious, however, is the button spider, which is readily recognised by its round black body and the characteristic 'hour-glass' marking on the underside of the abdomen. The bite inflicts local pain and the poison may cause severe generalised symptoms, particularly abdominal pain and vomiting. The mortality rate is very low but patients can be very ill. A specific anti-venom is available but should be used with circumspection.

There are other spiders, for example the violin spider, whose bite is venomous and causes some tissue destruction with ulceration. These spiders are not spontaneously aggressive but usually bite at night when they are rolled upon.

SPINA BIFIDA

The spinal vertebrae develop in such a way that in addition to the solid weight-bearing front part, an arch is formed enclosing the spinal cord. Sometimes this bony arch does not form properly and remains open. When the skin-covering is normal this condition is known as spina bifida occulta. It is usually detected only by X-ray examination and as a rule it causes no trouble.

The position is much more serious when the skin-covering is not intact. In such cases the coverings of the spinal cord, the meninges, may form a swelling in the area of the defect, the condition then being known as meningocoele. When the meninges, too, are deficient, the spinal cord lies open to the exterior, this condition being known as myelocoele. In such cases the nerves are imperfectly developed and varying degrees of paralysis and impaired sensation accompany the abnormality. Spina bifida is usually seen in the lower spinal regions but may occur at any level. It is often accompanied by hydrocephalus (water on the brain), which if not present at birth frequently supervenes later, especially if the defect is surgically closed. It can be corrected by insertion of a shunt that allows the excessive fluid to drain into the abdomen or the circulation.

With lower spinal deformities there is likely to be incontinence both of bladder and of bowels, and with the larger defects, severe paralysis of the legs. There may be other deformities of the spine. Careful clinical evaluation combined with commonsense must determine whether operative closure of the defect is worthwhile. Such operations protect the spinal cord and prevent infection but they cannot correct the neurological defects. Severe cases, therefore, in which the child would be left with appalling physical handicaps are best left untreated.

SPOILING

Is it possible to 'spoil' a child? Most people looking about them would give an unequivocal answer in the affirmative. But the spoilt child is a phenomenon of the beholder and the child who to others may be a 'spoilt brat' may to her parents be the perfect angel. It all depends what you want. Most of us do not like a child to rule her parents from dawn to midnight. Most of us expect children to be reasonably disciplined and well behaved, to show a degree of unselfishness appropriate to their age and to learn progressively that immediate gratification of every desire is not possible but is more likely to be achieved if an effort is made to work towards it. We must at all times look at children's behaviour in the light of their age and development. We must make allowances for social background and cultural habits as well as the financial standing of the family. A child who is indulged out of proportion to the family income is inevitably depriving other members of something, but the child of well-to-do parents who 'has everything' is hardly spoilt simply on this account. Such parents would feel guilty if they did not give their children every advantage they could afford. Such lavishness need not result in ingratitude, or over-demanding and bad manners.

No child can be spoilt by genuine affection. If you want to cuddle your baby for heaven's sake cuddle her. Do not be afraid that this will 'spoil her'. The time will come when she will not want much to be cuddled, especially in public, and then you will regret having missed your opportunities. Babies get lonely and if yours indicates that she wants your company, let her have it. In return, however, she has to realise that there are times when you have to do your own thing and she must learn consideration for you, because you, too, have rights and these rights she must at an early age be made to respect. You must decide early on how you want your child to behave and then consistently direct her along these lines. If you allow bad habits to develop these will be very difficult to reverse. Try to avoid head-on clashes but if one should develop, see that you win it. Having won, though, display no rancour but make it up immediately by a show of appropriate affection.

Some parents compensate for a lack of affection towards their children by physical over-indulgence. This of course is no compensation at all and simply encourages greed. Above all be fair; a child will accept almost anything if it seems to her fair, but you cannot expect her to clean her shoes if you do not clean your own; likewise she cannot expect you to over-indulge her at the cost of significant deprivation of yourselves. (See also *discipline.)

SPONGING

The small child who is running a very high temperature may be in danger of convulsing, and a useful way of bringing the temperature down is to sponge her with cool water. The water should be cool rather than ice cold, as the latter causes constriction of the vessels in the skin and diminishes blood flow. The skin therefore becomes very cold but the core temperature remains little altered. Placing in a cool bath is equally effective. (See *fever.)

SPRAINS

A sprain is a tear in a ligament surrounding a joint. It causes immediate pain and subsequently some swelling and after a day or two there may be bruising. This does not imply progressive injury but indicates simply that bleeding which occurred with the injury has now reached the skin, to cause discolouration. The ankle is the most common region affected. Severe ligamentous tears can be very incapacitating but in children particularly they always heal satisfactorily. Immediate application of cold, in the form of cold water or ice pack, helps to reduce the degree of bleeding and swelling. A supportive bandage will rest the joint and this assists repair. Prolonged immobilisation for minor sprains, however, is undesirable. More severe injuries should be seen by a doctor.

SQUINT

The axes of the eyes are normally parallel when looking at distant objects; when focusing on a near object it is normal to squint. The eyes should never diverge.

At birth the baby has poor control over her eye movements and squinting therefore is not abnormal. She is able to focus for short periods at a time, particularly on her mother's face. Eye control increases progressively and by 3 months of age she should be able to follow an object through her full range of eye movement. If squinting persists with a baby over 3 months of age she should be seen by a doctor. It is unlikely that anything would be done for a further few months but the eyes should be checked. Many babies give the illusion of squinting simply because the nasal bridge is wide, and there may be epicanthic folds over the inner aspect of the eye which will then give the impression that the eye is turning in. If in doubt, look for the reflection of a torch or a window off the cornea; the images should occupy the same place in each eye.

Squints are of two main types:

(1) Paralytic squints are due to weakness of one or more of the eye muscles and are usually evident when the child looks in a particular direction.

(2) Concomitant squints tend to be present no matter in what direction the child looks. They may be due to muscular imbalance or to errors of refraction. Such squints require expert attention.

STAMMERING AND STUTTERING

See *speech defects

STEALING

A toddler thinks she has a right to everything she sees. She can hardly be accused of stealing — though she nevertheless has gently to be taught to respect other people's property. The small child who 'lifts' a sweet or two from the supermarket cannot be regarded as a criminal but again the behaviour requires correction. The boy who pinches the neighbour's fruit is doing so for fun rather than with evil intentions and although the neighbour may rightfully be angry there need be no great cause for concern. The youngster who is stealing from his mother's purse and probably spending the money to buy friendship is crying out for affection, and although it may be difficult to understand and to respond appropriately, nevertheless such a child needs help. Stealing at school may get a child into serious trouble but punishment is not likely to cure the situation, which demands rather a sympathetic ear and probably psychological help. Stealing at a later age is more indicative of a criminal tendency and must therefore be taken very seriously. Should you encounter the problem of repeated stealing in your child, you may yourself be able to recognise the cause and deal with it appropriately but if your efforts are unsuccessful do not be tardy in seeking additional help from your doctor or from a psychologist. Simply hoping that the situation will improve is not enough. It almost certainly won't and will probably get worse unless the child's emotional problem is unearthed and remedied.

Above all make sure that your own standards are correct. You cannot expect your child to display complete honesty if she is aware that her parents are cheating the tax man, proudly evading customs duty, or defrauding their customers. If you have your little fiddles keep them concealed from your children unless you are specifically training them for the same crime!

STEAM

Inhalation of steam is often soothing and relieving in conditions such as sinusitis and croup. Moist warm air is less irritating than cold dry air, which is normally humidified and warmed by its passage through the nose. Humidification may be achieved by simply boiling a kettle or pan of water in the vicinity of the child, and the concentration of steam can be increased by directing its flow with a towel. Alternatively, the head may be held over a bowl of steaming hot water or hot water may be run into a bath and the child sat over it. It is of course extremely important to avoid scalds, especially in the case of restless young children with croup. The addition of medications to the water such as Friar's Balsam, camphor, eucalyptus, etc., does not significantly add to the efficacy, though it makes the procedure more impressive.

In hospitals, steam is now usually replaced by cold mist generated by a nebuliser. This is safer than steam but possibly less effective.

STERILISATION

Because germs are so readily spread by artificial feeding it is essential that for the first several months of the baby's life the feeds and feeding equipment be as sterile as possible. Bottles and teats may be sterilised either by boiling or by soaking in a sterilising fluid. For this purpose sodium hypochlorite (Milton) is ideal, as it is completely non-toxic. Bottles and teats should be thoroughly cleansed after use, the teats being rubbed with salt to remove any milk debris and clean water squirted through the holes to clear them. Bottles and teats must then be completely submerged in the hypochlorite solution for at least 3 hours. Be careful to avoid air bubbles, as the solution must come into direct contact with the surface in order to sterilise it. There is no need to rinse the bottles before filling them with milk.

If the boiling method is used, the bottles should be boiled for 10 minutes and the teats for 5, as excessive boiling causes deterioration of the rubber.

The feed itself should be prepared in a scrupulously clean bowl by adding the requisite quantity of milk powder to boiled water. It is usually more convenient to prepare the total quantity of feed for 24 hours but individual feeds can be prepared separately. Once the bottles have been filled and capped they should be stored in the refrigerator, as this method of sterilisation is not 100 per cent effective and standing at room temperature would enable germs to proliferate in the milk.

The method of terminal sterilisation is more effective and is used in hospitals. The bottles, having been thoroughly cleaned, are filled with the requisite quantity of feed and lightly capped. They may then be stacked upright in a pan of boiling water and maintained at this temperature for 20 minutes. After cooling, the caps are tightened. The contents of the bottle are then completely sterile. Refrigeration before use is therefore unnecessary.

How long should sterilisation be continued? Although some doctors advocate complete sterilisation for the first year, this is unrealistic. By 6 months a baby is putting all sorts of things into her mouth, many anything but sterile, and to continue to sterilise her bottles after this age is out of proportion. Cleanliness is desirable at all times and it is largely the lack of facilities or care for simple hygiene that is responsible for the devastating incidence of gastro-enteritis among the less privileged members of society. Cleanliness may for some be next to godliness but for us all it is vital to health.

STINGS (see also *insects, *scorpion stings)

Stings from bees, wasps and hornets are very similar in effect, but whereas the bee can sting only once, the others may make repeated attacks. A bee sting is barbed and therefore stays in the skin together with the poison sac attached. When removing it, therefore, be careful not to squeeze the poison sac as this will simply inject more venom. As a rule bees will sting only when they feel threatened and children should be trained to keep still and not to swat at bees when they come near. The stung child, being in considerable discomfort, will want something applied to relieve the pain. Whatever you do will have a psychological benefit but will be of little medicinal value. A cold compress will perhaps reduce the swelling to some extent.

Severe reactions may occur as the result of multiple bee stings, in which case the victim may be shocked and require medical help.

Of rather more concern is the person who is sensitive to bee venom, who reacts not just with a severe local reaction but with generalised manifestations such as urticaria, swelling of the face and throat with breathing difficulty, vomiting, etc. In such cases suitable precautions should be taken against the possibility of future stings. There are two alternatives. The patient or parent can be furnished with adrenaline to be given by injection immediately after a sting, augmented if necessary by an antihistamine preparation and a corticosteroid. If there should be a problem in maintaining the availability of such medications then the patient should be desensitised to bee venom. Whole bee extracts are not particularly effective but the pure bee-venom vaccine is a considerable improvement. Unfortunately it is impossible to tell when desensitisation has been effective (except by being stung) and it is difficult to know how long it should be maintained. In general, therefore, reliance is better placed on prompt administration of adrenaline when stings occur.

STRABISMUS
See *squint

STRAWBERRY MARK
See *birthmark

STOMACHACHE
See *abdominal pain

STOOLS
See *faeces

STREPTOCOCCUS
A small spherical bacterium growing in chains on culture and responsible for a variety of infections, particularly tonsillitis and impetigo. Some strains lead to nephritis and some to rheumatic fever in susceptible subjects. The streptococcus is always obligingly penicillin sensitive, and penicillin is therefore the antibiotic of choice in treating streptococcal infections.

STUTTERING
See *speech defects

STYES
These are really boils involving the hair follicles of the eyelashes. Like boils elsewhere they often tend to recur. Once a stye has formed there is little one can do but to wait for it to discharge and resolve. Traditional treatment is the application of warmth by hot sponging; a wad of bandage or other material is wound round a wooden spoon, dipped in warm water and applied to the eye repeatedly. This is comforting in that it at least gives the impression that something is being done, but the process of resolution is not significantly speeded.

Recurrent styes are best dealt with by daily application of an antibacterial ointment to the eyelids to prevent invasion by the staphylococcal germ responsible.

SUFFOCATION
This is the result of inadequate air entry through the nose or mouth. It may result from inhalation of noxious fumes or from mechanical obstruction. One of the commonest causes of suffocation in children is the plastic bag. Children find it very

tempting to pull these over the head and many fatalities have been reported. Do not therefore leave plastic bags lying around when small children are about and instruct your child at an early age regarding the dangers of such activity. Children also may suffocate in very confined spaces, for instance in disused refrigerators, the doors of which cannot be opened from the inside.

The danger of suffocation from bedding has been grossly exaggerated. Even small babies will turn their heads to the side and not keep their noses buried in the mattress. Pillows are unnecessary for small children, whose heads are nearly as big as their bodies.

SUGAR

The sugars are simple carbohydrates which are involved mainly in energy metabolism. Those of importance in man are of 2 main types.

(1) Monosaccharides. Of these, glucose is the most important as it is very readily metabolised, but others are fructose (fruit sugar) and galactose (derived from milk sugar, lactose).

(2) Disaccharides. Each consists of 2 molecules of monosaccharide. They include sucrose (glucose + fructose), maltose (glucose + glucose) and lactose (glucose + galactose). The disaccharides have to be split by digestive processes into their monosaccharide components before they can be absorbed. If not so split, e.g. as in lactose intolerance, they pass on through the bowel taking water with them and causing diarrhoea. All absorbed sugars are eventually converted into glucose.

Ordinary table sugar is sucrose. It is a good source of calories but has no other nutritive value. It is consumed in gross excess by nearly all populations and is responsible for much diabetes, obesity, dental caries and disease of the heart and blood vessels. You will be wise therefore to discourage sweet tastes in your children.

SUNBURN (see *burns)

Sunburn differs in no way from other burns but the burnt area is often extensive and therefore very uncomfortable. Sunburn should be prevented by graded exposure and by application of barrier preparations many of which are highly effective. Once the burn has occurred nothing will alter its course. It is difficult to do nothing, especially in the case of a child, but applications should at least not be too messy. A strong solution of sodium bicarbonate or simple calamine lotion is all that is required. Blisters should be left to rupture spontaneously as they afford some protection to the underlying raw area.

SUNSTROKE

This is synonymous with heat stroke and is not due to the direct effect of the sun's rays. (See *heat stroke.)

SWALLOWING DIFFICULTIES

Swallowing is a complex mechanism requiring remarkable co-ordination of the muscles of the throat. Difficulty in swallowing therefore may be experienced when the nerve supply is affected, for example in some cases of cerebral palsy or in muscular diseases. More commonly, swallowing difficulty arises as the result of a sore throat. Severe difficulty occurs when an abscess forms in the back of the throat, as in quinsy. Relatively sudden onset of difficulty in swallowing without sore throat suggests a foreign body stuck in the gullet. Any such case, therefore, should be seen promptly by a doctor.

SWEARING

Swearing, like nostalgia in the famous graffito, is not what it was. In a world in which profanities have become so fashionable it is difficult to know what constitutes swearing. Children exposed to the language not only of their parents and friends but also of the TV and cinema can hardly be expected not to emulate their heroes. When your child first utters a swear word you will probably be rather shocked and wonder where she might have picked up such an obscenity. Consider the possibility that it might have been from you! The small child will probably not know the meaning of the word and is only trying to experiment, simply because she has heard it or possibly in an attempt to shock you. Don't be shocked. This would give her the satisfaction she wants and encourage further similar experiments, particularly with other adults. A gentle explanation of the correct choice of social language is all that is required and punishment should never be applied.

At a later age, children, particularly boys, will swear in an attempt to impress, and again a non-reaction on your part is better than a tirade of disapproval. Set an example of restraint yourselves and explain to your offspring that there are more expressive adjectives than 'bloody', which usually adds nothing to descriptiveness, and explain to him that expletives overused lose their effectiveness as emotional deflaters. You can be reasonably confident that your child will adopt your own swearing habits.

SWEATING

Sweating is normal. It goes on all the time and only becomes noticeable when the rate of sweat-production exceeds evaporation. It is an extremely efficient way of cooling the body because in the process of evaporation considerable heat is lost. In very humid conditions, however, evaporation cannot occur and the body sweats in vain.

Excessive sweating may be seen in feverish states; during severe exertion, especially in hot, humid conditions; as the result of overdressing, particularly in small children; and in certain disease states such as thyrotoxicosis (excessive secretion by the thyroid gland), low blood-sugar levels, shock states, and in children with rickets and certain forms of congenital heart disease. Deficient sweating may occur in certain skin abnormalities with defective sweat glands, in severe protein malnutrition and in cystic fibrosis, in which case the sweat is extremely salty. Defective sweating may predispose to heat stroke.

Excessive sweating of the hands can be a handicap. It is common in schoolchildren as well as in nervous adults. The sweating can be reduced by drugs which block the sympathetic nervous system, e.g. propranolol.

SWEAT RASH

This is common in babies and infants and is usually the result of overdressing.

The rash occurs particularly over the shoulder and chest regions and in the neck. The relationship to the sweat glands is usually fairly obvious. The treatment is to keep the child cool by removing unnecessary garments and reducing atmospheric temperature by means of a fan. A simple application such as calamine lotion is as soothing as anything.

SWEAT TEST

This is a most useful test for confirming suspected cystic fibrosis. A sample of sweat is collected and tested for its sodium and chloride contents. High figures are diagnostic of the condition with an accuracy of 97 per cent.

SWEETS

The occasional sweet can hardly be denied or regarded as a menace but excessive sweet-eating cannot be condoned. Sugar around the teeth encourages the growth of caries-producing germs, and sweets are therefore a potent cause of dental decay. (See *caries.) Excessive consumption of sweets also adds unnecessary calories to the diet and may promote obesity with all its associated ills. Sweets are simply sugar and have therefore no nutritive value, except as a source of calories. You would be wise to curtail your children's sweet-eating habits to an absolute minimum and to encourage their tastes in other directions. Often grandparents and other relatives are the main problem. They naturally want to bring the children a treat, and sweets are the first thing they think of. Try to suggest alternatives such as fruit, dried fruits, biltong or better still small toys or puzzles.

SWIMMING

The proliferation of swimming pools bears ample testimony to the pleasures to be derived from swimming. It also, however, is responsible for several deaths of children per annum. However childproof you may try to make your pool it never seems to be infallible. The only safe way to ensure your child's survival is to teach her to swim. This can be achieved remarkably early. There are, however, as yet no statistics to prove that teaching babies to swim has in fact saved lives. Small children should never swim unaccompanied by adults and if you are fortunate enough to have a pool, please see that it is fenced as securely as possible.

Swimming does carry dangers other than drowning. Crowded public pools, no matter how well the water is kept, will inevitably cause some spread of infection, particularly of the numerous respiratory viruses but also of intestinal infections. Such places are therefore best avoided. Some children develop ear irritation as the result of constant sogginess of the external ear canal. Using ear plugs may help to prevent or reduce the trouble. Children with sinus infection or ear infections should not be allowed to submerge their heads in the water as the increased pressure is likely to aggravate these conditions.

Before allowing your children to swim in rivers, particularly those flowing into the Indian Ocean, make sure that there is no danger of bilharzia. These few precautions will make swimming both safer and more enjoyable for everybody.

TALKING

See *speech

TANTRUMS

It is normal for the 2-year-old to want everything and to want it instantly. He is a wilful creature to whom denial is almost incomprehensible. It is inevitable therefore that there will be clashes of will. Depending on the child's temperament some or many of these may lead to tantrums. If a child is allowed to profit from such exhibitions he quickly realises that they are a useful mechanism for getting his own way and he will then employ them quite deliberately. If therefore your child throws a tantrum see that he does not profit from it. The best thing is to walk calmly away — but not too far, so that he can reach you quickly once the tantrum is over — and to make it quite clear that you are thoroughly unimpressed by the show. Once he is deprived of an audience the tantrum will cease rapidly. A further stage in tantrum behaviour is *breathholding.

TAPEWORM

There are two kinds of common tapeworm. They consist of a tiny head, with which the worm attaches itself to the upper small bowel, and numerous segments, joined end to end and increasing in size as they mature. These segments are white, flattened, more or less rectangular in shape and possessing a degree of mobility. They may migrate out of the anus or be passed in the stools.

The life cycle of the tapeworm demands an intermediate host, either cattle or swine. These animals ingest the tapeworm eggs, which, when they reach the intestine, liberate the parasite, which then gains access to the bloodstream and becomes deposited in the muscles as small cysts. Meat affected in this way is said to be 'measly' but the condition of course bears no resemblance whatever to human measles. Upon human ingestion, the cysts are liberated and one or more may attach themselves to the bowel and develop into a tapeworm. The presence of one worm in some way seems to prevent the development of others. In the case of the pork tapeworm, the human may also serve as intermediate host and develop the cysts, known as cysticerci, in the muscles and also in the brain. In the latter situation, they frequently give rise to epilepsy, and during the acute phase may cause encephalitis. The pork tapeworm is particularly common in Transkei where the lack of sanitation and the fairly high pig population provide ideal conditions for its propagation.

Several preparations are available for treatment of tapeworm, including dichlorophen, niclosamide and mebendazole.

TEARS

Though tears are produced by the baby from birth they are not profuse enough to produce overflow tearing until about 1 month of age. This is, however, very variable. Tears not only lubricate the eye but contain protective substances to guard against infection.

TEATS

No artificial teat can emulate the suppleness and efficiency of the human nipple. Fortunately, the ability of manufacturers to produce ever-increasing variations in size, shape, colour and texture is usually matched by the adaptability of babies. The important thing about a teat is its hole. This should deliver milk at a sufficient rate for the baby to be able to consume an adequate quantity of feed before he tires of sucking. As babies vary greatly in their sucking ability as well as in their volumetric demands, it follows that not every teat will suit every baby. Weakly or premature babies with poor sucking ability require easier-flowing teats than stronger babies. Too large a hole, however, which allows the milk to pour in, may cause choking and drowning. Feeding difficulties in the artificially fed baby are very often due to inappropriate teats and are most usually due to too small a single hole. The correct flow rate is more easily obtained by having two or three holes which do not allow the milk to pour out but which yet give the baby better reward for his efforts than does a single hole. Remember that the human nipple has about 20 holes. Too slow teats can easily be modified by taking a fine needle, holding it in a cork, heating it red hot and plunging it quickly through the teat. Do not try to aim for the hole already present in the hope of enlarging it but simply make an extra hole or two.

Babies with particular feeding difficulties, for example premature babies and babies with cleft palate, may require teats which will deliver the milk with compression rather than suction. This can be achieved by cross-cutting the teat; be careful, however, not to make the cuts too big as otherwise the baby might drown.

Teats tend to deteriorate with time, and especially with boiling, and the holes become progressively larger. So, however, does the baby and he can usually cope with the increased flow as the teats age.

Needless to say, teats should be kept meticulously clean, washed thoroughly after each feed and rubbed with coarse salt on the inside to remove milk particles. They should then be flushed through with clean water and sterilised. (See *sterilisation.)

TEETH

The average times of eruption of the teeth are shown in the diagram. Teething is a very variable process, however. Some babies are born with one or two teeth already erupted and these may cause some initial difficulty in suckling. Very occasionally they might have to be removed. Parents often become concerned if there is delay in the eruption of teeth but it is not rare for the first tooth to appear towards the end of the first year and sometimes later.

Care of the teeth. Although some people advocate brushing from the time of the appearance of the first tooth, this is perhaps over-enthusiastic. By the age of 18 months, however, a child should be brushing his teeth regularly. He should be

20-30
10-16
16-20
8-11
6-8

Deciduous teeth
Usual times of eruption
(age in months)

upper jaw

5-9
7-10
16-20
10-16
20-30

lower jaw

17-22
12-13
6-7
10-12
10-11
11-12
8-9
7-8

Permanent teeth
Usual times of eruption
(age in years)

upper jaw

6-7
7-8
9-11
10-12
11-13
6-7
17-22
12-13

lower jaw

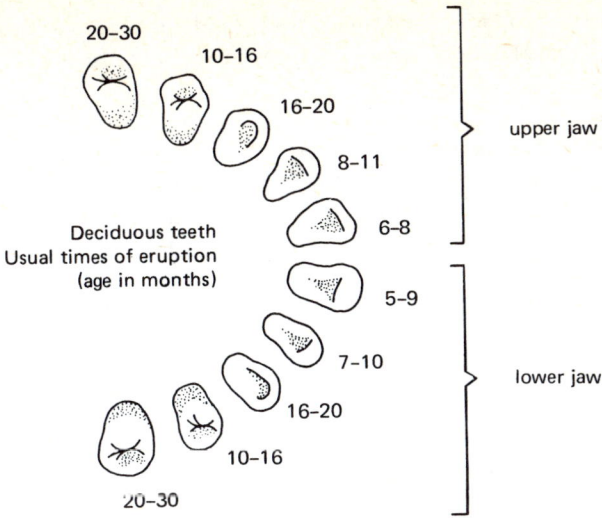

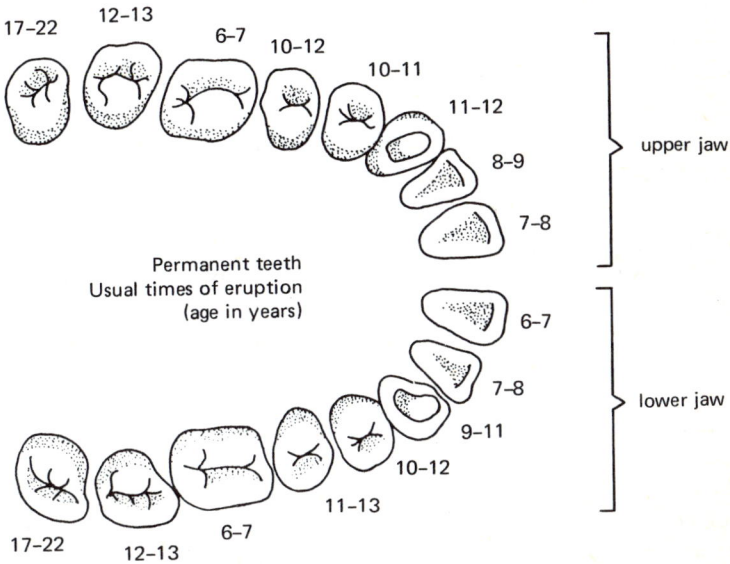

shown how to do this properly, brushing in a vertical rather than a horizontal motion. It is much easier to do this with a small toothbrush rather than a large one, even for adults. A thorough cleansing once a day is more effective than two or three cursory sweeps but ideally the teeth should be brushed to remove all food debris after each meal. Cleaning between the teeth with dental floss is also strongly advocated, especially when the teeth are crowded.

Dental decay is due largely to the adherence of sugars and starches to the teeth, thus promoting the growth of acid-producing germs. 'Bottle rot' of the upper incisors is particularly common in babies whose bottle-feeds are continued beyond 1 year, and especially when sugared drinks are given in this way. Refined starches tend to cling to the teeth and such foods should be kept to a minimum. In areas where fluoride is deficient in drinking water (and this applies to most of southern Africa), additional fluoride will help to prevent dental decay. (See *caries.)

TEETHING

Does teething cause symptoms? It certainly causes more distress to parents than it does to babies. It has to be admitted that some babies do get miserable when cutting a tooth, but teething should never be accepted as a cause of significant symptoms. It so happens that teething begins at the age when all the passive immunity to disease acquired from the mother has waned and the baby then becomes prone to every infection which he encounters. Colds, sore throats, vomiting and diarrhoea are due not to teething but usually to a virus which the baby has picked up. Significant fever is never due to teething and more serious manifestations such as convulsions can certainly not be attributed to this cause. Teething is a convenient scapegoat for every minor indisposition and there is no harm in comforting yourself with this explanation if explanation there must be, but do not delude yourself into imagining that teething is the cause of illness. This is just not so, and if your baby is really unwell another cause must be found.

Mothers often feel that they have to treat their babies for teething. Eruption of the teeth is a natural process which will occur without any help from you. There is no need to rub anything on the gums, give teething powders or administer any other concoction. In the past such medications have caused considerable harm and although they are now relatively innocuous they are absolutely unnecessary. Do not be taken in by commercial predators.

TELEVISION

Many parents worry about the amount of time spent by their children in watching TV, as well as by the influence this might have upon their lives. It has to be admitted that TV is a convenient dummy to make parents' lives more peaceful. A certain amount of information and stimulation might even be gleaned by children from some TV programmes, but much of the mindless trash that is served cannot even be regarded as entertainment. It seems a pity when time is the only commodity that is strictly rationed for each individual that so much of it should be wasted on gainless triviality. The child exposed to more stimulating personal contact will himself ration his TV viewing to those programmes that interest him or which he finds particularly amusing. This is the ideal. Other children, to whom the box provides the only entertainment and interest in life, will naturally resent its being rationed. It is perhaps better to have TV than nothing but emptiness, but do not imagine that it can replace the more satisfying and more stimulating close contact your child needs with you. If you have to ration TV time make sure that you replace it with something better.

Is television medically harmful? There is no evidence that TV strains the eyes, though it may strain the temper. The only adverse effect that it might have medically is to precipitate fits in certain epileptics. There is evidence that violence on TV breeds violence in real life.

TEMPER TANTRUMS

See *tantrums

TEMPERATURE

The normal temperature of the body is somewhere around 37°C taken in the mouth. The rectal temperature is slightly higher. Taking the temperature in the armpit is inaccurate: if taken there the thermometer should be left in position for at least 2 minutes. You can usually tell if your child is running a significant fever by simply feeling him, but skin temperatures are extremely inaccurate and may at times be very misleading. Small babies, particularly premature babies, have very unstable temperatures and have therefore to be kept in a stable environment. Small children when feverish often run wildly fluctuating temperatures. Body temperature normally varies during the day, reaching a low level during the early morning hours and rising during times of activity. Exertion can put up the temperature appreciably. Because exact temperature is of little importance and excessive attention to the thermometer often causes anxiety, it is probably better for the average household not to have a thermometer. The exception is in the case of the child liable to feverish convulsions, in whom the temperature should be kept at a sub-convulsive level, usually below 39°C, and in such cases a thermometer is useful as a guide to appropriate management. (See also *fever.)

TESTICLES

The testes are initially formed within the abdomen, and during the last 2 months of foetal life descend, passing through a canal in the abdominal muscles (the inguinal canal) to find their eventual place in the scrotum. In their descent they are accompanied by a protrusion of the abdominal lining (the peritoneum), a portion of which persists around the testis while the communicating portion disappears. When it persists it may give rise to an inguinal hernia. The testicles and scrotum may be rather impressively large at birth but in young childhood the testes are small and often very mobile, disappearing up towards the inguinal canal, particularly in cold weather. A testis thought to be undescended is often simply retracted in this way.

Maldescent of the testis. A testicle not present in the scrotum at birth may descend later but after the first year of life it will not descend spontaneously. A testicle left in an abnormally high position not only will not function but poses a threat because, being relatively immobile, it may be injured and there is also a chance of malignancy developing in it. An incompletely descended testicle therefore should be brought down into the scrotum surgically, and from a functional point of view this should be achieved by the age of about 3 years. The longer it is left in an abnormal site the more likely is its function to be impaired.

Occasionally the testis descends to an abnormal situation, e.g. the thigh or the pubic region; such testes should be returned to their proper place.

Hydrocoele. This is a collection of excessive fluid in the sac surrounding the testis. Such swellings may be unilateral or bilateral. Congenital hydrocoeles almost always disappear spontaneously during the first year and no treatment therefore should be attempted during this time unless they are of exceptional size. Hydrocoeles appearing later are a different problem and usually require surgical management. Pre-pubertal disease of the testicles is extremely rare.

TETANUS

The cause of this dread disease is a bacillus which grows best in an oxygen-deprived atmosphere and which therefore thrives in dead tissue. Any injury, however, may become infected with the tetanus germ and a particularly vicious form of the disease affects young babies who become infected via the umbilicus. The incubation period varies from 2 days to several weeks. The toxin causes increased nerve excitability resulting in spasm of the muscles. Involvement of the chewing muscles gave the disease its popular name of lockjaw. All muscles, however, may be affected and the slightest stimulus may cause severe reflex spasms. Involvement of the face muscles causes the typical sardonic smile. The disease varies considerably in severity, mild cases requiring little treatment, but in severe cases the mortality rate is high, even with elaborate management involving artificial ventilation.

Tetanus is preventable by adequate immunisation. Tetanus toxoid is incorporated in DPT given to babies as a rule from the third month onward. (See *immunisation.) Booster doses should be given every few years but if these are omitted a booster injection of toxoid at the time of the injury gives adequate protection. Temporary short-lived protection can be given to non-immunised patients suffering an injury likely to lead to tetanus, by administration of anti-tetanic serum. This is now derived from human sources and is free of the dangers of horse serum previously used. Serum is given to patients presenting with tetanus and they are usually also treated with penicillin to kill the tetanus germs, but this does little to alter the disease. Neonatal tetanus is preventable by adequate immunisation of the mother during the pregnancy, but the best safeguard is hygienic handling of the umbilicus and cord at birth. The spores of tetanus bacilli live for many years. They are passed in the excreta of animals, e.g. cows and horses, and the use of animal dung for such purposes as plastering floors greatly increases the risk of contamination.

THREADWORMS
See *worms

THROAT
The throat is a busy highway through which passes all the air we breathe as well as all the food we eat and the fluids we drink. In spite of all this traffic it remains remarkably healthy most of the time. Infections of the throat, however, are not uncommon and though frequently due to viruses may also be due to several other types of germs. (See *sore throat and *tonsillitis.)

THRUSH
This is a fungal infection commonly seen in the mouths of babies, sometimes also in babies' skin, particularly in the napkin area, and it is a common cause of vaginal infection. It causes white spots reminiscent of the breast of the thrush, from which the condition gets its name. In the mouth, white patches often coalesce, particularly on the inner surfaces of the cheeks. Lips, tongue and palate may be affected and the fungus may spread down the gullet. Administration of antibiotics often encourages thrush infection. When it affects the skin the fungus causes typical circular lesions with thin papery edges, but more confluent dermatitis is common, especially in moist regions.

Severe oral thrush does cause some discomfort which interferes with feeding. Often, however, there are no obvious symptoms. There are several forms of treatment. Gentian violet in a 1 per cent solution painted onto the thrush areas twice a day is effective but messy. Nystatin, an antibiotic effective against the thrush fungus, can be administered as drops after each feed. This has only a topical action and it is therefore important to maximise contact between the drops and the thrush areas by placing the drops in the correct place and administering them slowly so as to prolong the effect. Miconazole as an oral gel is extremely effective. Thrush of the skin responds to a variety of fungicides, including miconazole, clotrimazole and simple dyes such as gentian violet and mercurochrome lotion. The affected areas should be aired as much as possible.

Occasionally the thrush fungus is more invasive and in such cases treatment with a systemic preparation such as ketoconazole is required.

THUMB-SUCKING

Much needless parental anxiety focuses upon this relatively harmless habit. Sucking is a normal activity of babies and even *in utero* a baby may suck his thumb or hand. There is nothing you can do about it and there is precious little you can do about it later. Sucking of the thumb or fingers in babies is considered normal. It is likely to diminish if the baby is adequately fed and particularly if he is fed on demand. If it seems he has to suck something you may ask whether it is better for him to suck his thumb or a dummy. The thumb has the advantage of ready availability, it does not get lost and in the small baby it is reasonably clean. It cannot, however, be thrown away or even taken away, and attempts to occlude it by bandaging it up are usually futile. If your child wants to suck his thumb, therefore, he will go on doing so until he is ready to relinquish the habit. Sometimes excessive thumb-sucking after the teeth have appeared results in a degree of injury to the thumb. This, however, is never very severe as it is not allowed to become significantly painful. Dummies are not more hygienic than thumbs, often get lost, and produce an equal degree of dental distortion. They can, however, if necessary be removed.

The real question is why the child, beyond the age at which he is dependent upon sucking for getting his food, requires the solace of continued sucking. At the age of 1 year the child no longer needs a bottle and most mothers have abandoned breastfeeding. He should be living largely on solids with some milk by cup. He will, however, have fond recollections of the joys of sucking and it is perhaps therefore not surprising that at times of stress or when he is going to sleep, he will return to the habit for the comfort it brings. This in itself need not cause anxiety. If, however, the habit is indulged in to the exclusion of more interesting occupations, then the child probably has a security problem and this should be explored with him. If he is bored he should receive more stimulation and particularly the company of other children. Trying to shame him out of the habit will not work nor will attacks upon the thumb itself with vile-tasting applications or strapping. If there is a real problem its cause should be discovered and dealt with. In the vast majority of cases, however, thumb-sucking is simply a habit which the child will abandon when he discovers better things to do.

THYROID

The thyroid gland, situated in the front of the neck, controls the general rate of the body metabolism, deficiency of thyroid leading to sluggishness, loss of hair, etc., and in infants slowness in development with resultant mental retardation. Excessive thyroid results in hyper-excitability, tremor, rapid pulse and sometimes a protrusion of the eyes. This condition of thyrotoxicosis is sometimes seen in children. Thyroid deficiency, however, is more common and occurs as a congenital defect in about 1 in 4 000 births (slightly less frequently in Africans). Because it is essential to treat babies with thyroid deficiency from a very early age, many countries have adopted a policy of compulsory screening at birth. The test is simple, requiring only a spot of blood absorbed onto blotting paper, usually collected between the third and fifth day of life. If the screening test is positive, more definite and elaborate tests of thyroid function will be necessary for confirmation. Babies treated for thyroid deficiency within the first few weeks of life grow and develop normally.

TICS

These are common in school-age children. Also known as habit spasms, tics consist of repetitive movements of the face, with perhaps a shake of the head, lifting of a shoulder or movement of a hand. The movement is always the same, unlike that of chorea in which the movements vary all the time. Tics may be initiated by an irritation, such as a falling lock of hair which demands a particular movement for its correction. The movement then persists after the need has passed. Sometimes tics are imitative. They are usually associated with a minor emotional disturbance but seldom is deep psychological delving required for their termination. They are better simply ignored, as drawing attention to the habit tends to engrave it rather deeper. It may be difficult at times to restrain yourself from comment or reproof but remind yourself that it will do no good. The tic will stop sooner if it is totally ignored by everybody. If, however, the child is clearly upset emotionally then seek the help of a doctor or perhaps a psychologist.

TICK BITE FEVER

This disease, common in country areas, is due to a rickettsial organism which is somewhere between a virus and the larger bacteria. It is transmitted by the hard ticks which infest cattle and other animals. The tick causing the bite is often the larval form and therefore very small and difficult to see. There is an incubation period of 8–10 days, and typically symptoms begin on the Monday or Tuesday of the week following an outing into the country over a weekend. Initial fever and headache are followed by general body pains and severe malaise. The site of the bite may be inconspicuous but is usually found if sought. The lymph glands draining the area of the bite are enlarged and tender and there may be generalised lymph gland enlargement as well as enlargement of the spleen. The most typical feature of the disease is the rash, which appears soon after the onset of symptoms and consists of discrete pink spots distributed mainly over the extremities, including the palms of the hands and soles of the feet. The disease is self-limiting but is very unpleasant and causes significant debility. Fortunately it responds well to treatment with tetracycline antibiotics.

TIDINESS

For the sake of sanity it is wise to encourage tidiness in children but this should not become such a fetish that their activities are hampered. Tidiness is best taught by example. If your own things are in a mess you can hardly expect your child to keep his tidy. Tidying up after play is a thing best shared. To put this chore solely onto the child causes resentment. If you do it together it becomes fun. This applies to so much of domestic activity. If children have to share a room, a degree of tidiness is essential. They may have very different concepts as to what constitutes tidiness, and a good deal of refereeing may be necessary. If, however, you have taught your children consideration of others there should be no insuperable problem.

TOES

Minor abnormalities of the toes are common. Over-riding or under-riding toes may be the result of intra-uterine cramping and often correct themselves. In any case they rarely cause significant trouble. Often the condition runs in families.

Supernumerary toes also tend to be familial. The extra toe may be rather loosely attached or may have a strong bony articulation. Such extra toes are best removed but the optimum time for doing this will depend upon the precise anatomy.

Pigeon toes or turned-in feet are particularly common in babies who have slept mostly on their tummies, though many children tend to turn their feet in when they start walking. This is usually of no significance and is self-corrective.

TOILET-TRAINING

It is important to realise that clean toilet habits develop naturally and spontaneously in the child without any outside assistance. This statement may be disappointing to the mother who feels she has accomplished something when she has got her toddler trained and dry, but in fact all she has done is to supply the facilities for accomplishing his own inclinations. Before the age of 15 to 18 months a child has no real control over his excretory functions. Mothers, therefore, who boast that they have trained their babies from the first weeks of life because they have always managed to catch the stools in a pot rather than in the napkin, are deluding themselves. Some babies do have such regular bowel actions that it is possible to avoid napkin soiling but there is no question of training until the child knows what he is doing. Control of the bowels is achieved appreciably earlier than control of the bladder, for whereas the former will function once or twice a day the passage of urine is much more frequent. Although, therefore, most children will be clean by the age of 18 months they are seldom dry before the age of 2 to 2½. It is impossible to avoid wet napkins until the child has reached the stage where he can clearly signal his desire to pass water.

Bowel training. Towards the end of the first year an infant develops considerable interest in his excreta and if allowed access to them may proudly plaster them on every available surface. You have no need to share his pride in this performance but he should by no means be punished. He will later develop a normal desire to keep stools in their proper place. As the act of defaecation usually involves a mild degree of physical exertion the child usually indicates the impending event by ceasing whatever he is doing and developing that particular 'look' which mother soon recognises as a signal of this activity. If she then removes his clothing and sits him on the potty he is likely to oblige. An expression of pleasure at his co-operation encourages him to repeat the performance and once this stage has been reached a child will usually be rapidly trained. There may of course be the occasional subsequent accident, especially during periods of diarrhoea, but by the age of 18 months most children will be clean. They will still require napkins for urinary purposes. These they will be unable to remove without assistance but with normal bowel function a regular potting time, e.g. after breakfast, will usually ensure cleanliness.

Refusal to sit on the pot may arise from several causes. The child may have had a fright by falling off the pot and may then refuse to sit on it again for a time. A stable pot is therefore essential. The child may feel more secure on a small seat with the pot underneath. Baby seats placed on the adult toilet are often rather frightening, especially if the toilet is flushed while the child is still sitting, and he may then refuse to mount again. Forceful thrusting of the child onto the pot with the expectation that he will perform appropriately, and vigorous expression of displeasure when he fails to do so, may well put him against sitting on the pot at all. A very common cause of refusal is constipation. If the stool is large and firm its passage may cause distinct discomfort and may even tear the lining of the anus. In this case the child associates the pot with pain and will refuse to have anything to do with it. This situation must be handled with patience and the child's constipation overcome before trying to induce him to use the pot again. Pot training is really a matter of listening to your baby.

Bladder training. During the first year of life a baby has no voluntary control over his bladder, although the passage of urine becomes progressively less frequent as the bladder increases in size and capacity. The kidneys normally produce rather less urine during the night than by day and there are some babies who will be dry through the night by the age of 1 year. This however is rare. If the napkin is dry when the baby wakes, either after the night's sleep or after a nap, he may be sat on the potty and will almost always then urinate. Before the age of 12 to 18 months, however, this is simply a reflex action, though towards the end of this time suitable applause will encourage him to repeat the performance.

Most babies achieve awareness of their bladder function during the first half of the second year. The first indication usually comes after the actual event but in a short while the infant will indicate while he is actually passing urine, and shortly thereafter just before the act. When this stage has been reached, mother should help him to use the potty by removing his napkin and sitting him on it. The correct performance is then suitably applauded, though not to a ridiculous degree for this may lead to a temporary desire to repeat the obviously pleasing performance every few minutes. Training in no matter what sphere can be accomplished only by regular demonstration of approval of acceptable actions and disapproval of unacceptable actions. Until the child has control of his actions, therefore, no training is possible. Most children will be dry during the day between 2 and 2½ years of age but dryness at night is much more variable. The majority of children will stop wetting their beds by or shortly after 3 years of age. Boys on the whole tend to be somewhat slower than girls. It is important to realise that there is a wide range of normality and that you have to move at your particular child's pace. For bedwetting in the older child see *bedwetting.

TONGUE

The tongue is subject to few ills in childhood. It participates in infective conditions of the mouth such as thrush and herpetic stomatitis. A peculiar condition seen fairly commonly is so-called geographical tongue, in which irregular areas of the tongue become denuded of the papillae which give it its rough surface. These patches change, producing map-like areas. As a rule there is no discomfort but some children complain of increased sensitivity. The cause of the condition is unknown; it requires no treatment and it resolves spontaneously.

Tongue-tie is a hangover from the era of mythology. The length and thickness of the frenum which tethers the tip of the tongue to the floor of the mouth varies enormously. Sometimes the tip of the tongue can hardly be moved and cannot be protruded beyond the teeth. This does not interfere with sucking nor does it subsequently interfere with speech or any other ability. The frenum always stretches up and although there may appear to be a degree of residual tethering this is of no significance. It is quite unnecessary to cut a tongue-tie.

'TONICS'

The days are past when a doctor could prescribe any useless medication with the hope that the faith with which it was taken would probably do the patient some good. The modern parent is more discerning and rightly questions the need for medication when it seems unnecessary. Other parents retain such faith in medicines that they give their children regular so-called tonics, firmly believing that this will keep them healthy. These tonics consist mostly of vitamins, with some minerals thrown in to make them more impressive and perhaps some liver extract. A child on a normal mixed diet has absolutely no need of such preparations. Specific vitamin deficiencies should of course be treated appropriately but the random pouring of excessive vitamins down children's throats is unnecessary, extravagant and often psychologically harmful. The dose of vitamins is usually not sufficient to be frankly toxic but some vitamins in excess can be dangerous (see *vitamins).

Occasionally, preparations, like cyproheptadine, are given for their appetite-stimulating effect. Such medication is usually misguided but is easier to administer than parental enlightenment. If a child is thin because he is unwell the cause must be ascertained. If he is simply thin it doesn't matter.

Don't buy so-called tonics for your children — you are simply wasting money which could be better spent. Fortunes are spent annually on tonics, with benefits visible only to the manufacturers and distributors.

TONSILLITIS

The tonsils guard the entrance to the throat and are situated one on each side at the back of the tongue. They consist of lymphoid tissue, which is of great importance in body defence mechanisms. We are not sure precisely how the tonsils work but they are important in establishing immunity. It seems strange that structures which are concerned with defence should themselves be liable to infection, but such is the case, and acute tonsillitis is one of the commonest conditions in childhood. The tonsils become enlarged and red and covered in white spots. The tonsils, however, may participate in any throat infection and are then simply swollen and reddened, as are the surrounding tissues. As a result of repeated infection they often become scarred and craggy and are then more liable to further infection. There is, however, a distinct tendency for the frequency of tonsillitis to wane after the age of about 6. Frank septic tonsillitis is usually due to a streptococcal germ, and such cases require treatment with penicillin given in adequate doses for 10 days. In this way not only is the streptococcus cleared from the throat but the possible complications, namely acute nephritis and rheumatic fever, are prevented.

It is not abnormal for a child to have 3 or 4 attacks of tonsillitis a year. When the frequency increases much above this, however, there is usually a cause. It may be that other members of the family are also having frequent tonsillitis and the germs get passed around in circles. Even the family dog has been incriminated in this situation. It commonly happens that inadequate courses of antibiotic simply suppress the infection but do not eliminate the germs, which smoulder for a time but then cause further attacks, hence the need for a 10-day course of penicillin. If frequently recurring infection is due to chronically scarred tonsils these may be removed, but it is undesirable to remove the tonsils in a child under 4 years of age. An alternative to tonsillectomy is prophylactic penicillin given as a daily dose for a long period. This suggestion often causes parental anxiety but it is quite safe (except in the occasional patient sensitive to penicillin) and such prophylactic treatment may be continued for years if necessary. Rheumatic subjects may be kept on penicillin for life.

The size of the tonsils is usually irrelevant. When acutely inflamed they enlarge but rapidly subside again to their former dimensions once the infection is over. Chronically enlarged tonsils occasionally cause a degree of obstruction, with some difficulty in swallowing and difficult noisy breathing. This is a potentially dangerous condition with effects on the heart, and it forms one of the absolute indications for tonsillectomy. It is, however, very rare.

Though the adenoids are often removed together with the tonsils they should be separately evaluated. Adenoidal enlargement may lead to ear complications but there is often an underlying cause, such as nasal allergy, against which treatment should primarily be directed. Far too many tonsillectomies are performed. With knowledge of the natural history of the condition, together with adequate conservative treatment, the vast majority of tonsils, even when repeatedly inflamed, can be left where they are. Do not therefore pressurise your doctor into performing unnecessary surgery.

TRANSFUSION

Blood transfusions may be necessary in the treatment of severe anaemia, and children with certain forms of chronic anaemia may be dependent upon transfusions for survival. These are however rare situations.

Transfusions of certain specific blood components may be required in diseases such as haemophilia, where only the anti-haemophilic factor is required. Modern blood fractionation enables these specific components to be isolated and concentrated.

Exchange blood transfusion. This is indicated in severe haemolytic disease of the newborn due to Rhesus incompatibility (see *Rhesus) and also in severely jaundiced babies, when the jaundice cannot adequately be controlled by other means, such as phototherapy. In this procedure a catheter is passed into a large vein, usually via the umbilicus, and equal quantities of baby's blood are withdrawn and discarded and transfused blood injected. In this way the baby's blood is progressively replaced with transfused blood. It is, however, not possible to exchange the blood completely but an 85 per cent exchange is usually accomplished. In Rhesus cases not only are the baby's Rhesus positive cells replaced with Rhesus negative ones, which are then unaffected by the antibodies present, but in addition the antibodies in the blood plasma are removed and so is much of the bile which may have accumulated. Exchange blood transfusion does carry certain hazards but with careful technique the dangers are minimal.

Blood transfusion is not without danger. Apart from incompatible transfusion (a rare accident nowadays) and possible mechanical dangers such as overtransfusion, certain diseases may be transmitted — hepatitis, malaria, syphilis and, of course, the AIDS virus. Blood transfusion and administration of blood components should never therefore be undertaken needlessly.

TRAVEL SICKNESS

Some children regularly get sick when travelling, others never do. Babies are usually soothed by the motion of travelling and present little problem. It is as well to be prepared for the possibility of travel sickness by taking a few plastic bags with you. If previous experience indicates that travel sickness is likely, make sure that the unfortunate victim does not have too heavy a meal before starting off, though a light meal and snacks to chew *en route* are often helpful. There are several anti-emetic medications which are valuable in preventing motion sickness and there should be no hesitation in using one of these if the child is regularly afflicted.

TREMOR

Fine, rhythmical movements may be normal, such as the tremor of the lower lip in babies often seen when they are asleep. A fine tremor of the hands is characteristic of excessive thyroid secretion. Coarser tremors, increasing with intention, are found in diseases of the cerebellum, the lowest part of the brain. If your child has a pronounced tremor, get him examined by a doctor.

TRIPLETS

Triplets occur with a frequency of about 1:6 000 pregnancies. The use of the fertility pill has however increased their incidence. The three babies may be identical, all coming from one ovum, but this is rare. More often, two are monovular and the third different, and occasionally all 3 babies are dissimilar. Triplets are usually born prematurely and are often of disproportionately small size. They require no special management in the early days except that appropriate to their degree of prematurity. Thereafter, of course, the burden on the parents is considerable but their efforts are usually well rewarded. Joining the South African Multiple Birth Association is well worth while.

TUBERCULOSIS

In spite of the efficacy of modern drug treatment and the considerable efforts of public health authorities, this disease is still appallingly rife among the less privileged members of southern African society. The disease is due to infection by the tubercle bacillus, and although most often affecting lungs, it may spread to virtually all parts of the body. The lymph glands are often involved, particularly in the neck, where they may form large swellings. Involvement of the abdominal lymph glands often spreads to form tuberculous peritonitis. The disease may spread via the bloodstream to produce widespread dissemination, in what is known as miliary tuberculosis. More localised blood spread may result in tuberculosis of bones and joints, particularly the large joints such as hip and knee; it may spread to the spine resulting in a hunchback; and it may spread to the brain and the meninges, causing tuberculous meningitis, a very grave form of the disease. Tuberculosis may also involve the skin. Nearly all tuberculosis encountered nowadays is due to the human bacillus. In the past, abdominal and lymph gland disease was commonly due to bovine tuberculosis which spread to humans via milk supplies. Tuberculosis may also affect birds and other animals. Such atypical tubercle bacilli are sometimes the cause of glandular involvement.

The disease is spread largely by droplets, the result of coughing by people with open tuberculosis. Such patients should therefore be segregated until their sputum no longer contains tubercle bacilli. Children are seldom infectious and they usually acquire the disease from adults in the same household. If a case of tuberculosis is discovered in a household, therefore, it is extremely important that all contacts should be checked, not only clinically but also by means of tuberculin testing and a chest X-ray.

The tuberculin test. A person who has acquired the tubercle bacillus becomes sensitive to it and reacts to tuberculo-protein injected into the skin. Severe reactions nearly always denote recent infection. Sensitivity, however, does persist for a long time and moderate tuberculin sensitivity is induced by *BCG vaccination. There are several methods of injecting the tuberculo-protein, the most accurate being an intradermal injection with syringe and fine needle, the so-called Mantoux test. Other methods employ multiple needle punctures, e.g. the Heaf test and Tine test. The reaction is read after 48 hours and is graded according to its severity.

Treatment of tuberculosis. Several highly effective drugs are available. These are always given in combination, as the tubercle bacillus readily becomes resistant. Modern regimes are of much shorter duration than previous treatment schedules, and response is rapid. Surgery may be required for tuberculous abscesses and very enlarged glands, and orthopaedic measures will be required for bone and joint involvement. Tuberculous meningitis responds well if treatment is started early but many cases present when damage has already been done.

Prevention of tuberculosis. Effective measures include:

(1) Vigorous case-seeking. Anybody with a chronic cough should be screened for the possibility of TB.

(2) Isolation of open cases of pulmonary TB until the sputum is negative.

(3) Vigorous and effective treatment of all cases to prevent spread to others.

(4) Screening of all contacts and particularly children.

(5) Prophylactic treatment of, for example, babies of tuberculous mothers.

(6) BCG vaccination.

If you should encounter a case of tuberculosis in your household please see that all these steps are taken.

TURNER'S SYNDROME

This is a congenital abnormality due to one absent sex chromosome (XO). Such patients are stunted in growth and display certain physical characteristics such as webbing of the neck, increased angulation at the elbow and often raised blood pressure due to arterial abnormalities. Though morphologically female, cases of Turner's syndrome have vestigial ovaries and are almost always sterile.

TWINS

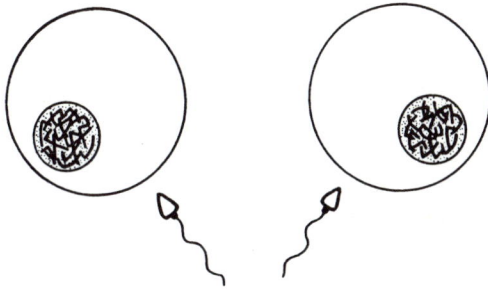

Origin of binovular twins from two separate ova individually fertilised.

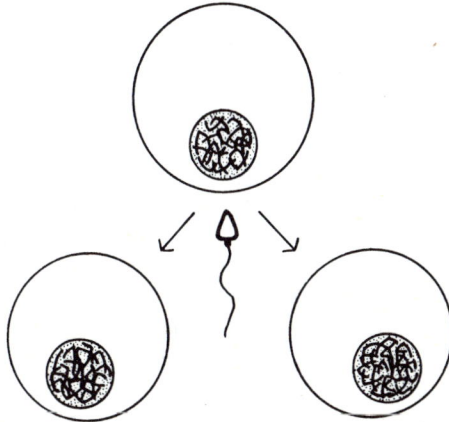

Origin of monovular twins (identical) from one ovum.

The incidence of twin pregnancy is about 1:80 but if there is a history of twins in the family and particularly if these twins are dissimilar (binovular) the risk is considerably increased. Twins may arise in one of two very different ways (see diagram). The mother may liberate two eggs at the time of ovulation and, if these are both fertilised, a twin pregnancy will result, with the production of babies who resemble each other no more closely than do any random brothers and sisters. They may be of the same or of opposite sex but in either case their genetic make-up is entirely different. In contrast, twins may result from the complete separate development of each of the two cells which follow the first division of the fertilised ovum. In this case the twins are identical in genetic constitution and in physical appearance. Sometimes, however, one baby is rather better nourished than the other and the difference in size may hide their similarity. Because such babies often share a common placenta there may be a disparity in blood content, one baby being purple and plethoric, the other pale and anaemic, and it is at times necessary to redress this imbalance.

Twins are often born prematurely and are usually of lower birth weight than singletons. Their behaviour, however, is determined more by their maturity than by their size. When one twin is very much smaller than the other he may demand special attention and care, and there is a tendency for the smaller of twins to become hypoglycaemic, i.e. for the blood sugar to fall, during the first few days of life. When one twin is not only smaller but decidedly less mature than the other it may be postulated that there has been 'super-fecundation' in which the less mature baby was conceived in the cycle following the conception of the first. This is a situation very difficult to prove. With ultrasound scanning twins are now diagnosed very early and this occasionally reveals that one twin dies at an early stage of development while the other continues to flourish. Such a twin situation would never be known without this specialised information, for at the time of delivery there would be no sign of the lost foetus.

Twins, while posing certain problems, are usually greeted with excitement and rejoicing. If, as is usually the case, you have been forewarned, you will have had time to prepare the necessary facilities as well as prepare other members of the family for their arrival. It should be made clear to older children that twins are a lot of hard work and that they will have to help. Toddlers, who normally feel a degree of displacement by the arrival of a new baby, may feel doubly deprived, especially as twins get a great deal of attention from everybody. Handled sensibly, however, the situation should not create too much of a problem. Later on, the close companionship of twins may result in a feeling of rejection by the other children and an impression that the twins, particularly when they are identical, 'gang up'. This is to some extent inevitable.

When preparing for the arrival of twins it is essential that you arrange some help for the first few weeks to prevent yourself becoming utterly exhausted and therefore missing the early joy of having twins. You may like to join the South African Multiple Birth Association, which gives considerable help.

Feeding of twins. Many mothers are able to breastfeed twins for a considerable time. They can be fed simultaneously, tucking one under each arm supported by a pillow. When they become dissatisfied with the quantity they are getting, and they will usually make this quite clear, then rather than giving each baby one breast and a bottle it may be more time-saving to alternate feeds, giving one baby both breasts and the other a bottle and reversing the situation at the next feed. Further time is of course saved if a helper gives the bottle-feeds while mother is breastfeeding. Like other small babies, twins may need extra vitamins and iron.

The relationship between twins. In the early years, as the result of being always together, twins develop an unusual degree of affection for and dependence upon each other. Their individual development is sometimes handicapped by the fact that they are regarded as 'the twins' rather than as individuals. This is less likely to happen in the case of dissimilar twins but similar twins who are always dressed alike, do exactly the same things and enjoy identical experiences, find it difficult to break away and establish their own identities. They should therefore be helped in this from an early age. It is fun to dress them alike and when they are small this does no harm, but later they should be encouraged to express their own tastes, even though these may be in fact very similar. Though they will in all probability start their schooling together, later on it may be wise to send them to different schools to avoid unhealthy rivalry and to encourage individual development.

The extraordinary relationship which develops between monovular twins is legendary. Endless stories are told relating the development of identical diseases at identical times and of apparent telepathic communication between them even at vast distances. The relationship is certainly a unique one. While providing much satisfying companionship and sympathy, the twin situation can lead to undesirable interdependence. Beware therefore of treating the twins as a unit instead of as two separate individuals, which they must become.

TYPHOID FEVER

This disease is due to infection by the typhoid bacillus. It is spread almost solely by the faecal–oral route, mostly via contaminated water supplies but also through milk or foods contaminated by carriers of the germ, who may not themselves be ill. Flies are also a common mode of contamination. Because of its means of spread, typhoid is largely a disease of rural communities, particularly those dependent upon streams for their water supply. Such water should always be boiled before drinking.

The symptoms of typhoid are rather vague. The onset is gradual with headache, fever, abdominal discomfort and often constipation. Diarrhoea supervenes later. At this stage of the disease, the germs abound in the bloodstream but subsequently they proliferate in the bile and the gut. Inflammation of the bowel may lead to bleeding or perforation. Patients become severely ill with high fever and mental torpor. After about two weeks the symptoms gradually subside but the patient is left considerably debilitated.

Treatment of typhoid involves general care, including maintenance of adequate hydration and nutrition, and administration of an appropriate antibiotic. Prevention of the disease, however, is of far greater importance than cure. This is dependent upon provision of adequate water supplies and general hygienic precautions. Patients recovering from the disease are checked for the possibility of a carrier state before they are allowed to return home. Immunisation with typhoid vaccine is only partly effective.

UMBILICUS
See *navel

URINARY INFECTIONS

Infection of the urinary tract — kidney, ureters, bladder and urethra — is relatively common and often deceptive. In small children who cannot complain of discomfort on passing urine, a diagnosis is dependent upon urine examination, and urine is often difficult to collect. Many cases of infection have passed unnoticed until considerable damage has been done. The symptoms of urinary infection are often vague, e.g. fever, loss of appetite, failure to thrive, vomiting and diarrhoea, and irritability. A child who is significantly unwell without obvious cause should always have her urine checked.

Whenever it is possible when visiting the doctor with a sick child, take a clean, fresh specimen of urine with you. Sometimes you will note that the urine smells strongly of ammonia or has a fishy odour and you may note that it is turbid. These features are of little significance in urine that has been standing for some time so the specimen must be fresh. It must also be cleanly collected into a sterile, clean container. To do this wash down the genital area, sit the baby on the receptacle and give her a feed. The most reliable portion of the urine is that collected midstream but this is possible only in the older child. If doubt exists regarding the reliability of urine specimens in infants it is sometimes necessary to aspirate urine directly from the bladder. This is a simple procedure which need not worry you.

The origin of urinary infection is often not clear. It may ascend from below and this situation is more likely in little girls, who have a shorter and more readily contaminated urethra. Sometimes germs may gain access to the kidneys via the bloodstream. Any obstruction in the urinary tract leading to stasis predisposes to infection. It is usual, therefore, when infection has been proved, to undertake investigation of the anatomy of the urinary tract to make sure that there is no predisposing abnormality. An intravenous pyelogram requires the administration of a dye into a vein and when the dye is excreted by the kidneys it renders them, as well as the ureters and bladder, visible on X-ray examination. To demonstrate abnormalities of the lower urinary tract, and particularly when ureteric reflux is suspected, a Voiding Cysto-urethrogram is performed. Radio-opaque dye is injected into the bladder and X-ray pictures taken as the child passes urine. More elaborate urological investigations are sometimes required.

Urinary infections are treated with appropriate antibacterial drugs and the immediate response is usually excellent. In chronic cases of recurrent urinary infection, such medication may have to be continued prophylactically. Where some anatomical abnormality is present, where there is obstruction, and in severe cases of ureteric reflux, corrective surgery may be required. Urinary infection in a child is always to be taken very seriously. (See also *cystitis and *pyelitis.)

URINE

A certain urinary output is obligatory but the quantity passed depends greatly upon the quantity of fluid imbibed. The concentration of urine therefore varies and the colour alters with concentration, dilute urine being pale and concentrated urine dark. Urine is normally more concentrated during the night, during periods of fever and in states of dehydration.

Urine may smell strong as the result of excessive ammonia, which is derived from the breakdown of urea by bacteria. If this occurs in the bladder as the result of infection then the ammoniacal smell will be present in freshly passed urine. More commonly, the ammonia is produced after the urine has been passed, and particularly when it has been in the napkin for some time. The significance of an ammoniacal smell therefore depends upon the freshness of the urine. An infected urine sometimes has a fishy smell. Certain foodstuffs, such as asparagus, impart a specific odour to the urine.

Urine is usually clearly transparent. Turbidity may be due to chemicals such as urates or phosphates and these are of little significance. Turbidity can also be due to infection, but without a microscope the cause cannot be determined.

The normal yellow colour of urine varies in intensity with urinary concentration. Other colours are sometimes seen. Pink or red urine may be due to dyes often found in red sweets. In certain persons beetroot produces red urine. Blood may make urine red or brown and, in black water fever, black. A pink stain is often seen on the napkin due to urates and this must be distinguished from blood. Dyes such as methylene blue may produce a blue or green urine and some other dyes, such a fluorosin, may produce spectacular hues. In jaundice the urine becomes very dark yellow or brownish and the froth is also discoloured. This is an important sign when the jaundice itself is so mild as to go unobserved.

Nowadays it is unfashionable to taste urine but in diabetes mellitus it would be found to be sweet.

URTICARIA (HIVES)

This is an allergic skin condition consisting of multiple itchy weals, often with a pale centre, usually widely distributed and sometimes accompanied by general symptoms such as fever, nausea, vomiting and joint pains. The individual skin lesions vary greatly in size and sometimes coalesce to form large swellings. There is often swelling too of the soft areas, such as the eyes and genitals. The cause of the condition is occasionally quite clear, for example an injection, medicine, an insect sting or ingestion of an unusual foodstuff such as shellfish. More frequently, however, the cause is difficult to determine and only repeated observation when the condition recurs may give a clue. Possible causes are foodstuffs such as fish, shellfish, nuts, chocolate, strawberries, tomatoes, pork, spices, contact with certain plants, stings and animal poisons. Some cases are induced by sunlight.

Treatment with antihistamine preparations is usually satisfactory but occasionally disappointing. In severe cases adrenaline by injection usually gives fairly prompt relief. Corticosteroids may have to be used. As a topical application to relieve itching, calamine lotion is as good as anything. Antihistamines should not be applied to the skin. (See also *allergy.)

VACCINATION

Vaccination against smallpox is no longer required as the disease has been eliminated. (See also *immunisation.)

VAGINAL DISCHARGE

In certain situations a vaginal discharge is quite normal. It is common in the newborn when it is due to the influence of maternal hormones on the baby. In addition to a mucoid discharge lasting a week or so there may be actual vaginal bleeding for a day or two. This situation need cause no concern. Just prior to the onset of puberty and menstruation, young girls may have a slight vaginal discharge due to normal hormonal stimulation of the mucus-secreting glands. This type of discharge is not offensive, irritating or profuse, but if these features are present, have the child seen by a doctor.

More significant vaginal discharge may be due to infection (and a variety of micro-organisms may be responsible) or to a foreign body in the vagina. Small girls often explore in this way. Superficial irritation may be due to threadworms or to trauma, for instance from tricycle saddles or excessive self-handling.

Do not try to treat a significant vaginal discharge in your child yourself. Until she can be seen by a doctor simply keep the part as clean as possible and perhaps protect it with a bland cream. Avoid irritating underclothes, cotton being preferable to nylon and other synthetic fibres.

VEGETABLES

Whereas it is quite possible to nourish oneself perfectly adequately with vegetables and fruits, the importance of vegetables in the diet tends to be overemphasised by many parents. It is not essential for your child to eat vegetables, especially if he is eating plenty of fruit. Vegetables do contain starch and protein, water and salts, some vitamins, particularly vitamin C, folic acid and, in yellow vegetables, the precursor of vitamin A — carotene. The main value of vegetables, however, is probably their fibre content. The undigested cellulose passes unabsorbed through the bowel and adds to the stool bulk. Undigested vegetable particles can often be recognised in children's stools. This does not mean that there is some impairment of digestion. Very rarely do vegetables cause any problem. Intolerance to the common vegetables is almost unknown. When introducing vegetables to your baby it is nevertheless wise to introduce one at a time so that if anything appears not to agree with him you will know what to suspect. An excess of yellow vegetables may cause *carotenaemia — a condition in which the skin becomes pigmented, and which may be confused with jaundice. The whites of the eyes, however, do not become discoloured. The carotene staining does no harm and fairly rapidly disappears when the consumption of yellow vegetables is reduced.

VENEREAL DISEASE

Venereal diseases are important as far as children are concerned because babies may acquire infections from their mothers at birth or even during pregnancy. Young children may be infected by perverts, and the promiscuity of adolescents leads to a high rate of venereal disease among them. The pattern of venereal disease is changing; old friends such as gonorrhoea and syphilis are still with us aplenty but in addition we have increasing cases of genital herpes, and probably much hepatitis is spread venereally. AIDS is not confined to homosexual men and may spread to children.

Syphilis is seldom transmitted to the foetus during the first half of pregnancy, but massive infections may cause stillbirth. The causative organism becomes widely disseminated throughout the body and congenital syphilis therefore has numerous manifestations. One of the earliest is *snuffles. It appears within the first 2 months and eventually causes destruction of the nasal bones. Various skin eruptions are common and may be present at birth. The bones are often involved and as this condition is painful, the baby tends to lie very still in a state of pseudoparalysis and resents handling. Anaemia and jaundice are common manifestations. Treatment consists of an adequate course of penicillin, to which, fortunately, the spirochaete of syphilis is constantly sensitive, and a complete cure is obtained.

Gonorrhoea often infects a baby's eyes at birth, causing a severe conjunctivitis and sometimes leading to blindness. Adequate prenatal treatment of the mother will prevent this condition. Gonococcal opthalmia requires intensive treatment, with appropriate antibiotics administered topically and sometimes systemically.

Genital herpes, a devastating condition because of its chronicity and its resistance to treatment, constitutes a grave danger to babies, in whom it tends to spread throughout the body, often resulting in death. A mother with active genital herpes will therefore almost certainly be delivered by Caesarean section in order to avoid infecting the baby.

In view of the gravity of these risks to the neonate, if you have any suspicion of having or having had a venereal disease, you must inform your doctor as early in pregnancy as possible.

Adolescents should be warned of the grave risks of venereal disease resulting from promiscuous sexual behaviour. Should they acquire such infections, immediate treatment is imperative.

VERNIX CASEOSA

At birth the baby is covered with a greasy white film which, while unflattering, seems to protect his skin from the watery uterine environment. The vernix is usually removed by the first bath but it would in any case be shed naturally.

VERRUCAE

See *warts

VESTS

A vest is simply a garment to be worn like any other, for comfort. The idea that a vest is in some way necessary for health dies hard. It must nevertheless be firmly killed. A vest does not protect a child from colds, bronchitis or asthma. It does nothing but keep him warm or make him uncomfortably hot, depending on the climate. Overclothing children does nothing but harm.

VIRUSES

Viruses are the smallest particles of living matter. Because they are so small they cannot contain all the chemicals needed for their own propagation and they therefore have to live within cells, whose chemistry they then utilise for their own purposes. In so doing they often cause the death of the cell and they then have to seek other havens. Viruses cause many of the common diseases. Common colds may be due to any one of about 200 viruses. Several varieties cause influenza. Other diseases due to viruses include herpes, hepatitis, chickenpox, measles, German measles, gastro-enteritis, poliomyelitis, aseptic meningitis, yellow fever and atypical pneumonia. Against the viruses we are almost powerless. There is no point, therefore, in going to the doctor when your child has a simple cold. All you will do is spread the cold to him and many of his patients and this is not a considerate thing to do. Many virus diseases of course are not so easily diagnosed and medical help may then be required, but do not imagine that your doctor will be able to cure a virus disease. He will not. He may be able to produce a degree of symptomatic relief and he will be able to help you by explaining the natural course of the illness, but he will not be able to modify it. Do not therefore demand an excess of treatment. Tons of antibiotics are wasted on virus infections with nothing but adverse effects. Cold and cough remedies are swallowed with enthusiasm but without benefit. Just accept that a virus illness will run its course and be content to know what it is.

VITAMINS

Vitamins are essential food substances which the body is incapable of manufacturing and which therefore must be provided in the food. A well-balanced diet contains quite enough vitamins, and supplementation by taking vitamin pills or syrups is not only wasteful but potentially harmful in large doses. Infants need proportionately larger quantities of vitamins because of their rapid growth, and premature babies require more than full-term babies. The important vitamins are as follows:

Vitamin A

This is a fat-soluble vitamin found in dairy products such as milk, cheese, butter, fortified margarine and eggs. High concentrations are present in liver, particularly fish liver, and the precursor of vitamin A, the yellow pigment carotene, is found in yellow vegetables and fruits. It is interesting, but of little practical importance, that the highest concentrations in nature of vitamin A are found in polar bear liver. This renders it extremely toxic, causing acute hydrocephalus. Never therefore be tempted to eat polar bear liver! Vitamin A is important in maintaining the integrity of surface membranes. This is seen particularly in the eye, where in vitamin A deficiency states the cornea becomes dry and sometimes ulcerated, a situation seen not uncommonly in children with severe malnutrition. Vitamin A is the precursor of a pigment in the retina of the eye essential for vision, and deficiency of vitamin A leads to night-blindness. Consuming heroic quantities of the vitamin, however, will not improve your vision. In vitamin A deficiency there is an increased tendency to infection as a result of epithelial degeneration, but again, excessive quantities of the vitamin will not improve resistance. Vitamin A in high doses is potentially toxic, causing depressed appetite, irritability, skin changes, bony changes and raised intracranial pressure with vomiting and headache.

Vitamin B

This is really a group of unrelated chemical substances which are often found in the same foodstuffs.

Vitamin B1 — thiamine. This is essential for normal carbohydrate metabolism. Deficiency leads to the condition known as beriberi, which may be manifest by peripheral nerve damage or, as is more common in children, by heart failure. The condition is seen most commonly in populations living largely on polished rice.

Vitamin B2 — riboflavin. Deficiency of this substance is rarely seen in pure form but constitutes part of a general state of malnutrition. It affects the eye and more particularly the mouth, with sores at the corner of the mouth and a painful red tongue.

Niacin. This is another component of the vitamin B group, deficiency of which leads to pellagra. This causes irritation, drying and pigmentation of the skin, especially in areas exposed to the sun and in pressure areas, troubles in the mouth similar to those produced by riboflavin deficiency, diarrhoea and mental disturbances. It is a common deficiency disease in southern Africa.

Vitamin B6 — pyridoxine. Deficiency of this vitamin is rarely seen, except under peculiar circumstances. Treatment of tuberculosis with INH may precipitate a state of pyridoxine deficiency manifest by peripheral nervous troubles and anaemia. Pyridoxine deficiency has caused convulsions in small babies. Very occasionally, infants with deranged metabolism require extremely high doses of pyridoxine and are said to be pyridoxine dependent.

Vitamin B12 — cyanocobalamin. This substance is necessary for normal blood formation, and lack of it causes a particular type of anaemia with larger than normal red blood-cells. Deficiency in childhood is extremely uncommon.

Folic acid. This substance is similar to vitamin B12 in its effect on blood formation. Deficiency of folic acid is relatively common and babies may manifest anaemia as a result of folate deficiency in their mothers. It is present in good quantity in leafy vegetables.

The group B vitamins — vitamin B1, vitamin B2, niacin, vatamin B6, vitamin B12 and folic acid — are found in dairy products, meat, liver, yeast, wholewheat, the germ of cereals and eggs. If foods were eaten in their natural state instead of in highly refined form, vitamin B deficiency would not exist.

Vitamin C — ascorbic acid

This substance is found in many natural foods, including fruit and vegetables, but it is destroyed by boiling, and canned foods are therefore deficient. Deficiency of vitamin C causes scurvy. There is a defect in the formation of collagen, the intercellular fibre found in nearly all tissues, and this leads to a bleeding tendency. In adults this is seen particularly in the mouth, with swollen, soggy, bleeding gums and loosening of the teeth. Infantile scurvy is characterised by bleeding around the bones. This is painful and leads to immobility and severe irritability. The condition may be mistaken for osteomyelitis and other painful bony conditions. There is a rapid response to administration of vitamin C. Infantile scurvy presents as a rule between the ages of 8 months and 2 years. It is entirely preventable by an adequate intake of fresh fruit or fruit juice or supplements of synthetic vitamin C, adequate quantities of which are found in all baby foods.

Vitamin C is non-toxic, being probably the only vitamin that is without some danger. The idea that massive doses help to prevent or cure colds has not been proved and there is no point in wasting your money in this way.

Vitamin D

The action of vitamin D is to increase the absorption of calcium and phosphorus from the bowel and to aid in the deposition of these salts in the bones. Lack of vitamin D causes rickets. It is a fat-soluble substance present in fish oils and in animal fat, with only a small quantity being found in milk. Vitamin D is also produced by the action of sunlight on the skin. One would not therefore expect to see much vitamin D deficiency in a sunny country but rickets is not rare in infants who have not been given adequate vitamin D in their feeds. Rickets at an older age is usually of more complex origin and related to kidney disease, to vitamin D resistance or to dietary deficiency of calcium.

Rickets is not uncommonly seen in premature babies, whose requirement of vitamin D is greater than that of the full-term infant. It is seen in babies fed ordinary cows' milk without vitamin D supplementation. The skull bones become soft, the fontanelle wide open, there may be deformities of the chest as well as bowing of the legs if a child is walking, and enlargement of the ends of the long bones. Confirmation of rickets is obtained from X-ray examination and blood tests, and these are usually repeated until the condition is cured. Except in vitamin D resistant cases the response to vitamin D administration is excellent.

Vitamin E — tocopherol

The tocopherols are present in milk, vegetables and a variety of foods so that deficiency is very rarely seen. It had been described in premature babies as a cause of anaemia.

Vitamin K

This is a fat-soluble vitamin, which is a precursor for more than one of the coagulation factors in the blood, and deficiency of vitamin K leads to a bleeding tendency. The vitamin is synthesised by the bacteria of the bowel. In the early days of life, before the bowel has been completely colonised, there may be a deficiency of vitamin K, leading to a severe bleeding tendency manifest most commonly by vomiting of blood or the passage of dark bloody stools. Blood transfusion may be necessary. Nearly all babies at birth are now given vitamin K in order to prevent haemorrhagic disease. Vitamin K deficiency in older children is very rare, except in states of severe malabsorption, but a similar bleeding tendency is seen in severe liver disease.

The need for vitamin supplements

The breastfed baby rarely develops vitamin deficiencies but the content of vitamin C and vitamin D in breast milk is sometimes precarious and supplements of these vitamins are advocated from the age of a few weeks. This is especially necessary in premature babies. It is customary nowadays to use multiple vitamin preparations to ensure against any form of deficiency, and these are convenient and usually well tolerated. Once a child is on a normal mixed-food intake, the need for vitamin supplementation falls away. Remember that whereas a little may be good, too much may be harmful. Do not therefore overdose with vitamins, and do not use them as 'tonics'. (See *tonics.)

VOMITING

Though vomiting can hardly be regarded as a normal activity, there are some situations in which it cannot be regarded as abnormal. It is important to distinguish acceptable vomiting from unacceptable vomiting, for the latter requires explanation and probably appropriate treatment.

What are the causes of acceptable vomiting?

In the first few days of life. Many babies vomit, especially when they are given unnecessary feeds of glucose water or milk before mother's lactation is established. This type of vomiting is more marked when the baby has swallowed a lot of blood during the birth process, and in such cases the stomach is often washed out with good effect. Babies at this stage vomit mostly gastric mucus, which is continuously being secreted by the stomach, and stomach washouts to remove it are unnecessary and misguided. The baby should be breastfed only.

This type of vomiting has to be distinguished from vomiting due to other causes, and in particular congenital obstructions of the digestive tract. Vomiting with bile has always to be taken seriously, so if the vomit is yellow in colour inform your doctor promptly.

Posseting. Many babies bring up small quantities of milk during or soon after feeds and this may continue for some time. Provided the baby is happy and is thriving satisfactorily such posseting can be ignored.

Habitual vomiting. Some infants have rather more exaggerated and persistent vomiting than the simple posseter. They vomit small quantities all the time usually right through from one feed to the next, with the result that mother is always a sour mess and every carpet is spotted. In spite of it all, the baby thrives and is thoroughly happy. This habitual vomiting is sometimes lessened by the introduction of solids and thickening of the feeds, either with a specific feed thickener or with a fine cereal.

Air-swallowing. The gluttonous baby may swallow a good deal of air with his feeds and his stomach may become very distended before satiety is reached. With the rather forceful burping this situation requires, some of the milk may be vomited. Excessive aerophagy can be avoided by feeding the baby in a sitting up position, for then he can burp whenever he wants to.

Vomiting as the result of coughing. A baby who chokes may well end up vomiting, and any severe cough such as whooping cough may lead to vomiting at the end of a severe coughing bout. Such situations are usually quite clear. The vomiting itself is of little importance, although with whooping cough, which is a serious condition in small babies, weight may be lost as a result of the repeated vomiting.

Serious causes of vomiting

Obstructions of the digestive tract. Congenital obstruction may occur at any level from the gullet to the anus. Obstruction of the oesophagus leads to almost continuous vomiting of saliva, with choking and blue attacks. Such symptoms demand urgent medical assessment.

Obstruction of the intestine. If the obstruction is below the level of the duodenum this leads to bilious vomiting, and if bile is present in the vomitus a serious view of the situation must be taken. Obstruction of the lower bowel usually produces abdominal pain and marked abdominal distension as well as vomiting, and there will probably be associated constipation.

Pyloric stenosis. In this condition vomiting usually starts at the age of 2 to 3 weeks and becomes increasingly forceful. It is due to muscular obstruction at the lower end of the stomach and usually requires surgical relief. (See *pyloric stenosis.)

'Gastritis'. Irritation of the stomach from poisons or dietary indiscretions frequently leads to vomiting, often followed by diarrhoea. It is best to withhold food until the vomiting has settled and to recommence feeding with small quantities administered frequently.

Gastro-enteritis. A combination of vomiting and diarrhoea usually implies an infection of the digestive tract. When vomiting is the dominant symptom it is more likely to be due to a virus infection rather than a bacterial one. (See *gastro-enteritis.)

Throat infection. Tonsillitis or the more common virus throat infections are often associated with vomiting. Sometimes the throat appears normal. A combination of fever and vomiting without other findings implies a viral cause and the condition may then be called simple virus vomiting.

Infections elsewhere. Some children seem to react to infection through their stomachs and present with vomiting in conditions such as ear infection and urinary tract infection. The combination of fever and vomiting therefore demands a complete medical examination as the underlying condition may require active treatment.

Meningitis and encephalitis. Vomiting is a characteristic symptom of these conditions, which usually present also with headache and fever. Stiffness of the neck and back are valuable associated signs. Any child presenting with these symptoms must be seen by a doctor as soon as possible.

Intracranial causes. In addition to meningitis and encephalitis, anything causing a rise in intracranial pressure is likely to cause vomiting. Headache is almost always an accompanying feature. Such conditions include collections of blood as the result of trauma, brain abscess, brain tumour, vitamin A poisoning and, rarely, certain drugs.

Psychological causes. A particularly harrowing experience or severe emotional upset may well make a child vomit. The occasional disturbed child may use self-induced vomiting to attract attention.

Recurrent vomiting. Occasionally, vomiting occurs in attacks with perfectly well periods in between. Such episodes may be due to recurrent infections or a series of unrelated conditions. Two other causes bear considering:

(1) *Cyclical vomiting.* This condition, perhaps better known as the periodic syndrome, is characterised by repeated attacks of a set of symptoms which may include vomiting, abdominal pain, headache and fever. No cause for the attacks is

apparent and in between them the child is perfectly well. It is important to check for such conditions as recurrent tonsillitis and urinary tract infection but, these having been excluded, one is left with no alternative diagnosis but cyclical vomiting. The attacks usually cease after a few years. A suitable anti-emetic drug usually helps to shorten the attacks.

(2) *Migraine*. Recurrent headaches associated with vomiting, the latter often producing relief, are characteristic of migraine. The condition is usually familial and it is a diagnosis difficult to make in the absence of a family history. (See *headache.)

WAKEFULNESS
See *sleep problems

WALKING
See *development

WARTS
Warts are due to a virus infection of the skin and are therefore contagious to some extent. They often appear in crops. They may occur on any part of the body but are particularly common on the hands and feet. Plantar warts are painful because the wart is continually pressed into the foot by the pressure on the sole. They are best managed by softening with a salicylate plaster until the base of the wart is reached, when it may then be chemically cauterised. Warts in other situations are best left alone, as they will almost always disappear after a year or two. When in embarrasing or inconvenient situations, however, they may demand treatment. Freezing is effective but it has to be skilfully done to avoid scarring. The same applies to cauterisation, which usually leaves a scar and often fails to cure the wart. The daily application of a mild preparation such as glacial acetic acid, if pursued with with patience, usually leads to cure without scarring.

WAX (in the ears)
The skin of the ear canal normally secretes wax and there is therefore no shame attached to having wax in the ears. It gradually finds its way to the surface and falls out. Sometimes it accumulates sufficiently to cause deafness or discomfort and may then have to be removed. Left alone, however, it will nearly always look after itself. If, however, the wax is repeatedly pushed back into the ear by the use of cotton buds it becomes impacted against the eardrum and may then cause trouble. Never therefore poke things into your children's ears. Whatever is visible may be gently removed but do not explore further. Occasionally the doctor may find it necessary to remove wax mechanically, otherwise ear wax can be dissolved by means of solvent eardrops.

WEANING
The termination of breastfeeding is best accomplished after the age of about 9 months when the child can be weaned to a cup instead of a bottle. There are no rules about weaning and you may continue to breastfeed as long as it gives you pleasure. Beyond the age of 18 months or so, however, the child is probably getting very little nourishment from the breast and the child's continued suckling

becomes more of an addiction than a need. (See *breastfeeding.)

WEIGHING

Weight charts are useful in detecting deviations of growth but an obsession with weight, without due attention to other parameters of growth and development, often does a disservice to babies by removing attention from far more important and interesting observations. There is nothing the matter with confirming a baby's adequate weight progress but this is usually apparent without weighing her and it is of far greater importance to know whether she is happy and well. If this is the case, there is almost certainly no need to weigh her. A baby's weight should always be considered in relation to her other dimensions. In spite of these remarks, mothers will continue to weigh their babies and to extract from the result either satisfaction or anxiety, either of which may or may not be justified. Probably no harm will be done provided you look at your baby as being something other than 5 or 7 kg of flesh. (See *growth.)

Test weighing. The practice of weighing a baby before and after a feed to determine how much she had taken is both seldom necessary and thoroughly inaccurate. It is often a fanatical occupation of maternity departments and, in general, causes more harm and anxiety than good. When employed it should be used for a specific and well-defined purpose. As a routine it can only be condemned.

WEIGHT

For appropriate weight at various ages see *growth. Remember that children as much as adults are individuals and what is appropriate for one may not be appropriate for another. In evaluating the significance of a child's weight, cognisance must be taken of her height and other dimensions, and successive weights are far more informative than any isolated reading. (See *growth and *weighing.)

WHEEZING

Wheezing is a symptom, not a disease. While characteristic of asthma it has many other causes. Wheezing implies some obstruction in the respiratory passages below the level of the larynx. It may be due to inflammation (bronchitis, laryngo-tracheo-bronchitis), to a foreign body, to compression of the trachea by cardiovascular abnormalities, enlarged glands in the chest or tumour, or it may be the result of chronic chest disease such as cystic fibrosis. Wheezing therefore calls for careful evaluation. (See also *asthma.)

WHOOPING-COUGH

See *pertussis

WIND

Of all the innocent culprits blamed for babies' ills, wind vies only with the teeth. When anybody feeds, child or adult, it is normal to swallow air. Some of this rests as a bubble in the stomach, some passes on down the bowel and is passed as flatus. That which stays in the stomach occupies space which would be better occupied with food and is therefore usually brought up as a burp. Some people seem to get satisfaction from burping loudly, others do it more discreetly. Babies are the same. It is a pity that they cannot share the pleasure they give the mother and granny when they burp impressively. To them there is nothing very impressive about it except that it may make room for more food and this they will then demand.

There is absolutely no need to spend ages beating your baby to get wind out of her. This is a largely Anglo–Saxon fetish. After the feed, or during it if she voluntarily asks for a rest, she should be placed in a vertical position and given the opportunity to burp. Whether she does or not is up to her. Afterwards she should be put back to the breast or offered the remainder of her feed to make sure that she has had all she wants. Feeds, whether breast or bottle, should not be interrupted in order to bring up wind. This simply irritates the baby, sometimes to the point where she may refuse further feeding. The giving of medicines to help 'wind', particularly such misguided preparations as those which alter the surface tension in the hope that making one big bubble out of several lesser ones will facilitate eructation, is as unnecessary as it is fatuous. Don't be taken in by such wanton commercialisation. To ascribe symptoms to wind is bad enough, to make money out of it is even less justifiable. (See also *colic.)

WORKING MOTHERS
Some mothers work because they have to, some because they want to. Whatever the reason, there need be absolutely no guilt attached to working. If for financial reasons you are forced to work to survive or to provide a reasonable standard of living for your family, surely this is to their advantage. If you work because you enjoy working and it makes you a happier person than does domestic drudgery, then this too is surely to your family's advantage. The fact that your child might have to spend much of the day in the care of others — nanny, crèche or pre-school — does not mean that she has been abandoned or deprived. You are still her mother and occupy a unique place in her life — a place that can be usurped by nobody. This she knows full well and though she may have a great deal of affection for nanny or teacher it will not by any means be the same sort of relationship she enjoys with you.

For the mother who has to work, whether because she is a single parent or divorcee or is faced with an income insufficient for her family's needs, there is no alternative. She may be fortunate enough to be able to take her baby to work with her so that breastfeeding may continue; and employers should realise that they are likely to get better service out of a contented employee than from someone who spends her day worrying about her child. Institutions which have a significant number of working mothers should have attached crèches where the children can be left but visited as frequently as possible during the day by their mothers. Failing such an ideal situation, mother will have to find someone to look after her child and this may of course prove difficult. Grandparents may help out and give themselves much joy and satisfaction in the process. If the child is left in the care of a nanny she should conform to your standards but above all should be able to love the child, not as a mother substitute but as a mother aid. If no suitable crèche is available, several mothers may be able to club together on a rotation basis and this often provides a very happy solution.

The mother who would like to work but feels guilty about 'abandoning' her child need not have such qualms. Some women find great satisfaction and fulfilment in domesticity, others are bored by it. Boredom does not lead to happiness and it is probable that your child will get more benefit from a few hours of happy contact with you daily than from full-time mutual irritation. Be honest with yourself and recognise what sort of person you are. Be assured that your child will adjust to almost anything. What matters is not whether you work or not but the sort of relationship you have with her and she with you. This is likely to be much better if you lead an interesting and fulfilling life than if you stay at home resenting the drudgery. And when your child grows up she will be proud of her working mother and probably wish to emulate her example. The same justification cannot of course be applied to the idle socialite who sheds her children in order to play bridge or laze by the pool but here we are discussing the working, not the shirking, mother.

WORMS

The common worms to afflict children apart from *tapeworm are roundworms, hookworms, threadworms and whipworms.

Roundworms (Ascaris). These are the common worms, rather resembling earthworms, which may be passed in the stools or sometimes vomited. They are spread by faecal contamination, the eggs of the worms being ingested in food or water. In the intestine the eggs hatch and the larvae penetrate the intestinal wall, enter the bloodstream and are swept to the lungs. There they break through the alveolar walls, are coughed up and swallowed. On reaching the intestine again, the larvae develop into adult worms.

In their passage through the lung the worms may cause respiratory symptoms, with coughing, breathlessness and wheezing. Adult worms in the intestine seldom cause symptoms unless the parasite load is very heavy. They may then become entangled in a mass, causing intestinal obstruction. They may also cause symptoms by migrating into unusual places such as the bile ducts, where they may give rise to jaundice, pain and sometimes liver abscesses. Occasionally, worms which have been vomited are inhaled and cause respiratory obstruction.

Treatment of roundworm infestation is simple, unless complications are present. Several drugs are effective, e.g. piperazine, levamisole, pyrantel, thiabendazole and mebendazole.

Hookworms. These are common in warm, moist climates. After being passed out in the stools, the eggs hatch under favourable conditions, to release a small larva which is able to penetrate the skin. Small children sitting in contaminated muddy soil are particularly liable to pick up these worms. The larvae enter the circulation and are swept up to the lungs, which they traverse; they are then coughed up and swallowed. On reaching the bowel, the worms mature and attach themselves to the lining of the upper small intestine. They may cause some intestinal discomfort but the main effect of the worms is to cause anaemia as the result of chronic blood loss. Hookworms are small, only about 1 cm long and are not seen in the stools. They may be treated with bephenium hydroxinaphoate, mebendazole or pyrantel.

Threadworms (pin worms). These are common in temperate rather than tropical climates. The worm is spread more by overcrowding than by poor hygiene. The eggs, which are very light, are easily spread about a home. The life cycle is simple — the eggs, having been swallowed, hatch into worms which mature in the intestine. Female worms crawl through the anus, particularly at night, to deposit their eggs on the perianal skin. This causes itching, the child scratches and if she then, as commonly happens, puts her fingers into her mouth, a new load of eggs is swallowed and the cycle is repeated. Threadworms resemble a 1 cm long piece of white cotton and may be seen around the anus at night if looked for.

As multiple members of the family are likely to be infested it is wise to treat the whole family at the same time. In addition to an appropriate drug (piperazine, pyrantel, thiabendazole or mebendazole), hygienic measures should be vigorously applied to prevent reinfection. The home, especially the bedroom, should be thoroughly cleaned and vacuumed to remove eggs in the dust, finger nails should be cut short and kept meticulously clean, and bedding and clothing and the night clothing should be thoroughly laundered and changed frequently during the period of treatment. If this is not done, reinfection almost always occurs.

Whipworms (Trichuris). These worms are so called because they resemble a whip, having a long, thin anterior portion and a short, thick posterior end. Ova passed in the faeces are ingested and the worms mature in the intestine without any migration to other regions. In the large bowel the worms burrow into the lining, and a heavy load of worms may cause dysenteric symptoms with blood and mucus in the stools, often resulting in severe anaemia. Heavy loads of worms in the rectum may cause rectal prolapse. Effective drugs for treating whipworms are thiabendazole and mebendazole.

X-RAYS

The discovery of X-rays gave medicine a powerful diagnostic and also therapeutic tool. Recent years have seen further refinements of radiological capability with the invention of the image intensifier, followed by computerised tomography, which enables soft tissues to be well demonstrated by means of X-rays. Ultrasound examination has replaced X-rays in certain areas, notably in the examination of early pregnancy. This is a considerable advance because X-rays can be harmful to the foetus whereas ultrasound appears to be completely innocuous. Advances continue with, for example, nuclear magnetic resonance, which produces even clearer pictures of the brain than does CT scanning. Standard X-ray examinations, however, are still extremely valuable not only for fractures and bone diseases but for examination of the chest, and, with the aid of contrast materials, of the gastro-intestinal tract and urinary tract.

X-rays have a damaging effect upon cells and for this reason over-exposure must be avoided. Especially when children are being examined in several places, a tally may not have been kept upon the number of exposures, and a safe dose may easily be exceeded. Mention this to your doctor if you feel that your child is having too many X-ray examinations. X-rays of the pelvic area should if possible be avoided during the first 3 months or so of pregnancy.

X-ray treatment is used for localised malignancy, usually in conjunction with cytotoxic drugs. Such treatment is nowadays used with discretion and with full awareness of possible ill effects. It is not very long since radiotherapy used for treatment of an 'enlarged' thymus (now realised to be perfectly normal in children) was found to produce cancer of the thyroid. Such errors are not likely to be made again but it does illustrate the need for circumspection in administering any form of treatment.

YELLOW COLOUR

Some children have normal sallow skins, but frank yellow discolouration is usually due to one of two causes, namely jaundice or carotenaemia. Jaundice affects the eyes as well as the skin whereas carotenaemic staining affects the skin only, and particularly in areas where the skin is thick, for instance on the palms and soles. Certain dyes may also produce a yellow discolouration. (See *carotenaemia and *jaundice.)

ZINC

Zinc salts are often incorporated into topical applications as soothing and mildly antiseptic constituents. Zinc deficiency sometimes occurs and may need correction with zinc supplements. Zinc has been of some value in the treatment of acne and is specific in the rare condition of acrodermatitis enteropathica.

First published in Great Britain in 1996 by
ANCHOR BOOKS
1-2 Wainman Road, Woodston,
Peterborough, PE2 7BU

SB ISBN 1 85930 049 9

CONTENTS

REVENGE IS SWEET

Sitting on a bar stool
Evil eye on command
Easy victim I can pull
Another one just at hand

Revenge! Revenge! I hear the call
Adrenaline flowing free
Poor victim, I've had it all
No-one can master me

Money in my pockets
Dreams for me come true
Bracelets, rings and lockets
Poor sucker join the queue.

Helen Bain

BROKEN DREAM

I feel a bit winded now
In a dream constantly out of breath.

When I heard the woman's name
Cried out at midnight from the bell tower.

And over yonder her baby cried
'When I hungered who did feed me?'

And in a dream I saw a person
Descend a winding stair.

It was with an aura of mystery
That be it he or she was destined
Ne'er to reach the floor.

Paul Byrne

1

JUST A CURTAIN

Just a curtain, that's all there is,
just a curtain, so don't despair.

A curtain made of silk so fine,
that's all there is, with me behind.

Just think of me and know I'm there
still here with you,
and still here to care.

Talk to me and I will hear.
Don't cry for me,
don't waste your tears,

for I am here do you not see,
behind this curtain listening I'll be.

Just call my name and I'll be there
do not cry, do not despair,
I have not gone, for I am here,
just by this curtain, for you I'll be,
by this curtain, happy and free.

May Strike

A VISION

I have a vision in Two thousand and Sixty-five
No human being will be left alive

Everyone reaching sixty will be put to sleep
Because no-one will want to pay for their keep

Mental patients and the sick will be put down
Because on these people the rest will frown

Any woman having a baby will have to abort
If not her life will be cut short

War and disease will do the rest
Starvation and famine will do its best

Animals and mammals will also die
In flames of fire that will light up the sky

Oceans will rise and cover the land
Leaving nothing behind but just the sand

But somewhere a man and woman will mate
For those that died it will be too late

J Doyle

GO THROUGH THE DOOR

To understand has been my driving passion
Since I can remember.
This I learned to do
As I lived in troubled regions
In the midst of contradictions.
But reason and understanding
Have had their season.
It is time to let understanding die
And be alive in the darkness of faith.
Blind now, please, take me by the hand
Through the door.
I risk leaving behind this side of the moon
And enter mystery.
With You I am ready to go through any door
Since only You have the power
To address me with the gift of your liberty and turn
My dark well, or whatever it may be,
Into your testament.

Angela Matheson

THE WHISPERS OF ANGELS

Out of the darkness,
    Came incredible light
        Its warmth pulled me closer
            And held onto me so tight

I didn't know where I was going
    Or where my journey would end
        Yet I felt no fear or panic
            For the light seemed like a friend

I walked through eternities
    And saw people that I once knew
        Their love reached out and touched me
            And my heart rose high and flew

In the distance I could see a garden
    Its beauty was far beyond compare
        Green grass grew in abundance
            And flowers seemed to dance in mid air

A fountain stood proud in the centre
    A cascade of shimmering light
        I could hear the whispers of angels
            Though their presence was beyond my sight

I wanted to remain in this paradise
    But a voice told me that I couldn't stay
        I had to return to where I had come from
            The light would show me the way

I felt so sad to leave this place
    For it was here my spirit felt free to roam
        But a voice kept telling me that it wasn't my time
            And I had to go back home

It was then that I saw a stranger
    She was lying motionless from what I could see
        And as I drew nearer to this woman
            I discovered this stranger was me!

Lin Jane Pearce

BEYOND THE BEYOND

Beyond earth, and space,
Moon, and the stars above
Time and motion, seem to stand still
When love, embraces everything
With light and good
Then, all therein, responds to it
A golden crown, emits a wondrous aura.
As if all the world were lit up with fire.
Suddenly a rainbow of colour
Paints every mountain, valley, and spire
Often, changing with rhythm to music and sound
Rising up higher! Ever higher!
And all are happy with no worry, or care.
For the spirit realms have no pain, or suffering there,
The sky above, remains ever blue
Whilst the fresh soft grass gives a deep emerald hue
Beyond the beyond, rests a silver sea
That shimmers thru' depths of tranquillity
With healing waters to bathe in each day,
Calming all ills and stresses away.
Here lives the spirit of all life
In being at peace, with creation,
Soul joined with soul, united in the celebration
Of eternal being, and in freeing
The spirit of earthly limitation
In the joy of seeing, that there is no death!

Geraldine Madden

THE PROMISED LAND

There is a land beyond the stars
Where peace and happiness reign
Where the sick of body, spirit or mind
Are made whole once again.

Our loved ones and our beloved pets
Who travelled on before
Are waiting there to greet us
On that far distant shore.

We shall be healed and cleansed of sin
Forget all our earthly strife
For we shall know love and contentment
And everlasting life.

P Worth

CONFUSION

Many years ago from now
When I first went to school
I could not really understand
A certain kind of rule
My left hand was the reason
I was chastised every day
And in the end the right hand
Was the one I used at bay
I realise after all these years
The damage it has done
My brain got so confused it seems
Life was not too much fun
So now I have come to the conclusion
I am as good as all the rest
So I have discarded that old label
And enjoy life at its best.

Rose Froud

6

THE BOY

The little boy with the dusky skin,
Opened the gate to let me in.
Stepping into a world so bright,
Full of flowers and beauty and light.

Taking me through ferns and trees,
He showed me over the mountains and the seas.
And everything was so quiet and still,
As I gazed in wonder from the top of a hill.

Only the soft cry of a bird,
Was the only sound that could be heard.
For we were travelling on and on,
Seeing loved ones, long since gone.

They stood silently as we passed by,
On our strange journey through the sky,
Until we came to a land so green,
The most beautiful I had ever seen.

And there before my very sight,
The house I'd dreamed of, all in white.
Then the little boy with the dusky skin,
Opened the door to let me in.

But I waited for it was so,
It wasn't the time for me to go.
For he was showing me the way,
Which I would travel on My Day.

So with sadness in my heart,
We returned and had to part.
Then promising to meet at a later date,
We said our farewells at the meeting gate.

W Booth

NOVEMBER 24TH 1921

When on my way to daily toil one November winter day
A scene of beauty I beheld and it cheered me on my way.
The sky above was brilliant blue till Mother Nature softened it
with tints of every hue
Then sprinkled it with shining gold, still more lovely to behold.
My work seemed less monotonous throughout that wintry day,
It seemed brightened with those tints of gold that nature cast away
But the beauty soon was sadly gone the sky was leaden grey
Those brilliant colours couldn't last throughout advancing day
But memory keeps that joy in store as I recall it o'er and o'er,
Though the year was nineteen twenty one I still can see that morning sun.

Nettie Stoddart

CHRISTMAS SOCKS

Claire a diligent Brownie, aged nine,
Was learning knots at Christmas time.
Among her Christmas shopping prizes,
Were coloured socks in varying sizes.

Packing them up with festive string,
Their lacy tops seemed just the thing
To thread and tie with different knots,
To decorate her sisters' cots.

The knots were good and turned out right,
And held the socks up very tight.
Alas, in the tops some holes were seen,
And ladders appeared where they shouldn't have been.

Claire, a diligent Brownie of nine
Must now darn socks at Christmas time.
Has Father Christmas a darning kit?
Poor Claire would be very glad of it.

Mary Allen

8

WHEN THE EXAMS ARE OVER

When the exams are over,
I shall be full of relief,
Long gone will be the days,
When I had to revise with grief.

When the exams are over
I'll be over the moon.
I look forward to that day
And hope it comes very soon.

When the exams are over,
I can do what I want, it's up to me.
My diary will be empty,
My days will be free!

Andrea Jane Blue

WAR AND PEACE

War takes over
Devastation and anger forever spreading
Sorrow
Revenge wanted
Screams from the nightmare outside
The bitterness of innocence
Hopelessness
Everywhere
When the dove is set free
The white flag is raised
Undisturbed truce
Satisfaction
People come together
Dreaming new dreams.

Sheri Moule

MISCARRIAGE

As I lay in my pain
the baby with no name
had died before I could
give it one.
I had no idea of the loss
I would bear at losing
an unknown loved one.
I felt such despair
that I could no longer care
to think of anyone else
but this one.
But it suddenly dawned
that I wasn't really alone.
I had dreamed that my baby
had been born.
A beautiful child it had not
really died its time simply
had not come

Carol Sweeney

MY VACATION

For this year's vacation
Kenya was my destination.
Dirt track roads and dust galore
T-shirt and shorts was all we wore,
Getting up at dawn many animals to see
Stirred great excitement inside of me.
Elephant, lion, rhino: all were there
On the great plains, they do share
In their land as it should be
All the animals are roaming free.

L J Male

FRIENDSHIP

It means a lot to have a friend
Who is reliable and true,
A friend to share all heartaches
And troubles through and through.

A friend is there to ease the pain,
When a loved one has passed on.
A kindly word, a sympathetic ear,
A shoulder to cry on.

When one is lost and far away
Feels so forlorn in every way
The hand of friendship is not far behind
It is like a saviour to mankind.

A friend is always there to talk
And listens with compassion
A pillar of strength in every way
And points in the right direction.

Friendship lasts throughout the years
As sturdy as a rock
So loving and protective
It never ceases to amaze
And is there for all to see.
A wonderful combination
Of truth and honesty.

One day when all the world is still
That friend will stand upon a hill
Stretch out a hand of might and main
The world will just be right again
The hand of friendship
Shall regain
An understanding not in vain.

Nancy Rees

PEMBROKESHIRE PUB DRIVE

for eighty quid we get a caravan
and fill it up with booze and food and junk.
we go for drink with my dad and
he takes us on a pembrokeshire pub drive:
you need headlights, you need the wipers on,
you need someone sober at the wheel, and
you need to know the leafy corridors
like your own back garden -
my dad manages all this and gets us
to a pub by a canal, miles from the sea
I recognise it, I remember being here one summer when
people gathered and held contests.
imagine it, adults playing with water.
now here I am, all grown up,
strolling into this pub bold as a regular -
some of the real regulars look round
I'm decked out in mustard suede, we're not from these parts
but my dad knows the landlord, so maybe we are.
we sit down. the local firewater is actually
called firewater, so I have to try it, and
at the bar I notice a chalkboard. my dad
explains that it's so you can stand someone
a drink even when they're not there.
my dad tells me I've got a distant uncle that lives in this village:
so I think, I could buy this man a drink
and never meet him at all, and he could sink it
and never have met me, and still know who I am,
just by who I'm related to.
'You can't do that in Bridgend,' says my dad,
and he's right.

Gary Owen

WORKING LATE

The tension eases
this day's near done,
now time to sit and
think of one,
or two mistakes
along the way,
that shouldn't have happened
in the fray.

Peaceful now
the phone's not ringing,
the cleaner's in
as usual, singing,
time to clear
the odds and ends,
and phone home
just to make amends.

To say that you're sorry
in work you're embroiled,
to go by herself
another time soiled,
you had to work late
a deadline was tight,
but there's no answer
she left last night.

Robert Douglas

LOVE

My heart melts
as he touches my face.
His sweet cheek to mine
his breath in my ear,
The quiver in my legs.
He talks in a whisper
declaring his feeling for another.
My soul shattered beneath me.
He took my hand
friends forever
nothing more.
My heart alive with hurt,
he takes another in his arms
his lips meet hers.
My pain rises up
his hands take her side.
My love is broken
never to heal again.
Love is hurting me.

Claire Jennings

REFLECTIONS OF THE SCILLY ISLES

When I leave Trescoe, a part of me will forever wander free,
and take the paths which for a time felt as though they were always mine,
To savour once more the spell on my heart for this fair land will not let me
depart,
But I must leave some part of me to wheel with the gulls when the winds blow
free,
To ebb and flow with the restless tide for here my heart is and will ever abide,
Its charm and its magic will call me it seems, to return to this wonderful isle of
my dreams.

Alice A Morton

14

WHAT I HAVE TO SAY

There was no time to say goodbye
The day you went away
You left the world so suddenly
Many centuries ago today

There'll always be a heartache
And often a silent tear
But always precious memories
Of days when you were here

We hold you close within our hearts
And there you will remain
To walk with us throughout our lives
Until you'll come again

For all the love you're giving us
In all these lovely years
The comfort of your presence
In days of joys and tears

Each sacrifice you made
Along the path you trod
Is remembered by us always
As you sit beside God

A resting place we visit
And put flowers with care
But no one knows the heartache
As we turn and leave you there

So Jesus will be treasured
In God's garden of rest
Because in this cruel world of ours
He was the best.

Blink

DWIGHT YOAKAM, CMT
(Dedicated to a famous country singer)

I hear your music on CMT,
A fine performer, it's true to see.
Your songs touch many, near and far,
Dwight, you're truly a first class star

You have such talent beyond compare,
A special gift which is so rare,
A style which stands out from the rest,
Dwight, you truly are the best.

The joy you bring, not just to me,
Also to my boy of three,
Listening to your music, from morn till night,
Then he'll say, 'Mammy, call me Dwight.'
With his guitar and mike, he'll sing aloud.
I'll stand and watch, oh, so proud.

So many more, just like me,
Will watch you daily on CMT.
Just like your music, is so rare,
So is your character, beyond compare.
That's why Dwight, you'll always be,
The best performer on CMT.

Sheila Farrer

REPRESSED MEMORIES

In my mind, I travel the distant paths of childhood
Meandering images appear like haunting dreams
Of a time before life could ever be truly understood
An era of peaceful harmony and tranquil scenes
A golden age, before the violence and stricken screams

16

I battle my inner soul to keep the visions from my mind
But the repressed memories infiltrate every trace of emotion
To the limited joys of my childhood, I am blind
As the faces of my family are viewed with condemnation
My brain dwells on those teenage years of bitter confrontation

Youthful innocence was torn from a beaten body
Vampiric, happiness was sucked from a child's eyes
Joy existed, only in a world of created fantasy
Reality was a series of harsh words and angry cries
Thus, now, I live with the permanent scar of my family ties.

Steven J Smith

AN INVITATION
(To a Charfield Garden)

Will you come into my garden in the twilight of the day
And listen to the birds' song they're singing while they may?
Can you hear the blackbird singing in the tree
Mingled with a thrush in a chorus just for me?

That's the plop of the frogs as they find our little pool
They're making the most of the evening in the gentle cool.
That's Mr Frissel, my rooster, getting ready for his rest,
The contented cluck, cluck, clucking of the hens lain about his breast.

The sniffle, snuffle, of the hedgehog coming out to play
And the to and fro-ing of the little owl searching for her prey.
If you're very quiet you may see a fox intent upon a kill,
Or even a baby badger. Now that would be a thrill.

Can you smell the honeysuckle twining on the wall,
Or the sweet perfume of the wallflower now it's grown quite tall?
Will you not stay a while, take a glass of wine?
I've yet to show you so much more, oh, you haven't got the time?

Patricia M Jones

THE ANALYST AND I

Quickly through the half lit streets
Through the rain in icy sheets.
Feeling like a disconnected phone
I wandered home alone.
When I reached my stately shambles
Thinking of those clifftop rambles.
I fell asleep upon the chair
Drifted dreaming free of care.
Come the morning the sun shone bright
My sleep was wakened by the light.
As I pondered over my morning excrement
I decided on some analytical treatment.
Waiting to scc the analyst is very trying
When you're called the butterflies start flying.
He beckoned me in and offered a seat,
I felt so strange like two left feet.
His voice was low, soft and calm
I felt the sweat run on my palm.
Sitting like sphinx he scanned the sea of trouble
From the summit of my mind in clifftop rubble.
Snake-like he slithered, slowly searching for truth
Hawk-like he watched from sub-conscious roof.
From panther-pose he pounced upon the answer
He freed me from my self-inflicted cancer.
I felt so good I went insane.
I'll never go back there again.

Nigel D Luton

LOOK TO THE QUIET HILLS

Streaks of sunlight dapple the ground;
Frost, as yet unreached,
Hides in its own shadow,
Waiting.

Still, sharp, clear, the day wakes and
Rises,
Rises to the death which is autumn.

Withered apples cling to branches which hang
Their last leaves
Like broken fingers, silently, into the still, cold air.
Suspended, they defy gravity and death,
Mock science and nature;
For a few, stolen, moments,
Fend off the inevitable.

The sharpness of this autumn morning
Etches against the sky,
The hills;
God's walls.
Curling like a protective arm around the land beneath;
Remote, yet somehow present too.

Atop the ridge of hills
Stand trees too full of leaf to know
The strife of those below:
Evergreens, tall and proud and full.
Watchmen upon thy walls.

Stephen Robinson

TODAY

Echoes in the ripples,
of the fountain of today.
Speak to me of your day.
I now understand,
your moon reflects
upon the water,
glistening with your touch.
Your want gave life,
to the lovers,
who now caress in a boat,
below your gaze.
You peered into their soul,
vanquished their fears,
let them rest together,
in peace,
contented with each other,
their arms locked
in passion
ignited by your
ripple across the sea.

Murray Pannett

PARADISE LOST

I sit by the lakeside
and see
the tall pines reflected
in the mirror
of the water
and think of yesterday
and you . . .
and all the yesterdays
we shared.

But now today -
the present moment -
becomes a sad intrusion
as our stubborn pride
ruined our enchanted lives
and I am left an empty void -
a husk . . .
filled with the memories of you,
as the rising mist
obliterates the lake.

Stephen Gyles

CLOUDS OF DARKNESS

There is no light where we are.
Darkness comes from inside.
Blinded eyes cast shadows
When our hands touch emptiness.
We march between walls,
Silent brick and stone.
No echo fills the ruins.
There's no space to weep.
The heaps of rubble
Rising like a pall of death,
Mask the light of our hope.
Children aged before their time,
Huddle together,
Clasping shattered limbs,
Tremble in the freezing dust.
Lies and broken promises
Fill the giddy air.
Will they retrieve faith and trust?
Their friends of yesterday
Betrayed them with each step.

Ingrid Riley

YESTERDAY'S MEMORIES

I remember it as yesterday when we used to walk,
I remember it as yesterday when we used to stop and talk,
I remember it as yesterday when I proposed to you,
I remember it as yesterday you replying 'Yes I'll marry you.'
Then one day disaster struck,
A barbarian ran over you with his huge big truck,
The next thing I remember is hearing the vicar say
'Earth to earth, ashes to ashes, dust to dust.'
That's the last thing I remember from all those years ago,
But I remember it as clearly as I remember yesterday.

Neil A Holbrook

LIMBO

Drifting on a sea of belated tides,
Lift I drowning eyes of emerald green to blue and black.
Clouds of pity rain tears;
Tiny, sharp darts,
Seeking, searching me.

I am sun, moon ever watchful, ever wakeful,
For you,
For your smell,
For your touch.

Float I on memories sublime to meet your presence;
But the tides are ruthless,
Time is our enemy;
I can only drift and drift along impotent,
Afloat in my desperate despair.

Nicole E Ingleton

NIGHTLY PRAYER

O God! Oh thanks mate.
Full belly,
Blaring telly,
Water, warmth and air.
Phone ringing,
Daughters singing.
Constant wear and tear.
Good clean bed,
Roof overhead,
Memories we can share.
Thanks mate, that I'm not out on the streets tonight.

Eileen Donachie

PATTERNS IN A LANDSCAPE

These are the patterns in this landscape November Estuary:

Grey levels of mud shores, shattered boat wrecks,
the dreams of men, to sail,
to reach upward and outward.
Drowned not by sea, but sand-earth that will not hold.
And here, still grey water where heron stalk,
and white sky broken by a plane tree.

                                      (My hand enfolds the sky)

These are the dimensions in which smaller voices play:

The bubbling trill voices of curlews,
and herring gulls wheeling and screaming in the invisible wind.
Our laughter distilled to a simple wonder, a breath sucks in the world.
I lean against a wall,
and the world may tip this way or that.

Kim Green

CHRISTMAS

The magic season's here again
A time when old and young
Gather round the Yule log fire
And hear the carols sung.
By children singing in the choir
By carollers outside
Standing in the midnight air
Heralding Christmastide

And in the house, the fire glows
The Christmas tree shines bright.
The presents, wrapped with coloured bows
Sparkle in the light.
Upstairs the little ones sleep sound
Their day will soon be here
As Santa journeys on his round
With presents, far and near.

It's Christmas Day, the bells ring out
To celebrate anew, our Saviour's birth in Bethlehem
And so, for me and you
The gift of giving, once again,
Bringing so much pleasure
Makes Christmastide a lovely time
With joy in fullest measure.

Doris Cowie

CANDLES ARE BEING LIT

Candles are being lit in the Holy City,
Shining in the dark they're very pretty.
People celebrating the very special birth
Of Jesus Christ's first sight of this earth.

The oxen are lowing quietly in the manger;
Christmastide will see many a stranger -
Folks from many lands paying respects to the babe:
Centuries later, still a cavalcade.

Does Mother Mary gaze fondly now on her son,
Although so many centuries have gone?
At Christmas, He is a babe in arms to the world,
As around everyone's heart He had twirled.

To Christians, Christmas is a very special time
For quiet thoughts as well as pantomime.
Over our world falls a sense of peaceful content
And we can relax 'midst the enjoyment.

J Millington

PEACE IN MY LIFETIME

I wonder in my lifetime,
If I will ever see,
Everybody in this world,
Promising to agree.

Every day, in the papers,
It is always filled,
With news, that people all over the world,
Are being maimed, or killed.

The leaders in some countries
Always seem to need,
To be invading their neighbour's land,
For either Power, or Greed.

So wouldn't it be wonderful,
If people, from different lands,
Could meet, at a Peace Conference,
To be friends, and all shake hands.

Jean Hendrie

25

UNTITLED

The weekend is here oh what a drag
The curtain rail's beginning to sag
Some paint is flaking from the kitchen door
Downstairs loo is blocked it's all such a bore
Sitting room rad has sprung a leak
Why couldn't it happen another week?
That broken glass it has to be mended
Back garden weeds just have to be tended
The linen cupboard has started to squeak
Professional help I'm not allowed to seek
That dripping tap in kitchen sink
Blocked 'U' bend too has started to stink
If only that floorboard hadn't come loose
It would save me putting my new hammer to use
One dining room chair has wobbly legs
Our lampshade is held together with pegs
The pilot light on the boiler is out
A freezing shower makes my wife shout
The wallpaper's coming unstuck again
This DIY is becoming a pain
If only I could get just motivated
To start these jobs that are so hated
Should I start on the back gate latch
No sod it all I'm off to the match.

C P Sparkes

LOSS

Soft as the stars remote in diamond distance
The very face of heaven shining clear
Soft as summer wind through green trees blowing
My mind creates your form and brings you near.

So very long since you were here with me
Your warm strong presence eternally dear
I feel once more your tender spirit glowing
I am released from pain released from fear

Just once more to have you really with me
For just an hour you could be really here
All that I have and all my time remaining
Would be small price to pay to hold you near.

Pat McAtee

HEART

My love. When we
began to do all the fun
things that feel brand new.
That makes each day a sweeter
day that other people see and
say, that love is blind, what
do they know, they cannot see
the shiny glow we feel when
ever we are near, and all
I can do is stand and
stare but this is a
feeling that we
create with a
sigh, we're
loved and
love my
lover
and
I

Ted Harrison

HARVEST FESTIVAL

Ochre marrows like marmalade cats bask on the stone window sill,
Puddled in sunbeams shimmering bright as rivulets under a mill.
Map-skinned apples arranged in line along an old oak ledge,
Cheek-by-jowl with fruit and flowers from garden, field and hedge.
Michaelmas daisies grace the aisle their faces looking East,
To greet the morning radiance that adorns this Holy Feast.

The organ croons about a flock 'He tenderly doth feed,'
A robin on a tombstone sings 'ecstatic'ly' for seed.
The scene is something fragile . . . mark it well before it fades,
Absorb its truth illumined in the stained-glass windows' shades.
The Psalm affirms it boldly . . . with carillon-like ring,
'The valleys stand so thick with corn, that they shall laugh and sing.'

Past the creeper-glowing font the processing choir sings,
Of thankfulness for Harvest and the bounty that it brings.
Basses and sopranos . . . and some uncertain tones of voice,
Sing in exaltation their compulsion to rejoice.
The ploughman's hope of plenty . . . a hope fulfilled again,
'To Thee O Lord our hearts we raise' extols the swelling strain.'

Gamboge carrots, well-scrubbed potatoes, amaranthine beet,
Purple grapes encircling the lectern's brazen eagle's feet.
On every chancel step a sheaf of ears of golden wheat.
Brilliant autumn berries bejewel the side sedilia seat.
The sight demands an artist to record the showy scene,
In Burnt Sienna, Crimson Lake, Vandyke and Hooker's Green.

Beneath the stained East window's hues - the damask altar cloth,
Silken and embroidered - as the wings of the tiger-moth.
The Cross and lighted candles, the brocaded chalice-veil,
Here the Eucharist is offered within the altar rail.

In sacramental gratitude . . . the faithful to avail,
Knowing 'While the Earth remains the Harvest shall not fail.'

Eric P Wilks

AUTUMN

Is it the melancholy me
Who really wants to be
And makes me love the sad brown leaves
Of Autumn falling from the tree

Is it the mellow wistful warmth
Which nestles deep inside
And gives to me a knowing glow
As by the warm sweet fire I hide

Or is it just the need to rest
After the summer's active fun
The walks and frolics of new found love
And knowing that its course has run

Whilst sitting in my cosy nest
I dream of halcyon days just past
The longing for that sundrenched youth
And knowing that I'm old at last

Did I hear the front door click
The patter of footsteps down the lane
Had he been in whilst I had slept
Had he held my hand again

I dream too much I know 'tis true
Of all that youth which once was me
I nod and as the clock strikes four
I sip my cup of Earl Grey Tea

Harry Bedborough

ENVIRONMENTAL FEARS
(To the Cumbrian trees)

How long have you been here
Majestic and so strong?
How old must you be, before you're old?
Did you see the borders being born?
How many wars have you seen,
From swords and shields
To air-raids and bombs?
Stripping yourself off in winter,
Letting frost be your garment,
Dressing up again in spring
In fine green apparel,
Are you going somewhere?
Going nowhere, you never move.
But you see everything,
And everything you have seen.
The heat and the storms
Rivers swell and rivers dry
You remain the same.
Beware now you're under threat,
Threat from acid rain.
It's the waste age,
Paper throw-aways.
The age of pollution,
The age of the bomb,
Fast trains and motorways.
Cumbrian tree let's say a prayer
Today, let's say a prayer
For you stand against a nuclear plant,
Nuclear waste, and,
The weak spot in the ozone layer.

Jan Howes

RULE BRITANNIA?

Massive English oak on, and in, whose fissured bark
Innumerable creatures live and die,
Each day, each week, each month,
As seasons flow from snow to snow.
Its crevassed skin is summer's host to eggs,
And winter's hibernating parasites
Which hatch, or wake, perpetuating life
To feed the birds in transitory occupation.

Massive English oak in Tudor times
Framed timbered cottages and stately homes alike,
Still extant in their glory, they shame
Modern crudity - so unpleasing to the eye.
Their great trunks crucked or sawn in beams
Were dressed with adze and simple tools -
Then joined by mortises and tenons,
And firmly held by wooden pegs, in holes,
Slowly auger bored in iron hard wood.

Massive English oak in Queen Elizabeth's day
Made 'men o' war'
For men like Drake to sail the world
When Britain ruled the seas
And built an empire which made us proud,
And rich, and great and kept our foes at bay.
We beat the Spanish - we beat the French,
We were the greatest in the world.
But now it's all been given away -
The 'Brussels lot' rule us today!

Ron Watts

NIGHTMARE ON DREAM STREET

Creaking doors, uneven floors
A fireplace that no longer roars
A missing rail, undelivered mail
A kitchen that's beyond the pale
Ancient plumbing, water running
A coldness that is stark and numbing
Rubbish piles, missing tiles
A problem house on agents' files

Decisions made, plans laid
A mortgage granted, a client paid
Estimates galore, architects to the fore
Can we really afford any more?
Woodwormers drilling, damp-proofers proofing,
Someone is banging away at the roofing
Out goes the bath, pull out the hearth
Re-lay all the slabs down the garden path

Finishing date's overdue, there isn't a loo
Next week the in-laws are coming to view
Last minute panic, finished the attic
Work day and night, like someone manic
Completed the task, finished at last
Hopefully achieving re-vamping the past
Relax in chair, without a care
Is that a stain on the ceiling up there?

Terence Raymond

THE SEA

Let the sea shine blue and bright.
In the paths of the liquid light.
Shining like grapes in the beam
Rippling like a world of dreams.
Beauty shining over there
A presence in the summer glare.

Bearing through the azure waves.
Pearly white foam in the lave,
Leaping waves ready to pour
Like rainbows lightening up the shore.
Gushing waves cascade the rocks
Like unfurled flags streaming the locks

They say the sea is like a child
Torrently and ever wild.
Roaring seas going fast
Erupting, howling like a blast.
The mighty sea with smothered sighs
Tired, tangled but never dies.

Mary Myles

FRIEND

A friend is a person who is always there,
Who will always support you and always care.
When you are sad they will make you feel bright,
The things they do are always right.
Even when things aren't going their way,
They push things aside to cheer up your day.
A comforting hug when you are feeling blue,
You know that your friend will be there for you.

Dawn Scanlon

EDINBURGH

Edinburgh was fun,
But I really missed my mum.
The castle was sensational,
And very educational.
When I heard the bagpipes play,
I said I ought to stay,
But instead we went on,
From dusk to dawn,
But we heard them play,
All the way,
And the trip just went on and on.

Laurie Cooper (11)

SUMMER

A cloudless sky, blue and clear
Always glad when summer's here
Hanging baskets colours ablaze
Relax and enjoy those lazy days
Brightly painted scented flowers
The noise of strimmers and lawn mowers
Grass needs trimming twice a week
If it's perfection that you seek
Buddlea attracts butterflies and bees
The colourful bloom of Acer trees
Cricket played on a village green
A typical summer's evening scene
Picnics beside a cool quiet lake
Swans glide by in their wake
Why go travelling abroad on holiday
When in England you can stay?

Helen Saunders

THAT CHRISTMAS

We'd wake around one o'clock,
Drag ourselves up for 'Neighbours,'
Then the chain of 'phones would lock.

I would 'phone her,
She would 'phone him,
How together we were.

At 8pm the cars would pick us up,
We'd travel to the pub,
And the cheapest thing there, we'd sup.

By 10pm the room would spin,
And strangers talked as old friends,
She didn't know his name, but she liked him.

After last orders we'd leave
By foot, carried, or dragged by everyone else,
'For God's sake, get him in the car, *heave*!'

As no time passed we'd travel home,
Laughing, talking, ignoring the smell of sick,
Never realising how far we'd come.

At home the key turned in the door with care,
We'd stumble, laugh, and pick ourselves up,
Hoping no-one had noticed we were there.

Then fall, weightless, onto the bed
Hope the room would slow overnight,
And sleep until we felt the throbbing head.

Carol Fearnall

HOME

1650 was the date my house was built so records state.
A lofty house in town's main street -
a wealthy merchant's needs to meet.
And down the years as pictures show -
it looks the same as long ago.
Visitors will come each year
to see the treasures that are here.
A timbered house with rooms so old
with hidden secrets never told.
But when inside it's plain to see
that changes there have had to be.
The kitchen once so dark and cold
is just a pleasure to behold.
An inglenook that now reveals
an Aga cooking all the meals!
The massive beams were treated their beauty brings a sigh -
to think they've stood the test of time through all the years gone by.
The sitting room is now upstairs with windows looking down
on a winding cottage garden in the middle of the town.
They've fixed the central heating to keep us warm at night
And now the bedrooms 'neath the eaves are cosy snug and bright.
It's given us some problems and taken many hours.
But oh the joy of looking round and knowing that it's ours.

E Warner

BELLS
(Venice, May 1995)

Swinging high in wild delight,
Brazen tongues kissing brazen lips,
Ringing out across the lagoon,
Echoes of Venetian might,
They sway to rest above domes and square,
Silent once more in their lofty tower.

Franca Warrington

36

EYES DOWN

Bingo is my passion
with its 'flyers,' links' and 'lines.'
My pen is poised, my hopes are raised,
that the 'national' will be mine.

So, eyes down, here we go,
now we're all on red alert!
At marking off those numbers
everyone here, is a bingo expert.

With felt-tip pens of every hue
our eyes are fixed and glazed.
Number nine, number four,
we mark our way through the maze.

Now I'm 'sweating' on just one number,
yes, yes, yes it's me!
I've called, I've done it, it's all paid off,
I've *won* the 'national' on number three!

Ann White

ONE FALLING LEAF

I looked up to the sky
The afternoon sun was slowly passing by
A quiet fluttering rippled the air.
Now the trees dared to whisper over here.

A feeling of good times
That is the clear sign.
So now that Autumn grows near
We can see and always *hear*.

Horizon Domino

37

HOME IS WHERE THE HEART IS - A WARTIME POEM

But where *is* my heart?
Is it high in the clouds,
The distant clouds of memory,
Moments seized and precious
For their glowing joys -
Knowing that all was changing
The world - the sky - the moon?
And that soon the roar of war
Would separate and deaden . . .
But my heart is still here
In the dim light of the fire
The cosy chairs, the teacups
And here it stays because
This is my home and where
I will wait for news
From distant lands
Or may be even from the docks.
But a sign - a sign
That you are thinking
And that is all that
Home can mean -
A settled place to which
Your thoughts will turn
And will find me
Just as you left - but wiser far.

Juliet A Thorne

ORPHANAGE

living in an orphanage, all look sad
can an orphanage really be that bad

when you think of all we eat
a treat for them is a piece of meat

38

all our clothes and all our treats
they're lucky to have shoes on their feet

why does it have to be this way
if everyone gave a penny each day

which I'm sure they would and i'd give more
c'os there's nothing worse than being poor.

Carla Jones

OIL LAMPS REMEMBERED

On the cliff-top
Deserted cottages stand
Roofless
And broken
Like fossilised eggshells
Only the sheep
And birds
Live there now
But in the evening
When the sun slips
Down the sky
It shines
Through the old
Broken windows
Like the ghosts
Of the old oil-lamps
Burning
To make the cottages
Feel lived in
And wanted
Once again.

Paula Weare

WARS OF PEACE

If the pain you gave;
Was something that you care to forget,
Why are you so worried?
Don't be scared;
Just lie in your bed.

Find us in our graves;
And face the nightmare.
You can write our epitaphs,
Now that we are lifeless,
But you are still here.

Sign your name in my blood,
So you can remember their fate.
Suddenly you feel so sad,
Don't grieve for us anymore
Because I'll be waiting at the gate!

All the graves are open now,
Which one will yours be?
I can see the blackest one;
Befitting for you says we.
Unlock the door now,
And let Lucifer take thee:
So the innocent souls
Will be set free.

Jagdeesh Sokhal

THANK YOU

Peace and contentment given to me
Beauty of life in all I see
Warmth and love for all I feel
Oh how I know that God is real

Thank you Father for all these things
The flowers that bloom, each bird that sings
The quiet country with its feeling of peace
Love from you that will never cease.

I pray all others may find you
That they may feel the love I do
And when this earth I no more roam
I know there is a heavenly home.

A M Pearson

LITTLE BOOTS
(Borneo 1962-5: The North Yorkshire Light Dragoons)

There they lay.
Lined, in a row.
A blanket, for a shroud,
With little boots, sticking out.
Who were they?
A voice enquired.
The lads turned round.
And, Yorkie, to the Yank
Replied:
Honour is their name -
Valour is their fame
They fight not with you
Nor will they ever,
For they fight for the British
In far flung lands,
Like here, you see.
Aye, to the world
They are the Ghurka
Little men, with little boots
But to me and the lads
They were *mates*.

Peter Read

WATER COLOUR

Across the stillness is seen a gathering of trees.
You speak of their structure,
transmission of light from winter-cold waters
which picture their image with faithful clarity;
oblique lighting from late day sun.

I marvel at dun coloured shadings
tinting late autumn leaves still clinging,
delicate beauty
set against grey blue whiteness above
and meadow green carpet.

The sun now fallen below the horizon,
this side of the world lies in shadow.
Dark indeed in the night
save when illumined
by constant moon and stars.

You offer the light from your eyes
to guide my way.
Loving is giving: I accept you gift
perceiving your deeper vision within
and understanding that in accepting

I too am loving.

Louise Rogers

THINK ABOUT IT

Lives are lost,
Friends and lovers too.
Kill *AIDS* before it kills you.

Don't be afraid,
Just wake up to the truth,
The cruel reality of death.

It's spreading too fast,
But we can still try.
Be safe and save yourself

Don't kill the love;
Live the love.
Kill the killer.

Natalie Roth

A CORNISH CONCLUSION

The bay beyond,
Half Turner dawn
Tinctures the slow,
Twin-shadowed wallow.

Now at the neap
So stony still,
Save scavenger gull,
Square-rigged fulmar;
Dinghy and launch
Make little stir.

Such an un-Cornish lull
Wild west of Tamar!
Why no combers
Ogre-tall
Sand shelves rending . . .
Having lugged to doom
Into ocean's charnel ground
Lifeboat and sail,
British tar, matelot,
Irish slaver,
Breton trader,
And Celtic saints
Fiery with the Word
Of a bleak ascetic God?

S Hoskins

YOU'RE ALL I'VE EVER WANTED TO BE

You're all I've ever wanted to be
I wish I were you and you were me,
You are strong in whatever you do
When there's a problem you fight your way through.

I would be strong like a concrete wall
Bounce back from any pain, no need to cry at all,
I'd be stronger and wiser and know so much more
I'd find the key to all my locked doors.

You've taught me through from right to wrong
Guided me on the path I walk along,
You shine the light on my darkest days
The love we share is ours for always.

But there's only one of you and only one of me
Although we share the same family,
You're like a shadow, always by my side
For when I need a little help at times.

You're all I've ever wanted to be
Except you'll always be you and I'll always be me,
But you're one of a kind, there could never be another
You're older and much wiser and you're my *big* brother.

Louise Taylor

THIRD AGE

How do I feel at sixty plus?
The same as I did at nineteen,
I may be a little bit slower,
But I'm certainly not a has been.

Age hasn't stopped me working,
I'm as busy as can be,
I've learned to use a computer,
I'm compiling my family tree.

I've won a prize for my painting,
Had some poems published too,
Now I am writing my life story,
There's no time for feeling blue.

So when at sixty you retire,
Don't into gloom descend,
With some sort of recreation,
Old age could be your friend.

C E Cannon

STORMS DAWN

The aftermath is frightening
All have suffered in its path
Flattened and crashed down trees
with terrifying ease
The tree still managing to stand
With wrenched off leaves and torn off bark
So tragically stark naked
Screams and shouts with such despair
Now men are roofless in their homes
Caused by the gale with one large wail
The chimney tall erect no more
Becoming debris on the floor
It scampers on creating havoc
Till all its strength is spent
It never turns its back and looks
At all the damage rent
It floats on down to secret crags
Its energies to charge
When he is large and loathsome
Again he will be at large

Connie Barker

LITTLE TREASURES

The lottery of life creates great favours for a few
The treasures of life are cast anew
But the most precious gifts in this world are not just ermine or gold
It's the birth of new life as we grow old.

As the grandchildren grow with their little faces aglow
We are privileged to share once again in their ascent.
Through life to become teenagers,
although not always do they wish us present.

Perhaps we are wiser, or think we are, that's true
Sometimes not, the newest generations have an entirely different view.
In time we get used to the new wordspeak,
'It's cool' and 'Right on man,' the clothes and hairstyles that they seek.

The realization of age is all too clear
When the chance remark from the grandchild happens to appear.
Whilst Grandad hoists Alex in play above his head
'You'll be able to lift *me* up like this when you get older'
'Of course not Grandad, 'cos you'll be dead!'

But the best thrill of all is to pick up the 'phone
and hear little voices intone:
> Happy Birthday Grandma
> Happy Birthday Grandad
> *We love you*

Hazel Broadbridge

ORDINARY PEOPLE

My small world of people
I come across each day.
Are special
Because of their differences
Of life, blended in many a way.

Different generations
Different emotions
Sometimes similar goals
Of general life.
But each hoping for happiness
In love, companionship,
Their working lives.

All people's a magic of living
Characters separating us
Beauty of a loving heart.
We are all people
Of this earth, a special part.

Victoria Joan Theedam

NIGHT

The moon spreads her beams of silvery light,
Spotlights the moth on silent flight.
Awakes the creatures from hole and lair,
They stretch and yawn and sniff the air
The fox, the badger, hedgehog and vole,
Are ready now for their night patrol.
The sharp eyed owl from his lofty view
Swoops, snatching a shrieking shrew,
The others stop; at the chilling sound.
Their hearts in bodies loudly pound.
Quietness now, and silently they move to their fate
To find food, death or a mate.
A nightingale sings in a bush close by
Serenades the moon as she rides the sky.
Tonight her work is nearly done
And must make way for Apollo sun
The creatures homeward make their way
Before the night meets up with day.

M Crossman

LANDSCAPE OF ESSENTIALS
'The Sixth Continent'

Earth - Romney marsh:

The seabed once, now tacked on
to Kent, a green plain nestling
between hills ribbed by ancient tides,
and the grey concrete of seawall.

Air - South-east coast:

Mirror-smooth or frothing, sea
fringes this sheep-speckled land
crushed by a sky, greedy
for space and light.

Fire - Sunrise, sunset:

Midas moves, just watch his course
first yellow then magenta.
One touch: the water's gone; gold,
the marsh's dyke-net stole.

Water - Strait of Dover:

Neptune advances, retreats,
shingle missiles at his will
pound the indictment of theft:
both sides contest the sea-wall.

Barbara Dordi

LONELY!

It's not so good being lonely.
There's always time to think.
Too much time I must admit,
It can leave you on the brink.

Even when there's someone there.
The thoughts are still the same.
And whatever happens in your life,
You always take the blame.

And when you go to bed at night,
You'd think at least you'll sleep,
But nothing ever works out right,
'Cause you end up counting sheep.

C A Shepherd

CONTEMPLATION

The children have gone back to school today.
The house seems empty, without them at play.
No more toys littering the floor,
Silent the garden, except for crows caw.

Sat with my breakfast, toast and tea.
Contemplating my day till three.
When once more, they will pour through the door,
Shouting and dropping their bags on the floor.

So what shall I do, for the next six hours?
Just sit here, and look at the flowers,
Or go down to the shops, and money spend?
Perhaps have coffee, and cakes, with a friend.

Suppose that I had better housework do,
Or hubby will come home, and take a dim view.
If breakfast pots are still in the sink,
He will throw a paddy, and kick up a stink.

So now I've got to roll up my sleeves,
Haven't time to spend as I please.

G W Bailey

OLD MAN EARTH

I am born and then torn
By the wind to the hills.
Now
I am Old Man Earth
Who stands firm
By the cam stones
And loose heartings
And ancient granite rings.
I am Rock
Dimly seeing still
The lambs with dull, brown fleece
Graze on moorland grass.
I am Well Worn Stone
That rears up in Helvellyn's arms
And watches an easing dew
Shift from fells
And tells the caw
Of circling crows.
I am Mountain
That hears crickets wake
And chant their mantra
On the lichen and the moss
To butterflies
In priestly hues.
I am Walls and Ways
Where Roman Legions trod
Past rosaries of pearl and pink.
I am formed.
Foundation
Think.

Robert Eggleston

OH THAT COUNTRY LIFE

Oh to travel through the countryside, through villages serene,
And travel through the dapple shade with trees all gold and green.
A-spy those country cottages along that lonely track,
See whitely painted walls, oak beams all painted black.
And see those country cottages, with flowers all out in bloom,
And fields of golden corn, caressed by harvest moon.
See the farmer at his ploughing with his horse, that grandly beast,
And see that country table with its mighty farmers' feast.
As the corn is gathered in, leaving lonely golden sheath,
Just watch the fox come creeping, like some common garden thief.
See the sheep all at their grazing, and the cows with mellow call.
With cobbled roads to walk upon, and dark gray slated walls.
See the horse, with cart he's pulling, as he slowly ambles by,
And with all the birds a-singing you can hear the curlews cry.
Life just seems to be so calm, as they go along their way,
They never seem to hurry, for they'll be another day.
Everyone will greet you, doesn't matter who you are,
And they never seem to fly about in dirty smoky cars.
They seem to like the life they lead, with days just drifting by,
It's a life that makes a townee want to heave a woeful sigh.
But life's not all a picnic, they have their trials and their pains,
Especially when they lose a crop through heavy falling rains.
See cows that make their gentle way, as milking time comes round.
Hear the noise of busy milk-maids, as they clatter churns around.
You'll always get a welcome from those people living there,
Who seem to go around each day without a single care.
But life is slowly changing from that calming country way,
As everything is mechanised to clatter out the day.
But no matter how life changes, all those memories are still there,
The farmer's wife will go along with happiness to spare.
And that friendly little woman says 'Well I'm just a farmer's wife.'
But it makes me want to change my way for that gentler country life.

Eric W T Ogle

SOUL MATES

He loved her mind he really did
Soul mates.
That's what they said.
She longed for him
To be with him
Lust to them.
Was not the thing
To see such love
Within their eyes
Never would they sacrifice
Such feelings for each other
Not wanting just a lover
They knew each other well
Such feelings growing stronger
Both began to wonder
About a little chapel
Within they'd
Take their vows
That day to them was magic
Their love shone in their eyes
For them it was no sacrifice
They stayed together
Until they died

J M Weller

SIXTY SOMETHING

Growing old is not so bad
when your family have all grown up.
And when you're blessed with grandchildren
it overfills your cup.

They know that you will pamper them
and give them of your best,
but then you can send them home,
and have a well earned rest!

You can make an effort to move yourself
because you can if you try,
get on your bike and go for a ride
or watch the world go by.

So, growing old is not so bad
if you're not prepared to die!

Elizabeth Goodwin

BECKONING HAND

She called to me at dead of night
A lady dressed in purest white
With beckoning hands she waves to me
And threads her way through fern and trees.

My reason tells me to be aware
My heart, says go, dare.
I hurry after the fleeting figure
Of this beautiful lacy floating shadow.

In the church-yard cold and damp
I lose her in a haze of fog,
Out of breath I spy a seat
Then rest awhile my thoughts to gather.

And see her standing in the lychgate shadow.
Her face is familiar, I must see it close
I slowly rise to meet my host
And close my eyes when the face I see
It is the face of one so dear to me.

With quickening steps, I return my way
I will not rest until I see
My lovely wife in her bed
Because I'm warned, she will soon be dead.

Sheilagh Benson

WALK WITH ME . . .

Walk with me into the unknown,
And I will hold your hand.
Follow me along the path that has no name,
And I will be your guide.
Stay beside me through the heat and dust of the day,
And in the coldness of the night's unspoken terrors
Hold fast to me, and I will not desert you.
Cling to me when the mists of dawn breathe cold and chill
Onto the new-born day,
And when the stars burn pale and clear at the day's death,
Before the rising of the moon,
I will be your eyes and your strength.
As you falter and slip along the muddy roads of unkindness,
I will hold you up, and make steady your feet.
When tiredness overcomes your worn and warring senses,
I shall sing to your heart, and caress your soul with gentleness.
When you are all but overcome by fear,
And when despair becomes your constant and untiring companion,
I shall give you the sunrise of a new morning,
And the rainbow of tomorrow . . .
And when your soul outwears the old,
The tired, and the frail, that is your humanness,
I will set free your immortality,
Deliver you from the transience of evil,
And give you the peace of an endless night,
Together with the promise of an undying day;
For I am your Eternity,
Saith the Lord, our God . . .

Comfort ye, comfort ye my people, saith your God.
Isaiah, Ch. 40, v.1.

J Margaret Service

HOLIDAYS OVER

October, where is the sun?
It is fading now just like the fun.
The promenade is quietening down
traffic slowing in the town.

Hoteliers are sweeping down the steps
counting their profits, sometimes debts.
Donkey rides are at an end
the last postcards now we send.
No candyfloss, no ice-creams
they have even closed the slot machines.

Caravans are stored again
the tents are down because of rain.
How quiet now our golden sands
no children playing, no brass bands.
Our Punch and Judy have gone away
it is much too cold for them to stay.

But winter time will come and go
traffic once again will flow.
We will arrive pale and wealthy
only to leave, tanned, broke, but healthy.

So get the brochures out once more
and book a holiday by the shore.
We will all be there so very soon
in April, May or it could be June.

Carol Shaikh

ADVICE TO JOE

He shouldn't rush rant and rave
It's not good for a man of his age
He's not very big but quite small
But he does shout swear and bawl
He throws his hat to the floor
Then in temper jumps on it once more.
Just one extra loud big shout
Then his light it will flicker out.
When at the pearly gates will St Peter let him in
Or the Devil make a grab at him?
It will be said poor old Joe had his lot
When worked with he is a man not to be forgot
This is Joe under a workload of stress
A tot or two of malt whisky and fishing would suit him best.

D J Newman

THE SWAN

The Queen of all birds.
Her feathers beautifully white,
her beak yellow so bright.
She glides gracefully across the water,
to find her long lost daughter.
Her daughter is a grey colour,
almost the colour of the night but duller.
Her feathers so soft and downy,
the colour sort of browny.
And while she searches for her long lost daughter
and glides gracefully across the water.
She cries for the something she lacks
and tear stains left behind streaks of black.
The Queen of all birds.

Rebecca Matkin (11)

THOUGHTS ON RETIREMENT

I'm supposed to be retired,
I'm sixty now you know,
I had a super special meal
With friends at the 'Tallyho.'
They lifted high their glasses,
And toasted 'lucky me!'
But am I really lucky -
Let's wait, and you'll just see.

The pills and potions I dispensed,
Will be dispensed no more,
The pestle and the mortar rest
On the shelf beside the door.
Glass stoppered bottles stand erect
Like soldiers on parade,
I'll never lift them down again,
Or use the oil of cade.

So what comes next, I ask myself,
Will each day be a bore?
Will my feet rest on the mantle shelf,
Will my brain be changed to straw?

Oh no! Retirement's not like that,
It's busy, busy, busy!
Help here, help there, help everywhere -
It makes you feel quite dizzy!

With flower arranging, decorating, selling bric-a-brac
At the jumble sale next week - oh dear -
Remember to tell Pat!

So if you want a quiet life, do not retire my friend,
Just stay at work, and help the boss,
Right up until the end!

Brenda Bastin

THE MORNING AFTER

The alarm goes off
I crawl out of bed,
I make for the bathroom
Feeling half dead.

I look in the mirror
What a horrible sight,
A reminder to me
Of what happened last night.

All of a sudden I'm feeling quite weak
I'm going to burst if I don't take a leak.

Well I seem to be peeing
For I don't know how long,
Wondering where the hell
Was it all coming from?

I can hardly stand up
I'm feeling quite queer,
I swear that's the last time
I drink so much beer.

I reach for the sink
I try to be quick
'Cos any minute now
I'm going to be sick.

Too late!
It lands on the floor,
Oh Lord I don't think I can take any more.

Surely no more can happen to me
But just how wrong can anyone be?
Just at that moment
She walks through the door
Slips on the sick
And falls on the floor.

Oh god it's the Mrs resembling a dragon,
From now on I'm definitely on the bandwagon.

P M Cronick

THE LEAN AND SLIPPER'D PANTALOON?

Being sixty shouldn't be too bad,
there'll be plenty of years ahead.
Unless you live in Samoa,
when at that age you'll be dead.
The same applies in Grenada,
Mauritius and Paraguay,
according to this book in the library
but it doesn't tell you why.

It went on to list achievements
of people of this decade.
By now I was extremely interested
and continued through the book to wade,
seeking the feats and inventions
of my contemporaries of yesteryear
for an inspiration for me to follow
to assuage my ageing fear.

There were sundry PM's and artists,
Oscar winners and one pope
but I don't possess an Equity card,
as for my drawing there's no hope.
Then my spirits sank to an all time low;
another blow for me.
I'll never surpass the invention
of barbed wire and the frozen pea.

Pauline Brennan

LIFE AFTER SIXTY

I used to be sixty - let me remember
It happened quite suddenly one September
I'd barely got used to the last fifty-nine
And only just bought my first jeans at the time.
The last of the kids had flown from the nest
Parental misgivings as usual expressed
Everyone needs to become independent
Free - and from apron strings no longer pendant.
Becoming a gran was the next advance
When I'd newly discovered the disco dance,
Just seventy (going on forty-five)
And you thought it had all gone out with 'jive'
I sailed to the seventies with great aplomb
wondering when the 'decline' came along
Re-shaping my plans causes no dilemma
Sailing the Amazon - waltzing Vienna
Forgetting the dreams that were once my objective
And viewing the world with a different perspective
I thought about all the tales I'd been told
Who invented the myth that *sixty* is *old*?
No longer spring chicken, now that's very true
Seventy year chicks may be 'chic' but few
The years are a bonus to be enjoyed
Resources available still employed
If with family you're blest, they'll have flown from the nest,
If you're single you've topped your profession
What knowledge you've gained at the age you've attained
And wisdom's a valued possession
Who cares if we haven't amassed great wealth
It we're sick, there's always the National Health.

M F Morrow

MAVERICK

I was born to be a maverick,
They all said I was slow and thick,
I'd ask lots of awkward questions,
That cut them to the quick.

They said I had to play the game,
Though my spirit they could never tame,
for I'd be searching taking pains,
To learn the secrets through
The snow and rains.

For you have to be the master of
the knowledge that you gain,
I will not bend and yearn to lend,
Life's enigmas to my courage end.

Society's conditioning does not serve,
my prepositioning,
as I use all my free spirit,
As sixty seconds in every minute,

So I will conquer in my quest and
put the 'secrets' to the test,
They say they are 'National Security,'
Well that's just all hogwash to me.

For the people want to know the truth,
They do not sign in mispent youth!
So do not treat them as uncouth,
Respect them in their search for proof.

And let's together stand tall and straight,
And eye to eye,
And wield our courage to the skies,
To find the honesty from lies,
Before our last breath of honour dies.

Thomas Hartley

BIRTHDAY GIRL

Approaching sixty,
No elation,
Tears of sadness,
Trepidation;
Chances missed,
Life passing by,
Alone until
The day I die;
Stiff upper lip,
And painted smile,
Heart that's breaking
All the while,
Future looking
Bleak and grim,
Hair turning grey,
Eyes growing dim;
Hating every passing
Day; Oh, to sleep,
And fade away!

Dorothy Neil

POETRY DAY

Poetry Day of October the 6th
Is certainly not a day to miss
The poets from far away and near
Should get together and make it clear

And say to people throughout the world
Listen to poets known and some yet unheard
Would make them think of good things in life
Of happy days without stress and strife

One writes of animals, birds and the bees
Of places around the world, you will agree
From the north south west, and the east
so in writing and reading one finds peace

Old poets wrote with pens dipped in ink
Better the curly writing than typing, I think
so to poets young and old to poetry stick
And enjoy Poetry Day on October the 6th

Joan Middleton

FREEDOM

What is freedom?
Freedom is running barefoot
Through the sand, with no cares
Of feeling the wind and rain
And sun on your face and
Enjoying every moment
Of feeling happy to see
Someone else happy.
Freedom is also freedom from
Doubt, jealousy, fear, vanity
Blind prejudice and all negative things
That is true freedom
An openness of mind
And a sensitivity towards others
A turning away from self
To others
Of looking inwards *and* outwards
Not just the freedom to do simply
What you want when you want.

Karen J Hardman

THE GOLFER

Your eyes they focus on the ball,
The way you stand you are not so tall,
Knees slightly bent, hands on the club,
Very soon you will hear a thud.

Your stance correct with feet apart,
To keep your balance from the start,
Never hold the club too tight,
Relax and you will be alright.

With leading arm as good as straight,
The club comes down with maxim weight,
The follow through you must complete,
Then ball direction will look so neat.

You now have started from the tee,
This game of golf you will agree,
By taking part you are so wise,
It is so good for exercise.

With gents and ladies taking part,
They all enjoy it from the start,
It is much better in the sun,
It's one's great way of having fun.

Just one bad stroke may make one cringe,
But never let your mind unhinge,
For if you do you'll start to flap,
Then up will go your handicap.

At times one's work can be a bind,
But golf could help your peace of mind,
So when you get out on the green,
Forget the week where you have been.

G D Marsh

SIXTY EIGHT

The years pass by.
Sixty-eight, dear me!
Put the kettle on,
And make a cup of tea.
What shall I do now?
Quietly sit by the fire.
Put my tired feet up.
And rest for an hour.
I must go to the shops,
Just along the street.
Better take the walking stick,
The one with the seat.
Then I can sit to talk,
If someone I meet.

What am I thinking!
Almost three score and ten,
But I do not feel old,
Forget the aches and pain.
Limber up the body,
Life must begin again.
Get out the passport,
Pack the travel cases,
I am off to see the world,
And find some lovely places.
Round the Bay of Biscay,
On to sunny climes,
To view majestic mountains,
And have exciting times.

Eugenie Barker

GOODBYE

To all who there around me sat
to wish goodwill and last goodbye,
'midst food, drink and bright format,
brushed I a tear there from my eye.
Faces that I long had known
were there again for me to see,
with friendships we once had sown
nurtured by mirth and familiarity.
With firm handshake, parting word
fleeting kiss or warm embrace,
last goodbyes may long be heard
like echoes in a mountain place.
For gift, cards, wholesome fare
and speech rendered so heartily,
may each and every one you share
my thanks conveyed gratuitously.
Some goodbyes are not forever
just till we meet again.
As scents borne from the heather
memories will remain.

Bill Fisher

THOUGHTS OF A LAYMAN REGARDING THE UTTERANCE FROM THE BISHOP OF BATH AND WELLS (COHABITATION)

My first thought, is scrumpy jack to blame for pickling the cleric's brain?
Second thought, it seems unfair to blame old jack for this affair.
Could the answer lie on Glaston Tor, an ancient press in some old store?
A bishop's apples crushed each autumn, through leaden sluice the thought's quite awesome.
Our cleric's brain has lost its use, through drinking leaden cider juice.
Unable now to comprehend, all rational thought is at an end.
He shouts, put marriage in a bin.
Cohabitation, that's no sin.

Ivan Langham

PAST AND FUTURE

Desolation.
Deep and black.
Pills and whisky.
Escape with death.

It's not over.
Swallow now.
A voice I heard.
Came from afar.
Drowning with a fluid word.

Drifting freely,
Must escape.
Please don't save me.
This is my fate.

My throat is raw.
At last the tears,
Must rid my rage,
From long lost years.

In foetal position I sit
like a bird.
Silent tears fall unheard.
Such shame so deep, and terrible.
How can I rid my pain?

Memories with tears.
Wash away my age old fears.

The bitter truth held in my hands.
In a bottle of pills and a whisky brand.

But now I see a future clear.
The choice is mine.
The time is here.

Heloise Annette McManus

67

SOFT WIND IN MY SAIL

O gentle one
Where have you gone?
It isn't quite clear
Where I go from here.

No child should ever be
Without one such as thee.
You never did fail,
Soft wind in my sail.

You were always there
To defend me.
You were always there
To mend me,
Whenever
Something tore at my spirit.

Fairytales you would peruse,
With a voice that would soothe,
But now
I can no longer hear it.

As your warmth fades from us
And the chill wind cometh,
Your path I wish to follow.

You found release,
You found your peace.
A sigh of relief,
A moment of grief.

At that moment
Fate was kind.
At that moment,
Your hand in mine.

I am not really sad,
The right word is 'glad,'
for pain can no longer hurt you.

As surely as your spirit rose,
Deep inside this son knows,
No one could ever replace you.

Douglas Kent

KISS

A kiss is so much more than just a form of salutation,
    an expression
        of reverence
            or of love;
It's more than the boundaries of physical expression,
    it is deeper,
        it's wider.
            so much more . . .

A kiss is where it happens for the first or hundredth time;
    on a blanket -
        in a field -
            a summer's day.
It's where your lips will meet me for that first or hundredth time;
    on my lips,
        in my palm;
            such ecstasy . . .

A kiss is how you move me - and we generate a spark;
    the welling
        of a groan
            from deep within;
It's that which is within me rising up to touch a star;
    so limitless -
        we meet
            in the ether.

Pat Severn

EDENHOLM

Light and space and flying cloud
Far away from the madding crowd
Is the stuccoed house beside the road
Where the system planners don't maraude
Geranium and such flowers arrayed
In portico and hall displayed
Beneath the old carillion tower
Was heard for miles, each clanging hour.

But time goes on and so do we
To phase us out inevitably
Somehow too, we take our turn
Touching the tape to where we yearn
To leisurely sit and watch the world
In its myriad cycles hurled
So I could wish that I could be
Sedately sewing or taking tea.

Collectors' pieces I would store
How better complement the decor
Oval dishes and drop leaved stand
Tea in the lounge is very grand
Comes gently squeaking on its wheels
The trolley with the loaded meals
And softly draped the large window
Views a velvet lawn below.

Compacted in a tri-colour show
Begonias and the annuals grow
A frilly queen of peonies fair
Scatters hyacinth petals where
Picked into shallow basketry
The withered stalks and flowerheads be
A mimicking Lisa leans to pull
And gathers her wee basket full.

Hail' to the passer-by and say
'Hello' and pass the time of day
Engage in incidental chatter
Some rustic or parochial matter
The rugby lads and cricketers
Throw up the coin for 'whose beginners'
Across the bouncing green they run
All whiteness in the gleaming sun

The echoes of the parrying teams
Recalls to mind those ancient dreams
Of such a game played long ago
For village teams in old KO
Beyond the pitch the rolling weald
Where here a tree fringed stead concealed
Goes back beyond the Solway Plain
To Eastrigg Towers and Scots domain
Such a place where I could spend
My days when closing to an end.

Geraldine Taylor

A POEM FOR LIZ

Like the summer sun on my face,
Like a dewdrop on a blade of grass,
Like a song that makes you cry,
And the sea crashing against the rocks,
Like birds singing on the 9th of June,
Like Miles playing 'Kind of Blue,'
Like the smile on your face,
When I tell you 'I love you,'
All these things I couldn't be without,
I hope you couldn't too.

Russ Meehan

REFLECTIONS OF THE WHITE ROOM

You are my truth
You are my world,
and I lie within the creased pages
of your closed book.

Cover me in white paper bags.
Up to the neck, stitched
white cotton, by silver needles
in the maiden's hand.

When I hear,
I am not real.
Block off my passages
and I'll stay inside,
happily inside
On my own, inside,
waiting.

I curled up inside
underneath thick white blankets
of cotton and paper
 - my first anniversary inside -
Reality inside.
Me, inside, reality.

The mirror reflected
me. All white.
Pale features inside
white eyes under white pillows
of paper cotton.
White eyes under white pillows
of paper cotton.
White nails, white hair
all remains of my days inside.
Reflections of inside,
white reflections of me.

H Pisarska

THE HURT, THE PAIN

Over the years
the tears I've cried
would fill a river
deep and wide.
So much hurt
so much pain.
The tears keep falling
just like rain.
Where they come from
I don't know
all they do is flow.
On the outside
I show I'm hard
but deep inside
I'm badly scarred.
The hurt stays with me
all the time
it never goes away.
When I'm sad
and get down
it's carried through the day.
The tears fall
and the rivers get deep.
I go to bed
and cry in my sleep.
When I awake
and remember the pain
the tears start to fall
again like rain.

Linda Roberts

BUDDY

You stood by me through a world of rejection
You offered me comfort, much valued affection
I tried to cling onto this thing that I loved
I fell at my feet the more she shoved

You never passed judgement, I told you no lies
You listened intently to this weak man's cries
I owe you much more than I could ever repay
My brother my friend day after day

We're ships that sail two opposite seas
We're birds that fly straight past in the breeze
Magnets that always seem to repel
Yet the only man of this I could tell

I know you my friend, you know me too
We're on opposite sides yet we have the same view
I could never impose on you my pain, my fear
I hold you close, you're someone too dear

One day in the future I'll understand
But now in this present we both fear this land
I'm always here I'm sure you'll know
There's nowhere left for me to go

I'll try to be with you and comfort you well
I'll try to understand we're all going through hell
My apologies remain with you I hope you'll forgive
This is one more journey we both must live

M Collins

THE CRINGE GAME

This time it'll be the same
No one makes any changes
Sacrifice again all the small people
Leave them all behind

Risk the drop of expectations
Living on a social star
Credit to all those who sail the system
They've broke through their own way.

The bomb again about to blow
We all stand round and wait
And scurry in to get our small vote
Get there quick, don't hesitate

Sorry if I don't get off your scream
But there's plans, your plans to be made
One day it'll all seem for nothing
How long do we have to wait?

Get out now make a clear run
A clear victory against mankind
Nothing round here changes
Tories win again

And all their followers strike poses
And give out blue boring smirks
This messed up world scares me, run by
A party of toffee-nosed suited burks.

It all goes on like years before
Homeless, jobless at the bottom of the list
Their heads spinning with crap
Their faces pushed into the floor

They talk about changes and fees
Another five years of misery.

Philip M Dalton

LATE ON DUTY

Excuses they come thick and fast
For being late none can surpass,
Did not sleep, the car broke down.
Domestic problems they abound,
Children at home are sick and in pain.
Husbands left to wax and wane.
Trains on strike, buses not running
In-laws arrived did not know they were coming.
I overslept, the clock stopped again
Accident on the way, helped in the pouring rain.
There is always one quiet and serene,
Who wanders in as if in a dream.
The time on duty is half-past eight
Cannot believe once again she is late.

Ivy Rhodes

DON'T

Don't try to tell me you understand,
Don't even try to comprehend.
For I have been there and you have not,
And you can't just pretend.

Don't say you know all the answers,
When you don't know what the questions will be.
Don't try to be smart and outdo me,
For I have been to places you've not yet seen.

Don't tell me some misguided tale,
You think it will help me to hear,
Don't try to remove this burden,
When you can't know of my fears.

Don't tell me that you're sorry,
Don't say that time will heal,
Don't try to salve your conscience,
When you don't know how I feel.

Karen Hullah

THE MACCLESFIELD TIMES

When me work is over
Shortly after five
The London Inter-City
Roars through alive.

Our local is awaitin'
   Out on platform 3
I wish that it would go now,
And take me home to tea.

A little while later,
At eleven past the hour,
The West-of-England stops . . .
And goes ahead full-power!

Our local is awaitin'
   Out on platform 3
I wish that it would go now,
I'm thinkin' of me tea.

As the fingers of the clock,
Bend to five-thirteen
The Wolver'ampton dawdles in:
Commuters can be seen.

Our local is awaitin'
   Out on platform 3
I wish that it would go now,
I'm desperate for me tea!

K B Newman

PRISON

The door unlocks - the jail begins
A mind hides from a heart that's crying
Which one may guide your steps
As cracks of conflict appear on your path
Survival has no treaty with a heart that sears

Threadbare emotions gasp for breath
An atmosphere thick with apathy
Trust has no cell in which to bide
As morning's faces proclaim their sorrows
Old Nick departed smiling at dawn

Too long my spirit seeks this light
'Tis a narrow path obscured by pain
Only uncertainty holds out its hand
A brave heart does dare to grasp -
Its journey promising only my fears

Dreams only scale these walks
Frustration it brings to haunt me
Failure constantly befalls my search
My questions halted by authority's face
- Only I count -may tell me.

Every game my heart does question
The prison gate for lies will open
Heaven's gate will open for the truth
Which one? My heart and mind argue
The door unlocks - I try to smile

Frank McKinlay

ARTIFICIAL

Synthetic,
False,
Fake . . .
Unreal,
The words I associate with an Artificial Queen
The kind of person
who thinks carrots come from cans,
And fresh, ripe Mangoes
not from foreign lands,
But appear overnight,
Magically themselves
to be there next morning
stacked neatly on shelves
in our local supermarket.
That's right - you heard it,
Heat wrapped - packed foods,
And rubber ball eggs,
A veritable feast
for those with legs that work on junk,
And nasty foul tasting foods
that can be cooked from frozen
For those on the move . . .
In a hurry - their least worry
seems to be not what they eat,
Not what's dragged in off the street . . .
Chopped up - heavily seasoned
and put in their meat
pie,
But what can be devoured with strong taste,
In the least amount of time.

Simon Collister

WILL YOU LISTEN

Will you listen when I'm telling you
There's no way I can go
I won't tell you all my problems
Because you don't want to know

Will you listen when I'm telling you
There's nothing I can do
There is no way, someone like me
Can help someone like you

Will you listen when I'm telling you
I cannot afford to give
What I get is just enough
For us on which to live

Will you listen when I'm telling you
I haven't got the time
What is left after I finish work
Is what is known as mine

Will you listen when I'm telling you
It's nothing to do with me
So all those people need some help
But I am only me!

L A Wright

BABY

I cuddled you and kissed you
I sang you off to sleep
I sat a while and missed you
I crept up to take a peep

I knelt beside your cradle
I touched each golden curl
I listened to your breathing
To make sure that you were

I saw your eyelids flicker
I tried to sneak away
I watched the smile light up your face
I knew I had to stay

I cuddled you and kissed you
I sang you off to sleep . . .

Kathryn Russell

MORNING GLORY

A tiny crack in the darkness
Where the dawn comes
Peeping through
Followed by clouds
Mottled with white
And a blue grey hue,
Streaks of fiery red and orange
Stretch o'er the mountain crest,
Like flames
Not flames like fire
Leaping up and down
But flames
Laid down to rest,
Glorious is the only word
Befitting such a sight,
As the sun comes
O'er the hill
And spreads its rosy light,
That tiny crack in the darkness
Brings the dawn
Of another day,
As the sun climbs in the sky
And night-time slips away.

Nora Cooper

THE TREE

You think it cold in the ground where I grow
Yet the sun when it shines makes me aglow
Warms me all over down to my roots
I am really majestic as all my young shoots
A silver birch and proud to be tall
I can see you you're so very small
You carved your name on my bark this day
There's no knowing when you next pass this way
The woods that I live in the forests and parks
Getting much smaller no room for the larks
Birds whistle and perch on my branches up high
Pussy cats chase them fly or you die
My life I give to the air that you breathe
Cut me down and you may have to leave
Some cut my friends no reason at all
Why not think and use bricks for your wall
The environment stands on the life that I give
Do me no harm so your children can live
Carelessness makes for mistakes you must know
If the sun stops shining how will I grow.

John Barker

MY LOVE

The day is grey
Rain fills the air and winds blow cold
Yet should I hear your voice or
Find your hand to hold
The song birds sing
All the sky is filled with colour
And the wind is stilled
Joy fills my heart
But - if once more we part
Again the day is grey.

Mary Llewellyn-Amos

FLEXIBLE ENEMY

They wash our brains, they advertise.
They tell us how to run our lives
They totally convince us, this is what you need
They make our world material, they fill us with greed.

You'll be healthy and wealthy if you eat this food
To be seen without this, would show you are crude
You're a man of the nineties, if you drive this car.
Women will love you, seen drinking this at the bar.

Enhance your home, it is truly amazing,
Fifty percent off our latest double glazing
You'll be cool and trendy, if you wear these jeans
Buy one of our homes, realize your dreams

Wear one of these watches, with digital time
Buy another phone and extend your line.
Install our new heating, you know it's the best
Get it now, pay later, twelve months free of interest.

Buy with your plastic card, you don't need cash.
But hurry now, don't think about it, the offer won't last
If you buy a product and quickly get bored
Buy something else that you can't afford.

At the end of the day, when you're in above your head
The grass is no greener and you wish you were dead.
You can't take heart, from the knowledge that you're not alone,
You're a product of today, a twentieth century clone.

Paul Lamb

FOR YOU MY LOVE

Reach out and touch me,
Like a rose from a stem,
I need to feel you near me,
My hero, my lover, my friend.

You are my light in the darkness,
My star at night,
You are my sunshine in the rain,
Shining twice as bright.

You came into my life,
Giving me pleasure and care,
You came to offer me,
This precious love that we share.

I feel unique and alive,
A bursting bud in spring,
You're gentle, strong, kind,
You make my heart sing.

Searching for your face in my mind,
Repeating the words that you say,
You are the reason for waking
And wanting to start a new day.

Hands and hearts entwined,
In snatched moments of time,
It hurts to say
You can never be mine.

A fleeting glance,
A shy wave,
The pain of others,
Is what we save.

Our elusive love,
Can never be,
Because you belong
To another you see.

Dianne Borien

THRILL

We get ready
Now go, go go!
Gallop uphill beneath green canopy
on narrow chalky path
Exhilaration - aaah!
Sudden rush of legs and feet clashing
Lickety split
Feeling like a proper jockey
Knees dug in
Body down low
Over hot neck
Horsehair soft beneath my hands
Straining reins
Mud specks flying from those before me
Keep mouth shut!
Breath urgent -
both mine and my mount's
gasps and rasps -

Phew! At the top
calm down
sit back
and rest
walk out
relax the neck and reins
Have a good stretch, Mystery -
you deserve it.

Jane Pietrusiak

I WISH!

I wish, I wish that I could write
A verse without a rhyme,
But in my head keeps tumbling
Same sound words all the time.

Narrative verse is what I like
It tells what we have done,
But I don't always want to rhyme
Although it's sometimes fun!

It's like an inbuilt pattern
Right inside my head,
Why can't I write sweet sounding verse?
Just lovely words instead.

But rhyme they must, they will insist
On sounding near the same.
I've tried and tried but rhyme they will
I'll never win this game!

Try as I will, move them around
Use a variety of words,
They still come out, not beautiful
But rhymes, often absurd!

I've no desire - it's just as well!
A poet great to be.
I'd just like to be in charge of words
Instead of them of me!

Why do you ask! These simple lines
Do you bother then to write?
They just keep jumping in my head,
Must go down on paper white.

Pat Rees

WALKING WITH MUM AND DAD IN DERBYSHIRE

My dad said the same thing every time, 'Beautiful Derbyshire,' with a smiling
face.
'How much further?' we complained, walking behind, keeping the pace.
Calver to Grindleford seems a long long way, when you are quite small,
'There's a lemonade spring down in the woods,' teasingly dad would call.
He always said children needed lots of fresh air, to keep them well,
I remember, stonewalls, sheep, softwinds, the fresh county smell.
Walking with mum and dad in the summer, Kim and I trailing behind,
Collecting sticks and leaves and things, anything we could find.
Every outing an adventure, to Lathkilldale or Monsal Head,
We'd all walk down to the waterside, climbing the hill, feet like lead.
Searching the grass for flat stones, to skim across the river,
Enjoying all the simple pleasures that nature could deliver.
What a hard climb up to Abrahams Heights, 'Don't go near the edge you two'
In matching hand-knitted cardigans, sit near the edge, admire the view.
Hopping and skipping across the steps at Dovedale,
Making boats from lolly sticks, in clear cool water we let them sail.
Walking with mum and dad in Derbyshire, how simple life seemed then,
Oh! Turn back the clock thirty years, and let me do it all again.

Gaynor Stillings

IF I WERE A GROWN UP

If I were a grown up, then I could please myself,
I'd leave my books untidy, not neatly on the shelf.
I wouldn't clean my teeth each night,
or wash behind my ears, or do the things
that children should, in their tender years.
Though, if I were a grown-up, with children
of my own, and they were this untidy
I would be the first to moan!

Andrew Simmonite

WINTER'S NIGHT

A sparkle, a twinkle!
A shout of delight!
Glistening frost
On a snowy night!

Glittering stars
Brilliantly shine,
Vivid and clear,
Huge and fine.

Above and below
Night, like day,
Gleaming white
Invites to play.

The sparkling snow,
The moonlit night,
Together make
A ring of light.

And so we play
And shout and sing
Tumble and slide
Like anything.

The night is ours,
The breathless fun
In snow and frost
Has just begun.

Margaret Ballard

SMILING THROUGH

The smile on the face of the pansy
As it lifts up its head to the sun
To bring joy to the heart of the gardener
With the message that spring has begun.

The smile on the face of a mother
Looking down at her newborn child
Has a radiance that nothing can equal
And a power no monarch can wield.

The smile on the face of old Santa
As he stands in the busy town store
And hands out his gifts to the children
Who come crowding around by the score.

The grin on the face of young Johnnie
Arriving home late from his school
With mud on his clothes and a story
As tall as the trees by the pool.

Growing old and the knowalls will tell you
That schooldays are your happiest time
And the laughter that comes from the playground
Fades away with the passage of time.

You go home and get out the album
With its pictures of days that have gone
And you grin at the young smiling faces
Which remind you of things that you've done

There'll be smiles on the face of the angels
Who'll wait at the heavenly door
To welcome you after life's journey
And take you to peace evermore.

Reg Turner

THE TWIN

The crimson gilted two mirrored sword
Time keeps ticking, tossing, turning
'Are you coming to play?'
Why all these questions
to be answered?
A part of me, a tiny part
Gnawing, scratching, hurts
I never reach, never can
They don't want to know
My inner soul
Sometimes it's still, but
Never quite
The thirst for knowledge
A why, wherefore, curtained
Did you see the sun whirls?
Dance inside my mind.
I called but you ran on
I'm old inside, I miss you
Missing, that you are
Posters of the missing you
Don't say that, pain is deep
Chokes me sometimes
Paint the sky black
Then dip in silver
Part black, part silver
Don't touch, keep out.
What do they know
Not as much as I
Never can, doesn't cease
Only god can give
Me peace

A S Sanderson

SKIT ON CHANGE

The world is changing, it has to be said
Not the world, just the people in it instead!
What do we want from the world today?
Is it greedy persons who do not pray?
Yes, someone said they'll prosper more
So come out in the open, and shut the door.

Start with the animals and nature for fun:
The bears to have spots, the leopards none.
Cats not to each fish - kitty be kind
The fish will eat cats, and the birds won't mind;
The goats and cows to give milk in tins
So eliminate bottles thrown in the bins.

Killing and fighting is now forgiven
Persons in prison mistake it for heaven!
No need for brains to decipher what's said
Just ask a machine to tell you instead!
With honour and love and marriage to end
What can one do to be a good friend?

Females in pits and out to sea
Or up in the pulpits - now they be
Males at home, their muscles unused
Making the beds and feeling confused
When humans play with guns and money
Eating their salads with unsweetened honey

They'll be there on top of the world indeed
Looking down on changes which cannot succeed
We were proud to be *us*, and know the right way
To cope with our lives all the next day
Modern change is something to really deplore
Think we - who are sixty years or more!

Marrianne Warby

91

UNTITLED

With magic in their eyes
They pass me by
And call a distant memory
Which serves only to remind
Of a passing place
That smiles in the distance
Bringing hope to this empty existence.

This mindless, rotting day
It so slays
A person of their wishing soul
It is the essence of their whole
That is driven from them
So far into a passing place
That defiantly they face.

Such passage of oblivion
So steals a heart of all rebellion
As its reminiscent shadow smiles
On the sultry touch of a lie
That shimmers in remembrance
It breathes upon frosted air
Which dangles, slowly, dying there.

This vacuum packed hindrance
So defeats that which calms within us
As a childish hope finds a way
In which to pass this raping day
It is the ghostly haunt of life's romance
That reminds a heart of its story
And the echo of reality, passes by any glory.

This ease of wicked pretence
So bleeds a heart of all defence
As the gloom of reality walks by
It is the stance of despair that survives
This cruel world, where only a moment is spared
For a bitter sweet moon that cries as he stares
Upon this place so desolate
Of once grand state
A wilderness a far that pays for Man's mistakes.

V Lloyd-Williams

MY OWN WORLD

In the midst of my dreams, as my own world uncurls,
There'd be tall handsome men, and beautiful girls,
No-one would be fat, or ugly or gay,
Yes they'd exist, but be accepted that way.
There'd be no regulations, no rules or no laws,
But there'd never be need, in my world there's no flaws,
There'd never be fighting, or anger, or grief,
Never be need for famine relief.
There'd be sunshine and laughter, but no tears or no pain,
There'd be snow every Christmas and there'd never be rain.
But the fields would stay green, and the flowers still bloom
There'd be happy ever after, for each bride and groom.
No-one would grow old, or wrinkled or grey,
Youth would be eternal, I'd like it that way
Suddenly I'm woken, by alarm bells that ring
No more are the birds that usually sing
I peer through the curtains and watch the rain fall
Reality looms, it isn't my world at all.
It's only a dream, but how nice it would be,
I wish you could join us, my world and me.

Dawn Speakman

THE TREE AND THE GIRL

He felt the wind move in his branches
a whisper lingered, then slipped from his leaves
Almost like a lie.
An emptiness crept slowly through his very fibres
A hunger, seeping in, draining the lifeforce.

Grow straight and strong, for if you lean
You will reap too much of one thing and too little of another
Shelter and protect the ones that dwell beneath your branches,
For they bring you gifts.

Give forth only pure fruit and guard against thieves,
For there are those that need, and those that want.
Give love to the precious one and protect her with your life
For she has the nourishment your lifeforce needs.

The weariness left me dwelling on the lines
The real meaning's only just coming to light
after all these years.
And a distant feeling, that maybe it is only I . . .
That could, or ever will, understand.

The girl was so pretty, she stirred something inside me.

Paul Nevard

DAY DREAMING

Wandering off, deep in thought,
Creating images in my head,
How wonderful the mind is,
Letting me dream, and fly free,

Imagination, giving me freedom,
Taking me anywhere,
Be anything, my heart desire,
Achieve any ambition, all one could wish for,

In thought there's no limits,
You set your own agenda,
Space and time does not exist,
Your thoughts can take you to the stars,

Within my own mind,
I have achieved many things,
I've just returned from Africa,
Among the wild and free in my day dream,
Not bad, for a Sunday afternoon,
Now I must make the tea.

D Goldbold

THE PATIENT

Past the barricades of bedscreens,
Beyond the garrison of glass he lies,
Wan with the wariness of the besieged
But, lord of his body, will not lightly lose
The lovely agony of his life.
When he wanted to parley in the midst of pleasure
He was brought a present of pain:
When he sued for a settlement
Advancing forces did not flinch from their foray.
Surrounded by his advisors, who have donned
The white coat of right, that mystical secret; uncertainly secure,
He awaits the struggle of the night.
To his fortress of fortitude, out of the twilight
A new champion is coming.
What gleams in the darkness, what sound surfaces
In the far shadows?
Bright and blood bearing,
Night softens his advent. Life give or taker? . . . Inexorably advancing.

Valerie Baxter

A FAVOURITE DAY

When you say to children, what's your favourite day
So many will say, Easter, Christmas, and my birthday
Teenagers say, it is the day they saw
A personality they idolise and adore
Romantics then will tell you it's when they fell in love
Or when they wed with eyes all full of stars from up above
For new parents this must be
The first time we held our tiny baby
For me it's each of these I favour in my head
And I am sure for all of us, many lay ahead
So which could be one's favourite day
When so many we've had along life's way

Merril Morgan

WHEN THE EARTH AWAKENS

At sunrise the sun shines down on us as we awaken,
Then slowly and brightly it reveals the earth's beauty.
It blasts its early light against our faces through the glass stained window.
And almost in an instant the sun blows its full power.

The people are burning their feet on the scorching paths,
Of the foul and infested streets of London.
Everyone is trying to quench their thirst,
For a trickle of water which shall end their craving.

The day's finally ending,
And the sun's dying down,
The stars are shining in the night brightly,
The day's ending and the stars are twinkling,
Tomorrow shall be another day,
And another hot summer's day.

Aliya Hanif

BEHOLD THE BEAUTY

There once stood a Church
With a tall, tall steeple
Surrounded by houses
There lived many happy people
Within the valleys
Beyond tall mountains
There was a cool running stream

Within the valleys behold
Such beauty ever seen
There once stood a Church
With a tall, tall steeple
But gone - are all the houses
And where are all the - people?

Within the valleys
Beyond tall mountains
There was a cool running stream
Within the valleys
Behold - such beauty
That now is just a dream

J M Weller

WAR

Alchemy - a chosen juncture,
  A fortuous right fought
    A war of idealists,
      As to what ought.

Inanimation prevails,
  Assumingly unbiased,
    The cost of life,
      Lost in the details.

Natalie Cavens

THAT DAY OF WONDER

Kids at Christmas I often think,
always put you in the pink.
Presents wrapped so prettily,
grandchildren so full of glee.
That look upon their faces says it all,
pretty cards upon the wall.
The tree with lights, stands so tall,
as I reflect on years gone by
and wonder, with a little sigh;
A silent tear fills my eye.

My thoughts drift back
to when I was a child,
I ponder for a little while
to think of my parents;
And how they smiled.

Those happy days where they have gone,
so wonderful every one.
Outside snow falls so evenly, and covers the hills and trees
the night so still; and children slumber.
Snow slides off the roofs like distant thunder,
up the stairs I creep, round the bedroom door I peep.
Are the children fast asleep, presents hurriedly left in a heap,
that Day of Wonder has arrived, oh! So happy I can't describe.
It's the time of year I will always treasure.

Brian Taylor

MOONLIGHT

Pale moon drifting and rising in the void
Like a ship on the crest of a wave.
Your background of black and navy blue
Enhance your paleness as you climb
Across the sky.

Smoky, wispy scudding clouds
Gathering now in misty shrouds
Momentarily hide you from view.

Sphere of light in silent flight
Across the universe you ride
Beacon of the night
Master of the tides.

The stars are your companions now
Golden sequins winking and blinking
A peaceful reassuring sight.
You never cease to captivate those
Who gaze in wonder at a scene set so
Perfectly in God's sky.

Linda Caunter

YESTERDAYS

If I could give up all
Of my tomorrow's for just
One yesterday, oh how happy
I would be to laugh and to walk
In the sunshine once again. I'd
Even smile in the rain just to
Have you back again. Oh! Why did
You have to go away and such a
Dreadful day, you decided just on
That mother's day. Oh! What an awful
Day and I was so happy too. Oh,
I would give up all of my tomorrows
For just one yesterday. In fact,
I'd just love it if I could just
        Be with you!

Eileen Ashbridge

PARADISE FOUND

I stand upon this deserted shore
Gazing out at an endless sea
I feel the enchantment of this magic place.
Slowly weave its spell for me.

No golden sands await me here
This is a grey and lonely shore
But this is the place I hold most dear
No spot on earth could I love more.

No eerie cry of seagull reaches me
No titbits await them at this rocky place,
For no humans spread a picnic here
Here, where there is limitless time and space.

I sit there quietly, a boulder for my chair
Silence and infinite peace washes over me
This awe inspiring landscape bleak and bare
Is all the beauty I would wish to see.

And so I watch a darkening sky
As the sunset tinges it with red
Slowly another day begins to die
And it is time for me to seek my bed.

Slowly, I walk back up the lane
My spirit is tranquil, my mind is still
And I reflect on what I always gain
As I turn once more and drink my fill.

Dorothy N Davies

THE THOUGHTS OF GRINDLE - OH! MAGNOLIA VILLA!

So emptying his glass of Green King bitter
And calling for another, Grindle said:
'I'll tell you what I know about Magnolia Villa,
Magnolia Villa stands at Mullet's Corner,
Highly respectable, later nineteenth century,
Symmetrical red brick, trim slate, grey tiles,
Conservatory (of course), porch, white veranda,
Smooth laurel hedges, rosemary, lavender,
And a startled monkey puzzle tree,
Built by an over-speculative local dealer
Who failed and hanged himself,
His nonagenarian father,
Once parish sexton, dug two hundred graves
Before he lost his foothold picking apples
And broke his neck. Oh! Prim Magnolia Villa!
Your looks don't tell the half of it, last week
That smart executive, the present owner,
Church goer, golf club member, 'And by gad!
Politically sound, just one of us,'
Locked his front door, piled up the boot and sped
Over the hills and far away with someone's bread
And the blonde wife of Colonel Bollicks, (Ret.)
Who blew his brains out in the potting shed,
Later we learned, that smart executive
Began a stretch as prison librarian,
And the gallant Colonel's wife,
Fine yellow hair outspread, eyes quite unseeing,
Went floating down the river. Oh! Magnolia Villa!

Enough about it,' Grindle said, and went
To spend an urgent penny in the Gents.

Norman Sinclair

WINTER THOUGHTS

As autumn turns to winter,
And the snows begin to fall,
I can feel the cold winds call,
And see the leaves of golden brown fall,
Only the pines keep their cloaks of green,
At heights of forty feet they seem
Iron clad in perennial themes.

The sheep are in the fields as the
dogs fight through the drifts to get them penned,
The farmer crooks his shotgun bent and
Prepares to end the foxes' chicken run
Cordite from twelve cartridges smokes
before he's done.

The swans skate on the lake,
Frozen over in their wake,
The cygnets, their mothers waddle
they attempt to imitate.

The people on their skis clap their hands
As their breath begins to freeze,
Bright colours are their smocks
As they trundle past the docks.

What are their thoughts of winter
As they jumble through the grey clouds
As the myriads of snowflakes begin to fall
like white shrouds.
Are they seeking shelter as the driving rains
helter pelter?

Do they scramble for the log fires as their
Heart strength falters, fires?
Do they reach for roasted chestnuts
And recline on check bedspreads
In their wooden huts?

The snow again falls thick and fast
And the winter season deepens as the
cold sleet slowly steepens
What are all their thoughts of winter?
As the ice they tread begins to splinter?

Thomas Hartley

AN ANNIVERSARY

A dozen years have passed away
    Since down the aisle you came
To stand serene at my left side
    To take my heart and name.
My heart was mine alone to give
    And on that April day
I placed it in your tender hands
    Forever - come what may.
My darling you have cherished it
    With tender love so true.
That's why it beats as true today
    As then, when love was new.

A dozen years of joy and peace
    Of war and strife and pain
But with my loved one by my side
    God give me them again.
The name I gave it was my sires
    He set its value high.
That you have but enhanced it more
    None can in truth deny.
If God gives me a hundred years,
    Upon this earth to bide,
I pray my love, my mate, my wife
    Be ever by my side.

H G Achard

WARRIOR

Destiny is the warrior,
Made strong,
Armies,
Of soldiers,
Battle,
Destiny.

K Pearce

PHILOSOPHY

If whales eat plankton
And plankton are very small,
Then what do plankton eat,
If plankton eat at all?

The microbes that live on ear lobes
Endlessly chew away at skin.
And household dust falls from all of us,
So consign your vacuum to the bin.

The infinitely tiny creatures
That occupy our gastric metres,
Form football teams and hold debates
Before devouring our tea-time cakes.

So, praise to them all!
The tiny, microscopic and small.
They're so small it's unbelievable,
If I was a germ I'd be irretrievable.

But if you had a magnifying glass,
You'd spot me chomping on the back of your hand.
The world of the parasite
Is truly a well fed land.

Marcus Pond

THAT OLD DEVIL MOON

Softly she sang a song of the silver moon and how hauntingly it shone.
Her eyes sparkled with salty tears, sad that her lover had gone.
I knew not then of her special moon, or indeed about true love,
For I am a vagabond! A wayward travelling man? Directed by the stars
above.
I tote my wares from town to town, I meet damsels by the score!
What need have I for just one true love? The world is my pearl, my oyster.
Travelling these fair isles for three and thirty years singing happy songs,
Leaving many broken hearts behind me, for this canny lad no wedding
flowers,
No tying that dreaded knot, just milling with the happy throng.
None of these long goodbyes, no longing for that '*one and only'*,
I load my cart, talk softly to my pony, ready to bewitch in some other town,
how can I be lonely?

There she sat, she caught me by surprise! Singing a sad lament of her lover
now long since departed,
Her misty eyes the bluest of blues, her rosebud mouth sweetly parted,
She asked me of my direction? Was it to be left or right?
Her flame red hair hung like flower fronds around her shoulders milky white.
We'd tarry here a while and talked of this and that, we ate by the fire's glow,
Chatting as good friends do of the ways of this wicked world,
And as 'Demelza' smiled her smile the strings which held my selfish heart
So fast, against my will, did now unfurl!
We sat by fire glow all of that night until the break of day,
My tongue was also now bewitched as I asked, 'Demelza will you stay?'
And stay she did and stayed so long my mind the years have forgotten well,
As we travel the roads o'er vales and hills no longer sad songs she sings
As she cradles our son to her loving breasts she sings tenderly of birds
And flowers and of our years together, and of all our blessings,
For sunshine and flowers and gentle winds and the coming of each spring
Can make a wandering vagabond forget all manner of things!
So many songs of that silver moon have been sung by many a damsel I fear,
But none so enchanted by it as I, my friends, as I hold my 'Demelza' near!

Joyce Hefti-Whitney

SPEED DEMON

Onto the dark road
Come the creatures of the night
Innocent and naive to the roadside theatre.
It must be full of magic
For they come as if drawn by a magnet,
Scampering and swooping from the safety of the hedgerows and trees,
Some to act in the play, others to watch the performance.

Death is in the wings
Strumming his humming song,
Bright spotlights announce him to roaring applause.
The curtains fall on the final act,
The roaring subsides to an eerie silence.
Perhaps a feeble flutter or a sigh,
Empty stage.

Next day
Fragments of fur and feather float away,
Fat crows feast on the flat corpses.
Poor little bodies, bent and bloodied.

And you?
Bloodied wheels, bloodied conscience?
Your Dance of Death is the winning act,
Congratulations, another award.

Deborah Hubbard

YOU

Far away in a time we forget
still lives an Illusion in me
Far away in a place that's no more
still lingers a dream from the past
Far away, yet standing up close
you remain a ghost at my side

106

Don't tell me things change
I know that they do
Don't tell me memories are
distorted - rose coloured

No. Don't tell me
I don't want to know
Just leave me alone
I'm a young man *Again!*

Walter V Sinclair

COME IN SHE SAID, INTO MY GREEN MOUTH

'Come in,' she said, 'into my green mouth.'
Into the tumbling bay of poor sailors
I will not carry a monster here.
In all my green days, safe as milk
From the cracked breast. I will lay you down.
Up bracken hill I'll wind your bobbin on,
In the groin of my ways, within his ivy arms
I will shape your living. Under the white owl
Floating as soundless as seeds, on a great wind.
That drives the sharp spark on.
I shall be Bridget then.

'Come in,' she said, 'into my green mouth.'
I have known you all my days,
In the lowered lids at owl time,
By the saps sign, at the mayfly madness,
When the rain rattles in Holly-Hole.
I shall be your forgetfulness.
Into the tumbling bay of poor sailors
I will not carry a monster here.

T H Nockolds

ACROSS THE COUNTRYSIDE

I stand in a field without a care,
I feel and breathe in the countryside air,
the hills and valleys go a long way,
it's a lovely scenery, is what they say
you listen carefully, to the sound of wildlife,
some are as sharp, as a butcher's knife,
all around, it's quiet and green,
there's holes in the ground, where the hunt have been.

J Titchener

CUTS

Near where I live, just across the road
There stands a building big and bold
It's a place where old folk can have a rest
They are nursed with care, it's really the best

Cashes Green Hospital is its name
Without it this place just won't be the same
Because next year they're knocking it down
What a pity and tragedy for our town

The nursing there is excellent, the food is just fine
The care that is given is just so sublime
The beds are comfy, the atmosphere is gay
Patients can relax, and feel fears fade away

The Government again are having a field day
With all the cuts that are coming this way
Education and Health are most affected it seems
This country really is going to seed

Old folk will suffer, and children too
It's more than enough to make you feel blue
The rich will get richer, the poor more depressed
We must do something to get us out of this mess

J M Campbell

A TRIBUTE TO BOB MARLEY

Brother Bob Marley
Our beloved Bob Marley
He made a clean way for the nation
He teaches and sings the truth to the young generation
He taught us things like we must always unite
And we must always stand up for our rights
Brother Bob could sing and sing all day
Because he got so much good things to say
Brother Bob never separated himself from the people
He taught us that good is always over evil
Brother Bob was born in the ghetto
And he was always there to help the poor
Brother Bob also said we must be one love
Because there is only one almighty God above
Brother Bob said the things that politicians do is a rat race
And the way they treat poor families is a disgrace
Bob Marley sings words of wisdom
And helps fights our way to freedom
Brother Bob also said don't jump in the water if you can't swim
I remember he singing this in a reggae redim
Brother Bob said it's time to know our culture brother man
And if you know our history then you will know where you are
coming from
Bob was sent to this earth to do the works of Jah
Brother Bob flesh die but his spirit lives on and he has gone so far
Lots of heros die and their history go with them
But Brother Bob is like he still alive before you
And when his music plays you think he is playing in front of you
Bob Marley is a freedom fighter
Who hates to see poor people suffer
God could not have given us anything better

Michael Sylvester

VIRTUAL UNREALITY

I must admit that
I felt pretty good.
Nothing could faze
A chap that had
Flown the Atlantic
In a Microlite,
And snow-boarded
Down the Eiger
In one short Saturday
Morning.

I removed the headset
To thick black smoke
Of burning stew,

A pile of yellow feathers,

And a note
By the telephone,
Which screamed
'I couldn't stand any more . . . have gone to mother's!'

Please don't adjust
Your heads,
There is something wrong with
Reality!

David Robinson

CHRISTMAS

Snowflakes fall, gently they settle on the ground,
Everywhere you look you can see it is crispy, cold and white.
Trees look fragile, hedges are a beauty to behold.
The snow makes everything beautiful for miles around.

'Jack Frost' makes your face and fingers tingle,
Blustery winds make you wrap up to keep out the cold.
You're building a snowman, a wonderful sight to behold,
Your nose wrinkles with delicious smells that mingle.

Mince pies, sausage rolls, Turkey and stuffing all blend in,
Apples, oranges, bananas too . . . pine trees all add to this
With lights and tinsel, balloons and jokes that make you grin,
For Christmas is here again; Oh what *Bliss*.

Helen Thompson

DAD

Perhaps there are some tears
that I need to shed
as I think of him now.
A thin man. All alone.

Needing nothing, but his books
Sharing nothing but his time.
A clock ticking. Peace.
Time for a quiet read.
Time, time
Tick, tock, tick, tock
Time whisping away.

Life slowly ebbing by a man
An old man. A hunched back.
Two matchsticks legs.
Watery blind eyes. Behind blind glasses.
Funny old man. Funny creature.

Why did I have to love you?
Why do I miss you so much?
Because now I see how like you I am.

Janis Eastwood

HE WITHOUT LOVE

Genius of music, tortured internal peace,
Spiralling downwards, the life to cease.
Artist of perfection, rarely without bloom,
Golden marigolds in gloom.
Decades of humorous comedy, masking fractured life,
Cruelly twisting of the knife.
The fatal strike, the lethal blow,
Broken hearted lovers know,
The man who carried the world upon his shoulders without love.

Philip Weber

THE DWELLING

Inanimate I stand awaiting impact from an iron ball, men toil to destroy what
once they strove to build,
Seeing nought before them but a vandalised shell, a candidate for
bulldozed earth,
The value of the land on which I stand my worth.
They are not to know, that once my plaster walls absorbed the joys of
brides and grooms,
Children's' happy laughter, joy, pain or small talk that led to violent
disarray,
Forgotten at the dawning of another day.
From bleak wind and ravening cold protected all who lived within,
Opened my eyes in summer to those that sought the sun, sweet scents
provided from my garden's flowers,
Shared with them the sunlit hours.
Once the family hub no matter what the length of spoke, happiness and
sorrow raw has rested neath my roof,
Mute witness I retain the sounds of joy and groanings of despair,
My plaster walls absorbing both foul and fair.
Those that once lived within, would see me as ill used,
Remember me as once I was, a haven from which unity of family shone,
But alas they too are gone.

R H Higgins

112

TO MY DAUGHTER

It happened some years ago now, it's true
but little Jess, I still miss you.
I see you every other week
but that's nowhere near enough for me.

I'd love to see you every single day
And watch you asleep each night.
To see your face, and your beautiful hair
Spread over your pillow in the morning light.

To share your thoughts, and feel your fears
to help you when you're moved to tears.
This divorce has cost me more than you'll ever know
but my love for my little girl will never go.

You must have been confused and so lost
when your parents separated to your cost
You were taken on a ship, it must have been bad,
To meet the man who was to become your new dad.

Your brother Kevin, so strong, so brave
sometimes I have to yell 'Behave'
He has been so long without his mother
It seems he won't settle for any other.

When you grow up so very soon.
I hope I'm not asking for the moon.
If you could visit me fairly often
Before I'm carried off in my coffin.

Danny Price

SOMEBODY

I really would like to meet somebody,
As I am feeling very lonely.
I would like to meet someone kind,
Someone who is always on my mind.
I'd like to be loved,
And understood.
I'd like to meet someone to enjoy happy days,
And we would love each other always.

Alison Rainsford

UNTITLED
(For L K)

There you are - just lying, on my bedside table, all long and lonely.
Your head prevents you from lying quite flat.
You could scratch my name on the surface on which you lie.
You could gouge and tear the most delicate silk.
You would break and shatter when forced into leather.
You could be my enemy, you could pierce my snow white skin, and
bead my blood on the surface. Such pain you could inflict.
You could blind, or open a vein. Would you dance for me? If you had
a partner, a (horseshoe) magnet perhaps.
You could help me hold the pattern to the cloth, or a note on the
board. Still you lie, still silent quietly. Do you think you could
hear yourself drop?
You could make holes in my ears for gold rings to hang through.
You held my poppy, you were there when a splinter caused pain
and tears. What am I saying? Why you're nothing but a . . .

   Dress Pin!

Bunny

PLANET EARTH - 20TH CENTURY

The Lord said that the meek will inherit the earth;
Food, famine, murder and rape, self destruction
As billions from this madness wants to escape,
Disease, polluted lakes, rivers, slaggies and pitheaps,
As deprivation and Aids insidiously creeps, the
Poisoned air. Polluted seas, and murdered land,
With filth, garbage and graffiti up to your knees, the
Decaying forests, run down cities, an underclass as
Our politicians behave like *'Walter Mitties'*, Oh
Lord with thy infinite mercy hear our prayers, and
Release thy people from their despair, so disinherit
The common folk from these abominations, only you,
The solutions find to cure us from these pollutions,
This, we beseech you, God deliver us,
Your chosen people.

Duncan Robson

YOU ARE MEANT TO DIE

The night is much too warm for this behaviour.
Intelligence will never blind the eye.
I would not countenance your skinny structure
did I not know that you were meant to die.

I much prefer the act of kiss and wrestle
in pointed grass or covered by a sky.
Four walls and trumpets in the aged mattress
are useless save that you are meant to die.

Sometimes you're better with your wretched labours
stowed out of sight away from where I lie.
But as it is I bear you in your postures
for I have guessed that you are meant to die.

John Atkins

115

WHY?

Why do teapot lids have holes
And yet some do not?
Why do bubbles form on things
When they're boiling hot?
Why do prunes have wrinkles
All dried up and black?
Why aren't our arms long enough
To wash right down our back?
Why are wasps so spiteful
Land on you and sting?
(There's so many 'why's' you know
in most everything)
Why - when young and you get smacked
Do you start to cry?
I suppose that you could say
'Not ours to reason 'why'!

L K Taylor

SNOWSTORM

Softly falling, downwards hurtling,
Nothing stops its ceaseless circling,
On and on throughout the land,
Whiteness gleams on every hand.
Slowly winding through the air,
Twisting turning here and there,
Over houses, streets and towns,
Rolling hills and endless downs -
Miles of beauty here is found.

Ruth Calder

116

EVERYONE'S DAY

I'll die someday
I'll be no more,
It won't be painful
It won't be sore.
I'll be somewhere else
Not here anymore,
It won't be painful
It won't be sore.
I'll be peaceful
With my solitude and more,
It won't be painful
It won't be sore.

I'll die, everyone will.
It won't be painful
It won't be sore

Lee Broadrick

ON SECOND CHANCES

Love is the second time around
The carefulness of holding hands
The finger tipping touching of understanding how lucky we are,
able to grow old.
Easily forgetting frittered youth carping at expectations unresolved,
and past failures of wanting and not giving.
Now comfortable communication is made easy by recognition of being close.
Nothing needed.
No past. No future.
Just enjoying lengthening time in doing things together.
Confident in knowing, that there is no end.

Rhona Bennett Pointon

TIME

The sands of time are running slow,
Each grain is like an age.
With more above than gone below
I feel I'm in a cage.
As if the walls enfolding me,
Were like a timer's glass.
But to hurry time just cannot be,
For time has time to pass.

Each second of each lonely day,
Is like an hour gone.
And the many more to come my way,
Will echo one by one.
But even time cannot stand still,
And I must look ahead.
To the time when time will do my will,
And work for me instead.

In future time this time will seem,
As but a fleeting glance.
But time is time and can't redeem,
Its favours for romance.
The sands of time are running slow,
I know this cannot be.
For time it time so now you know,
The fault must lie in me.

Neil Shedden

118

A DIFFERENT PLACE

The night sky
Cold as a bell jar;
Covering dew lay gentle
Like a soft silk skin.
The rustling of leaves
From the disturbing winds
The silence of life
Crept all around.

Man lay asleep
In hibernation.
The darkness of night
Smothered with glitter,
By all tranquillity
Surrounded.
Tomorrow, another night
May bring peace
On earth once more.
If man could sleep forever
This peace would remain.

The hustle and bustle
Of everyday life,
Man always rushing:
But the calm and beauty
Of real life on earth
Takes its time
As the clock of life slows.
Man has no care
In the wilderness of this world.

Joanne Quine (15)

WHEN I WAS YOUNG

When I was young I fell in love.
I sadly didn't know.
Yet after she had left my life
I knew I'd loved her so.

I missed the way she held my hand
And made me feel a king.
She'd meant so much to my whole life.
A part of everything.

I missed her silky long dark hair.
I missed her large brown eyes.
The greatest sadness of my life,
I'd lost so rich a prize.

I cherished every thought of her.
Each loving memory.
For deep inside my heart I know
That she had cared for me.

Oh that the clock had been put back
And I'd had time again.
So many things I would have said.
So much I would explain.

For if I'd known without her love
My heart with pain would ache,
I would have held her oh so tight,
Nor ever her forsake.

Oh love. Dear love. Where are you now?
On wings you flew away.
Yet locked within my heart remain
Your echoes till this day.

John Christopher Cole

BOOKS

Today is the day I go to town,
Steeping out smartly on the way down,
The air is fresh and bright and clear,
And soon I see the building quite near.
My heart skips a beat as I hurry my pace,
To reach at last my favourite place
    The place of Books.

All day long my time is spent here,
Glancing to the right and left and to the rear,
Gazing in awe at the neatly stacked rows,
Of wonderful reading and sometimes of prose.
Hard books mostly, paper backs too,
Making my mind up is a hard thing to do.
    In the place of Books.

I look for the authors, under their headings
Which will I choose for my own special readings?
I marvel at words, as I flip through the pages,
Love and romance, tales through the ages,
All kinds of stories of travel and thrillers
Of rich men, poor men, carpenters and millers
    All to be found in the place of Books.

No time to be bored, no time to be losing,
The marvellous array, get on with the choosing,
Something to study? One to get lost in,
Humour maybe, a macabre with frosting,
Whatever I take I know I'll be thrilled
To read a book, penned by one so skilled.
    From the place of Books.

Madge Thomas

OLD MR BARRATT

He was of the time when people said 'Please'
And had lacy cloths for Sunday teas,
And polished boots and '*Sunday best*',
With time to chat and time to rest.

He taught her all he'd ever known
About the produce he had grown.
His garden, tended by fingers green,
Flourished, with beauty like she'd never seen.

His hints made sense and she learnt a lot
Of the flowers and veggies that grew in his plot.
In autumn, he thrived - his favourite time -
His Michaelmas daisies now all in their prime.

These daisies he loved - their pinks and their blues
He collected varieties - soft, misty hues.
The bunches he gave her, she set near her chair
And saw his dear face, with his silvery hair.

The winter came, and the tender flowers
Could not withstand the freezing hours,
And the gardener tired and he needed rest
And she lost the friend
Whom she'd loved the best.

On his grave she placed every bloom she had,
From her garden picked, with a heart so sad.
Next autumn she'd make sure there'd be
Dozens of daisies - perhaps he'd see!

Linda Blakey

A VISIT TO MY GRANDFATHER

As I sleep, the nightly journey begins.
The train moves through the black of night.
My sister and I sit in different compartments,
Travelling together, yet apart.
My station arrives long before hers,
I get off to find some precious words.
A porter stands blocking the way,
He utters a caution about my stay.
My grandfather sits alone,
Living in a room for all to see.
There is another room,
But that's for the chosen few.
I sneak a look and realise a truth,
I am not one of the chosen few.
My father must have known of this room,
And I think my mother too,
A fire burns here in the dark,
Twisting their shadows and leaving its mark.
Thoughts turn to my father,
What did he learn in this room?
How often did he come, or was even allowed to come?
What parts of him were burned in the fire?
I visit a different room now,
My father's room echoes
To the sound of my footfalls,
Its emptiness suddenly filled
For a fleeting moment I see
A ghost of that other room,
Occupied by someone I never really knew.
Now it is me who comes to call,
In my dreams He is me,
A messenger from a distant but near shore,
Ah! The father stream begins to fade,
No longer am I catching the night train.

Steve Scott-Marshall

SUN DAY

Sitting on a sand dune
The sun against my face
I feel the warmth wash over me
In this special place.
I close my eyes, I hear the sea
Rushing to the shore
Here and there I hear a voice
Then I dream some more.
I'm on a desert island
Toes buried in the sand
The sun is like a sleeping pill
Someone takes my hand
Come on Mum, hurry up
Lottie's caught a crab
Rosie's dropped her ice cream
And Sam has buried Dad.

Sue Watts

IN HIS DEN

Ah yes, but you have a silver band on your finger
And I am older than you!
But it was heavenly with your
Eyes cloudy with love
And my hair glittering with wet dew.
And I could feel your physical youngness
As it surrounded my fragile frame
And I knew his moment of madness
Would not visit us again.
So why am I older than you love
And your handsom face remains?
Hard on your finger is silver
As lost is once gained!

Lesley Brown

RICHARD

It was you that I left.
You introduced him to me.
Not the man of my fantasy or delusion you see.

It was the man you had made.
That I could not accept.
Though I still love you.
I have to forget.
I keep trying to make the man I want you to be.
As in my mind's eye you are perfect you see.
But the realities not so . . . and so you must be . . . the
man of my past, not my future.

You are into games.
You are moody, and tight.
You keep your eyes closed so you won't see the light.
Seen from my point of view.
That's now how I see you . . .
So you are of my past.
Not my future.

Signed.
She . . .

Sheila Mack

WHY ME

So many ordinary every day jobs
That I've no wish to do
But even so they must be done
By either me or you.

I suppose it will be me again
It always is my turn
And like a fool I do it all
Why will I never learn.

Amelia Canning

UNTITLED

Why take no for an answer,
When no is no answer at all.
I never took no for an answer,
Even when I was quite small.

Why when I questioned my parents,
Did they both give the same old reply.
They looked with disdain when they answered,
Because I have said so, that's why.

Why did they think I was awfully bold,
When a reason they'd often deny.
Not surprising I grew up completely confused,
Little wonder I always asked why.

My teacher would say if you don't understand,
Put your hand up and I'll make it plain.
If I did, she asked? Didn't you listen,
Then why did she never explain.

Why when I'm told that I can't,
Do folks stare me straight in the eye.
Saying, well I would not if I were you.
And I'm left still wondering why.

From the very first day I came into this world,
It was destined that one day I'd die.
I know as I take my very last breath,
I shall still be wondering why.

Dorothy Roberts

CHILDHOOD MEMORIES

Bullying boys, not letting me pass.
Having a picnic on damp, summer grass.
Wearing school uniform, striped green and white.
Trying to sleep on a hot, humid night.

Feeding the cows in the field down the track.
Catching small tiddlers, then putting them back.
Wearing school berets, we hated those hats!
Hours by the river, spent watching the rats.

Looking for black slugs in wet country lanes,
Riding on horses and gripping their manes.
Going for bike rides, as far as we could.
Picking the bluebells in Dingledown Wood.

Out on our roller skates, whizzing down roads,
Frog spawn just hatching and warty, brown toads.
Going to parties and eating ice creams.
It only cost twopence, or was that a dream?

Sweets were on ration, bananas were rare,
We didn't miss them, we didn't care.
So much to remember, no time to go on.
My memories of childhood, treasured though gone.

Jacqueline Johnson

HOPE YOU UNDERSTAND

It takes millions of years
For a diamond to grow,
But it's taken too little years
To destroy our lands,
So on your birthday
I won't buy you a diamond,
I'll buy you a plot of land
Hope you understand.

J F Edwards

MELANIE BEGINS TO PLAY

When Melanie begins to play
Soft cascades of sound
Ripple round the room -
Joy and Life abound -

Waterfalls of notes rush down
To fill the woodland streams,
Rising in crescendos then
Diminuendo - ing to dreams.

Roses, violets, sylvan glades
Dance before your eyes,
Butterflies and laughter
And the blue of summer skies.

Then she'll slow the tempo
To the trickle of a brook;
And the stars begin to twinkle
With the change she subtly took

Till you see the pale moon gliding
Over beds of flowers
And you hear the soulful sound
Of the passing of the hours.

The golden hair showers over
Her shoulders round and bare,
The fingers gently touch
And caress the keyboard there

And we are breathless, longing,
Waiting for another day
When we can sit enchanted
As Melanie begins to play.

Dorothy Thompson

CHILDHOOD MEMORIES

Around our piano oft on Sunday
We loved to sing some hymns of Sankey.
'Throw out the lifeline' next we sang,
Or 'Will your anchor hold.' our voices rang.
Then 'Jesus bids us shine,
You in your small corner, I in mine.'

When Springtime came around
Kingcups by a marsh we found.
Bluebells made a woodland carpet,
Forget-me-nots blue could not forget.
Hazel catkins in hedgerow seen,
Celandine and Coltsfoot graced the scene.

Good Friday made the annual trek,
Taking tea in cottage by the beck.
Those wooded banks used to climb,
Gathered Primrose posies every time.
Crossed that wooden plank to other side
Where ruined Ayton Castle we espied.

Knew a pond edged with Meadow sweet.
Heard a Yellow Hammer sing, 'Teet, teet, teet.
On patch of grass played at cricket,
Taking turns to bat at wicket.
Learnt the names of many flowers
Throughout those sunny summer hours.

Gathered brambles on Autumn days,
Elderberries picked by other ways.
Winter sledged on hills snowbound,
Or skated when the Mere icebound.
From January through to dark December.
Treasured childhood days to remember.

Florence Needler

GRANDCHILDREN

You know the score
they are yours forevermore,
grant this wish
that nothing comes amiss,
for down the years
there have been tears
and tantrums round the clock.
And now it's peace
and we take stock.
Teddy bears have gone
many games been won,
and at the going down of the sun
we praise their wicked ways
and we are there
to comfort and to bless
when rooms get in a mess.
This motley crew
will turn to you
an angel in disguise
till at last they see
the beauty and the wise.

Joan Hands

LABOUR OF LOVE

Junk shop hunt I look to find
Piece's of furniture to look better in my mind
A desk a chest, a rocking chair
An old chaise lounge filled with horse hair.

Strip it back, down to the wood
Old lead paint does it no good
Scratched distressed layers of paint
Sand, stain, varnish, curse of a saint.

Furniture polished, fabric lilac and mint
Stencilled animals, stars clouds a subtle hint
Lemon carpet, Roman blind
Everything you'll need to find
Feathered my nest, finished the roost
Contented appraisal gives me a boost
Hard work, love harmony
This is how it's meant to be
My first baby's nursery.

Beverley McLoughlin

THEME IN BLACK AND WHITE

White snow cold. Black coal.
Heat of contest in dominoes,
Black and white keys of pianos
White and black sides in one's soul.

The contrast in black and white 'snaps'
of photographers' negatives develop unsure.
The reversal of images in one's eyes -
Until the picture is sharp and clear.

Night and day. Passing - white and black pawns
Move across the chequered board -
like life, the ploy in chess games
play the struggles that through one has clawed.

Black and white may be opposites -
But like the ebony and white keys
of that piano, in composition and concertos,
Music and Harmony are in black and white notes
        So in Harmony
Black and white are necessities.

R Peter Smith

I LONG TO BE FREE

Searching for my inner self as I walk,
Along the garden path

Softly blows the wind
As the trees whisper together

Birds in the high branches
Singing sweet songs of melodies

Water fowls flapping their wings
As they flow across the pond

How fresh and clean is the air
My nostril inhale the sweet fragrance of flowers
Blooming with their blossom

How I want to be free
Honey bee how sweet honey bee
Buzzing from one flower to another
Gathering nectar for the making of the honey

Which God has made pure
God Has created everything beautiful
pure and free

In this garden there is life
In man's world there is only destruction
I long to be free.

Patricia Jones

THE DEATH OF A CHARMER

'He hasn't got long.' The nurse spoke quietly.
I look at him, and quell a wave of pity.
He wasn't always so helpless, I remind myself.

'Your husband is such a charmer' they told my mother
She'd smile, and agree, call him a 'gentle giant'
'How did you get those bruises?' 'Oh, I walked into a door'
'And the broken ribs?' 'I tripped, and hit the floor.'
And the charmers legend continued.

I loved him once, when I was a child
Before fear and awareness turned love to hate
And when she died aged forty-five
I vowed I'd get my revenge.

But he died alone and the pity came
His own children didn't want to know
But I think the charmer fooled me again
Pity was the last thing he deserved.

Because the nightmares didn't stop when he died
He always re-appears when my life is going well
Beating my mother, giving her hell.

But I have got revenge, he must realise
Because he's dead

But I am alive.

Tracy Hartshorn

MY VISITOR

It was first thing in the morning
The night had flown away.
Just the song of early birds
At the start of another day

Then as I looked at misty dawn
A fox came trotting up the lawn
And as I stood by watching him
He jumped up on my wheelie bin.

I stood and saw just what he did
As he tried to lift the lid,
He aimed to lift it with his head.
Lost his grip slipped down instead,

As if to say 'It's not my day'
He scrambled up and dashed away,
I was sorry to see him fly,
Left me alone again you see,

Tonight I think before I go to bed,
I'll leave out some bits of bread
When he comes to satisfy his need
Perhaps I will just see him feed.

Gordon Dungey

THE RAG AND BONE MAN

The clanging of the bell
Was all we needed to hear
To gather all the rags we had
And wait for the cart to appear.

The old horse would stand quietly
Only its tail would swish
As we handed over our old rags
And in return got a goldfish.

134

We'd run inside and show mum
And her eyes would usually roll
I suppose you realise she'd say
We've got no goldfish bowl.

We'd put it in Mum's best fruit dish
That always did the trick
Mum would send dad down the pet shop
To get a bowl pretty quick.

Susan Stevens

WASTED TEARS

Tears hath no place in my heart, or dreams,
Regrets are not for me,
For you can be all that it seems,
But please don't cry for me,

It's love I want and not your tears,
I don't care if I am unkind,
For I've had it up to here for years,
All I need, is peace of mind.

So hide from me your lovely face,
Go then from my life,
If I can't have you in good grace,
There's no sense in your being my wife.

I'll miss you dear, for I love you so,
I think you're simply grand,
But I tell you now, you are free to go,
Back to your husband.

David D Brodie

I WONDER HOW HE FEELS

I wonder how he felt, when she walked out and left him
alone with four children, all under eight
Did he cry? We never saw it.
But he must have, he's that type of man

And I wonder how he felt, when she came and took me
And although I was only six,
There was a pain in his eyes I'll never forget
But he smiled and said, 'That's alright.'

And I wonder how he felt when I married
As he watched another give me away
The other insisted it was his right, I was torn
So my father smiled and said, 'That's alright'

And when my mother died, he came to pay his respects
But was told he wouldn't be welcome
So he smiled and said, 'That's alright.'

And I wonder how he feels when he's alone
When we're all getting on with our lives
We take him for granted, just like she did
But he smiles, and says, 'That's alright . . . '

Sally Quilford

IT'S A MAD MAD WORLD

The world is going crazy
It's getting really bad
An awful lot of people
Must be really mad.

There's fighting and there's squabbling
There's stealing and there's looting
There's wars and there is bombing
And there's too much bloody shooting.

There's rape and abuse
There's an overdose of drugs
These people think they're really brave
But they really are just thugs

It's not a children's world today
And for their futures we do fear
When I think about our life today
It brings, to my eye, a tear.

E Riddoch

CHOICES

She's grown up in the nineties
not knowing nature's limits
on her sex.
If she wants to climb a mountain,
travel the world,
or just go swimming every day,
she will.
The world's her oyster;
she'll find its pearl
and wear it or give it away
according to her whim.

Her mother never knew
the oyster held a pearl
for her - she thought
she was just supposed
to swallow it.

And her granny was
allergic to sea food
anyway.

Gill Wistowsky

MY VANDALISED HEART

You ripped it
You tore it
You broke it and burned it
You clipped it
You wore it
You poked it and spurned it

You aged it
You crushed it
You slashed it and mugged it
You caged it
You rushed it
You trashed it and slugged it

You kicked it
You stopped it
You jabbed it and starved it
You pricked it
You dropped it
You stabbed it and halved it

You clawed it
You maimed it
You stunned it and nailed it
You gnawed it
You shamed it
You shunned it and failed it

You captured it!

Mark Ringsted

ON BEING HUMAN

It is hard to be a human in a crowd that's polychrome,
I find it hard to be a special light as round the world I roam,
So in *our* imaginations, *yours and mine,* I'd like to try,
To conjure up a *Social task* for *all* beneath the sky.
We do not need a pulpit where no one may contradict,
The opinions of a preacher mind with many dogmas trickt.
All we need is just one microphone so all around may hear,
The causes and the remedies for all of us being here.

Human life's a very strange affair or so it seems to me,
We can fathom how we got here but the *Why's* a *Blank* to me,
I have read the sacred scriptures but I'm frankly not impressed.
Some say that God invented us millennia ago but on that my answer's *No*
I think that we invented God and here is something very odd
I think we face the greatest *Mystery* beneath the shining *Sun*
All Gods are *myths* and *we don't know* how *The Cosmos* was begun

This is the clue we need to clear the way to knowing what is *True*
This *Basic Truth* is what the early minds all *failed* to have in view,
They were treating ancient writings as being based on *real fact,*
When all the time the *Basic truth* was hid behind an *invented artefact*
So we must live with *mystery* on how the *Cosmos* came to *be,*
That thought proved the vital clue of what is *right* for *you* and *me.*
We must educate our children to be *patient* while *humans think,*
Of some new ways to rule ourselves or into murdering nations sink

We must see ourselves as *people* and not *nations* from today,
One *blinding truth of mystery* can help us on our way,
What say we try to *fathom out* the *truth* we do not know,
This will give us all a *global task* for a really *human show.*

Edward Graham Macfarlane

THE GREAT ESCAPE

Maybe someday I'll kick the booze
And live my life the way I choose.
Maybe someday I won't need drugs,
Or live in a squat surrounded by bugs.
It gives me hope if I can dream
In this situation I could scream.
I'm educated and very well read
I must leave the streets before I'm dead
It's almost like reaching for the moon
Trapped inside a wondrous cocoon
And yet I wish to get away
But all the time I simply stay
Until one night I had a dream,
About God in such high esteem
Next day I staggered to the church
And gave my soul a thorough search,
I felt a sudden surge of power
To reach the summit of this tower
I flowed with great determination
To evade this deterioration
And now although it's living hell
I'm on my way to being well.

Sylvia Lowe

NO TOMORROWS?

Where do you go when there's nothing to live for
What do you do when the world's all at war
When people are killing and people are dying
When children are starving and mothers are crying.

Do you know what to do when your brain is awash
With spirits and drugs and you just want more cash
To drown out your memories and kill your tomorrows
And try not to remember all of your sorrows

I know where to go and I know what to say
Because all my tomorrows are really today
The Lord will provide what I need to survive
He will comfort my sorrows and help me to live

So turn to our God with heart open wide
Don't turn your face nor e'en try to hide
'Cos His love conquers all from the small to the tall
If you let him come in he will succour us all

F Higgins

CIGARETTE BURNS

The old man sits down, the clock ticks away
no visitors arive and the room fills with smoke of his
cigarette.

He begins to cough as the smell lingers on
no washing is ever done, no clean clothes are worn.

The windows are shut, the fire is on, the
cigarette begins to fall as his snoring is heard.

The telephone rings as the wire does burn, the
room fills with smoke and his curtains come down in flames.

A deep sleep he's in but, wakes as he burns
piercing screams are heard and photo's burn the memories
as the neighbours rush to help.

They find him lying dead, with a tear down his cheek
and a coffee stain upon his shirt, while his
hands remain burned, the neighbours are
guilty for leaving him alone to cope in
a death trap of smoky rooms and
carpets of dust.

Sandra Ann Banks

BRITISH DISEASES

British Education.

I don't want something new-fangled or flashy
or something called Jocasta or Ned.
I want a Miss Protheroe - old fashioned and reliable -
someone to get me from A to Z

British Justice.

Thirty days hath a first offender:
Great Dane-buggerer or jewelry-fencer;
second offenders hath thirty one;
excepting rapists alone who
hath twenty eight days in the nick
but twenty nine if they didn't wear a prophylactic.

British Censorship.

Just as when I was a child
there's still a fairground in our park.
Nowadays, they're called Dodgems
- they used to be called Bumper Cars.

British Sign of the Times.

The paddling pool is now a boating pond
in exactly the same park,
with a large vandalised notice
saying *Beware of Broken Glass* . . .

Andrew Pye

DARKNESS

Why can't the world understand me ?
Why must I seem insane?
Why this choking darkness,
Why all the fear, the pain?
Why will no-one help me,
Why is it always a game?
How many dead does it take,
And why do they laugh when they maim?
Why must I cry now, old, choked and dying?
Why does the world hide its shame.

Bill Brammar

TO MAKE THEIR MARK

Bubble of light
New men run at you
Trailing metal mirrors of their manhood,
Locked in filing cabinets
Labelled, stored
Refrigerated.
They glimpse you
Through advancing Macro mumble
And, richer now, fatter now
They lie in the arms of their formulae,
Their productivity deals,
Improved economy.
Still seduced,
They grow old in your light's brilliance.
Reaching for your beam,
They drink the wine of your existence
And sleep at last,
Drunk in the joy of success attained,
While dead men poke the bubble
To burst it.

Ann McCloud

SPINACH SPILLAGE

Yawn groan stumble
From slumber I mumble
Into movement bumble
Feet on floor tumble
Touching carpet but wait
Something wrong too late
Leaves of green everywhere
In the wardrobe on the stair
Skiing from room to room
On vegetable matter brain is doom
Am I frazzled or awake
Is this all some elaborate mistake
There has been a spinach spillage
Everywhere but there is no advantage
In pretending I can explain
Anything in life the stain
And mess of insanity
Will remain confusing permanently
I lie surrounded by spinach leaves
As time ducks and weaves
Around me no strength to worry
Only to exist in sleep and let reality be.

Stephen Neal

AFTERMATH

Poised on the edge of time the shell lies still
In harbour, calm because the storm has passed.
The water mirrors how the shattered will
Withstood so many tempests till the last.
That moment, when death's fingers scratched out hope
And agony had stalled the engine's glow,
How could the tiring life-force cope
When quashed by searing blast and overthrow?

The treasure of the memories that are left
Of grace, and hands, and plans, and happiness,
Gives comfort and some help to those bereft
Whose heartache must reflect the emptiness.
The essence of the vessel now sails free
Exploring far horizons out at sea.

Pam Clarke

A CHILD OF WAR

Every night I tread my dreams
And drown them in my tears
When awake my yearning long
Is to return to my yesteryears
Golden memories come to mind
As step by step I trace
A picture in my inner eye
Of a child with a battered suitcase
That September day my world fell apart
Transported by reason of war
To a village that would be my home
Maybe for a year or more
Fields of corn and grazing cows
We played on grass so green
A house with straw upon its roof
I'd never see before
Now through the quiet churchyard
I see the names I knew
How I wish I could say to them
I really did love you
I will go back of that I'm sure
And recall the things I did
I wonder if there is anyone
Who remembers that small cockney kid.

Annie Kilgour

CHAMPAGNE BUBBLES

I've drank the champagne bottle dry
I'm much too drunk to weep or sigh
It was meant to celebrate
Our first kiss on our blind date
I paced up and down for endless hours
Clutching a bunch of wilting flowers
I felt so sad and wanted to cry
So drank the champagne bottle dry
She arrived much too late
And left me in my drunken state
I couldn't weep or even sigh
That champagne bottle was really dry
Dreams of love kisses and cuddles
Lost in a mist of champagne bubbles.

Norman Neild

JULY 1995

Ice melts and
water warms dusty in
this heat - Gasping,
you swallow hot air
like sawdust tickling
bronchials and branching
through the brain - A
terrible see-saw dangerous
heat that laughs at the
city madness it spreads and
hunts down the hunted
with those all or nothing plans -
That leave small children murdered and
a little girl lost without a nightie.

Tania Jacklin

RAPPING IN THE NINETIES

I'm a fast raping dude
And I'm here to make you see
What life is like in
the nineteen nineties.

Computers, CD's,
Virtual Reality,
Information superhighway,
Results of our technology.

A fast paced world
No time to stop.
You've gotta play tough
To make it to the top.

The elderly are neglected
And youngsters feel rejected
Who are we to blame
politicians we've elected?

There's a hole in the ozone
And pollution's everywhere
Chemicals in the sea
Carbon monoxide in the air.

So open your eyes
Though you may not want to see
That this is the life
In the nineteen nineties.

Heather Campbell

CARE IN THE COMMUNITY

The new flat is quiet.
I hear the dogs barking next door,
But I've only seen the woman once.
Most days, I don't get up till dinner.
I keep the telly on all night.

Sometimes a man called John
Knocks on my door, and takes me shopping.
I like riding in his car.
He brings me back to the flat,
And then he goes away again.

The nurses used to change my bed,
And give us our tea in the canteen.
They used to tell me when to take my pills,
And I used to tell them about my old dad.
He worked on the railway.

When I went to the hospital,
He gave me a postcard of a train.
I brought it with me to the new flat.
I lived there for a long time -
For birthdays and birthdays.

The new flat is quiet.

I keep the telly on all night.

Susanne McCafferty

MY SEA

Restless as the Sea, my troubled thoughts crash upon the
shores of life's realities.

Pounding the spray of question on the edge or reason only to
return again to torment my mind with mere grains of sand in
answer to the meaning of my existence.

Wave upon wave seeking out the weakness of my nature
whilst ever eroding the veneers of my vanity.

With each ebb the maelstrom leaves the debris of life at my
feet and a cold feeling of futility in the harbour of my
heart.

Old age is the Sea.

Graham Griffiths

ASCENT OF THE MAN OF SUMMER

When the weather is fine
I will be ready to shine
When the weather is fine
For sure, it will be truly mine

I stand tall amongst the daffodils
and sway with a soft breeze
I go this way . . . I go that way
But always on the right track
Even if it breaks my back

The past of my tears of sadness
are behind me now
And I won't look back
I shall only go forward . . .
With tears of joy and happiness . . .
For the weather is fine now
and it's truly mine

Behold, for the Man of Summer
is in the historicity of now . . .
I am within the greatness of the love rays
Beaming upon my sweet head
Behold, for the Man of Summer is now . . .
For the weather is fine
and it truly will be mine

Stephen Rusby

HE

He is gorgeous, he is fun,
he loves everyone.
His eyes shine with joy.
He can be a pest, his sister says,
But she loves him just the same,
and so do I.
He is kind, he is adorable,
Formidable, irrepressible,
thoughtful, cute and kissable,
and he's just *My little boy!*

Isabel Bray

WISHING

Lying here in our bed
wishing you would turn your head
whisper sweet nothings in my ear
and make believe you really care.

What happened to that passionate man
who made me feel that we were one,
you came into my life that day
I changed direction and went your way.

I've been through all the highs and lows
and listened dearest to all your woes,
to share with me your love and life
but not to hear you call me wife.

Ten long years have now gone by
and was it all such a lie,
we've laughed and cried tears of pain
could we really try again.

So turn around, I am quite near
hold me close and love me dear.

Ann Sherley

LONELY

How lonely the hours seem to pass,
when we are parted.
The long nights we wish will pass,
until we are re-united.
So cold and desperately afraid,
we sit and silently we weep.
The bedside pilgrimage is laid.
Lying, praying till were tired,
enabling you to sleep the night away.
Morning comes far too early,
bringing fresh sorrow too clearly.

Jo Smith

I DIDN'T ASK HIM

I didn't ask him
if he would stay that night.
He camped quite happily
his feet aloft
a cup of tea for nourishment.
He held my hand
a soft embrace
then he grabbed at my breast
but I moved quicker than he guessed.
It was not his rudeness
that opened the door;
nor bashfulness, nor frigidness
that closed it shut.
His own complacency had
turned the key. Expectation
is a short-lived quest.

Elizabeth Kerl

THE PARTING

And so, our love affair must
end at last,
Becoming in our hearts, the
cherished past
We both knew it could not be
otherwise.
For our bonds were those strong,
yet silken ties.
But, although there is bound to
be regret,
And it will not be easy to
forget,
How could we ever build
true happiness
On someone else's heartbreak,
and distress.
Yet, though you may be very
far away,
You'll linger in my thoughts
by night and day.
To heart and soul, mere
time and distance are
As nothing; one looks up and
sees a star
Millions of miles away and a
whole age
Can be spanned by a single
thought. A page,
Or complete chapter I might
pen, but know
That just a glance from me
would tell you so
Much more than I could write
in any book.
For you can read my mind
with just one look

But it's goodbye, goodbye, for
all time, dear.
I have one souvenir of
yesteryear.
Those primroses you picked
that morn in May
Are memory's blossoms, and
your last bouquet.
And they will never lose
their fragrance, they
Will be all mine, forever and
a day.

Pauline Ransley

WAITING

Ray of sunshine
Not yet born
Smothered cries
Into emptiness.
Alone and lonely
For there's no other
Alter ego
Who is mine.
Senses gone
But alive.
Waiting
For the future to progress
Into the past,
And present to take form
For the ray of sunshine
Has begun
To glow, brighter.

Humera Khan (16)

RADAR MAST, VENTNOR, 1950'S

With taut steel tendon and girder bone,
Unclothed in the solid flesh of stone,
These obelisk skeletons stand and sift
    The sea-cloud's drift
As it swirls and swoops above the town
And breaks on the round firm breast of the Down.

What alien spectral shapes are these
That dwarf the hills and flout the seas?
No monolithic granite hewn
    With magic rune,
To boast great deeds of valour done,
Of empires gained or battles won; -

But grimly functional ugly, vast,
Built for use, not made to last;
Carefully costed, nothing spent
    On ornament, -
Fit symbols for this age unsure
That builds so little that may endure.

But yet these bolted girders stand
Watchful guardians of this land,
Since from them questing pulses flow
    That come and go,
Probing sky and scanning sea
To thwart a prowling enemy.

Oh, shall we ever ages see
When use and beauty wedded be,
And the offspring of man's intellect
    With no defect?
Or in tomorrow's world instead
Must we still live uncomforted.

Alwyn Trubshaw

ONE LOOK

Piano player play.
Soulful eyes,
Make me stay.
Music waft away
The heart's decay.

Bernadette O'Reilly

LIFE

Life is a wonderful thing
Unique and one of a kind.
Life is what you want it to be,
Take the days just one at a time.
Count your blessings not your troubles
And you will find a way,
With courage, love and happiness
To be stronger every day.
So many dreams are waiting,
So many paths to tread,
Decisions too important to leave to chance instead.
Live a life of serenity,
Not that of regret.
Put your problems far behind you
And try hard to forget.
Life is so precious and rare
With someone to love and someone to share
And realise it is never too late
To wish upon a star.
Life is a wonderful thing,
Whatever, whoever you are.

Carole Mills

WARWICKSHIRE

W here I was born
A long time ago
R ight at the beginning of the thirties
W hat was in store for me?
I did not know.
C ould you even guess?
K ids I wanted, animals too
S o my life was planned.
H ere I am now
I n my sixties, sure
R ewarded by kids and animals too
E njoying my life.

I M Burgess

RETIREMENT

If I could live my life again
I would do the very same
For love and life go hand in hand.
The laughter and the pain
For all the joys and troubles
Are the meaning of your life
The happiness, the sorrows
The troubles and the strife
Then in the evening of your life
You have your memories
The sound of children's laughter
The very best of these
And growing old together
The sharing of your lives
Brings peace, love, and contentment
        A retirement of ease.

E Hopkins

156

TO SOFIA

If I by chance should fail
Don't take my spirit too
A slight upon a hope so frail
Would fragment deepest blue
Upon a canvas
Paint my mind
For all the world to see
But if you have a thought that's kind
Then leave this poor wretch be.

Ken Starks

EYES

Have you seen the naked eyes of the crowd?
Eyes that look, not conscious of one's gaze,
        at nothing.
I have seen the scooped eyes,
        blind as Persophene's
            in the earth's darkness.

Guarded eyes,
        what are your secrets?
Then have you seen the lilting eyes
            that twinkle out?
Eyes that are happy
            because they are looking,
                seeing the hurdy-gurdy world.
Have you seen the wondering eyes
                    of children?
Open and amazed.
        I have seen them
            and my eyes have danced to the music
                    of their innocence.

Olga M Momcilovic

157

SPACE

Restless, you said we needed space, that
I should take some time away, alone - so
I became Belfast's first woman to
Take a package trip to outer space.
At the start, thinking of home, I
Wrote a flippant postcard, saying that I
Missed you, felt that I'd lost weight, that
Food tasted like dry powder and there
Seemed to be no atmosphere, but the
Day when I was taken on a
Guided tour of the moon I
Stopped to think of what it was I missed.
I walked across the face of moonlight,
Questioning my weightlessness, so
Far away from all those sunset scenes we'd
Thought made happiness compete;
Floating up from arguments and tears I
Saw our love as gravity to
Drag me down to earth, and
When you sent the spaceship up to
Bring me home I wondered if I'd
Stay in space, alone.

Caragh Devlin

YOU

I skulked in the gloom of my youth
Till the field of your gladness
Lit up my life.
Puzzled and blinking
I did not understand at once
And am still learning
To tan without burning.

Ali Cohen

158

CARRY ON

Carry on living
As well as you can
Whether you're woman
Or whether you're man.

Carry on loving
Though it may be
Different for man,
Look at history!

Carry on learning
How best to stay
Friendly with both sex
And not go astray.

Carry on wooing
And doing your part
To show to your partner
You have a good heart.

Carry on seeing
Romance in the air
Whether you're youthful
Or showing grey hair.

Carry on believing
To love and to care
Is the best medicine
To have and to share.

Carry on being
All that you should
To give life true meaning
From child to adulthood.

June Rampton

ALONE

I eat there once a week.
It is convenient.
The food is good,
wholesome and cheap.
Most customers are couples
past *retiring* age.

He and she seldom pass a word.
She sits crumpled, depressed,
munching stoically 'till her plate is clean.
Every so often she spoons
more veggies on his plate.
These seem invisible as
he chews on and on and on
staring blankly at his food,
then all about. On a round trip
his eyes pick me up.
A woman alone! First a quick glance, then
glances back and forth, then the stare
his food got first.

Bored eyes flutter a signal:
'you're animated, interesting . . .
wish you were here instead of her.'

My response is gratitude
that I am not. Or I too
would be crumpled, depressed and . . .
he wouldn't notice how or why
I faded.

Ruth I Johns

WHERE ANGEL FEARS TO TREAD

I need not NHS upbraid
For lack of beds, appointment cuts;
Go private? No. I am afraid
I'm passionate and simply *nuts*
And privacy is home with thoughts
You never would believe of me.
Although, through love, I'm out of sorts,
I doubt there's any remedy.
When, confident I knew my bloke,
Considered secrecy had flown,
I noticed that when last we spoke,
Some reticence came down the phone.
It seems I'm on pin and needle
At something of reserve, opaque,
For, however hard I wheedle,
He'll merely *fetching* twinkle make
Inscrutable as Cheshire cat;
Behind that winsome grin of his
My boggling mind supposes that
Much deep deliberation is.
Does he feel that Aphrodite
(Or Joanna Lumley at best)
Makes me, in my see through nightie
Come bottom in the glamour test?
I'm told 'look on the side that's brighter'
And though I'm three score years and ten,
He may think I'm the *tops,* the blighter;
When shall we understand our men?

Ruth Daviat

THE BOAST HOUSE

It was a rest house
by title *The Haven*
and this one had a waiting list

those waiting to gain entrance
others a'waiting heaven's call
although
with central heating
maintained at 84
destiny gave future
another twist

in summer, a gazebo-like attachment
held in daytime
a horseshoe of helpless women

they vied with one another
with tales of . . .
My son is in charge of the Patents office

Our eldest daughter is a JP

You've heard of Tottenham Hotspur . . .
well, my grandson . . .

. . . lead at Birmingham Sadlers Wells

none of these depositions
won the day
but each left its speaker
important in her own eyes

Cato

SAMANTHA NESBIT

Young naiad of Portsmouth Northsea's team,
place in Atlanta Olympics Samantha's dream.
Look cool in *Speedo* royal blue sportsuit,
hoping British swimming team soon recruit?

That Mayville High School pupil 13 aspire,
At Youth Olympics Bath four gold acquire.
Possible medals in Atlanta '96 wish!
brilliant talented swimmer like fish.

At National Age Group in Leeds event,
impressive bravado swimmer not relent.
Great performances at championships; yes.
dashing like a wonderful dolphin I guess.

In 400 metres medley, 15 min 1.89 seconds win,
breeze through wonderful, victory Nesbit grin.
In butterfly 69.07 seconds leg so excellent,
reward trained hours in Victoria pool spent.

Northsea speedster won 200m butterfly; yes,
and made winning double, 400m freestyle; yes.
Triumphant victory in 100m breast stroke
and made eight titles, 200m back stroke.

Earned silver medal in 100m freestyle,
winning time 61.38 seconds, sure smile.
This young naiad has promising future,
Portsmouth folk watch Ms Nesbit mature.
So remember Samantha Nesbit name,
this splashing swimmer such fame.

Young naiad of Portsmouth Northsea's team,
place in Atlanta Olympics Samantha's dream.
Look cool in *Speedo* royal blue sportsuit,
hoping British swimming team soon recruit?

George Woodford

SCATTER THE ASHES AT HOLKHAM GAP

A cry breaks from silent dunes
    and wings towards the pines
    muffled by thickening mist
    rising out of pastures.
    Whispers at the shoreline
    are from a tired sea
    as the shadows slide to darkness
    in the marram.

    Grass skirts soft thighs
    stars skim on cooling shoulders
    whilst meltdown in the eyes
    make our actions bolder.
    We meld
    now rhythm takes control
    I play you firmly as the song begins
    a flood of sound
    that the years locked in
    wells from lips
            flies
          across
              the dunes

    to await reunion
    with my strewn remains.

Ivor Murrell

LIGHT OF LOVE

So much in words a never ending tone
    as nectar is the food of Gods

Transcending all a search pursued
    prefix insidious to extremity

The clash of sabre
    the art of rapier thrust

A walk of set paces
    a duel of pistol fire

Bear us not to part awhile
    would play and players play

And poets of song would cleave
    to stir each flowing line

But to catch the gleam the bright
    that would pertrude the woman's eye

Who but the brave would bare the soul
    then lay each ruin, an altar, at her feet.

George

TIDE OF LIFE

Stormy weather, calm weather,
                  fuel the tide of life
Slowly, quickly, buffeted
               from side to side
From angry to calm
Eagerly awaited, showers of heavy rain, the balm
Where re-echoes, of thought
Are the memory so often forgot
Where the meantime, and the middle, ebb and flow regardless
And the modes, of thought, we often bless
Now at last, life floats along
Amid the tranquil water, singing its own swan song
Where, every time and tide, and season
How its own echo and reason
Where tempests, sometimes take control
Of our being, and soul
Constantly being tossed, from one extreme, to another
Where the tide, is constantly aware

Denise Walker

PARTING

Instinctively we knew and though we tried
when the darkness fell - we cried
gushing with the wind and rain
cocooned in each other's pain.

With morning from the depths we rose
in broken tears deep around:
the shining sun greeting the damned
as if differently, we could have chose.

J Calkin

THE PRICE OF POWER

What cost is the price of power?
To Humanity: suffering, death,
Destruction: *Much too high.*

People lying, torn apart, down trodden,
Weary, losing heart.
What price Power?

When there's no cities or
People left to rule, only,
The remains of once normal
Life, of peace, and quiet
      and less strife

So think again, the *Powers that be*
Before you ruin and destroy
The price of Power
    Much too high

Catherine Scales

A BAD DAY

all I see
is the knowledge
of worlds
turned harder

louder
and colours
so bright
they hurt

100 types
of sugar
salt
well balanced
preservatives

and families
that love
to hate
and own
everything
except
themselves

Lisa Michelle

HELLO HEART!

How's your beat?
Are all those scars and patches
wholly healed? Have you renounced
all chance of leap or break?
Have you announced
your vow? Who watches
if you're not awake?
And can I quote your thump on that?

James Hall Thomson

ALMOST A SONNET - TO T H

That night, you stoked the grate, got up
And made some cocoa in your favourite cup.
You took your knitting and gathered your thread,
And made your way on up to bed.
I heard your tread, soft on the stair,
And there on the landing, the light in your hair.
You bade me farewell without a word,
Save a scarce few mutterings I barely heard.

At the funeral they called me a *poor old chap*
With no-one to wake him from afternoon nap.
I go about the house remembering your ways;
You are no longer here to lighten my days.
So here I am now, my whole life diminished,
And there in the chair: your last crossword, unfinished.

Simon Walsh

ALCOHOL ABUSE

Abusing alcohol?
Consider - you might lose control!
One drink - maybe two
'Till - one day - it's got a hold on you
Blurring vision
Scorching the mind
Entering dimensions
Of a different kind
Encouraging the soul's demise
'Till - ultimately - thro' despairing eyes
Despising the vessel from which you sip
You're compelled to raise it to your lip
In nauseous intoxication
Consider the risks being taken.

Anna MacDonald

LET MUSIC FLY

Play me a tune Keith
On the body of your flute
Through stops and starts
Let your fingers descale that silver flying fish
Drop your notes like mercury
Let them slide off fish scales
Release the arpeggios drumming in your heat
Play me that music to die for rhythm
Pull it up through your spine
Stretch it out to reach mine
Play me that close your eyes
Reach into your belly
Driven by your seed
Procreation and need
Love and then die music
Smooth out the petals
Reach for the nectar
Conjure up birds, lakes, forests
Spin webs for spiders
Make rivers cascade
Let notes glide
Let sounds collide
Let breath and fingertips
Connive with flute and lips
Let music fly
Reawaken memories
Don't let them die Keith
Don't let them die
Squeeze sound from your lips
Let the music feed mine
Drip honey notes and fill me
Let your moist breath slide down
Warm up cold metal
Play music to love and die for
Play music to move me.

Maureen Roberts

YOU WILL COME

You will come, that when
you're gone forever, you'll
find no trace, or a tear,
while I wept.

I saw you, sleeping, with
the same sorrow, that
brings morning.

Surely you will come, at
the dawning of the day,
were tomorrow, not still to
come.

You will come, you said
and with it Spring.
I'll meet you there in
the morning, with your
cup of dancing rain,
that plays with Summer,
were it not gone.

As you say, it is spent
my youth, with idle chatter
the birds, the bees, the
hive swarms, in the warmth
of Summer.

Robert Robb

AGEISM

I was me when I was three
And I'm still me at sixty three.
Though sixty three is outwardly: merely.
It's the inner me who is still three,
Yet sixty three and three are both me.
        The same me: essentially.

Of course my bones do not agree.
They are not three.
Definitely and definitively not three.
Nor is my whole anatomy
Or Physiology
For, you see, my age is three,
Psychologically.
Yes my psyche is three.
So which is the real me?
I think: it's my psyche!

Maureen Dodd

BLUE MIST

Early morning wind,
Reflection,
Sparkles the soft dew,
Operatic larks croon,
Silent fading moon,
Young minds occupied,
Triumphant,
Eyes glare,
Noise,
Iron carriages unaware,
Relinquish the thought.

The great deity has chosen,
Now,
Friends of the morning depart with a frown,
No knowledge,
No pain,
No thoughts of why,
Onward from mortal life,
Unto paradise they safely fly.

P MacKenzie

TO BABY

You came into the
world,
with a single piercing
cry,
and one slight
imperfection,
that made them all
ask, why?
But your soul is
what's important,
and that little
loving heart,
with these you
are accepted,
without them
you're apart.
So don't place too
much on beauty,
this world was
made for you,
and if you give
it love,
the world will
love you too.

M Turner

BEST DAYS

Waking with a start is the only way
To start those little important days.
One vaguely engendered with recall
Replays days clouded with challenge and turmoil.

Youthful heart pumping one's rises,
As one hundred vague surprises
Enfilled the mind: the light
Merely dream-troubled night's extension.
But stiffen sinews, summon courage,
For days lay waiting, cold and merciless:
One must gain ground, believe, progress,
Wait not on future, now is her test.

She occurs here, now, while the past dwells,
Our repast a little daily diminution, dissolution:
Our task to promote effort over apathy, here
Where defeatism is hope living in dread of fear.

Michael Soulsby Williamson

JANE

Summer
  Bathed you
  In youthful expression

Autumn
  Coloured your hair

Winter
  Bestowed her complexion

Spring
  Gave us a maiden fair

My eyes are your mirror

  And reflect
   The beauty there . . .

G A Judge

BRAVE ONES

Look out at the world, bronze effigy of distress
In depictions of sister, daughter, mother, and wife
Mid Conisbrough's fair green, display and impress
The uncertainty of mining, the reality of strife.

Expressed is your pain, in your stark overt stance
The epitome of hardship, dwells cold 'neath your shawl
When earth's moody tempers, brought tragic discontinuance
Of kins loving presence, through merciless pitfall.

Yes! I witness your sorrow, your mute angry stare
Unparalleled its message, to the kithless of coal
The recipients of fatality, you denote solitaire
The women of miners, whose men folk pits stole.

And you poor black soul, I with heavy heart - gaze
You tired human mole, in nature's dark shroud
Who toiled where the brave, seek no reason for praise
Yet in brotherhood's gallantry, abundantly proud.

Reach from your circumstance, I understand your plight
That pleads for all men of arduous task
Now laid as they perished, still void of light
Let your outstretched hand, their raw courage unmask.

I see not the dust, that invaded your lungs
Nor the blue scars of mishap, vividly stained
In your face an anthology, of heroes unsung
Reminding mankind of the deeds they attained.

And who can deny both, full public array
One painstakingly gained in that black subterrain
And the other who waited, and blessed every day
That the mine failed to claim a loved one again.

Benny Wilkinson

MEMORIES

When I look back at *memory time*
When winter winds so chill did blow.
Residing by an open grate
Protected from the snow - we sat.
All was at peace within our halls.
The firelight flickering on the walls,
Upon the china, sparkling in the shade
Of the old rack, that long ago was made.
We'd dream of all the pleasant hours spent.
Of times, when we could scarcely pay the rent.
But we came through, to see a happier time.
To hear our children chant a nursery rhyme.
When tears were shed. To rescue comfort came.
You, were that comfort, I was just to blame -
Which often was.
At even when the toil of day was done.
You would come home, ere the set of sun.
Me in the porch, my hair a little grey.
But it was you, who charmed my cares away.
Your face, serene, a solace to my woes.
Your nature, sweet, as natural as a rose.
I know I have my memories to reflect upon.
But now my heart is broken. You are gone.

E Rathbone

MAGPIE

Hands behind black
satiny back
you stalk

important
airborne commander
cock-of-the-walk

your bright white
cardboard shirt-front
neat in the light

blank button eye
staring blind
on its little pin

mad-monocled
monster-surgeon
touring your wards

the raw slither
fresh in your maw,
your trained brain

scanning the range
Maestro Diabolo,
Paganini

in patent leather
your prints of darkness
devour the sun.

Len Rix

RE-BIRTH

Smooth and wet
The clay turns on the wheel
Yielding to the potter's will;
But the rhythm wavers,
And the vessel, once so promising,
Fades into shapelessness.

Patiently the potter
Holds the shapelessness,
Feels the wetness of the tears
That smooth the clay,
Supple in his hands,
Ready to be refashioned.

But the clay, re-moulded
Falters on the wheel that spins
Relentlessly, ceaselessly;
The vessel twists, contorts,
Lies broken
In his hands.

Lovingly the potter
Holds the brokenness,
Feels the ruptured dough
And deftly works until the clay responds,
Supple again,
Compliant.

And through his skill, his care,
A vessel now is fashioned
In simpler form, more lasting than before.
A better shape from which to pour
His living water
Into other lives.

Diana Hardiman

INFORMATION

We hope you have enjoyed reading this book - and that you will continue to enjoy it in the coming years.

If you like reading and writing poetry drop us a line, or give us a call, and we'll send you a free information pack.

Write to

Anchor Books Information
1-2 Wainman Road
Woodston
Peterborough
PE2 7BU